SOCIAL THOUGHT
FROM LORE TO SCIENCE

In Three Volumes. Volume III.
Sociological Trends throughout the World
to the Start of
the Twentieth Century's Seventh Decade

Third Edition

by *HOWARD BECKER*

Late Professor of Sociology, University of Wisconsin;
President, 1959-1960, American Sociological Association

and HARRY ELMER BARNES with the assistance

of Émile Benoît-Smullyan and Others

With an introductory note by Merle Curti, prefaces to all three editions,
1960 addenda for all chapters, a terminological commentary, a 1937-1960
appendix on contemporary sociology; 1960 bibliographies,
notes and subject indexes.

Dover Publications, Inc., New York

Published in Canada by General Publishing Company, Ltd., 30 Lesmill Road, Don Mills, Toronto, Ontario.
Published in the United Kingdom by Constable and Company, Ltd., 10 Orange Street, London WC 2.

This Dover edition, first published in 1961, is an expanded and revised version of the second (1952) edition of the work originally published by D. C. Heath and Company in 1938.

The work has been previously published in two volumes, but the present edition is published in three volumes. Volumes One and Two of this Dover edition comprise the original Volume One, whereas Volume Three of this Dover edition comprises Volume Two of previous editions.

Professor Howard Becker's articles from the various issues of the *Britannica Book of the Year* are reprinted through the courtesy of Encyclopaedia, Britannica, Inc.

Standard Book Number: 486-20903-2
Library of Congress Catalog Card Number: 61-4323

Manufactured in the United States of America
Dover Publications, Inc.
180 Varick Street
New York, N.Y. 10014

To
Those Sharing the Privileges of Membership in
Professional Sociological Associations
Who Are Concerned about Duties Owed
Mankind

CONTENTS

Authorship and editorial responsibility for each chapter and section is indicated by the following marks:

Barnes,   edited by Becker ....*
Becker,   "   "   "   ....†
Barnes and
   Becker, joint,   "   "   "   ....‡
Others,   "   "   "   ....§

When chapter is not marked, see the section markings; when section is not marked, see the chapter marking.

XXIV. SOCIOLOGY IN THE UNITED STATES

XXV. SOCIOLOGY IN ITALY.†

XXVI. RUSSIAN SOCIOLOGY.†

Sociological Trends
Throughout the World
to the Start of
the Twentieth Century's Seventh Decade

CHAPTER XXI

British Sociology

HILLS AHEAD. — The present chapter marks a turning point in the method of exposition we have thus far followed. It seems inadvisable to skip from country to country in tracing the more recent development of sociological theories; henceforth we shall permit national boundaries or the limits of language to define the fields surveyed. Undoubtedly the gain in unity possible within each chapter is partially offset by the inevitable lack of connection between chapters, but alternative methods impose even greater costs. Science should of course recognize no restrictions other than those imposed by its own nature, and in a number of the natural sciences, particularly physics and chemistry, it makes little difference whether a theory is set forth in England or in France. These sciences, however, possess an elaborate set of symbols that carry the real burden of theoretical communication; the various languages on which these symbols are suspended, as it were, merely serve as scaffolding. The situation in the social sciences is at present altogether different. Here the central core of any theory one cares to name is almost inseparably connected with the language in which it is formulated; even statistical generalizations provide only a partial exception to this rule. Not only this: the cultures of the different countries in which the social sciences have developed possess a number of aspects other than language which vitally affect the sociological theories that develop within them. It may some day be possible to transcend such " cultural compulsives " — indeed, works like this history of social thought may eventually provide the necessary international or supranational footing upon which we may erect social sciences that are not so historically relative as such sciences now are. Until that great day comes, however, we must continually remind ourselves that the cultural settings in which sociological theories are placed oftentimes make writers whose points of view are widely separated, but who share the same culture, much more like each other than like those holding apparently similar views in widely contrasting cultures.

Not only does the present chapter mark a turning point in the respects just noted, but it also involves a transition to a somewhat higher plane of description and analysis (marked by the omission of chapter " summaries," among other things). We have heretofore directed our discussion to the intelligent reader who possesses no specialized knowledge of sociology, and it is hoped that our aim has been measurably successful. We also hope that this and succeeding chapters will not too frequently pass beyond his interest, but some sections will appeal primarily to the sociologist as such. Even for those already having some background, however, discussion will seem over-brief at times, and criticism scanty. But manifestly a whole library cannot be jammed within the covers of one book, and we assume that auxiliary use will be made of treatises such as Sorokin's *Contemporary Sociological Theories,* House's *Development of Sociology,* Karpf's *American Social Psychology,* and Parsons's *Structure of Social Action,* not to mention the *Encyclopedia of the Social Sciences* and the original works of the various writers named.

Lack of Sociology per se *in Great Britain.* — It is disconcerting to begin a survey of sociology in Great Britain with the necessary statement that it is almost as rare as gold in sea-water. There are doubtless many reasons for this, but we shall restrict ourselves to the consideration of two: (1) the general cultural setting of university education; and (2) the handicap under which sociology has suffered because of its early association with Spencer and other thinkers outside the pale of the Oxford-Cambridge tradition.

We hope that we shall not incur the charge of over-estimating the importance of our discipline through our assertion that inclusion of sociology in the subjects of academic instruction is one symptom of contemporaneity in curriculum and pedagogical ideals. Now with the notable exception of the University of London and a few other municipal universities such as those of Liverpool, Manchester, Leeds, and Glasgow, British education is still strongly medieval and humanistic, being chiefly concerned with the classics and recondite speculative disciplines. Oxford may be the place where all good German philosophies go when they die, but it nevertheless enjoys great prestige. The idea is still to train the cultured gentleman, in terms of the older criteria of " culture." That is to say, the objective is to prepare the university man to move easily and urbanely in formal social circles rather than actually to understand the processes of human society — to be in polite society rather than to understand social life. The more aristocratic groups in the colleges look forward to public life, and the rhetorical and dialectical technique is viewed as the main means of worldly success — and not without reason. Men are trained to argue with charm and lofty detachment rather than to investigate with precision. The subject-matter may be trivial, but if the literary finish is glossy, all is well. The whole process is a dignified and seductive flight from reality. In contrast to this polishing process undergone by the British gentleman and literary philosopher stands the specialized training of those going into the civil service and the various professions. These persons seldom have either time, inclination, or capacity to work out for themselves any general theory of the fundamentals of social life, and there is nobody to work it out for them. Further, the entrenched position and prestige of history, political philosophy, and economics in Great Britain have made it difficult to press the claims of a science which seemingly infringes upon the jurisdiction of these older disciplines. Again, the social reformers, engaged in partisan struggle, cannot well be expected to pause for sociological orientation unless they have previously been accustomed to such assistance by systematic instruction, and the same is true of the social workers. The upshot of it all is that there is little or no public demand for the offerings of sociology.

Let us now try to discover why there has been such slight demand within academic circles themselves. Early in the 1920's, it was said that looking for snakes in Ireland after the ravages of St. Patrick was a hopeful task in comparison with the search for British sociologists having official status. This may seem extreme, but Harper's recent survey (1932) reveals a somewhat discouraging state of affairs:

Modern scientific and academic sociology was discovered to be in a rather undeveloped and even moribund condition. It was a distinct shock to learn that only a single chair of sociology existed in the universities of Great Britain. The professional association seemed below par and its journal certainly not up to the standard of the earlier *Sociological Papers*. Some work was being done along the line of local studies, but on the side of theory, research, and teaching, sociology in England appeared definitely weak. Perhaps it would be fairer and more exact to say that it appeared to be rare.

After several months spent in visiting classes, reading publications, and consulting teachers, officials of the " Institute," and others, the following conclusions were reached: First, that " official " sociology in England at the present moment is largely non-academic. Further, that most of the writing labelled sociological during recent years has been of a general philosophical and individualized type rather than scientific, and that professional interest has centered largely in practical applications, non-technical local community investigations, and training institutes. Secondly, in so far as it is academic, with the single exception of the London School of Economics where there has been a steady development, sociology is not to be found as such but only in the institutional disguise of " social science " (social work), or in such related departments as anthropology, ethics, political science and philosophy.[1]

How has this come to pass? There has been no lack of eminent individuals: Carver, for example, still declares that Spencer's *Principles of Sociology* is the greatest work ever written in the field; Laski proclaimed Graham Wallas (1858–1932) to be " the wisest of sociologists " after the latter's *Our Social Heritage* appeared in 1921; and as recently as 1929, the year of his death, many American sociologists would have placed Hobhouse in the foremost rank of the world's contemporary sociologists. Nevertheless, the stubborn fact remains that only Ginsberg, occupant of the Martin White chair at the University of London, and one or two German émigrés such as Mannheim, can now be classed as sociologists in the strict sense, if we mean by that either comprehensive systematizers like Park or specialists with a previous broad training in sociology like Bernard or Ogburn.

The reasons for this are not far to seek. As we have already seen, Spencer was really a cosmic philosopher who turned his attention to sociology as one phase of the application of his evolutionary formula. He called this department of his evolutionary encyclopedia " sociology " only because Comte had used this Latin-Greek hybrid to christen the socio-theological utopia embodied in the *Positive Polity*. This is not to belittle Spencer, who undoubtedly was one of the greatest thinkers of his time, but it is intended to show that he was not a professional sociologist, and that only a portion of his writings were even incidentally sociological in character. Similarly, Hobhouse was primarily a philosopher, although his outlook was freshened and his materials rendered concrete and vital by the great range and depth of his information in biology, psychology, anthropology, and political science. It would certainly be difficult to prove him more definitely a sociologist than John Dewey or Bertrand Russell.

The mere fact that he held one of the sociological professorships at the University of London does not prove that he was any more of a sociologist than the ethnographer, Edward Westermarck, who held the other Martin White chair. Indeed, the very existence of these two professorships was but a fortunate academic accident, and the funds available have so dwindled, relatively speaking, that they now support but one exponent of sociology, Ginsberg. Once more, Graham Wallas was first of all a " publicist " with a penchant for a somewhat archaic psychological type of analysis; his specialized knowledge related almost exclusively to the social philosophy and public figures of Bentham's period and to the evolution of English local government. Still further, the London Sociological Society derived the greater part of its spiritual heritage from the French social philosopher, Comte, from the French social economist, LePlay, and from the French anthropogeographer, Demolins.

Likewise, although much valuable work has been done by specialists in other brands of social science having sociological implications, hardly one of these specialists has been adequately oriented in any of the various types of sociology, and as a consequence the problems selected and the results achieved fall far short of sociological requirements. As a consequence of all this, any effort to write the history of sociology in Britain must be chiefly a record of the development of more adequate knowledge, more precise methods, and more fundamental orientation in the special fields of anthropogeography, biology, psychology, anthropology, history, economics, political science, and social reform. Such specialized endeavor has led to the accumulation of a wealth of material that may be utilized by contemporary and future British sociologists, but a tremendous amount of labor will have to be expended before the harvest.

The Development of British Social Science before 1850. — Although the line is necessarily vague, one may divide the development of British social science into two general periods. The first, from the middle of the eighteenth to the middle of the nineteenth century, marks the gradual transition from an almost exclusively speculative type of social philosophy to social sciences granting a fairly large place to empirical investigation. The second stage extends from approximately 1850 to the present time, synchronizing with the increasing sway of the evolutionary theory of man's origin, the growth of the genetic method of dealing with social issues and sociological problems, the advent of more accurate and profound psycho-sociological analyses of human motives and behavior, and the introduction of the more exact statistical methods of dealing with social phenomena.

Among the tendencies in social philosophy before 1850 that have proved sociologically relevant were Deism and rationalism, for they helped to generate interest in the study of man's secular conduct and in " the quest for secular salvation." One of the first sciences to yield hypotheses of sociological import was anthropo-geography, which in the eighteenth century escaped from the occult realm dominated by astrology and Hippocratic medicine. Mead and Arbuthnot developed a sort of " meteorological de-terminism " which was not without its effects on Montesquieu and Ferguson. British explorers also played a large part in that ex-tension of geographical knowledge which eventually enabled Rit-ter to establish scientific anthropogeography. Social biology was another outstanding development, particularly in the field of pop-ulation theory. In addition, a great deal of spadework for later evolutionary hypotheses was accomplished, and the early physical anthropologists, among them Barclay, Grattan, White, *et alii,* helped to found anthropometry, so indispensable for any scientific study of race.

As was abundantly demonstrated in earlier chapters, British thinkers made numerous contributions toward the isolation and analysis of psychical factors in social life. One need mention only the names of Hume and Smith, among a host of others, to sub-stantiate this statement. The modern time-perspective of social development, so different from belief in the chronology of Gene-sis, was greatly furthered by British geologists (Woodward, Hut-ton, and Lyell were among the most important), biologists, ar-chaeologists, and physical anthropologists. Ferguson's work was a great step forward in historical sociology from the standpoint of both scope and attitude, and Burke helped to initiate the genetic point of view with respect to social institutions through his sweeping criticism of the rationalistic social philosophy of the French Revolution. The accuracy of historical method and docu-mentation was notably furthered, in the interval between the Humanists and Ranke, by Gibbon, Robertson, Hallam, Mackin-tosh, and Grote.

The economic philosophy of the age, associated chiefly with the writings of Adam Smith and the classical economists, was rich in sociological implications. Smith, for example, was defi-nitely a forerunner of Sombart, Weber, and other economists who have recently insisted upon the necessity of a sociological orientation in economic analysis as opposed to the exclusive em-phasis upon rarefied speculations concerning value and distribution for which Ricardo and his successors were responsible. Again, Malthus's famous studies of population were an outgrowth of his attitude toward welfare economics, and the deep concern of his contemporaries with the problems of social legislation can be un-derstood only in the light of the contending economic interests of the time. The studies conducted by the factory investigating committees and like bodies brought together a vast amount of information of relevance to social economics, and indirectly, to sociology. In the field of political philosophy, the varied types of speculation and analysis that were current had a common denominator in the tendency to look upon political institutions as outgrowths of more general social situations. Again, the great increase of social problems forced upon the attention of Great Britain by the onset and course of the Industrial Revolution suggested to Bentham the necessity of working out a science of social reconstruction that was later to stimulate writers like Graham Wallas. The same social problems also impelled Chalmers to formulate those principles of case work which later exercised so powerful an influence on social technology.

The Place of Spencer in British Social Science. — The development of the social sciences in England since 1850 has consisted essentially in further progress along the lines of the specialisms just described, but before resuming the story we may pause to indicate the contributions to sociology made by Herbert Spencer in his cosmic philosophy as applied to an interpretation of social processes.

In an earlier chapter we quoted at length from Hankins's cogent summary of Spencer's theories, and the reader will probably agree that his estimate is both just and comprehensive. It might be well, however, to recall to mind the fact that in another summary we emphasized, somewhat more than did Hankins, Spencer's persistently reiterated generalization that social or institutional evolution is part and parcel of cosmic evolution as a whole, and hence cannot be successfully controlled by artificial human intervention and guidance. This is the core of all of Spencer's sociological and political writings. Again, it is necessary to insist upon the utterly inadequate impression of Spencer's sociological theory which is offered by such presentations as those of Small, where Spencer's sociology is represented as largely identical with the elaboration of the organismic analogy. The discussion of society as an organism was but an incidental, unimportant, and rather illogical phase of Spencer's social philosophy. Finally, the writers believe that not enough has been made of Spencer's general observations on sociological attitudes and methodology in his *Study of Sociology.* This little work will probably come to be regarded as Spencer's chief, if not, indeed, his only enduring work in the field of sociology.

Spencer affected but little the growth of sociology in Great

Britain, yet he had a tremendous influence on its subsequent development elsewhere. Not only did he have enthusiastic followers on the Continent, but the early American sociologists — Ward, Sumner, Giddings, and Small — were profoundly influenced by him. Giddings's early work was chiefly an original synthesis of Spencer's physical philosophy with the psychological conceptions of Adam Smith and Gabriel Tarde. Carver seems to retain as fresh and unabashed an enthusiasm for Spencer today as Giddings exhibited toward him in 1894. Nevertheless, Spencer's influence on academic social science in Great Britain was almost negligible. The prevailing trend toward somewhat narrow and uncoördinated specialization was not paralleled by a more general systematic tendency. Moreover, the one British writer on sociology since Spencer who made any effort to systematize, Leonard Trelawney Hobhouse, differed diametrically from him in nearly every phase of his doctrine except in the adoption of the evolutionary approach. While there were many factors which help to account for Spencer's strange lack of influence in Great Britain, it would seem that the following are the most important: (1) the type of mind which tended toward calm reflection and broad generalization in the field of social science was still under the spell of Thomas Hill Green and the Scottish dialecticians; (2) the specialists were too narrow or too absorbed professionally to interest themselves in Spencer's sweeping generalizations and grandiose formulas; and (3) the reformers and uplifters were repelled by his harsh, uncompromising, and mechanical individualism. Hence Spencer remained a lonely and isolated figure in British social science.

Sociologically Relevant Phases of British Social Science after 1850. — We shall now endeavor to trace briefly and concisely the outstanding developments since Spencer, keeping in mind the general background of: (1) improved techniques in social research and analysis; (2) a vast increase in social data; (3) the growing complexity of social phenomena; (4) the steady advance of the secular *Weltanschauung;* and (5) better differentiation and distribution of scientific labor.

There have been numerous contributions to better techniques in social science. The outstanding development here is to be found in the field of social statistics, founded in large part by Jevons, Galton, and Pearson. The most productive figure has been Bowley, who has trained and inspired a large body of students and associates. Even more abstruse theories have been set forth in this field by Yule, Keynes, and others. The most important specialized phase of the quantitative method as applied to sociology which has been worked out in England has been due to Karl Pearson, whose biometrical concepts and coefficient of correlation are world-famous.[2] Statistical techniques for " social measurement " have been applied to contemporary social problems by a host of English students; and we have seen in Chapter Twenty that Hobhouse made an effort to introduce statistics into the study of material culture and social institutions.

Frédéric LePlay, the French social economist, exerted a wide influence on British social science. His technique of the social survey was elaborated and applied in patient detail by Booth, Rowntree, and others in their classic investigations of poverty in London and York. His regional plan for social reconstruction was warmly espoused by Geddes, Branford, and others, and as we shall later note, Geddes achieved no little practical success in applying these doctrines in Edinburgh and elsewhere.

The study of the influence of geographic factors on social processes was initiated in the modern period by a philosophical historian, Buckle, a much misunderstood and misinterpreted man. Writing to prove the growing primacy of cultural and psychological factors in human society, he has most frequently been interpreted and condemned as an unthinking and uncritical apostle of geographical determinism. In anthropogeography the trend since Buckle has been away from the well-intentioned efforts of amateurish physicians, philosophers, travelers, and historians toward the work of well-trained and socially oriented geographers. Herbertson, Cowan, and Fairgrieve have presented illuminating and balanced descriptions and analyses of the manner in which the history of human culture has been *conditioned,* rather than *determined,* by geographic factors; George has dealt with the geographic conditioning of military history; Payne has written on the geographic factors involved in the European settlement of the New World; and Newbigin and Mackinder have elucidated the geographic influences in the ancient and modern history of the Near East and the Balkans. Mackinder especially stresses the crucial importance of the possession of this pivotal area in the Near East for any state desirous of maintaining supreme political power in the Old World. Lucas has inspired and edited an extensive work on the geographical basis of British colonization and imperialism. Geddes and Branford have accepted the geographic basis of LePlay's regionalism as one of the chief clues to the reconstruction of contemporary urban and industrial society, and Chisholm and McFarlane have treated in detail the geographic basis of modern commerce and industry. Especially important has been the introduction of the basic concepts of Paul Vidal de La Blache relating to the regional technique in human geography by Herbertson, Mill, and Fleure. This represents the most advanced phase of development in physical and human geography, and it will doubtless be conceded that Fleure is one of the outstanding exponents of up-to-date human geography in contemporary Britain.[3]

In the realm of biology it will probably be granted that the most sociologically significant and far-reaching development was the triumph of the evolutionary hypothesis and the proof that man, as a higher type of mammal, is a definite part of that process. This not only laid the basis for a realistic study of human origins, but also provided the scientific and methodological justification for the biological approach to social problems. In other words, evolutionary biology helped to create the time-perspective and further the secular attitude essential for any scientific consideration of human society. (This was far more important than the social Darwinism which, among other things, regarded war as the social analogue of the struggle for existence.) The evolutionary analysis of man naturally led to a more detailed and precise study of the mechanisms of human heredity, thus helping to establish the science of genetics. Out of this has arisen the social program of eugenics, chief exponents of which have been, in succession, Francis Galton and Karl Pearson, the former the more seductive prophet and the latter the more skilled technical scientist. Among the discriminating recent students of genetics in relation to medicine and social science we may name Lancelot Hogben.

This interest in the qualitative aspect of the population problem has been paralleled by further developments of the quantitative analysis founded by Malthus. The Neo-Malthusians have apparently shown that the Malthusian doctrine, when accurately interpreted, has been fully vindicated by the history of modern population growth since 1800. They have also given considerable scientific support to the belief that artificial restriction of the population in the interest of general social well-being is far more needful today than when Malthus penned his famous essay. Marie Stopes and other leaders of the birth-control movement have discovered methods for restraining population increase which are far more effective than the expedient of delayed marriages suggested by Malthus. The striking work done on the psychology and sociology of sex by Havelock Ellis and others has rendered the general attitude toward birth-control and other sexual aspects of social improvement less hostile. Neo-Malthusian writing in England has varied from the erudite and specialized work of Carr-Saunders to the effective propaganda of Swinburne and Cox and the introductory but comprehensive textbook of Wright. As indispensable data for both quantitative and qualitative social biology, students have been able to draw on the vital statistics ever more accurately and thoroughly compiled by government agencies and sifted and analyzed by such authorities as Newsholme and Hogben.[4]

In the study of the psychical aspects of social phenomena the most important development in the last three-quarters of a century in Great Britain has been the annihilation of the intellectualistic psychology, exemplified by the Benthamite " felicific calculus." This not only furnished the philosophico-moral basis of Bentham's elaborate series of social inventions and reform schemes, but also constituted the foundation of most of the so-called psychological economics and political science. Destruction was imperative; it came through the spectacular labors of Graham Wallas, in his *Human Nature in Politics,* of McDougall, with his emphasis on the importance of non-rational impulses, of Tansley, Rivers, Hart, and others who have exploited those types of social psychology which stress the importance of " subconscious " factors in human behavior, and of the social psychologists and anthropologists who, from Bagehot's day onward, have emphasized the importance of custom, habit, and convention in conditioning the thought and conduct of man. One of the earliest dissenters from the orthodox doctrine of instincts promulgated by McDougall was Ginsberg, whose *Psychology of Society* appeared in 1921. Important also has been the defense of the social importance of sympathy and altruism by Drummond, Kidd, Sutherland, and Spiller, all of whom oppose, rightly or wrongly, the egoistic premises of the " felicific calculus " and the bellicose assumptions of social Darwinism.[5]

As in America, the cultural analysis of social processes and institutions has been established chiefly by the ethnologists. The older evolutionary or comparative approach was espoused by Avebury, Tylor, Frazer, and others. The opposed or diffusionist position has been exploited moderately by Haddon and Rivers, and with naïve exuberance by Smith and his disciples, such as Mackenzie and Perry. A more critical and tentative viewpoint, roughly resembling that taken by Boas and the American school of historical ethnology, has been maintained by Marett, G. Lane-

Fox Pitt-Rivers, Malinowski, Radcliffe-Brown, and Bartlett. There has been no British sociologist to take over and utilize the technique of cultural analysis for sociology after the manner of Ogburn and his followers in the United States, although Hobhouse was cordial toward the cultural point of view and made wide use of it in his writings.[6]

The genetic study of social institutions and cultural development has been pursued by a varied group of scholars. John Richard Green repudiated Freeman's episodical political history and his dictum that " history is past politics," and wrote a history of English social life and culture. Following his lead, the contributors to the Traill and Mann series have compiled a vast social and cultural history of England; Maitland and Pollard have founded an institutional approach to English political history; and the Webbs, Ashley, Tawney, the Hammonds, Slater, Knowles, and others have made precious and voluminous contributions to our knowledge of the social and economic history of England.[7] The ethnologists previously mentioned have amassed a vast body of material on cultural and institutional origins, and physical anthropologists such as Arthur Keith, as well as a large number of competent prehistoric archaeologists, have clarified the complicated problems relating to human origins. The history of institutions has been ably dealt with by Maine, Maitland, Pollock, Vinogradoff, and others in the field of legal origins; by Hobhouse and Jenks in tracing the evolution of the state; by a large number of competent economic historians and genetic economists, led by Archdeacon Cunningham, in analyzing the evolution of economic life; by Westermarck and Briffault in their studies of the evolution of the family and human marriage; and by Lang, Frazer, Marett, and others in the field of the history of religion and comparative mythology. Marvin has done more than anyone else in England to arouse an interest in the " new history," associated in this country chiefly with the work of Robinson and his disciples. Wells, in his *Outline of History,* has effected a juncture between the competent professional study of the history of civilization and the popular appreciation of his novel type of historical writing. Of epoch-making significance for historical sociology is Toynbee's projected twelve-volume work (of which three volumes have appeared), *A Study of History* (2nd ed., 1934). As was pointed out at considerable length in Chapter Twenty, his conception of " challenge-and-response " coincides closely with recent analyses by ethnologists and sociologists of the stimulating effects of culture contact. The range of historical data covered by

Toynbee is simply stupendous; he can be compared only with Max Weber and Sorokin. This range enables him to employ with marked success a method of culture case study essentially akin to that advocated in the chapter just noted. In studying " the stimulus of penalization," for example, he takes the obvious instance of the Jews and compares and contrasts it with a number of others far from obvious that provide almost an experimental check on his generalizations. American sociologists must at once avail themselves of his methods and data if they are to continue to act as " the grammarians of the social sciences "; otherwise the historians will take over that function, to the general detriment of the scientific division of labor.

Certain contributions to contemporary British economics have been of some indirect significance for sociology. Among these we should perhaps list Ashley's achievements in genetic economics and economic history; the institutional economics of the Webbs, Tawney, Clay, and others; the work of Pigou and Hobson in welfare economics; and the functional approach to socio-economic life represented in the methods and assumptions of Cole and the guild socialists.[8]

There have been many phases of British political science which have brought forth material usable by sociology. Maitland, Pollard, Jenks, Hobhouse, and others have devoted themselves to the study of the historical evolution of political institutions. The pluralistic revolt from the conceptions and practices of the absolute and omnipotent state and from the doctrine of unified, concentrated, and unlimited sovereignty was organized in England by Maitland under the inspiration of Gierke. This movement has been further developed with particular reference to ecclesiastical groups and interests by Figgis, and in relation to professional and vocational groupings and programs by Laski. Particular emphasis has been laid by Maitland and Figgis on the " real personality " of the corporate group, and this dubious contention has been utilized as the basis of a skillful argument for a certain amount of group autonomy.[9]

The psychical factor in politics was discussed with great acumen, if with imperfect psychological knowledge, by Walter Bagehot in his *Physics and Politics,* where he stressed in particular the operation of imitation and discussion. Graham Wallas dealt the death blow to political rationalism and intellectualistic psychology, but his efforts to suggest a constructive way out of these perplexities were less successful than his critical work. We cannot fail to mention here the important work of MacIver on the place of the community in social and political life which has so profoundly influenced Cole and the guild socialists in their political doctrine. (Although now at Columbia University, MacIver, a Scotsman by birth, was at Aberdeen and Toronto for some time after his *Community* appeared.) The question of aristocracy *versus* democracy has long been one of the staples of British academic controversy, with Maine, Stephen, Lecky, Mallock, and others defending the aristocratic tradition; whereas Hobson, Hobhouse, and Bryce have espoused the cause of democracy.

A viewpoint owing much to sociology has been introduced into ethics through Leslie Stephen's attempt to restate ethical theory in terms of the evolutionary hypothesis and through the comparative·and historical studies of Hobhouse and Westermarck.[10] The Webbs and others have done a great deal to emphasize the contention that social ethics should be concerned with the establishment of a comprehensive scheme of "social justice," and have buttressed their case with quasi-sociological analyses. The repudiation of the theological assumptions underlying conventional English criminology and penology is in part due to insights that may be called sociological, and the sociological cast in such contemporary English literature as the works of Shaw, Wells, Bennett, and Galsworthy should not be overlooked. (In the notes of this chapter we have listed a large number of quasi-sociological writers, literary and otherwise.)

The Social Philosophy of Hobhouse. — Spencer was the outstanding defender of the old *laissez faire* liberalism; Hobhouse was one of the chief agents in transforming that liberalism into the newer type which espoused a modified collectivism and an extensive program of social reform.[11]

He began his work in conscious revolt against the current Hegelianism of Green; even while a student at Oxford he had been deeply impressed by the impotence of idealism when confronted with the problem of evil. As a consequence, a kind of rational empiricism proved most attractive to him, and he did much to establish realism in Great Britain. His search for facts led him to the study of animal behavior, and out of this came his *Mind in Evolution* (1901), which established him as one of the first of British comparative·psychologists. The next stage in his investigations was in the field of social anthropology, and after the analysis of a great deal of data by techniques considerably in advance of those used by many of his contemporaries, *Morals in Evolution* appeared in 1906, a treatise which Ginsberg describes as a "broad

study of human evolution in terms of psychology and anthropology." [12]

The title of the book last mentioned gives us a clue to the general theory underlying the greater part of Hobhouse's work.
Like Spencer, he developed his sociological system as a part of a
general philosophy of evolution. There is a still more intimate
similarity between the two systems, in that although Spencer conceived of the evolutionary process as one of progressive differentiation and adjustment, Hobhouse viewed it as a growth in
correlation and harmony, and both looked upon society as an
organic unity. But here the resemblance ceases. Spencer held
that the course of evolution moves on automatically regardless
of the interference of man, believing that the latter could at the
best have only a slight beneficial effect and was extremely likely
to hinder the process. Hobhouse claimed, on the contrary, that
however much the evolutionary process may depend upon " automatic " factors, such as the struggle for existence, social evolution has come more and more to rest upon conscious control. He
held that, from this stage on, progress must depend primarily on
the conscious direction of social conduct by the " social mind."
Again, while Spencer's conception of the organic nature of society rested on a large use of organismic analogy, Hobhouse es-
chewed the use of biological terms and implied only the essential
unity and interdependence of social life. One thus finds in Hobhouse the interesting combination of a writer who approached
his problems from the standpoint of a philosopher of evolution
of the most thorough and recent type, of a social philosopher unsurpassed in any country for breadth and profundity of learning,
and of a liberal democrat in politics.

Hobhouse carried his general evolutionary doctrines over consistently into his sociological system as a means of interpreting
social processes. His specific sociological doctrines are to be found
mainly in his suggestive little work on *Social Evolution and Political Theory* and in his more recent *Social Development,* which
may be said to bear much the same relation to Spencer's *Study
of Sociology* that Hobhouse's volumes in the philosophy of evolution do to the *Synthetic Philosophy.*

In the first place, as to the general field or scope of sociology,
Hobhouse holds that it may be regarded chiefly as the science of
human progress. He says:

To form by a philosophic analysis a just conception of human progress,
to trace this progress to its manifold complexity in the course of history,

to test its reality by careful classification and searching comparisons, to ascertain its conditions, and if possible to forecast the future — this is the comprehensive problem towards which all sociological science converges and on the solution of which reasoned sociological effort must finally depend.[13]

Progress, which is the prime object of sociological study, is not synonymous with social evolution.[14] The latter term is the wider, and may include retrogression as well as advance. " By evolution I mean any sort of growth; by social progress, the growth of social life in respect to those qualities to which human beings attach or can rationally attach value." [15] Nor is social progress primarily dependent upon biological factors. It is almost exclusively a result of psychical and social forces:

> That is to say, there is progress just where the factor of social tradition comes into play and just so far as its influence extends. If the tradition is broken, the race begins again where it stood before the tradition was formed. We may infer that while the race has been relatively stagnant, society has rapidly developed, and we may conclude that, whether for good or for evil, social changes are mainly determined, not by alterations of racial type, but by modifications of tradition due to the interactions of social causes. Progress is not racial, but social.[16]

Social progress, in last analysis, Hobhouse regards as the growth in the harmonious adjustment of: (1) man to society, (2) the different types of social organization to each other, and (3) society as a whole to its environment. " Social progress may be regarded as development of the principles of union, order, coöperation, and harmony among human beings." [17] The ideal society toward which social progress should lead is one in which harmony is realized. " The ideal society is conceived as a whole which lives and flourishes by the harmonious growth of its parts, each of which in developing on its own lines and in accordance with its own nature tends on the whole to further the development of others." [18]

This growth of harmonious adjustment in society, which is the essence of social progress, is not, however, solely the result of blind forces; it can only be completely achieved by the conscious action of will and intelligence. " But in all its meaning, harmony, as already hinted, is something which does not come of itself, but is achieved in greater or less degree by effort, that is to say, by intelligence and will." [19] " The growth of rational control by society over the conditions of life may thus be taken as the measure of social progress." [20]

The most significant fact in the modern stage of civilization is that we have now reached the point where the social mind has obtained control over the external conditions of life. "The distinguishing characteristics of our time are that civilization for the first time has the upper hand, that the physical conditions of life have come and are rapidly coming more and more within human control, and that at least the foundations have been laid for a social order which would render possible a permanent and unbroken development." [21] (These lines, it should be remembered, were written before the outbreak of the World War.)

The aversion for sustained thought manifest among many contemporary American sociologists has led them unduly to discount Hobhouse because of the marked philosophic cast of his researches; the emphasis upon "work" as opposed to "armchair speculation" has gone so far that it is considered quite proper to be wholly ignorant of the really great minds of the past if only one knows the number of fireplugs in Ashtabula on January 16, 1934. Let it be proclaimed from the housetops that for all the social philosophizing in which Hobhouse indulged, he never was guilty of mere speculation: "He fed on factual material which he digested with the aid of brilliant hypotheses." [22] Social philosopher he undoubtedly was, and not a sociologist in the strict sense, but the most rigidly scientific of social scientists can learn much from Hobhouse.

Westermarck, Darwinian Ethnologist. — Although not a Britisher by birth, the Finno-Swedish scholar, Edward Westermarck, was a colleague of Hobhouse for over a quarter of a century, and hence may properly be considered here.

In the academic year of 1903–4, Westermarck, Hobhouse, and others gave several short lecture courses on quasi-sociological subjects at the London School of Economics, and the following year Westermarck was appointed University Lecturer in Sociology for a three-year period. Shortly thereafter a Maecenas in the person of a Scottish merchant and member of Parliament, Martin White, endowed the chairs of sociology to which we have already referred. Westermarck was also at this time professor of moral philosophy in the University of Helsingfors, and since Hobhouse's death in 1929 he has devoted all his efforts to the latter institution. [23]

Unlike Hobhouse, Westermarck was not rationalistically inclined; instead, he was dominated by those phases of Darwinism most clearly evident in *The Descent of Man.* Curiously enough, however, he became interested in the nature of morality at about

the same time that Hobhouse was applying the genetic method
to the analysis of " the rational good," and the result was his
Origin and Development of Moral Ideas, appearing at about the
same time as Hobhouse's *Morals in Evolution,* but independent
of it. It is also interesting to note that although the methods used
in the two treatises differ considerably, similar conclusions are
reached.

Westermarck was not interested in setting forth a coherent
sociological system; he was content to study more or less disconnected social institutions. His biologistic Darwinism was quite
marked in his persistent attempt to find the " causes " of institutions in the instinct of jealousy and like psychical factors supposedly perpetuated by the survival value of the institution in
question. Failing to distinguish between institutions and social
structures, he defined the former as forms of social relationships
regulated and sanctioned by " society." Society, in turn, was
vaguely described as a grouping characterized by some degree of
coöperation, but in which spatial nearness is not an absolute essential. The origin of the coöperative activity that constitutes
society, said Westermarck, was probably the parental impulses
(here the reader will recall John Fiske) and the mutually beneficial activities of food-getting and other joint enterprises.

Almost ten years before his association with the London School
of Economics, Westermarck won a considerable reputation
through his pioneer work, *The History of Human Marriage*;
this was the first well-rounded attack on the theories of promiscuity and group marriage set forth by Morgan and like devotees
of unilinear social evolution. Westermarck maintained that the
evidence presented by the social evolutionists really had to do with
cases of fraternal polyandry and polygamy instead of unregulated
promiscuity. Of recent years, Briffault, a Communist who has attempted to revive the doctrines of Morgan, has made a frontal
attack on Westermarck's position, but has encountered a stubborn defense and slashing counter-attack. Inasmuch as both writers make use of the illustrative method, the critical sociologist is
necessarily somewhat wary of taking up the cudgels in behalf of
either opponent. Nevertheless, this much can be said: Briffault is
wrong in thinking that Westermarck had theological or traditionally moral reasons for his hypothesis, inasmuch as he has been
an unsparing critic of religion and the church, and has recently set
forth, in his *Ethical Relativity,* a theory that runs counter to all
forms of moral, ethical, or religious absolutism.

Branford and Geddes. — The French social economist Fré-

déric LePlay (1806–1882), of whom we shall later have more to say, was a contemporary of Comte. His name is mentioned here because his formula for description and analysis — Place, Work, Folk; his interest in regional studies; his emphasis on the family as the basic unit of society; and his zeal for social reform, were all absorbed by the English railway director turned social reformer, Victor Branford (1864–1930), and the Scottish naturalist and mystic, Patrick Geddes (1854–1932). Branford devoted his energies and personal fortune to LePlay House in London, a sort of settlement which also serves as a sociological laboratory, and Geddes established the Outlook Tower as an experimental center for " sociology and civics " on the Castle Hill of Edinburgh.

There can be little doubt that the strongest force behind British sociology of recent years has been the Sociological Society of London. This has done much to promote sociological discussion in the strict sense, and in addition to encourage social reform and bring prominent persons together for at least the ostensible purpose of dealing with social problems. Moreover, until the establishment of the Institute of Sociology in 1933, it had control of a useful journal, the *Sociological Review*. We may therefore say that the name of sociology, at least, has been kept alive in Great Britain by Branford and his associates, but we must also say that the society has done little to make the substance of sociology more acceptable to the British academic world. To begin with, until quite recently it has been rather provincial and out of touch with sociological developments elsewhere. Further, it has been heavily handicapped by discipleship; many of the members have been so engrossed in making genuflections before the great god LePlay and his prophet Demolins (with an occasional bow toward Comte and his emotionally surcharged Positivistic religion) that strictly scientific endeavor has been slighted. Moreover, the overmastering interest in social reform, particularly in regional planning for urban reconstruction, and in the various phases of social work has prevented theoretical discussion of major sociological interests from gaining headway.

After the death of Branford in 1930 the Sociological Society and LePlay House were merged to form the Institute of Sociology. The vigorous policy of Farquharson, the interim editor of the *Sociological Review,* the election of the ethnologist Marett as president, and the setting up of an editorial board composed of eminent social scientists has led to an extension of interests and activities that augurs well for the future of the Institute. The

Sociological Review, for example, has been rejuvenated; moreover, its dilettantish flavor is in process of disappearing.

Geddes earned a great biological reputation through his early work with Huxley, Haeckel, and Virchow, and his later collaboration with James Arthur Thomson. In the latter half of his life he threw himself into the study of the social sciences, led an onslaught on the slums of Edinburgh, preached the gospel of workers' education, helped to found the eugenics movement, became the first outstanding exponent of city planning, and greatly advanced the method of the regional survey. When the Great War stultified his work in Europe he turned toward the East, spent several years in India as a teacher and social planner, and then found at Jerusalem the opportunity of designing the Hebrew University and its environs. His last enterprise was an attempt to revive the old Scots College at Montpellier, France; he hoped to relate it directly to such organs of a " renascent Asia " as Tagore's international college in Bengal.

Here certainly was a Diogenes Teufelsdröckh in the flesh, an unrivalled example of the Professor of Things in General. The flaming energy of Geddes seems, to the academic sociologist at least, to have been tragically wasted through incessant change of direction. Nevertheless, we cannot impose academic criteria upon a man whose genius was primarily inspirational; as an ardent follower has put it:

> He was wonderful and inexhaustible: a brilliant intelligence, a spirit of the finest temper, a maker of visions, a weaver of spells. And for some thousands of men and women scattered about the world his memory is a possession that can never fade or be impaired. He used to say that he was known as the fellow who pulled the bell and ran away. His friends were apt to put it otherwise. They said he had foreseen more, and started more creative enterprises, than any man of his epoch.[24]

Undoubtedly this is all true, and it is well for the world and to the undying credit of Geddes that it is true. Still — and here is the nub of the difficulty we have repeatedly confronted in this chapter — the very genius of Geddes provided still another reason for the persistent neglect of sociology by British universities. It was inevitably regarded as a science, a philosophy, a religion, and a social program primarily dependent upon Messianic leadership. No discipline can win a foothold when these things can be truthfully said of it.

Ginsberg. — To the present writers it seems obvious that only the type of sociology represented by Morris Ginsberg can even-

tually gain acceptance in Great Britain. When Hobhouse died and Westermarck retired from England in 1929, Ginsberg, who had been closely associated with them both, became the successor of both in the way already indicated. His works show a wide range of interests, for they include a *Psychology of Society, Dialogues on Metaphysics,* a painstaking statistical study in collaboration with Wheeler and Hobhouse, *The Material Culture and Social Institutions of the Simpler Peoples,* and recently a biography, *L. T. Hobhouse: His Life and Works* (with J. A. Hobson). He is on the new editorial board of the *Sociological Review,* and is also one of the editors of *Politica,* a promising new social science journal sponsored by the University of London.

Ginsberg's definition of sociology shows the influence of Hobhouse (and secondarily of Westermarck), for he regards it as " the science of social institutions." Nevertheless, and although he severely criticizes Simmel, he qualifies this definition in such a way that it closely approaches Simmel's conception. To wit: Sociology is ". . . the science dealing with the forms or modes of social relationships. . . ." Let us hastily add, however, that he does not agree with Simmel's restriction of sociology to the study of these forms, for he feels that sociology runs a grave risk if it assumes that the content of social relationships is the same as that dealt with by other social sciences. In other words, he does not agree that sociology should restrict itself to data which are also utilized by such special social sciences as economics or government, merely dealing with this material in its own characteristic way by subjecting it to sociological categories — e.g., to competition, conflict, and so on. He therefore qualifies the clause just quoted by adding " as they are exhibited in the civilization or culture of a people." From this it is clear that he lays considerable stress on content: sociology, he holds, should collect its own typical data and also apply sociological analysis to social data in general. The upshot of this and similar qualifications is that sociology is not regarded as a special social science, as in Simmel's version, but as " the science which deals with social life as a whole in contradistinction to the special sciences which deal with special aspects of human life." Ginsberg therefore may be regarded as in favor of a type of sociology which utilizes the results of the more specialized social sciences, but assigns them to their appropriate niches in a frame of reference composed of the " broader principles of social organization which often escape the specialist." This is not mere encyclopedic eclecticism, however; he aims at the interpretation of social life as a whole, not at a summary of the findings of the other sciences. Instead of synthesizing their generalizations, sociology, according to Ginsberg, must furnish generalizations which they either do not or cannot make. From this point of view, therefore, such specialisms as ethnology and political science may be regarded as subdivisions of the broader sociological field.[25] To quote Harper's interpretation of Ginsberg:

> Specifically the objectives of sociology are: (1) To determine the nature of the various social groupings and trace their development; (2) to determine by comparative method and quantitative measurement, as far as possible, interrelations between institutions; (3) to formulate empirical laws; and (4) to interpret these laws in the light of the more ultimate principles of life and mind, and discover the relation of social facts to civilization as a whole, primitive and modern.[26]

Many American devotees of raw empiricism would probably use the rubber-stamp term " philosophical " to characterize Ginsberg's approach. Properly understood, philosophical it may indeed be, but it certainly is not arbitrary fiat or groundless speculation. Factual material plays a large part in Ginsberg's work, as witness his use of ethnographic data. Moreover, he possesses sound knowledge of psychology, and it is interesting to note, in passing, that he is quite sceptical of the doctrine of instincts or propensities advanced by McDougall and still reverentially accepted by many British psychologists. Again, he commands a great deal of historical information and has provided some of the most thoughtful analyses of the relation of history and sociology now extant. Finally, he manifests great familiarity with the writings of the German systematic and historical sociologists, and his present associations with Karl Mannheim will probably render this *rapprochement* even more fruitful.

With all due respect for Ginsberg, however, we cannot help voicing the fear that the very catholicity of his sociological theory may operate against its acceptance in academic circles, for differences from the older sciences are thereby minimized and affinities with social and political philosophy stressed, leaving little or no place for sociology as a strictly delimited science with a field exclusively its own. Nevertheless, we sincerely hope that these forebodings are unjustified.

Much that seems relevant for this chapter is covered in the 1937-1960 Appendix on Sociological Trends. Attention should be called, however, to W. J. H. Sprott's summary, from a rather special perspective, in Howard Becker and Alvin Boskoff, eds., *Modern Sociological Theory in Continuity and Change* (New York: Dryden Press, 1957), pp. 607-22 (MSTICAC).

CHAPTER XXII

Sociology in the French Language

I

RETROSPECT AND PROSPECT. — French sociology has been notably characterized by that logical keenness and subtlety which has often been asserted to be typical French thought generally. From this follows three of its major peculiarities: first, a great dependence on analysis and abstraction, and comparatively little aimless fact-gathering; second, an awareness of the full implications of a theory, and hence a tendency to push it to its extreme, thus ending in a position which is apt to be startling to naïve common sense; third, a markedly controversial tone, the clear recognition and elaboration of theoretical differences, and the tendency to line up in opposing schools.

No country has played a more important part in the origin of sociology than has France. Descartes, in his proud reliance on human reason, his methodological doubt, his insistence on universal, invariable law, prepared the stage for a break with traditionalism in social matters, for a felt need to rationalize political and economic institutions, and for an attempt to extend to the domain of social facts the same systematic modes of interpretation in terms of natural law which characterized the emerging physical sciences.

Montesquieu, in his *Considerations on the Greatness and Decadence of the Romans* (1734) and his *Spirit of Laws* (1748), insisted that political and social phenomena are subject to general laws much as are those of physics. In particular he stressed and popularized the rôle of climatic and geographic factors, being in this way an important precursor of the LePlay school and the social geographers. Voltaire's *Essai sur les Mœurs* and his various historical works offered a general history of civilization and embodied important sociological theses as to the rôle of religion and war in social development. He conceived them, moreover, in a thoroughly naturalistic spirit, insisting on explanations in terms of efficient causation, and challenging directly Bossuet's interpretation in terms of a providential final causation. This general point of view was characteristic also of Diderot, D'Alembert, D'Holbach, Helvétius, and the other leading Encyclopedists, who, in addition, brought into the open the attack on traditionalism implicit in Descartes's rationalistic insistence on rigorous demonstration in all things. Helvétius and D'Holbach, moreover, insisted on the importance of the cultural factor in the shaping of human personality, the latter suggesting a theory of the social importance of imitation foreshadowing the one later elaborated by Tarde.

The Physiocrats — Quesnay, Mirabeau, Mercier de la Rivière, and the others — concerned at first with narrowly practical economic interests, were led in the elaboration of their views to wider theoretical analyses of considerable sociological significance, dealing in particular with the social rôle of the institution of private property. Somewhat later Saint-Simon, developing a hint of Condorcet, insisted on the importance of prevision and prediction as a test of our understanding of social phenomena, and attempted to discover a law of history which would make such prevision possible. With this objective he worked out a " law " of the alternation of periods of organization or construction with those of criticism and revolution. He also envisaged the profound social changes to be brought about by the rationalization of society in accordance with modern science.

Auguste Comte has been generally considered the intellectual father of French sociology. He contributed the first clear view as to the nature of sociology as a specific science and its place in the hierarchy of the sciences. His discussion of sociological methodology is distinguished by catholicity and insight, and is vastly superior to many recent one-sided theories in this field. His insistence on the specific reality of the social fact, its irreducibility to the physical or biological reality, coupled with his omission of psychology from the list of the sciences (except as a part of physiology), is an essential factor in the rise of the sociologistic school in France. Also important in this connection was his theory of consensus, which had very important biologistic implications. The famous theory of the law of the three stages is a brilliant analysis of the rôle of basic ideas, and in particular of supernaturalistic and naturalistic *Weltanschauungen* in social development, having direct present-day usefulness for the sociology of knowledge. If one drops out the metaphysical stage (which is only negatively conceived and sketchily treated), then the antithesis between the theological and positive stages corresponds roughly to the familiar ideal-typical antithesis of the sacred and the secular society, *Gemeinschaft* and *Gesellschaft*, and similar dichotomies. The importance of these and other contributions of Comte will perhaps become more manifest as we trace out his influence on his French successors.

For purposes of convenience we may roughly classify all French sociology under four main heads: (1) geographic and environmentalist theories, (2) biologistic theories, (3) sociologistic theories, and (4) psychologistic and individualistic theories. Our principal attention will be focused on the two latter groups, which have probably been the most important in contemporary French sociology. In the second division of the chapter we shall deal only with sociology in Belgium [1] (French Switzerland being included in the first division for the sake of simplicity and convenience).

Evironmentalist Theories: the LePlay School.[2] — By environmentalist theories we mean all those which use as an ultimate explanatory principle in sociology some condition of the cosmic or physical milieu, whether astronomic, topographic, climatic, agronomic, or the like. It seems wisest to classify the LePlay School and its modern followers, *L'École des sciences sociaux,* among the environmentalists, in spite of their considerable eclecticism. The basic formula of the school, " Place, Work, Folk (Family)," means that the general characters of the physical environment dictate the economic life of the people, which in turn determines the form of the family and the general characteristics of the society. This is, in a wide sense, historical materialism and economic determinism; it is in many respects similar to the logical structure of Marxism. Never, however, have systems starting with common methodological premises arrived at such startlingly different conclusions. LePlay, Catholic and extreme conservative, defended all the typically conservative institutions: religion, parental authority, nationalism, and hereditary social classes. The method by which the divergence occurs is not difficult to perceive. Marx focused his attention on social classes and the class struggle; LePlay concentrated on the family as an essential element in social solidarity and stability.

Perhaps the most important and certainly the most celebrated contribution of the LePlay school is to the technique of social research. The family is selected as the unit of investigation, and the family budget is systematically analyzed as a quantitative expression of all aspects of the family life.[3] This clearly reflects the materialistic presuppositions underlying both the methodological and substantive doctrines of LePlay, which have attracted some criticism even among his own followers.

LePlay and his followers prepared a large number of monographic studies of the socio-economic aspects of family life in specific regions of France and elsewhere, and LePlay embodied the practical and theoretical results in a number of extensive works, among the more important of which were: *Les Ouvriers Europeens* (1855); *Les Ouvriers des deux mondes* (1857); *La Réforme sociale en France* (1864); *L'Organisation de la famille* (1871); *L'Organisation du travail* (1870); *and La Constitution essentielle de l'humanité* (1881). LePlay also founded, in 1881, a journal devoted to social and industrial problems, *La Réforme sociale*. In the hands of LePlay's chief followers, his methodology was considerably transformed: it was given a broader and more systematic character and a comprehensive nomenclature. A defense and characterization of the revised method and nomenclature from the pen of Paul Bureau (1865–1923), one of the latest of the followers of LePlay, follows:

Just as it stands, this brief questionnaire is . . . a valuable instrument of analysis and doubtless this will soon be realized if students will consent to follow LePlay's recommendation to study the working-class family. I am aware that this method seems to some discredited and antiquated. Nevertheless, the analysis of wisely chosen samples remains the favorite and most certain method in all empirical sciences. . . . As has long been said, the working-class family, that is to say, the family which draws its means of subsistence largely from the manual labor of its head or of its members, furnishes an excellent introduction to the general study of society as a whole. Since the organization of private life occupies such an important place in the general economy of society, no better avenue could be found to the interior of society itself; and the choice of a working-class family is likewise justified by the fact that, alike because of its work and because of its means of existence, this family, more than any other, is under the influence of determining elements of the group under observation. By virtue of their intellectual culture or material resources, families in moderate or good circumstances can raise themselves above the action of these elements. The working-class family is more the prisoner of circumstance, and by reference to it one can best perceive the action of the environment. Moreover, to recommend the monographic method is not to say that the completion of a single monograph is sufficient. On the contrary, it is advantageous to renew observation of the first study. All that can be said is that the scrupulous analysis of a well-chosen sample, better than any other procedure, permits the penetration of those mysterious fastnesses . . . where the social life of a people is developed and organized.[4]

Demolins (1852–1907) specialized on the effect of the physical environment on society and the history of civilization. His *Comment la route crée le type social* would appear from the title to be a specialized treatise dealing with the social influences of routes of travel, but it is a far more comprehensive affair, being really a suggestive manual of anthropogeography with emphasis on topographic factors. With Demolins, *la route* tends to become practically the whole physical environment. In his *The Growth of Modern Nations,* DeTourville gave special attention to the development of the chief types of the family and social groups, devoting himself particularly to the origins of the modern family among the Teutons and its triumph over the patriarchal family organization. Paul Bureau, in the generation following Demolins and DeTourville, still further improved the methodology of the LePlay school and freed it from the somewhat narrow materialistic limitations which had characterized its earlier implications.

The LePlay approach secured many converts among British sociologists, the leaders here being the distinguished Scottish biologist, Patrick Geddes, and the English social philosopher, Victor Branford, whom we have already discussed. Geddes and Branford's *The Coming Polity* (1919) is the best British adaptation of the LePlay conceptions. The Sociological Society of London as a whole has shown much interest in the LePlay methods, and members of the society have recently prepared an English edition of Demolins's classic work. Highly significant is the revival of LePlay in America by the eminent rural sociologist and authority on family budgets, Carle C. Zimmerman. In a recent book [5] he includes a condensed translation of a large part of LePlay's most important work, *Les Ouvriers Européens,* and attempts to apply its fundamental ideas to an analysis of some urgent contemporary problems and to a severe criticism of some of the rural reconstruction policies of the present political régime in this country.

Human Geography in France. — The LePlay system gave a definite impulse to the further introduction of statistical techniques. Moreover, it also had a great deal of influence on the establishment of regional geography. Paul Vidal de La Blache, the founder of French regional geography, was as much influenced by the regional orientation of the LePlay socio-economic investigations as he was by his work in physical geography. The other chief stimulus to human geography in France came through the more natural and conventional channel of physical geography. The great figure in the establishment of physical and descriptive geography in the French-speaking countries was the Belgian, Élisée Reclus (1830–1905), who combined in his work much the same achievements as those made by Ritter and Ratzel respectively in Germany. His physical and descriptive geography, perhaps unequaled as to scope and precision by the work of any other single author of his period in this field, was embodied in his monumental series, *La nouvelle géographie universelle*. His chief work on anthropogeography, which also contains much physical geography, is *L'Homme et la terre,* in some six volumes. The ablest and most discriminating modern French adaptation of this rather generalized anthropogeography of Reclus, Ratzel, and Ritter is probably to be found in Camille Vallaux's two books, *Le Sol et l'État* and *La Mer,* which make up the two parts of a general *Géographie sociale.*

The reaction against this ambitious effort to present a highly generalized anthropogeography was led by Paul Vidal de La Blache, regarded by many as the leader of French anthropogeography in the generation after Reclus. It was the contention of Vidal that geographic science was not yet sufficiently developed to allow of the sweeping formulations of a Ratzel. Not only did the doctrines of Ratzel and Reclus rest upon inadequate information; they were so generalized as to admit of many exceptions, and they tended to make the followers of such writers satisfied with accepted formulas instead of eager to test existing hypotheses by the accumulation of additional facts. The regionalist criticism of the Ratzel method is well summarized in the following quotation from Lucien Febvre's *A Geographical Introduction to History,* the work of an enthusiastic follower of Vidal, and the best treatment of the theoretical principles of the regional anthropogeography:

Man's customs, particular characteristics, and his mode of life are not the necessary consequence of the fact that he is situated in this or that " environment." . . . They are the consequences of his own nature. It is no longer possible to repeat blindly: " Such a region inevitably forces such a mode of life upon its inhabitants." Under the powerful action of organized and systematized habits, which continually wear deeper and deeper grooves and impose themselves with increasing force upon successive generations, putting their mark on mentality and turning all the forces of progress in a definite direction, the features of a country may be changed, may be profoundly transformed. . . . Here is another aspect of reality which geography does not have the right to neglect . . . for without due regard to this human aspect it would turn into a sterile routine, to a monotonous chant of old Ratzelian litanies or of astrological formulas inherited from the distant past. We also feel justified in saying that geography has a duty to history, for the progress of the two disciplines is closely connected; they must march side by side. . . .

Against the spirit of premature generalization, Vidal de La Blache long ago said that the best defense is to make analytic studies, monographs where the relations between geographic conditions and social facts are viewed at close range on a well chosen and limited field. This program is still excellent. It remains only for us to be inspired by it.[6]

Vidal de La Blache first stated the basic conception of regional geography, with its insistence upon intensive study of natural geographic units and their effect upon society and culture, in an article on *Les Divisions fondamentales du sol français,* published in the *Bulletin littéraire* in 1888. He set forth the program of work much more thoroughly later in his *La France: tableau géographique,* and his followers have executed a large number of remarkable studies in the regional geography of France and outlying districts. His general principles of work and such generalizations as he brought out of his researches and those of his pupils are contained in a posthumous treatise, *Principes de géographie humaine* (now available in English translation). Vidal's regional approach has been broadened to reject the notion of geographic determinism and to accept the cultural point of view of the historians and of Durkheim and the cultural sociologists. In this process of amending the methodology of Vidal's school, the best general presentation has been provided by Lucien Febvre in his above-mentioned work.

It will probably be conceded that the outstanding living representative of French anthropogeography, conceived of from the newer regional and cultural point of view, is Jean Brunhes, whose chief general treatise, *La Géographie humaine,* was translated into English in 1924. He also collaborated with Vallaux, who has of late come to espouse the regional approach to anthropogeographical problems, in an extended interpretation of history from the geographical point of view, *La Géographie et l'histoire.* The regional conceptions and methodology in geography have been adopted not only in France, but in England, Germany, the United States, and elsewhere. Ferdinand von Richthofen has been the leader of this movement in Germany, A. J. Herbertson in England, and J. Russell Smith in the United States. Nowhere in the world today is anthropogeography more highly developed or more extensively cultivated than in France. The movement launched by Bodin and Montesquieu has traveled far to bear fruit in the works of Reclus, Vidal, Brunhes, Febvre, Vallaux, and DeMartonne.

Biologistic Theories in France. — By biologistic theories we mean those which base their explanations of social facts on some element of an essentially biological nature, or which interpret social reality in terms of analogies drawn from the science of biology. Historically there have been four main varieties of biologistic theories: social organicism, social Darwinism, social demography, and racialism.

As we have already noted, several French writers followed the false lead of Lilienfeld and Schäffle in turning sociology into a recondite branch of biology by the use of the organismic analogy. Curiously enough, however, the second of the earlier manifestations of biologism in sociology, namely, social Darwinism, was never espoused by any prominent French sociologist. In part this may have been due to the fact that the theories of the *Rassenkampf* and of the struggle for-existence were extensively popularized by Germanic writers. But it was probably much more largely the result of the unremitting warfare started in 1884 by Gabriel Tarde against all forms of biologistic sociology, and especially to two brilliant articles by Célestin Bouglé in the *Revue Philosophique* in 1900 and 1901 which disposed, with remarkable controversial skill, of the whole social Darwinist position. These arguments were later elaborated and expanded in his *La Démocratie devant la science.*

The closest approach to social Darwinism is to be found in studies of biological and social selection, best represented by the writings of Paul Jacoby and G. Vacher de Lapouge. In his *Études sur la sélection dans ses rapports avec l'hérédité chez l'homme* (1881), Jacoby took the position that civilization is antithetical to biological "progress," that social evolution is accompanied by biological deterioration. As culture advances, the upper classes tend to restrict births and to indulge in modes of life which result in biological deterioration, and hence the more important parts of the social structure steadily crumble until the whole finally topples in ruin. Out of the chaos another culture arises, and the process is repeated.

Lapouge arrived at equally pessimistic conclusions. His chief works are *Les Sélections sociales* (1896); *L'Aryen, son rôle social* (1899); and *Race et milieu social* (1909). Holmes has thus set forth his leading conceptions:

Lapouge has described the operation of several forms of social selection, i.e., military, political, religious, moral, legal, economic, and systematic, all of which are brought into play as a consequence of the development of civilization. Military selection, according to the author, eliminates the best of the race; political selection, through the effects of civil war, the prison, the scaffold, and exile, gets rid of the more independent spirits and tends thereby to render the population submissive and tractable; religious selection, through the celibacy of the clergy and by persecution, tends to effect the elimination of the more intelligent and independent minds; moral and legal selection in general produce dysgenic effects; and economic selection, while operating in many different ways, acts on the whole, in the most destructive manner, upon the superior elements of the race. As civilization becomes more advanced, the evil effects of the various forms of social selection become more intense. The racial influence of civilization is therefore bad. . . .

There is only one way by which these destructive forces may be overcome and that is by conscious, systematic selection, or, as we should now call it, eugenics; but Lapouge is not sanguine over the prospect that human beings will ever bring themselves to supply this remedy in a really effective manner.[7]

Lapouge, like most writers of this school, intertwined the notion of socio-biological selection with conceptions of racial superiority. Essentially similar in his basic outlook to Gobineau, although perhaps a bit more sophisticated in matters of method, he identified the social and biological élite with the " Aryan race." He then went on to show, to his own satisfaction at least, how the process of social selection operates with a peculiarly disastrous effect on the " Aryans " or Nordics, gradually leaving the unprogressive and generally inferior brachycephalic Alpines in a position of social ascendency. It has been unfortunate that Lapouge, like Ammon, Schallmayer, and even Pearson, confused the fertile field of research into the biological history of man and the physical effects of cultural evolution with the vague notion of definite bio-psychological differences (in terms of superior-inferior) among the sub-branches of the white race.

Other influential studies in social biology have been in the field of demography. One of the most prominent French representatives of this subject during the late nineteenth century was Adolphe Coste (1842–1901), whose doctrines are presented in his two books, Les Principes d'une sociologie objective (1899), and L'Expérience des peuples et les prévisions qu'elle autorise (1900). As set forth by Coste, the degree and the type of social evolution are causally connected with the growth and density of population. This bears some similarity to the thesis defended by an earlier writer, Paul Mougeolle, who in his Statique des civilisations (1883) maintained that the progress of civilization is correlated with the growth and density of population. Whether or not Mougeolle influenced Coste is uncertain, but we can at least say that it was on the basis of an assumption much like this that Coste set forth an equation of " social power " in relation to the rapidity of increase and density of population in the various states of the world. He also used this formula to construct an index of national power, with France as the base of 100. Coste represents one of the most extreme developments of demographized sociology and of the opposition to Neo-Malthusianism, and he did his share toward arousing French public opinion to the alleged dangers of the discrepancy between the birth-rates of France and Germany. A viewpoint essentially similar to Coste's is at present represented by the eminent Belgian sociologist, Eugène Dupréel.

Another famous French student of population problems was Arsène Dumont (1849–1902), promulgator of the so-called " law of social capillarity " of population growth. This was advanced in his book *Dépopulation et civilisation: étude démographique* (1890). Briefly stated, Dumont's " law " is to the effect that the tendency to restrict the birth-rate bears a direct relation to the degree of opportunity for individual achievement and advancement in the social scale, i.e., the greater the degree of freedom to rise through individual effort, the greater the tendency to limit the number of offspring. This seems to be simply the French equivalent of Spencer's " individuation *versus* genesis."

The French demographer and social historian Émile Levasseur (1828–1911) was quite optimistic regarding the relation of dense population to social well-being. Although he did not deny the evil effects of overpopulation where it actually existed, he contended in his three-volume work, *La Population française,* that the remarkable technological developments of the nineteenth century had increased productivity, potentially at least, so as practically to suspend indefinitely the operation of Malthus's law. Noneconomic considerations, particularly of a military sort, probably bulked very large in inclining these theorists to such a favorable view of the effects of population density. Such considerations are of course not lightly to be dismissed, but it would seem to be preferable to present them explicitly.

Sociologistic Theories: the Comtean Tradition. — By sociologistic theories we mean, in general, theories which assume that society is a reality *sui generis,* and that sociology must adopt as its ultimate explanatory principle some element which is itself social. It is obvious that what is understood by " society " and the

" social" is of the greatest importance in this connection. It will be maintained here that the sociologistic tradition in France has confused in varying degrees two different senses of these key terms. In the *first* sense, the " social " is to be contrasted primarily with the " psychological." Within the human being there are two elements which are *analytically* but not empirically separable. One is native, genetic, hereditary, comprising such things as instincts, prepotent reflexes, inherent capabilities, and the like — in short, the generic element of " human nature." This is the psychological element. The other is intrinsically *cultural,* i.e., transmitted from individual to individual and from generation to generation, not through the germ plasm, but by means of imitation, teaching, and deliberate imposition. It is this element which is thought to be social; and it comprises such things as religions, sciences, philosophies, arts, mores, practical techniques, and institutions. In a *second* sense, the " social " is opposed not to the " psychological," but to the " individual." The social is that which is not individual but characteristic of the *group;* it is an entity *sui generis,* an emergent reality created by the association of individuals. Thus in the *first* sense, " social " means *cultural;* in the *second* sense it means *collective.* The sociologistic school has in general, as we shall see, tended to confuse these two senses of the social, and has therefore fought two different antagonists simultaneously; it has been at the same time anti-psychologistic and anti-individualistic without attempting to distinguish between the two.

Comte is the true founder of the sociologistic school in France, and both these elements are clearly present in his thought. The *first* view of the " social " is implicit in his omission of psychology (except as a part of biology) from his original classification of the social sciences; and in his conviction that each level of reality must be understood in terms of the laws of its appropriate science, and that therefore social facts must be understood primarily on the basis of sociology and not of biology. The central explanatory categories of his own sociology, the supernaturalistic and naturalistic *Weltanschauungen,* are completely cultural and are precisely " social " in this first sense. The *second* view of the social is implicit in his thoroughgoing anti-individualism (inherited no doubt to a large extent from DeMaistre), and in his quasi-organismic view of society as an independent reality, individuals being only abstractions from that reality. It is evident in his insistence that in so far as there is any social unit, it is the family and not the individual. It also lies back of his profound preoccupation with the problem of social control and the reëstablishment of social consensus.

Neo-Comtean Theories: DeRoberty.[8] — Eugène Valentino-vitch de Roberty (1843–1915), the Russian Neo-Positivist and inventor of the " bio-social hypothesis," was educated partly in Germany, and lived and taught in France, Belgium, and Russia. The reasons for treating him in this chapter are at least two. First, most of his work was written and published in French. Second, his *sociological* work is an essential part of the French socio-logical tradition, and could hardly be understood in abstraction from it. It is deeply influenced by DeBonald and Comte, and forms a connecting link between the system of Comte and the system of Durkheim. DeRoberty's main sociological contributions may perhaps be summed up under three heads: (1) the bio-social hypothesis; (2) the classification of the four types of collective knowledge; and (3) the sociologistic theory of morals.

In 1872, DeRoberty became one of the two foreign members of the first *Société de sociologie,* a circle of Neo-Comtean positivists headed by Littré. In 1878, he first sketched the ground plan of his " bio-social hypothesis." [9] He took a firm stand on the specificity of the social and its irreducibility to the biological. Over and above the biological and hereditary faculties of memory, association, and sensation, there is, he claimed, a social or cultural element which cannot be reduced to it. The mind as we now perceive it, *in concreto,* is the result of the interaction of both elements. The science which studies the concrete mind as a whole is therefore a subsidiary and dependent science resting on biology on the one hand and sociology on the other. This science he calls psychology.

So far the analysis has run roughly in terms of the distinction between original nature and culture. At this point, however, we have a reversion to the second type of distinction, that between the *individual* and the *group*:

> Surely the biological individual, or the individual isolated from his fellows, manifests only elementary psychic properties. . . . However, as a result of association, which belongs to the particular order of phenomena studied in social science, the psychic phenomena of all types show a remarkable growth and development; the biological individual himself brought into this milieu, is radically transformed in his intellectual and affective faculties; he becomes a social atom.

Commenting briefly: this second distinction by no means follows from the previous one and is even incompatible with it, for strictly speaking, there is no biological individual, but only a biological *element* in the human being, which must be supplemented by a cultural element if we are to have a total person. The historical cases of various feral children demonstrate that, lacking contact with a culture, a truly human personality cannot develop. Now this contact with a culture is not the same thing as mere association; there will arise no culture through association unless the individuals in association are already *social* and not merely biological (or, as we would say, psychological).

In a discussion with DeRoberty, Tarde once expressed this objection very decisively:

If you pretend to found social science on simple *biological,* or — *à fortiori* — *physical* interactions of organisms, you are mistaken; from the physiological fact of association, if nothing intermental [i.e., social] is added to it, you can get forth absolutely nothing which differs essentially from the other intraorganic facts.[10]

We have seen that Comte made intellectual evolution the primary factor of general social evolution. Here DeRoberty remained in basic agreement with him.[11] But Comte had thought it was ultimate philosophical ideas, naturalism or supernaturalism, which played the dominant rôle. DeRoberty, on the contrary, insisted on the primacy of scientific thought.[12] Philosophical systems *resulted* rather from scientific ideas, the gaps of which they filled up and the conclusions of which they synthesized.

DeRoberty divided the totality of culture into four great classes, ranked in accordance with their evolutionary importance and causal priority.

We can, we believe, distinguish four principal categories of facts forming the framework of four kinds of intellectual evolution: (1) the evolution of ideas which have for their object the analysis of phenomena of all sorts, and their partial synthesis . . . in smaller or larger aggregates [science]. (2) The evolution of ideas which are concerned with the unity or the universal synthesis of phenomena [philosophy]. (3) The evolution of ideas which tend to reproduce in an artificial manner the emotions naturally evoked in us by the objects of the two preceding evolutions [art]. (4) The evolution of ideas which seek to satisfy the needs engendered by the three preceding evolutions and their objects [applied science, technology, or " action "].[13]

A third important contribution of DeRoberty was his sketch of a sociologistic theory of morals. Comte had already given the hint by suggesting that morality equaled sociability, that the degree of the moral was also the degree of the social. It is obvious that here he was thinking of the social in the second sense. Morality is the subjection of the individual to the exigencies of group welfare and his regulation in accordance with the facts of group structure. DeRoberty further explores the implications of this view, concluding that morals is a science of empirical observation which does not rest on any absolute, but on the sociological data:

> Truly, it seems to me impossible not to perceive that the only acceptable objective basis for the principles of morality . . . can be nothing else than the organization and detailed structure of the society and the laws which regulate this structure and its natural functioning.[14]

We have here the essentials of the *science des mœurs* later elaborated by Lévy-Bruhl, Durkheim, and Bayet.

The Development of Social Realism: Espinas and Izoulet. — Similar in many respects to the theories of DeRoberty were the sociologistic theories advanced by Alfred Espinas (1844–1922). An early and classical study of animal societies,[15] strongly organismic in flavor, was much influenced by Spencerian evolutionism. He even goes so far as to state that " a society is a living consciousness; or an organism of ideas." [16]

While Espinas never repudiated this early organismic approach, he moved closer to the sociologistic position, and later devoted himself to a number of brilliant empirical studies in which the sociologistic assumptions emerged more and more clearly. In his *Origines de la technologie* [17] he adopts a strongly anti-individualistic point of view, insisting on the rôle of the collectivity in the formation of technics. The arts are collective habits, analogous to instincts in the biological realm, and sociology is in part the study of these collective habits. The reverence for a given stage of technique as sacred, necessary, and immutable, found among preliterate peoples, consists at bottom, Espinas imagines, " in connecting what is orderly and permanent in the individual will with the will and the wisdom of the *group*." [18]

Perhaps exceeding even Espinas in moral earnestness and deepseated hatred of individualism was Jean Izoulet (1854–1929), author of *La Cité moderne, métaphysique de la sociologie.* Here DeRoberty's bio-social hypothesis was exploited with intense zeal and with considerable deficiencies in caution and perspective. Association, in itself, is invested with mysterious or even magical powers. On a biological level, it is the association of unicellular organisms which is responsible for the evolution of animal intelligence. Similarly, man in isolation is only an anthropoid:

> Primitive man . . . does not yet have reason or language. He does not think and does not speak. Like the animal he has sensation and vo-

cal expression, not reason and language. How do reason and speech arise. . . ? In and through association. . . . By an inexplicable miracle, society, which is constructed out of anthropoids, in the very act of constructing itself, transforms its materials and changes " anthropoids " into " men " — like a building which builds itself and nevertheless transforms its material from ordinary rock into precious marble.[19]

The individual, then, owes to association, to the group, his very mentality, his soul, as well as his real liberty — herein anticipating Mead and Cooley. Nevertheless man often shows himself ignorant of his debt to society and ungrateful for the benefits it has conferred on him. He revolts against group restraints, scorns group mores. He supposes that society is merely a convenience, a device for economic coöperation, which can be repudiated without any spiritual loss. Izoulet never tires of denouncing and castigating this view, which he takes to be characteristic of the individualistic tendencies in modern thought.[20] (A more detailed discussion of the ways in which association has developed human intelligence, treated in another chapter, is the main contribution of the Rumanian writer, D. Draghicescu.)

The Sociology of Durkheim.[21] — There can be little doubt that the dominating individual figure in recent French sociology was and is Émile Durkheim (1858–1917), formerly of the Sorbonne. In spite of the opposition of vested educational interests (he was the son of a Lorraine rabbi), he rose to one of the most important professorial positions in France. His influence on his contemporaries and on later French sociologists has been enormous. Most of the latter have been either *pro-* or *anti*-Durkheim, and very few of them have been unaffected by him. He gathered in his train a group of capable and energetic collaborators, many of them specialists in the allied fields of ethnology, history, psychology, juristics, economics, languages, and religion. The members of the " school " formed a well-disciplined and coöperative research group, guided for the most part by the main framework of his thought. One of the fruits of their joint labors was *L'Année sociologique,* edited by Durkheim from 1898 to 1912, and taken up again for a short period by Mauss in 1924–1925. This may legitimately be considered one of the most comprehensive and scholarly sociological reviews ever published.

Durkheim's own work is marked by extraordinary logical and dialectical gifts, coupled with a quite unusual erudition, attested by the wide range of empirical material found not only in his books but also in his numerous studies and reviews in *L'Année sociologique.* His originality is great, though his dependence on his sociologistic predecessors, particularly on Comte, is undoubtedly very considerable. (The influence of German sociology, made so much of by Deploige in *Le Conflit de la morale et de la sociologie*, is perhaps less important.) From Comte, Durkheim probably inherited the two central and basic tendencies of his own thought, i.e., positivism and sociologism. Comte, however, was primarily interested in social dynamics, whereas Durkheim is almost exclusively interested in essentially static problems of social structure and social control.

Sociology, according to the view held by Durkheim, is more a system or a method of investigation of social phenomena, permeating all the social sciences, than it is a definite and independent body of knowledge. The fundamental task of the sociologist is to infuse into the special social sciences the sociological method of procedure. This would prevent the social sciences from being detached, isolated, or *a priori* bodies of knowledge, and would weld them all into a coherent system and allow them to contribute to their mutual improvement. Though there may be in the future a place for " general sociology," in the sense in which this word is used by Giddings, Small, Wiese, and others, its data must be provided in advance by the special social sciences.

Certain interpreters of Durkheim have insisted that his general theories have been generated primarily out of certain basic methodological assumptions or intuitions.[22] Beyond doubt this element is important. Durkheim begins with a strong desire to make sociology a " positive " science. In line with a positivistic theory of methodology he wishes to treat social facts " as things," *comme des choses*. As in the physical sciences, all explanation must be mechanical; teleology is to be excluded. On this basis it is easy to understand Durkheim's clear-cut opposition to the use of introspective psychology.

By a second line of thought [23] starting from the same methodological assumptions, Durkheim arrives at an equally vigorous antiindividualism. The sociologist in treating social facts *comme des choses* treats them as having an objective nature of their own which is not affected by him and does not respond to his wishes. In an unconscious transition, Durkheim now shifts the center of reference from the scientist who is *studying* society to the individual who is *acting* in society, and assumes also that the social facts are similarly independent of and unresponsive to the volitions of individuals. They are *sui generis,* in a realm which is different from and *external* to the realm of individual phenomena; and just as the scientific facts *constrain* the scientist to think in certain ways which are conformable to the order of these facts, so the social fact must be understood as *constraining* the individual to conform to them. Some critics, thinking of the large part that constraining ritual observances play in the life of the orthodox Jew, have called Durkheim's system " Talmudic sociology." What has already been said about the irrelevance of origins with regard to validity should be recalled here.

Thus we have here what were for Durkheim the two distinguishing characteristics of the social fact, " exteriority " and " constraint." He arrives at them not only by the indirect route we have just sketched, but also as a direct implication from his sociologistic position itself. Society is viewed as an emergent reality, rising out of the collocation of individuals but with properties which do not depend on those individuals. This new reality *sui generis* is primarily a psychical, though *not* a psychological reality. As a *conscience collective,* it has ways of " acting, thinking, and feeling " different from the ways of the individual minds. Hence psychology, as the study of individual minds, can give us no clue to it. It is " exterior " to the individual mind only in the sense that the two are numerically distinct and on different planes of reality, *not* in the sense of *spatial* exteriority, which would be a meaningless kind of relationship between two psychic, nonmaterial entities.

Society also " constrains " the individual, and here Durkheim uses the term in at least two senses. First, the *group coerces* the individual and forces him to obey legal and moral rules by the fear of sanctions to be applied by the police courts, and public opinion respectively. Second, the *culture determines* what ethical ideals and what conceptual formulations the individual will have and hence indirectly how he will act.

From this there follows the methodological corollary that a social fact must always be explained by another social fact and never by a fact of an individualistic or psychological order. Thus the various elements in Durkheim's thought are synthesized in such a fashion as mutually to reinforce one another. The manner in which they are applied to the interpretation of concrete social phenomena we shall now examine.

The Division of Labor in Society: a Theory of Social Solidarity. — Individualism itself is a social phenomenon in the sense that it is an emanation of the morphological characteristics of the social group. This is the challenging conclusion of Durkheim's first major work, *De la division du travail social.* The respect for individuality and personal development, the tendency to judge men on the basis of innate worth rather than hereditary status, the narrowing down of moral and legal responsibility to the acting agent himself apart from his affiliations with family or regional groups, the right of the individual to express and embody his personal volitions in contracts, and the enforcements of such contracts by the legal system — all these are elements in one particular kind of group solidarity which Durkheim calls " organic " solidarity. This kind of solidarity is necessitated by and functionally dependent upon a particular state of group organization, namely, upon the extensive development of the division of labor (one of the characteristics of our " secular society ").

When division of labor is relatively undeveloped, the individuals are undifferentiated and largely lacking in individuality. Hence the solidarity which binds the group together is " mechanistic," based on the mental and moral homogeneity of the component individuals. Since the members of the group lack individuality and self-determination, moral and legal responsibility is collective, social status is apt to be hereditarily fixed, and a relatively small part of social life is ordered by the contractual principle (thus resembling, in *some* measure, our " sacred society "). The " mechanistic " and the " organic " types of solidarities thus characterize two antithetical types of social orders.

Individualism is inevitable and necessary in a society constituted, as is ours, on the basis of the division of labor. It teaches the individual to develop his own particular potentialities and to respect those of other men. All this looks at first sight very much like an apology for individualism. But it must be noted that this is a very special kind of individualism. It is a new kind of duty which the group *imposes* on the individual whether he likes it or not; it is thus exterior to him and constrains him. Moreover, Durkheim is quite insistent on demonstrating that even this kind of individualism is not by itself a sufficient principle of social cohesion, and is not an adequate explanation of the forms of social organization, even in our contemporary society where it does have such a large place. In an intensive analysis of the most typically individualistic of institutions, i.e., *contract,* he attempts to show that even here there are present important non-individualistic, institutional elements. Individual interests cannot in themselves create an enduring solidarity. They bring individuals together only temporarily and create only an " external " bond.

The obvious question now arises as to what has caused the great increase in the division of labor. It was difficult for Durkheim to find a truly sociologistic answer to this question. His system is monistic and static: it is society itself which explains everything. But this makes it difficult to explain diversity, and above all to explain change. Moreover, it was necessary for Durkheim to distinguish his position carefully from that of the utilitarians (e.g., Adam Smith and Spencer), who also had insisted on the central importance of the division of labor as consciously adopted for economic efficiency. Durkheim's objection to this sort of explanation is that it involves both individualism and teleology. Hence, as his first step in establishing a sociologistic explanation by the process of elimination, he feels it necessary to destroy the theory that the division of labor has resulted from the pursuit of human happiness.

The main argument is that the division of labor and the complex civilization which it makes possible have not in fact made mankind any happier. Primitive peoples seem just as happy as we. This argument appears decidedly weak; and considering how central the point is, it is astonishing that Durkheim could have been satisfied with it.[24] Failure to reach a goal does not necessarily mean that efforts toward it have been lacking. His subsidiary arguments, though more subtle, are likewise shaky.[25]

Having thus dismissed individualistic and psychological explanations of the division of labor, Durkheim gives his own explanation. The division of labor varies according to the size and density of a society, that is to say, in accordance with the number of people in the group and the number and intensity of social interactions. The basic cause of the division of labor is a great increase of population, which intensifies the struggle for existence, increases " social density," and makes further division of labor necessary if the standard of living is not to be depressed. That Durkheim should have picked on population increase and intensification of the struggle for existence as the basic explanatory factor is highly interesting, and shows how central was his anti-individualistic bias. But a demographic fact is, after all, biological and not social in the mental or cultural sense of the latter term. The use of this type of explanation has caused Durkheim, over his vigorous protests, to be classified as a materialist in certain quarters.[26]

Not only is this demographic explanation incompatible with important elements in Durkheim's own position, but it is also very weak in itself. In the first place, we cannot any longer believe in a universal natural tendency for population to increase. As was pointed out in Chapter One, recent ethnography has shown that most preliterate peoples use abortion, infanticide, and other devices for maintaining a stable population.[27] In the second place, any *de facto* increase in population might just as easily be dissipated by emigration and warfare as by division of labor. In the third place, in so far as division of labor is deliberately adopted as the most desirable of possible alternatives by which to mitigate the severity of the struggle for existence, it involves teleological activity in the pursuit of happiness. It is just this type of explanation which Durkheim rebuked the utilitarians for adopting.

Social Pathology and Therapy.[28] — Although Durkheim insisted on the autonomy of objective and impersonal scientific research in sociology, and warned against subordinating this element to the demands of social practice, his fundamental interests were moral in nature. He insisted that sociology would be of no value if it did not offer some guidance for action, and he was tremendously concerned with the problem of social control and the maintenance of social stability. The primary criterion of the health or "normality" of a social fact was, he decided, its generality. *On this basis he classified crime as normal and not pathological.* We now turn to Durkheim's diagnosis, on the basis of this theory of pathology, of the ills of contemporary society and his suggestions for their cure.

If the later and more advanced type of organic or functional solidarity is prevented by external or artificial interference from developing in proportion to the decline of repressive or "mechanical" solidarity, social cohesion and social control will be weakened and abnormal conditions will arise in society. The individual accustomed to the external and authoritative control of the sacred society finds it hard to adjust himself to the extremely complicated relations of modern secular life, and the functional solidarity of the secular society either has not developed enough as yet to furnish the necessary guidance for the individual, or else it has assumed such repugnant, forced, and unnatural forms that the individual rebels against it. We have in modern society, therefore, the growing prevalence of suicide, the antagonism of capital and labor, social anarchy, and general social maladjustment. This being the case, the abnormal conditions of modern society can be remedied only by strengthening the functional type of social solidarity and by making it possible for it to assume more adequate and equitable forms. Since the family is too narrow and unstable a group upon which to base a firm and comprehensive system of control, it is to an improvement of the occupational group that the practical reformer should direct his efforts. The occupational group is not only well adapted to enforce an adequate type of social control, but in addition this is likely to be more agreeable to the individual than the authority now inadequately exercised by the state, in that the individual can always be much more conscious of his interests in the occupational group. This last point leads directly to the proposal to strengthen the occupational group at the expense of the economic functions of the state, and to make it the basis of representation in the lawmaking body. The similarity of Durkheim's suggestions to those of syndicalism should not be taken to imply any agreement with socialism, guild or otherwise, on his part, although he had from the beginning been interested in socialism, and gave a course on the subject in 1895–1896 (edited by Mauss and published in 1928).[29] Durkheim finds himself in opposition to socialism because its main goal is the maximation of individual-want satisfaction; it differs from *laissez faire* theory only in supposing that government ownership and control is more efficient. In sharp contrast to socialism Durkheim conceives " communism " as interested in the state regulation of the economic life, not in order to make it more efficient, but to prevent its naturally anarchic character from destroying social stability. In this sense, Durkheim's sympathies are clearly with " communism " as opposed to " socialism," and it is here that the possible influence of Tönnies comes to mind (see Chapter Twenty-three).

A Sociologistic Theory of Suicide.[30] — We have seen how, in his previous book, Durkheim boldly challenged individualism and psychologism on a decisive issue by proposing a sociologistic theory of contract, and hence of individualism itself. Now suicides, which are usually conceived as individual acts of intentional self-destruction, seem at first sight equally unsuited to any but an individualistic and a teleological explanation. Yet it is characteristic of Durkheim's intellectual courage and insight that he should have again waged his controversy with psychologism and individualism over a particular issue which at first seems most favorable to their position.

To begin with, Durkheim refuses to define suicides as *intentional* acts of self-destruction. Intentions, he objects, are capricious, unreliable, and not scientifically observable. Moreover, he wishes to include as a special type of suicide, " altruistic suicide," deaths resulting from the willing *sacrifice* of the victim. (Charles Blondel has formulated some crushing retorts to these objections.)[31]

What are the causal factors on which suicide rests? Durkheim

is probably at his best in his brilliant statistical refutations of
theories which allege racial, hereditary, cosmic, or psychopathological factors to be the exclusive or main explanation of the
suicide rate. There is also an excellent criticism of theories of
imitation (which we will take up in the section on Tarde). His
assertion that individual motives, such as disappointment in love,
failure in business, and so on, are not real causes of suicide, is,
however, less plausible, and it is significant that his disciple, Halbwachs, refuses to follow him on this issue.[32]

In Durkheim's own theory, suicide results mainly though not
exclusively from conditions relative to the structure and functioning of groups. He makes first a number of statistical observations.
Catholics have a lower rate of suicide than Protestants, who in
turn have a lower rate than freethinkers. Married people with
children have a very low suicide rate, and childless couples and
widowers have a lower rate than the unmarried. Periods of political crisis and consolidation of in-groups, such as are produced
by wars and revolutions, are characterized by abnormally low
suicide rates. By a series of extremely ingenious statistical and
logical arguments, Durkheim then tries to demonstrate that these
facts can be explained in only one way: *the suicide rate is a function of the degree of integration of the group.*[33]

Insufficient participation by the individual in the life of social
groups, or insufficient integration of the social groups of which
he is a member, is in Durkheim's opinion the main cause of that
variety of suicide he has called " egoistic." The intellectual, the
dreamer, the sceptic, are peculiarly liable to this form of suicide.
Side by side with this is another form of suicide which Durkheim
calls " normless " (*anomique*) ; this is more apt to attack the
worldly man of affairs, particularly the business man. It arises
from an insufficient regulation of the individual's moral life by
the norms of a collective order. Rapid changes or crises may
shake this collective order so that it is powerless to regulate the
individual's aspirations; " normlessness " (*anomie*) prevails. Suicides following business depressions are the perfect example. It
is not the loss of wealth itself, however, but the moral disorder
incidental to the crisis which Durkheim thinks is basic. He attempts to bolster this by the assertion that " crises of prosperity,"
economic booms, also increase the suicide rate.[34]

The anti-individualistic thesis of Durkheim's study must now
be quite clear. Suicides, he insists, are caused by " suicidal currents" (*courants suicidogènes*), which act mechanically, and must
be conceived as strictly analogous to physical or chemical forces.

The action of these suicidal currents predetermines for each society a fixed and necessary yearly quota and distribution of suicides. The individuals who commit suicide are merely those who oppose the least resistance to these currents.

A Sociologistic Theory of Religion and of Knowledge. — Durkheim's last work, *Les Formes élémentaires de la vie religieuse* (1912), carries the sociologistic point of view into the explanation of religion, and sketches a new theory of knowledge. Religion is defined by two elements. First, it establishes a complete and absolute heterogeneity between the two realms of the sacred and the profane. The sacred is that which is set apart and forbidden and which inspires a particular sort of reverence (not in all respects the same as our usage of "sacred"). Second, a religion unites its adherents into a *group* or a moral community which is called a church. As usual, Durkheim's first step is an attempt to do away with the rival individualistic and psychologistic theories in the field, in particular with the animism of Tylor and Spencer and the naturism of Müller (see Chapter One).

Durkheim attacks these theories on a great many points, but only his fundamental objections can be noted here. First, these theories do not explain the absolute heterogeneity between the sacred and the profane. Second, they view religion as founded on illusion; they "explain religion away." He contends that on the contrary an adequate theory of religion must explain the sacred-profane antithesis, and must assume that anything so wide-spread and so long-enduring as religion has some basis in reality and in experience.[35]

With individualism and psychologism disposed of to Durkheim's satisfaction, he proposes his own sociologistic explanation of religion. We noted in an earlier chapter his social evolutionism, true to which he searched for the origins of the sacred in the "social protoplasmic" traits of Australian totemism (cf. Chapter Twenty). The analysis proceeds about as follows: depending on the season of the year, Australian life is either intensely solitary or intensely associative, i.e., the natives either wander about in small family groups or they assemble for the periodic orgies called *corroboris*. When in the semi-solitary state, life is "uniform, languishing, and dull," but when the natives are massed together for a *corrobori*, "everything changes." Crowd stimulation brings on a condition of intense emotional excitement in which all the ordinary restrictions of life are cast aside, everyone is carried beyond himself, and the idea of the sacred emerges.[36]

Durkheim goes on to discuss the way in which the idea of souls or spirits finally develops from the matrix of the sacred, and also attempts to show that the belief in immortality issues from the same source.

The sacred therefore is not illusory; it is not generated by any cosmic, individual, or psychological phenomena. Its true nature is *symbolic,* and there is only one thing it could symbolize: society itself — for it is only society which produces in the individual that mixture of awe and respect which is characteristic of his attitude toward the sacred. Thus the concepts of God and of other religious entities are only symbols; their proper reference is to society.

It is easy to perceive how scandalous such a conclusion has appeared to genuinely religious people. They insist that by God they emphatically do *not* mean society, and that Durkheim's sociology is merely a new and ingenious form of atheism. The Protestant and Catholic objections to Durkheim's sociology of religion may be found in P. de la Boullaye's *L'Étude comparée des religions,* and in G. Richard's *L'Athéisme dogmatique en sociologie religieuse.*

The other main feature of *Les Formes élémentaires de la vie religieuse* is the attempt to found a new theory of knowledge on sociologistic principles;[37] Durkheim commits himself to the by no means unambitious attempt to derive the fundamental categories of thought from the nature of society itself. First he criticizes the rival views which have so far dominated the field: empiricism and apriorism. Empiricism, he asserts, cannot explain how particular and contingent experiences could suggest the universality and necessity which seem to characterize the categories. Apriorism cannot explain where the categories have come from except by invoking some supernaturalistic principle. The Kantian alternative he dismisses without any very decisive objections. His own explanation is offered as combining the sound features in both the empiricistic and the aprioristic theories. It is society itself, he claims, which is at the origin of the categories: the categories reflect the very nature of society, and society imposes them upon the individual. Thus he agrees with the empiricist position that the categories have a natural origin, and reflect a natural reality (since society is a part of nature), but he shows also a possible source for their generality and necessity (since they affect the broadest features of society, and society forces them upon the individual mind).

Using this general approach, he seeks to reconstruct the origins of each of the main categories separately, giving special attention to time and space:

The category of class was at first indistinguishable from the concept of the human group; it is the rhythm of social life which is at the basis of the category of time; the territory occupied by the society furnished the material for the category of space; it is the collective force which was the prototype of the concept of efficient force, an essential element in the category of causality. However, the categories are not made to be applied only to the social realm; they reach out to all reality.[38]

This is clearly an excursion into philosophic territory, and Durkheim exposes himself to philosophic counter-criticism, which runs as follows: To bring in society adds nothing new whatever, for in so far as the categories reflect society alone, they are inadequate for understanding nature; and in so far as society itself is only a part of nature, there is no need to give it special consideration.

In favor of Durkheim's position, it must be said that it has undoubtedly helped to start a number of important investigations. In Germany, Mannheim and Scheler (also influenced by Marx) have developed the "sociology of knowledge." In France, mention must be made of the interesting studies of the development of Greek thought by Abel Rey and Pierre-Maxime Schuhl. In the same tradition is Marcel Granet's recent work on Chinese thought in which certain Chinese notions of space, time, number, totality, and the like are incontestably shown to bear the distinct impress of Chinese social institutions; our chapter on the ancient Far East is heavily indebted to Granet. Another of Durkheim's disciples, Alexandre Moret, has placed us under obligation to him in the Egyptian sections of the chapter on the ancient Near East.

Immediate Followers of Durkheim: Davy, Mauss, Fauconnet. — There can be no doubt that all of the sociologistic sociologists following Durkheim have been enormously influenced by him. Not all of the sociologists, however, who are usually listed as of the "Durkheim school" have been equally orthodox. Here we deal with the work of three of Durkheim's immediate followers and collaborators who have remained most faithful to both the general trend of his thought and the particular formulas in which it found expression.

The most resolute and intrepid defender of the Durkheimian sociology has perhaps been Georges Davy, of Dijon. In a very useful compilation of excerpts from the writing of Durkheim, and in various articles [39] he has jealously defended the master from all criticism, and has even given certain realistic tendencies in Durkheim's thought a more extreme and less guarded expression. For him the group is literally a separate being, above and beyond its constituent individuals, with its own mind, habits, and character.

Davy's main empirical investigation, *La Foi jurée,* is an important contribution to juristic sociology, and offers a completely sociologistic interpretation of contract. Durkheim, in his study of the division of labor, had been concerned to show that contract contains non-individualistic elements and presupposes a solidarity which it cannot itself generate. Continuing along this line, Davy finds that the earliest forms of contractual relationship grew out of the phenomena of adoption, blood brotherhood, and marriage; these united individuals in familistic relationships and gave them reciprocal rights and duties. The characteristic form of the contract, and the individualistic quest for personal prestige and power do not emerge, however, till we come to the phenomenon of the *potlatch,* the obligatory exchange of gifts in the interest of social prestige, as practiced by the Kwakiutl Indians of the Northwest American coast, by the Trobrianders, with their *kula* giving, and many other groups. In fact, says Davy, all advanced societies have had, at one stage in their development, some institution resembling the *potlatch.* In conclusion, he sums up as follows:

> Contract is thus not an invention of juridic individualism, it is an objective institution. . . . The evidence we have gathered does not give us any justification for the radical, and too frequently proposed, opposition between contract and status, and consequently between the individual and society. Quite on the contrary, we have observed contract rise out of status and borrow from it its obligatory force. It has finally succeeded in freeing itself from status. But its origin itself requires us to suppose that between these two institutions there exist necessary affinities.[40]

Marcel Mauss, of the Collège de France and the University of Paris, is one of the most direct and loyal of Durkheim's successors. After the World War and the death of Durkheim, he endeavored to reconstruct the school, and undertook the editorship of the new series of *L'Année sociologique* (published only during 1924–1925). He has also taken up the very important and arduous task of editing Durkheim's unpublished works. On assuming the editorship of *L'Année sociologique,* Mauss published an article entitled " Divisions et proportions des divisions de la sociologie," in which he discussed the advisability of retaining the categories Durkheim had used in classifying the materials published, and came to the conclusion that most of them were still well suited to the purpose. He added two categories, however, which partially cut across the old: " social physiology," which treats persons acting as parts of social structures, and " social morphology." This latter notion, so central in Mauss's thought, seems to have a somewhat varying content. Sometimes it is conceived in a very materialistic fashion. It is " the science which studies . . . the material substratum of societies, that is to say, the forms that it takes in establishing itself on the soil, the volume and the density of the population, the manner in which it is distributed, and thus the totality of things which form the seat (*siège*) of the collective life." [41] At other times it appears as concerned primarily with spiritual or cultural phenomena. The material entities studied by social morphology, says Mauss, include moral elements. Since these ideal or cultural elements are essentially collective rather than individual, however, they remain the subject-matter of sociology and not of psychology.

Embodying these methodological principles, Mauss has written several important monographs in ethnographic sociology.[42] Perhaps the most important of these is his study of Eskimo society. As a result of morphological factors, the Eskimos have two different moral, juridic, and economic systems and two kinds of religious life. " To a real community of ideas and interests in the dense agglomeration of the winter, to a strong mental, religious, and moral unity, there is opposed an isolation, a social atomization, an extreme poverty in moral and religious life during the scattering that occurs in the summer." [43] The similarity of this monograph to Durkheim's study of Australian totemism is quite striking.

Paul Fauconnet, another of Durkheim's collaborators and disciples, is the latter's immediate successor at the Sorbonne, where he is the present incumbent of Durkheim's chair of education and sociology. His main empirical investigation, *La Résponsibilité*, is a direct continuation of some of Durkheim's work, and is markedly similar in certain respects to the master's study of the evolution of criminal law.[44]

Casting aside our present philosophical and juridical conception that responsibility exists only in the case of a criminal " free agent," Fauconnet shows that historically children, insane people, idiots, corpses, animals, and even chattels have been held responsible at various times and places. This is explained by reverting to the Durkheimian theory of crime as an act which disturbs a strong and definite state of the collective conscience. Punishment is in its origin an endeavor to restore the emotional balance by a group-sanctioned act of retaliatory violence, but the question of *who* is to be punished is very secondary. The primary purpose is to wipe out the crime itself, and this is achieved by destroying some person, or even some *thing,* which is made to symbolize the crime. The true function of responsibility, then, is to focus and give a point of application for the felt need of inflicting punishment. It is only after a long course of social development bringing about a high degree of individualism and a serious concern for the individual conscience that society achieves the more spiritual and subtle notions characteristic of developed ethical reflection.

A Sociologistic Theory of Social Classes, and of Memory: Halbwachs. — Maurice Halbwachs, of the Collège de France, is one of the most eminent and productive of the Durkheim group. He has an unusual capacity for theoretical and psychological analyses, and is also the most able statistician among contemporary French sociologists.

His first major work, *La Classe ouvrière et les niveaux de vie* (1913), written somewhat under the influence of the French economist François Simiand, is a sociologistic interpretation of social classes and differential standards of living. Halbwachs insists, in the first place, that a social class cannot be defined solely in terms either of vocation or of income. Each society has a hierarchy of values which determines its particular idea of the good life. The higher classes are those who are enabled to live a life in conformity with these ideals, to achieve the major social values, or, as he prefers to put it, to lead a more intense social existence. There may be, however, groups whose mode of life bars them from the achievement of these values, either because of the smallness of their incomes, or the arduousness and peculiar characteristics of their occupation.

An intensive study of certain German labor statistics and budgetary data discloses that the members of the wage-earning class spent on the average a smaller proportion of their income on rent than the salaried employees, even when the respective total incomes were the same. This is not in conformity with Engels's earlier generalization that the proportion of income spent for rent (and also for clothing) remains approximately the same for all incomes. Halbwachs finds on the other hand that in the cases studied an increase in total income is spent ordinarily on food, not on rent. Halbwachs explains this by the fact that the proletarian is desocialized by the mechanical and socially isolated nature of his work. The smaller proportion of the total budget spent on rent reflects a lower valuation placed on domestic life and on the cultural amenities associated with it. This study fills in one of the most obvious gaps of the Durkheimian sociology. It shows how social classes and standards of living may be explained as a reflection of a set of common values and collective representations.

Turning now to a sociologistic explanation of memory, *Les Cadres sociaux de la mémoire* (1925), Halbwachs seeks to show that even this apparently irreducible psychological property of the individual mind must be explained as a product of group life. This study pushes the sociologistic thesis very far indeed, and is one of the most significant contributions to the growing literature of what has been called the sociology of knowledge, the linking up of the forms of knowledge themselves with social factors. Epistemologists have repeatedly pointed out that memory is an essential constituent or condition of knowledge as we experience it. A sociologistic explanation of memory is thus a very important step in a general sociology of knowledge.

Halbwachs begins with the alleged fact that memory, properly speaking, does not exist in dreams, that our dreams never reproduce in full and exact detail any episodes of our life. " The operation of memory depends upon the constructive and rational activity of the mind, of which the latter is entirely incapable during sleep." [45] Now it is in the dream that we are furthest from the influence of society. " Almost entirely detached from the system of social representations, the images are only raw material, capable of entering into all kinds of combinations. . . ." He concludes that it is this escape from the collective representations which makes it impossible for us to remember in our sleep. It is because " the dream rests only on itself, while our memories depend upon the memories of all our fellows and on the great framework of the memory of society."

The manner in which we attempt to localize and fix our memories further confirms Halbwachs's thesis, " To localize a memory, it is necessary to link it up with a group of others, the temporal locus of which one knows." [46] These memories which serve as the basic framework of memory, and by relation to which we locate our individual memories, are not themselves individual. They are memories common to groups. Thus, for example, we localize an individual memory by relating it to the history of our family, by placing it in relation to some of the important episodes, births, marriages, deaths, and the like, which have occurred in it. Essential to memory as we experience it, moreover, is the use of words and concepts which we acquire solely as members of society.

Halbwachs's recent study of suicide, *Les Causes du suicide* (1930), treats the subject in a less original but in a more balanced and conciliatory way than did Durkheim. Although Halbwachs strives to minimize the extent of his divergences from the work of his predecessor, he differs from him on several important points. In the first place, he makes a very important concession to individualism and psychologism. Instead of seeking to bar out individual motives of suicide as irrelevant, Halbwachs admits that individual motives are real and causally important, but insists that they themselves reflect the larger social forces. Social forces work through individual motivation. He also makes a noteworthy concession to psychologism by admitting that *all* suicide has a psychopathic aspect.

He differs clearly from Durkheim on a number of specific points. He refuses to define suicide so as to include the phenomenon of deliberate self-sacrifice, takes a less pessimistic view of the importance of the rising suicide rate, and presents evidence to controvert Durkheim's assumption that suicides increase in times of prosperity. Although he substantiates Durkheim's contention that Catholics have ordinarily a lower rate of suicide than Protestants, he points out that Protestant rates vary greatly, that urban Catholics may have a higher rate than rural Protestants, and that the Catholics Durkheim studied had a higher concentration in the rural regions.

In addition to these critical observations, Halbwachs has made certain interesting original discoveries about suicide. First, he finds that the suicide rate is losing in acceleration and approaching stabilization. Second, he notes that in each country the increase in the total rate is almost entirely due to an increase in the rate of those rural regions which have previously had the lowest rate. Thus all the regions tend to approach one another and to stabilize at a common upper level. From this he concludes that a low rate of suicide is fundamentally correlated with the rural way of life, with the whole complex of peaceful and uneventful traditionalism, of sacredness (in *our* sense) associated with the life of the village or the small town. The rise of a secular, urban civilization produces a great increase in complexity, mobility, and change, exposing the individuals to many more shocks and rebuffs, and to frequent feelings of maladaptation. It is this factor on which a rise in the suicide rate must be blamed.

The Sociology of Democracy: Bouglé. — Célestin Bouglé, of

the Sorbonne and the *École Normale Superieure,* has been most
influenced by Durkheim and Simmel. While he has always been
more or less affiliated with the Durkheim school, he has been severely critical of the master on several issues. He early warned
against any theory of the group mind, and definitely refused to
accept the sociologistic theory of knowledge. Together with
Richard, he has insisted that the pathological cannot be adequately
defined in terms of the abnormal, and that sociology cannot of
itself generate ethically valid norms for action. He has also
claimed, on methodological grounds, that it is necessary for sociology to coöperate with psychology, to make use of introspec-
tion, and to interpret its material teleologically rather than mechanically.[47]

Bouglé's main interest has been in egalitarianism and democracy. His definition of egalitarianism is itself important. The
" egalitarian idea " is above all an ideal or value. It does not
assert that men are in fact equal, but that they ought to be. But
note that by equal it does not mean identical. It clearly recog-
nizes ineradicable differences between persons, and accordingly
holds that social rewards ought not to be uniform, but rather proportional to the value of the individual's merits and social contribution. The individual's merits, however, can be fairly measured only when the external conditions of competition are equal
for all, and the equality demanded by egalitarianism is therefore
an equality of *opportunity,* the abolition or severe restriction of
all non-genetic hereditary advantages.

The main thesis of *Les Idées égalitaires* (1899) is that the success of egalitarianism in our society has resulted from the influence of certain social forms; namely, increasing population, mobility, centralization, and social complication.

The increase in population and in the size of the social group
has lessened ethnocentrism, increased the number of social contacts, and made it necessary to judge people in accordance with
their individual merits rather than their family status. Social
complication makes it possible for the individual to belong to
several intersecting social groups. This makes for individuality
and a richer and more diversified personality. Social mobility,
which results in the individual's passage from one social status
or set of social relationships to another, encourages egalitarianism
in a similar fashion. Again, centralization or unification of a society helps to free the individual by lightening the tryanny of the
small, local group.

Turning now to the study of the completely anti-egalitarian society of India, Bouglé finds, in his *Essai sur le régime des castes* (1908), that the caste system is distinguished by certain predominantly morphological characteristics; namely, hereditary specialization of profession, a rigid social hierarchy with an unequal division of rights, and the separation of society into sharply demarcated, mutually repellent groups. The explanatory factors on which Bouglé finally comes to rest are clearly ideological, namely, a set of religious and magical beliefs — *karma, samsara, mukti, dharma* (see Chapter Two). The caste hierarchy is based entirely on the exalted position of the sacerdotal Brahmans, and the preoccupation with the preservation of religious purity makes caste atomism necessary and supplies a criterion of caste status. The whole anti-egalitarian social structure is given an ethical justification by the fundamental Hindu belief in reincarnation.

In 1900 and 1901 Bouglé wrote for the *Revue Philosophique* a series of two articles which seriously challenged the new movement of social Darwinism and exposed its weaknesses with extraordinary controversial ingenuity.[48] The attack on biologistic sociology was extended and given more specific and concrete shape in *La Démocratie devant la science* (1903), which attempted to meet the criticism that the democratic ideal is in fundamental opposition to biological processes (e.g., differentiation and the struggle for existence) and is hence "unscientific" or utopian. It has been claimed by opponents of democracy that the evolution of organisms is closely dependent on the increase in differentiation, and that egalitarianism halts or reverses the trend to increasing social differentiation. Against this Bouglé urges the following objections: (1) on the biological level, differentiation is not always an advantage, and must always be kept within certain limits of the possibility of integration; (2) societies are not organisms; (3) in society, the proper analogy of biologic differentiation is not a caste-like separation and hereditary specialization of large social groups, but an increase in the differences among *individuals* and a proliferation of free special-interest associations.

Our present class system has often been supported as stimulating competition and being in accord with the Darwinian principle of the struggle for existence. Bouglé points out that this principle, even on a biological level, has been overstressed. The inheritance of property and status has falsified the whole analogy to natural and sexual selection, since the success of the individual or his marriageability depends not on his personal qualities but on the social advantages which he has acquired by birth. From this point of view, hereditary social classes rather restrict than augment the area of competition, and democracy is precisely the attempt to extend such competition and make it socially useful. Bouglé has also succeeded in showing how new ends and aspirations and the liberation of new social forces enable society in a way to " surpass " nature. He seems definitely to have refuted the social Darwinistic arguments against democracy — though he has not attempted, in this book, to answer criticisms on other levels.

In *Leçons sur l'évolution des valeurs* (1922),[49] Bouglé adopts a moderate and tempered sociologistic position in the explanation of the genesis of human values, and attributes to them a very considerable rôle in social existence. His latest book, *Bilan de la sociologie française contemporaine* (1935), is an excellent little study of French sociology in recent years, with special emphasis on the interrelations of sociology and the other special social sciences.

A Sociologistic Theory of Insanity and of Volition: Blondel. — Charles Blondel of Strasbourg, while perhaps primarily a psychologist, has been deeply influenced by sociological thought: his work may be viewed as a remarkable convergence of the influences of Bergson and Durkheim. In an extremely interesting clinical study of insanity, he comes to the conclusion that insanity is primarily the result of a desocialization of the mental life, an abandonment of the mental framework, which is collective in origin.[50] The psychotic case loses the power of conceptualization and the ability to control the flow of his private impressions. He loses his hold on a common language, and his emotions become more and more ineffable and incommunicable. He finally comes to lack even the power of volition.

This last point is connected with Blondel's theory that even the individual will is a social product.[51] Blondel views the act of will not as a purely internal phenomenon but as a tendency striving to exteriorize itself in action. It is society which provides the instruments, the tools, and techniques by which the fulfillment of the tendency becomes possible. But it does more than this: it provides the *ideal* which sets the action in motion. It is just this which distinguishes human action from the instinctive life of the lower animals; the presence of an ideal is necessary before there can be *human* volition.

Blondel's methodological theses are given fullest expression in the *Introduction à la psychologie collective.* He believes that psychology falls into three departments: physiological psychology, collective psychology, and individual psychology, and that individual psychology is dependent upon and anterior to collective psychology. This, he attempts to show, is also the opinion of Comte, Durkheim, and Tarde. It is, he feels, a task of the most pressing importance for psychology to disentangle the collective elements in the functioning of the individual mind, and he performs preliminary analyses of this sort with respect to memory, perception, and the affective life. In a recent study of suicide, *Le Suicide* (1933), Blondel changes his position somewhat and criticizes the sociologistic interpretation of suicide. He insists that only a psychopathological explanation can be adequate. Especially effective is his criticism of Durkheim's definition of suicide.[52]

The Science of Morals and the Theory of Primitive Mentality: Lévy-Bruhl. — Lucien Lévy-Bruhl, of the Sorbonne and editor since 1916 of the *Revue Philosophique,* is a loyal disciple of Comte. His sociological contributions have been along two lines: a sociologistic " science of morals " and a theory of primitive mentality.[53]

In *La Morale et la science des mœurs* (1900), he developed certain ideas which we have already seen put forth by Comte, DeRoberty, and Durkheim with regard to a science of moral facts. Beginning by an attack on speculative moral or ethical philosophies, he insists on the need of an empirical study of the *facts* of moral judgment in particular societies. Such moral judgments and their variation in different societies must be taken as sheer *data* by the sociologist of morals.[54]

Each social type has its own appropriate set of moral judgments expressive of its peculiar nature; it would be vain to suggest an alternative morality. Here we have agreement with Sumner's contention that the mores can make anything right. Does this mean that the science of morals is purely descriptive and can offer no guidance for action? Is Sumnerian *laissez faire* the last word? " This conclusion does not necessarily follow at all. Science procures us means of modifying physical reality to our advantage. There is no reason, *a priori,* why it should not give us the same power over social reality when it has made sufficient progress." [55] Thus there will be an *applied* science of morals which will be a guide for action, just as are the applied sciences of medicine, hygiene, and engineering.

As a program of research, Lévy-Bruhl's suggestion has already had some interesting and valuable results in the works of Albert Bayet,[56] especially as embodied in his *La Suicide et la morale* (1922). This remarkable work is a veritable mine of erudition; as a piece of " empirical " sociological research it far surpasses in significance and permanent value most of the projects which customarily assume that title.

It is Lévy-Bruhl's theory of "primitive mentality," however, which has provoked the most intense controversy, a controversy in which psychologists and anthropologists as well as sociologists and philosophers have joined. Lévy-Bruhl feels that preliterate man's magical, animistic, and supernaturalistic beliefs cannot be explained as solely due to deficiencies of knowledge and mistaken association of ideas. They must be attributed rather to a unique type of thinking characteristic of "primitive mentality," a type of thinking which is dominated by collective representations of a thoroughly "mystical" nature. Lévy-Bruhl defines mysticism as a "belief in forces and influences which, though imperceptible to sense, are nevertheless real." [57] As a result of this mysticism, preliterate man is "pre-logical," "impervious to experience," living in a world quite different from our own. This world is not integrated, as is ours, by logical connections, but rather by what Lévy-Bruhl has called the "law of participation." The fundamental postulate of our logic, the law of contradiction, is blithely disregarded.[58]

In support of these adventurous theses Lévy-Bruhl has gathered an enormous amount of ethnographic data bearing on preliterate man's systems of classification, his belief in contagious and homeopathic magic, and his conception of time, space, causality, death, omens, the soul, the dream, the supernatural and similar matters.[59]

But although the sheer mass of the data is imposing, Lévy-Bruhl's interpretations have been seriously challenged by the Durkheimians. By making a complete antithesis between "primitive" and "civilized" thought, and insisting that there is no possible connection between them, he has come into sharp conflict with Durkheim's view that "civilized" scientific thought was generated out of "primitive" religious thought.[60] Moreover, the rôle of the group and of purely morphological factors has not been sufficiently indicated to satisfy Mauss.[61]

Other critics, particularly Goldenweiser in the United States, Malinowski in England, and Leroy in France, have been inclined to hold that preliterate man does think logically and does act rationally in at least certain areas of his experience, and particularly in his technological and industrial life. Raoul Allier, in his *La Psychologie de la conversion chez les peuples noncivilisés* (1925), and in his *Le Noncivilisé et nous* (1928), assembles much evidence to disprove the assumption that there is a complete gap between "primitive" thought and our own, and that in "primitive" society the individual is wholly dominated by the group. These objections are further reinforced by Daniel Essertier in *Les Formes inférieurs de l'éxplication* (chap. v). Many of the philosophers, particularly Parodi, Belot, Lapie, and Brunschvicg, have also made numerous objections.[62]

Psychologistic and Individualistic Theories: Tarde.[63] — Psychologistic theories attempt to explain social phenomena by some elements in the *hereditary nature* of mankind. Individualism, on the other hand, insists on the importance of the individual in society; it denies that a *group* of individuals constitutes a new emergent reality, that mind can exist dissociated from a biological organism, and hence that there can be in any strict sense a group mind. It denies that association in itself has fundamental creative powers, or that it can become an adequate principle of sociological explanation. We have seen how the sociologistic school in its common antagonism to both psychologism and individualism has tended to confuse them with one another. Unfortunately, the antagonists of the sociologistic school have in general defended both psychologism and individualism and have not distinguished the two doctrines any more successfully than have their opponents. Nevertheless, the distinction is an important one. A psychologistic element such as the asserted "instinct of imitation" is *not* individual, but is common to all the members of a social group, or a plurality of social groups. Similar in this respect are the sexual instinct, the parental instinct, and a great number of other drives, tropisms, and forms of mental activity. An individualistic sociology, on the other hand, should ideally concern itself with the *total* human being, not merely with the psychologistic or "hereditary nature" element in the individual. It therefore treats as an essential part of its explanation the cultural element, and insists that culture can exist only in the minds of individuals and has no existence outside of the totality of individual minds.

In France psychologism has on the whole tended to remain on the defensive. The two most important positive psychologistic systems are those of Tarde and LeBon. Tarde of course is the most eminent protagonist in France of both psychologism and individualism, but LeBon combines a definitely psychologistic slant with a theory of the group mind, thus confirming our assumption that between psychologism and individualism there is no necessary logical affiliation.

In France, individualism has been on the whole much more

important than psychologism. It is from the individualists that the most acute and cogent criticisms of the Durkheim school have come. In fact, the best statements of the individualistic position are to be found in the large literature of Durkheim criticism in France.

We turn now to the work of the man who, in recent French sociology, has shared the center of the stage with Durkheim, who has given one of the most spirited and original defenses of both psychologism and individualism, and who has produced a classic sociological system. This system of Gabriel Tarde (1843–1904) centers around the sociological importance of the principle of psychological imitation. Taine has called it the key which opens all doors.

To be sure, the idea of imitation as a factor in sociation was not new; a century and a half before Tarde, Hume had emphasized its action in his brilliant essay on *National Character,* in which he defended the idea of imitation as producing those uniformities of culture attributed by Montesquieu to geographic influences. The emphasis placed upon imitation by Bagehot and Huxley is also well known. Finally, at about the same time that Tarde was elaborating his doctrine, similar views were being put forward by a number of writers, among them Bordier, Espinas, Baldwin, James, and Royce.[64] But no one has approached Tarde in the completeness and thoroughness of his analysis of imitation, and he alone has constructed a well-knit and elaborate sociological system on this basis. Wiese has summarized this aspect of his doctrine:

From his point of view, imitation is simply a manifestation of personal influence exercised by one human being upon another: A gives B occasion to imitate him. Tarde regards the influence exerted as different in degree only from that exercised by the rapport of the hypnotist, hence imitation is " a mild sort of somnambulism." The sociologically important point in Tarde's theory is the assertion that all new culture traits, e.g., words, mythological images, ritual acts, etc., emanate from creative " individuals " and are imitated by the " crowd." In order for new kinds of social behavior to arise, two processes are therefore necessary: the creative process in the individual and the imitative process in the group.

The trait imitated Tarde terms an " invention "; this is always the product of a creative mind. The basic theme of history is invention and imitation.

Tarde further asserts that the creative man is qualitatively different from the crowd of imitators. The latter are passive, credulous, and impressionable, and in addition do not know that they possess these traits. The innovators, on the other hand, appear odd or even monomaniac; an impregnable self-confidence is characteristic of most of them, and hence the gaping imitators often regard them as " madmen of an odd kind." The ideas of the inventor, says Tarde, do *not* originate in the society surrounding him; the process of invention is the secret of genius, cannot be rationalized, results from free combinations, and is not the result of scientific method.[65]

Imitation, however, was only the central theme of Tarde's system of sociology, and it now remains to examine the whole structure. He finds that social processes consist fundamentally in the intermental activities of a group of associated persons. These intermental activities take place through the three fundamental processes of *repetition* (imitation), *opposition,* and *adaptation*; and these in turn operate upon the beliefs and desires of individuals and societies.

In other words, beliefs and desires are the raw psychical material of sociation; intermental activity is the general process through which sociation is achieved; and repetition, opposition, and adaptation are the special processes through which intermental activity accomplishes its work.

Tarde finds that these three principles of repetition, opposition, and adaptation will serve as the basis of a cosmic philosophy as well as for the foundation of a system of sociology. They are the three great factors in the development of all sciences and all phenomena. His general thesis is twofold: (1) in the thoughts and observations of men regarding the operation and existence of these three fundamental processes, historic progress has been from the observation of the large-scale and sometimes fantastic examples of repetition, opposition, and adaptation to the discovery of the minute and fundamental examples which go to make up the greater; (2) in the actual world of phenomena the repetitions, oppositions, and adaptations proceed in the reverse order from the minute and fundamental to the great and extensive.

It will be impossible in this place to do more than summarize his main points concerning sociology and sociation. In the field of social phenomena one may discover the same inversion of order between theory and fact in regard to *repetition* as was noticed in regard to phenomena in general. Beginning with the earlier superficial observation of picturesque social repetitions, such as the classical theory of the cycles of government or the triads of Vico and Hegel, the scientific sociologist has now come to regard as fundamental the repetitions of two persons in a state of association. In the same way, the reversal of observed progress to actual progress in repetition is manifested by the fact that social repetitions proceed in a geometrical ratio from the fundamental one of two persons (here Wiese's emphasis on the pair is anticipated) to that of international repetition or imitation. As it is under the head of repetition that Tarde would include the fundamental process of imitation, it might be well at this place to interpolate a brief summary of his analysis of the mode of action of this principle in social life as developed in his *Les Lois de l'imitation*. Davis sums up his treatment thus:

I. The source of social action is in individual initiatives expressed in new ideas of procedures called *Inventions*. II. The essential social and socializing act is *Imitation*, by which Inventions become more or less socially accepted and socially influential. III. The *origin* of an Invention is influenced by: (a) The inherent difficulty of combining mentally the ideas whose combination *is* the invention; (b) The grades of innate mental ability in the society; (c) The social conditions favoring mental alertness and the expression of ability. IV. The *imitation* of an invention is affected by: (a) The *general law* that imitations spread from their initial center in geometrical progression, with regard to the number of persons affected; (b) *Physical and biological* inferences, including race characteristics; the general law being that " Imitations are refracted by their media "; (c) *Social* influences: (1) *Logical:* the agreement or disagreement of the new invention with the inventions already more or less socially accepted (imitated); (" Logical causes operate whenever an individual prefers a given imitation to others because he thinks it is more useful or more true than others, that is, more in accord than they are with the aims or principles that have already found a place in his mind."); (2) *Extralogical:* (x) Ideas are transmitted before means; imitation goes *ab interioribus ad exteriora;* (y) Imitation proceeds from the socially superior to the socially inferior; (z) Ages of custom, in which the past has peculiar prestige, alternate with ages of fashion, in which prestige is possessed by the novel and the foreign.[66]

In regard to the principle of *opposition* in sociology and society, the earlier oppositions observed by students of society were the mythological struggles between the forces of good and evil. Next came the idea of the conflict of races and nations, softened by the economists into the notion of competition. Finally, however, the sociologist has reduced the matter so that he correctly understands that " the really fundamental social opposition must be sought for in the bosom of the social individual himself, whenever he hesitates between adopting or rejecting a new pattern offered to him, whether in the way of phraseology, ritual, concept, canon of art or conduct." [67] The three main types of social opposition are war, competition, and discussion, mentioned in the order of their historic predominance. Each of these forms has tended to develop on a larger scale, and again verifies the thesis that the order of the progress of phenomena in fact is the reverse of the order of the observation of these facts.

With respect to the third great principle, *adaptation,* the sociological observation of this principle was first confined to the somewhat fantastic ideas of the philosophy of history, whereby the path of history was looked upon as the result of the adaptation or harmonizing of the work of one nation to that of the nation which had preceded it or was to follow it, thus making the advance of historical action appear as a harmonious and teleological whole. These ideas were gradually made more scientific until now, according to Tarde, we know that " we must seek the fundamental social adaptation in the brain and individual mind of the inventor " — a harmony among the ideas in the minds of the individuals in society is essential to a harmony of the minds of the different members of a society. Following the usual rule, the adaptation of social phenomena proceeds from the lesser to the greater — from those in the individual mind to those adaptations between nations upon which must be based the expectation of eliminating war in the future.

In summing up the interrelation of the action of these three principles of repetition, opposition, and adaptation, Tarde says:

These three terms constitute a circular series which is capable of proceeding on and on without ceasing. It is through imitative repetition that invention, the fundamental social adaptation, spreads and is strengthened, and tends, through the encounter of one of its own imitative rays with an imitative ray emanating from some other invention, old or new, either to arouse new struggles, or to yield new and more complex inventions, which soon radiate out imitatively in turn, and so on indefinitely. . . . Thus of the three terms compared, the first and third surpass the second in height, depth, importance, and possibly also in duration. The only value of the second — opposition — is to provoke a tension of antagonistic forces fitted to arouse inventive genius.

The mutual relations of our three terms — repetition, opposition, and adaptation — are easily understood when we consider successive repetitions as operating sometimes in favor of adaptation, which they spread and develop by their own interferences, sometimes in favor of opposition, which they arouse by interferences of another sort.[68]

The Durkheim-Tarde Controversy. — For a quarter of a century there existed a spirited and brilliant controversy between

Tarde and Durkheim. This has been extensively deprecated by those who are perturbed at controversy in the social sciences, but it was inevitable and desirable that two such bold and honest thinkers should have realized the points at which their respective systems clashed. We may, however, admit that the followers of Durkheim and Tarde have often exhausted themselves in mutual denunciation instead of showing appreciation of the sound elements in the opposing theories. Unfortunately, there is lacking as yet any definitive treatment of the controversy which brings out the basic issues and synthesizes the partial truths involved in both sets of negations and affirmations. We have space here for only a mere sketch of one central aspect of the controversy: the nature of the social fact.

Durkheim's essential criticism of Tarde is well expressed in a section of *Le Suicide* in which he discusses imitation.[69] That concept, he notes, is customarily used to include three sets of phenomena: (1) the similarities of social thought or behavior which are the result of the working of similar forces on all the individuals; (2) the similarities of behavior which come from the acceptance of customs, traditions, or fashions; and (3) the reproduction of actions which we have seen or heard about merely for the sake of imitating them — "aping for its own sake." Obviously enough, it is only the third class that should strictly be called imitation, for in the first there is no reproduction, but merely a number of similar results flowing from similar causes, and in the second no mechanical reproduction and no evidence of any instinct of imitation.[70] "There is imitation only when an act has for its immediate antecedent the representation of a similar act previously accomplished by somebody else without there being, between the representation and the execution of the act, any implicit or explicit intellectual operation relative to the intrinsic characters of the act reproduced." [71] In this sense imitation cannot be used either to define the social fact or to explain any extended range of social phenomena.

Durkheim has here put his finger on the essential weak spot of the Tardean system (anticipating Faris's critique, be it noted, by twenty years). By a loose use of the concept of imitation, Tarde is enabled on the one hand to make it cover a whole range of *cultural* phenomena, and on the other hand to retain certain specifically *psychological* connotations. By the use of this concept he can pretend to explain social or cultural phenomena by appeal to certain fundamental traits of "original nature," i.e., explain them psychologically. But, in fact, if the concept is used in its

strict psychological sense, it cannot explain the cultural phenomena in question; and if it is used in a broader sense, it is no
longer a psychological explanation. Tarde himself goes far beyond the strictly psychological significance of imitation in
most of his sociological thinking. Quite incompatible with the
psychologistic conception of imitation as " a mild form of somnambulism " is his insistence on the basic character of consciousness in social facts:

> Consciousness is the postulate of sociology as movement is the
> postulate of mechanics. . . . The elementary social fact is the communi-
> cation or the modification of a state of consciousness by the action of
> one conscious being on another.[72]

Moreover, Tarde clearly distinguishes the social from the
merely physiological:

> Not everything that the members of a society do is social. Many of
> their acts, I might say the larger part, are purely physiologic or purely
> psychological. To breathe, digest, wink, move the legs mechanically . . .
> these acts have nothing of the social, except in the case where they are
> the effect of a habit contracted in commerce with other men and born of
> a wish or a belief which they have communicated to us. But to speak to
> someone, to pray to an idol, sew a garment . . . these are social acts, for
> it is only man in society who acts in this fashion, and without the example
> of other men which he has copied, voluntarily or involuntarily, ever since
> the cradle, he would not act thus. The common character of social facts,
> then, is to be imitative. They alone have this character; and, when an act
> which, ordinarily, is purely vital or mental, becomes by exception social,
> it is insofar as it has received a special imprint by virtue of imitation.[73]

It is therefore clear that the distinctive character of the social
is that it is based on contact with other men or " born of a wish
or a belief which they have communicated to us." This latter
point may very plausibly be understood to refer to a tradition,
a value-system, or a set of beliefs, possibly crystallized and preserved in some impersonal super-organic medium (science, religion, law, literature, philosophy, art, and the like). And this is
precisely what we mean by culture.

This interpretation is reinforced by Tarde's point that over
and above men's differences in physiological substructure there
exists a unifying realm. " There is psychologically a common substance, so to speak, namely a belief or a desire transmitted from
mind to mind." [74] Tarde is here no longer thinking of the psychological *mechanism* by which culture is transferred from one mind

to another, but of the *content* of the particular acts of "imitation," i.e., of culture itself.

Further, it is significant to note that Tarde divides the realm of imitations into two main classes: desires and beliefs. It should be observed, however, that Durkheim's strict definition of imitation makes it relevant only for *acts,* not for desires or beliefs. And, indeed, strictly speaking, we do not *imitate* other peoples' beliefs and ideals. They are transmitted to us, they arouse in us comparable states, but they are not imitated. It is apparent then that there is an important non-psychologistic aspect of Tarde's thought, and some re-interpretation of his work from this point of view would be highly desirable.

Tarde's criticism of Durkheim centers around the latter's conception of the social fact as essentially characterized by exteriority and constraint. The social fact is external to the individual and imposes itself upon him. It is, as Tarde asserts, *common* to the members of a group, but this fact must be explained by the coercive and constraining power which as a social or collective fact it exercises over them.

In respect to the first of these criteria (exteriority), Tarde makes the shrewd and telling comment that the (partial) externality of the social fact to any one individual does not prove its externality to all the individuals in a society taken together.[75] Durkheim's assumption of the externality of the social fact in this latter sense fatally involves a wholly unscientific hypostatization of the group mind.

Tarde's second criticism is of the notion of constraint. He asserts that this unduly limits the range of social facts, confining it to such phenomena as political conquest, master-slave relationships, and related types of conduct. This objection may seem shallow to the Durkheimians, who may reply that Durkheim means *moral* more often than physical constraint. But this response in turn requires examination. If what is meant here is the intrinsic appeal of certain ideals and ethical norms to the individual's conscience, it is doubtful whether the term "constraint" is appropriate. There is an important theoretical difference between coercing the individual's will by the application of penalties, and forming or determining his will by suggesting to him ideals and ethical norms which lead him to act voluntarily in the way desired. This distinction should not be allowed to be blurred because in some cases, such as in obedience to the laws of the state, both elements may in fact be present and hard to distinguish empirically.

Without attempting to state any positive conclusions on the issues involved in this famous controversy, we may hazard a couple of negative conclusions which the discussion seems to have generated. First, social facts are not genuine examples of psychological imitation, and while they may be mental or *psychic* are probably not, in a narrow and precise sense, *psychological* at all. Second, social facts are not external to the individuals in a society, but internal, and in large part they influence these individuals in a fashion not properly characterized by the term " constraint."

The Psycho-Sociology of LeBon. — Gustave LeBon (1841–1931) was one of the most versatile and popular *and* one of the most superficial of all French social thinkers outside the ranks of the avowed publicists. His works have had a great vogue, though probably more in non-scientific than in scientific circles. He is properly to be regarded as a popularizer of the more striking ideas of others, especially of Tarde's views on imitation and Durkheim's notion of a collective consciousness.

LeBon's first considerable work in the field of psycho-sociology was the volume entitled *Lois psychologiques de l'évolution des peuples.* Its main theme is the nature and importance of mentality of peoples, or " the soul of a race," in the explanation of social processes. LeBon contends that races may be classified psychologically as well as anatomically on a scale ranging from inferior to superior. Of the latter, the Indo-European peoples are the best examples. It is national character and not intelligence which is the dominant factor in social evolution. In LeBon's view, history is nothing more than a product of racial character, and political institutions are particularly expressive of national character. Sentiment rather than reason is the main motive force in history, and for this reason religious beliefs have played a predominant rôle, particularly in social control. Dramatic social changes are brought about by fanatics who appeal to sentiment, but real progress depends on the intellectual élite.

LeBon's best-known work is his study of crowd psychology in *La Psychologie des foules.* In defining what he means by a crowd, LeBon makes it clear that he does not regard it as a mere multitude assembled in physical contiguity, but rather as an aggregation organized in such a way that a " collective mind " is formed and the conscious individuality of the assembled persons practically lost. He then proceeds to enumerate the main traits which characterize crowds. A crowd possesses a type of mental unity which alters the normal emotions, thoughts, and conduct of the individual to a considerable degree. The resulting " crowd mind " is not the average of the minds of its members, but is rather a body of new traits which arise from the combination. The subconscious mind plays the predominant part in the psychic activity of crowds, and as the subconscious is mainly charged with highly emotional qualities, with the archaic social inheritance of the race, and with the more common and instinctive content of the mind, these very qualities are brought to the front in the mental operations of crowds. In a crowd, therefore, the individual members are assimilated to a common mediocrity; the crowd is never capable of engaging in activities requiring a high degree of intellectual effort.

The Sociology of Maunier. — The sociology of René Maunier does not appear to have received adequate recognition (in part, perhaps, because he has been an adherent of no school). Maunier combines an unusual ability in logical classification with a fine erudition and a remarkable bibliographical memory.[76] His work shows the influence of both Durkheim and Tarde, whose rival insights he has combined in an interesting fashion. Reminiscent of Tarde's theory of imitation is Maunier's characterization of the social fact as " repeated " and " general." " The social fact is not original and invented; it is a repeated fact." [77] It occurs only in a social milieu, and is " borrowed " by one individual from other individuals. " Thus, social facts are general facts . . . common to a multiplicity of individuals. . . . They presuppose a group. . . . Contracts and religious rites are, therefore, social facts in so far as they reproduce other contracts and other rites — that is to say, in so far as they are only examples of a generic type." [78] " The social is the opposite of the personal, the *common* and the *vulgar* are of its essence — the *public* as opposed to the *private*." [79]

But Maunier realizes that all repeated human acts are not necessarily social; instinctive, habitual, and hereditary acts do not fall in this category. The further qualifications are definitely Durkheimian: the social must be " traditional " and " obligatory " for the individual. These two sets of characteristics are not necessarily opposed to each other, for it is the traditional and obligatory character of these acts which is responsible for their being repeated and common.[80]

Maunier is an exponent of the concrete as opposed to the abstract view of the social sciences. Social science must study a given concrete social complex in all of its aspects — herein bearing some resemblance to our " culture case study." This program is reflected both in his study of the morphology of towns and in his ethnographic studies of certain North African societies.[81] His study of towns, *L'Origine et la fonction économique des villes,* is an excellent example of the potentialities of a morphological and ecological interpretation of collective facts. The first part of it has been translated by L. L. Bernard.[82] In his recent *Essai sur les groupements sociaux,* Maunier gives us an excellent analytical classification of social groups. His most recent work has consisted mainly in opening up the new concrete science of " colonial sociology," of which he is now professor at the University of Paris.

Richard and Other Critics of Durkheim. — Gaston Richard, for many years at Bordeaux, was one of the leading collaborators of Durkheim on *L'Année sociologique* from 1898 to 1907, but since that time has been one of the severest and most effective critics of the main presuppositions of Durkheim's sociology.

To begin with, says Richard, Durkheim has endeavored to work out two entirely different and mutually inconsistent programs for sociology. In the first, sociology is the study of " social morphology " or the " internal social milieu ": density and mass of population, composition of secondary groups, and their divisions in social space. Neither Durkheim nor his collaborators, however, remain faithful to this naturalistic and materialistic [83] conception of sociology. They abandon social morphology, and espouse the sociology of religion — or, more strictly, the theory of collective representations — as the directing science.

As a philosophic disciple of the Neo-Kantian, Renouvier, Richard has consistently defended the importance of the individual and has insisted on the scientific necessity of a study of the individual's psychic processes in any science of man. Durkheim's " collective representations " and the like appear to Richard as essentially metaphysical speculations bearing a striking resemblance to the Romantic idealism of Hegel and Schelling. As for Durkheim's sociology of religion, Richard, who is a liberal but sincere Huguenot, finds it particularly disturbing. In *L'Athéisme dogmatique en sociologie réligieuse,* he criticizes it as an attempt to replace the traditional belief in God by a new form of atheism, and to discredit theism by making it appear an inadequately understood symbolism of that very secular reality, society. As a part of the criticism he attacks the evolutionary presuppositions of the study in essentially the same way as we have done in Chapter Twenty. How can Durkheim be sure that Australian totemism is really the prototype of the religious phenomenon? Is totemism even a religious phenomenon at all? Sir James Frazer, who first suggested the idea to Durkheim, later changed his mind on the point. Moreover, even if it were a religious phenomenon, why should it be any more revelatory of the true nature of religion than religion's more developed, differentiated, and purified forms? Richard has also given us some incisive and detailed criticism of Durkheim's social pathology, and particularly of Durkheim's appreciation of crime.[84]

Richard's thought has always been firmly opposed to all forms of empiricism and materialism, and he has therefore consistently opposed positivism and biologism in sociology. This is already apparent in an early work directed against Spencerian evolutionism: *L'Idée d'évolution dans la nature et l'histoire. La Sociologie générale* (1912) is a persuasive plea for the necessity of a general sociology. Richard observes that the special social sciences must be subordinated to a more general social science which they help to form; otherwise they tend to overstep the proper limits of their subject-matter. The distinction between community and society, which corresponds in a general way to Tönnies's distinction between *Gemeinschaft* and *Gesellschaft,* and to the distinction made in this book between the sacred and the secular society, has been accepted by Richard as the guiding hypothesis, or central principle for general sociology. In Richard's opinion, general sociology should be a comparative study of social institutions, using primarily historical material, and guided by the ideal-typical distinction between community and society. It should cast its theories in terms of tendencies, not of iron-clad laws, and should attempt no more than probable and approximate prediction. These methodological views are given concrete application in two brilliant empirical studies, *La Femme dans l'histoire et chez les différents peuples* (1907), and *L'Évolution des mœurs* (1924), in which Richard is particularly concerned to point out the rôle of the individual in effecting the transformation from community to society.

A number of other critics of Durkheim have made significant contributions to sociological theory and must be given at least passing mention. René Worms (1867–1926), jurist and philosopher as well as sociologist, was the founder and first editor of the *Revue internationale de sociologie,* which has served as the chief organ of expression of the anti-Durkheimian sociologists in France. He also founded the *Institut International de Sociologie* and was its general secretary. Both the editorship of the *Revue* and the secretaryship of the *Institut* passed to Richard upon the death of Worms in 1926 (Richard has now been succeeded by Émile Lasbax as editor of the *Revue*). Worms began as an organismic thinker (as we saw in an earlier chapter), but under the influence of Tarde's criticisms he later adopted a moderate individualistic and psychologistic position. His monumental *Philosophie des sciences sociales* (1903) pleads for a general sociology synthesizing the one-sided conclusions of the various special social sciences, making use of historical data drawn from widely divergent sources, granting a proper place to the rôle of the individual, and treating philosophical and other ideological systems as important sociological data.

A Franco-Swiss, G.-L. Duprat, present incumbent of the secretaryship of the *Institut International de Sociologie*, brings out into the open the struggle between the full-fledged sociologistic school and those who maintain that psychology is coördinate with and complementary to sociology. Author of numerous books and articles, he holds throughout that no ontologically real existence can be attributed to society *à la* Durkheim, and that individual consciousness cannot be regarded as a mere medium through which collective consciousness enunciates its fiats. Social psychology, in particular, must take its point of departure from the study of psycho-biological behavior, and must pay equal attention to psychical and social functions. Duprat is a somewhat irenic and eclectic writer, endeavoring wherever possible to reconcile opposing points of view and utilize theories coming from the most divergent sources, but on the issues above named he is adamant.

To Daniel Essertier, another critic of the Durkheimian sociology, we owe one of the most systematic and useful digests of recent French sociology as yet available: *La Sociologie* (1930). Its discussion is centered about the psychologistic-sociologistic controversy. In an earlier annotated bibliography of the controversy, entitled *Psychologie et sociologie*, Essertier makes a number of interesting criticisms of Durkheim from a somewhat Bergsonian point of view.[85]

Durkheim's methodology has been intensively analyzed and brilliantly criticized by Roger Lacombe.[86] Elaborate methodological precautions in dealing with external data are wasted, Lacombe believes, unless there is an equally rigorous procedure in passing from them to the internal psychic reality lying behind them (a point ably upheld in the United States by MacIver). But this is just where Durkheim is weakest. It is impossible to proceed without some psychological notions, and Durkheim is continually falling victim to implicit psychological assumptions of an uncritical and common-sense variety.

The utilitarian position, against which Durkheim directed so many attacks, has been ably defended by Gustave Belot, who has in turn given a searching criticism of many of Durkheim's theories, and particularly of his sociology of religion.[87] Léon Brunschvicg has criticized the sociologistic theory of knowledge from a more or less empiricist point of view. He asks how it is that the categories which are supposed to reflect society nevertheless coincide so well with nature.[88] André Lalande has protested that the group as such cannot create the norms either of truth or of morality.[89] Frédéric Rauh has insisted on the importance of the individual consciousness in the formation of collective ideas.[90] Dominique Parodi has criticized the Durkheimians for an irrationalism which leads them to a self-defeating relativism, and has pointed out certain very conservative implications of their doctrines which gives them a certain affiliation with such men as Charles Maurras, Maurice Barrès, and Paul Bourget. Finally, some mention should also be made of the Catholic school, which numbers among its members Legrand, Deploige, Maritain, Belliot, Dèlos, Doucy, Lemonnyer, Riolle, and Troude. The school engages in fierce criticism of the theories of Durkheim and seeks to reintroduce the general ideas of Thomas Aquinas. In particular, its members wish to prevent sociology from intruding into the field of ultimate value-judgments.

Recent Relations between Sociology and the Special Social Sciences in France.[91] — Although there are comparatively few chairs of sociology in French universities, the situation is not so altogether unfavorable as it might appear, since there is considerable interaction between the various social sciences. In consequence, there has been a high degree of diffusion of sociological ideas, and a great many psychologists, historians, jurists, economists, and students of language have done much work of definitely sociological significance.

Among the psychologists, in addition to Charles Blondel and Daniel Essertier, we may mention Georges Dumas, Henri Delacroix, and Henri Wallon. Dumas is the editor of two monumental treatises, *Traité de psychologie* (1924) and *Nouveau Traité de psychologie* (1930–34), which bring into collaboration members of the two major sociological schools. Dumas himself is a moderate partisan of the sociologistic type of explanation in psychology, and has contributed a particularly interesting analysis of the social elements in laughter. Delacroix has been more critical of the sociologistic point of view. In *La Langage et la pensée*, and in his section of Dumas's *Traité*, he maintains that "society does not create intelligence," that the mind of the individual is by no means merely a reflection of environing social structures, and that the collective enthusiasm generated by group association is not so considerable or significant a factor as the Durkheimians have supposed. Wallon, in his study of *L'Enfant turbulent*, has interpreted the psychological processes of retarded or abnormal children in a fashion strongly resembling Lévy-Bruhl's interpretation of primitive mentality.

Among the historians special mention must be made of Paul Lacombe (1839–1919), Henri Berr, and Marcel Granet. Lacombe, a disciple of Tarde, strove to write history with a proper emphasis on sociological and institutional factors. In his *De l'histoire considérée comme science* (1894), he distinguished between the unique inexplicable event, and the social institutions, composed of common and repeated phenomena, which form the basis of "scientific" history. Berr, the founder and editor of the *Revue de synthèse historique* (now the *Revue de synthèse*) has performed a signal service in bringing together a number of specialists from different fields in a coöperative attempt to write synthetic history. Granet, who is one of the most eminent living Sinologists, has been profoundly influenced by Durkheim. In *La Civilisation chinoise* he has applied the Durkheimian conceptual scheme to the interpretation of Chinese life with remarkable success. His recent study of Chinese thought applying Durkheim's sociologistic theory of knowledge to the interpretation of fundamental Chinese categories — time, space, number, and the like — has been of much use in Chapter Two.

Léon Duguit, one of the most celebrated of recent French jurists, has based his "realistic" or "objective" theory of law directly on Durkheim's conception of "organic solidarity." Seeking to avoid any subjective or ethical foundation for the authority of law, Duguit finds its origin in a necessary solidarity based on the division of labor.[92] Duguit's theories have been severely criticized by Maurice Hauriou who, apparently influenced by Tarde, has insisted on the importance and primacy of the ideals, values, and beliefs of the individuals composing the society.[93] Emmanuel Lévy was one of the original collaborators of *L'Année sociologique*, and his theory of law leans heavily on a sociologistic conception of the collective conscience.

Among the economists it is necessary to mention François

Simiand, who was an important collaborator on both the old and the new series of the *L'Année sociologique*. He made many acute criticisms of the classical and mathematical schools of economics, and claimed that economic phenomena are above all an expression of collective judgments of social value. He applied this point of view in several heavily-documented statistical studies of wages and prices in which the rôle of various institutional factors was made clearly apparent.[94]

The students of comparative language in France have been much influenced by sociological thought, and particularly by that of the Durkheim school. Antoine Meillet, in *Les Langues dans l'Europe nouvelle* (1918), and in a memoire for *L'Année sociologique*,[95] maintained that if the philologist wishes to *explain* his facts he must go beyond the realm of pure linguistics and must study the influence of the interaction of groups. Ferdinand Brunot, in his monumental *Histoire de la langue française,* has brought to light a great many social facts influencing the development of the French language. In a more theoretical study, *La Pensée et la langue* (1922), he has constructed on a linguistic basis many suggestive sociological theories. Jacques Vendryes, a student of Brunot and Meillet, has been particularly influenced by Durkheim. He has found that the rules of language well exemplify Durkheim's conception of a collective reality exterior to and constraining of the individual.

Summary of Trends in Current French Sociology. — " The battle of the schools " is a feature that first strikes the outsider's attention: antagonisms of method, basic concepts, and interests lend a peculiarly polemic character to much of the discussion; it sounds like a debate in the Chamber of Deputies. Durkheim's thesis concerning the specifically emergent character of social phenomena is countered by the doctrine that these phenomena do not differ in nature from those which have the " individual mind " as their point of support; almost exclusive attention to the data of ethnography on the one hand is confronted by the doctrine that sociology should make use of data derived from historical and contemporary Western society; to the conception of sociology as an autonomous science is contrasted the position that it is a synthesis of the general results of the other social sciences. But after all, these differences, so striking at first glance, should not blind us to tendencies toward agreement, even though they are of rather recent origin. We have already mentioned the monumental treatises on psychology edited by Georges Dumas, these brought into collaboration members of the two major sociological schools, and gave evidence that the two separate factions are gradually drawing together in the common recognition that mental phenomena can be fruitfully studied from the standpoints of both psycho-physiology and sociology. A further resemblance, which may or may not be creditable to both parties, is that the use of statistics in generalization is very rare, although there are of course a few exceptions such as Halbwachs. At the same time, no one can deny the fact that French sociologists have a good appetite for empirical data, and that assimilation is thorough; the " raw empiricism " so often characteristic of American sociology is refreshingly absent.

The Official Status of Sociology in France and French Switzerland.— We have already pointed out that there are relatively few chairs of sociology as such in France, for the traditional division into faculties is so ossified that there is not even a separate faculty of the social sciences. Economics is usually under the patronizing tutelage of the faculty of law, history is in the domain of letters, and philosophy takes psycho-sociology and like specialties under its wing. There is no chair of sociology in any law faculty in France (although the late Paul Bureau, formerly professor in the *Faculté libre de Droit de Paris,* was primarily a sociologist). The faculty of letters provides a chair of sociology at Bordeaux and another at Toulouse. In Paris the faculty of philosophy at the Sorbonne has a chair of sociology. A few courses bearing the label of sociology are given in France, mostly in normal schools (which train future university professors as well as teachers for the secondary schools), graduate schools, and special institutes, and psycho-sociology is also taught here and there. This is a bit depressing at first view, but it should be borne in mind that the numerous social scientists who apply sociological theories in their work disseminate a good deal of sociological knowledge. Moreover, a sociologist, Bouglé, is director of the *École Normale Supérieure, the* graduate school for professorial training. The highest academic posts in France are therefore filled by men who have had some contact, at least, with high-grade French sociology.

In Switzerland there has been a favorable break with the past in the creation of an independent faculty of the " economic and social sciences " at Geneva. Moreover, the degree of Doctor of Sociology is conferred there.

At the same university a number of courses in sociology are given by G.-L. Duprat and his daughter, Jeanne Duprat. (It should also be noted that sociology the world over is greatly in-

debted to M. and Mlle. Duprat for their efforts in connection with
the *Institut International de Sociologie,* a federation of sociological societies that takes in most of the important national organizations.) At the *Institut J.-J. Rousseau* in the same city Jean
Piaget, who is also a professor at the University of Neuchâtel,
offers a type of instruction in child psychology that has many
sociological implications. For example, it goes far toward bearing out certain theories of Mead, Cooley, and Faris.

In 1900 Durkheim made the proud boast that " sociology is a
science essentially French." Whether or not this could have been
successfully challenged then is perhaps debatable; it is in some
danger of refutation now. French sociology has brilliantly con-
solidated· the ground once gained by its daring raiders, true
enough, but too little is being done in the way of original theo-
rizing, and discipleship is rampant. The French, however, have
a way of rising to the occasion. . . .

II

BELGIUM

The position of Belgium as a buffer state and its intensely
industrialized economic life both played their part in influencing
the social theory of Guillaume DeGreef (1842–1924). In fact,
we entirely agree with Dorothy Douglas's contention that his
work cannot be entirely understood unless the Belgian background is taken into account.[96]

A Radical Start and an Academic Finish. — As a young man
DeGreef was profoundly stirred by the philosophical anarchist
Proudhon, then in Brussels as a political refugee. From this
thinker, DeGreef and his fellows, greatly exercised over the in-
justices of Belgian industrialism, absorbed the theory that all
exchange should be on a basis of mutual equality (" mutualism ")
and that mankind could be saved only by setting up a framework
of autonomous *syndicats,* combining the functions of trade unions
and producers' coöperatives, and bound together by a system of
interest-free credit. Under the sway of this doctrine, DeGreef
and his classmate Hector Denis " joined forces with the workers " by editing various radical journals.

To Proudhon's idea of free-credit groups, DeGreef and Denis
added the idea of occupational representation. Members of these
groups were to be organized, trade by trade, in each locality, not
only for the purpose of carrying on the usual union activities,

but also for the eventual taking over of the functions of the political state itself. Such an idea bears witness to great originality, but it also reflects the amazing economic development of Belgium, which in many respects outstripped the rest of Europe. More than a generation before the modern French syndicalism or British guild socialism gained headway, DeGreef and his friends were advocating a syndicalist society.

The doctrine had strong competition, however, and it lost ground both internationally and nationally as Marxism gained in strength. As a consequence, DeGreef found it more and more difficult to function effectively in the labor movement, and he therefore directed his energies along academic lines. His *Introduction de la sociologie* (1886–1889) was so well received that he was appointed to the first chair of sociology in Belgium, at the University of Brussels, but because of a struggle over the issue of academic freedom involving the eminent geographer, Elisée Reclus, who was dismissed because of his philosophic anarchism, DeGreef and Denis led an exodus from the University and founded a new institution. This was called *L'Université nouvelle,* and was devoted to social science, at the same time maintaining close connection with the workers' educational movement. Here DeGreef taught quietly, occasionally emerging from his academic seclusion to advocate reforms, particularly with regard to occupational representation, until his death in 1924.

Syndicalist Sociology. — From the point of view of contemporary significance, by far the most important of DeGreef's works is the three-volume *Structure générale des sociétés* (1908), although DeGreef himself attributed great importance to several small monographs which combine empirical research with a vision of the syndicalist state he so ardently desired.[97]

The practical program he set forth in these works is based upon a transformation of the credit system and the setting up of collective bargaining on a nation-wide scale. Both require the establishment of strong trade unions, and these in turn are to furnish a foundation for occupational representation in parliament.

By these measures DeGreef sought to build a system that would not only vitalize parliamentary processes by linking them with vital social functions, but that would also, through the educational effect of collective bargaining, bring those functions within the scope of labor control. As already noted, he expected to see the *syndicats* absorb the employing function and exercise the remaining fragment of political power.

Classificatory Sociology. — Comte's classification of the sciences provided a foundation for DeGreef's " pure " social theory, but he rejected the " law of the three stages " and the doctrine that " ideas rule the world or throw it into chaos." At the same time, he took over bodily Comte's theory of a necessary and irreversible serial development of the sciences. DeGreef claimed that his own originality lay in projecting that series over the social field, or in other words, in the discovery that not the mere thoughts but the activities (what he called the " factors ") of social life themselves develop serially, with the more complex always dependent on the less. The series DeGreef set up runs as follows: (1) economic phenomena, (2) genetic (sexual-reproductive), (3) aesthetic, (4) psycho-collective, (5) moral, (6) juridical, and (7) political.

This is " classificatory sociology " with a vengeance, but it is nowhere nearly so complex as it would be if the " law of serial causation " were taken seriously by DeGreef himself. If it were, social influences would have to be traced from one link to another along the entire chain of the hierarchy, but in virtually every case DeGreef merely describes and illustrates the effect of the " lowest center of coördination," namely, the economic, on every other " factor." No matter where he begins, he ends by reaffirming economic determinism, and all the influences he traces are evaluated in terms of " good " or " bad," i.e., as they make for or against the development of the world syndicalist state he so ardently desired.

Evolution toward Syndicalism. — Such social evaluation gives us the clue to his theory of social evolution. Spencer maintained that all forms of life, including social organization, are passing from homogeneity to heterogeneity, are evolving from a less to a more complex, more " highly organized " form. DeGreef took over this formula, and then, characteristically enough, applied it not to " organization " in general, but to the kind of voluntary, contractual organization which Proudhon had taught him to cherish. This shift of meaning made it possible for him to " prove " the " higher " organization of almost anything, and the result was a full-fledged theory of progress under the guise of dispassionate social science.

This theory, stated in terminology less recondite than DeGreef's, is about as follows: (1) an evolutionary change in forms of human association is generally observable; (2) it consists, as a rule, first in growing complexity of structure with increasing for-

mal control, and then, somewhat more slowly, in growing autonomy of the differentiated parts; (3) in any society, the various
forms of association will show a time-lag with respect to each
other; and (4) the interdependence of these forms is so close and
the influence of the economic variety upon the rest so powerful
that it is hopeless to try to push the others far in advance of it.
The practical conclusion he drew from all this was that the
remedy for Belgium's ills was concentration on those economic
reforms that would make advances in the other spheres possible
and safe. *Ergo,* syndicalism.

*Quetelet's Theory of "Oscillation" Applied to Interest-
Groups.* — This syndicalist society, the goal of progress, is also
the contractual state. For DeGreef, "contractualism" meant
something quite different from the complete individualism of
Proudhon; he used the term to designate the free give-and-take
of *interest-groups.* Concentrating on the process of "contractual-
ization," he concludes that it is basically a *débat,* a balancing and
weighing of contending interests. It is the function of syndicalist
organization to raise this *débat* to a rational and methodical
level; instead of letting interest-groups struggle until the weaker
are exterminated and the stronger are exhausted, the clash of interests should be adjusted by the use of the proper contractual
machinery.

In this it is plain that although DeGreef's debt to Proudhon,
Comte, and Spencer was great, still greater was his obligation to
his fellow-countryman, the great statistician Adolphe Quetelet.[98]
Although like Proudhon an internationalist, Quetelet's approach
was vastly different, governed as it was by his deep interest
in the problems of Belgium as a buffer state. A pioneer in the
application of statistical methods to the problems of human
life, he conceived of the differences between individuals in terms
of variation from an abstract "average man," not only in physical traits but also as regards mental and social reactions.[99] Quetelet believed that as social contacts increased and racial stocks
mingled with each other, differences between men would grow in
number but lessen in intensity. Most frequently he spoke of the
tendency as a steadily developing equilibrium, an ever more complete balance of forces. As he put it, civilization "more and more
contracts the limits within which the different elements relating
to man oscillate."[100]

DeGreef took this conception of the process of oscillation or
equilibration making the progressive levelling of human differences possible, termed it *débat,* and, true to his usual practice,

applied it to groups rather than merely to individuals. The result was his famous theory of frontiers, the most original and important of his contributions.

Buffer-State Sociology: the Theory of Frontiers. — With regard to international relations, he uses the concept of a moving equilibrium of forces to show that the political boundaries of peoples are perhaps the least important thing to know about them. They are only derivative, the transitory result of the real *débat* of interest-groups within and thrusts and resistances without. Frontiers, DeGreef insists, are never primarily geographic; they are social and equilibrative, the point at which the social forces of one constellation of groups strike a momentary balance with those of another. No matter how strong a " natural " barrier may lie in the way, it will be superseded if social conditions demand it. Moreover, the advance of culture means that such barriers do not remain constant in their influence; for example, large rivers may at one time serve as dividing lines and at another become powerful aids to communication.[101]

The frontier has great social significance; in early times it was frequently not a line but a more or less neutral zone, oftentimes a natural or artificial desert. Eventually such desert wastes are peopled by traders, freebooters, government outposts, and perpetual pioneers of all kinds. Once settled, it commonly becomes the place of the community's intensest life, for it is the point where political contacts are concentrated. Moreover, it is the frontier that commonly stamps national life with its double aspect of political separatism and economic expansiveness, for it is at the frontier that military force must be exerted and also there that peaceful intercourse is unavoidable.[102] (Those who have attended Robert E. Park's famous lectures on " The Crowd and the Public " at the University of Chicago will at once recognize how much Park's analysis of such organizations as the California Vigilantes has been influenced by DeGreef — an influence which Park himself would probably be the first to admit.)

The Mission of Neutrality. — The " buffer state " of modern times may be said to be descended from earlier frontier zones. The concept of neutrality has slowly developed because some safety zone between powerful antagonists has appeared more and more essential to *their* survival.

DeGreef, incorrigible optimist that he was, went on to say that once the leading nations have made a start at internal reorganization (i.e., when syndicalism gets under way), they will agree to make all the great transit zones of the world neutral, and when these zones ultimately become linked together, they will form the beginning of a world state that will be truly pacific and international. He perpetually insists, however, that the international reorganization of each nation must precede these changes of broader scope, and consequently he continually returns to syndicalism as an integral part of his theory of frontiers.

In spite of all the exceptions we are now inclined to take to his practical program, there can be no doubt that he anticipated a great deal of modern sociology, especially human ecology, in this theory, and that human geography and the "new history" might still profit by a closer acquaintance with it.

Overlapping of Frontiers Buries the National State. — The expanding social forces to which DeGreef trusts for the breaking down of political barriers are of course the familiar seven "factors." Each of these is pictured as having a figurative "frontier," namely, a limit to its activity or sphere of membership *which usually is not the same as the geographic frontier of the nation.* The result is that the economic factor crosses the political boundary, eventually bringing the others with it, until finally the political is itself ready for a new adjustment, and the geographic boundary shifts. There is normally a time lag during the adjustment of the successive frontiers, so that the political always brings up the rear — an anticipation of at least one aspect of Ogburn's doctrine of cultural lag. For all his economic determinism, however, DeGreef was careful to avoid undue dogmatism: he admitted that once the non-material factors begin to follow the economic factor, they may penetrate into foreign territory much farther than it does.

The trend of his discussion makes it quite clear what DeGreef thought of the nature of the factors themselves: at bottom they are interest-groups with a group consciousness strong enough to support a definite organization. By perfecting the internal organization of each of these subsidiary groups, with their inevitable crossing of material frontiers through foreign affiliations, the super-group — i.e., the national state — will lose its attribute of sovereignty, becoming for the citizen only one of many possible centers of solidarity. We shall have "new groupings in a new world." [103]

Summary of DeGreef's Theories. — The unity of DeGreef's work is easy to see, constituted as it is by the essentially syndicalist conception that political activities are but the remote reflexes of economic life, and that "natural" economic divisions along functional lines are the necessary centers of real power —

if not in the present, then in the future. This was Proudhon's idea, but DeGreef went far beyond his master, for he coupled with it Proudhon's originally anarchistic conception of political " contract," added Quetelet's theory of " oscillation," and worked in the fruitful idea of the waxing and waning of opposed groups through " frontier contacts," as demonstrated by his own experience of the actual process of interest adjustment in the courts.

The result was a new and enlarged contractualism, vastly different from Proudhon's, for its core was the essentially judicial (or psycho-sociological) process of *débat* oscillating its way to an equilibrium through group rather than through individual pressure.

So it is that we can follow Dorothy Douglas in saying that DeGreef, with his syndicalistic internationalism and his theory of " contract " and " frontiers," fitly represents the sociology of Belgium, " at once the buffer state of Europe and the center of a highly class-conscious and interdependent economic life."

Waxweiler, Analyst of Social Processes. — Émile Waxweiler (1867–1916) was for many years (1901–1916) director of what is still one of the best organized and financed institutes of sociology to be found in Europe — the *Institut de Sociologie Solvay* in Brussels. His chief work, *Esquisse d'une sociologie,* appeared in 1906, and for a long time received very little attention. Perhaps one reason for the neglect into which it fell was its too exclusive limitation to the biological aspects of behavior.[104] There is no doubt that Waxweiler erred in this respect, but his work is nevertheless far too important to be overlooked.

He regards sociology as the science of the processes of reaction resulting from the mutual stimulation of individuals of the same species. Otherwise expressed, it is the theory of the adjustment of these individuals to each other. The central concept is " social affinity." He stresses observation of the individual *acting* in his environment, and never wearies of pointing out that this activity is to be analyzed as a social process rather than as a means for bringing about various results — economic, political, or what not. In other words, he emphasizes form rather than content. The organism has multifarious relations to many environments, but the sociologist is interested only in its relation to the *living* environment. This is not to be conceived of as a mere collection of discrete organisms, but as a network of relations based upon specific affinity between organically similar individuals. This specific social affinity, the special object-matter of sociology, is complemented by sexual affinity and "vegetative" affinity (manifesting itself in the life of the cells).

Social affinity is not to be explained by a particular gregarious instinct, or by emotions such as sympathy or altruistic feeling, or by any other teleological influence. Moreover, the family instinct and the play instinct do not explain it; neither does imitation. The sole explanation is the physical sensitivity of the organisms in question; they are capable of reacting to stimuli from other animals of the same species in strict accordance with the degree of development reached by their nervous systems. Here we see a marked resemblance to Giddings's behavioristic reworking of his "consciousness of kind" formula: "Like response to like stimulus." As Waxweiler put it a decade earlier, the specific affinity of the organic structures in question is the external cause of social affinity.[105]

Behaviorism before Watson. — A remarkably modern note in Waxweiler's treatise is struck by his insistence that the concept "social" must be divested of its popular connotations, so far as the sociologist is concerned, and must be used only to denote actions and reactions (active or passive as the case may be) as they are manifested by individuals in their reciprocal relations.

He distinguishes nine principal forms of social action. These are: (1) conjunctive actions which are immediately consequent upon physical proximity; (2) actions tending to protect or to injure others; (3) competition; (4) efforts to evoke in others behavior like one's own; (5) spontaneous gregarious association, independent of conscious imitation, and dependent upon fear and similar emotions; (6) repetitive actions, which are placed in four subdivisions — (a) imitation, a type in which the initiative toward repetition is furnished by the imitating person, (b) suggestion, in which initiative proceeds from the person whose action is repeated by another, (c) contagion, in which there is no conscious initiative on the part of either imitator or imitated, and (d) reproduction, which occurs when repetition is for the purpose of duplicating in every respect a particular social action; (7) initiative action, taking place when an individual behaves in any respect differently from the way to which education and prior experience have accustomed him; (8) acquisitive action, a type particularly important in the economic zone; and (9) selection.[106]

In studying these social actions, the interest of the sociologist will of course center itself primarily on human beings, although, says Waxweiler, a sort of rudimentary social affinity is also pres-

ent in the higher animals and is the determining factor in their
sociology. The much more complex nature of the human organism, however, has led to strikingly different phenomena;
namely, those associated with the fact that human beings steadily
become more dependent on each other as they become more
skillful in organizing their social world. Indeed, the human being
has become the only animal whose sole primary " instinct " inheres in the capacity and the inclination to learn (a position implicitly taken by many of the American behaviorists, and explicitly
expounded by the British writer, Spiller). Physical receptivity
for social stimulation has reached such a peak of development
in the human being that social affinity now makes itself evident
in an actual need for other individuals of the same species. In
short, the human being transmutes social affinity into *associativeness.*[107]

Waxweiler's work was remarkable for its period because of its
precise restriction of sociology to the study of processes by which
adjustment (in the broadest sense) of individuals to each other
takes place. The data are to be gathered from the specific modes
of behavior which externally manifest the mental fact of adjustment. Here is one of the points in which Waxweiler's influence on
the German sociologist, Leopold von Wiese, is most apparent.
Waxweiler elevated these processes of adjustment to the rank
of the sole means by which social life is to be explained. Because
of this delimitation and unification his sociology is markedly different from the majority of other works that use biology as a
starting point.

Organicism Rejected. — Another very significant phase of
Waxweiler's theory is his express rejection of the notion of society as an organism and the correlated doctrine of " parallelism " between organismic systems and social institutions. He calls
this doctrine " a shameful abuse of terms which usually covers
a confusion of facts." [108] He does not make biology the foundation of sociology because he assumes society to be an organism,
but rather because the social processes issue from individuals
who, being organisms, must be dealt with from the biological
viewpoint. He goes on to say that it is not the task of sociology
to explain what " society " *is;* such abstractions run counter to
the methodological principles of a science based on observation
rather than speculation. When the general condition of sociology
in the early 1900's is held in view, Waxweiler's originality becomes evident, for the assumptions he rejected were the common
coin of his day. Furthermore, he refused to use phrases that had

been worn meaningless by careless usage, and for better or for worse he avoided, with at least a consistency seldom found elsewhere, every teleological element.[109]

Further evidence of Waxweiler's originality was his proposal to develop sociologically usable materials through intensive analysis of words denoting social actions and related phenomena, and he appended to his *Esquisse d'une sociologie* (1906) a collection of over two thousand words made by an associate under his direction. The collection was only tentative and no claim to completeness or system was made, but it provided a hint which was not without its effect on Wiese's famous table of social relations.[110]

In spite of all these important anticipations it is nevertheless true that Waxweiler's work for a long time exercised little influence, probably because of his failure to take other than biological factors into account. He was too much convinced that the natural sciences of his day, and particularly biology, were the only sources of materials and methods for the sociologist. Had he included data of more directly social nature, his advances in viewpoint and methodology would not have been so late in bearing fruit.

The Brussels Institute of Sociology. — We have already referred to the *Institut de Sociologie Solvay,* which Waxweiler directed for fifteen years. This is a sort of Russell Sage Foundation on a very small scale, but, because of its concentration on more strictly sociological matters and its unusual type of organization, is an excellent place for the research sociologist to work. It was founded in 1901 by Ernest Solvay (1838–1922), an industrialist who was also a far-seeing sociologist, and is now an integral part of the University of Brussels, retaining its own director.[111] Worthy of special mention among the staff of the institute is Daniel Warnotte, whose remarkable *Chronique du mouvement scientifique,* an elaborate annotated bibliography appearing quarterly in the organ of the institute, *Revue de l'Institut de Sociologie,* is an indispensable part of any well-equipped social science library. Warnotte also has charge of the documentation and information service of the institute, which is conducted as follows: several hundred leading sociologists throughout the world have been and are being requested to indicate those phases of their subject on which they are willing to give information, and as soon as anyone asks a question which cannot be answered by the staff of the institute, it is relayed to one or more of the listed sociologists, who rarely fail to furnish the aid requested.[112] In addition to all this, a series of monographic studies in the social sciences has been financed and published by the institute; of special interest to sociologists are those by Petrucci on the gap between animal and human societies, Wodon on errors of method in studying the social life of preliterates, Houzé on the Aryan fallacy, and Varendonck on children's groups.[113]

When compared with many larger and wealthier countries, Belgium is a far from somber spot on the sociological map. Had we more space at our disposal we could offer further justification of this assertion by describing the recent work of Henri De-Man, director of the bureau of social statistics of the Belgian Labor Party, of Émile Vandervelde, leader of the Socialist party, of W. Malgaud, professor at the University of Antwerp, of J. P. Haesert, professor of the University of Ghent, and of Fernand Van Langenhove and Eugène Dupréel, professors at the University of Brussels. And where the past is concerned, Quetelet, DeGreef, and Waxweiler by no means exhaust the list: we might profitably consider the sociological implications of the theories of Charles Perin (1815–1905), the great economist; Émile de Laveleye (1822–92), the political scientist, economist, and historian; Victor Brants (1856–1917), the Social Catholic reformer, economist, historian, and sociological follower of LePlay; Hector Denis (1849–1921), the friend and colleague of DeGreef whom we have already mentioned; and Adolphe Prins (1845–1919), the criminologist who exposed the fallacies of both the classical and the Lombrosian schools of criminology when the latter, in particular, still had the upper hand throughout Europe. We repeat, therefore, that Belgian sociology has an honorable past and a hopeful future.[114]

Here again some relevant remarks are provided in the 1937-1960 Appendix on Sociological Trends, especially for 1946, 1951, 1953, 1954, and 1958. Really first-rate coverage is offered by Jean Stoetzel and his coworkers in Howard Becker and Alvin Boskoff, eds., *Modern Sociological Theory in Continuity and Change* (New York: Dryden Press, 1957), pp. 623-57 (MSTICAC). Attention may also be called to the remarkable bibliographies issued under UNESCO auspices on sociological publication and research appearing in the French language.

Sociology has never been granted appropriate academic recognition in the French-speaking countries, if by recognition is meant university posts for sociologists as such—and this in spite of the pioneer efforts of Comte, Tarde, Durkheim, and other able men. Nevertheless, public recognition is widespread, perhaps because of the outstanding ability of many French sociologists as top-quality publicists. Raymond Aron, renowned as one of the chief writers for *Le Figaro,* is among the most recent examples of a long and distinguished line.

CHAPTER XXIII

Sociology in the Germanic Languages

PORTMANTEAU PRACTICE. — Here again our chapter title points to the language used as the basis of classification. Germany, Austria, Holland, Norway, Denmark, Sweden, and Finland are so diverse that almost no other basis could be regarded as " with malice toward none and with charity for all." (Finnish, of course, is not a Germanic language, but Finnish scientists almost invariably publish in one or another of the Germanic languages.)

With seven countries to be surveyed in one chapter, it is indeed fortunate that our discussion of sociology in Germany and Austria can be kept within close bounds. This possibility of relative brevity arises from the fact that much of the framework and a considerable part of the content of the present volume has been influenced by German writers. Tönnies has had a great deal to do with our guiding concepts of the sacred and the secular, as well as with the allied ideas of mental immobility and mental mobility. Thurnwald's analysis of the mentality of preliterates has been of no small significance, particularly in Chapter One. Max Weber? Almost all-pervasive! We may single out for special mention, however, these themes: traditional, charismatic, and rational domination; secularization; the ideal-typical; functional interdependence; abstention from value-judgment; the importance of non-material culture; and culture case study. Moreover, it should be noted that his culture case studies in the sociology of religion have played parts so large in Chapters Two, Three, and sections of Eight that even the numerous references do not do full justice to him. Troeltsch provides the backbone of our treatment of Christian social philosophy; Chapter Six would be very little indeed without his contribution. Simmel's " sociology of the stranger " is evident throughout the description of the mobile Greco-Roman world in Chapter Four, and the frequently-recurring theme of culture contact shows marked traces of the same influence. Wiese remains somewhat more in the background, but his estimate of various thinkers has rarely been disregarded;

further, his definition of the central field of sociology has often had weight in the distribution of space and selection of topics.

And when we turn to those relatively recent German and Austrian writers to whom a high degree of influence on this book cannot be attributed, but to whom a good deal of attention has already been paid in previous chapters, a long list confronts us. Confining it to approximately the past hundred years, we have Heeren, Hegel, Marx and Engels, Thibaut and Savigny, Lilienfeld, Schäffle, Gumplowicz and Ratzenhofer, Oppenheimer, Alfred Weber, and Spengler. Many more to whom less space is devoted might have been mentioned, and later chapters give notice to one or two important figures, notably Krause, who have been honored abroad instead of at home. It should therefore be evident that we can design the German and Austrian division of this chapter along the lines of a portmanteau rather than a trunk, and that it might well bear a label worded about as follows: " Those Phases of Sociology in Germany and Austria Not Yet or Not to Be Adequately Discussed or Utilized by Us."

I

GERMANY AND AUSTRIA

Slow Growth of Sociology as an Academic Subject. — Any survey of German and Austrian sociology that follows chronological lines falls naturally into two main divisions; namely, the periods before and after the World War.[1] This is primarily the result of the sudden emergence of sociology as a recognized academic discipline; until the early 1920's there was very little except that expounded by " left-handed sociologists," i.e., by men whose professional duties lay almost wholly in philosophy, economics, and similar non-sociological realms. Even during the Weimar Republic and Viennese Social-Democracy relatively few chairs were maintained exclusively in the interests of sociology, but the subject was admitted as a *Lehrfach,* and a fairly large number of professors added " and Sociology " to their titles.[2] Since the advent of the National Socialist and the Christian Socialist régimes, however, growth has once more become slow, to say the least, and prospects are decidedly uncertain.

But ignoring current events for the moment, it must be said that even under relatively favorable circumstances a very halting development of the subject could hardly have been avoided in countries where academic boundary lines are so sharply marked.

Further, the vested interests of a professional caste operated against the admission of a subject largely cultivated, not only in Germany and Austria, but elsewhere as well, by amateurs. Comte had no professional standing after his expulsion from the *École Polytechnique;* Spencer remained out of touch with university circles all his life, and added insult to injury by refusing to make use of the honors showered upon him by learned societies; Ward had no academic affiliations until he began his work at Brown University at the age of sixty-five; the Russo-German, Paul von Lilienfeld, was a jurist, as was also Gabriel Tarde; Albert Schäffle never overcame the distrust evoked in his colleagues by his journalistic and political activity; Gumplowicz was a Jew from Austrian Poland whose conflict theory of the state ran directly counter to the Hegelian apotheosis of that institution; and Ratzenhofer, the Austrian field-marshal, was a gifted dilettante whose positivism and monism made him highly suspect. Moreover, the flaming nationalist, Heinrich von Treitschke, declared war on " the so-called science of society " as early as 1859, even going so far as to link it with socialism, and the ammunition thus furnished was ceaselessly discharged by the professors of history, political science, and philosophy.[3] To cap it all, sociology was declared to be " Western," filled with the poison of the Enlightenment. Small wonder, then, that only the most courageous or foolhardy spirits avowed sociological interests.

Early Psycho-Sociology. — The failure of the earlier varieties of sociology to strike deep root probably would not be too strongly deplored by an adherent of the doctrine that sociology is a special rather than a universal social science, for they were all universal or " encyclopedic " in character.[4] One of the earliest attempts to discover those processes basic to human association and dissociation — an attempt therefore quite congenial to those opposing sociological encyclopedism — was that of the educator, Johann Herbart (1776–1841). His earlier writings were directed toward the analysis of the social aspects of personality and the effects of communication (*Allgemeine praktische Philosophie,* 1807), whereas his later efforts were less psycho-sociological in nature, largely consisting of studies in the statics and dynamics of the state and society.[5]

Herbart's interest in personality, and the Romantic conception of the " folk-spirit " given prestige by Hegel, eventually led to the development of " folk-psychology " by Lazarus and Steinthal. These writers were particularly interested in manners and customs as expressions of underlying uniformities of folk character which, true to the Hegelian tradition, they held to be something ineffable and hence not to be finally explained in causal terms.[6]

About ten years after the founding of the Lazarus and Steinthal periodical for the study of *Völkerpsychologie*, Gustav Lindner (1843–1919) announced himself as a direct opponent of the obscurities of folk-psychology in his *Ideen zur Psychologie der Gesellschaft als Grundlage der Socialwissenschaft* (1871). Lindner is of some historical importance because of his influence on Schäffle, but especially because of the undeniable traces he left upon the thought of Georg Simmel, the fountain-head of sociology as an independent social science.[7]

Wundt and Social Prediction. — Before dealing with Simmel, however, we must pay attention to the man who salvaged a considerable portion of the " folk-psychology " of Lazarus and Steinthal and added to it many novel contributions of his own. Wilhelm Wundt (1834–1920) was primarily a philosopher-psychologist, but he was so deeply interested in the psychical phases of social life that he might almost be termed a psycho-sociologist.

" Almost." The term is not fully applicable because he insisted on operating with psychological rather than sociological categories — a mode of thought for which Mauss, among others, repeatedly took him to task. Reacting against the intellectualism of the English associationists, Wundt built up his psychological system on the basis of will, volition, conation. Instead of the mere " perception " of the associationists, he worked with the concept of " apperception," in which the original endowment and experience of the willing, apperceiving mind creates something that did not exist before this " creative synthesis " occurred. In other words, mind has an active rather than a merely " recording " function; man constructs his meaningful world out of elements that in and of themselves are meaningless.

The psycho-sociological relevance of these psychological considerations appears when two derivatives of " creative synthesis " are studied. One of these is the " transformation of motives " and the other is the " heterogeneity of purposes." Societal life may remain to all appearances the same even though the motives that engender and sustain it undergo radical change, and old structures and institutions may be adapted to purposes for which they were not originally designed. To take contemporary examples: the Nazis have retained some of the external forms of parliamentary democracy in spite of the fact that their motivating content is now party dictatorship; conversely, the old foreign policy of " Berlin to Bagdad " is being adapted to Nazi yearnings for Ukrainian wheat and Roumanian oil.

A further consequence of the " transformation of motives " and the " heterogeneity of ends " is that social conduct is unpredictable over a long time-span. The end originally sought as gratification of a given motive is seldom if ever attainable as first envisaged; it usually presents itself in plural form as a set of alternatives. The alternative chosen is then considered as a means to the original end, but the means chosen inevitably modify both the end and the motive. When repeated choices are necessary, the goal " finally " achieved may be in a direction quite opposite from that initially intended, and the purpose may have been drastically altered in the process.

It should be plain from the foregoing that Wundt's analysis of " means," " ends," " motives," and " purposes " has nothing mysteriously teleological about it. " The ' end ' or ' purpose ' is nothing more than the consequence of antecedent conditions to which a particular value has been assigned, and this consequence or result is held to be end-achieving or purpose-gratifying — i.e., teleological — because of its value-component. The antecedent conditions, therefore, become the ' means ' with regard to the value, and in the measure in which they have functioned as emotional or cognitive factors they are assigned rôles as ' motives ' of the teleological happening."[8]

From this it follows that the same occurrence may be interpreted in two different ways. From the standpoint of the " end " involved, a sort of " forward-looking " conceptual schema may be constructed, while from the standpoint of the " motive," a " backward-looking " analysis results. A further complication is introduced by the element of value. The limits of motivational fluctuation and mutation of ends are set by the hierarchy of values prevailing in a given period and culture, but this hierarchy is itself transformed by the vicissitudes undergone by its incorporated motives and ends, and a new cultural epoch eventually dawns.

In Wundt's day the sociology of knowledge under that name was unknown, but he drew conclusions of high importance for this new subdivision of the sociological field. The growth of the scientific habit of mind, said Wundt, has given a measure of persistence of motives and stability of ends that, in eras dominated by this mentality, permits of a considerable degree of social prediction. But even science is relative, and if ever a general shift in the social and cultural framework occurs, this scientific persistence and stability will *ipso facto* yield to something else. In fact, the prevailing scale of values may be so altered by science itself, through its own mutation of motives and transformation of purposes, that science may, so to speak, kill science.[9]

Mentality and Romanticism. — Wundt therefore held that his major psychological principle, creative synthesis, is responsible, through its immanent fluctuation of motives and ends, for the never-ending succession of cultural epochs. Manifestly too little importance is given to intrusive social and cultural factors in this analysis, but in justice to Wundt it should be said that he did not permit his psychology, paradoxically enough, to distort his great *Völkerpsychologie*. In fact, his psychological principles greatly aided him in avoiding the pitfalls of evolutionism into which British writers, dominated by the associationist psychology, so readily fell.

This is clearly shown in his discussion of " primitive mentality." Instead of the arid intellectualism of the associationists, we find Wundt upholding emotion, volition, and creative synthesis. When the preliterate calls a flash of lightning a snake, there is no process of associating jagged lightning with wriggling snake or a rational *Analogieschluss* that " anything like that must be a snake." Instead, there is a direct response in which the lightning is " apperceived " *as* a snake; this Wundt calls *mythological apperception*. It will readily be seen that explanation drawing upon the intellectual realm is abandoned; the emotional, volitional, and intuitive functions of the human mind are given the decisive rôle.[10]

This sounds the Romantic note, but Wundt vigorously asserted that he was exceedingly sceptical of, or even hostile to, certain phases of Romanticism. For example, he often inveighed against the vague notions of *Geist* current in the Germany of his day (and not of his day only). True to his psycho-physical parallelism, however, he draws a sharp distinction between physical and psychical causality, and asserts that the creative synthesis which is the mind's highest function brings forth effects which, so to speak, are greater than their causes. Here again, in spite of the mechanistic clatter of his parallelism, a Romantic overtone can be heard. On the other hand, he not only was sharply critical of the general misuse of *Geist,* as noted above, but also attacked the conceptions of " folk mind " and " folk soul " disseminated by Lazarus and Steinthal. For Wundt the group, of whatever character, is not " a whole of a higher order," but simply a functional unity woven from the relevant aspects of the minds of its members. These aspects, however, are in a certain sense constituted by group membership; the relation is reciprocal. Mind and group are inseparable, but there is no group mind.[11]

Evolutionism and Völkerpsychologie. — Group relations are especially important for three phases of culture: language, myth (inclusive of religion), and the mores. As Wundt uses these terms, they include virtually all of non-material culture except the arts and techniques intrinsically bound up with material culture, and it is highly significant that he should begin his enormous ten-volume *Völkerpsychologie* with topics so much favored by the Romantic writers against whom he thought he was reacting. The work also includes lengthy analyses of social organization and of law, and concludes with a treatise on culture and history.[12]

The present-day drift away from evolutionary preconceptions has led, in Germany and elsewhere, to an undue disparagement of Wundt's achievement. His utilization of materials also drawn upon by the evolutionists has unfairly counted against him. To be sure, he does not wholly escape the pitfalls of evolutionary schematism, particularly in his attempts at popularization; nevertheless, he is far more critical than the members of the classical school. For example, he nowhere applies the principle of unilinear evolution; if for no other reason, his stress on creative synthesis forces him to leave room for alternative developmental sequences. Moreover, the constant emphasis he lays on the interaction of motives and purposes and the " transvaluation of values " generates a pattern more complicated, and yet in closer touch with happenings as they actually took place, than that traced by the social evolutionists *per se*. Finally, his basic psychologism saved him from positing a rigid sequence of cultural stages; the recurrent regularities of human development he held to be of psychological rather than historical character. Historical events as such are of necessity unique; their general traits derive only from their exemplification of psychological principles. That is to say, historical occurrences are subject only to " singular laws "; they remain unique even though they may have aspects that demonstrate the workings of the transformation of motives, the heterogeneity of ends, or like psychological possibilities.[13]

Dilthey, Anti-Naturalist. — Wundt's extreme caution *vis-à-vis* social evolutionism was in part due to the general German distrust, in academic circles at least, of the philosophical naturalism with which evolutionary doctrines are so compatible. This caution was open-armed enthusiasm, however, in comparison with the exceedingly critical, anti-naturalistic attitude adopted by Wilhelm Dilthey (1833–1911).

This brilliant philosopher, successor of Lotze at Berlin and antagonist of Simmel, is famous for his attempt to establish the social sciences (*Geisteswissenschaften*) on a basis different from that of the natural sciences. Approaching the problem of human conduct at its most complex levels, he rejected both the positivistic and the Neo-Kantian metaphysics so popular at the close of the nineteenth century in favor of the sort of vitalism of which Bergson has since become the chief representative. Upon the foundation afforded by this vitalism, this *Lebensphilosophie,* Dilthey erected his " *geisteswissenschaftliche* psychology," and this in turn provided the basis for both the methodological considerations and the concrete researches in the social sciences for which he is so widely known.

For Dilthey there is no cleavage between mind and matter; mind is organic to nature *and nature is organic to mind.* The ultimate unit of social life, man himself, is not a disembodied mind nor a fortuitous concourse of atoms; he is a psychophysical entity inseparably linked with the world of nature, animate and inanimate, because he is part of it and it is part of him.

But in spite of man's oneness with nature, the natural sciences are quite different from the social sciences. The natural scientist constructs *explanatory* ultimates, such as the electron or the quantum, which in some degree, at least, are abstractions from the " raw data." The social scientist, on the other hand, finds his *understandable* ultimates directly in his raw data, in the concrete manifestations of human life. These are not abstractions, but aspects of ultimate reality itself, and as experienced bring with them a sense of immediacy and profundity that is all-persuading and a conviction of knowledge that is unshakeable. " We explain in the natural sciences; we understand in the social sciences." [14]

Social Science Necessarily Subjective. — The entire realm of social relations, both statically and dynamically considered, can be understood only to the degree in which the social scientist is prepared by native endowment and experience to understand it. There is no substitute for insight, and insight cannot be imparted by the methods of natural science. Humanistic and artistic approaches alone can yield valid results. One must in some sense " live himself into " (*nachleben*) events and eras which he is endeavoring to understand, and this he can do only when he achieves identification, partial and temporary though it may be, with their key values and meanings. Clearly, it is impossible to identify oneself with everything to be found in a given cross-section of social and cultural life; there must necessarily be selection. Here again the relation to the social scientist himself is determining; what he selects is what he regards as meaningful. Hence, says Dilthey, there can be no valid sociology of the objective, Comtean, natural-science type; the understanding of personal and societal life is an endless task that shifts to ever new and higher levels of insight as the social scientist in question *subjectively* acquires the capacity to understand at these levels. Understanding can never be dissociated from the particular " I " that understands.[15]

It should be noted here that the " *geisteswissenschaftliche* psychology " sponsored by Dilthey is not wholly devoid of resemblance to the kind of psychology upheld by DeRoberty and like advocates of the bio-social hypothesis, by Durkheim, and by others who maintain that sociology is directly based on biology rather than psychology. For them psychology is a concrete, descriptive science dependent on the abstract social sciences, and particularly upon sociology, for its explanatory principles. In fact, it might well be called psycho-sociology, or something similar, in order to indicate its place in the structure of the sciences. In thus calling attention to *one* point of resemblance between Dilthey and DeRoberty *et alii,* however, we have no intention of obscuring fundamental differences. After all, Dilthey's insistence on aesthetic sophistication, on vividness of description (*Anschaulichkeit*), and on evaluational re-living of events and eras puts him many removes from the matter-of-fact positivists with whom he has just been compared. He was first of all an artist, and a Romantic artist at that.

Rickert and the Logic of History. — Moreover, Dilthey laid so much stress on understanding that, in spite of his vitalism and his frequent assertions to the contrary, he tended to draw a sharp line between nature and mind. Wundt, as we have seen, also stressed the cleavage between the two in his principle of creative synthesis.

Heinrich Rickert, however, has challenged both Wundt and Dilthey, asserting that the practice of distinguishing between the natural and the social sciences at the point where the human mind enters is logically questionable and methodologically useless. (It will be recalled that we have already referred to Rickert in Chapter Twenty in connection with the Windelband-Rickert distinction between the idiographic and nomothetic sciences. It is necessary to omit consideration of Windelband here.)

The natural-scientific procedure, says Rickert, is quite as well justified in the realm of the psychical as it is in that of the physical.

To be sure, the achievements of the physical sciences surpass those of the psychical, but this is simply a difference of degree, not of logical character. There is no logical warrant for assuming that the difference cannot be notably diminished or even wholly overcome.[16]

There is, however, a genuine contrast between two types of science: (1) the natural-scientific; and (2) the historical. The first aims at generalization, at nomothetic laws; the second, at individualization, at idiographic description. One attains its generalizations by dissecting wholes as empirically experienced into abstract, conceptualized units that are relatively simple and uniform; and then recombining them into clearly-articulated structures. The other achieves its individualizations by placing complex wholes within the context of larger wholes or otherwise demonstrating their uniqueness and non-duplicable ramifications. Further, when a given historical whole is considered in its connections with another, more inclusive historical whole, it is not thereby assigned a niche in a classificatory schema of the variety-species-genus variety, as in certain of the natural sciences. On the contrary, it becomes an individualized, perpetually distinguishable part of a new individualized whole which is in every respect as unique and unrepeatable as each of the less inclusive wholes comprised in it.[17] Once more, in still another dress, Romanticism steps forth.

The antithesis between the natural sciences and history, moreover, is not between the abstract and the concrete. The historian must abstract from the full empirical reality in determining which complexes of personages and events shall be considered as historical wholes and which of the many determinable wholes are to be regarded as worthy of attention. Reality as given in immediate experience is transmuted into manageable constructs by the historian as well as by the natural scientist. There is always selection, and it always takes place with regard to meaningfulness, or better, to significance.

Selection in terms of historical significance is determined by the relevance of the particular aspect chosen to some supreme cultural value. This does not mean that the historian must evaluate by calling this good and that bad in accordance with the degree to which the realization of the supreme value is furthered or checked. It is possible, for example, to say that Bismarck was a significant personality in relation to the supremacy of the German state, considered as an ultimate value, without approving either of Bismarck or of the doctrine of state-supremacy.

There may eventually be a science of history, says Rickert, but it will not follow the pattern of the natural sciences. If sociology aspires to be a natural science, then it must relinquish all claim to the establishment of "historical laws." The very essence of history is individualization, and where individualization reigns, generalization cannot.[18] So Rickert.

Beginnings of Systematic Sociology as such: Tönnies. — Let us now turn for a time to more strictly sociological writers. The history of social thought makes at least one thing fairly clear: it is exceedingly difficult to say when any specific trend actually began. We must have landmarks on our journey, however, and for this purpose we can do no better than choose Ferdinand Tönnies (1855–1936) as the initiator of that type of sociological analysis which has recently been christened systematic sociology.

Tönnies is interesting for at least two things. First, he paid little attention, if perusal of his chief writings affords any ground for conclusion, to the methodological controversies resounding all around him during his youth. Second, his most important work was written while he was still a young man; the plan of his *Gemeinschaft und Gesellschaft* dates from 1880–1881, and the first edition from 1887.

This book has recently enjoyed a tremendous vogue; the eighth edition appeared in 1935 and has been reprinted since then. *Gemeinschaft und Gesellschaft* is devoted, as the title indicates, to the analysis of "community" and "society," terms which Tönnies uses to denote social structures such as are found in the isolated peasant village on the one hand and the highly accessible urban center on the other. (American sociologists implicitly recognize this distinction, not only in their writings but even in the organization of their annual programs: a section is frequently devoted to "folk sociology" and another to "urban sociology." We have already called attention to the marked influence Tönnies has exercised on several of the concepts basic to the present work.) Inseparably linked with this distinction between forms of social structure is the division of the volitional aspects of personality into *Wesenwille* and *Kürwille*, i.e., into essential will and arbitrary will. This is not mere scholastic word-juggling: some idea of the empirical implications of the dichotomy can be gained by calling attention to the fact that *Wesenwille* is practically equivalent to non-rational, vitally determined acceptance of existing social arrangements, whereas *Kürwille* corresponds

to calculating choice dictated by egocentric considerations that
may run directly counter to prevailing standards.[19]

The significant thing about Tönnies's work is the close association it establishes between personality and social structure, thus
anticipating Baldwin, Cooley, Durkheim, Mead, and a number
of related thinkers. It is probable that Tönnies was to some extent influenced by the folk-psychology of Lazarus and Steinthal,
as well as by that promulgated by Wundt, who delivered his first
lecture on the subject in 1874 — over six years before the first
outline of *Gemeinschaft und Gesellschaft* was drafted. It will
also be recalled that Lindner's Herbartian social psychology had
appeared in 1871. Whatever the influences on Tönnies's " folk
sociology " may have been, however, there can be little doubt
that Karl Marx had a great deal to do with his analysis of urban
society and mentality.[20] Indeed, it seems clear that Marx's resolute exposure of the seamier sides of competition in *Das Kapital*
exerted an influence on Tönnies second only to that of Hobbes,
with whose " war of each against all " he had early become familiar.[21] He wrote a number of important treatises expanding
the ideas contained in *Gemeinschaft und Gesellschaft,* as well as
several others which do not derive directly from this source.
His influence on German sociology has been so all-pervasive that
it is difficult to single out any one disciple or school that may be
regarded as representative, although he possesses an outspoken
and gifted proponent in his son-in-law, Rudolf Heberle.[22] From
1921 to the late summer of 1933 Tönnies was president of the
now defunct *Deutsche Gesellschaft für Soziologie.*

The Study of the Forms of Sociation: Simmel. — The contribution that Tönnies made to German sociology has proved to
be of great significance, but although his sociology was quite
self-contained, he did very little to establish the science as an
independent academic discipline. This task fell to Georg Simmel
(1858–1918), a philosopher whose literary and forensic gifts
eventually made him the most popular lecturer at the University
of Berlin in spite of the handicap imposed by his Jewish ancestry.
He possessed a keenly analytical and highly critical mind — indeed, Simmel's first writings manifest the peculiarity of being
more analytical than constructive, and in addition fail to reveal
any positive standpoint of his own. Gradually, however, he began to devote his efforts to the definition and construction of
a variety of sociology in striking contrast with the all-inclusive
systems of cosmic philosophy put forward under the name of

sociology by Schäffle and similar encyclopedists. The way in which he effected a separation of sociology from social philosophy, the philosophy of history, and allied methods of dealing with social life was to concentrate on the modes of social interaction, on the manner in which human beings associate and dissociate. His researches along these lines extended from 1890 to about 1910, although a distinct ebb in his interest seems to have set in at approximately the period when his chief sociological work, *Soziologie: Untersuchungen über den Formen der Vergesellschaftung*, was finally published in book form (1908). After this time, aesthetics and metaphysics claimed his attention almost exclusively, but he had already done enough to start sociology on its way to acceptance as a social science coördinate with the others.[23]

He was able to do this because of the sharp delimitation he succeeded in establishing, a delimitation ostensibly based on the Kantian antithesis between " form " and " content," but actually of a different character. For Simmel, the forms of sociation are simply those uniformities of human interaction that occur in social groupings of widely varied nature and in conjunction with diverse purposes. For example, the social phenomena of supraordination and subordination appear in ecclesiastical organizations, criminal gangs, associations of business men, and military bodies. The highly discrepant purposes or ends of action held in view by the members of these markedly different groupings make up the " content " of the behavior in question, and this content is proper object-matter for the student of religion and theology, the criminologist, the economist, or the military tactician. The sociologist, on the other hand, considers the highly variable content of human interaction only in order that he may discover the relatively invariable forms. A few of the topics dealt with by Simmel will further illustrate his meaning: " The Intersection of Social Circles "; " The Number of Members as Determining the Form of the Social Group "; " Secrecy and the Secret Society "; and " The Sociology of the Stranger." [24] In all such topics it is possible, said Simmel, to isolate uniformities that are relatively independent of historical and cultural setting and of specific motivation.

These recurrent regularities of interaction Simmel termed forms, and thereby gave the name " formal sociology " to the trend he initiated. This name has been exceedingly unfortunate because of the erroneous connotations it evokes, e.g., formal logic, rigidity, barren abstraction. Critics who have apparently understood very little of Simmel's work have even gone so far as to equate his exclusion of content, in the special meaning attached to that term, with " emptiness." *Ergo,* say these writers, Simmel's sociology is a hollow shell; the warm, pulsing life of society is to be sought elsewhere. Now the amazing thing about Simmel's work is precisely his ability to lend color and movement to the most abstract type of sociological analysis; there is far more content in his sociology, using that term in its ordinary meaning, than is to be found in the work of many if not most of his critics.

At the same time, it cannot be denied that Simmel's sociology has many defects, chief of which are its unsystematic character, its use of an illustrative rather than a truly comparative method, and its lack of emphasis — the unimportant is dealt with in minute detail, and Simmel's delight in subtleties and nuances of meaning buries his main points under the resulting sediment. As Wiese puts it, " From his numerous theories of the manifold forms of sociation there has arisen no unifying theory of sociation and its forms." [25]

The Hibernation and Sudden Emergence of Sociology. — This concludes our hasty survey of psycho-sociology and sociology during the period before the World War. To be sure, a number of the writers of whom we shall speak had definitely aligned themselves with the sociological movement at least as early as the founding of the *Deutsche Gesellschaft für Soziologie* in 1909, and several, notably Max Weber and Sombart, were already widely recognized at that time. But — and here is the decisive factor — this recognition was accorded them as economists or exponents of other social sciences, *not as sociologists.* The consequence was that the distraction of public interest by the war and the general delay in publication made many persons think of sociology as a mushroom growth, cultivated by dexterous opportunists, when it once more attracted attention in the early 1920's. This effect of sudden emergence was intensified by the new problems thrust upon the German and Austrian peoples by the collapse of the Empire and the Dual Monarchy, the framing of new constitutions, the rise of the Social-Democratic parties to power, the Spartacist revolt, and the ferment of the Youth Movement. Topics that had long before run through the mill of public discussion in other countries became questions of the hour in post-war Germany and Austria, and to many of these questions not even the hitherto omniscient professors of philosophy and the *Staatswissenschaften* could return satisfying answers. Sociologists, spurious and genuine, began to be accorded a respectful hearing. The most prominent, for the time at least, were Werner Sombart, Max Weber, Ernst Troeltsch, Alfred Weber, Othmar Spann, Max Scheler, Alfred Vierkandt, and Leopold von Wiese. In addition to these professorial sociologists we must mention Oswald Spengler, whose " morphology of world-history " (discussed in Chapter Twenty) is undeniably a sociological treatise, whatever one may think of its validity.

Sombart and Interpretative Sociology. — This brilliant writer, known in the United States primarily as an economist, began to develop sociological leanings early in his career. Strongly influenced by Marx and the historical school, he executed a number of amazingly penetrating studies in the sociology of economics, among them his famous *Der Bourgeois* (translated as *The Quintessence of Capitalism*), *Die Juden und das Wirtschaftsleben*, and *Luxus und Kapitalismus.*[26] These specialized studies really constitute Sombart's greatest claim to sociological eminence, but the sheer size and sweep of his socio-economic treatise, *Der moderne Kapitalismus,* has led many people to deal with him as if he were a man of one book, and hence to lose sight of other examples of his sociological method. Sombart's basic sociological approach is difficult to isolate or characterize, but some idea of it can be given by the following quotation, in which the influence of Dilthey is apparent:

> I have termed the concept of " understanding " the most important in our science, for the reason that it is a cultural science. All observation in cultural science strives toward " understanding," i.e., toward knowledge from within outward. The natural sciences, on the contrary, can only " explain," i.e., must infer inner states from outer. All truly scientific sociology strives to become " understanding " sociology. What we do not " understand " is either philosophy, in the sense of metaphysics, or crude science. . . .
>
> We cannot call it anything less than unpardonable intellectual provincialism when we are time and again enjoined to apply the principles of mechanics or some other natural science to the phenomena of culture. Such naïve folk seem to have the delusion that the methods of the natural sciences alone enable us to arrive at " true " knowledge. As a matter of fact, the situation is precisely the reverse: we have " true " knowledge insofar as we " understand "; i.e., our knowledge is limited to the sphere of culture and fails us in the realm of nature.[27]

The position here defended is dealt with more explicitly in his *Die drei Nationalökonomien,* where he maintains that the only valid economic theory is that erected on the basis afforded by " understanding " or interpretative sociology. In a book review of this work, Robert E. Park has stated Sombart's position as follows:

> Looking at a chess game in operation, observing it objectively as a natural phenomenon, one may discover how, in general, the different pieces may be expected to move. If one is ingenious and patient enough he may be able to calculate, within limits, what the result of a certain line of play may be. But he will never be able to find out as long as he merely seeks to describe objectively, that is, in mathematical and statistical terms, the changes taking place upon the chess board, just what the game is about or what the different players are trying to accomplish. The *Wesen* of a chess game, as Sombart would describe it, is identical with the general rules and purposes of the game — rules which at once guide and limit the player in his playing. This *Wesen* can be understood quite apart from the specific purposes which any player at any point in the game may happen to have. The moves and tactics of every individual player as well as the general plan and purpose of the game become intelligible only when one understands what each player is trying to achieve. The general purpose is common to both players, though each has his own individual notion of how to play to win. . . .

> To understand a thing in this sense is to take account of the reason, the purpose, and, in general, the function which it performs in a given cultural complex. We understand a tool as we understand a language, not by descriptions of the parts of speech of which it is composed, nor of the rules of syntax which describe how words are put together, but by interpreting these formal symbols in terms of the sentiments and ideas they are intended to express.[28]

In *Die drei Nationalökonomien,* and in several of its forerunners as well, there is also apparent the influence of Rudolf Stammler (1856–   ) and Max Scheler (1874–1928), both of whom contributed toward the development of " noölogical sociology." Except for the anti-naturalistic animus evident in Sombart's, Stammler's, and Scheler's usage of *Geist,* it might be said that " noölogical sociology " is simply the study of the effect of the prevailing mentality of a given people on the processes of social life, and hence is closely similar to the analyses carried out by Granet, Max Weber, and others.

Recently Sombart has done a good deal of backing and filling in methodological matters related to *Geist,* and has not been uninfluenced by the political considerations surrounding German intellectual life under Hitler.

Interpretation within Ideal-Typical Schemas: Max Weber. — Another sociologist who has made use of the idea of understanding, albeit in a more cautious and less dogmatic way, is our ubiq-

uitous Max Weber (1864–1920). Indeed, it was he who gave
the first outstanding example of its application in his famous
study, *Die protestantische Ethik und der Geist des Kapitalismus*
(first version 1904–1905),[29] and who also published the first
article attempting to define and show the further possibilities
of this kind of sociology.[30] So great has been Weber's influence
that practically all present-day German sociology directly or
indirectly makes use of concepts he formulated, among them his
well-known definition of social action:

" Action " . . . denotes that type of human conduct (overt or covert,
passive or active) to which a *meaning* is assigned by the acting person
or persons. " Social " action differs from this in that it is carried out, according to the intention of the acting person or persons, with reference
to the behavior of others and is oriented toward the behavior of those
others throughout its course.[31]

(It must be granted, however, that in spite of the precise meaning that Weber himself attached to each word in this definition,
those who now incorporate it in their sociological systems interpret it in ways that are sometimes quite discrepant.)

We have already discussed Max Weber's use of the ideal-
typical method in historical sociology; hence we shall not devote
much space to it here. It seems necessary, however, to point out
that Max Weber's conception of understanding led him to use
an ideal type in his sociology that has evoked some criticism.
This type is framed with the aim of embodying in it the greatest
possible measure of rationally purposeful action, on the assumption that we must first discover what conduct would be rational in
a given situation before non-rational factors preventing or distorting such conduct can be determined. This emphasis on " the
rational man " has led to the unjustified criticism that Max
Weber's sociology is rationalistic; his express denials of this
have been willfully ignored. We therefore quote at length one
of his most illuminating utterances:

Human conduct, whether " overt " or " covert," manifests patternings
and regularities of sequence just as do all other happenings. Nevertheless, the patternings and regularities of human conduct differ from all
others in one important respect: they alone may be " understandingly "
interpreted in the full sense of the term (*verständlich*). Now all interpretations of human conduct that produce this intelligibility have a certain inherent plausibility; we incline to regard them as self-evident.
But such evidential validity (*Evidenz*) is after all qualitative and extremely variable; the mere fact that a particular interpretation is un-

usually plausible is no warrant of its empirical accuracy. Instances of conduct which, externally considered, run the same course and produce the same effects may be based upon extremely diverse motives, and of these possible motives or constellations of motives the one which is most " understandable " (and therefore plausible or self-evident) is not necessarily the one actually operative.

Hence it cannot be too strongly emphasized that any " understanding " of or insight into the conduct in question must be carefully verified by the customary methods of causal inference before it can be raised to the rank of a valid " understandable explanation." The greatest degree of self-evidence attaches to interpretation in terms of rational purpose (*zweckrational*). Conduct may be termed rationally purposeful when it is completely centered upon means *subjectively* viewed as adequate for the attainment of ends *subjectively* conceived to be unambiguous.[32]

The last sentence perhaps requires comment and illustration. *Objectively* conceived, the means chosen to attain a given end may be wholly inadequate, and the end itself may be self-contradictory, but so long as the person or persons in question *believe* the means to be sufficient and the end to be definite, the conduct must be called rationally purposeful. For example, a military leader may count upon the certainty and value of victory as the end he pursues, and may shape his means, his military tactics, accordingly; his conduct is rationally purposeful even though defeat is certain and victory useless — *objectively*. In other words, Max Weber insists that the sociologist must assume the standpoint of the subject as a necessary step in the achievement of " understandable explanation."

In laying stress upon rationally purposeful conduct Max Weber does not, however, deny that a large measure of intelligibility also attaches to ordinary emotional processes and the influences they usually exert upon ourselves and others. There may be emotional " understanding." This of course does not mean that all conduct is equally intelligible: ecstatic states, mystic experiences, the inner lives of children, and above all, certain psychopathic conditions are at least partially closed to us. But, says Weber:

For the empirical disciplines the " understandable " has elastic limits. . . . The " abnormal " as such is not beyond the bounds of intelligibility. . . . One need not be Caesar to understand Caesar. . . . On the other hand, there are many ordinary, " normal " psychical processes lacking in that peculiar qualitative self-evidence from which " understanding " derives. Quite as opaque as many psychopathological processes are the sudden transitions from one plateau of learning to another. Consequently the social sciences must deal with such determinable but non-" understandable " psychical regularities in exactly the same way as they deal with the " laws " of physics.

From the foregoing it is apparent that in spite of the high degree of intelligibility attaching to interpretation in terms of rational purpose, it is not in any sense the goal of sociological explanation. Indeed, the knowledge we possess concerning the predominance of non-rational factors such as emotions and moods . . . makes it possible to say that an exactly opposite goal might be quite as easily reached.[33]

Here it is apparent that Max Weber explicitly disavows any conception of man as a " rational animal," as *Homo rationalis*. In the same context, however, he points out that ideal types incorporating rational conduct are often of the highest value in strictly sociological analysis, *which in spite of its " understanding " method is not to be confused with psychology.*

Avoidance of Value-Judgments. — Weber drew many of his methodological leads from Rickert, and among others was the conception of " relevance to value." All selection of data in the social sciences is determined by the relation of the particular data to some supreme cultural value or value-system. Inasmuch as the sociologist, of all men, should be aware of the multiplicity of possible and actual value-systems, how was it possible for Max Weber to grant so much to relativism and at the same time to champion the cause of valid, objective knowledge? Or, as Parsons puts it :

How then does he escape being drawn into a closed relativistic circle so that " knowledge " becomes a function only of the subjective values of the scientist, an expression of his valuations (*Wertungen*)?[34]

Max Weber's way out of this dilemma was to assert that it is possible to separate the scientist's subjective preferences from the logical, universal elements in his thought which cut across discrepant, particular value-systems. There is a formal schema of proof which is at least potentially universal, and it can be isolated by sifting out the scientist's likes and dislikes. It is therefore possible to uphold a certain type of historical relativism and at the same time to maintain that this relativism can be transcended under certain circumstances and for certain purposes.

In order to achieve this type of universality, however, the scientist must renounce all extra-scientific pretensions. He must cease posing as the high-priest of modern life, with answers to all problems. Further, the layman must be taught not to expect more from science than it can legitimately offer. If anyone approaches science in the expectation of receiving solutions for his most urgent problems, says Weber, he is mistaken and he will be sorely disappointed. All that science can teach it teaches in the conditional form: If you wish to produce this particular effect, then you must use these particular means. Whether the effect is desirable as a goal, however, science cannot decide. It can, however, do something else: it can discover that the means which must be used produce certain secondary effects that may not have been considered when the goal was chosen. But whether these unexpected effects are so bad that they invalidate the original intention, or whether the intended effect is so desirable that the secondary consequences seem comparatively negligible — here again is a problem that science cannot decide.

Why? Because, as Weber goes on to say, the values involved cannot be quantitatively measured, and if they conflict, they cannot be reconciled by proportional mixture. Moreover, no hierarchy of values fixing qualitative ranks for the multitude of irreconcilable human preferences has yet been accepted by mankind, and there seems no likelihood of such acceptance in the foreseeable future. The conflict between values can be decided only by an arbitrary choice which is ultimately based on the kind of person the chooser happens to be and the culture in which he has been molded.

Max Weber shows with the accuracy of the scientist what science can and cannot do. First, it can supply the technical instruments for the realization of purposes. Second, it can consequently reveal more thoroughly the exact spot where the vital decision lies. Third, it can analyze the structure of decisions and show that irrational or non-rational factors swing the balance, that final, vital decisions are not and cannot be based on reason. In so far as the scientist is a genuine scientist, he will have to admit, to himself and others, that those decisions on which life in its fullest sense depends cannot be finally made by science. That is to say, he will have to grant, says Weber, that science has no normative validity.

This of course does not mean that the scientific sociologist is barred from dealing with values as data; they lie in the very focus of the sociological lens. It does mean, however, that he is barred from *judging* the ethical rightness or wrongness of human conduct. He may say, in effect: If such conduct continues, the social structure within which it occurs will be destroyed. But he may *not* say: You must stop such conduct because it will destroy the social structure of which you are a member. Perhaps it is a good thing that it should be destroyed, or perhaps it is bad; the sociologist *as sociologist* has no value-*judgment* to make.

We should also note, however, that Max Weber never denied the sociologist the right of asking what function a given process, etc., serves within a given structure. He may with entire propriety seek to determine what functional value that process has in the maintenence of that structure; i.e., he may make " inductive evaluations of functional appropriateness," to use Woodard's phrase. This is not value-judgment; in stating the fact that *esprit de corps* is essential to an efficient regiment, for example, we are not committed either to approval or to condemnation of the " military virtues " or the ends military organization serves.

In barring value-judgments to the sociologist in his strictly sociological capacity, however, Max Weber did not counsel passivity or indifference. His own life as political thinker and doer shows clearly that it is possible to differentiate between analysis and action without injury to either. To be sure, the scientist cannot wholly compartmentalize himself if he wishes to avoid schizophrenia. His function as specialized scientist is continually interfering with and contributing to his function as rounded, human personality, and *vice versa*. He is to be pitied, in fact, if this reciprocal relation does not hold, but that is no reason for saying that the two poles between which the relation exists cannot and should not be distinguished by the scientist himself.[35]

The most convincing demonstration of the validity of Max Weber's position on the value-judgment issue is an examination of his own work. His opponents can seldom stand the same test. But we must say no more about this matter, for we do not wish to give the impression that the slogan " Freedom from value-judgments " is all that sociology and the social sciences owe to Max Weber. He has provided modern research with so many other methods, tools of analysis, and attested results, that we cannot even begin to list them all here. We have several times acknowledged our indebtedness to him, but we are so deeply obligated that still another statement is in order. Few if any German sociologists more amply repay intensive study, and his influence, although probably on the wane in contemporary Germany and Austria, is likely to become increasingly important in other countries.

Troeltsch and the Sociology of Religion. — The philosophy of history of Ernst Troeltsch (1865–1923) was included among our " rejected types " in Chapter Twenty, but it would be a mistake to assume from this that so eminent an author could be so summarily dismissed. Troeltsch marched side by side with Max Weber in several fields. For example, he attacked the extreme historical relativism against which Weber also protested; in *Der Historismus und seine Probleme* (vol. I, 1922) he surveyed the whole range of " historicist " doctrines, and effectively punctured many of them. Unfortunately, Troeltsch died before he could complete the second volume of *Der Historismus;* in it he planned to set forth his own constructive theory. Again, Troeltsch provided a mass of corroborative detail for the Calvinism-capitalism thesis that Max Weber's activity in other fields did not give him time to supply. Moreover, Troeltsch worked out in detail certain fundamental differences between the branches of Protestantism, notably Lutheranism and Calvinism, at which Weber had been able only to hint. A sample of Troeltsch's cogent analysis should be quoted:

Things are not simple in this matter. . . . Thus when Luther calls men to be " diligent in their calling," it is viewed as a Christian justification for profit-seeking, which will have received a great impetus from this justification. In taking this view one forgets that this vocation-doctrine had already been Catholic doctrine for a long time under the guise of the graded contribution of all workers to the purposes of society imposed by the law of nature. For Luther only the monastic limitations dropped away, and this strengthened the secularizing of princely property and the rational economic policy of governments. Above all it is forgotten that the Protestant idea of a " calling " in the Lutheran sense corresponds closely to a conservative, class-organized society. It kept each man in his class and bade him expect only protection of life and a minimum subsistence from the authorities, while suffering with patience the unrighteousness of the world. It is the same traditional attitude towards life that Catholicism prescribed. It is least of all a spur to the upward movement of modern economic life. . . .

On the other hand, Calvinism has much greater importance in this matter. Here, as in politics, it is a force standing closer to modern life. . . . This has recently been demonstrated by Max Weber, who attacking the great problem of present economic history — that of the nature and origin of capitalism — has raised the question of the intellectual, ethical, and philosophical presuppositions of the system. Without a certain intellectual basis such a system cannot achieve mastery. Or as Sombart expresses it, in dealing with the same problem: The great mass of those who carry it on, and especially its founders, must have a certain economic attitude as well as external stimuli, compulsions, and drives. From the capitalistic system there is to be distinguished the " capitalistic spirit " without which the former would never have attained its power over the mind. . . .

This spirit, according to Weber, did not come of itself with industrial inventions, the discoveries, and profits of trade. It did not develop in the money economy of the later Middle Ages, in the capitalism of the Renaissance, and in Spanish colonization, for here it had to fight and conclude compromises with a counteracting spirit, the Catholic-nurtured conscience. Hence he has formed the conjecture, in view of the fact that capitalism did flower upon Calvinistic soil, that the Calvinist religio-ethical spirit was of special importance for the development of this capitalistic spirit. With penetrating scrutiny he shows how it is precisely the Calvinistic asceticism which produced not so much capitalism as its prerequisite spirit, and formed the basis upon which its unnatural expansion took place. . . . On the basis of this economic attitude the early capitalism of the Huguenots, the Dutch, the English and Americans, arose, and it is yet visibly associated with it in America and Scotland and among English Dissenters in the period of " high capitalism." The various pietistic and Anabaptist groups influenced by Calvinism have nurtured the same attitude.

Weber's demonstration is in my judgment successful, although one may perhaps emphasize more strongly that this special sort of reformed asceticism was supported by the particular conditions of business life in western Europe, and especially by the exclusion of the Dissenters from the state and from political culture. In like manner the traditional position of Lutheranism was supported by the economic decline of Germany due to the Thirty Years' War. It is, however, clear that the contribution of Protestantism to modern economic development is not due to Protestantism as a whole, but to Calvinism, Pietism, and the sects, and even in their case it is indirect and was not intentional.[36]

We do a certain injustice to Troeltsch, however, in considering his contributions to sociological theory only in conjunction with those of Max Weber, for he was an original thinker of high rank. Instance the fact that he was among the first to distinguish clearly between the ecclesia (which he calls *Kirche,* thus depriving himself of an inclusive concept) and the sect. This distinction has proved surprisingly fruitful, as numerous monographic studies based upon it demonstrate. In essence Troeltsch proceeds as follows:

(1) The social structure known as the ecclesia is a predominantly conservative body, not in open conflict with the secular aspects of social life, and professedly universal in its aims. The phrase "Come ye out from among them and be ye separate" has no place in the ideology of the genuine ecclesiastic; "Force them to come in" is likely to characterize his thinking. The fully developed ecclesia attempts to amalgamate itself with the state and the dominant classes, and strives to exercise control over every person in the population. Members are *born into* the ecclesia; they do not have to *join* it. It is therefore a social structure

somewhat, although remotely, akin to the nation or the state, and is in no sense elective. Membership in an ecclesia is a necessary consequence of birth into a family, folk, or similar structure, and no special requirements condition its privileges. . . .

Two main varieties of the ecclesia can be distinguished: international and national. The Catholic Church is the most outstanding example of the first, whereas the Lutheran and Anglican varieties illustrate the second. . . .

(2) The sect is in marked contrast to the ecclesia. In the first place, it is a relatively small structure that has abandoned the attempt to win the whole world over to its doctrines; the phrase, " Come ye out from among them and be ye separate " is followed literally. It is readily seen that the sect is an elective body which one must join in order to become a member. At bottom, the sect is exclusive in character, appeals to strictly personal trends, and emphasizes ethical demands; it frequently requires some definite type of religious experience as a prerequisite of acceptance. It therefore attaches primary importance to the religious experience of its members prior to their fellowship with the sect, to the so-called " priesthood of all believers." It frequently rejects an official clergy, preferring to trust for guidance to lay inspiration rather than to theological and liturgical expertness.

In many instances sects are persecuted, but this persecution only reinforces the separatist and semi-ascetic attitude toward the world inherent in the sect as a social structure. At times it refuses participation in the government, at times rejects war and other resort to force, and at times seeks to sever as much as possible the bonds which tie it to the common life of the larger social structure within which it develops. In general, the sect prefers isolation to compromise. . . .

Sects exist in great variety at the present time, but they were to be found even before the period of the Reformation, as evidenced by the Cathari, the Waldensians, the Wyckliffites, and others. Since the Reformation, of course, many such bodies have come into being: Anabaptists, Mennonites, Huguenots, Presbyterians, Baptists, and scores of others dot the pages of history.[37]

Troeltsch does not add the further useful distinctions of the denomination and the cult, but they really grow out of his analysis. The concepts of ecclesia and sect were incorporated in his massive treatise, *Die Soziallehren der christlichen Kirchen und Gruppen,* the first edition of which appeared in 1912; it is now exerting profound influence on the sociology of religion throughout the Western world. An English translation appeared in 1931, and it is to be hoped that as this becomes generally known American analyses in this field will not be confined, as they usually are now, to preliterate faiths on the one hand and the threadbare Fundamentalist-Modernist controversy on the other.

Neo-Romantic Universalism: Spann. — The Austrian prophet of so-called " universalism," Othmar Spann (1878–   ) traces his intellectual lineage as far back as the social philosophers of the ancient Orient, notably those of India. His more recent ancestry, however, he declares to have been furnished by the members of the German Romantic school, and particularly by Adam Müller, a sort of German DeMaistre.[38] The few mild traces of Romanticism we have from time to time noted in the work of other contemporary German thinkers pale into nothingness when contrasted with the highly-colored doctrines of Spann.

All of Spann's sociological thinking is in terms of the antithesis between " individualism " and " universalism." For him, individualism is a doctrine derived from the French rationalists. The upholders of this " Western " heresy are charged with asserting the absolute self-sufficiency of the individual. More, they are accused of promulgating the fallacy that society is an artificial aggregate based upon a contract between these autonomous individual entities. Nearly all contemporary German sociologists are branded as individualists by Spann, *and for good measure he places all Marxians in the same elastic category.* In this as in other respects he has furnished valuable ammunition for the Nazis: their condemnation of " liberal-Marxist ideology " is in close accord with his Neo-Romanticism (a term adopted by Spann himself).

The universalists, on the other hand, taking seriously Aristotle's dictum that the whole is logically prior to the part, maintain that the individual has reality only as a part of society, from which it follows that although the existence of others is a mere accident for individualism, with its " essential solipsism," it is a vital requisite for the development of *human* nature according to universalistic doctrine. To quote from an exposition of Spann's teaching by Landheer, one of his most loyal adherents:

. . . The heart of universalism is . . . that it finds the first, primary, original essence from which everything proceeds, not in the individual, but in the totality, in society. From this it follows: (1) that society itself is the true reality; and (2) that the whole is primary, and thus that the individual exists only as a component or member of the whole. The human being cannot develop out of himself, but only in spiritual community with others, in mutuality, or polarity — " *Gezweiung,*" as Spann calls it. This conception is necessary in order to understand that the world is an intelligible whole where nothing exists without relation to something else and where not blind chance but purpose governs as the final cause. Spann gives many examples — friendship, love, sociability, the family, education, and the like — to show how the human mind comes to expression only in relationship with other minds. He shows that we cannot understand the human mind as a spontaneous growth but only as something created and stimulated into existence, as *lumen de lumine,* where another mind is always the igniting torch, the beaming light out of darkness, the midwife of the mind, to use a Socratic figure. All mental life exists through the being of others. . . .[39]

Spann's Totalitarianism. — Except for the fact that Spann arrives at these conclusions about the human mind as a social product through a process reminiscent of Thomas Aquinas's method rather than of modern empirical science, there is little with which psycho-sociologists such as James Mark Baldwin, Cooley, Mead, Faris, Young, and others could quarrel. Further, several of these writers would find themselves in essential agreement with Spann's theory of society as an organic unity mentally constituted, although they would certainly take issue with his anti-naturalistic interpretation of *Geist.* It is to say the least doubtful, however, whether they would follow him in his totalitarian deductions from these principles. Here is a relevant sample:

   . . . the totality is something superindividual, something which is above and beyond the individuals, a creative force which does not belong to any single member. The totality, therefore, is a reality on its own account; and so it is most accurate to speak of the objectivity of the community or of the whole.[40]

Spann also maintains that sociology is necessarily normative, i.e., that it cannot avoid value-judgments, because of a principle complementary to Aristotle's " the whole is logically prior to the part." This principle is that " the perfect necessarily precedes the imperfect." In comprehending society as a totality, higher than the existence of its members, one comprehends a higher stage of perfection, and thus gains an objective standard of value. In understanding how society *is,* one therefore understands how society *ought* to be. (Needless to say, we are here engaged only in the task of exposition.) Thus equipped, the sociologist can easily determine the kind and relation of the concrete social structures in which the ontological-ethical reality, society as a totality, should be temporally and spatially actualized. Spann's own proposals, as set forth in his *Der wahre Staat* (3rd ed., 1930) and elsewhere, are as follows (we add comments in [ ]):

The basic principle of a universalistic community is justice instead of freedom. The latter is the ideal of liberalism. . . . Justice has not the meaning of equality, but of *suum cuique,* the distributive justice of Aristotle. This idea that everyone has to perform a certain function, which defines his position in the community, gives society its organic character. The performance by the individual of the task he is best fitted for gives the highest possible degree of vitality to society. . . . The inequality of functions causes the structure of society. Society has not the purpose of neglecting existing differences; on the contrary, it should be a true representation of the unequal natures of men as they really are. . . .

" Freedom " means in the individualistic sense the liberty to be free *from* others, not free *to* achieve some function. Freedom in the universalistic sense is only valuable as the possibility to follow the path which gives guidance to the individual, not as isolation. . . .

Another conception which has little structural value is " equality." . . . In nature we do not observe equality; every part of an organism has its special function. . . . It is clear that even in the most perfect democracy no such thing as entire equality has ever been realized. . . . But besides the fact that equality cannot be realized, it is not desirable according to a universalistic doctrine of society. The true structural laws of society are equality among equals and obedience of those low in the spiritual scale toward those more highly developed. . . . Between the different parts there has to be a certain balance which is best realized through a hierarchical structure. . . . Man is a spiritual being [here again we have *Geist*], and such a hierarchy must be built according to a scale of spiritual values.

Every individual belongs to a certain group. Every group has its place in the whole of society. This causes a structure of ranks in which all parts are given their place. . . . [From this it is easy to see why Spann has predilections for *dharma* and the Hindu caste system.]

The best form of society is the one which brings the best elements to leadership. The leadership of the best means the leadership of the spiritually and mentally highly-developed individuals. Organization from the top down [the *Führerprinzip* of the Nazis] is therefore the only truly totalitarian possibility. Social groupings should be kept open, however, by admitting capable individuals to higher education [thus leading to a " circulation of the élite "].

The following ranks, in an ascending scale, may be regarded as the necessary elements of an ideal society: (1) workers — their function is to procure the material means of the community; (2) skilled technical workers or artisans, and intellectual workers of the repetitive type; (3) industrial and business leaders — their function is the organization of the community activities necessary to material existence; (4) leaders of state, army, and church; (5) spiritual leaders and creators. . . .

Such a hierarchy, it is evident, would lead to a stabilization of the economic system. Property will be held in feudal tenure, as in the Middle

Ages. [Nazi laws regarding the inheritance of peasant estates now follow this principle.] Private property will remain, but its use will be regulated by law, as is already largely done today in some European countries. . . .

Group-ownership would check egotism and develop the more altruistic attitude which is a necessity for every higher type of culture. The Middle Ages were ideal in this regard. . . . Every group which performs a very important function in society ought to be subject to severe regulation to curb individualism and the pursuit of private interests. Inasmuch as the mentally highly-developed individuals would get the higher positions, there would be no hardship in this system, because they are by nature inclined to live in a more spiritual atmosphere [Plato's philosopher-kings in unexpected guise!]. . . .

Organization of the economic system could take place through labor unions on the one hand and employers' unions on the other. . . . In this way organic groups would be formed which would shape the life of the community. In every industry a representation of workers and employers ought to be built up which could be united in a central body. . . . [Guild socialism raises its head here.]

Civic activities could be transferred to these social groups. All decisions about legal problems in each industry should be made by the groups functioning in that industry. Special courts for the separate industries could develop their own codes. [The late NRA followed a pattern strangely like this.] Such a system of codes would create a very wholesome decentralizing tendency, and at the same time it would cause a much greater consciousness of civic duties. Further, the financial regulation of the various industries ought to be given over to them. . . .

All the different organizations of employers and workers in agriculture, industry, and trade ought to be united in one general representative body (*Ständehaus* — House of Estates). For the state only cultural activities such as religion, education, and law ought to be reserved. [This bears some resemblance to totalitarian or corporative ideas, but the similarity to the pluralistic type of guild socialism is too strong to be overlooked.]

The rich community life which would develop in a hierarchical system of corporations would solve the problems from which individualistic, egotistic society suffers. . . .

Sociology reveals the egotistic cause of social conflict very clearly, and therefore is able to contribute to the creation of a better type of society. . . . Only the over-development of the exact sciences and the concentration of mankind on economic pursuits can account for the existence of individualism. Rationally we may still understand the arguments advanced in its support, but their fundamentally erroneous character has been proved by the course of history.[41]

We have devoted to Spann an amount of space altogether out of proportion to his scientific importance because his puerile arguments show what happens when empirical science, with its freedom from value-judgments, is abandoned. But incredible· as it may seem, " with the tide of Fascism on the Continent, Spann has received fame and recognition. His advocacy of state corporativism and his teleological absolutism have provided the rationale for the politics of the extreme right." The sociology of knowledge has much to gain from a study of cases like that of Othmar Spann.[42]

Phenomenology and Scheler. — Neo-Romanticism of a markedly different type was once represented by the erstwhile leader of the Catholic intellectuals, Max Scheler (1874–1928). This protean personality ran the whole gamut of religious possibilities, from devout Catholic mysticism to a belligerent anti-Catholic position that bordered on atheism. Similarly, his philosophical system underwent many changes, and had it not been for his premature death he might have reversed his original postulates. His sociology was always integrally bound up with complex metaphysical structures and value-judgments of one or another type, and can hardly be dealt with properly in abstraction from the rest of his thought — yet we are forced to do so to a large extent. At the very least, however, the general phenomenological background against which Scheler's theories are outlined must be filled in, more especially as it is also essential for the comprehension of Vierkandt's " formal " sociology and of Mannheim's sociology of knowledge.

Phenomenology is realistic (in the sense of ontological realism). In so far as any trend of thought can be said to have an " origin," it takes its rise from the Austrian psychologist, Franz Brentano (1838–1917). This thinker derived from his studies of Aristotle, scholasticism, and Bernhard Bolzano the conception that mind is " intentional." Psychical activity " intends " or is primarily directed upon *objects;* only secondarily, and as it were in retrospect, does it regard itself. The objects thus intended may exist or not exist, but the fact that they are intended lends them their objective character.

Alexius Meinong (1853–1920), one of Brentano's students, developed a " theory of objects." In Meinong's generalized sense this includes *more* than both that which exists, e.g., a physical thing, and that which merely subsists, such as qualities, numbers, or propositions. " Object " takes in *anything* that can be referred to and thought about, i.e., anything that can be intended. Therefore even a " round square," which can neither exist nor subsist, can be dealt with as an object.

Objects are inherently hierarchical; those of one kind are founded upon or presuppose those of another. For example, " the difference between red and green " presupposes both " red " and " green," and these in turn presuppose " color." Consequently the theory of objects not only discloses objects which may be nonexistent, such as values, but also grades these subsistent objects in terms of " higher " and " lower."

Another student of Brentano's, Edmund Husserl (1859–), established phenomenology under that name. This is a descriptive study of consciousness-of-objects, which in view of the phenomenological assumption of the nature of mind as intentional, is really a study of consciousness as such. It differs from psychology because of the peculiar phenomenological attitude (*Einstellung*) which, in contrast to the ordinary conscious act taking its object as existent, " reduces " or devitalizes it. The consequence is that the question of existence is not raised; the object appears simply as the objective aspect of the act. As Perry puts it, " It is like the difference between believing in God and thinking of myself as believing in God. In the latter case the belief is not asserted but simply noted — God becoming only the objective component of the act."

The phenomenological relation of subject to object implies that the object is approached or addressed, rather than constituted, by knowledge. Herein Husserl takes issue with idealisms of every kind, and particularly with the Neo-Kantianism dominant in German scientific circles. For phenomenology the particular physical object, for example, cannot be intended except in partial aspects or in perspective; there is therefore a large amount of uncertainty and error in the intention of particulars. What *is* intended, however, is definitely a part of the object, and the remaining parts can in turn be intended, until finally the complementary aspects form a whole. Universals, on the other hand, can be completely " given " in a sort of intuition or " envisagement of essences " (*Wesensschau*). Moreover, the phenomenologist claims not only to be able to isolate universals, but also unfailingly to distinguish between universal and particular because the latter are always founded upon or presuppose the former.[43]

For all of Scheler's phenomenological predecessors, the act of " reduction " and the " envisagement of essences " remained primarily in the cognitive realm (if we may be permitted the use of a psychological term). The novel element in Scheler's phe-

nomenology lies in its stress on emotion. The act of " preferring " (*vorziehen*) is held to be intentional with relation to objective values as universals, and the result is the discovery of
an emotional scale (of what are essentially likes and dislikes)
which takes on the character of a universally binding value-hierarchy culminating in the *unio mystica*.

The work incorporating this theory, and the one on which
Scheler's philosophical reputation chiefly rests, is *Der Formalismus in der Ethik und die materiale Wertethik* (first version
1913). This is a destructive critique of the Kantian categorical
imperative and a vigorous assertion of the counterclaims of a
hierarchy of values ranging from the gross objective satisfac-
tions of vital impulses, such as hunger and sex, to God as the
object of all-consuming love. Emotional discriminations of lower
rank are presupposed in those of higher rank.

Scheler's phenomenological ethics, interesting as it may be,
is of importance here only because it is accompanied by a remarkably minute and penetrating analysis of emotional states.
Scheler was a curious combination of man of the world and
ecstatic mystic, of roué and saint. In another connection, Troeltsch
says that Scheler's doctrines are much more the result of " the
phenomenologically interpreted instincts of this Catholic Nietzsche than of the normative concepts of the Husserlian school." [44]
His power of living himself into other periods and personalities
was stupendous. The present writer once attended a series
of Scheler's lectures on the fundamental forms of personality,
and witnessed a display of histrionic virtuosity that the greatest
of actors might have envied. And yet it was not " histrionics "
in the usual derogatory connotation of that term; Scheler literally *was* by turns the ascetic, the repentant sinner, the hero,
and the exalted devotee about whom he spoke.

Scheler's outstanding analysis of emotional states was contained in a relatively small book published during the same year
as his major ethical treatise. This book at first bore the title of
*Zur Phänomenologie und Theorie der Sympathiegefühle und von
Liebe und Hass* (1913); it was later altered to *Wesen und Formen der Sympathie* (1922). We shall use the second version, in
spite of the fact that the first is more exactly descriptive.

The *Nature and Forms of Sympathy* was designed to support
Scheler's ethical doctrines, but it really stands in its own right
as a profound study of the social rôle of sympathy and of emotional understanding. Following Pascal, Scheler called it a " logic

of the heart." Beginning with a forthright attack on Adam Smith, Herbert Spencer, and like "sympathy theorists," Scheler expounds his own doctrines as follows:

We must distinguish between *genuine* sympathy and all conduct which serves only the apprehension, the understanding, and eventually the emotional imitation of the experiences of others. . . .

Another's experience can be fully present to perception as a result of emotional imitation or "mimpathy" without prior sympathetic feeling of any kind being present. A man means something very definite when he says "I can feel just as you do about the matter, but I have no sympathy for you." Such emotional imitation remains in the realm of *cognitive* conduct. The historian, the novelist, and the actor must possess in high degree the gift of "living themselves into" other selves and situations — they must be able to mimpathize. They do not, however, need to sympathize with their characters. . . . We comprehend by feeling, when we mimpathize, only the *quality* of the other's feeling — altogether without its passing over into us or creating a similar real feeling. . . .

Moreover, the imitation of another's gestures is of no real help in understanding him. . . . The fact that an experience going on in me is similar to that going on in others has very little if anything to do with understanding those others. Further, it is not necessary to evoke an emotion in oneself in order to understand such an emotion in others. In understanding the death-terror of a drowning person we do not in the least need to experience a real (but weaker) death-terror, as some writers assume. Such a theory contradicts the self-evident fact that in understanding we really do not experience that which is understood at all. . . .

Let us now turn to sympathy, which is founded upon or presupposes the components of mimpathetic understanding with which we have just dealt. . . . Four entirely distinct facts must be recognized: (1) immediate sharing of the same emotion with someone; (2) sympathy "in" something; e.g., rejoicing in another's joy or having pity for his suffering; (3) mere emotional contagion; and (4) complete emotional identification. These may also be termed: (1) compathy; (2) sympathy; (3) transpathy; and (4) unipathy.

(1) Father and mother stand by the corpse of a beloved child. They feel with each other the *same* sorrow, the *same* pain. This is not a case of "A feels sorrow and B feels it also, and in addition they both know that they both feel it." . . . They compathize in the sense of feeling and experiencing in solidarity not only the same value-complex but also the same emotional susceptibility in relation thereto. Sorrow as value-complex and sorrow as quality of function are here one and the same.

. . . Only psychical suffering can thus be felt, and not a physical pain, a sense-initiated feeling. There is here no " symagony," no physical pain felt through emotional contagion, *à la* Adam Smith's so-called sympathy. . . .

(2) Quite otherwise is the case of genuine sympathy. Here also suffering is not simply the effect of the perceived suffering of another. . . . The sorrow of B as belonging to B is first of all present in an act of understanding experienced as such an act. Upon the content of this act the original pity of A directs itself; i.e., *my* pity and *his* sorrow are phenomenologically *two* different facts and not *one* fact as in the case of compathy. Instead of emotional solidarity there appears emotional participation — sympathy in the only genuine sense. . . .

(3) Entirely distinct from both these cases is mere emotional introjection, contagion, or transpathy. . . . An example is the " infection " of a group of persons by a wail or lamentation set up by some one of them. . . . They weep in unison without any understanding of the values involved; transpathy remains on a physiological level. . . . This transpathy is what Adam Smith and his successors miscalled sympathy. . . .

Of course this has not the least thing to do with genuine sympathy. An emotional *intention* toward the sorrow (or joy) of the other does not occur, nor does any sort of participation in his experience. Characteristic of transpathy is the fact that it takes place between emotional *states,* and that it in no way presupposes any understanding of the emotion of the other. For example, one may detect only subsequently that a mournful emotion which one finds in oneself rests upon emotional contagion deriving from a funeral visited a few hours before. There is nothing in the grief itself that shows whence it came. . . .

Peculiar to this process of emotional contagion is the fact that it has a tendency to return . . . to its point of origin. . . . This circular process is especially evident in crowd phenomena; the *reciprocity* of the self-cumulative contagions leads the crowd members to extremes far beyond anything they would have undertaken as single individuals. . . .

(4) Last in this series is genuine emotional identification, or unipathy, of self with other. It is really only an intensified form or marginal case of transpathy, for just as in transpathy, the identification is quite as involuntary as it is unconscious. (Lipps thought, quite erroneously, that such cases are parallel to aesthetic empathy.) . . . There are instances on record in which such unipathy seems to be complete. Moreover, not only may it lead to momentary manifestations of genuine ecstasy, but may also endure for long periods — indeed, it may result in a sort of habitual euphoria throughout whole phases of an individual's life. Two polar types are found: idiopathic and heteropathic. In the first, unipathy may be so oriented as to cause complete absorption of other by self. [To quote a Sufi saying: " The macrocosm abides in me; eternal Allah's

naught but I."] . . . In the second, orientation may be such that " I "
. . . no longer live in " me," but entirely in " him." [The language of
Christian mysticism abounds in these heteropathic turns of expression.] . . . Empirical examples of unipathy are afforded by widely
divergent phenomena:

(a) One type is found in the " mystic participation " of certain preliterates. This has been dealt with by Lévy-Bruhl, and even though his
explanation in terms of " prelogicality " may not be satisfactory, there
can be no gainsaying the existence of such emotional identification. . . .

(b) Genuine unipathy of the heteropathic type was integrally bound
up with certain religious mysteries of the Greco-Roman world. The
mystery-worshiper, when he entered the ecstatic state, " knew " himself truly identical with the being, life, and fate of the *heros* — he " became " the god. . . .

(c) The relationship of hypnotizer and hypnotized is also an example
of genuine unipathy when the relationship is not merely of the transient,
exhibition type, . . . but where it becomes a stable and lasting relationship of such nature that the subject is continually drawn into all the attitudes of the hypnotizer's self. . . .

(d) The psychic life of the child also manifests unipathies. . . .
What in an adult is empathy is unipathy for the child; what is play for
the adult is for the child serious and at least momentarily real. When
a little girl " plays mama " with her doll, the play character of the play
(i.e., acting as if she were the mother) almost certainly exists only for
the adult spectator. The child herself feels herself in the instant of
" play " through and through one with her mother, and her doll one with
herself. . . .

(e) Further, we should designate as genuine unipathy the phenomenon of " mutual coalescence." . . . The most elementary form of
this unipathy is without doubt found in the love-suffused sex act. . . .
This lay at the root of the Dionysiac orgies . . . in which the coalescing
believers thought themselves immersed in the one primal source, the
natura naturans, in which their own personalities were once more dissolved.[45]

Scheler deals with several other forms of unipathy, but for present purposes they are less important than those noted; the number and kind of varieties surveyed suffice to give some idea of the
great significance of this kind of emotional identification.

Another point of interest is Scheler's scale of emotional preferences, for on this he establishes his " objective value-hierarchy."
The phenomenological " envisagement of essences " necessarily
involves, it will be recalled, the ranking of these universals; similarly, Scheler's " emotional preference of emotional fundamen-

tals " simultaneously yields the order in which these fundamentals stand. Unipathy is the basis or presupposition of mimpathy; mimpathy is the basis of sympathy; sympathy is the basis for love of one's fellowmen (*humanitas*); and love of humanity is the basis for " acosmic " love of God and " persons " (Scheler's substitute for " souls "). Psycho-sociology and Neo-Romantic Catholicism are stirred together.[46]

The balance of the *Nature and Forms of Sympathy* is taken up with efforts at unraveling the metaphysical web; with searching analyses of love and hate; with " spiritual-organismic " theories of the knowledge of other minds that remind one of Krause (see Chapter Twenty-eight); and with turgid discussions of Freud's naturalistic conception of love. The most determinedly devoted admirer of Scheler would probably be compelled to admit, if he retained any critical judgment whatever, that " the Catholic Nietzsche " perpetrated a good deal of incidental nonsense while arriving at his valid psycho-sociological insights. Much chaff, little wheat — but it is good wheat! Scheler's contributions to the analysis of sympathy and understanding cannot be ignored, regardless of what one may think of the phenomenological trimmings.

The Forms of Knowledge and Society. — In addition to his work in psycho-sociology, Scheler did much to extend the German and Austrian interest in the sociology of knowledge beyond the confines of Marxian and anti-Marxian controversy. His attention turned to this type of sociology during the World War, primarily as a result of his effort to understand English mentality, and resulted in a striking study of " cant " as related to English social history and social structure. (Some hints of *Wissenssoziologie* are to be found as early as 1913, however, in his attempt to show that the Kantian categorical imperative was a joint product of Pietism and Prussian discipline.) Not until 1924, however, did Scheler make published use of the term *Soziologie des Wissens*. In rapid succession thereafter a number of articles and books from his hand appeared on this topic, and the interest he aroused helped to create an audience for many writers who had been working along similar lines. After Scheler's premature death in 1928, the leadership passed to Karl Mannheim. The references to Mannheim's studies in the sociology of knowledge which we shall make in later sections will provide opportunity to say something further of Scheler's work in this field.[47]

Scheler also set forth many novel ideas in so-called " philosophical anthropology," the sociology of culture, historical sociology, and the sociology of war, but we must omit consideration of them here.[48] Suffice it to say that few more fertile minds have appeared in twentieth-century Germany, and that in spite of the absurdities of which he was often guilty, an intensive study of his thought will repay the effort.

Vierkandt and Cultural Sociology. — We have said, in effect, that Scheler's psycho-sociology and sociology is stronger than the flimsy phenomenological scaffolding which he believed to be its prop and mainstay. This fortunate state of affairs is not the case, however, with the work of Alfred Vierkandt (1867–), an ethnologist who later developed sociological inclinations.

To Vierkandt's early work in the field of cultural analysis the criticism implied in the foregoing paragraph does not apply, for in his *Die Stetigkeit im Kulturwandel* (1908) he remained within the limits of empirical knowledge, and worked out a masterly theory of cultural continuity and cultural change. In fact, he anticipated virtually everything of importance to be found in Ogburn's *Social Change* (1923) and Wissler's *Man and Culture* (1923). Vierkandt's central idea in this early work was that nothing in the realm of culture develops spontaneously, that everything is the product of gradual accumulation. In addition to setting forth the ideas of cultural continuity, inertia, and so on, he gave empirical examples such as the development of the bicycle (here we have Ogburn's use of invention foreshadowed), of economic institutions, languages, religion, and art. Further, he showed his essential agreement with the later cultural determinists in minimizing the rôle of " the great man " through calling attention to multiple inventions and similar phenomena. Once more, he was well aware of " cultural lag " as a characteristic typical of transitional periods, particularly of modern civilization, although he did not erect upon it a whole theory of social change, nor infuse it with value-judgments. Finally, he attacked the mechanical theories of diffusionism advanced by some of Ratzel's uncritical followers, pointing out that in order for any given culture trait to diffuse there must be a certain readiness for its acceptance, and that mere spatial proximity is a condition wholly insufficient in itself to explain the transmission of culture.[49]

Phenomenological Futilities and " Holism." — Had Vierkandt continued to develop these highly significant although perhaps one-sided ideas, a German variety of cultural sociology, profiting by a decade's priority, might have eventually overshadowed the luxuriant American growth. Unfortunately, he abandoned this line of investigation, and under the joint stimulus of Simmel,

Husserl, and McDougall (strange combination!) tried to work out a "phenomenological sociology." Vierkandt, like Simmel, wished to isolate the unchanging forms of social relations from the varying empirical modes of social interaction "in and through which they are manifested." But instead of focusing on the external uniformities of such interaction — as Wiese, for example, does — Vierkandt attempted to pierce to the presumably constant mental nucleus from which each variety of outward conduct was assumed to issue. Using the "phenomenological reduction" of Husserl, which enables every investigator to find "universals" that strangely resemble the notions he had before the "reduction" began, Vierkandt found that the universals underlying all social processes and structures are emotional.

This reminds one of Pareto's "sentiments," but Vierkandt apparently knew not Pareto. The emotions revealed by phenomenology are feelings of fellowship, shame, abasement, gratitude, power, and so on. Here is where the link with McDougall was forged, for McDougall regards the emotional core of instinct (or, to use his latest term, propensity) as its distinguishing element.[50] The propensity of flight may express itself through the climbing of a tree, the swimming of a stream, or in manifold other ways. The emotion of fear, however, enables the investigator to recognize (but without the fine discriminations of phenomenology) all these different methods of utilizing motor mechanisms in the service of a propensity for what they are; namely, the outward expressions of a determining inner impulse. Vierkandt even went so far as to say that McDougall's theory of instincts was the great Copernican turning-point of sociology, needing only to be extended and refined by the formal analysis of Simmel and the phenomenology of Husserl.

Another of Vierkandt's doctrines has to do with "the group mind." Impressed by the revelations of *Gestalt* psychology, he attempted to apply them to social life, and in so doing developed a doctrine something like the social realism of Durkheim, Spann, and others; viz., that social "wholes" have a "real" existence over and above the sum total of their members and the web of relations in which those members stand. This enthusiasm for "wholes" has also led Vierkandt to give an ethical twist to Tönnies's theory of community and society. Tönnies himself repeatedly asserted that *Gemeinschaft* is not necessarily of higher ethical value than *Gesellschaft,* but the fact that the former type of social organization is more homogeneous than the latter, and hence more nearly a "whole," has led Vierkandt to inject his private value-judgments into his sociological analysis to such an extent that the analysis is at least partially vitiated.[51] (Recently, however, Vierkandt has acted as editor of an excellent *Handwörterbuch der Soziologie*; with a catholicity oftentimes regrettably absent in German thinkers, he has assembled a corps of writers who have made the handbook an indispensable aid.)

Wiese the Systematizer. — Of all the sociologists of contemporary Germany, Leopold von Wiese (1876–) is the least open to the charge of scientific ethnocentrism. In fact, some of his blatantly " German " colleagues reproach him for paying too much attention to " Western " thought.

After winning recognition as an economist, his sociological interests, which had manifested themselves early in his academic career,[52] again came to the fore, and a series of fortunate circumstances made it possible for him to become editor of the *Kölner Vierteljahrshefte für Soziologie,* where some of the articles later incorporated in his *Allgemeine Soziologie* (Vol. I, 1924, Vol. II, 1929; second edition, one volume, 1933) first appeared. This treatise immediately placed Wiese in the front rank of German sociologists, a position which he still maintains.[53]

The chief influences on Wiese's sociological system were undoubtedly the writings of Georg Simmel, but Waxweiler, Ross, Spencer, Thomas, Max Weber, and a number of others have also played significant parts.[54] Wiese's effort is first of all to present sociology as a science that is clearly differentiated from other social sciences and that is empirical and systematic in its approach. The basic concepts are those of social process, social distance, social space, and social structure.[55] (The augmented adaptation of his major treatise, entitled Wiese-Becker, *Systematic Sociology* [1932], uses a slightly different set of categories; the essential points, however, are similar.) Instead of endeavoring to discover *inner* uniformities issuing in externally observable actions, as Vierkandt does, Wiese concentrates on those regularities of human interaction that are primarily *outward* phases of social action. The following schematic summary gives the gist of his system (approximately as set forth in the adapted first edition of the work mentioned above; the second edition differs in some important respects, but the broad outlines remain the same) :

   I. Sociology, as the science of interhuman relations as such, has two main divisions:
      A. The systematics of social relations;
      B. The systematics of social structures.

II. The most important element in both divisions is that of the social process.

III. The systematics of social processes in turn has two main divisions:
   A. Social processes between human beings relatively uninfluenced by social structures, i.e., common-human relations;
   B. Social processes within and between social structures, i.e., circumscribed relations.

IV. All social processes may be studied in two ways:
   A. As existent;
   B. As functional.

V. All social processes are sociative in one of three ways:
   A. Associative;
   B. Dissociative;
   C. In certain aspects associative and in others dissociative.

VI. All social structures may be divided into three main categories:
   A. Crowds (patternings of the lowest power);
   B. Groups (patternings of the intermediate power);
   C. Abstract collectivities (patternings of the highest power).

VII. The total process of sociation comprises all social relations, whether associative or dissociative, circumscribed or common-human.

VIII. The two fundamental processes of association and dissociation may be divided into principal processes, which may in turn be divided into sub-processes, and these in turn into single processes subsuming concrete social actions.

IX. In the systematics of social processes, all the inclusive and single processes, whether common-human or circumscribed, are to be dealt with as follows:
   A. Conceptually delimited and described;
   B. Assigned places within the total system;
   C. Analyzed as
      1. Objective phenomena if they are common-human;
      2. Subjective phenomena. . . .
   D. Ranked (" measured ") according to the degrees of association and/or dissociation they manifest;
   E. Compared with other social processes.

X. Social structures and single human beings do not stand in the position of earlier and later; neither has any priority; they are simultaneous and of equal importance and validity.[56]

This highly condensed outline of a wide-ranging system is necessarily abstract, and it must not be assumed that Wiese remains perpetually in the realm of abstractions. Not only does he deal with such concrete matters as exploitation, favoritism, bribery, and commercialization, but he also comes to grips with the problems of the pair, the family, the organized group, the

class, the state, and the church.[57] It is unfortunate that the studies
carried out by himself and his students in the fields of rural and
urban sociology are not widely known in the United States, for
if they were, it would be impossible to assert that he does not
deal with " facts." [58] Quite the opposite is the case; no present-
day sociologist is more consistently empirical in his method.
The contrary impression probably derives from the fact that he
abhors " raw empiricism," an abhorrence apparent in the high
degree of systematization which he has successfully brought into
his empirical investigations — but systematization is not synonymous with groundless speculation or arbitrary dogma. The type
of sociology presented by Park and Burgess is the closest American analogue of Wiese's work — indeed, inasmuch as both the
Cologne and the Chicago writers gained a large measure of their
methodological orientation from Simmel, the resemblance could
hardly have been avoided unless Vierkandt's erring example
had been followed.

Systematic-Empirical *Analysis.* — Wiese's lack of dogmatism,
consistent regard for empirical evidence, and conviction of the
necessity of systematization are all shown in the following
adapted and augmented quotation:

[We] . . . attempt to set forth a method by which the total process
of sociation can be observed, analyzed, and systematized. The assertion
may confidently be made that contemporary society abounds in gen-
eralities concerning social life, but that a method of observing the
specifically social zone has hitherto been lacking. To be sure, most sociologists have not been aware of any such deficiency; they have naïvely
believed that they could borrow the methods of other sciences or that
common sense would be sufficient. So far as the latter is concerned,
there is no doubt that it is the final and most important source of all
knowledge, but it is complex and composite and is essentially untransferable in its original form. It must be made accessible to all minds by
the method of delimitation, definition, comparison, and classification.
The lack of a single, unified method of studying the specifically interhuman produces disastrous consequences which are all too apparent
when we look at the chaotic conglomeration of preachments, dogmas,
legislative proposals, philosophical doctrines, statisticoid flights from
reality, and what not, currently offered as sociological knowledge. . . .

[With regard to the present treatise] . . . it must be emphasized that
no conclusions are stated as final, for if they were it would be quite
superfluous to recommend the application of the [systematic] method.
The results of previous analyses are announced only to the end that they
may be verified by others; there is no intention of adding to the already
far too numerous class of prejudices and premature judgments.

Such restriction of purpose affords some consolation for the deficiency inherent in this as in all general systems; namely, that a logically compelling, empirically demonstrable proof cannot be adduced at every point. There has of course been a consistent effort to refrain from all assertions that cannot be proven adequately — which is to say, immediately and in the same context. Nevertheless, such requirements can be entirely met only in monographic studies; a treatise dealing with the state, church, crowd, group, and similar plurality patterns would have to be expanded into a whole library if more than simple indication of possible lines of proof were attempted. The mere observer advocating a completely Baconian or " inductive " method (best exemplified by Steinmetz or Ogburn) loses sight of the fact that deductions and schematic constructs must be judged and tested with reference to the carrying power of the scientific " scaffolding " they represent rather than to the exhaustive knowledge of single factors manifest in them. No doubt it is vitally necessary to strive toward such exhaustive knowledge, but in the very nature of the case the goal can never be reached. It is much more important to erect a scaffold which can be used in working out the minute details of the sociological structure than first to perfect those details. As Jaspers says: " In order to deal with any problem with the maximum theoretical exactitude, it is absolutely necessary to construct frames of reference. Otherwise one remains aphoristic, devoid of any fruitful method of discovering gaps and interrelations, and unable to survey the ground already covered." [59]

Sociation and Understanding. — In the preceding sections of this chapter a great deal has been said about sociology as an " understanding " science. So crucial a question, and one to which so much attention has been paid in Germany, naturally called forth a statement from Wiese making clear his own position with regard to it:

In . . . agreeing with Max Weber . . . however, we by no means agree with Sombart! We wish only to " understand " the meaning *subjectively* assigned to the social action by the acting person or persons — in other words, we wish to gain insight into a certain aspect of motivation. . . . Sombart, however, claims that sociology should search for the *objectively* valid meaning because, forsooth, " sociology is a *Geisteswissenschaft,* a science of objective Mind." But we answer that a sociology which attempts to lay bare the objective, true, and valid " significance " of social actions is not sociology at all, but rather social philosophy and philosophy of history. The sociological method of observation and generalization is not philosophical, for it does not attempt to determine the " worth " or " significance " of social actions in the ethical or metaphysical sense, but merely describes, classifies, and, wherever possible, places in rank order the degree of association and/or dissociation they represent.

For fear of misunderstanding and imputation of a crudely naturalistic philosophy, let us hasten to add that the rank-order determination of intensity of association and dissociation here proposed is not "quantification" and "measurement" in the usual sense. Social processes cannot be "spatialized" altogether, and as a consequence the most that can be done is to construct a scale grading them from the weakest to the strongest and to assign arbitrary symbolic values to the various points of the scale, i.e., to *rank* them. . . .

Hence, although it is not the province of the sociologist to determine the significance of social actions in the ethical or metaphysical sense, he must "understand" them in some measure if he is successfully to rank them. He must describe the unique essence of each separate empirical process as well as discursive thinking in general permits; he dare not disregard the qualitative peculiarity of such relations as, let us say, friendship when compared with the inner nature of the erotic, parent-child, master-servant, or similar relations. Connection with the qualitative essence or "kernel" of relations can be established only through sympathy. . . . This connection once established and "understanding" achieved, the relation in question should then be viewed in and through its effects upon association and/or dissociation, and the degree of association and/or dissociation resulting should then be stated in terms of rank order, and if possible numerical or similar symbols should be used. This of course means that comparison with other kinds of relation resulting in different degrees of association and dissociation must be practiced; ranking necessarily involves comparison.

When we have thus ascertained the relative strength of the bond with which a given associative relation unites human beings, or conversely, when we have thus determined the relative strength of the barrier with which a given dissociative relation separates human beings, we have also achieved a more complete "understanding" of the relation; we have, paradoxically enough, come nearer to its essential quality by centering upon its comparable aspects. This quality, however, should not be analyzed by the scientific sociologist beyond the point necessary for comparison, for it is in large measure scientifically incommunicable to others even if, as is entirely possible, it can be brought extremely close to our own subjective feeling and desiring through the agency of sympathy. No matter how well developed our sympathetic capacities are, however, we cannot persuade others, who do not or cannot establish the connection as we do, that our description of the subjective aspects of a given case of exploitation, for example, is the "true" one; the exact way in which the exploiting or exploited person feels may be "self-evident" to us but not to others. But what we *can* do is to determine in a great number of observed cases the approximate degree of association and/or dissociation resulting from exploitative actions, and we can therefore say, in relative independence of the personal equation, a good many definite things about the nature of the social process of exploitation.

[One of the fundamental postulates of this system is that] . . . the "kernel" of the human being is [not] amenable to sociological reduction; . . . [moreover,] the qualitative "kernel" of the empirical relation cannot be assumed to be rationally explicable. In the monographic analysis of any single empirical relation we must of course attempt to resolve its particular traits into rationally explicable factors as far as possible, but we must always reckon with the possibility that it is in its essence unique. . . .

To repeat: the scientific sociologist cannot assume that the special quality of any empirical social action can be entirely grasped by scientific means; his only reason for paying any attention at all to this quality is in order to determine the degree of association and/or dissociation which the relation brings about or because of which it is called forth. This degree can be determined with some accuracy by the rank-order method and the comparison it entails, and when this is accomplished, *partial* rational comprehension of the relation is achieved. . . .

And this is the place of "understanding" in the system.[60]

In this characteristically precise statement Wiese makes it clear that his rejection of philosophic naturalism as the metaphysical basis of sociology does not commit him to the Neo-Romanticism of Dilthey or Spann. (This juxtaposition is unfair to Dilthey and flattering to Spann!) Although much more friendly to the natural sciences than was Max Weber, Wiese is in very close accord with him on a great number of basic sociological theorems, and there seems reason to agree with Abel when he says, in his estimate of systematic sociology in Germany:

. . . the foundation of the science, as laid down particularly in the sociological systems of . . . Wiese and of Weber, must be regarded as secure.[61]

Subdivisions of German and Austrian Sociology: Historical Sociology. — Now that we have hastily glanced at a few of the leading figures, it seems advisable to round out our survey by noting various subdivisions: (1) historical sociology; (2) the sociology of knowledge; (3) systematic-empirical sociology; (4) psycho-sociology; (5) ethno-sociology; (6) encyclopedic eclecticism; (7) sociosophy; (8) Marxian sociology; and (9) Catholic sociology.

It is evident that the above classification overlaps sections and even chapters already set before the reader. Our primary purpose here, however, is merely to gather up a few loose ends or to deal with figures like Mannheim, who has frequently been mentioned but nowhere considered in his own right.

Historical sociology has had the benefit of all of Chapter Twenty and of numerous references elsewhere. Only a few thinkers of any importance have been omitted, among them Hans Freyer. Hegel's influence on Spengler was commented upon; it is also evident, although in a different way, in Freyer's work. In his *Soziologie als Wirklichkeitswissenschaft* (1930), he uses Hegel's forms of freedom — the family-community, civil society, and the state — in a "realistic" rather than a "logical" way, and following Marx's example, treats them as a dialectic sequence of historical epochs, each of which negates and engenders its successor. Freyer's treatise itself exhibits a dialectic structure: the systems of a number of sociologists are presented, and in the familiar triangular interlinking of thesis — antithesis — synthesis, Freyer builds up a case for his own system. Altogether apart from the undue reverence for the Hegelian formula which the book manifests, it is dangerous because of its excellent style and the pseudo-objectivity with which the systems of other writers are presented. For example, his discussion of Simmel, Dilthey, and Wiese seems so clear and fair that the unwary might be persuaded, but anyone who knows what these writers actually said rather than what Freyer makes them say will reject at least half the book. But for all the gross errors of which he is guilty, Freyer has properly pointed out one thing: the historical sociologist should not approach his data with the intention of forcing them into a rigid framework of "timeless" categories that are *a priori* generalizable. If his concepts prove to be generalizable *in spite of* the fact that they are intended to be fully adequate for the shorthand description and analysis of the social processes and structures permeating and, as it were, sustaining a particular historical happening, era, or what not, so much the better, but such generalizability must not be the controlling aim of the endeavor.

Among the historical sociologists who in some measure adhere to the social evolutionism once so popular, we should mention Kurt Breysig (1866–) [62] and Hermann Schneider (1874–).[63] The same evolutionary emphasis, modified somewhat by the Schmidt-Koppers *Kulturkreis* theory, an Austrian product, is evident in the work of Franz Oppenheimer (1864–),[64] whose conflict theory of the state we have already dealt with at length.

The Sociology of Knowledge. — The fact has already been noted that Max Scheler was one of the first German sociologists to carry on work in this field; his only important predecessor seems to have been the Austrian, Wilhelm Jerusalem (1854–1923),[65] and the latter exerted no great influence.

The objective of the more moderate exponents of the sociology of knowledge is the determination of the precise ways in which the social organizations within which thinkers develop condition the form and content of their social thought in general and their sociological theories in particular. Studies of the sociology of Platonism, Nominalism, and Marxism — to name only a few — have already been made. It must be realized that such studies are not mere efforts to discover the " historical context " of this or that type of thought; the sociology of knowledge must not be confused with intellectual or cultural history. The historical phases as such are of secondary importance; the outcome should be the construction of a sociological frame of reference that is usable in any historical period, once the unique configurations of particular events are adequately analyzed.

As part and parcel of this effort to find just what the sociological conditions for various types of thought are, there is also the effort to indicate how far the sociological critique of the forms of thought may go. In other words, the student of the sociology of knowledge not only tries to see where and how social and cultural influences affect or fundamentally determine mentality, but he also seeks to discover whether or not it is possible to transcend the barriers of nation, class, and historical epoch in making theoretical generalizations of various kinds, particularly in the social sciences. Among other things, the whole question of so-called judgments of value *versus* judgments of fact must be confronted.

Karl Mannheim (whose chief work, *Ideologie und Utopie,* has recently been published in English translation by Louis Wirth and Edward A. Shils) ; Karl Wittfogel; Paul Honigsheim; Paul Landsberg; the Marxian scholar, Max Adler; Kuno Mittenzwey; and a number of other writers have helped to define the field,[66] and several of them are busily at work extending and consolidating the boundaries of this latest border-province of sociology.

Mannheim's Wissenssoziologie. — Inasmuch as Mannheim is the only member of this group whose major contribution is likely to be readily accessible to American sociologists, it seems well to deal with *Ideology and Utopia* (1936) at some length, more especially as the translation incorporates several important additions and revisions by Mannheim himself. Any future changes are likely to be of a wholly secondary nature.

Wirth's preface is appreciative and in no sense critical or constructive (in the sense of making positive additions to Mannheim's thought), and therefore may be disregarded here. This is by no means an adverse judgment, for the primary function of an introducer is to " stand up, shut up, and sit down," and Wirth accomplishes his task gracefully.

Mannheim's own introduction stresses the fact that there are modes of thought that cannot be wholly understood if their social bases are hidden — a position that few modern thinkers, of whatever school, would think of disputing. He goes on to point out that the " great man " theory is as false in the intellectual realm as it is elsewhere, that without a culture base of appropriate type a Marx or a Spencer could produce nothing noteworthy. Here again there would be widespread agreement. Next, he calls attention to the fact that in the modern world there is a " confusion of tongues," and that we are all keenly aware of a multiplicity of possible ways of thinking without being in possession of any clue to the correct one. And, says Mannheim, " Only when horizontal mobility is accompanied by intensive vertical mobility, i.e., rapid movement between strata in the sense of social ascent and descent, is the belief in the general and eternal validity of one's own thought-forms shaken." [67] This is going a bit too far, for horizontal mobility alone, in certain cases, may generate mental mobility, as our chapters and sections dealing with mobility and culture may have done something to show. Nevertheless, Mannheim is pointing in the right direction, and we have no wish to quibble about minor matters. He then offers cogent criticism of traditional epistemology and psychology, and rightly says that without the offerings of psycho-sociology and sociology the genesis of ideas having to do with social life cannot be understood. This is certainly true of the *genesis* of ideas; their validity, however, is another thing.

But enough of introductions; let us turn to the central theses. In process of doing so, it is well to contrast Scheler and Mannheim. Scheler's Catholicism probably had much to do with his early interest in the sociology of knowledge; he shared with many other thinkers of his type the belief that Lutheranism arose primarily because the German princes did not wish to send a substantial part of their revenues south of the Alps. Luther simply provided a rationalization for this reluctance. But another strand in Scheler's thought was perhaps inserted when intense anti-English feeling pervaded Germany shortly after the outbreak of the World War; his study of " cant " expressed his deep-rooted aversion for what he conceived to be Anglo-Saxon hypocrisy. [68]

Whether Marx markedly influenced his initial work in the field may well be doubted, and as late as 1926 he was paying more attention to the French studies of cultural compulsives being carried on in the Durkheim tradition than he was to the hackneyed themes of Marxian controversy. Mannheim, on the other hand, was for a long time identified with German Social-Democracy, and is said to have owed his appointment at the University of Frankfort not to his Jewish ancestry but to the fact that he had done much to make Marxism *salonfähig*, i.e., socially and intellectually respectable. (Scheler's appointment at Cologne was as a representative of Catholic social philosophy.)[69] Mannheim's technique was to exalt Marx and disparage his *epigoni* — a not altogether unjustified procedure. Thereby enabled to say, " I am not a Marxian, but — ," he popularized the Marxian conception that " It is not the consciousness of men that determines their being, but their being that determines their consciousness."

Yells from the idealistic camp at once arose when this slogan of *Seinsgebundenheit* resounded through the placid Vale of Academe, and the clamor was answered by the somewhat reedy war cries of Social-Democratic intellectuals. In the ensuing tumult a third group saying " A plague o' both your houses " went unheard; its members were inclined to give Mannheim full credit for his work in what may be called *substantive Wissenssoziologie* while at the same time challenging his more sweeping epistemological conclusions. Alexander von Schelting is one of this group's outstanding representatives, and we shall later present his critique of Mannheim.

The Marxian note in Mannheim's study appears at once in his discussion of ideology. All systems of thought that aim merely at the justification and maintenance of a *status quo* are ideologies; they are essentially static and defensive. The well-known " bourgeois ideology " is of this type, but so also is socialist thought that shirks its revolutionary mission. There are two chief types: particular and general. A particular ideology may range all the way from a conscious lie to consistent self-deception, but its nature is essentially psychological. That is to say, the bearer of a particular ideology might have been able to think otherwise had he been willing to renounce his prejudices or cast off his biases. Far otherwise is the case of him who has fallen prey to a total ideology. Here the very categories of thought are at fault; no matter how honest or how willing to attempt impartiality the bearer of a total ideology may be, he simply cannot think in other than total-ideological terms. His " false consciousness " is false through and through, and absolutely nothing can be done about it.

At the opposite pole stand the utopian thinkers. A utopia is " a vision of things hoped for, the substance of things not seen." Its function is to disrupt the order which the ideologists are attempting to preserve, and to usher in a new order that will in some measure, at least, incorporate its own utopian features. As utopia, however, it stands in eternal contrast to the topia; it is always nowhere, whereas the topia is always here. Here again the Marxian element is present; all formulas of progress with a fixed goal are rejected by the genuine Marxian, and all detailed pictures of the future Communist society are steadfastly avoided. In the dialectic process itself is sought the criterion of truth. " The movement is everything, the goal nothing." The truth of a utopian theory, says Mannheim, lies in its rôle as " pacemaker of history," in its " explosive force." If it aids in its own realization, then it is " true " in the only sense that is socially significant.[70]

These relatively simple ideas Mannheim has decked out in the language of phenomenology and other recondite subjects. Moreover, he has tried to avoid the charge of " Relativism! " hurled at him by the absolutists by creeping into the shelter he has named " relationism." He means by this simply that knowledge is always related to time, place, and circumstance. Wherein this differs from relativism in any significant degree is difficult to perceive, in spite of the dozen-odd pages Mannheim devotes to the distinction.[71] Not willing, however, to admit that his theory cuts both ways, and that if one man can say " Ideology! " so can another, he tries to find a criterion of truth in the conceptions held by the intelligentsia, by the " socially unbound intellectuals." All ideas are sadly relative except those held by the possessors of " free-floating intelligence "; these are merely relational.[72] In short, Mannheim the relationist seeks an absolute *in the social grouping with which he can identify himself.*

Mannheim Criticized by Schelting. — The foregoing exposition has also contained a good deal of explicit criticism, but it seems well to present some of the ideas of Alexander von Schelting, most distinguished heir of the Max Weber tradition and most effective critic of Mannheim. We quote brief excerpts from his lengthy review of *Ideologie und Utopie*:

It is clear . . . that this [totalistic] conception of ideology originated in the sphere of social struggle in its various forms. . . . Where there is no possibility of discrediting the opponent's position by common logical reasoning or by reproaching him with ideological thinking in any of its less inclusive forms, it may appear desirable . . . [to assert] that his whole turn of thought and its fundamental forms are " mere ideology." . . .

Since . . . the total structure of consciousness is included in the ideology concept, and since, consequently, *there cannot be any thinking but ideological thinking,* therefore even scientific thought, and especially in the social sciences, falls under this concept and becomes " functionalized " with respect to social factors. Consequently, according to our author, its objective, impartial validity is altogether destroyed. This is surely the more astounding in view of the fact that Mannheim himself apparently claims to be offering scientific truth. What else does he think his sociology of knowledge is? . . .

. . . we can formulate Mannheim's thesis as follows: The process of history realizes by stages an immanent meaning. Thinking participates in this realization. Certain conceptions, certain " structures of thought," fulfill a " function " at every stage of this process. They contribute some part to the " next phase " of the " meaningful process." *The value, the truth, of social conceptions is bound to their actual rôle in the historical process.* Not every kind of efficacy bestows the value of truth upon them, however; only such efficacy as lies in the direction of the " next step " in the realization of the meaning of the historical process confers this dignity. . . .

This sociological theory of knowledge contains two [exceedingly dubious] implications . . . ; namely, (1) that the meaning of the historical process, or at least the direction of its realization, is knowable, and (2) that it is possible to ascertain that a concrete historical change is the " next step " of this development. . . . [Moreover, these propositions carry] the assertion that there is a possibility of objective cognition of historical facts and their relationships. Mannheim himself explicitly declares that it is possible to ascertain the contribution to historical development of every " utopia," every " social-historical conception." It is clear that no kind of " social functionality " can bestow validity on such an ascertainment. . . . It must be correct and true *in itself.* . . .

[Yet there seems no basis for the criteria that Mannheim proposes as substitutes for the older conceptions of truth] . . . but that of the intelligentsia itself; *i.e., the fact that a conception comes out of the brain of a socially unbound intellectual is the guarantee of its validity.* This then would mean that any decision as to the value of a given conception presupposes the solution of a complicated scientific problem; namely, the problem of whether or not, and in what degree, the situation of " social unboundness " is . . . [actually present], and whether or not it accounts in the concrete case for the conceptual creation. Yet what are the foundations and criteria for a valid solution of *this* problem? Mannheim offers none.[73]

Hopeful Prospects for the Sociology of Knowledge. — Yet in spite of all this adverse criticism, there can be little doubt that the sociology of knowledge has a brilliant future before it. Mannheim himself has ably demonstrated, in his studies of intellectual competition, German conservatism, and the like, how much *Wissenssoziologie* can accomplish in aiding our understanding of ideas and their social functioning. With considerably less furor, however, the French school of Durkheim successors has achieved as much as or more than the German sponsors of the sociology of knowledge. Its members have been able to do this because they have avoided the epistemological pitfalls into which many of the Germans have fallen. For all their *sociologisme,* the Frenchmen have not drawn the whole realm of the philosophical and social sciences into their orbit; a saving common sense has enabled them to cultivate their own gardens with some measure of success.

At present, of course, there is no German sociology of knowledge in Germany. All that is permitted is a biology of knowledge: if " Aryan," you think one way; if " Semitic," another. Consequently Mannheim and others like him are compelled to work abroad. Perhaps relative freedom from the traditional methodological and political controversies will enable an internationalized sociology of knowledge to follow the promising paths of moderate, substantive research.

Systematic-Empirical Sociology. — A number of currents can be traced in the stream of that type of sociology which is insistent upon relating its researches to a comprehensive frame of reference, but which is at the same time anxious to keep those researches within the limits of empirical knowledge and a sharply-defined discipline. Such systematic-empirical sociology was earlier exemplified by Tönnies, Simmel, and Max Weber, and more recently by Wiese. With these examples before us, it seems unnecessary to attempt further description; we shall merely list certain other writers and take note of the subdivisions.

Johann Plenge has done a great deal in the way of systematizing the knowledge of interhuman relations already available, and has reduced much of his system to schematic and tabular form.[74] The great drawback of Plenge's work, however, is that he is not content to limit sociology to the study of human relations as such. In his view, sociology occupies the place of philosophy and religion as well as science. For this reason he has not had much influence on contemporary German sociology, in spite of his profound insights and the ingenious formulas he has developed. Wiese, for example, makes relatively little use of even those portions of Plenge's system most closely related to his own. Another writer who attempted, more or less unsuccessfully, to work out a systematic frame of reference for the guidance of empirical research was the Russo-German, David Koigen (1879–1933).

The empirical research carried on under Wiese's influence was for a time quite extensive. There developed a " Cologne school," among whose members may be noted the following: Wilhelm Stok, Wilhelm Vleugels, Hermann Haemmerle, Willy Gierlichs, Willy Latten, Hanna Meuter, Elsbeth Linpinsel, and Boris Ischboldin.[75] No longer so active as it was before Hitler's advent, and hampered by lack of funds and official encouragement, the Cologne school may decline in importance, but a great deal of good work has already been done.

The directions that systematic-empirical research has taken with most satisfactory results have been: (1) crowd sociology; (2) the sociology of the organized group; and (3) the sociology of locality patterns (*Siedlungsgebilde*) such as the village, the small town, the " natural area," and so on — what American sociologists call human ecology. Crowd sociology numbers among its contributors Wiese, Theodor Geiger, Gerhard Colm, Wilhelm Vleugels, Edward Fueter, Georg Sieber, and Gerhard Lehmann. The sociology of the organized group is intensively cultivated by the Cologne school, a number of the followers of the late Karl Dunkmann in Berlin, the Marxian sociologists (in so far as social classes may be regarded as organized groups), Vierkandt, Tönnies, and a recent writer of great promise, Max Graf zu Solms.[76] The sociology of locality patterns has been markedly furthered by the Cologne school, of whom we may name in particular Willy Latten and Willy Gierlichs.[77] Andreas Walther of Hamburg has also accomplished a great deal in this field, particularly in the construction of sociological maps somewhat like those used by American human ecologists. Adolf Günther has made a unique study of a whole region in his *Soziologie des Alpenlandes,* a work which combines human geography, human ecology, and a number of other specialties in an interesting although somewhat unsystematic way.[78] Max Rumpf has provided one of the best recent sketches of urban sociology with his " *Die Grossstadt als Lebensform und in ihrer sozialen Prägekraft,*"[79] and is also doing splendid work in the analysis of peasant life.

Closely related to this type of research is the " sociography " so ably carried on by Rudolph Heberle [80] (who has also made an excellent study of mobility in the United States) and others under Tönnies's influence. The best American analogues of sociography are probably the Lynd's *Middletown* and *Middletown in Transition*, Blumenthal's *Small Town Stuff*, and the various ecological studies of Chicago. Sociography makes extensive use of statistics in both the descriptive and analytic senses, and for this and other reasons we should also mention a number of statisticians whose work has notably advanced the precision of sociological research: Georg von Mayr and Ladislaus von Bortkiewicz among the earlier writers, and among the more recent Adolf Günther, Helmuth Wolff, E. Würzburger, F. Zahn, and Franz Zizek.

Psycho-Sociology. — As our earlier section-titles would suggest, and as our references to Wundt, Tönnies, and Vierkandt showed, there has long been a strong psycho-sociological trend in sociology and related disciplines. We must here content ourselves with hasty notice of a few of the more important figures in this movement (in addition to those already mentioned).

Theodor Litt (1880–), in his *Individuum und Gemeinschaft,* has applied phenomenological methods to the analysis of the interdependence of personality and social structure. His conclusions are in some respects similar to those of Cooley. Aloys Fischer (1880–), and Willy Hellpach (1887–) have also done significant work in this general field.

Hans L. Stoltenberg (1888–) is the author of several important books and articles on the psychical aspects of social life. One outcome of his work to which American sociologists might well give heed is the distinction between socio-psychology and psycho-sociology.[81] In addition, he has also worked out an elaborate set of terms for the designation of various types of awareness of self and others; Cooley's notion of the " looking-glass self " has thereby been expanded and traced to its remotest implications.[82] It is unlikely, however, that much use will be made of Stoltenberg's undeniably important innovations until he abandons his terminological acrobatics. He is so much interested in coining neologisms on the basis afforded by Germanic root-words that German-speaking persons themselves cannot always understand him, and needless to say, he is quite untranslatable.

Richard Müller-Freienfels (1882–) has recently published an *Allgemeine Sozial- und Kulturpsychologie* in which, along with other influences, traces of those parts of Schäffle's thought which were not vitiated by his organismic analogy are evident.

Were space unlimited, it would be desirable to include in our survey of psycho-sociology a conspectus of psychoanalytic theories. Certainly the measure of popular interest taken in them cannot be lightly disregarded. There are available, however, so many excellent résumés of Freudian, Jungian, Adlerian, Rankian, and similar psycho-therapies that there seems little reason for burdening our already overloaded pages.[83] We shall therefore rest content with only a brief comment on Freud's trinity of Id-Ego-Superego.

The Id may be thought of as man in his unsocialized, relatively unmodified biological aspects, as a bundle of desires and impulses that have merely been overlaid, not transformed, by culture. When cultural controls disintegrate, or are relaxed in the dream, etc., the Id steps forth to achieve the gratifications denied it by the watchful Ego and Superego. Although the extreme behaviorists scout any such theory, it seems clear that the phenomena of release bear witness to the probable correctness of this part of Freudian doctrine. Men, even the best of men, are but imperfectly socialized, and under stress sufficiently great will follow patterns much more elemental than those prevailing in any organized society. Our discussion of " The Effects of Liberation " (pages 264–265) follows a line of analysis not irreconcilable with this aspect of Freudian thought.

The Ego is a bit more difficult to characterize. It is the conscious self, yes, but in a peculiar form. Perhaps the best brief characterization is to say that it is that part of the bundle of Id-cravings which has been woven into some sort of unity and is acceptable in the light of prevailing cultural standards. In a sense it is the more or less precarious subjective balance between unregulated animality on the one hand and the objective rigidities of social constraint on the other. What distinguishes the Ego, however, is its relative integration, persistence, and continuity. In some respects it is like the " looking-glass self " of Cooley and the " me " of Mead, but the relatively sharp line which Freud draws between the Ego and the Superego makes this comparison not wholly tenable.

The Superego replaces what Freud once called " the censor "; it may be thought of as the whispering of social control that has not been sufficiently incorporated in the Ego to be regarded as the voice of self. " Conscience," " the demands of society," " decency," " propriety," and all other demands that represent an imperfect introjection of social imperatives make up the Superego. Herein lies a marked resemblance to Durkheim's *conscience collective,* with its two criteria of exteriority and constraint. A strong Superego means that its possessor, or better, its possessee, lacks identification with the social patterns within which he has developed. A strong Ego, on the contrary, means that the degree of correspondence between the ensemble of social imperatives entering into the person's socially real world and his individual impulses is high — in other words, there is a stable equilibrium between Id and Superego, and the result is an Ego relatively free from conflict.

There is notoriously a great deal more than this in Freudian theory, but it is best left to treatises of a different character. Scepticism as to whether the far-flung claims of psychoanalysis can be even partially substantiated is growing, and where it is impossible to make one's position unmistakably clear, omission is the better course, for both reader and author.[84]

Ethno-Sociology. — The only contemporary German ethnographer who is also of importance as a sociologist is Richard Thurnwald of the University of Berlin. Associated with Gumplowicz early in his career, and translator of Ward's *Contemporary Sociology,*[85] he founded, in 1925, the *Zeitschrift für Völkerpsychologie und Soziologie.* From the title chosen for this journal, it would appear that he may also have had some connection with the work of Wundt, the earlier exponent of *Völkerpsychologie.* Thurnwald has written relatively little of a strictly sociological nature, but his articles on personality, on the psychology of acculturation, his numerous encyclopedia contributions, and his recent five-volume work entitled *Die menschliche Gesellschaft in ihren ethno-soziologischen Grundlagen* have certainly put him on the sociological map. If Lippert's *Evolution of Culture* or the Sumner-Keller *Science of Society* is sociology, there can be no doubt that Thurnwald's methodologically more reliable treatise is sociology of a considerably better brand. Sorokin has reviewed the work as follows:

. . . he correctly indicates the shortcomings of various methods used by ethnologists, and comes to the conclusion that the best way is to use a kind of typological method, so as to give an undistorted and representative picture of the main forms of primitive societies, their real *Gestalt,* life and organization. . . .

His selection of peoples to represent each type, his description of these, and, finally, his analysis of each type are almost irreproachable. They convey a living *Gestalt* of each of the peoples described; and when one has finished reading about the main variations of the same type of society, one possesses not only an excellent individual picture of each of the several peoples, but a general idea as well of the most important characteristics of the type of society as a whole. In this way, Dr. Thurnwald has succeeded in combining the plusses of B. Malinowski's works, for instance, with those of such works as the statistical study of primitive peoples by Hobhouse, Wheeler, and Ginsberg.[86]

Minor Trends. — Our classification also included encyclopedic eclectism, sociosophy, Marxian sociology, and Catholic sociology, but inasmuch as none of these sub-varieties exert any great influence in present-day Germany, we shall merely characterize them and mention a few representatives. Encyclopedic eclecticism is best exemplified by Oppenheimer, to whom we have already referred several times in other connections. For him, sociology is the crowning synthesis of all the sciences, just as it was for Comte, Spencer, and Ward. Further, he also regards sociology as a program of social reform, again following the example of predecessors like Comte.[87] Franz Müller-Lyer may also be placed in this category, although his " phaseological " method also classes him with the social evolutionists.[88] The sociosophists, i.e., those persons who, like Othmar Spann, continually intermingle sociology and social philosophy without setting forth a clear conception of either, are best represented by Karl Dunkmann, Gerhard Lehmann, and the like.[89] Avowedly Marxian sociology possesses one writer of distinction in the person of the Austrian Socialist, Max Adler, who has done noteworthy work in the sociology of knowledge from the Marxian point of view,[90] and has also been an incisive critic of so-called bourgeois tendencies in German sociology. Mark Abramowitsch may also be mentioned,[91] but he is an altogether insignificant figure in comparison with Adler. Catholic sociology now has no prominent exponents (Scheler might have been placed in this category before 1923) ; its existence is vouchsafed more by the manner in which sociology is taught in Catholic schools and seminaries than by a particular body of sociological doctrine.

At the beginning of this division on German and Austrian sociology we said that for a long time the new discipline was cultivated only by amateurs. Perhaps our survey has done something to show that after the amateur stage was passed a number of exceedingly promising beginnings and several well-advanced schools of thought, together with the usual proportion of false starts, made their appearance. If, however, present tendencies in Central European academic circles continue unchecked, there is real danger that Germany and Austria may become lands in which knowledge of sociology is promulgated not only by amateurs and dilettantes, but also by time-servers and political spoilsmen.

II

HOLLAND

The Present Status of Dutch Sociology. — Although they are masters of a great colonial empire, the homeland of the Dutch covers no great area. Moreover, although the population is relatively dense, it still is not large enough to maintain universities of sufficient size to admit of consistent and thoroughgoing specialization in the various subdivisions of the social sciences. Consequently sociology is a stepchild of philosophy, economics, or ethnology; it does not receive the undivided attention of any Dutch scholar. Steinmetz, to whom we shall later refer, is an excellent example of this: his best-known book was entitled *The Philosophy of War* when it first appeared (1908) ; only in a later edition, published in Germany during the 1920's when sociology was enjoying some popularity in that country, was the word sociology included in the title. (Both editions were written in German.) Further, Steinmetz's chief interest is in the field of ethnology, and not one of his graduate students has written a strictly sociological treatise. Another reason for the lack of independent sociology in Holland is the prevailingly practical emphasis of Dutch culture; concrete descriptive studies rather than abstract analyses have been most in favor, but such studies can provide only the indispensable foundation upon which the structure of sociology *per se* is erected. Finally, the fact that many of the early representatives of sociology were socialists meant that the entrenched academicians were not especially friendly.

Nevertheless, one should not be too pessimistic about the prospects for Dutch sociology. In 1921, sociology was made one of the required examination subjects for the doctorate in social geography and an elective subject for the doctorate in Dutch law. Moreover, a statute permitting these concessions also provided for the doctorate in sociology, although up to date very few candidates have presented themselves.[92] Further, recent developments, among them the founding of the first Dutch sociological society, augur well for the future.

Christian Social Philosophy and Sociology. — As might be expected from what we have already said, the history of sociology in Holland must be drawn from the main currents and side streams of the history of other disciplines.

In 1863 an *Introduction to the Science of the Community* was written by Kemper,[93] professor of law at the University of Amsterdam. This work was dominated by a Protestant social philosophy. Kemper viewed mankind as the ultimate product of the world-order, destined to carry out a God-given function. All social activity was held to be teleological, and once in possession of the set of norms upon which Kemper's system was based, all conduct, it was held, could be evaluated according to the degree in which it furthered the sway of these norms.

In addition to the dominant Christian theme, the legal motif was prominent in Kemper's work. In fact, he was convinced that the study of society found its chief *empirical* justification as a prerequisite for sound legal practice, and in particular explicitly said that his social theory was an introduction to the theory of public law. In this introduction Kemper defines a science " which aims at the understanding and betterment of society," but refuses to name this science sociology because the term is a " barbarous compound of Greek and Latin." The first part of the introduction deals with the kinds of knowledge on which sociology is based. Philosophy stands in first place, immediately followed by a heterogeneous array of gleanings from every field that in any way borders upon social life, and the resulting composite is squeezed within the confines of the Christian philosophy of history already mentioned. In fairness to Kemper, however, it must be said that his " encyclopedic eclecticism " was remarkably full and thorough; he dealt, by implication at least, with practically everything that present-day encyclopedists include in their province. Needless to say, however, he did not develop any special type of theory that would now be regarded as definitely sociological.[94]

Another form of Christian social philosophy that has some sociological relevance is the Catholic conception set forth by Aengenent, professor at the Catholic seminary of Warmond at Leyden.[95] His *Textbook of Sociology* (1909) is primarily concerned with the discussion of social problems dealt with in the encyclical letters of the recent popes. He distinguishes two types of sociology: philosophical sociology, which is a branch of moral philosophy or ethics; and positivistic sociology, in which the ethical problem is not central. Aengenent of course casts his vote for philosophical sociology, and defines it as that branch of ethics which deals with the rights and duties of man as a member of society. This obviously includes a great deal, and he consequently defines sociology in a narrower sense as well. It then becomes the study of " the social question," which may be subdivided into five different questions or problems: (1) the labor problem; (2) the agrarian problem; (3) the problem of the bourgeois class; (4) the problem of industrial labor or the proletariat; and (5) the question of woman's proper place in society. He then goes on to discuss the three schools of thought offering solutions: first, individualism; second, socialism; and third, Christian solidarism, i.e., class coöperation on a functional basis under the guidance of Catholicism. The points of view set forth in the encyclicals are [96] faithfully mirrored by Aengenent, and he also draws on other Catholic writers.

Another opponent of positivistic sociology is Bruine, who like Aengenent advocates Christian solidarism, but on a Protestant instead of a Catholic basis. True to the individualistic heritage of Protestantism, Bruine denies the rule of the church in social matters, transferring some of its authority to the state, and limiting the activity of the latter to the protection of " common human interests " in such a way that private initiative will not be stifled and a maximum degree of " decent liberty " vouchsafed. The producers' and consumers' coöperative movements Bruine views as the best economic example of solidaristic aims.[97] Although a great deal of sociology in the United States and elsewhere has been quite as thoroughly pervaded by ultimate value-judgments and immediate reform programs as this Dutch counterpart, candor compels us to say that the sociologist who spreads himself over so large a slice of life runs the risk of being all things to all men without saving any.

Sociology in the Shadow of Law. — A curious variant of our science was set forth by Anema [98] in his *Fundamentals of Sociology* (1900). He dealt with it as a branch of law, for his Calvinistic predilections [99] led him to declare that no purely causal science dealing with social life could be established, and that sociology was therefore normative only. Following this false lead, he divided law into a general and a special part, the general comprising its philosophy, " encyclopedia," and history, and the special falling into three subdivisions: (1) criminal law; (2) public law, international law, and administrative law; and (3) sociology, in its turn made up of private law and economics. Plainly enough, only the name of sociology survived Anema's normative dissection.[100]

Jonge, while by no means so bizarre a " sociologist " as Anema, likewise represents the legalistic approach.[101] In his *Politics of the Future* (1917) he declared that he had provided "an objective study of social processes in their inner connections," and that by the same token he had set forth a political system highly desirable for the enlightenment of the statesman. In view of the latter pronouncement, it can occasion small wonder that the whole work is dominated by juristic notions. Further, Jonge's zeal for classification and criticism of the ideas of others lends his treatise the character of a loosely organized survey rather than an independent investigation.

Criminology may quite properly be regarded as a legitimate field for the application of sociological theories, and therefore does not cast so blighting a shadow upon them as do the strictly legalistic, normative philosophies above mentioned. Bonger, Van Kan, and Roos are at present the outstanding Dutch criminologists.

W. A. Bonger in particular is well known for a number of interesting statistical studies.[102] In his *Crime and Economic Conditions* (1905, recently published in a revised and expanded English version), he took the position that economic factors almost exclusively account for crime. This inference in part derives from his adherence to the Marxian theory of history, in line with which he concludes that capitalism has engendered an enormous increase of "anti-social conduct." This comes about because the materialistic outlook on life favored by capitalism weakens fellow-feeling and stimulates criminal motives through its inherent egoism and brutality, embittering the life of the poor and corrupting the rich. Steinmetz has criticized Bonger for his neglect of hereditary differences and his failure to complement his undoubtedly thorough and penetrating statistical analyses by making use of psychosociological interpretation.[103]

Another of Bonger's studies is concerned with the correlation between religious belief and crime — *Belief and Misbehavior* (1913) — and in it he concludes that religion exercises no perceptible influence. To be sure, he shows that the crime reports of the Netherlands and Germany evidence a higher rate for the Catholics than for the Protestants, whereas the latter in turn have a higher rate than the Jews, and that the types of crimes committed also differ: more cases of burglary among Protestants and Catholics, more financial trickery among Jews. These discrepancies in crime rate, however, Bonger holds to be economically determined. For example, the Roman Catholic population of southern Holland is very poor and lacking in education, with a corresponding prevalence of the cruder but perhaps less socially damaging crimes. In another study, *The Social Factors in Crime* (1912), he arrives at like results: the economic element is held to be almost all-important.

The two other criminologists mentioned, Van Kan and Roos, had earlier reached similar conclusions. In 1903 Van Kan published his *Les Causes économiques de la criminalité* which, in addition to being for its time an excellent example of careful statistical technique, contains a critical review of the European literature of the problem that is still worth reading.[104] Roos's *Etiology of Misconduct* (1908) is largely confined to an analysis of Dutch criminal statistics.[105]

Sociology and Ethnology. — The most famous of all Dutch sociologists is Steinmetz, who was also one of the first (1895) to declare his allegiance to the new and unpopular science.[106] Fortunately for his own academic standing, he had already attracted much favorable attention by his work in ethnology, particularly through his *Ethnologische Studien zur ersten Entwicklung der Strafe* (1892) and *Endo-Kannibalismus* (1895). Shortly thereafter (1899) he published an article, *Der Krieg als soziologisches Problem,* that marked the first stage in the construction of his chief work, *Soziologie des Krieges.*

In this treatise war is dealt with as a sociological phenomenon, and its function within the total process of sociation is defined and analyzed. The general conclusions are roughly in accord with the tenets of social Darwinism. To begin with, Steinmetz holds that those preliterate groups which try to avoid conflict necessarily remain on the lowest level of culture; war forces all tribes which have the requisite ability into the armor of political organization, thus creating the state. As this institution develops, the smaller units (such as clans) which it incorporates lose in importance. But if expansion proceeds more rapidly than the development of internal relations which supply the cohesive force formerly due to clans, *et cetera,* the state collapses under attack from without, and the process begins over again. War is therefore the creator of homogeneous societies, and eventually of nations as we now know them. Further, its rôle in compelling migrations has been of tremendous importance in the contact of cultures and consequently in that increase of cultural complexity ordinarily called progress. No matter how great the loss and suffering caused by warfare, its scope and intensity have steadily increased. Steinmetz considers war to be one of the expressions of the cruel, covetous, and aggressive nature of man, and there-

fore as something that will end only when mankind is either wiped
out or transformed into something *biologically* pacific, for although we now pin our faith on education as a preventive, the
history of the world offers scant hope of success.[107]

In addition to this and similar specialized studies, Steinmetz
has also devoted considerable attention to general methodology.
He defines sociology as the positive science which deals with all
human groupings: their development, forms, conditioning factors, and decay. It is not the science of culture, for this would
mean that sociology would have to include almost the whole
range of human knowledge. The forms which social groupings
assume are numerous: clan, tribe, nation, village, town, church,
sect, army, gang, club, and so on. All these groupings and their
modes of change must be described and functionally analyzed
by use of the inductive method. Induction is of great importance,
for it enables that coöperation in research which is an essential
characteristic of genuine science as distinct from the peculiarly
personal and untransferable function of philosophy.[108]

Sociology must take account of man's physical nature and his
relations with the " natural " environment, but the social environment is of much greater importance. In other words, the
primary task of sociology is the study of social relations, not
only in their outer but also in their inner aspects. The inference
to be drawn from this is that psychical factors are inseparably
bound up with social behavior; hence psychology is the science
upon which sociology most heavily leans, and *vice versa*.[109] Another indispensable adjunct of sociology is sociography, a concrete descriptive science (which we have already discussed in
connection with German and Austrian sociology) bearing much
the same relation to its abstract counterpart as ethnography does
to ethnology.[110] The chief difference between the two is that the
phenomena dealt with by ethnography are not so complex, and
hence a wider field can be covered than is the case with sociography. Further, the mass of material confronting the sociographer forces him to make extensive use of statistics, whereas
the ethnographer can make more use of direct description.

There are many other interesting phases of Steinmetz's work,
but space forbids their consideration here. His strategic location at the University of Amsterdam, together with his renown
as a researcher and teacher, has brought to him a number of
gifted students, among whom may be mentioned Nieboer, Van
der Bij, Ronhaar, Van Deursen, and Fahrenfort.

Among the prominent Dutch sociographers and ethnographers

who have not been pupils of Steinmetz we may mention Wilken, Blonk, and Heere.[111] Wilken has done a great deal to acquaint his Dutch colleagues with the newer ethnological theories developed elsewhere in Europe and in America, and has also made more generally available the rich ethnographic material derived from Holland's colonial possessions in the East Indies. Blonk has written a sociography of a Dutch industrial town that will stand comparison with many American surveys, and Heere has attempted to introduce into Dutch social science LePlay's study of regions, family budgets, and similar methodological devices.[112]

Other Dutch Trends. — So-called practical or applied sociology, in some respects similar to the social philosophies of Aengenent and Bruine, has been elaborately dealt with by Kohlbrugge of the University of Utrecht. His eight-volume work ranges over the fields of social education, child welfare, social legislation, and a number of other problems of social well-being. Not only does he provide a conspectus of practically everything done in these fields in the Netherlands, but he also makes detailed comparisons with the methods of social technology in other countries.[113]

Collective psychology, corresponding to some phases of American psycho-sociology, is represented by Visser. In *The Mind of the Crowd* (1911) he gives a survey of the crowd theories of a number of sociologists, with particular attention to those of Tarde, Sighele, LeBon, and Stoll. In 1916 appeared his *The Collective Mind in Law and Government,* which is primarily a study of public opinion. His most recent book, *Character as an Element in Culture* (1922), discusses character-education, and advances the theory that reward and punishment must always be the chief methods of motivating socially acceptable behavior. Visser is an exceptionally erudite person, but he flits from point to point without discussing any exhaustively, and he seems to feel no need of precise analysis and definite proof.[114]

The late Clara Wichmann provided an interesting social philosophy with Communist leanings in her *Introduction to the Philosophy of the Community* (1917), but although her book is of high literary merit and well calculated to stimulate interest in social matters, it takes no account of previous research, and will hardly lead anyone to engage in strictly sociological study. Steinmetz is probably right in saying that " This little book, for all its vividness, is more dangerous than useful, so far as the positive side of our science is concerned. Only genuine research can carry us onward." [115] Another type of social philosophy closely related to the Neo-Romanticism of Othmar Spann has been set forth by Landheer. His study of Plato is an attempt to revive the supposed universalism of the Greek philosopher and to show its essential agreement with Spann's doctrines.

Thus far practically all the writers we have been considering, with the possible exception of Steinmetz, bear only an incidental relation to sociology in the narrower sense. There are two writers, however, who limit the field more closely. Gerretson published a *Prolegomena to Sociology* (1911) in which he sharply separated this science from history, political science, economics, anthropology, and so on, and stressed the importance of the inductive method. He divided sociology into three parts: (1) sociography or descriptive sociology; (2) comparative sociology, in which the data gathered by sociography are classified and related to one another; and (3) sociosophy (not the same as that designated in Germany by the same term). This third form utilizes the results achieved in the first two divisions for the construction of a theoretical system harmonizing with the principles of philosophy and all the other sciences. Gerretson also granted a place to "practical sociology," in so far as this is simply the application of sociological principles to "reality." Thus sociology is essential to scientific politics and similar technological activities. Unfortunately, this promising beginning (many of the ideas of which Gerretson seems to have derived from French and Italian sociologists) has not led to anything further; he has since published nothing in the sociological field. The rapid developments in German systematic sociology since 1918 have not been without their effect on Dutch thinkers, for in 1931 Endt, of the University of Leyden, published a small *Sociologie* dealing with social processes in a way closely similar to that represented by Wiese, and there seems some evidence that this type of sociological analysis has been favorably received in Holland. Most important, it is sufficiently empirical to appeal to the Dutch interest in the concrete. On the other hand, it provides a means of classifying and interpreting the wealth of material already accumulated by the Dutch ethnographers and sociographers.[116]

The Netherlands Sociological Society. — To judge by the very latest developments, Dutch sociology has taken a new lease on life. In 1936 a sociological society, the first of its kind in Holland, was established, and gives every sign of vigor and serious purpose. DeNood has given us news of this development in a recent review:

In this address to the first meeting of the Netherlands Sociological Association, the distinguished criminologist, W. A. Bonger, briefly summarizes the history of the social sciences, states the aims of the Association, and discusses the qualifications required for membership. From the beginning of the nineteenth century, states Professor Bonger, the "streams of the social sciences have become constantly broader and deeper." Social Economics, History, Ethnology, Social Statistics, Social Geography, *Wissenssoziologie*, and Sociology have all reaped rich harvests in their respective fields. Although a synthesis of these sciences lies in the remote future, it is hoped that the Association will, in however small degree, ably play its part in the process. Among the topics to be discussed at the next meeting are: (1) Social Science Methods; (2) Changes and Consequences of Changes in the Tempo of Societies; (3) The Sociology of the Formation of States; (4) The Social Structure of Ancient Empires; (5) Imperialism, Observed from the Historical and Sociological Point of View; (6) *Wissenssoziologie*. That the Association has serious intentions is evident in the qualifications required for membership. Politicians, jurists, and others "who are concerned exclusively with practical applications of the social sciences" are to be excluded. Dilettantes and professional "joiners" are also banned. Equally undesirable are social philosophers who insist upon asking such questions as "What is society?" and "What is sociology?" To be admitted, a candidate is required to demonstrate in published work that he is a serious scholar in one or more of the social sciences. . . .[117]

We heartily join our reviewer in his closing phrase, "Long live the Netherlands Sociological Society!"

III

SCANDINAVIA

Current Condition of Sociology. — Here again it is the old story: sociology under that name has been quite neglected in Norway, Denmark, Sweden, and Finland. Nowhere is there a chair of sociology as such. From 1883 to 1918 the University of Copenhagen had one for philosophy and sociology, but since then the teaching of sociology has been the task of one of the professors of economics, so that the attention it really receives is quite negligible. In the universities of Lund and Uppsala, sociology is included in the philosophical division, being classed as a branch of practical philosophy. Some of the professors have dealt with sociological topics, but always in the highly speculative manner reminiscent of Schäffle and other writers of the nineteenth century.[118]

The University of Gothenburg is in somewhat better case, for it now possesses a chair of economics and sociology, and candidates for the doctorate in either discipline are examined in both.[119] This fortunate situation is largely the result of the influence of one man, the late Gustaf Steffen, an outstanding economist, sociologist, and political leader. Whether the example of Gothenburg will be followed by other Scandinavian universities is still in doubt. The very fact of Steffen's prominence (he was a power in the Socialist party) may make other academicians of differing political faith reluctant to admit any new science that has had such a champion within their sacred portals.

The University of Åbo in Finland has the advantage of the services of Edward Westermarck, who accepted a position there after his retirement from the University of London. He is now very old, however, and can hardly be regarded as an active sociologist. Rafael Karsten, professor of moral philosophy in the University of Helsingfors, does a good deal of interesting work in ethnography, and a member of the same institution, Hilma Granqvist, has made a remarkably able study of marriage conditions in Palestine. All of this, however, merely borders on sociology, the central fields of the discipline remain uncultivated, and it has no official recognition.

This lack of " official " sociology makes it necessary to follow the course we have pursued before: namely, to garner the scattered grains of sociologically relevant thought and research regardless of the fields in which they fall.

Early Literary and Philosophical Studies of Social Phenomena. — Ludwig Holberg (1684–1754), a dramatic and philosophical author frequently called " the father of modern Norwegian and Danish literature," has sometimes been placed among the earliest ancestors of Scandinavian sociology. This assumption is tenable only if we grant that social satire of the type later set forth by Ibsen, Strindberg, and others may be called sociological. On the whole, it seems better not to confuse the issue by too free use of the term. Holberg also published historical and philosophical works of a moralizing tendency and with some analysis of the caste and class relations of his time. Whatever may be said of the claim that he was a sociological writer, there can be no doubt of his significance for Scandinavian social thought in general.

Samuel Grubbe (1786–1853), a Swedish philosopher, was the author of two unfinished works of a sociological nature, *The Concepts of the Science of Society: An Attempt at Clarification*

(1826), and *Philosophy of Law and Society* (1839). Grubbe defined society as any human grouping, of which he listed three types: family, state, and mankind, distinguished primarily by their differing extent in space and time. Every society, said Grubbe, has a moral-religious content and a legal-external form, and true progress consists in the harmonious development of both sides of societal life. Grubbe opposed Kant and Fichte in their separation of morals and law, asserting that the goal of social development is the greatest possible ennobling of all the members of society. The whole system is anchored in religion: for example, Grubbe maintained that patriotism derives its significance from its essential harmony with God's plan for the world.[120]

Christopher Jacob Boström (1797–1866) was one of the most original of Swedish philosophers; he worked out a system of his own at a time when most of his compatriots were looking to other European countries for their leading ideas. In some of his writings he dealt at length with social theory, notably in his *Outlines of the Philosophical Study of the State* (1859), and *Introduction to the Philosophical Study of the State* (1874). He definitely belonged to the organismic school; in his attempt to justify constitutional monarchy, he conceived of the state as a living organism endowed with intelligence and ultimately dependent upon God for its existence. A monarch is the defender of the vital interests of this organism. Representative government was also subjected to the organismic formula, for Boström regarded the prevailing separation of electors into four classes with differing rights of franchise as a functional necessity of the national organism. Although he found a place in his system for the family, the association, the community, and the folk, Boström thoroughly developed only his political theories.[121]

His influence during his lifetime was considerable, but two of his pupils, Sahlin and Björklund, greatly extended it after his death.

Carl Yngve Sahlin (1824–1918) developed, with some modifications, certain aspects of Boström's theory of personality. The human being has individuality but not totality, whereas society may be said to represent totality but has no individuality. Men become human, in the fullest sense, through social intercourse, and the more fully the personalities of all the members of society are developed, the more thoroughly integrated a totality does society become. It is readily seen that this bears some resemblance to the theories advanced by Cooley. Sahlin classified human groupings in five main categories: (1) the *oikos* or household (equivalent to the family in the broadest sense); (2) the association based on one or another phase of a common culture; (3) the state; (4) the federation of states; and (5) the world-empire. Each of these five forms is divided into two subclasses: first, the marriage group and the family; second, the community and the organized group; third, the folk and the government; fourth, the race and the interrelated system of governments; and fifth, mankind and the federation of governmental systems. This curious preoccupation with combinations and recombinations of states and governments reflects the separation of the Scandinavian race and culture into political units that cut across more fundamental bonds of union; Sahlin was forced to recognize the fact that government and state are not the same, and that these in turn have no essential connection with race and culture.[122]

Gustaf Björklund (1846–1903), pursuing a somewhat similar line of thought, took over Boström's organismic ideas (with Spencerian reinforcements), and attempted to show that nations are organisms of a type that must necessarily grow together, just as coral polyps are forced by their very nature to cohere and consolidate. Impressed by the unification of Germany as exemplified in the customs union and the federation of kingdoms, and contrasting this with the political discord among the Scandinavian states, he maintained that the growth of trade relations represented a sort of organismic intertwining in the material realm that should lead to the evolution of ever larger political organisms, eventually culminating in a world society. Björklund further developed these ideas in his attack on what he termed " evolutionary anarchy "; he was a savage opponent of protectionism and militarism because to him they represented pathological hindrances to the beneficent process of social evolution. Thus Björklund united in a peculiar way the philosophy of Boström and the biological theories of his own time.[123]

Utopians, Reformers, and Their Critics. — Under this somewhat vague section-heading we shall have to include a number of exceedingly diverse figures.

Nils Herman Quiding (1808–1886) is the only systematic utopian socialist that Sweden has produced. Influenced to some extent by Plato, he embodied in his criticism of the *status quo* a number of sociological theories which, although current elsewhere before or during his period, apparently were not directly derived from any other writer. Quiding set forth a conflict theory of the state: brute force created law, and law consolidated the position of the dominant class. He seems to have introduced the terms " upper class " and " lower class " into the popular vocabulary, and he presented a lengthy analysis of all forms of " social servitude ": property, government, marriage, education, money, etc. He was also a bitter critic of urban life; for him large cities were parasitic fungi on the trunk of society. He therefore proposed a system of decentralization: no communities numbering more than about five thousand persons were to be permitted (here we have Plato's proposal to limit the *polis* to 5040 citizens). In this way, said Quiding, the earliest form of social life, the commune, would become the last and best.[124]

Anton Nyström (1842–1926), physician, social reformer, teetotaler, was the earliest adherent of Comte's social philosophy in the Scandinavian countries, translating most of his writings. In addition to accepting positivism in both the scientific and quasi-religious senses, he was active in struggles for religious freedom, separation of church and state, and so on. Moreover, he did a great deal to establish folk schools along lines similar to those laid down by the Danish bishop, Grundtvig.[125] Christen Collin, professor at the University of Oslo, represented in Norway ideas akin to those of Nyström; these are set forth in his *Religion of Brotherly Love and the New Sociology,* and in numerous other writings.

The Scandinavian countries have been the scene of perhaps the most bitter feminism and anti-feminism to be found anywhere. There are probably good reasons for this in the background of Scandinavian culture, but it is difficult for the outsider to discern them.

Ellen Key (1849–1926) was a feminist of an uncommon type. Instead of laying special stress on woman's " equality " with man in all lines of activity, she deplored indiscriminate rivalry, maintaining that women are fitted primarily for motherhood. In spite of bitter antagonism from feminists of a different stamp, she succeeded in realizing many of her specific aims, such as motherhood insurance, " labor vacations " before and after childbirth, legitimation of children born out of wedlock, and a number of other reforms. She was an upholder of solidarism; believing fervently in Guyau's " irreligion of the future " she championed a type of humanitarianism that was religious in every respect but its heterodoxy.[126]

August Strindberg (1849–1912) is famous as the most uncompromising opponent of the emancipation of women; he seems to have taken seriously Nietzsche's injunction, " When thou hast to do with woman, do not forget thy whip." At the same time, Strindberg's interest in the class struggle should not be overlooked; his autobiography, *The Son of a Servant Girl,* clearly evidences that anti-feminism was of secondary importance as compared to his preoccupation with caste and class. Further, his opposition to the existing social order found expression in a book castigating the hypocrisy and discrimination practiced by the upper classes.[127]

A more direct opponent of Ellen Key's program was Vitalis Nordström (1856–1916). He criticized modern culture because of its inner poverty; quantity, as manifested in and through the mere material satisfaction of mass needs, has debased quality. The impersonality, uniformity, and disunity of modern culture are symptoms of degeneration, and modern mass morals have submerged personality. Nordström foreshadowed the cultural pessimism of Spengler, but unlike the latter he saw hope of salvation in the imminent revival of religion. That is, although the quest for secular salvation is doomed to futility, the sacred in its ancient garb will one day regain its power.[128] Sorokin's theories of social and cultural dynamics are in basic agreement with Nordström's.

Marxians and Anti-Marxians. — As we noted in the chapter on revolutionary socialism, Marx owed a great deal of his social analysis to Lorenz von Stein. This was also true of Erik Gustaf Geijer(1783–1847), a historian in the University of Uppsala. In 1844, long before the appearance of *Das Kapital,* Geijer predicted the increasing dominance of the bourgeois class, the victory of mobile over immobile capital, and the rising power of the proletariat. He advocated the solidarity of the disadvantaged classes, but hoped to find a solution for the class struggle through gradual reform. Originally a conservative, his conversion to a type of liberalism remarkably similar to that represented by Hobhouse almost three-quarters of a century later created a great sensation.[129]

Geijer was in a way a Marxian before Marx — at least, he foreshadowed several aspects of Marxian thought. A real follower of Marx is to be found in Axel Hägerström (1868–), whose *Social Teleology in Marxism* (1909) lays special stress on the optimistic phases of Marx's thought.[130] Sven Helander (1889–), an opponent of Marxian theory, has attempted to show that it is precisely this optimism which distorts Marx's social analysis. In other words, the very fact that Marx wished not to interpret the world but to change it for the better is the reason for the fallacies in the theory of surplus value and other specific doctrines.[131] Excellent analyses of the relation of political parties and social classes in Sweden have been presented by E. H. Thörnberg. They are especially valuable because of their thorough discussion of the ideological as well as the economic foundations of political alignments. Thörnberg has been much influenced by American sociology and, in conjunction with his work as emigration investigator for the Swedish government, has studied the problem of Swedish emigration to America and the processes of assimilation in considerable detail.[132]

The Beginnings of Sociology Proper.—It is to a chemist who in later life became a journalist and Social-Democratic politician that sociology owes whatever academic standing it now has in the Scandinavian countries. Gustaf F. Steffen (1864–1929) became prominent as a Revisionist about the turn of the century; he had spent some time in England, and had been much impressed by the Fabian Society. In 1903 he was called to the professorship of economics and sociology in Gothenburg, a chair expressly designed to suit his interests and capabilities. In 1910 he published a large four-volume work on sociology in which many modern trends are represented. For Steffen social life consists of mental interaction; society is not an organism, nor anything remotely like it, but simply a network of relations between persons. As a consequence, the relation of sociology and psycho-sociology is particularly close. Because of the influence of Bergson's philosophy, Steffen rejects the idea that sociology is a natural science, maintaining that it must be based on a sort of intuitive insight that will render possible the understanding of the social actions of others. The point of view set forth in the larger work Steffen later embodied in a small, popularly written volume, and this has gone through numerous editions; hence a fairly large section of the educated public is acquainted with systematic sociology as conceived by Steffen.

He was also active in the field of historical sociology; his three-volume work, *The Ages of the World* (1918–1920), represents an attempt to lay down an ideal-typical series of stages valid for all peoples and periods. This work is particularly interesting for methodological reasons, inasmuch as it represents the utmost possible extension of the ideal-typical mode of presentation.

These more narrowly sociological treatises failed to give full scope to Steffen's energies, and he published a series of studies dealing critically with the problems of democracy as related to various phases of modern culture, as well as with a number of social-philosophical questions (one essay is entitled "The Purpose of Life"). Further, he dealt with the sociology of war: his *War and Culture* (1914–16) attracted a great deal of attention, in part because of his vigorous advocacy of the cause of the Central Powers. Once more, he analyzed the theories of Marxism at some length, and his forthright criticism of what he believed to be the arbitrary dogmas of the Marxian interpretation of history led to his expulsion from the Social-Democratic party. Finally, Steffen's zeal for social reform caused him to make intensive investigations of the housing problem in Sweden and of the various English and German measures for the socialization of insurance, unemployment relief, and so on. The peculiar merit of his work in this field was due to the fact that his proposals were concrete as well as theoretically justifiable in the light of his broader sociological generalizations. It is not to be wondered at, therefore, that he has been called the Swedish Hobhouse. Moreover, there are other points of similarity between Steffen and the British social philosopher, not the least of which is their common catholicity of thought.[133]

The Specialists and Their Sociological Contributions.—But even though Steffen is almost a solitary figure so far as sociology in Scandinavia is concerned, several scholars and scientists who do not bear the label have provided data and formulated hypotheses of some sociological significance.

For example, Oskar Montelius (1843–1921) carried on archaeological studies that were utilized to great advantage by Steffen in his historical sociology. Not only was Montelius's research unsurpassed in accuracy, but its results were also presented in a form that made their sociological utilization easy. All too often archaeologists and like specialists treat their discoveries as ends in themselves, apparently caring nothing for those aspects of their work that can be linked up closely with the other social sciences. Montelius, however, used a typological procedure that admitted of comparison with culture areas other than the Scandinavian, and that in addition was methodologically in harmony with the ideal-typical method upon which Steffen's studies in social change were based.[134]

Another writer utilizing a typological means of investigation was Pontus E. Fahlbeck (1850–1923), a Swedish political scientist and statistician. He studied at the University of Lund, taught there throughout the whole of his academic career, and in 1918 established the Fahlbeck Foundation for the study of economics, political science, and statistics. His work in the social studies mentioned was of much importance — witness the fact that he founded modern statistics as an independent science in Sweden — but for our purposes his last and unfinished work, *The Classes and Society,* is paramount. It is markedly similar in some respects to Sorokin's *Social Mobility,* although not based on European and American data in general (as is the case with Sorokin's researches), but primarily on Scandinavian material. Fahlbeck presented an ideal-typical set of stages in class development, and attempted to show that the upper classes are superior to the lower in terms of all vital indices. He also maintained that class stratification is culturally as well as biologically conditioned, as evidenced by the fact that social differentiation has been inseparably associated with the development of complex cultures. His writings are exceedingly suggestive because of the profusion of ideas they display, and his style is incisive.[135]

A political scientist of somewhat different stamp was Rudolf Kjellén (1864–1922), professor at the University of Gothenburg from 1890 to 1916, and thereafter at Uppsala. He was a member of the organismic school, and in addition was markedly influenced by Ratzel's anthropogeography as applied to politics.[136] In *The State as Organism* (1916) he set forth what he designated as a sociological system, but which he later incorporated in his *Outline of a System of Politics* (1920). His use of the term " politics," however, is not in the sense of practical political action, but in the Aristotelian sense of the science of the state, thus bringing it very close to sociology. Kjellén's system is a highly original combination of doctrines previously espoused by other political scientists, economists, geographers, and sociologists,[137] but originality is its chief virtue. All the fallacies of organismic thought are perpetrated, and in spite of the interesting array of concrete descriptions embodied in his theoretical discussions, they are not sufficient to save his work from superficiality. Some aspects of his geopolitics (a term he used to designate those problems and conditions of life in the state which arise from geographical factors and natural environment) have been enthusiastically adopted in Germany.[138] This is readily understandable, for the organismic notions therein contained provide excellent rationalizations for Pan-German schemes; almost any kind of national expansion can be justified on the ground that the state, as an organism, must grow or die. Kjellén's disciples would be greatly deflated if recent sociological refutations of their organismic gospel pierced their armor, but this happy result is not likely to ensue — men never hear what they do not want to heed.

The Danish scholar, C. N. Starcke (1858–1926), the second successor of Harald Höffding at the University of Copenhagen, was primarily a philosopher, but his ethnological interests justify mention of him here. His *Conscience: A Study in the Principles of Human Society* (1894–1897) is perhaps the most profound of his many treatises, as well as the most definitely sociological, but *The Primitive Family in Its Origin and Development* (1889) is his best-known work. This was somewhat influenced by the social evolutionism then current, but a note of caution or even scepticism is plainly apparent, and in some respects Starcke may be regarded as a Westermarck who wrote too soon. Tönnies has called his work " sociological in nature," and it is quite true that he was not so wholly engrossed in descriptive detail as to lose sight of those broader phases of social structure that most interest the sociologist. A recent Swedish work on the " primitive " family is that by Sven Lönborg of the University of Gothenburg.[139]

A philosopher also making liberal use of ethnographical material is Esaias Tegnér (1843–1925; not to be confused with the great poet of the same name). He may be regarded as a forerunner of modern sociological linguistics and of the sociology of knowledge, for in 1880 he published *The Power of Speech over Thought,* a work in which these trends are clearly in evidence. Many of the insights of Dewey, Mead, and other students of communication and " vocal gesture " were anticipated by Tegnér.[140]

The students of comparative religion have made a number of contributions of sociological interest. We may mention here the work of Martin P. Nilsson, Director of the University of Lund, who has written on preliterate religion and the religion of the Greeks. Archbishop Söderblom's studies in preliterate and comparative religion are world-famous. Not so well known, but of great importance, are the writings of Reutersskiöld, Wicklund, and others on the religion of the Lapps. But most significant for our purposes is the work of the Danish scholar Svend Ranulf, *The Jealousy of the Gods and Criminal Law at Athens: A Contribution to the Sociology of Moral Indignation* (2 vols., 1934). This is an erudite study of the peculiar jealousy manifested by the believers in the Athenian gods. Ostracism and prosecution on the charge of impiety were two of the chief modes of wreaking vengeance on a fellow-mortal who had been guilty of *hybris,* of presumption that incurred the jealousy of the gods themselves. A sample of Ranulf's Scheler-like manner of analysis [141] seems worth giving:

> . . . the tendency to inflict punishment and the propensity to envy can be seen to have disappeared simultaneously in a definite social group. That group is the upper class at Athens in the latter half of the fifth century, more precisely, that part of the upper class which was of noble descent and possessed intellectual culture, and which had taken advantage of the chances of enrichment offered by the growth of the Athenian Empire. It was in this social group that the sophists found their public. . . .

> . . . the old view was no longer the predominant one, and this was probably due to the fact that envy, the foundation on which it rested, was less prevalent owing to the newly acquired wealth. The idea of justice, too, was less respected at Athens during the Peloponnesian war than it had hitherto been. This would seem to confirm the assumption that there is a causal interdependence between poverty, envy, and the zeal for justice.[142]

Swedish ethnography had until recently a distinguished representative in the person of N. E. Nordenskiöld (1877–1932). He dealt chiefly with the technological aspects of culture, but also took some interest in recording myths and social conduct. His chief contributions appeared in English under the general title of *Comparative Ethnographical Studies* (9 vols., 1919–1931). Eric von Rosen and Gustaf Bolinder should also be listed.[143] Finland claims Westermarck, who has two outstanding disciples in Rafael Karsten and Gunnar Landtman.[144] A Finnish ethnologist with strong sociological leanings is Ragnar Numelin, who in 1918 published an interesting study of the causes of migration on the simpler levels of culture; he has also written a small volume on the history of Scandinavian ethnology.[145] Danish ethnologists include H. P. Steensby, Knud Rasmussen, and Daniel Bruun.

Most of the work in criminology in the Scandinavian countries has been carried out by psychiatrists and psychologists. Of sufficient sociological importance to call forth an enthusiastic review article from Robert E. Park [146] was Andreas Bjerre's *The Psychology of Murder*; this is available in English translation. It is a psychoanalytic study of three cases, and is in many ways a remarkable work. David Lund, a Swedish criminologist, made in 1917 a thorough study of juvenile delinquency on the matched pair basis; the control group was drawn from the same sort of environment as the delinquents. It was published in German:

Über die Ursachen der jugendlichen Asozialität. In 1936 Olaf Kinberg, professor of psychiatry at the University of Stockholm, received the Lombroso Prize for his *Basic Problems of Criminology.* He draws on sociological material to a considerable extent, but the stress is biological and psychological.

Karl Arvid Edin is outstanding among Swedish demographers " for his imaginative grasp of important problems, for his manifold explorations in the population field, and for his patient manipulation of Swedish data." [147] In collaboration with E. P. Hutchinson, some of his recent analyses have been made available in English.[148] At an earlier period, sociography in Sweden was notably furthered by Gustav Sundbärg (1875–1914). Internationally known as a statistician, he was also director of the official studies of Swedish emigration, and in addition wrote one of the most unique and penetrating works in folk sociology extant. Primarily a social reformer, he was sharply critical of his own people, but chiefly because of his intense conviction of their essential worth.[149]

Social reform in the Scandinavian countries has contributed, as elsewhere, to the slow deposit of soil for the growth of sociology. Gustav Cassel, the well-known economist, wrote a popular book on social problems early in his career, and is still avocationally interested in reforms of various kinds. Gösta Bagge, present Conservative leader in the Swedish parliament, is head of the flourishing *Socialvetenskapliga Institutet* (Institute of Social Science) in Stockholm. This is a school designed for furthering child welfare, social welfare work in local communities, and the like.

In general, sociology and bordering fields are tilled in the Scandinavian countries chiefly with the tangible and the practical as anticipated harvests. Theoretical analysis is not favored, herein offering a marked contrast to Germany and Austria.

Sociology in all the countries discussed in this chapter survived World War II and its immediate aftermath remarkably well. The Appendix for the years 1946, 1949, 1951, 1952, 1953, 1957, 1958, and 1959 bears witness to this, as does also the MSTICAC referred to on pp. 814 and 877.

In Germany, the period after World War II was for a long time marked by an astonishing failure of the sociology of the "classical 1920's" to revive effectively. Indeed, only in the late 1950s were there other than trivial indications of re-establishment of continuity. Of course, continuity may be of little value in and of itself, at least where science is concerned— but the lapse mentioned did seem to some observers to be accompanied by real scientific loss. Today, however, many younger men are responding to those of their colleagues who survived the Nazi terror, and are discriminatingly blending the worthwhile old with the worthwhile new.

CHAPTER XXIV

Sociology in the United States

A N EARLY START. — Sociology has had many antecedents in the United States,[1] most of them similar to its European forerunners. Even in the literature dating from before the Civil War distinctly sociological interests and types of analysis are to be found in history, the law of nature and of nations, moral philosophy, political economy, public law, geography, ethnology, " social science," as well as in the Classics and Biblical literature. We cannot deal with all of these here; let us take a few of the more important examples at random.

As early as 1754 instruction in " The Ends and Uses of Society " was offered by the College of Philadelphia, and in 1794 Columbia College had a course in " Humanity " taught by the professor of Greek. The catalogue description of the latter reads surprisingly like those provided for elementary classes in sociology a century later.[2]

These are isolated instances, however; the earliest continuing influence is to be found in the courses in moral philosophy which from 1750 until well past the middle of the nineteenth century were offered in nearly all colleges, oftentimes by the president himself where the denominational schools were concerned. (Gladys Bryson and Bernard have demonstrated the importance of this trend.)[3] The English theologian Paley was the author of *Principles of Moral and Political Philosophy* (1785), of which large portions were concerned with essentially sociological data and were on the whole sociological in principle. Textbooks written to replace Paley's work, such as Wayland's *Elements of Moral Science* (1835) and Combe's *Moral Philosophy* (1840), were very popular and somewhat more definitely inclined toward sociology. To be sure, the sociological phases of these treatises were bound up with all sorts of theological presuppositions, but it was possible to organize the sociological material more or less in its own terms.[4]

Apparently the first American to do this was Robert Hamilton Bishop, who from 1834 to 1836 taught a course at Miami University called "The Philosophy of Social Relations." Bishop was trained at Edinburgh, and may have been influenced by Thomas Chalmers, to whom we have already referred in discussing the antecedents of social work. Of course, Chalmers was not the only scholar of this earlier period who contributed to the development of moral philosophy — was not the great Adam Smith himself professor of moral philosophy at Edinburgh? And is it not possible to show that Giddings was by no means the first American thinker to borrow largely from *The Theory of Moral Sentiments*? But however this may be, one of Bishop's former associates, W. H. McGuffey of the famous McGuffey's Readers, taught a course at the University of Virginia from 1850 to 1858 entitled "Philosophy of Social Relations, or Ethics of Society," and other instances of Bishop's influence are not lacking.[5]

Not only were these and many other harbingers of sociology in existence before the Civil War, but the term sociology itself was also in use. The first book ever to carry the word sociology on the title page was written by a Mississippian, Henry Hughes, who in defense of slavery developed *A Treatise on Sociology, Theoretical and Applied* (1854). Hughes made an impassioned plea for the "warranty system" (slavery), as against the wage system, and in so doing gave evidence of considerable acquaintance with the writings of Comte. In the same year, George Fitzhugh of Virginia announced the purpose of his book by calling it *Sociology for the South, or the Failure of Free Society.* This acquaintance with European thought bears witness to the practice, then common in the South, of sending the scions of the aristocracy abroad rather than North for their training. The Civil War broke off these tender sociological shoots, however, and nothing of any importance to sociology came out of the South for many decades thereafter.[6]

"Social Science," and the Philosophy of Evolution. — Another significant precursor of sociology, perhaps the most important after moral philosophy, was a curious hybrid called "social science." The first work in this field was that by Henry C. Carey, *The Principles of Social Science,* published in 1858–60 in three somewhat discursive volumes (which have been much praised by some sociologists, notably Oppenheimer). Carey had been influenced by the German protectionist, Friedrich List, who in opposition to the classical English and Scottish economics of his period dealt with the chief influences affecting social life and social policy as well as with the more formal analysis of rent,

wages, money, and so on. The example set by Carey gave rise to the American Social Science Association, which was organized to promote a more or less " synthetic " view of social life and also had a strong social reform bent. Perhaps this was because leadership came largely from Frank Sanborn who, with Theodore Dwight, E. C. Wines, and others, founded the American Prison Association in 1870 and played a prominent part in the setting up of the National Conference of Charities and Corrections in 1879.[7] As we shall see, this reform trend in the currents that later coalesced to form sociology was opposed by Sumner and zealously furthered by Ward, author of the first American sociological treatise to attract wide interest.

" Social science " instruction began to be offered at Williams College in conjunction with A. L. Perry's course in economics in 1865, the same year that the American Social Science Association was founded, and in 1868 Robert E. Thompson, a disciple of Carey, gave an independent course in social science at the University of Pennsylvania. Soon other courses were established: Sumner at Yale (1872), Laws at Missouri (1876), Mayo-Smith at Columbia (1878), Dunster at Michigan (1880), and Sanborn at Cornell (1885). Most of these dealt with what we now call " social problems," i.e., race, immigration, poverty, crime, alcoholism, divorce, and so on.[8]

During this period the writings of Spencer became widely known in the United States, partly because of his prestige as the great cosmic philosopher expounding the doctrine of evolution, and partly because of the enterprise and enthusiasm of the publishing house of Appleton, which brought out an elaborate American edition of his works. His vogue soon passed beyond a mere fad; he developed a stable following through his intrinsic merits as a lucid and cogent expositor, as well as through the labors of his brilliant disciple John Fiske, who also did much to spread the knowledge of Darwin.[9] (Henry Drummond and Benjamin Kidd also labored at the task of deodorizing evolution — and with some success.) The result of all this was that Sumner, Laws, and some of the other teachers of social science began to use Spencer's writings as reading matter in their courses, and at the same time lessened or abandoned the social problems emphasis.[10] This not only made the term sociology — which Spencer used — quite widely known, but also narrowed the data upon which sociological generalizations were based primarily to the field of ethnography and biology, with unfortunate results. American theoretical sociology has not yet wholly recovered from the ethnographizing and biologizing to which it was subjected at this early date.

Thus it came to be that the chronological order of Comte and Spencer was, as it were, reversed. As we saw, the pre-Civil War fruits of Comte's teaching withered because they were the outgrowth of a social system that was soon uprooted, whereas Spencer's evolutionary and individualistic doctrines coincided with the vogue of Darwinism, the growth of biological science, and the tremendous burst of expansion through private enterprise that characterized the period between the spanning of the continent by rail in the middle 'sixties and " the passing of the frontier " in the 'nineties. We shall therefore begin our discussion of American sociological theories with the Spencerian and Darwinian lines of development, leaving the later Comtean impulse for subsequent sections.

The Philosophy of Sumner. — Among the first generation of American sociologists there is little doubt that the late William Graham Sumner, of Yale, was the most vigorous and striking personality, and probably the most inspiring and popular teacher. Consequently, in even a brief sketch of his contributions to sociology, an attempt to interpret his personality and methods is more essential than it would be in the case of any other American sociologist.

In spite of the fact that Sumner frequently emphasizes the necessity for an objective point of view in social science and decries any attempt on the part of the sociologist to moralize,[11] it is impossible for the dispassionate reader to examine closely his economic, political, and sociological writings without becoming convinced that Sumner, trained originally for the ministry and serving for a short time as an ordained curate of the Episcopal Church,[12] was primarily a preacher in the true sense of that term. His *Social Classes* is, above all, an exhortation to independent thought and action, self-reliance, and individual initiative, and the element of the preacher is not entirely absent even in *Folkways*.[13] If one adds to this initial zeal the influence of genuine love for aspiring young students, commanding personality, wide learning, splendid dogmatism,[14] and mastery of incisive English which makes his essays models of terse nineteenth-century critical prose, it is not difficult to understand Sumner's reputation.

Sumner was always primarily a sociologist in method and point of view,[15] but there can be no doubt that he built up his academic and literary reputation in the fields of economics and political science as a vigorous advocate of " hard money," free trade, and *laissez faire*.[16] Again, while Sumner may claim priority of practically a decade over any other American teacher in introducing a well-defined and continuing course in sociology (under the name of social science or " the study of societal matters ") into the university curriculum,[17] he never published a systematic exposition of his sociology, and his great monograph, *Folkways*, did not appear until three years before his death. It is only since his colleague, Albert Galloway Keller, has utilized Sumner's classroom lectures and notes to build the massive Sumner-Keller treatise, *The Science of Society* (1927), that the nature of Sumner's system (*and* Keller's) has been fully revealed.

Sumner's sociological views were colored by his economic and political predispositions and were inspired by the general thought and methods of procedure of Darwin, Spencer, and Lippert.[18] An evolutionary view of social life and development, a feeling of the plasticity of society (" the mores can make anything right "), a rigid economic determinism, a slight predilection for the use of biological concepts, and a firm conviction of the preëminent value of ethnography as the " data " and to a large extent the substance of sociology are the dominant features of Sumner's sociological thought. He seems to have been little influenced by, or acquainted with, the systematic sociological literature of America or Europe, and Keller states that he had little respect for such works.[19] On the whole it was probably fortunate that Sumner specialized in the descriptive and ethnographic, rather than the theoretical, phase of sociology, as his power of (or inclination toward) sustained and logical abstract thinking was not great. Fortunately his disciple, Keller, is more gifted in this respect, and their joint work, the *Science of Society,* has greatly benefited by his collaboration.

Folkways and Mores. — Nevertheless, Sumner's *Folkways* has already exerted far more influence, it seems safe to say, than will ever issue from the cumbersome *Science of Society* or Keller's epitome of the latter, *Man's Rough Road*. We shall therefore restrict our discussion of Sumner's writings primarily to *Folkways*. Of this it is not inaccurate to say that it is unsurpassed as a sociological treatise on " usages, manners, customs, mores, and morals." [20] No extended analysis of it can be attempted within the scope of the present chapter, but it is essential that certain fundamental conceptions be pointed out.

Folkways is essentially an attempt to explain the origin, nature, value, and persistence of certain of the most important and characteristic group habits. Briefly, Sumner's theory of the folkways is that, guided in a *general* way by instincts inherited from animal ancestors and by the psycho-physical capacity to distinguish pain from pleasure, man has built up gradually, by a process of trial and error, certain types of group conduct which have been found by experience to be conducive to a successful issue of the struggle for existence. These group habits or folkways function primarily on a subconscious level, and acquire greater power, as time passes, through the force of tradition, habit, and religious sanction. When the folkways reach the stage where they are raised to the level of conscious reflection and are regarded as adapted to securing the continued welfare and prosperity of the group, they are thereby transformed into *mores*. The mores, as supported by group authority, are the chief agency through which societal selection operates. The mores determine what shall be regarded as right and wrong modes of conduct in any group, morality thus being not absolute and universal but relative and local. The question of the evolution of the mores is not dealt with by Sumner at any length, but he furnished leading ideas which were developed by his disciple Keller, and which we shall later discuss as an integral part of the general point of view Sumner represents. Further, Sumner devoted no extended analysis to the problem as to whether the mores can be consciously changed by society, although time and again he makes it plain that he did not believe that members of any group are competent to discuss and criticize the validity of their own mores, much less to change them by predetermined action. The following selected and rearranged quotations from *Folkways* epitomize Sumner's theoretical position:

Men in groups are under life conditions; they have needs which are similar under the state of the life conditions; the relations of the needs to the conditions are interests under the heads of hunger, love, vanity, and fear; efforts of numbers at the same time to satisfy interests produce mass phenomena which are folkways by virtue of uniformity, repetition, and wide concurrence. The folkways are attended by pleasure or pain according as they are well fitted for the purpose. Pain forces reflection and observation of some relation between acts and welfare. At this point the prevailing world philosophy suggests explanations and inferences, which become entangled with judgment and expediency. However, the folkways take on a philosophy of right living and life policy for welfare. When the elements of truth and right are developed into doctrines of welfare, the folkways are raised to another plane. They then become capable of producing inferences, developing into new forms, and extending their constructive influence over men and society. Then we call them the mores. The mores are the folkways, including the philosophical and ethical generalizations as to societal welfare which are suggested by them, and inherent in them, as they grow. They are the ways of doing things which are current in a society to satisfy human needs and desires, together with the faiths, notions, codes, and standards of well living which inhere in those ways, having a genetic connection with them. By virtue of the latter element the mores are traits in the specific character of a society or a period. They pervade and control the ways of thinking in all the exigencies of life, returning from the world of abstractions to the world of action, to give guidance and to win revivification. At every turn we find new evidence that the mores can make anything right. What they do is that they cover a usage in dress, language, behavior, manners, etc., with the mantle of current custom, and give it regulation and limits within which it becomes unquestionable. The limit is generally a limit of toleration. The mores set the limits or define the disapproval. The most important fact about the mores is their dominion over the individual. Arising he knows not whence or how, they meet his opening mind in earliest childhood, give him his outfit of ideas, faiths, and tastes, and lead him into prescribed mental processes. The mores are therefore an engine of social selection. Their coercion of the individual is the mode in which they operate the selection. It is vain to imagine that a " scientific man " can divest himself of prejudice or previous opinion, and put himself in an attitude of neutral independence towards the mores. He might as well try to get out of gravity or the pressure of the atmosphere.[21]

The Powerlessness of Mind in Evolution. — In addition to his notion of the mores, the other fundamental conception in Sumner's sociological theory is the assumption that social as well as organismic evolution is almost wholly an automatic, spontaneous, unilinear, irreversible process which cannot be extensively altered by social effort. In the light of Sumner's admitted obligation to Spencer, it seems reasonable to suppose that this view of social development was either directly derived from the latter, or was strengthened by Spencer's vigorous exposition of this doctrine, particularly in his *Study of Sociology.* The following passage is the best summary of Sumner's views on the subject of the automatic evolution of society and the futility of social initiative:

If this poor old world is as bad as they say, one more reflection may check the zeal of the headlong reformer. It is at any rate a tough old world. It has taken its trend and curvature and all its twists and tangles from a long course of formation. . . . If we puny men by our arts can do anything at all to straighten them, it will be only by modifying the tendencies of some of the forces at work, so that, after a sufficient time, their action may be changed a little and slowly the lines of movement may be modified. This effort, however, can at most be only slight, and it will take a long time. In the meantime spontaneous forces will be at work,

compared with which our efforts are like those of a man trying to deflect
a river, and these forces will have changed the whole problem before our
interferences have time to make themselves felt. The great stream of
time and earthly things will sweep on just the same in spite of us. . . .
It will absorb the efforts at change and take them into itself as new but
trivial components, and the great movement of tradition and work will go
on unchanged by our fads and schemes. The things which will change it
are the great discoveries and inventions, the new reactions inside the
social organism, and the changes in the earth itself on account of changes
in the cosmical forces. These causes will make of it just what, in fidelity
to them, it ought to be. The men will be carried along with it and be made
by it. . . . That is why it is the greatest folly of which a man can be
capable, to sit down with a slate and pencil to plan out a new social
world.[22]

It would be interesting to know to what extent Sumner's support of *laissez faire* was derived from his reading of Spencer, and
how far it was the outcome of his practical experience in American municipal politics early in his career. At any rate, Sumner's
opposition to the doctrine that social reform can be effected
through the agency of political machinery is readily understandable, for it would be a rare individual who could emerge with
any other viewpoint after undergoing the simultaneous influence
of Spencer's *Study of Sociology* and three years' experience in
American city politics.[23]

Darwinism and the Mores: Keller. — We have seen that in his
discussion of the mores Sumner treated their genesis as he would
a fact of nature. They arise to meet the necessities imposed upon
the group by nature, and their evolution and domination are produced by a struggle and selective process akin to that governing
the genesis of biological types. Although this essentially Darwinian idea occurs several times in his writings, Sumner did not
attempt to elaborate the analogy between organic evolution and
the development of the mores. This task has been executed by his
disciple, Keller (1874–), to whom we have already referred.[24] For the same reason that we chose Sumner's *Folkways*
rather than the Sumner-Keller *Science of Society* as a vehicle for
analyzing Sumner's basic theories, so will we use Keller's *Societal
Evolution* as a means of getting at Keller's elaboration of Sumner's fundamental postulates. Historical importance, conciseness,
and trenchant formulation are all in its favor.

Keller holds that as far as the formula of evolution has been
adopted by sociologists it has been the doctrine of evolution elaborated by Spencer, which, he thinks, is not a scientific but a

philosophic concept.[25] Hence, it is time that the really scientific formula of Darwin should be appropriated by sociology, and that the doctrine of the " transformation of the incoherent homogeneous into the coherent heterogeneous " should be displaced by that of " variation, selection, transmission, and adaptation." [26]

Keller begins by asserting that societal [27] evolution is primarily mental and not physical, inasmuch as the mores are analogous to the germ cells and embryos in the organismic world; they are " raw material " upon which and through which societal evolution operates. The next step is to discover whether or not the main factors in the Darwinian theory of evolution — variation, selection, transmission, and adaptation, are also exemplified in the evolution of the mores.

Variation in the mores is shown by the fact that no two groups possess identical codes of customary procedure. These variations arise from the differences between groups in their mental reaction to the stimulation of their environment.

Keller finds three types of societal selection — automatic, rational, and counter-selection. Automatic selection involves no conscious adaptation of means to a preconceived end, but is effected through the general processes of war, subjection and class-conflict, and competition. He has some harsh words for those who would put an end to this natural process of the elimination of the " socially unfit " that sound much like some of the passages from Spencer's *Man Versus the State,* or Sumner's *What Social Classes Owe to Each Other.*

Rational selection, the social analogue of the breeder's art, takes place in society, but in different degrees among the various classes of mores. (In the second edition of his work [1931], Keller says, " I do not see in rational selection as much as I then [1915] thought I did " [p. vi]. Because of its historical importance, we use the first edition; moreover, Keller's rational emphasis was never very strong.) To a limited extent the leaders in thought can determine the direction which changes in the mores will take, but even such persons are held in check by the domination of public opinion. The degree to which the mores are amenable to deliberate change varies with the particular variety of the mores — it is never great, and those connected with matters of sentiment like religion and sex are most difficult to change. Those not thus entangled open a somewhat wider field for improvement. In general, rational selection in the mores is accomplished in an indirect manner. Those connected with the processes of the self-maintenance of society are the least wrapped up in sentiment, and in them beneficial changes are more obvious and demonstrable. Hence it is in the economic field that rational selection in society finds its least limited range of application. But every important change in the economic organization is necessarily followed by a consequent, though not necessarily equal, transformation in the other mores; and thus, though it is usually impossible directly to modify derivative social institutions, the process can *occasionally* be achieved in this roundabout manner. Keller's answer to the question as to whether society can control its own evolution therefore issues in a simple version of economic determinism, which he is careful to dissociate from his interpretation of Marxism.

By counter-selection Keller means that type of societal selection which renders the individual biologically less fit. He summarizes the modern social factors described by Lapouge and Schallmayer as resulting in the survival of the biologically unfit: these are mainly war, modern industry, celibacy, late marriage, and the sterility of the better classes in society. But counter-selection, while disastrous biologically, may have more than equal social compensations. Societal selection in the form of warfare, for example, operates primarily between groups rather than among individuals, and hence in so far as it secures social advantages which are greater than the biological loss, it is to be commended. Keller has many doubts concerning the practicability of the eugenic program advanced by Galton and Pearson, since he believes that it involves interference with mores of a type most resistant to rational control.

Societal transmission is not possible in the sense of biological heredity, for the mores are "acquired characteristics." The transmission of the mores takes place through the medium of tradition, which operates automatically by means of imitation and artificially in the process of education.

Adaptation in the mores is the outcome of the operation of the processes of variation, selection, and transmission. Every social custom or institution is the result of an adaptation of the life of a people to the environmental condition which confronted them. Even though the particular adjustment may later be an anachronism, it should not be condemned absolutely, says Keller, for it must have once been useful or it would not have existed.

Keller thus applies the Darwinian formulas to the processes of social evolution in a broad general way. He has performed the task so well that any similar exploitation of this field is likely to be very unfruitful, but the question arises as to whether or not he has simply outlined a novel variation of the old organismic anal-ogy.[28] At any rate, Keller has certainly done more than justice to the thought of his master — indeed, he has devoted so much effort to giving Sumner a posthumous personality that he has les-sened his own chances for sociological immortality. A comparison of *Societal Evolution* with *Folkways,* and further comparison of them both with *The Science of Society,* leads to the conclusion that we are probably justified in treating the topic of the evolution of the mores as an integral part of one of the most impassioned American preachments of the nineteenth century.

Classifier and Environmentalist: Ward. — The great nine-teenth-century era of ruthless private exploitation of the re-sources of the United States, of governmental inefficiency and corruption, and of boundless confidence in the automatic workings of " manifest destiny " was not attended by complete intellectual acquiescence. Sumner himself, with characteristic lack of consist-ency, attacked the protectionism and plutocracy of the time so vig-orously that one might be inclined to believe that he expected the " futile pipings " of one man to bring down the walls of a Jericho reared by the " great spontaneous forces of nature." Other thinkers, even more convinced that the times were out of joint, grimly took up their *verdammte Pflicht und Schuldigkeit* in the effort to set them where they should be, and among these was the first effective disciple of Comte to appear in the United States, Lester F. Ward (1841–1913). A product of the frontier, almost wholly self-taught, Ward represents an almost complete antithe-sis in background to the erstwhile Episcopalian curate with whom we here contrast him.

Of all American writers there can be no doubt that Ward pro-duced the most imposing and comprehensive system of sociology. His *Dynamic Sociology,* which many critics consider his *magnum opus,* appeared in 1883, about a decade after Sumner launched his course in " social science," and approximately midway be-tween the publication of the first and the last volume of Spencer's *Principles of Sociology.* In addition to many articles in periodi-cals, Ward's sociological system was embodied in six volumes.[29] Whatever may be the estimate of the future regarding his place in the history of sociology, it is certain that no other writer has approached the subject with an even approximately equal body of natural-scientific knowledge. Herbert Spencer's *Synthetic Philos-ophy* undoubtedly displays more profound reasoning powers and a greater talent for the logical marshaling of evidence, but the data he commanded were not at all comparable in quantity to those possessed by Ward. Ward's formal scientific career was passed as a government expert in paleobotany, to which he made contributions only second in importance to his work in sociology.[30] His predilection for introducing his botanical terminology and the fruits of his linguistic studies into his sociology often gives the latter as strange, technical, and repulsive a tone as is to be found in the writings of the extreme organismic theorists. Some of his scientific terms, however, such as "sympodial development," "synergy," "creative synthesis," "gynaecocracy," and "social telesis" are less barbarous and have been absorbed to some extent into conventional sociological thought and expression.

An extended or comprehensive exposition of Ward's sociological system within the scope of the present chapter is manifestly impossible. Attention will be confined to a few of his cardinal contributions.

The Outlines of the System. — In Ward's view, as in Comte's, sociology is a general social science to which all the others, and the natural sciences as well, are merely contributory. This is not to say that they are unimportant, but it most decidedly is to say that they are subordinate. To quote:

It is not quite enough to say that it is a synthesis of them all. It is the new compound which their synthesis creates. It is not any of them and it is not all of them. It is that science which they spontaneously generate. It is a genetic product, the last term in the genesis of science. The special social sciences are the units of aggregation that organically combine to create sociology, but they lose their individuality as completely as do chemical units, and the resultant product is wholly unlike any of them and is of a higher order. All this is true of any of the complex sciences, but sociology, standing at the head of the entire series, is enriched by all the truths of nature and embraces all truth. It is the *scientia scientiarum*.[31]

As to the subject-matter of sociology, Ward says: "My thesis is that the subject-matter of sociology is human *achievement*. It is not what men are but what they do. It is not the structure but the function."[32] As nearly all the earlier sociologists had been concerned almost wholly with an analysis of social structure, Ward's point of approach was novel, and epoch-making in its significance. The divisions of sociology are two — pure and applied. Pure sociology is theoretical and seeks to establish the principles of the science, whereas applied sociology is practical and points out applications. Specifically, the latter "deals with the artificial means of accelerating the spontaneous processes of nature."[33] Ward accordingly divides the body of his sociological system into genesis and telesis. The former treats of the origin and spontaneous development of social structures and functions, and the latter of the conscious improvement of society. In the department of social genesis, Ward's most important contributions may be summarized under these headings: sympodial development, creative synthesis, synergy, the law of parsimony, the functions and biological origin of mind, social statics and dynamics, and the classification of the social forces.

The natural or genetic development of society is " sympodial." By this Ward means that type of development found in certain plants in which the trunk, after developing to a certain extent, gives off a branch or sympode, which from that point onward virtually becomes the trunk, until it is in turn displaced by another sympode. The doctrine of " creative synthesis," which Ward adopted from Wundt, he explains as denoting that " each combination is something more than the mere sum of its component factors." [34] Every synthesis of nature is, like the chemical compound, a new creation. " Synergy " is defined as " the systematic and organic working together of the antithetical forces of nature." [35] This is one of the basic conceptions underlying the theory of the spontaneous development of society, and we shall refer to it again. Finally, the " law of parsimony," which is the basic law of social mechanics, is described as the tendency of natural forces to work along the line of least resistance or greatest attraction. The identity of this with Spencer's Newtonian principle of motion along the line of least resistance is obvious.

With his characteristic daring and confidence, Ward describes the origin of life and the biological creation of the mind. Life originated through the process of " zoism," which was a creative synthesis taking the form of the recompounding of the highest known chemical properties. The mind was also a creative product of " zoism "; it originated in the fact of " awareness," and its irreducible element is the capacity of detecting and differentiating painful and pleasurable stimuli which come from the environment. Feeling and desire, which are of an earlier origin than intellect, are the dynamic and impelling forces of mind; intellect, which is a later and higher product, is the directive faculty.

Ward considers his distinction between social statics and social dynamics and his discussion of the nature of each of these aspects of the social process to be one of his most important theoretical contributions [36] — although Comte anticipated him in many points. Social statics deals with social equilibration and the establishment of a social order — i.e., the building up of social structures. The development of the social order is a " struggle for structure " rather than a struggle for existence. The best structures survive.[37]

The Mystic Force of Synergy. — In the growth of social structures synergy is the most important principle, for it is the force which creates all structures and explains all organization. Through this principle of synergy there is brought about a working together of the antithetical forces of nature in a sequence of processes: collision, conflict, antagonism, opposition, competition, interaction, compromise, collaboration, coöperation, and organization. Synergy, in the development of the social order, operates mainly through the process that Ward calls " social karyokinesis." This is the social analogue of fertilization in the biological field, and is manifested in the contact, amalgamation, and assimilation of different social groups. All the processes enumerated in the foregoing sequence are exemplified in this process, which ends in the production of a homogeneous nation. As we saw in the sections on conflict theories of the origin of the state, Ward is here in fairly close agreement with the theories of Ratzenhofer and Gumplowicz regarding " the struggle of races " as the main factor in state-building.

This stress on the clash and conciliation of antagonistic forces through synergy seems to be a positivistic adaptation of the Hegelian theory of social development, although Ward in general pays very little attention to Hegel, and what he does say about him is disparaging. " Synergy " has the same occult odor that hovers about " the dialectic "; indeed, it has been called animistic — and so has the dialectic. It should also be noted that there is more than a little resemblance to the Marxian adaptation of Hegel as regards the function of the conflict of political parties, although Ward does not use the term " class struggle " and thinks in parliamentary forms. The fundamental principle underlying such conflict is that of synergy; it brings about a coöperation (synthesis) between antithetical forces (thesis — antithesis) which secures their working together toward an end of which they are unconscious (or, as Marx put it, socialism grows out of capitalism). Ward's contention runs as follows:

The vigorous interaction of the two forces, which looks so much like antagonism, strife, and struggle, transforms force into energy and energy into power, and builds political and social structures. And after they are constructed, the same influence transforms them, and it is this that constitutes progress. Political institutions — the laws of every country — are the product of this political synergy, the crystallized action of legislative bodies created by political parties.[38]

Moreover, Ward takes quite as positive an attitude toward the state as does Hegel; the following dithyramb sounds for all the world like a passage from the *Philosophie des Rechts:*

We thus see that the state, though genetic in its origin, is telic in its method; that it has but one purpose, function, or mission, that of securing the welfare of society; that its mode of operation is that of preventing the anti-social action of individuals; that in doing this it increases the freedom of human action so long as it is not anti-social; that the state is therefore essentially moral and ethical; that its own acts must necessarily be ethical; that being a natural product it must in a large sense be representative; that in point of fact it is always as good as society will permit it to be; that while thus far in the history of society the state has rarely performed acts that tend to advance mankind, it has always been the condition to all achievement, making possible all the social, industrial, artistic, literary, and scientific activities that go on within the state and under its protection. There is no other institution with which the state may be compared, and yet, in view of all this, it is the most important of all human institutions.[39]

The Rôle of Psychic Factors. — Social dynamics, says Ward, deals with social progress or the changes in the structure of society. In social dynamics there are three fundamental principles: difference of potential, innovation, and conation. The difference of potential is manifested in the crossing of cultures which takes place in social assimilation and amalgamation. Progress comes from a fusion of unlike elements. Innovation, which is the social analogue of the sport or mutation in the organic world, is the product of psychic exuberance. Conation, or social effort, is that application of social energy from which achievement results. This achievement takes the form of the satisfaction of desire, the preservation of life, and the modification of the environment.

Ward classifies the social forces as ontogenetic or preservative, phylogenetic or reproductive, and sociogenetic or spiritual. It is in connection with the discussion of the phylogenetic forces that Ward develops his famous theory of " gynaecocracy," according to which he holds that the female sex was the original sex in nature, and was the most important until subordinated by the social restraints imposed upon it after man discovered his relation to the child. (This theory has been attacked by Knight, upheld by Briffault, and, rightly or wrongly, regarded with indifference by most American sociologists.)

In his exposition of the principle of social telesis Ward lays down the fundamental proposition that energy must be controlled if evolution is to result. There are two possible methods of control: the unconscious control by the unconscious forces of nature manifested in genesis, and the conscious direction by mind, the conscious force of nature, in the broadest sense, involved in telesis. The conscious method of control by mind is manifestly superior to unconscious control. Nature is wasteful in providing an immense mass of raw material and leaving it to be improved very slowly through natural selection. The tendency of mind is to economize through foresight and the adjustment of means to ends. This control of the dynamic forces of nature and society through the adjustment of means to ends is what Ward designated as "telesis," for which our modern catchword "planning" is a less mysterious substitute. In this process of conscious or telic control of the social forces, the development of the state and its agency, government, was the most important step ever taken by man or society.[40]

Governmental Control, the Manifestation of Social Telesis. — In view of the central importance of Ward's ideas of the state and government in his system, it is necessary to consider this aspect of his thought in some detail.

As the basis for a general classification of the forms of government, Ward proposes the terms autocracy, aristocracy, and democracy. Within the general category of democracy he distinguishes three distinct variations: physiocracy, plutocracy, and sociocracy. Physiocracy is that type of government which developed in Western Europe as a result of the teachings of the Physiocrats and Adam Smith, and the individualistic writers like Humboldt and Spencer. It is that sort of *laissez faire* government which is based upon honest but wrong-headed individualistic political philosophy. Plutocracy is the perversion of physiocracy which came about when, early in the nineteenth century, "the corrupt and selfish vested interests" appropriated the individualistic political philosophy for the purpose of maintaining themselves in their position. This perversion of individualism is still the current form of contemporary political theory and organization.[41] Sociocracy is the next logical stage in political evolution. It is in reality the ideal democracy from which the present partisanship, ignorance, hypocrisy, and graft have been eliminated. Sociocracy does not lay stress primarily upon the form of government but "goes to the substance, and denotes that, in whatever manner organized, it is the duty of society to act consciously and intelligently, as becomes an enlightened age, in the direction of guarding its own interests and working out its own destiny." [42]

In his theories regarding the sphere of the state Ward was the most vigorous and consistent opponent of Spencerian and Sumnerian *laissez faire* individualism to be found among the sociological writers of his day. He never lost his faith in the efficacy of government as an agent of social reform, declaring that it could be put on a scientific basis and purged of its corruption and stupidity.[43]

Ward enumerates four chief functions of government: the restraint, protection, accommodation, and amelioration of society. The first of these has never been a legitimate function; the second will be necessary so long as men do not refrain from injuring their fellows; the third is, and always will be, an indispensable function of government; while the fourth, which is the most important of all, has scarcely been put into action as yet.

In carrying on its restraining, protecting, and accommodating functions, government has not directly aided or promoted progress. But, while possessing no directly progressive element, it has been the indispensable prerequisite of all progress, and if legislators will only become sociologists or be guided by them, they may directly improve the condition of society in accord with social telesis.[44]

Ward's whole defense of government as the most effective instrument of society in promoting progress rests primarily upon his distinction between honest and intelligent government and its past and present perversions. In his essay on " False Notions of Government," [45] Ward points out the unfortunate results which have come about as a result of the failure to distinguish between the true principles and the actual practice of government. The deep-seated popular distrust of government was very beneficial in the earlier periods of despotism, but the modern democratization of government has removed the need of this suspicious attitude toward political direction and control, and its persistence is detrimental. Accordingly, Ward severely criticizes as obstructionists those " misarchists," of whom the most conspicuous examples among sociologists have been Spencer and Sumner, for their strenuous attempts to perpetrate this " pernicious view of government." [46]

The basic principles of Ward's sociology are nowhere better displayed than in his doctrines regarding the solution of social problems through governmental activity. In his *Psychic Factors of Civilization* Ward summarizes what he regards as the indispensable prerequisites for the successful operation of social or collective telesis through the instrumentality of government. Like Comte, to whom Ward was greatly indebted, Ward placed his reliance on sociology as the source of the information which is preliminary to any extensive development of scientific government. Ward's legislators, like the priests of the Positivist régime, were to be trained sociologists. Hence a diffusion of the knowledge of fundamental sociological principles must precede the scientific development and application of governmental activity in behalf of social reform. The legislators must be thoroughly acquainted with the nature of, and method of controlling, the social forces.[47] In an article entitled "The Way to Scientific Law-Making," published in 1877, five years before Jevons's classic exposition of the same subject, Ward clearly and forcefully argued the value of statistics in scientific legislation.[48] Later (1903) he set forth essentially the same arguments with regard to the usefulness of statistics for sociology, pointing out that sociological knowledge is in a very imperfect and undeveloped stage — about analogous to the physics and chemistry of the fifteenth century.[49]

Education, the Assurance of Things Hoped For. — Once achieved, this indispensable sociological knowledge must be imparted by an improved system of education. No other sociologist, not even of the "educational sociology" variety, has approximated in emphasis, thoroughness, or optimism Ward's treatment of the sociological importance of education. He takes as his point of departure the thesis that social forces can be directed into safe and useful channels only if their nature and the manner of their control is understood.[50] Education should thus be valued in proportion " as it gives to its possessor correct views of life, of his relation to society, and to nature." [51] The educational system which embraces this useful type of information should be carried on by the state and should be universal. The whole sociological problem and significance of education he sums up in the following characteristic paragraph:

It is the question whether the social system shall always be left to nature, always be genetic and spontaneous, and be allowed to drift listlessly on, entrusted to the by no means always progressive influences which have developed it and brought it to its present condition, or whether it shall be regarded as a proper subject of art, treated as other natural products have been treated by human intelligence, and made as much superior to nature, in this only proper sense of the word, as other artificial productions are superior to natural ones.[52]

When this revised and universal system of education is put into effect, government, which will be sociocratic in form, can be conducted on truly scientific principles, and it will then be possible to promote progress by the telic method of " social invention " and " attractive legislation." True social invention " consists in making such adjustments as will induce men to act in the manner most advantageous to society," and therefore must take the form of " attractive legislation," which would aim not to check or restrain the vital energy of society, but rather to divert it from harmful expression and direct it into useful channels of expenditure. The following paragraph is Ward's best summary of this position:

As a scientific investigator, the legislator would then set for himself the task of devising means to render harmless those forces now seen to be working evil results, and to render useful those now running to waste. Not only would the present prohibitive legislation, which seeks to accomplish its ends by direct, or brute, method, be rapidly supplanted by attractive legislation accomplishing its purposes by the indirect, or intellectual, method, and thus fulfilling the protective functions of government at a saving of enormous loss through the friction of opposition, but the accommodative function would now be in condition to advance toward the position of a truly ameliorative one. Society, possessed for the first time of a completely integrated consciousness, could at last proceed to map out a field of independent operation for the systematic realization of its own interests, in the same manner that an intelligent and keen-witted individual pursues his life-purposes. Not only would protection and accommodation be secured without loss of liberty and at the least possible cost to society, but directly progressive measures would be adopted looking to the organization of human happiness. Fully realizing the character and mode of operation of the truly progressive agencies of society, government would not simply foster and protect these, but would increase and intensify them and their influence. No longer doubting that progress upon the whole must be in proportion to the degree and universality of intelligence, no effort or expense would be spared to impart to every citizen an equal and adequate amount of useful knowledge.[53]

Ward's prophetic vein was not entirely exhausted by this eloquent affirmation of his faith in the coming of that glorious day when scientific legislation will make of the earth a pedagogue's paradise. He even dared to predict that in the still more remote future, with the perfection of the intellect, the completeness of knowledge, and the ministrations of the teacher, the state and government may disappear![54] This is a denial of his assertion, mentioned above, that society will never outgrow the accommodating function of government, but consistency is a petty virtue. Just as Hegel let the dialectic come to rest when the final stage of perfection, as outlined in the Prussian state of 1820, had been attained, and just as Marx thought he foresaw the day when the class-struggle, the mainspring of history, would be eliminated by the abolition of classes and the consequent cessation of struggle, so Ward wandered into the far future to find that the perfect society will be made up of philosophical anarchists, wearing necklaces made of Sigma Xi and Phi Beta Kappa keys. " The owl of Minerva begins her flight." " The kingdom of necessity ends; freedom itself has become a necessity."

In conclusion, one may safely say that Ward's salient doctrines were his assertion of the relation between cosmic and social evolution, and his proclamation of the superiority of the conscious over the unconscious control of the total process of sociation. Of these two theories, the former is but picturesque and eloquent guesswork, and must remain so until the range of human knowledge is greatly extended. The latter, for all its dubious character, is nevertheless within the range of refutation or verification, and if true is certainly the most important single contribution sociology has yet made to human thought. Ward's significance must therefore rest chiefly upon the fact that his presentation of this conception (which he shared with many forerunners) has been the most powerful ever penned by any sociologist. Giddings has thus summed up this aspect of Ward's teaching:

Throughout all Ward's work there runs one dominating and organizing thought. Human society, as we who live now know it, is not the passive product of unconscious forces. It lies within the domain of cosmic law, but so does the mind of man: and this mind of man has knowingly, artfully adapted and readapted its social environment, and with reflective intelligence has begun to shape it into an instrument wherewith to fulfil man's will. With forecasting wisdom man will perfect it, until it shall be at once adequate and adaptable to all its uses. This he will do not by creative impulse evolving in a void, but by constructive intelligence shaping the substantial stuff of verified scientific knowledge. Wherefore, scientific knowledge must be made the possession of mankind. Education must not merely train the mind. It must also equip and store, with knowledge.

This great thought Dr. Ward apprehended, expressed, explained, illuminated, drove home to the mind of all who read his pages, as no other writer, ancient or modern, has ever done. It is his enduring and cogent contribution to sociology.[55]

Summary of the Divergent Views of Sumner and Ward. — Both these men lived through what was perhaps the age of greatest corruption and inefficiency in American state and national government during the entire nineteenth century, and for all of this both had unlimited contempt. But, although agreeing as to the hopelessness of expecting constructive policies from existing governments, there was a fundamental divergence between them with regard to the possibility of improving political intelligence. Sumner insisted that governments were always likely to remain inferior to individual initiative and enterprise, whereas Ward contended that with the improvement of sociological knowledge and its wide dissemination through an adequate system of education, the state would become the chief instrument in advancing group welfare and in anticipating the natural course of political and social evolution. It may reasonably be doubted whether this difference of opinion was as much due to congenital optimism on the part of Ward as it was to the basic divergence of their views regarding the nature of social evolution. Sumner was convinced of the accuracy of the Spencerian notion that it is an automatic process not amenable to social control and direction, and also subscribed to the Darwinistic idea that it, like organismic evolution, is a blind process ruthlessly crushing all things, even the most skillfully planned institutions, that fail to meet its inscrutable requirements. Ward was equally convinced that although social evolution began as a spontaneous development it has at last reached a point where the human mind can comprehend its trend, can control it, and can thereby artificially direct and accelerate social progress.

It scarcely needs to be pointed out that although Sumner's views were perhaps more characteristic of the generation in which the two men lived, Ward's opinion, right or wrong, has received the acclaim of most sociologists in the period since 1910.

The Social Sciences Move Forward. — Interesting and important as the skirmishes of these sociological guerillas were, they are not sufficient in and of themselves to account for the advance that took place along the whole sociological front in the last decades of the nineteenth century. Moreover, plenty of sociological ammunition was available aside from that furnished by Spencer and Comte, as we shall see when surveying the range occupied by Small, Giddings, and others. In order to understand the success of the sociological assault on the bastions of the older disciplines, it is necessary to get a bird's-eye view of the whole field of the social sciences at that time. Granted, the academic history of American sociology is the record of the difficulties of a new social science in breaking through the outworks reared by vested curricular interests, not the least important of which were other social sciences already in a favorable position or less likely to arouse prejudice. Nevertheless, it would be a great mistake to assume that the founding of departments of sociology in the 'nineties was made possible only by the single-handed victories of daring sociological raiders; if there had not been a remarkable series of advances in the social sciences generally, it is difficult to see how sociology could have won its way. Further, even though it is obvious that sociology would still have developed outside of university walls through the efforts of such men as Ward, there can be no doubt whatever that its growth as an academic discipline was bound up with the increasing recognition of the social sciences as a whole.[56]

A growing attention to the facts of history was early manifested at Michigan and Cornell, due to the influence of Andrew D. White and Charles Kendall Adams. At Harvard scientific history was introduced by Henry Adams and MacVane. But far the most active and influential school of history in this country prior to the twentieth century was that which was organized by Herbert Baxter Adams at Johns Hopkins about 1885. This was based on the historical concepts of Droysen and Freeman, combining scholarly precision with obsessive beliefs in the superiority of the Teutonic political genius and in the exclusive importance of the affairs of the state. Political science itself received its chief impetus from the activities of the famous faculty of political science established at Columbia by Herbert A. Burgess and his former students and friends at Amherst College. Economic science received encouragement in many centers, the most notable of which were Harvard under Dunbar and others; Yale under Sumner and F. A. Walker; Johns Hopkins under R. T. Ely (who later removed to Wisconsin) ; Chicago under J. Laurence Laughlin; and last but not least, at Pennsylvania.[57]

The institution last named was kept on the *qui vive* by the broad intellectual range of Simon N. Patten, as well as by his interest in the economics of consumption, for these inevitably led him into many types of sociological investigation and analysis, though he has always been technically regarded as primarily an economist. He also stimulated some of our most active " social economists," such as Edward T. Devine, S. M. Lindsay, Scott Nearing, and Rexford Guy Tugwell, while the work of his students who have remained officially and departmentally economists has served to advance the sociological point of view in economics, not only at Pennsylvania, but in many other American universities. Patten himself, in such works as *The Theory of Social Forces, Heredity and Social Progress, The New Basis of*

Civilization, and *The Social Basis of Religion,* contributed many innovations to the field of sociological theory, and some of them have retained their popularity.[58]

Thorstein Veblen, for a time at the University of Chicago, did much in psycho-anthropological analysis of sociological and economic import. *The Theory of the Leisure Class* (1899), to name but one of his many brilliant books, will long remain a landmark.

Psychology and anthropology were also promoted at Clark University by G. Stanley Hall, who held until his death a conception of the interrelation between the psychological and social sciences at least as broad as any that has been possessed by other American psychologists.[59]

The American Historical Association was founded in 1884; the American Economic Association in 1885; the American Academy of Political and Social Science in 1889; and the American Political Science Association in 1903. The American Sociological Society was not founded until 1905.

With the exception of the work of Sumner, whom historians regard as primarily a historian, whom many economists call the "father of American economics," whom political scientists class as distinctly one of their number, and whose course in "social science" was for a long time regarded as incidental to his more technical and intensive work in economics and political science, the more outstanding advocates of sociology in the United States were men whose first interests and achievements in this field were developed outside academic circles. John Fiske, Lester F. Ward, F. H. Giddings, and J. H. W. Stuckenberg [60] all came to an interest in sociology from their personal studies and preferences rather than from academic connections and assignments. Professional interest in the field of sociology led Giddings into a distinguished academic department and made Ward lecturer in sociology in an important American university a few years before his death, but the genesis of their interests in the field dated back to their pre-academic days. A. W. Small was the first true academic sociologist in the United States, and also the first head of an independent department of sociology, which he established at the University of Chicago in 1892.[61] This department and the one established at Columbia a few years later by Giddings were the two most important influences in the further spread of academic sociology in America.[62]

(Before going further, we must announce that within the confines of this chapter it will be impossible to provide even extended expositions, to say nothing of criticism, of the theories of the American sociologists who will be mentioned from this point on. Moreover, the fact that this book is designed primarily for American readers means that we can assume the availability of the standard American journals, reference works, textbooks, and similar auxiliaries, to say nothing of the works of the men themselves. The notes at the end of the chapter list a number of primary and secondary sources.)

The Columbia Department. — The earliest work of Franklin H. Giddings (1855–1931), aside from his extensive experience in journalism, was primarily in economics and political science, but his interests soon turned toward sociology. In this field he was first stimulated largely by the writings of Spencer and Tarde, and by the personalities and writings of Sumner and Patten. Dean Herbert A. Burgess of the faculty of political science at Columbia University was much less narrow-minded than most of his associates in the field of political science in this country, and in 1894 he called Giddings from Bryn Mawr (where he had succeeded Woodrow Wilson) to become professor of sociology, to which chair the title of the history of civilization was added in 1906.[63]

A man of great mental power and wide erudition, with an impressive but kindly personality, a fine stage presence, and remarkable hortatory powers and forensic capacity, Giddings exerted great influence on both the subject-matter of sociology and the minds of his students. From an early day Giddings had associated with him, in addition to related statisticians and economists, Alvan A. Tenney, whose unselfish devotion to the graduate seminar was primarily responsible for the high quality of the dissertations in the Columbia department. Giddings and Tenney made an admirable pair of associates because of Giddings's unusually original, stimulating, and suggestive mind, which served to start his students along many interesting and original lines of investigation, and Tenney's scholarly precision and painstaking editorship, which prevented them from publishing undisciplined and undocumented vagaries. It was extremely unfortunate, however, that during Giddings's lifetime the department was not more adequately manned, and that it did not present a wider range of interests, more varied types of approach to the problems of sociology, and rather less dynastic sense and loyalty. The graduate students of the Columbia department have until recently occupied the greater number of the sociology positions in the East, in the same way that Small's students moved into most of the chairs of sociology throughout the Middle West.[64]

Giddings's name will always be associated with the phrase

" consciousness of kind," or, as he later reworded it under the impact of behaviorism, "like response to like stimulus" and " pluralistic behavior." This doctrine was derived from Adam Smith's theory of moral sentiments and Herbert Spencer's doctrine of evolution, and its essence is simply that association is primarily dependent upon a feeling of similarity or a like response to like stimulus in associated beings — " Birds of a feather flock together." That is to say, human beings become conditioned to respond to like stimuli by communicating and associating, by acting upon one another through suggestion, example, and imitation, and they thus develop similar feelings and likemindedness. Becoming aware of these similarities and of contrasting conduct, consciousness of kind or type emerges, and this converts mere associativeness ("gregariousness") into discriminative association. Moreover, " herd habits" are thereby transmuted into norms and customs through which society, by utilizing social constraints and incentives, maintains social cohesion and perpetuates the adequate. So strong was Giddings's emphasis upon association that the definition of sociology he finally adhered to was " sociology is the science of the relation of human beings to, for, and with each other." [65] Observe that nothing whatever is said about dissociation, i.e., about certain aspects of competition, opposition, and conflict — *against* each other. This is in fact the weak point of Giddings's sociological system. So hypnotized was he by the alliterative melody of " consciousness of kind " that he failed to pay due heed to what might facetiously be called " unkind consciousness." The concept can of course be modified to include the phenomena of dissociation, and Abel, one of Giddings's former students, has done so by incorporating it in the idea of social distance,[66] but nevertheless the net effect of " consciousness of kind " was to limit the range of Giddings's system.

Time may show, however, that the most important influence Giddings exerted upon American sociology was not through his famous formula, but rather through his early interest in demography and statistics. Under his leadership the Columbia department inspired or brought into relation with it a large number of able statisticians; among them may be mentioned Chaddock, Ogburn, Rice, Frank Ross, and Hankins.

Another important result of the training provided by the Columbia department was the close relation it established with anthropology. Although Giddings himself made little use of the great advances in ethnographical and ethnological knowledge achieved by Boas (who came to Columbia from Clark Univer-

sity, where he had been the occupant of the first chair of anthropology in the United States), the greater number of Gid-
ding's students and associates assimilated enough to start
cultural sociology on its way. Ogburn, Willey, Chapin, and
many others arrived at the conviction that the products of man's
hands and brain, i.e., material and non-material culture, are far
more important in the course taken by social change and social
processes than the climatic, topographic, and biological factors
once rated so highly. In this they came partially to approximate
the position of the Durkheim school, but it would be difficult to
show that there was any direct influence worth mentioning. Although the cultural trend now includes adherents of the Sumner-
Keller school such as Leyburn and Murdock, as well as persons
whose training has been almost exclusively anthropological —
numerous pupils of Lowie, Sapir, Kroeber, and Wissler may be
instanced — it seems safe to say that the Columbia department
of sociology has been of preponderant influence among sociologists.[67]

Since Giddings's death in 1931 (he had retired only a short
time before), a marked change that was already under way at
Columbia has begun to make itself strongly manifest. R. M.
MacIver, a Scottish sociologist who came to Columbia by way of
Aberdeen and Toronto, has taken charge of the department,
with interesting results. We have already mentioned the handicaps under which the department labored, especially during Giddings's declining years; these have in some measure been overcome. While granting a place to the statistical approach and doing
justice to the claims of ethnography, MacIver is chiefly known
for a broad outlook in political philosophy (in which he has done
distinguished work), thorough knowledge of the Continental
sociologists, particularly the German, and an intimate acquaintance with the type of sociology represented by Hobhouse and
Ginsberg.

MacIver's theoretical contributions are many, but those for
which he is best known are his development and application of
the concepts of community and association,[68] and his effective
defense of a type of sociological method akin to the *verstehende
Soziologie* of Max Weber or the "subjectivism" of Mikhalovsky.[69] Of an analytic and logical turn of mind, he is in some respects closely allied with those who regard sociology as the basic,
value-free science of interhuman relations as such, but he also
preserves what for lack of a better term may be called the Hob-
housian tradition of viewing social life in its total setting and in

its relation to a scale of values. The two positions are by no means incompatible, and they are thoroughly harmonized in MacIver's work.

MacIver has been fortunate in having associated with him a number of competent men, some of them appointed during the Giddings era and some during his own. We may name Theodore Abel, penetrating exponent of systematic sociology; Robert S. Lynd, student of American culture; Robert E. Chaddock, well-known statistician; Alexander von Schelting, author of the best study of Max Weber's methodology extant; Willard Waller, prominent student of family relations and practitioner of a sophisticated " insight " technique in psycho-sociology; and Bernhard J. Stern, student of ethnology and researcher in the history of American sociology.[70] At the present moment it may be said that Columbia has gone a long way toward winning back its high reputation for graduate work in sociology.

The Chicago Department. — It is now time that we return to the other early graduate center, Chicago, which has the distinction of having the first department of sociology to be founded as an independent unit anywhere in the world. Albion Woodbury Small, its first head, possessed a more thorough academic training for his position than could have been boasted of by Giddings in 1892, but had less practical contact with social and public problems. Small's chief mentor in his early days as a sociologist was Lester F. Ward, but in later years he found more stimulation in the writings of the Scottish philosophers and of Ratzenhofer and other Germanic sociologists.[71] He had been trained thoroughly in Germany by Schmoller and other German *Kathedersozialisten* or professorial socialists, and was also in touch with the general development of the social sciences in Germany and Austria, together with the progress of social economics in England from the time of Adam Smith onward. He also spent a year (1890–91) as a mature man in the seminar of Herbert Baxter Adams at Johns Hopkins University. This gave him a more than usually thorough preparation in the fields of history and government. Shortly afterward (1892) he retired from the presidency of Colby College, where he had introduced one of the early courses in social science, to become head of the department of sociology in the newly-founded University of Chicago. His training and background doubtless account for the fact that his sociological interests were always strongly tinged with a preoccupation with economics and state intervention.

While Small, though a person of great charm and kindliness,

was a man of less personal force and impressiveness than Sumner or Giddings, he was at the same time a man of greater doctrinal tolerance and mental flexibility. This led him to associate with himself at an early date distinguished colleagues, such as Henderson, Vincent, Thomas, Park, and others, who gave to the Chicago department a variety of abilities and points of view never in any sense attained at Columbia. In the work of such students as Hayes, Ellwood, Gillette, Bernard, Bogardus, and many others, the attitudes and interests of the Chicago school were carried throughout the Middle and Far West.

Small's chief contributions to American sociology were undoubtedly in the fields of organization and editorship. Not only did he set up a splendid department, but he also did more than anyone else to organize the American Sociological Society and bring it through its first difficult years. Further, he was the editor of *The American Journal of Sociology* from its first appearance in 1895 until over twenty years later, thus performing a service of inestimable value for the new discipline. In the pages of this journal many of the most significant writings of Ward, Simmel, DeGreef, and other sociologists of world-wide reputation were published, and the book review section was for a long period one of the most catholic and at the same time one of the most discriminating to be found anywhere.

At the same time Small's own writings had a good deal of influence. His adaptation, in his *General Sociology* (1905), of the interest-struggle theory of social development presented by Ratzenhofer found many followers, and his methodological articles, although inconsistent when followed over a period of years, were usually timely and to the point. Further, his studies in the history of social thought and sociology are still decidedly worth reading, notably those dealing with the Cameralists, Adam Smith, the Germanic antecedents of sociology, and the development of sociology in the United States.[72]

During the first two decades of the twentieth century the Chicago department enjoyed the services of W. I. Thomas, an ethnologist, psycho-sociologist, and sociologist of great distinction, who is still so much a Chicago tradition that we feel justified in dealing with him here. His *Source Book for Social Origins* (1909) first won him wide renown, but this was soon eclipsed by *The Polish Peasant in Europe and America* (1918–1920), a work written in collaboration with Florian Znaniecki, eminent Polish sociologist. The life-history technique in American sociological research owes its initial stimulus to Thomas and Znaniecki. Further, their work did more to raise the study of immigrant mal-adjustment to a scientific level than anything else that has yet appeared. Again, numerous concepts (discussed in the section on Znaniecki in Chapter Twenty-Seven) utilized in their monumental treatise have proved so valuable in many kinds of sociological research that they have become common coin among American sociologists. Once more, Thomas and Znaniecki fathered " the four wishes " — response, recognition, security, new experience — that have been so much invoked, praised, and condemned as keys to human motivation. Some over-zealous disciples at once reified these wishes (perhaps misguided by Thomas's *The Unadjusted Girl* [1922]), making them virtually equivalent to clear-cut, separate, virtually unmodifiable instincts. Thomas and Znaniecki warned against reification soon after the tendency appeared, and themselves made little use, after about 1925, of what they felt to be an excessively dangerous tool. There seems no good reason for going to this extreme, however, and American sociologists will probably continue to use " the four wishes " as useful classifications. In collaboration with Dorothy S. Thomas, who later became his wife, Thomas brought out *The Child in America* (1927), one of the most profound studies extant of the whole range of information bearing on the psychical and social development and functioning of the American child. Recently Thomas has revised (in fact, rewritten) the ethnological source book mentioned above, and under the title of *Primitive Behavior* (1937) it is enjoying well-deserved popularity. Thomas is engaged in finishing a study of the Swedish peasant; he has been doing research in this field, both here and in Sweden, for a number of years. The sociological world awaits the result with interest.

After Small's death in 1926 Ellsworth Faris took over the chairmanship of the department. A former missionary in a Bantu-speaking region of Africa who has also done outstanding work in psychology, Faris has been associated with the department since 1919, and has done much to acquaint Chicago students with recent developments in psycho-sociology. Greatly influenced by the philosopher, George H. Mead, he has done much to engender a catholic receptivity to fruitful ideas. His stimulating seminar in social attitudes not only carries on the kind of painstaking analysis exemplified by Thomas and Znaniecki's *Polish Peasant in Europe and in America,* but also evaluates critically all the important work being done in psycho-sociology. For example, at a time when Pareto was largely unknown in the United States (which is to say before 1928) Faris was serenely attempting to

acquaint his students with the mysteries of residues and derivations. He is also well versed in ethnology, and does a great deal
to develop an interest in this field among his students.[73]

Associated with the Chicago department for many years, Robert E. Park, former journalist and aide to Booker T. Washington, has been one of its greatest assets. Trained in German universities and possessed of a profoundly original and reflective
type of mind, Park represents the unusual combination of literary
ability, wide range of experience, insight into personality, keen
appreciation of empirical evidence, and a gift for systematic
thought.[74] In collaboration with another member of the department, E. W. Burgess, he published in 1921 what has probably
been the most influential textbook in the history of American
sociology, *An Introduction to the Science of Sociology*. This presented, among other things, a synthesis of theories in methodology, " collective psychology," and " human ecology " that had
already demonstrated their value as guides to research. Although
theoretically far from bullet-proof, the human ecology in particular was to prove a fruitful lead. It involves the study of the
spatial distribution of population in conjunction with other social
phenomena such as urban land uses and values, division of labor,
transportation, mobility of residence, and various forms of personal disorganization, all rendered vivid by a highly-developed
type of social map. A series of excellent dissertations guided by
the Park and Burgess frame of reference and enriched by the
contributions of other members of the department began to
appear in the early 1920's and has continued ever since. Among
the most outstanding may be mentioned those by McKenzie,
Thrasher, Hiller, Wirth, Zorbaugh, Mowrer, Cressey, Cavan,
Shaw, Blumenthal, and Robert E. L. Faris.[75] Park's recent retirement, with Ellsworth Faris's to follow in the near future, may
diminish the remarkable fruitfulness of the Chicago school. Much
will depend on their successors.

Since 1927 another important member of the department has
been W. F. Ogburn, formerly of Columbia. His interests are
varied: abnormal psychology, ethnology, the history of invention, the family, and the processes of social change have all engaged his attention, but the contribution for which he is the best
known is probably his emphasis on quantitative method.[76] A
gifted statistician, he has done much to arouse in his students a
genuine if perhaps at times immoderate enthusiasm for measurement, although we hasten to add that Ogburn himself is oftentimes well aware of the pitfalls that await those obsessed by

mathematical incantations.[77] His own work in the field is marked by considerable caution and judicious interpretation, although his *Social Change* (1922) is not free from serious flaws. Open to criticism on some points, the report entitled *Recent Social Trends* (1933) executed under Ogburn's direction, is nevertheless a landmark in the history of American sociography.

Among the other members of the department at Chicago should be mentioned Herbert Blumer, philosophically-minded methodologist and psycho-sociologist, foe of statistical dogmatism and friend of judicious quantitative method; Louis Wirth, leader in the study of Germanic sociological theories; and Samuel Stouffer, one of the best of the younger social statisticians. Although perhaps no longer so unapproachably supreme a graduate center as it was from 1915 to 1930, Chicago still enjoys and deserves the highest reputation among the sociological departments of the United States and, one may even say, of the world.

Other Outstanding Early Departments. — Until very recent years academic sociology, outside of undergraduate work, has been largely monopolized by the Columbia and Chicago departments. But even a brief account of the establishment and development of the first important departments in the United States cannot omit mention of those at Wisconsin, Michigan, Brown, Yale, and Pennsylvania.

The development of sociology at the University of Wisconsin has been associated primarily with the writings and teaching of one of the most striking personalities in American sociology since the days of Sumner, namely, Edward Alsworth Ross. A product of the Johns Hopkins economics seminar, Ross first began his academic work as an economist at Leland Stanford. He was driven out of this institution through a disagreement with Mrs. Stanford about Ross's courageous discussion of the utilization of cheap coolie labor by Mr. Stanford when building the Southern and Central Pacific railroads. Ross then went to Nebraska, and later to Wisconsin, which had been made a congenial field for the sociologist because of the friendly attitude of such economists as Ely and Commons.

Although Ross's influence may seem to have been exerted chiefly through his brilliant writings and forceful lectures, his academic work has for a long time included a large quota of graduate courses. He has trained many promising men who have taken their doctorates in the Madison department and have carried the spirit and principles of Ross into other institutions. Ross's interests were at first primarily in the field of psycho-sociology, where he adapted the doctrines of Tarde to an interpretation of modern society, particularly contemporary American life. Not only did he lay bare the roots of the phenomena of suggestion, prestige, fashions, and the like, but he had earlier made one of the most brilliant studies of the sources of social order that has yet appeared — his *Social Control* (1901). Later he turned his attention to the analysis and classification of social processes; his labors in this field resulted in the publication of his *Principles of Sociology* (1920). This book has been translated into several other languages, and has greatly influenced German sociology, particularly the variety represented by Leopold von Wiese.[78] (This scholar was visiting professor at Wisconsin in 1934–1935.)

Throughout all of Ross's career, and especially in more recent years, he has given much attention to the problems of social change and international relations, basing his views upon extensive travels in all parts of the globe. In addition to his activity in these fields, most of it in the rôle of a publicist, he came out strongly in the early 1920's against indiscriminate immigration to America and in favor of birth control and eugenics. Ross's work in the Wisconsin department has long been ably supplemented by the painstaking researches and numerous publications of his successor as chairman, J. L. Gillin, outstanding in the field of social pathology. Of recent years the eminent psycho-sociologist, Kimball Young, has been a member of the Wisconsin staff, and has notably increased the prestige of the department. Among the other members, J. H. Kolb, prominent rural sociologist, and Thomas C. McCormick, well-known social statistician, are particularly worthy of mention. Howard Becker, Ross's successor in the systematic sociology courses, also gives work in the history and interpretation of social thought. The excellent anthropological division numbers among its members Charlotte Gower and the author of *The Study of Man* (1936), Ralph Linton.

Of almost the opposite type of personality from that of Ross was Charles Horton Cooley (1864–1929) of the University of Michigan, son of Thomas M. Cooley, the famous Michigan jurist. Retiring, almost seclusive, Cooley made no extensive observations of man in the mass, but drew most of his sociological inspiration and insight from observation of his intimates and himself, together with a careful study of the writings of the major sociologists and psychologists and an almost unique assimilation of the social thought of the great literary figures such as Goethe, Montaigne, Shakespeare, and Meredith. He was most concerned with the psychical aspects of social life, and his trilogy, *Human Nature and the Social Order* (1902), *Social Organization* (1909), and *Social Process* (1918), is the clearest general statement of psycho-sociology yet produced in the English language. His guiding principles represent a discriminating application of the theories of Baldwin and James to the interpretation of the problems of modern society.

The general position to be found in his writings is that self and society are simply two sides of the same thing, inasmuch as selves are social products and society is the result of their organic, continuing interrelation. Cooley's use of the organic idea is perhaps the sanest that has yet been made, but it led him to a benevolent optimism that saw harmony where most sociologists would say it is absent or only partial. For this same reason he viewed democracy more hopefully than has recently been usual. Nevertheless, whatever corrections of Cooley's views are demanded by a less sanguine study of American democracy, it is certain that his books will always be admired and respected because of their high literary quality,[79] their dignity, and their fairness.

Among those who received their training in the Michigan department under Cooley may be mentioned Hamilton, Angell, Wood, Deardorff, Carr, Thompson, Lurie, and that vigorous, forthright thinker, Read Bain. After Cooley's death in 1929 the headship of the department passed to R. D. McKenzie, one of the earliest adherents of the Chicago school of human ecology, who has maintained the high standards of the department and launched an extensive program of ecological research and graduate study.

Brown University should also be mentioned, at least in passing, in connection with the earlier developments of sociology in this country. Here the leading figure was James Quayle Dealey (1862–1937), who came to his position in sociology chiefly from an interest in the sociological aspects of history and political science. He was early attracted by the writings of Lester F. Ward, and his sociological works have been chiefly an assimilation and interpretation of the fundamental theories of Ward.[80] In 1906 he prevailed upon Brown University to extend an invitation to Ward to accept a chair in sociology there, and at the age of sixty-five Ward began his teaching career, spending the last seven years of his life at Brown.

At Yale, in spite of its priority and the enormous popularity of Sumner, sociology has been very slow in getting under way, partly because it has suffered from the too ardent discipleship of Keller, and partly because of the equivocal position forced upon it by the persistent use of such terms as " social science " and " the science of society." Of recent years, however, there have been signs that the ice is breaking, for under the leadership of Maurice R. Davie, recently-elected chairman of the department, Yale is beginning to resume its rightful rank, and the excellent work now being done by Leyburn, Murdock, Bakké, and Davie himself gives ground for high hopes. In the Institute of Human Relations, splendid work of a sociological character is being done by Dorothy Swaine Thomas, John Dollard, and others. At the Yale Divinity School, Jerome Davis, expert on problems of social well-being and co-editor of the Davis and Barnes *Introduction to Sociology,* a popular textbook, had charge of sociological courses, and did much to expand the scope of sociology at Yale beyond the narrow confines of " Sumnerology." [81] The severance of Davis's connection with Yale (1937) was in many ways unfortunate.

Finally, we cannot pass over the University of Pennsylvania. Reference has already been made to the influential economist Simon N. Patten, who was also of considerable importance in the development of sociological theory from about 1890 to 1910. Not only did he devote much attention to sociological generalization in his lectures and writings, but he was also responsible for the liberal policy of *The Annals of the American Academy of Political and Social Science,* a journal which at an early date published translations of some of the works of Gumplowicz, Simmel, and other European sociologists, reviewed all the important sociological literature of the time, and devoted many issues to the analysis of social problems which are now regarded as within the sociological field. No independent department of sociology was established until 1905, when Carl Kelsey, later well known as author of *The Physical Basis of Society* (1915), became head. Kelsey has been a pioneer in the study of the relation of geographical, biological, and like phenomena to social behavior, and has assembled about him a strong staff. Among its members may be named J. P. Lichtenberger, well-known writer in the field of the history of social thought; J. H. S. Bossard, specialist in the uses of sociology for the solution of social problems; Thorsten Sellin, editor of *The Annals* and one of the most able criminologists in the United States; Donald Young, eminent expert on race relations; W. Rex Crawford, comprehensively-grounded student of the philosophical bases of sociology, and a number of well-equipped younger men; among them J. P. Shalloo, Ray Abrams, and Wallace Weaver.[82]

After the establishment of sociology in such important university centers as Yale, Chicago, Columbia, Pennsylvania, Wisconsin, Michigan, and Brown, the next stage of progress lay in its adoption by other institutions of higher learning. It spread rapidly in the State universities of the Middle West, and in some of these institutions there is today a far heavier registration in sociology than in the parent schools — in many it runs to more than a thousand, and in at least one case to more than two thousand. Sociology has also made considerable headway in many of the smaller endowed colleges, particularly in the West. Finally, one of the few remaining strongholds of opposition capitulated when in 1930 a division of sociology was inaugurated at Harvard University. This growing popularity of the subject has encouraged more students to enter graduate work in sociology, for it has offered greater prospects of desirable openings in the teaching of the subject. Likewise, the students trained in these institutions have provided a larger supply of graduate students for the more famous university centers. In other words, the last quarter of a century has witnessed the real establishment of sociology as an important university and college subject in the United States, and it should also be said that it is making some slight progress in the high schools.

The Spread of Sociology: Harvard. — Exceedingly significant for the further development of American sociology is the newly-established Harvard department. Its head, Pitirim Sorokin, was one of the leading sociologists of Russia before the 1917 revolution, and in the chapter on Russian sociology we shall attempt to say something about this phase of his activity. He fled from Russia in 1922, and after a short stay in Europe came to the United States, where he was welcomed by Ross and Chapin. Soon he took a position as professor of sociology at the University of Minnesota, where he remained until called to head the Harvard division. Associated with him at both Minnesota and Harvard has been the well-known rural sociologist, Carle C. Zimmerman, who has also collaborated with Sorokin on several important works, among them the monumental *Systematic Source Book in Rural Sociology* (1930–1932), and the new departure, *Principles of Rural-Urban Sociology* (1929). Zimmerman is also known for his fundamental studies of family budgets and for his text, *Family and Society* (1935, with Frampton).

Sorokin's basic sociological theories are difficult to characterize briefly, for they are far-reaching in their implications. (We shall discuss his pioneer work on social mobility in the

Russian chapter.) His *Sociology of Revolution* (1925) bears the impress of the " objectivist " neuro-physiology of Pavlov and Bekhterev, and takes the position that although revolution may be inevitable under certain circumstances, it is so destructive of cultural values and of life itself that practically any alternative is preferable. In his *Contemporary Sociological Theories* (1928), erudition is united with a methodological point of view that in *some* respects brings him close to the position of Pareto, although he grants more room for the operation of cultural factors in social life than is apparent in Pareto's writings. The work on rural-urban sociology mentioned in connection with Zimmerman vigorously attacks many current ideas regarding the superiority of the city population, and is one of the most consistent defenses of rural values and ways of life that has appeared anywhere, but also offers much objective interpretation of a mass of statistical and historical data. Latterly Sorokin has challenged some applications of the quantitative method, notably certain phases of the *Recent Social Trends* studies executed under Ogburn's leadership, and has himself undertaken studies in social and cultural dynamics (discussed in Chapter Twenty) which he hopes will demonstrate more fruitful ways of applying objective standards to the interpretation of social phenomena.

In addition to Sorokin and Zimmerman, a number of other able social scientists have been brought into relation with the Harvard department. Among them should be mentioned E. B. Wilson, eminent statistician, and Talcott Parsons, translator of Max Weber's *The Protestant Ethic and the Spirit of Capitalism,* excellent analyst of the sociology of economics and outstanding researcher in sociological theory. The prospects for extensive graduate instruction at Harvard are now good; the configuration represented by the old Columbia-Chicago struggle for intellectual supremacy in sociology may eventually become polygonal.

Minnesota, North Carolina, Northwestern, Southern California. — Moreover, the polygon will not be merely a triangle. The University of Minnesota, among others, also possesses a distinguished department which does a large amount of graduate work in sociology. Among its members may be named the head, F. Stuart Chapin, who has done outstanding work in the study of social institutions and cultural change, and was for the three years of its all-too-brief existence the editor of that remarkable publication, *Social Science Abstracts*. L. L. Bernard was once at Minnesota, as was also Pitirim Sorokin. Malcolm Willey, one of the pioneers in the establishment of cultural sociology as a major trend, is now connected with the department. Other valuable members are Wallis, well-known cultural sociologist, Monachesi and Vold, criminological researchers; Schmid, ecologist and quantitative researcher; and Clifford Kirkpatrick, penetrating student of the ethnological and psycho-sociological aspects of religion and a circumspect practitioner of quantitative method in psycho-sociological research.[83]

At the University of North Carolina there is an active department headed by Howard A. Odum, product of Clark University and the Giddings régime at Columbia. His particular interests lie in the fields of regionalism and " folk sociology," both of them conditioned by his Southern affiliations. Especially popular and interesting have been his unique narratives utilizing Negro stories and songs for sociological purposes, *Rainbow 'round My Shoulder* and *Wings on My Feet*. Associated with him are: Guy B. Johnson, connoisseur of Negro folklore; Ernest R. Groves, voluminous writer and specialist on the problems of modern marriage; Rupert P. Vance, an outstanding regionalist whose *Human Geography of the South* (1932) represents some of the most significant work that has been done in the field; and Katherine E. Jocher, managing editor of *Social Forces,* an excellent sociological journal controlled by the department.

Northwestern University is somewhat obscured by the proximity of Chicago, but it has an excellent department. Arthur J. Todd, the head, not only has had wide experience in probation and personnel work, but is also a gifted writer and lecturer. Moreover, his *Theories of Social Progress* (1918) occupies a position in sociological literature not likely to be challenged soon; both literary merit and richness of content place it beyond competition. Thomas D. Eliot, another member of the Northwestern department, has been a pioneer in the sociological exploitation of psychiatric discoveries, and has also done excellent work in social economy and the therapeutic and constructive prevention of juvenile delinquency.[84] Not the least of Eliot's attainments is his capacity for eliciting the loyalty, affection, and best efforts of the students who know him intimately. The department also has the services of Ernest R. Mowrer, product of the Chicago department and one of the most able students of the modern American family; William Byron, stimulating teacher; and W. F. Bailey, pioneer in urban sociology.

On the Pacific Coast, although excellent sociological instruction is to be found at the universities of Oregon and Leland Stanford, as well as at Reed and Scripps colleges, the only flourishing departments are those which have been built up by Emory S. Bogardus at the University of Southern California in Los Angeles and by Howard B. Woolston at the University of Washington. For undergraduate work they may be numbered among the largest and best-equipped departments in the country. Moreover, a good journal, *Sociology and Social Research,* is published by the Los Angeles department. One of the opportunities for a truly great graduate department of sociology on the Pacific Coast, namely, at the University of California in Berkeley, has been frustrated through the opposition of vested interests in the Berkeley faculty. This deficiency is in part offset by the sociological interests of the brilliant California ethnologists, Lowie and Kroeber, and the sociological orientation of the ablest historical methodologist in the United States, F. J. Teggart.[85]

There are undoubtedly several other departments of major rank in the country; omission should be regarded as evidence of the writers' ignorance and all-too-human fallibility. Did space permit, we should describe in detail the work being done at Smith, Vassar, Illinois, Iowa, Duke, New York University, Pittsburgh, Temple, Ohio State, Washington (St. Louis), and many other meritorious universities and colleges,[86] but inasmuch as we shall have opportunity to say something about outstanding individuals in the following sections, dealing with specialized trends in American sociology, we shall here conclude our discussion of departments.

Drifting into Specialization Stern Foremost. — Of recent years American sociology has more and more abandoned the older effort to work out a comprehensive system covering all phases of social life. Not only are there few younger contemporary synthesists such as Ward, Small, Giddings, Ross, Bernard, or Ellwood, but even the attempt to set forth a comprehensive frame of reference for analytic purposes has but a small body of supporters. MacIver, Park and Burgess, Thomas and Znaniecki, and Sorokin have many admirers but few real followers.

It has been customary to be enthusiastic over the trend toward minute specialization and " fact-gathering " that is characteristic of present-day American sociology,[87] but there are grounds for mixed feelings. True, there is probably less unfounded speculation at present than there has been in the past, and for this we may be thankful. But speculation is not the same as rigorous, comprehensive, theoretical analysis, and of the latter there is far too little. The naïveté of most American sociologists when confronted by basic epistemological and methodological problems is deplor-

able. Part of the difficulty arises from the tremendous increase in
the number of graduate students in recent years: no one can expect ability to wrestle with fundamental issues to be present in
every member of a whole swarm of would-be sociologists. Professors have too often dodged their responsibility for the elimination of " poor sticks " by assigning little " objective " problems
that require industry but no thought. Another source of our present difficulty undoubtedly lies in the splendid achievements of the
natural sciences; seeing that certain methods are applicable to
physical, chemical, and biological problems, we have jumped at
the conclusion that they can be carried over *en bloc* to sociological
problems. Our Comtean heritage has much to do with this, but
the general drift of thought during the nineteenth century is at
least equally to blame.

This is not the place, however, to indulge in criticism of current American sociology; a whole book would be necessary to
justify what we should like to say. Let us simply state once more
that there has been a marked trend toward specialization, or even
compartmentalization.[88] We shall now try to indicate what some
of the specialities are in the approximate order of their prevalence.[89] In so doing we shall also indicate some of the special interests of sociologists who are not afflicted with compartmentalization.

" *Social Psychology*." — Perhaps the most common tendency
in American sociology is concentration on the psychical phases of
social life to the neglect of larger questions of social structure.
This is usually called " social psychology " — a sociologically dangerous and fundamentally erroneous term as generally used —
or " psycho-sociology." The leads given by Ward, Giddings,
Sumner, Cooley, Ellwood, Ross, Thomas, and Patten, together
with the rise of behaviorism and psychoanalysis, in part account
for the prevalence of this interest; a certain intrinsic fascination
combines with the undeniable importance of psychical factors to
account for much of the remainder. The outstanding exponents
of the psychical emphasis in the United States today are: W. I.
Thomas, father of the famous " four wishes " and co-author with
Florian Znaniecki, the Polish sociologist, of the epoch-making
monograph, *The Polish Peasant in Europe and in America* (5
vols., 1918–20) ; Kimball Young, one of the few psycho-sociologists with adequate psychological training, who has been influenced by Mead, Terman, Park, the cultural sociologists, and the
psychoanalytic psychiatrists; L. L. Bernard, largely responsible
for the general disfavor into which crude instinct psychology has

fallen through his critical study, *Instinct* (1924); Thomas D. Eliot, one of the first sociologists to make use of the recent advances in psychiatry; Ellsworth Faris, irenic expounder of a well-balanced type of social psychology deriving from Dewey, Mead, Judd, Thomas, and his own keen insight; C. A. Ellwood, representative of an eclectic trend, who has recently made vigorous attacks on behaviorism; [90] and a number of others including Fay B. Karpf, E. S. Bogardus, A. G. Balz, F. H. Allport, E. R. Groves, Herbert Blumer, Read Bain, J. K. Folsom, Richard T. LaPiere, John Markey, E. T. Krueger, and W. H. Reckless.[91]

Quantitative Methods. — Another well-marked trend is the advocacy and use of quantitative methods. This too has roots in the general American situation, some of which we have already indicated. Ogburn, Rice, Lundberg, Chaddock, McCormick, Bain, and Stouffer [92] are perhaps the most prominent leaders, but the stress on measurement is so strong that by far the greater number of researchers at least try to make a passing bow to the coefficient of correlation. When used with full knowledge of its limitations, measurement (or even numerical statement, which is what much so-called measurement really is) may be of considerable value, particularly when the task of interpretation is not slighted. Now that the first excesses of uncritical enthusiasm are being condemned, there seems reason to expect that statistical techniques and like devices for attaining precision in sociological research will be used in such ways that their great potentialities will be realized.

Human Ecology, and Rural-Urban Sociology. — The making of social maps and their systematic interpretation, or human ecology, has had a remarkable vogue, a good deal of which has been justified. Studies of delinquency areas and other focal points of social maladjustment in Chicago and elsewhere have done more to show the possibilities of empirical sociology than any other type of research. In saying this we do not necessarily agree with the puerile interpretations sometimes indulged in by the minor figures in ecological research, nor do we hold with the fanciful analogies, some of them close to discredited organismic conceptions, that have been seriously advanced by a few of the major workers in the field. In discussing the Chicago department we have already mentioned a number of the leading ecologists, but McKenzie, Quinn, E. F. Young, Weaver, Steiner, Shaw, and a large number of others should be listed.[93]

Urban sociology has made much use of ecological methods in

recent years, and rural sociology, somewhat belatedly following the lead given by Galpin and others, is beginning to do so. Many other methods are of course applicable, as the work of Sorokin and Zimmerman, Anderson and Lindeman, Sims, Kimball Young, Gillin, Blumenthal, Carpenter, Kolb, and Ellis Kirkpatrick demonstrate. In fact, as Reuter has pointed out, there is no warrant for assuming that the fields arbitrarily defined as " urban " and " rural " should show any particular difference in methods of investigation from sociology at large. Sorokin and Zimmerman explicitly recognize this when they call their work in rural sociology the study of the farmer-peasant class.

Cultural and Folk Sociology. — Cultural and folk sociology are comparatively recent developments. When discussing the Columbia department, some reference was made to the antecedents of cultural sociology, and it is those antecedents which account for the fact that the data used and the questions posed throughout the earlier phases of cultural sociology were almost wholly derived from the Boas and the British functionalist schools of ethnology. There has been too much preoccupation with the simpler peoples to the neglect of the historical records of the more complex civilizations — a point dwelt on at length in the chapter on social evolutionism. Even studies of contemporary American life are made in accordance with ethnographic formulas (*Middletown* is an example), and although this brings with it demonstrable advantages, there are also serious deficiencies, most notable of which are the neglect of historical intangibles and the failure to isolate social processes as such. A valuable aspect of cultural sociology is its explicit or implicit criticism of crude geographical and biological determinism, but sometimes an equally crude economic or technological determinism has been substituted. At present, however, the cultural sociologists are becoming more temperate in their claims, and with the substantial results already achieved we may expect still more valuable contributions in the future.

Folk sociology is also making rapid strides. Somewhat difficult to define, in practice it is the study of groups such as the Kentucky and Ozark mountaineers, the Florida scrub dwellers, the lower strata of Negro society, those levels of American society at large described in the so-called proletarian novels, immigrant communities, Mexican and Indian groups in transition, and the like. Redfield has furnished the most adequate statement of the content of folk sociology, and has provided in his *Tepotztlan: A*

Mexican Village (1929) a splendid example of research in the field. Leyburn, Odum, Wallis, Vance, Mead, and others should also be mentioned.[94]

Social Pathology. — Problems of social maladjustment and disorganization of all kinds probably outrank several of the trends dealt with above in the attention given to them. Certainly the number of persons engaged in the study of poverty and dependency, family disorganization, crime and delinquency, public health, mental disease, hygiene, child welfare, nutrition, and a host of other " social problems " frequently regarded as an all-sufficient diet for sociology, makes any attempt at a comprehensive list out of the question. But there is little reason for attempting to make such a list, inasmuch as very few of these matters can be regarded as any more sociological than psychological, economic, medical, or what not. In countries where the lines between disciplines are more sharply drawn, such a helter-skelter conglomeration is simply unthinkable. True, it is possible to isolate a sociological aspect of many of these social phenomena, particularly in the cases of family disorganization, delinquency and crime, and a few others, but all too often rambling discourses on being " socially-minded " usurp the place of theoretical analysis. Most of the texts on social problems have very little strictly sociological framework: the only ones that conform to high standards are Elliott and Merrill's *Social Disorganization* (1934), Queen, Bodenhafer, and Harper's *Social Organization and Disorganization* (1935), and Gillin's *Poverty and Dependency* (3rd ed., 1937), although books by Bossard, Davis, and one or two others are acceptable. Courses using such texts are of considerable value as pre-social work training or for general orientation in the contemporary world, but no student should be allowed to restrict himself to a diet of this kind in the belief that he is becoming a sociological adept.[95]

Minority Groups, and Population Problems. — Race relations or, to borrow Donald Young's phrase, the study of minority groups, have always attracted much attention on the part of American sociologists. And rightly so: Negro–white, immigrant–native, and like configurations provide some of the clearest examples of the social processes associated with struggles of interest, amalgamation, domination, submission, and selection to be found anywhere. Most of the sociologists concentrating on minority-group processes also make recommendation for ameliorating conditions regarded as objectionable, but this does not have the disastrous consequences so often evident in the treatment of the other " social problems " discussed above. The reason for this lies in the fact that the analysis of inter-group relations can be led into sociological channels with comparative ease. Some of the best-known students of minority-group relations are Park, Miller, Dubois, Donald Young, Frazier, Charles Johnson, Hankins, Pauline V. Young, Wirth, Reuter, and Fairchild.[96]

Problems of population quantity and quality are the concern of a fairly large number of American sociologists. In other countries they usually fall in the province of economics, an independent discipline called demography, or social politics, but when they are bound up with sociological generalizations, as is usually the case, there seems reason to keep them in the domain of sociology. Certainly much less relevant matters are kept there.

Until about 1927 the bogey of overpopulation called forth shouts of alarm from Giddings, Ross, Baber, and Fairchild, but the recent work of Kuczynski, Dublin, Thompson, Pearl, and others has shown that, for the United States and all the European nations except Russia, population is likely to diminish rather than to increase. Aside from these questions of population quantity in gross, there is also a substantial body of American sociologists who are engaged in the study of differential birthrates, which involves considerations of both quantity and quality. Hankins, Fairchild, Bossard, Sorokin, and Himes are among those who hold that present population tendencies make for the deterioration of the innate capacities of the population because the upper classes, who are presumably more intelligent, fail to keep pace with the survival rate of the lower. In accordance with this conviction, most of those just mentioned advocate a program of positive and negative eugenics, for the present laying most stress on the negative phase. Other experts in the same field, among them Thompson, Reuter, Morgan, and Jennings, maintain that there is not sufficient proof of wide and transmissible difference in the various strata of the population, nor a sufficiently stable difference in survival rates, to warrant an extensive eugenics program. Most of the biologists enthusiastically back the sociological eugenists, whereas the behaviorists and psychoanalytic psychologists seem lukewarm to the movement.[97]

Analytic Sociology. — Turning now to less specialized fields, analytic or, as it has been recently termed, systematic sociology probably has the next most numerous group of practitioners. It is to be distinguished from the older synthetic sociology represented by Ward, Dealey, and like heirs of Comte and Spencer, for it regards sociology not as the *scientia scientiarum,* " enriched by all the truths of nature and embracing all truth," but as an abstract, basic, social science on which more detailed and concrete disciplines such as government and economics are erected. In other words, the analytic sociologists are the grammarians of the social sciences. We may divide them into two groups: those who at some periods or in certain aspects of their writing retain strongly synthetic tendencies, and those in whom the analytic bent is more consistently followed. In the first group we have Ross, Ellwood, Bernard, Sorokin, and Thomas. In the second may be placed MacIver, Park and Burgess, Reuter, Dawson and Gettys, Hiller, Abel, House, Wirth, Blumer, Case, Bogardus, Eubank, Spykman, Talcott Parsons, and Howard Becker.[98]

The History of Sociology, and Historical Sociology. — The history of sociology does not receive so much attention as it once did, but interest in it is fairly strong. Here we may list Bernard, who is undoubtedly preëminent for North and South America; Wirth, perhaps most at home in the Germanic literature, but widely informed elsewhere; House, systematic and penetrating; Sorokin, easily the most erudite; Barnes, thoroughly versed in the historical background of sociological theory; Todd, able to draw on an extensive knowledge of literature and the fine arts; Hertzler, specialist in the ancient civilizations and in utopian thought; Bryson, one of the first to show the full extent of the relation between sociology and moral philosophy, and also an expert in eighteenth-century Scottish social thought; DeGrange, well known for his study of Comte; Lichtenberger, author of a popular text which combines the approaches of Dunning and Giddings; and several others, among them Hankins, Bogardus, Crawford, Gillin, Odum, Bain, Lehmann, and Douglas.[99]

Historical sociology, or the study of social development and change over fairly long periods, does not have a very large following in the United States. Most of the studies are fired at point-blank range, and therefore permit virtually no generalizations about trends or cycles that can be followed over a long period. Perhaps our knowledge is not yet sufficient to permit this, but a beginning must sometime be made. One of the reasons for the scarcity of historical sociology in the United States is the reaction against social evolutionism of the nineteenth-century variety. This is understandable, but it does not warrant almost complete neglect of one of the most important branches of sociology. The consequences of this neglect are readily seen in the vogue of erudite journalists like Spengler, apostles of Pareto like Bernard DeVoto, mystics like Waldo Frank, and the multifarious expounders of the vulgar Marxian version of " the dialectic." Sociologists stand by while pseudo-historians, *littérateurs,* and " intellectuals " awe the multitude with borrowed and tawdry finery. If we are not to be dragged hither and yon by slogans such as " Civilization is the alternation of *speculator* and *rentier,*" "Every culture has a life-cycle like an organism," " History is the record of the urge to Wholeness," " Thesis, antithesis, and synthesis," and " History repeats itself," sociologists must cease to restrict themselves to the study of current events and history-less preliterate societies. Among the few workers in historical sociology may be mentioned Barnes, Teggart, Sorokin, and a number of social historians, who, although insufficiently interested in generalization, are nevertheless on the right track — Shotwell, Turner, Beard, Carl Becker, Preserved Smith, Dodd, Hayes, and Thompson.[100]

Philosophical Presuppositions. — The epistemology and methodology of sociology are not overwhelmingly popular subjects, as we made clear when discussing the stern-foremost drift into specialization. The most common epistemological notion seems to be that there are " lots of facts " lying about which when sorted into piles and counted will enable us to discover " laws " that exist independently of the observer. This essentially Baconian conception of scientific procedure is all-pervasive; it turns up even where it is explicitly disavowed. Pure Induction is a god to whom the appropriate genuflections must always be made. Linked with this is the belief that sense-data — things that one can see, touch, taste, smell, and hear — are and should be the sole object-matter of sociology. In the space at our disposal it is impossible to expose the manifold fallacies of such a position; we shall merely say that in our opinion it is sheer nonsense. Ironically enough, the most belligerent and dogmatic exponents of this metaphysical and epistemological conception are precisely those people who know nothing of metaphysics and epistemology and have no desire to know anything. Their own little home-made article suits them; why go shopping? The fact that it is quite impossible to engage in systematic rational discourse of any kind without making assumptions that cannot be proved by any amount of Pure Induction has never dawned on these philosophically innocent folk. " Don't think — try! " may be an excellent motto for some types of natural-science research (although we doubt it), but it is certainly pernicious when transferred to the field of the social sciences.

But to return to our task of exposition: MacIver, Abel, Sorokin, Crawford, House, Blumer, Jensen, and Ellwood seem to be among those most keenly aware of the necessity for a firmer philosophical foundation for present-day sociology.[101] With some of them we are not in entire agreement, but that is neither here nor there: they are quite right in insisting that unless American sociologists do a little " armchair " work, their research is doomed to sterility. It is notorious that men will go to any amount of trouble rather than think; they flock after any prophet who relieves them of responsibility by saying soothingly, " Let your Comptometer be your guide."

It would be unfair, however, to give the impression that all the advocates of so-called "fact-finding" are oblivious to the claims of sustained reflection. Bernard, Lundberg, Stouffer, Thurstone, A. F. Bentley, Bain, McCormick, and Rice are all earnestly engaged in the establishment of some sort of sound foundation for their researches. It is not these men who threaten the future of American sociology, but the sprinkling of the intellectually incurious to whom they unwittingly give aid and comfort.

This is the last of the classifications of trends in American sociology with which we shall deal. The various heads we have used are not systematically arranged or logically connected, and we should be the last to defend them on any grounds other than those of convenience and immediate usefulness. Many of them are used in the programs of the American Sociological Society, which is to say that they are catch-alls, and we have added a few more of our own. Many others could have been used: no mention has been made of the sociology of religion, educational sociology, sociological jurisprudence, and a host of other categories that for some purposes are just as good as ours. In extenuation we again use the well-worn phrase, " Space forbids."

Sociological Publications. — There are now several good periodicals devoted more or less exclusively to sociological publication in the United States. Of these the *American Journal of Sociology* is the oldest and had until recently the largest circulation, for membership in the American Sociological Society involved a subscription fee to that journal. A statistical study of the articles published in it has shown that there has been a marked trend away from the discussion of matters of general interest since Small's death; specialization is the order of the day. In all probability this is not the result of editorial policy alone; at about the time that Small's guiding hand relaxed the drift toward the minute subdivision of sociology was just becoming evident. A valuable feature of the *American Journal of Sociology* was its abstract service (recently discontinued); current literature in several languages was thus brought within the range of many to whom it would otherwise be unattainable.

The *American Sociological Review*, established in 1936 by vote of the American Sociological Society as its official journal, is yet too new to be characterized briefly. Up to date the articles have been largely quantitative and/or definitory, but this may be the result of the offerings available rather than of hard-and-fast editorial policy. One valuable feature is the frequent publication of articles and reports dealing with sociology abroad; another is the bibliography of articles in foreign periodicals that appears in each issue. The book review policy for a time inclined in the direction of lengthy critical reviews of outstanding books rather than all-inclusiveness at the cost of adequate treatment.

Social Forces once had a much better reviewing policy than the *American Journal of Sociology;* lengthy topical reviews quite exhaustively covering the respective topics appeared, but of late these have deteriorated in quality and diminished in quantity. In other respects *Social Forces* is a splendid journal; several articles of excellent quality are brought out in almost every issue.

The remaining general periodical, *Sociology and Social Research,* is not in the class of the others. This is readily understandable. The editorial control is on the Pacific Coast, and there is a selective factor in the manuscripts submitted and chosen that tends to make the journal somewhat sectional. It also suffers from the itch for brevity.

A specialized organ, the *Journal of Rural Sociology,* has recently begun publication. If it succeeds in maintaining the high standard of its first issues, not only rural sociologists but sociologists of every variety will be compelled to give heed.

Among the general " social science " journals, the *Southwestern Social Science Quarterly* deserves prominent mention. Bernard and a number of other sociologists have published in it. A relatively new arrival in the social science field, *Social Research,* published by the faculty of the University in Exile (a group of émigrés now living in the United States), bids fair to fill a very important niche. It is perhaps a bit too soon to say whether the high quality of its first two or three volumes can be maintained, but it at least gives more space to fundamental theoretical considerations than is usual in American journals. It covers a fairly wide range — psychologists, economists, experts in *Sozialpolitik,* political scientists, and sociologists are among its contributors — hence the amount of strictly sociological material in it is not very great. At the same time, it is one more medium of publication, and one having a policy that may affect the sociological journals *per se* for the better.

The Annals of the American Academy of Political and Social Science also covers a field much wider than sociology, and the sociological symposia it does publish from time to time are nearly all in the social problems category. Much as we may regret the absence of an occasional theoretical issue, there can be no doubt that the symposia mentioned conform to standards so high as to make *The Annals* an indispensable research tool. The book review section is notable, especially for promptness, range, and judicious selection of reviewers. The number of books reviewed is fairly large, but the review policy is so good that one wishes for twice as many. Two very useful social problems periodicals, frequently containing excellent factual articles, are published by Survey Associates: one is designed primarily for the professional social worker, and is simply called the *Survey;* the other has a somewhat more general appeal, and bears the title of *Survey Graphic.* Neither of them is wholly free from the slightly enervating aromas of cheery " good-will " and the " we-know-the-worst-but-we're-optimistic " spirit, but the social reforms advocated are usually in accord with the present state of sociological knowledge. The *Family* is of the same general type as the *Survey,* but as the title indicates, covers a more limited field. The same may be said of *Social Work Technique.* Criminology and penology are fairly well cared for by the *Journal of Criminology and Criminal Law,* although the legalistic phase necessarily occupies a good deal of space. It was this periodical which seven years ago published Thorsten Sellin's amazingly comprehensive topical bibliographies of current criminological and penological literature in a dozen languages.

The *American Anthropologist* frequently gives space to articles of sociological interest; most of them are highly technical and abstruse, but none the less useful. It is to be regretted, however, that so much space is devoted to the description of material culture and so little to the analysis of cultural processes. The *Political Science Quarterly* formerly published many articles of interest to sociologists, and occasionally one appears even now. The reviews are adequate, but usually fall somewhat outside the sociological field.

The *Journal of Abnormal and Social Psychology* and *Mental Hygiene* always have a few articles of importance to those sociologists who concentrate on the psychical phases of social life, but the *Journal of Social Psychology* is so thoroughly psychological (in the bad sense) that its value is much less. *Social Science Abstracts* is no longer published, but *Psychological Abstracts* continues, and in the section bearing the incongruous title of " Social Functions of the Individual " a good many items of importance are dealt with.

The *Philosophical Review* sometimes has valuable sociological articles; quite recently one on Troeltsch and another on Dilthey appeared, both of them excellent. The *Monist* is another philosophical journal of importance to sociologists; for example, Eliot and Bernard have published in it quite frequently. Two Marxian journals, *Science and Society* and the *Marxist Quarterly*, have just made their bow.

The most pressing need in American sociological publication would seem to be something like the *Archives of Psychology*, i.e., an organ appearing at irregular intervals containing longer articles and small monographs which do not warrant book format but which are too valuable to be confined to manuscript. There has been an effort to set up something of this kind, but the financial responsibilities placed on the authors involved have been so heavy as almost hopelessly to hamper the project.

The emphasis throughout the Appendix of this volume is so heavily on developments in American sociology that little need be said here. Further, the availability of Howard W. Odum's *American Sociology* (New York: Longmans Green, 1951), the Hinkles' *Development of American Sociology* (New York: Doubleday, 1957), and similar works makes detailed follow-up readily possible for the advanced student and professional sociologist. For most general purposes, however, the present volume is adequate.

Comment seems appropriate here, however, with regard to "social psychology." On p. 991, Becker remarked in 1938 that it is "a sociologically dangerous and fundamentally erroneous term as generally used." Beginning with the latter structure first: erroneous because, following McDougall's imperialistic example, every social science whatsoever—ethics, law, and similar judgmentally normative studies—falls under the rubric of social psychology as defined by many psychologists. "When something's everything, then nothing's anything." Sociologically dangerous because: (1) university administrators tend to think in terms of nouns, not of adjectives —social psychology is therefore handed over to psychology; (2) some social psychologists of sociological derivation define their field so broadly or even so loosely that any psychologist, whether an heir of McDougall or not, feels justified in taking over all the sociological territory that he can readily seize. The disastrous consequences for sociology have been in plain view on the American scene for a couple of decades.

CHAPTER XXV

Sociology in Italy

BEGINNINGS. — Penetrating and wide-ranging social thought has not been lacking in Italy.[1] Among many others, one need mention only the names of Machiavelli and Vico. The former analyzed the social phenomena of prestige, leadership, and clashes of interest, and the latter anticipated Comte's " law of the three stages," presented a schema of social evolution, and worked out one of the most plausible of the cyclical theories of history. As a whole, the ideas presented by these men of course fall in the realm of social thought, not of sociology proper, but it should be clear that sociology as a science did not spring full-panoplied from the head of any single thinker. Moreover, several sociologists have been at pains to trace the influence of these writers on later, more strictly sociological, thought. Pareto, for example, has shown how strikingly modern Machiavelli is in many respects, and Cosentini has done the same for Vico.[2]

Less well known than the famous author of *The Prince* or the expounder of *corsi* and *ricorsi* are Beccaria, Filangieri, and Romagnosi, but they have been scarcely less important as forerunners of Italian sociology. We have already discussed Beccaria, primarily as one of the founders of the classical school of criminology, but it must not be forgotten that he was a teacher of Cameralism in the last half of the eighteenth century,[3] and during this period, as Small has shown, Cameralism (at least of the German variety) established its claim to rank among the disciplines that ultimately issued in sociology.

Gaetano Filangieri (1752–1788) produced one of the most radical of eighteenth-century socio-political treatises, in spite of the fact that he was a paid apologist for the " benevolent despotism " of the Neapolitan state, one of the worst among the many thoroughly bad Italian régimes of his time. His radicalism lay in his rationalism. Although his *Scienza della Legislazione* (1780–85) was intended to be a continuation and improvement of Montesquieu's *De l'esprit des lois,* Filangieri, instead of concerning himself with what the prevailing laws were, attempted to determine what, according to rationalistic rules, they ought to be. For this, among other things, he won the admiration of Franklin. In all departments of life, from economics to religion, he applies the test of conformity to reason. Nevertheless, he is more cautious than many of the rationalists, particularly in regard to methodology, pointing out that even though it may help the social scientist if he assumes that causation in his domain operates as it does in the physical sciences, he nevertheless should not go to the length of directly applying the methods of mechanics and mathematics.[4]

Gian Romagnosi (1761–1835), writing several decades before Comte, expressed the idea that a synthetic science treating social life and culture as a "highly composite phenomenon" (*fenomeno compostissimo*)[5] would have to be developed, and he himself, through his synthetic studies in economics, ethics, and politics, strove mightily toward the building of this new science. So highly is his work regarded that he has been called *the* Italian sociologist,[6] outranking all others; his brilliant analyses of public opinion in several sections of his famous work on the foundations of cultural history go far toward justifying such an estimate.[7]

When Comte loomed on the horizon, he soon attracted followers in Italy — in fact he attracted one, Giuseppe Ferrari (1812–1876), so early in the development of positivism that Ferrari published an exceedingly radical book, *Filosofia della Rivoluzione,* in 1851, several years before Comte's *Positive Polity,* with its relatively conservative political doctrine, appeared.[8] The consequence was that for some time only the more revolutionary phases of Comte's thought were known in Italy, and sociology achieved a "subversive" reputation that clung to it until well in the twentieth century, and perhaps to the present hour.

The Christening of Italian Sociology. — The first sociological treatise in Italy definitely labeled as such was the great *Sociologia* of the positivistic philosopher Roberto Ardigò (1828–1920). This appeared in 1879, but nine years earlier Ardigò had already made his standpoint clear in a work on psychology as a positive science which clearly showed the influence of both Comte and Spencer. He adopted Comte's classification of the sciences, with the single exception of the status assigned to psychology, which, in agreement with Spencer, he placed between biology and sociology rather than in a position of complete dependence on the latter science.[9]

Soon after Ardigò's work appeared, a veritable flood of sociological systems arose, virtually all of them primarily influenced by Ardigò — relatively few showed any large *direct* carry-over of Comte's doctrines. One of the first was a critical introduction to sociology by Julio Vanni, *Prime linee di un programma critico di Sociologia* (1888).[10] Among the later followers of Ardigò may be reckoned Francesco Cosentini (1870–), a pupil of Ardigò, whose *Sociologia* (1912) was decidedly one of the best published before the World War;[11] another was Eugenio Rignano, famous editor of the general scientific journal, *Scientia,* and author of numerous unconventional and stimulating works in biology, psychology, economics, and sociology.[12]

The Impact of Biology. — In Italy as elsewhere the biological analogies used by Comte and Spencer exercised a hypnotic influence on some late nineteenth-century scholars, notably Salvatore Fragapane, a follower of Fouillée's doctrine of a " contractual organism," [13] and Enrico Pessina (1828–1916) an organicist somewhat resembling Schäffle.[14]

The evolutionists, of both Spencerian and Darwinian varieties, did not lack Italian adherents. Interestingly enough, however, " social Darwinists " in the narrow sense, i.e., believers in the inevitability or desirability of natural selection through an unmitigated struggle for existence, were relatively rare in Italy. Most of the Darwinian evolutionists were inclined in the opposite direction; instead of accepting as unavoidable or even glorifying the " survival of the fittest," they attempted to reconcile the findings of natural science with the needs of the lower classes and the latter's " ethical right to participation in the enjoyments of life." Their standpoint is well exemplified in the writing of Vadalà Papale [15] and Napoleone Colajanni,[16] both of whom maintained that biological evolution and social evolution do not conform to the same laws.

Michelangelo Vaccaro (1854–) provides a still better example of this standpoint.[17] In one of his early books, he attempted to reconcile the anthropometrical data presented by Lombroso, tending to prove that criminal activity is biologically determined, with social data tending to show that it may be forestalled or diverted into socially harmless channels.[18] His conclusion was that the struggle against the criminal will assume ever milder forms, thus following the evolutionary course making for mitigation of the struggle for existence.

In later volumes of a more general character,[19] Vaccaro held that all previous studies of adaptation are inadequate because of the failure to distinguish between the biological and the sociological varieties. Adopting a Lamarckian view, he maintained that since the environment is the chief cause of favorable modifications, and since man can transform the environment through his culture-building abilities, humanity can lift itself to ever higher planes — by improving environment you improve the breed and by improving the breed you improve the environment.

We need not stop to criticize this Lamarckian biology and the conclusions based upon it; let us examine other phases of Vaccaro's theory. He held that the struggle for existence has steadily become milder and adaptation more complete, e.g., control of conquered by conqueror steadily gives ground to more and more complete democracy. Hence, although still far from the goal, mankind marches toward abundance, brotherhood, and peace.[20] Here again comment is superfluous. Even those as tender-minded as Vaccaro himself have probably been taught by the years after 1914 to mix a little water with their optimism.

Somewhat more realistic work in a not too remotely related field has been done by Emanuele Sella (1879–), whose study of competition, *La Concorrenza* (1915–16), is the most important thus far published in any language.[21] The sections dealing with economic-biological competition are sober and penetrating, and the treatise as a whole clearly shows that although the struggle for existence has perhaps grown less bloody (although of this there is some doubt), it is certainly as all-pervasive and relentless as it has ever been. The chief defect of Sella's work, from our standpoint, is its primarily economic orientation; a host of important sociological questions remain unanswered.

One of the few Italian writers to be influenced by Gumplowicz's theories of group competition and conflict is Franco Savorgnan (1879–), who has done good work on the problems of homogeneity and heterogeneity.[22] It may be noted that Gumplowicz is about the only sociologist writing in German who has had any influence in Italy; his book on the sociology of the state was promptly translated and quickly went out of print.[23] For some reason no further editions appeared, but in radical circles his doctrine that the state is always a tool of the minority for holding the majority in subjection was eagerly adopted as a prop to the similar theory of Marx, and may even have had some effect on Pareto and Mosca (to be discussed later), whose political sympathies diverged widely from those of the Marxists.

Biologized Criminology and Criminologized Biology. — The impact of the new biology also made itself felt in the field of criminology. Cesare Lombroso (1836–1909) developed the theory of the born criminal who is easily recognized by various "atavistic stigmata," i.e., who bears traces of an earlier evolutionary stage — savage, cave-man, or what not. "The criminal is half-way between the idiot and the savage." Later Lombroso widened his dragnet to include defectives of all kinds who do not necessarily manifest primitive traits but are simply — defective. His doctrines, now ludicrous but then taken seriously, spread like wildfire, and all over the world people began to distrust the man with beetling brows or the woman with no lobes on her ears.[24] Later the so-called positivistic school of penologists arose. This, more or less incongruously, combined theories of Spencer, Lombroso, and Marx. As might be expected, the mixture proved unstable, and the school soon split into a radical, Lamarckian environmentalist wing headed by Enrico Ferri (1856–1929)[25] and a conservative led by Raffael Garofalo (1851–),[26] both of them advancing theories that have had much influence. Recent writers following somewhat similar lines of investigation are DiTullio, Ottolenghi, DeSanctis, Pende, Vidoni, and Grispigní.

It can be readily seen that criminological theories of this general kind are closely related to social biology. An excellent example of the closeness of the relation is provided by the work of Alfredo Niceforo (1876–), author of a biological theory of class stratification — "the anthropology of the propertyless classes," as he called it. Taking over the methods and conclusions of Galton, Quetelet, Bertillon, and several Italian researchers, Niceforo made measurements of "the skulls of a cemetery in Sepino" (southern Italy) and of school children from various sections of the city of Lausanne. On the basis of this scanty supply of data he arrived at the startling conclusion that the poor man (*l'uomo povero*) is a special "anthropo-biological species," and that poor and rich are therefore separated not only by property but by blood. The following quotation shows how this doctrine is connected with the positivistic school of criminology:

The older criminological school, which was highly metaphysical, limited itself to examining the crime, without concerning itself with the criminal. The newer researches in this field, on the other hand, following the example set by the revolution in methods in the science of medicine and especially of psychiatry, have struck out on new lines. They are concerned primarily with the man who commits the act, and only then with the deed itself, and make use of all the auxiliaries offered them by the natural sciences and by nature. From the day on which these new methods began to be applied dates the beginning of the scientific study of the criminal, his intellectual qualities, his passions, his inner organism, the potentiality of his heredity, his constitution, his temperament and his environment, past and present. Thus developed criminal anthropology. The same path must be followed in the study of the organism of the lower classes in the population, if we are to solve the problem of the economic misery of these classes. In this way alone can concern with the questions of pauperism be lifted to the ranks of an actual and independent science, a *natural* science, that is, the anthropology of the proletariat.[27]

Niceforo's extreme conclusion of two different " species " is not supported at present by any competent student of population, but that there are marked differences in the anthropometric characteristics of the various social strata hardly anyone will deny. The fundamental questions are: To what are these differences due? and, How much overlapping is there? Instead of dogmatic answers in terms of heredity and absolute disjunction, the modern social biologist (non-Italian), ignoring Niceforo, grants that both heredity and environment play significant parts and that the range of variation is so great that sharp distinctions between classes are impossible.

Variegated Social Biology. — The thesis that the lower classes contain a high proportion of degenerates (in the strict biological sense of this term) has been propounded by Giuseppe Sergi (1841–1929), whose studies of heredity are widely known.[28] A curious variant of biological sociology is represented by the work of Gina Lombroso, daughter of the famous criminologist and wife of the historian Ferraro. She maintains that the degeneration of modern man, which she considers demonstrable, has marked advantages in rendering him a more social being, and she also holds that the unhealthful environment to which he is exposed is ultimately for the benefit of humanity at large.[29]

The sociology of sex has been exhaustively studied by the jurist Pio Viazzi. One of his most striking conclusions is that there is a " war of the sexes " resulting from a basic biological antagonism of male and female.[30] Roberto Michels (1876–1936) has written several books in this field, two of the best known dealing with the fallacies of moral statistics and the limits of chastity.[31] Since 1920 Aldo Mieli has ably edited a periodical for the study of sexual behavior, *Rassegna di Studi Sessuali.*

Interesting studies of lower-class types, particularly of the vagabond and wanderer, have been made by Guido Cavaglieri and Eugenio Florian.[32] Because of Italy's former rôle as exporter of seasonal and unskilled labor, there is a wealth of material in this field, and a number of semi-scientific articles and books deal with it (cited in the work by Cavaglieri and Florian). There are not so many studies of the more stable elements in the lower classes, and still fewer studies of the bourgeoisie, although with regard to the latter the writings of Pietro Ellero [33] and Pasquale Turiello [34] may be mentioned.

Italian demography has long been carefully cultivated; in fact, the occupant of the first chair devoted to any social science in an Italian university, Antonio Genovesi (1713–1769), paid a great deal of attention to the theory of population,[35] as did also Giammaria Ortes (1713–1790) [36] and Melchiorre Gioia (1767–1829).[37] An excellent survey of the historical development of Italian demography in the nineteenth century is to be found in the readable little book by Filippo Virgilii.[38] Among present-day Italian demographers Corrado Gini (whose theories we shall later discuss in detail), Lanfranco Maroi,[39] and Filippo Carli [40] are well known.

Psycho-Sociology, the Crowd, and the Public. — One of the most strongly developed phases of Italian sociology has long been psycho-sociology and crowd sociology. Gioia, a contemporary of Napoleon, paid a great deal of attention to the phenomena of imitation and suggestion, and pointed out that there is probably a direct correlation between the intensity of these psycho-sociological phenomena and the number of persons in the crowd.[41] In 1859 Carlo Cattaneo (1801–1869) presented the outlines of a system of collective psychology or, as he termed it, *psicologia delle menti associate.*[42] In spite of their priority in this field, however, the Italian writers, although gifted with originality and insight, did not achieve such thorough systematization of their theories as did the French, particularly Tarde. Under Tarde's influence developed the later theories of crowd sociology associated with the name of Scipio Sighele (1868–1914), who charged LeBon with plagiarism. Whether or not the latter was guilty is an open question, but it cannot be denied that Sighele published an article on crowd sociology in 1894 which contained many of the ideas (attributed by Sighele to his teacher Ferri) elaborated by LeBon in his famous book on the crowd, *La Psychologie des foules,* which appeared a year later. In 1903 Sighele's own book on crowd mentality was published,[43] and shortly thereafter Pasquale Rossi brought out the best treatise on the psycho-sociology of the crowd and related social structures yet to appear in any language, *Sociologia e psicologia colletiva* (1904). It contains an excellent history of the theories of the field, and Rossi's own analysis gives evidence of great acumen.

In the nearby province of the psycho-sociology of public opinion, Romagnosi (mentioned above) was a pioneer. His famous book on the foundation of cultural history contains several sections dealing with the development and influence of public opinion as a spontaneous accompaniment of complex societies.[44] A few years later the Milanese patriot and philosopher Cattaneo (also referred to previously) made careful analyses of the connections between the ideology of the individual and that of the groups to which he belongs.[45] At about the same time, Giuseppe Pecchio made some remarkable comments, based upon his own experience, concerning the actual functioning of public opinion in English elections. Sighele and Rossi, the psycho-sociologists just considered, developed theories of public opinion that are still worthy of attention, and Giuseppe Sergi presented a novel doctrine having to do with the pathological or psychotic aspects of public opinion in times of crisis.[46]

Economists and Historical Materialism. — The economic approach to sociological problems has been frequently chosen by Italian scholars. We have already mentioned the names of Genovesi, Ortes, and Gioia — all of them eighteenth-century economists who frequently dealt with matters now falling in the province of sociology. Present-day Italian economists are as a rule not particularly friendly to the new science, although exceptions like Loria and Pareto (with whom we shall deal later) are to be found, and there are others such as Camillo Supino, Carlo Cassola, Amilcare Puviani, and Augusto Graziani who are very cordial. As is quite often the case, many of the economists who are most distrustful of sociology themselves adopt the sociological standpoint when confronted with problems in which the strict economic approach is inadequate. This is particularly true in studies of immigration and emigration: Giuseppe Prato, Luigi Einaudi, and Francesco Coletti are good examples.[47]

It may be that the antagonism of Italian academic economists, many if not most of whom are quite conservative, is to be traced to the fact that a large number of sociologists have been radically inclined. Indeed, a great many Italian academicians seem to identify sociology with the doctrines of historical materialism, i.e., with Marxism. Instance the fact that Augusto Graziani, writing in 1930 on the social sciences as disciplines in Italy, gives vent to these naïve remarks: " Chairs of sociology were established only in a few universities . . . [but although] political economists did not adhere to the materialistic interpretation of history, they constantly referred to the importance of the economic factor in the constitution of society and also devoted special courses of lectures to the sociological doctrines." [48] In spite of the justified amusement such confused utterances evoke, it must be granted that the academic opponents of historical materialism have not had an easy task; the doctrine is hydra-headed. Moreover, its Italian career did not begin with Marx; as early as 1826 the Milanese economist, Giuseppe Pecchio, maintained that productivity in art and literature corresponds quantitatively and qualitatively with economic demand,[49] a theory extreme enough to satisfy the most rigid Communist. After all, Italian economics has had a few *enfants terribles*.

Moreover, Italy can boast of two sociologists each of whom, at different periods, gained the reputation of being her leading economist and upon whom the title of Senator was bestowed — Loria and Pareto. The former was an ardent exponent of his own private variety of the economic interpretation of history, and believed that the lot of mankind could be bettered by altering the social institutions that mold him, whereas the latter held that the more human nature changes the more it is the same thing, and that institutions are powerless to cope with the sub-rational springs of conduct. Pareto was born almost a decade before Loria, but the younger man represents a type of social thought antedating the rise of Fascism, while the older was acclaimed as its ideologist. Consequently we shall deal with Loria first.

Free-Land Loria, Prophet of Secular Salvation. — Achille Loria (1857–) taught economics with great success at Siena, Padua, and Turin.[50] He is the author of a long series of works, many of them issued in successive editions and translated into many of the other European languages and Japanese.[51] His long career as author and teacher earned him an enviable reputation, and in addition he was named minister of labor during the hectic period between the end of the World War and the March on Rome. We shall not attempt to deal with the long array of his works here, for most of them are economic rather than sociological. Nevertheless, we are warranted in dealing with the man himself as a sociologist, for the idea fundamental to all his writing was the economic interpretation of history, which, right or wrong, is one of the theories with which sociology must concern itself. To be sure, his particular variety of " historical materialism " was rejected by Engels and by the leading Italian Marxist, Labriola, both of whom said that it was unoriginal and dangerous,[52] but such considerations are irrelevant in the present context.

In his *Le Basi economiche della costituzione sociale* (English translation available, made from second French edition) he most clearly set forth his sociological conceptions. Accepting as proven the twofold class structure of Western civilization, he asserts that this is not the unavoidable consequence of human nature, but rather the result of definite social processes which are destined to be fundamentally altered in the final stage of social evolution. These processes are linked with certain historical events. What they were and are become clear when it is realized that capitalism is impossible when there is free land. Only when the populace is prevented from access to the soil by slavery, serfdom, or undue concentration does capitalistic exploitation flourish. This comes about because the worker then has no other means of livelihood than the sale of his labor to the capitalist for a price which the latter fixes, and which is always so low that a substantial surplus remains as profit. With the lapse of time the machinery of profit-making is so perfected that the violent methods of slavery or serfdom are not needed. The low wages paid make forcible restraint unnecessary, inasmuch as the worker cannot save enough money to pay for passage to countries where free land is still available or for the high-priced land in his own country.

Thus held in subjection and forced to function as cog-wheels in the minute division of labor, the workers enormously increase their output, but get only slight benefit from such acceleration of production. This situation could not long endure if it were not for the fact that capitalist property sets up a series of institutions which guard against revolt or ensure the acquiescence of the victims. The chief of these are morals and religion, law, and the political constitution of society. In their present forms they are all indissolubly united with capitalism. If morality and religion are not able to persuade all the workers to act against their own interest, the law steps in, prohibiting everything that can shake the power of the rulers. Law changes as economic relations change, for it is only one of the means by which control is maintained. The ultimate sanction of law is always physical force, the political means *par excellence,* and it can readily be observed that in all the various historical forms of capitalism the owners of wealth appropriate political power — the military machine and the police force are always tools of class oppression.

Loria ventures the belief that the sociologist can today observe the symptoms of decay in Western civilization and can render easier the transition to a new society in which the peace and justice of the golden age (Loria says " primitive age ") will be restored by abolishing rent and profit. The theory has decided resemblances to that expounded in Henry George's *Progress and*

Poverty, but it is probable that when their early works were written neither knew of the other. The system of land ownership that Loria saw all around him in Italy undoubtedly entailed widespread suffering, and his sensitive and sympathetic nature led him to seek a way out through freedom from coercive control which would permit labor to enjoy in common the surplus rendered possible by the modern division of labor.[53] His disciples in Italy were many, and among sociologists he won enthusiastic support from the editor of *Scientia,* Eugenio Rignano. Franz Oppenheimer of Germany has advanced a similar program, and is still turning out learned works in support of the contention that the source of all social evil is the barrier that keeps the workers from the land. There is no doubt that Loria and others like him have drawn attention to a factor in socio-economic development that is frequently overlooked, but in spite of the brilliance and erudition with which his thesis is set forth, it is an outstanding example of the single-factor fallacy in sociological generalization. The economic interpretation of history in the form of vulgar Marxism is certainly one-sided enough, but it is catholicity itself in comparison with Loria's free-land formula. Engels may at times have shown a lack of theoretical acumen, to put it mildly, but he showed that he could recognize completely untenable propositions when he excluded Loria's works from the Marxist canon.

Sociological Jurisprudence and the Sociology of Politics. — It has been said that the Italians are a nation of lawyers, and although this is an exaggeration, it is still true that one of the most prominent features of Italian life is the lively interest taken in the problems of private and public law, the latter especially, among the most widely separated strata of society. The high development of this interest is partly traceable to the peculiar history of the country. The struggle between the papacy and the secular princes, the conflicting claims of the rival city-states, the relation to the Holy Roman Empire and later to Austria, the problems of jurisdiction and sovereignty raised by the *Risorgimento,* the struggle between parliamentarism and Fascism — all these influences have kept law in the foreground of public interest. It is perhaps for this reason that the philosophy of law as taught in the universities includes much material that in other countries is presented by sociology, political science, or the *Staatswissenschaften.* Here we may particularly mention Gian Chironi, *Sociologia e Filosofia del Diritto* (1901), Giuseppe Carle, *Il Comparire della Sociologia e la Filosofia del Diritto* (1901), Carlo

Nardi-Greco, *Sociologia giuridica* (1907),[54] and Giuseppe Mazzarella, *Les types sociaux et le droit* (French ed. 1908).[55] Sergio Panunzio, Cesare Vivante, A. Rocco, and Arrigo Solmi have also written in this field.[56]

Before the advent of Fascism, the Italian parliament was one of the best examples of the fact that parliamentarism nourishes lawyers, and this, together with the sociological content of the philosophy of law, may account for the large number of works on the sociology of political parties. The foremost treatise in this field is by the German-Italian, Roberto Michels, whose *Zur Soziologie des Parteiwesens* (1911), a convincing demonstration of the oligarchic tendencies of party organization, first appeared in outline form in the Italian journal, *Riforma Sociale,* in 1908. This anticipates much of what Pareto had to say about the development of *rentier* tendencies among the ruling class (see pp. 1021–22), and may conceivably have offered him some suggestions. Other writers in this socio-political field are Vincenzo Gioberti, Ettore Ciccotti, Celso Ferrari, and Gaetano Mosca.[57] Such studies of the sociology of political parties have not gone unnoticed, for even though they may have played no direct part in the initial rise of Fascism, they have furnished many of the literary missiles used in its defense. Let us now turn to a work that has provided many of these slings and arrows, and that draws a substantial proportion of its illustrations from French and Italian parliamentary history — Pareto's treatise on general sociology.

The "Marx of Fascism": Pareto. — Someone has said of Machiavelli and his best-known book, *The Prince,* that few men have ever entered the Hall of Fame with so small a volume in hand. Whether or not Pareto's fame will be equally lasting is a matter for prophecy, but if by some freak of fate he should eventually loom as large on the page of intellectual history as his great forerunner, some observer would be justified in saying that few men ever achieved such eminence through the fact of having written books so heavily padded, confused, and obscure as Pareto's *Trattato di Sociologia Generale,* the work on which his present influence rests. The amount of space we shall devote to this treatise here is fairly large, not because of its intrinsic importance, which is undeniably great, but because it has attracted a considerable amount of attention in " intellectual " circles, and a sober analysis may at least help to deflate uncritical enthusiasm. We have no quarrel with serious, qualified students of sociological theory who rate Pareto highly, but we do oppose and condemn the dilettantes who have rallied to what they think is his banner. As Talcott Parsons has aptly said, there has been too little examination of the substantive issues.

Vilfredo Pareto was born in Paris in 1848; his father was an exiled Genoese nobleman, whom he cordially hated, and his mother was French. Ten years later the family went back to Italy, where Pareto's formal education, partly Classical, partly mathematical and scientific, was completed. After graduation from the *Istituto Politecnico* of Turin in 1870, he took up the profession of engineer, holding several important positions on Italian railways, and also engaging in mining. For twenty years he remained an engineer, but during this time he was increasingly drawn into historical, philosophical, and mathematical studies, the results of which he applied to economics and sociology. His advocacy of free trade made him *persona non grata* to the protectionist Italian government, and he planned to retire and to devote himself to science. At this juncture (1893) his fame as disciple of Leon Walras, the mathematical economist, brought him an appointment to a professorship outside Italy, at the University of Lausanne, where he taught for the rest of his life.[58]

Pareto wrote a great deal, and we cannot even superficially discuss his important treatises in economic theory or in the history of political doctrines within our present limits. It is necessary, however, to point out that a work in the latter field, *Les Systèmes socialistes* (first published in French, 1902) contains the kernel of many of his more strictly sociological theories, in particular that of the " circulation of the *élites*," which is the capstone of the *Trattato* already referred to. The latter, a bulky *opus* of over two thousand pages, was the only book he ever published bearing " sociology " in its title. It appeared in 1916, and because of the fact that a French translation was issued almost at once (1917), it became widely known in a very short time. Therefore, although Pareto was well past the mark of threescore and ten when the *Trattato* came off the press, he lived to find himself famous. Without either his express approval or disapproval the Fascists claimed him as their ideologist, and Mussolini made him a Senator in 1922, a year before his death.

Goethe published his complete *Faust* when he too was an old man, and like *Faust*, Pareto's massive work is singularly disjointed. Indeed, even his friendliest commentators agree that it is one of the worst arranged books in the world. In the following summary we shall nevertheless follow the general order of his paragraphs (Pareto numbered them and insisted that all references be made in this form) because most of the available digests of his work, and all the translations,[59] use the same sequence.

The Logico-Experimental Method. — Pareto proposed to adhere strictly to what he called the " logico-experimental method," taking only experience and observation as his guides, and hoping at the most to achieve relative truth. He was exceedingly sceptical, and rejected all *a priori* assumptions (or thought he did, at least), maintaining that sociology as a science must proceed from concrete cases to general principles (par. 69). This procedure does not lead to the discovery of the " metaphysical essence " of phenomena, and it may not even produce anything socially or individually useful, but it is the only way in which any scientist worthy of the name can go about his work. The *Trattato* accordingly abounds in protestations of the purity of scientific spirit animating its author, and also in vehement attacks on those who do not possess so high a degree of disinterestedness. Pareto sharply separated truth and utility, i.e., he held that the truth may at times be socially harmful, and that there may be beneficent error, but that the genuine scientist must follow truth, though it lead him to hell instead of heaven. He was especially bitter against those tender-minded pseudo-sociologists who shaped their doctrines in conformity with *a priori* postulates such as solidarity or humanitarianism; his kindest word for them was that they merely wrote sentimental ethics. (Herein his rebellion against his " liberal " father is evident.) The only path to logico-experimental truth, said Pareto, is the resolute rejection of all sentiments and the resounding words that evoke them; sharp distinction must be made between all theories which are subject to experimental verification and those which are not, and the latter must be summarily thrown out of court, for their ultimate basis is non-logical.

This distinction sets the basic problem for the whole *Trattato*: given the whole range of human conduct to classify, the problem is to find categories that will separate logical actions (in which the means are logically united with the end) from the non-logical. To be sure, Pareto finds non-logical actions so tremendously important in human social life that he devotes nearly all his attention to them; the classification of the various kinds of logical actions is neglected. The chief drift of his argument is that we do what we want to do and find the reasons for it afterward (here closely agreeing with the Freudian doctrine of rationalization, although no mention of it is made). Handman has thus summarized the all-pervasive assumption that lends his work its distinctive character:

For Pareto, the whole problem of social life becomes a series of equations in which ineluctable sentiments mask their inescapable push by a series of accidental manifestations frantically trying to conform their non-logical character to an equally ineluctable necessity to appear logical to themselves as well as to others. . . . The history of mankind is therefore a succession of efforts to appear logical.[60]

Isis Unveiled: the Residues. — In fact, reasoning has so little force in producing action that it may almost be said that it must change into sentiment if it is effectively to determine conduct (par. 69). Behavior, B, depends upon an unknown psychic state, A, but is justified by a theory, C, which usually is far from being strictly logical in its connection with B. The example furnished by magic throughout the ages shows how thoroughly non-logical actions may be justified by theological or even "scientific" explanations. Instances such as these show that a certain kernel of acts and words is more or less constant, whereas the interpretations covering them shift with fads in thinking (par. 217).

With unwearied and unnecessary persistence, Pareto applies this insight to legends, the work of the forerunners and founders of philosophy, and literally scores of other intellectual constructs, concluding in all cases that they are contemptible examples of the way the human mind works under the influence of sentiment. On the foundation provided by this heap of empirical evidence, he rears his own contribution, namely, the theory that there is a constant kernel or core which is a part, let us say, of purification ceremonies, and a variable shell comprising the detailed methods used and the reasons advanced for their efficacy. The constant part he calls the " residue," and the variable part the " derivation." In his collection of essays, *Fatti e Teorie,* Pareto attempts to short-circuit some of the criticism of these categories by saying that they are merely convenient pigeonholes, and that they might just as well be termed x or y. As an explanation of his constants in human behavior, he provides nothing better than the phrase that " the residues are manifestations of sentiments," to be studied further by the psychologist but to be accepted as data by the sociologist. This is a way of dismissing awkward questions that will hardly commend itself to those sociologists who have learned to distrust the practice of " explaining " everything by reference to a few supposedly constant factors implanted in man by — what? The hand of God? Biological heredity? A universal culture pattern? Values held in common by men as men? It seems a bit crude to build a whole sociology on assumptions which are then handed over to some other science for verification.

Six Pigeon-Hole Explanations. — But let us go on. Residues, says Pareto, were " unconsciously " sought by sociologists of the past in an attempt to explain social equilibrium (apparently he was unaware of McDougall's — to name no other — highly conscious attempt to provide a list of " constants " in human behavior almost a decade before). He lists some fifty residues, but they all fall in the six following classes: (1) residues of combination — pars. 889–990; (2) residues of the persistence of aggregates — pars. 991–1088; (3) residues (or needs) of the manifestation of sentiments through overt acts — pars. 1089–1112; (4) residues in regard to sociability — pars. 1113–1206; (5) residues of the integrity of the individual — pars. 1201–1323; and (6) sexual residues — pars. 1324–1396. Although the strength and proportions of these residues vary from time to time and from social group to social group (of which we shall have more to say later), they are the *constant elements* of any social system.

The first class of residues result in our combining certain things, usually with no logical justification, although we may seek to give " reasons " for our faith. Thus men sometimes believe that dreams reveal useful information about winning numbers in a lottery, that certain days are lucky or unlucky, and so on. What is said about such beliefs is only a mask for the operation of a non-logical residue. Modern notions that good is always associated with material progress, democracy, and universal suffrage fall in the same class; the residues of combination embody the constants which account for them all.

Residues of the second class provide the inertia that causes aggregates, once constituted or personified, to be preserved with great stubbornness. All the survivals of customs which persist after their engendering forces have disappeared illustrate residues of this class, and in Pareto's thought they largely account for the amazing tenacity with which any *status quo* clings to the reins of power. The residues of combination and the residues of the persistence of aggregates form the two poles of Pareto's theory of social dynamics; first one set has the upper hand and then the other, and the resulting vicissitudes are the ups and downs of history.

Carli, in his *Le Teorie sociologiche* (1925), criticizes both these classes of residues on the ground that they are tautologous; they merely give a name to an alleged force behind the observed facts of combination or persistence, just as the older physicists had a *vis inertia* and a *phlogiston* in their explanatory equipment.

Another point made by Carli is that phenomena of every description are tumbled into the ragbag of the residues. To change the figure, the Procrustean bed of the scheme cuts and trims the most diverse data to a convenient length.

A relevant example is provided by the residues of class three, those bringing about the manifestation of sentiments through overt acts. With the utmost naïveté, Pareto regards shamanism, revivalism, and canine tail-wagging as all of a piece; with the appropriate formulas they can all be " explained " in the same way.

The residues which make man a social being are placed in the fourth class: sociability. The conduct to which they lead is instanced by every sort of " uniformation," by all the processes through which the social group molds its members into uniform patterns. In this connection, Pareto also discusses pity, cruelty, asceticism, and neophobia (the fear of innovations). The social processes bound up with such manifestations are given little or no attention, but this should occasion no surprise, for Pareto uniformly slights custom, tradition, and other cultural factors in human conduct (although his category of sentiment does not exclude cultural interpretation). As a consequence, there is ample warrant for the charge that, in spite of his discussion of the residues of stability, Pareto deals with individual psychology in at least three-quarters of his " sociological " treatise.

Complementary to the preceding class is the fifth, comprising residues linked with the sentiments opposed to the alteration of the social equilibrium (in some respects hard to differentiate from class one). The name Pareto gives to these is " residues of the integrity of the individual and of his dependents." At bottom, these unfamiliar turns of expression are closely linked with our everyday words " just " and " unjust," which, says Pareto, really refer to the preservation or destruction of an equilibrium. It is these residues, rather than rational thought, which lead us so strongly to resent every disturbance threatening to ourselves as individuals or to the society of which we are a part. The attempt is always to restore the old order, even though the means used are non-logical or pseudo-logical. Witness the fact that a given lynching may be logically absurd — indeed, the " wrong person " may be lynched — but *something* has rightly been done, and the " residues of the integrity of the individual " are thereby satisfied.

The analysis of the sexual residue concludes this portion of the treatise. It is in connection with the analysis of this sixth class of residues that our author is at pains to note that residues of different classes often unite in complex forms, such as the union of asceticism with the sexual residue, yielding taboos that are only intermittently observed and which help to develop hypocrisy and perversion. " Sexual religions " such as Catholicism are the chief objects of his attack. It is interesting to see how completely Pareto ignores all the work done on this general topic by Ellis, Freud, and thousands of others. Apparently he read very little outside of narrowly circumscribed fields: mathematical economics, French and Italian parliamentary history, politico-economic theories, and the literature of classical antiquity. In all of these he was a genuine *érudit;* elsewhere, zero.

Masks of Four Kinds: the Derivations. — Having thus analyzed the supposedly constant elements underlying the theories and ideologies of mankind, Pareto next turns to the devices men use to conceal the true character of their acts from themselves and others, namely, the derivations. He examines them closely, and concludes that they are only manifestations of the need to reason, are in no sense identifiable with logico-experimental science, and are of quite secondary importance. But erroneous as the derivations generally are, the task of the sociologist is more than the discovery of error; his special function lies in showing why the error is so frequently accepted as truth. Disregarding minor subdivisions, the classes of derivations are as follows: (1) affirmations — pars. 1430–1433; (2) authority — pars. 1434–1463; (3) accord with sentiment or principles — pars. 1464–1542; and (4) verbal proofs — pars. 1543–1686.

Under the derivations of the first class, Pareto places simple affirmations or statements which are not controlled by experience, although real or imaginary " facts " may be used to prop them up. The techniques of propaganda and advertising make much use of such derivations: " A clean tooth never decays," " The German army was never defeated," and so on. (Needless to say, these are not Pareto's illustrations.)

The derivations of authority also have a powerful effect, even though the competence of the authorities in the field in question may or may not be experimentally supported. Witness the fact that those who are sceptical in religion may nevertheless accept the poorest of authorities on the effects of alcohol.

The residues of sociability lend strength to derivations which appeal to sentiments and principles held by the majority, in spite of the fact that history shows that majorities have frequently been in the wrong. Included in these derivations of the third class are arguments of the type that would persuade us that conduct for the sake of others is really to our own interest. Kant, Bentham, and others provide excellent examples of the attempt to reconcile the logically antithetical principles of egoism and altruism.

Pareto gives a great deal of space to the limitless complexities of derivations of the type called verbal proofs. These are usually associated with other types, and may serve to rationalize residues of various kinds. Verbal proofs make much use of terms that do not correspond exactly to things, and the resulting indefiniteness makes all sorts of jugglery possible. A dexterous orator can get anything he wants out of terms such as liberty or solidarity. But the exposure of the fallacies of verbal proofs does not necessarily impugn their social utility; myths do not correspond to anything " real," but they may be useful.

Interrelations of Derivations and Residues. — Having discussed the nature of the residues and derivations, Pareto next considers at length the properties that may be ascribed to them in producing a given type of society. *The course of social events is due to fluctuations in the strength of the residues.* The residues of combination change only slightly and slowly, and those of the " integrity of the individual " scarcely alter at all, but some of the other classes may vary considerably. The condition of any given society can be easily diagnosed if the proportional distribution of the different groups of residues is known. In some social strata, the proportion of the residues of combination may be very high, while in others widely differing types may be dominant — for, says Pareto, the residues vary with occupation, physical environment, and social level.

This brings up the question of interdependence. In some parts of the treatise, the implication is that the residues are constants, but at the beginning of volume three of the Italian edition, Pareto explicitly says that social facts influence the residues as well as *vice versa,* although he very largely confines himself to illustrations of the latter process only. Other relations of interdependence are the action of residues on other residues or of derivations on residues and on other derivations. He uses the newspaper as an illustration of the action of derivations on residues. The arguments therein contained are usually scanty and seldom logical, yet they sway sentiments, and when a derivation comes into fashion, others like it spring up by a process of imitation, thus extending the general influence of derivations on residues. Pareto gives numerous illustrations and diagrams of the various interrelations possible, but space forbids any comment on them here. We shall cite only his remark that the majority of strong residues cannot be contrary to the welfare of any given society or it would cease to exist. Those who wish to preserve this society must see to it that the strong residues are perpetually reinforced by appropriate derivations, and the doctrine must be thoroughly inculcated that the following of these derivations — morals, religious precepts, and what not — conduces to individual happiness. As a maxim for statesmen, Pareto proposes to revive the Machiavellian aphorism: Talk about eternal justice, but act as if there were none. It is useful that a people should believe that the gods fight for them.

This is all perfectly good *Realpolitik,* but is it compatible with the theory that the residues are constants? Why pay any attention to derivations? Here we confront a difficulty that is latent throughout the whole treatise. In one chapter Pareto describes the residues as all-powerful forces, and in another states that they can be altered by derivations they have engendered. The logic of the whole thing seems much like that of vulgar Marxism, in which economic forces are taken as the sole causal factors in social development, while at the same time it is implicitly assumed that economic life can be made over through the political intervention of the Communist state. If the latter is true, the former cannot be; in the same way, the residues cannot be variables and constants at the same time.

The Societal Cycle: the Circulation of the Élite.—We now come to the only strictly sociological part of the *Trattato,* that devoted to the discussion of social equilibrium. It is fairly brief, but all the previous portions of the book point toward the cyclical theory of social phenomena it contains. (This theory might well have been considered in the sections on historical sociology in Chapter Twenty, but in order to preserve contextual connections is dealt with here.)

History, says Pareto, is a cemetery of aristocracies (par. 2052), for the social equilibrium is constantly being disrupted by the accumulation of inferiors in the upper classes or superiors in the lower. When the upper classes no longer have the residues necessary for governing, and the lower classes have, revolution is the inevitable sequel. No society can maintain itself by reason; all countries are governed by oligarchies using force. When such an oligarchy becomes soft-hearted, squeamish, humanitarian, when it has lost the capacity or willingness to use force, social equilibrium becomes unstable, and can be restored only when a new *élite,* rising from the ranks of the governed, forcibly wrests power from the effete rulers and does the governing itself.

Among the various factors in this process, Pareto thinks the most important is a division of society into two classes which can everywhere be observed. The members of these classes are the *speculators,* whose income is variable and depends on their sagacity and manipulative skill, and the *rentiers,* whose income is fixed, or nearly so, and hence non-speculative. In the former, the residues of combination predominate; they are innovators, experimenters, risk-takers, mentally mobile, " foxes." In the latter, residues of the persistence of aggregates have the upper hand; they are traditionalists, followers of routine, advocates of " sound methods," mentally immobile, " lions." The most prosperous society is one in which the most important residues are best distributed: the leaders should be strong in residues of combination, thus leading the society to innovate; the followers should be strong in the residues of the persistence of aggregates, thus consolidating all the advantages that may be derived from the new combinations.

Leaders manage to hold power for a time by the adroit use of force and of stabilizing sentiments and residues, but unless there is what Pareto calls a " circulation of the *élite,*" power cannot be retained. The reason why history is a " cemetery of aristocracies " is that sooner or later the ranks of the upper classes are closed to enterprising individuals from the lower, with the result that the former becomes prevailingly *rentier* and the latter is led by excluded *speculators.* The result is revolution. Although Pareto does not hold out much hope that any upper class can maintain itself indefinitely, he says that there are two methods that may give it a longer lease on life: first, the liberal use of force, and second, the absorption of lower-class *speculators* who constitute a threat to the existing régime by permitting them to acquire wealth or other requisites of upper-class membership. Sooner or later, however, one or both (usually the latter) of two things happen: the upper class becomes unwilling to resort to force and closes its ranks to aspirants from below. These enterprising outsiders, emboldened by their relative immunity from physical repression, generate among the masses the belief that their rulers should be set aside, and in due course the longed-for revolution takes place. The masses then have a new *élite* to dominate them. Thus the historical record can be described in terms of the " circulation of the *élites.*" Here is another cyclical theory to place beside those set forth by Aristotle, Ibn Khaldūn, Vico, Turgot, Spengler, and Sorokin.

The Basic Difficulty. — Pareto's grandiose structure, for all its wealth of particular insights and undeniable correctness in numerous details, suffers from the general shortcoming of all theories which attempt to explain social conduct by reference to motivation alone: they put something into human beings and then explain every kind of behavior by what they have put in. The "Karl Marx of the bourgeoisie" proclaimed to the world that he had discovered uniformities in human conduct; did he find them, or did he make them from countless scraps of hand-picked evidence? Perhaps, as Handman concludes, the *Trattato* is "monumental because of that very passion for a scientific approach which it does not reach and for the terrific blows it gives to the numerous preconceptions different from its own." [61] Or, as Crawford puts it, the "most imposing product of any mind in recent sociological writing, it is likely to remain a monument, rather than a stepping stone." [62]

Mosca Twenty Years Ahead of Pareto? — As in the case of Sighele and LeBon, questions of priority or even plagiarism have been raised in connection with Pareto and Gaetano Mosca. The latter scholar, writing in 1896, twenty years before Pareto's work appeared, energetically defended the thesis that the majority is always lacking in capacity to govern itself. Even if the dissatisfaction of the masses leads them to overthrow the ruling class occasionally, an organizing minority inevitably arises from the masses and takes over the reins of power in its own interest. Mosca also set forth a conception of the ruling class which is close to Pareto's notion of the *élite*.[63] Interestingly enough, he says that his basic ideas are largely the result of the influence of Hippolyte Taine and Ludwig Gumplowicz, but Saint-Simon, Comte, the French utopian socialists, and Marx, to name only a few, advanced similar doctrines. The influence of Mosca is great, although primarily limited to specialists, whereas Pareto makes a more popular appeal. Among the followers of Mosca may be mentioned Carmelo Caristia, whose study of modern constitutionalism is perhaps the best product of the Mosca school.[64]

In an earlier section some attention was paid to Italian works in social biology having sociological implications; we shall now consider the theories of a social biologist that not only incorporate a number of sociological doctrines but also have direct political significance.

An Organismic Population Cycle: Gini. — If Loria may be taken as in some sense representative of pre-war Italian sociology of radical bent, and Pareto as an outstanding sociological champion of anti-radical tendencies, Corrado Gini may be regarded as an exponent of that peculiar blend of conservative and radical currents of thought known as Fascist ideology.

Gini was born in 1884, and is professor of statistics at the University of Rome. He is best known as a demographer, but inasmuch as he mixes his specialized studies with large amounts of sociological generalization, he warrants attention here. In particular, his theory of the cyclical rise and fall of population is closely bound up with his major premises and conclusions in sociology, and it will therefore be sufficient for present purposes if we examine this one theory in detail.[65]

In speaking of the cyclical rise and fall of population, Gini is a bit misleading. What he actually means is not world population but the population of specific nations which, as did the generally discredited organismic theorists, he persists in considering as biological entities. These national entities have a definite curve of growth and decline. Families as well as nations show such a parabolic curve in their life-history; not only among the wealthy but in all classes of society vigorous growth is followed by rapid exhaustion. Gini, like Pearl, finds an analogy for this in the growth curves displayed by that laboratory maid-of-all-work, *Drosophila;* its societies supposedly show stages corresponding to the youth, adult age, and senility of the single organism. In the period of youthful exuberance each generation contains a greater proportion of prolific individuals than its predecessor, consequently average fecundity increases. Eventually, however, the ever-present tendency toward exhaustion of the germinal cells gains the upper hand, and the society becomes extinct.

Demographic Metabolism. — Applying this idea to the growth of nations, Gini concludes that three-quarters of the generation which survives descends from a smaller proportion, varying from one-third to one-eighth, of the generation which is passing away. Moreover, the fact that the birth rate is in inverse ratio to socioeconomic status, generally speaking, means that if the ratio between the classes is to be preserved, the upper must be continually recruited from the middle, and the middle from the lower. This process, named social capillarity by Dumont, the circulation of the *élite* by Pareto, and social mobility by Sorokin, is, in accordance with his organismic predilections, termed demographic metabolism by Gini. He draws a neat picture of its workings. In the youth of a nation, metabolism is sluggish and the lower classes must get rid of their superfluous members by war and emigration, thus causing the organism of the nation to grow. When adult age is reached, the lowered fecundity of the upper classes permits the absorption of nearly all the individuals rising from the lower, and inasmuch as the latter have lost their most prolific elements through war and emigration, their birth rate has also declined. When the nation begins to grow old, the gaps in the ranks of the upper classes grow wider and wider, and although the recruits from the lower increase in number, they are insufficient, unless supplemented by immigration, to maintain a real *élite*. Gini hastens to add that this beautifully clear diagram is occasionally disturbed by " temporary checks." Thus in England, until well along in the nineteenth century, industrial expansion gave the upper classes such advantages that they continued to multiply rapidly, whereas urban overcrowding and other handicaps kept the death rate of the lower conveniently high.

Unable or Unwilling to Reproduce? — We have implied but not explicitly stated Gini's contention that the downward turn in the curve of reproduction first becomes manifest among the upper classes. There seems to be a sort of providential mechanism for the elimination of " those family stocks which have fulfilled the cycle of their evolution." Birth control is not responsible; it is simply that the urge to reproduce has dwindled. " The primary cause of the evolution of nations must be sought in biological factors." It is statistically demonstrable, says Gini, that the decline of reproductive capacity is alone responsible, for the data show that conceptions decrease among the aging upper classes in the first three months of marriage. And, says Gini, it is clear that birth control is not practiced during this ecstatic period!

Thus nations die, new ones are born. Can anything be done to prevent or delay this biological process? Yes, says Gini: immigration from a young, prolific nation may be permitted; new blood thus enters the old organism. And thus it should be; those who interfere with nature do so at their peril. Speaking with reference to the contemporary world, it is implied that those nations which refuse to accept Italian immigrants do so at their peril. On the other hand, consistently continues our author, if many have taken their force and aggressiveness to the New World, Italy is only the gainer, for her unity is increased when the maladjusted depart. Another method of national revivification is cross-breeding, as is likewise its Italian equivalent, the abandonment of an unfortunate regionalism. Hence, says Gini, the biological basis of Italy's future greatness is being laid by " our magnificent Fascist centralization of government."

Our discussion of organismic theories in an earlier chapter makes it unnecessary to add anything to this presentation of what

Gini calls " neo-organicism." Although Duncan is perhaps a bit harsh in saying that Gini's doctrines are all borrowed, and that " they are interspersed with puerile arguments based on antiquated biological and psychological theories," [66] it is hard to develop much enthusiasm for *il Neo-Organicismo*.

A History and a Handbook of Sociology: Squillace. — A student of population problems, some of whose doctrines, although cautiously stated and in general less extreme, bear a resemblance to those of Gini, is Fausto Squillace. We mention him here, however, on altogether different grounds. He is worthy of special mention because he not only wrote what for its time was the best history of sociological doctrines,[67] but was also the author of the first encyclopedia (or handbook) of sociology.[68] So highly was the history regarded that it was translated into German by Rudolf Eisler, famous author of the monumental *Handwörterbuch der Philosophie*. The classification of sociological theories worked out by Squillace is still valuable, and for the older sociological writers his presentation, although condensed, leaves little to be desired. Unfortunately, a similarly favorable opinion cannot be expressed concerning his encyclopedia. First of all, he did all the work himself instead of calling for the collaboration of specialists. This is especially to be deplored in the articles bearing on the sociological aspects of economics, for although Squillace was quite well trained in philosophy and jurisprudence, he had little grasp of economic problems. Moreover, the work is blemished by a large number of errors, unavoidable in a one-man enterprise. Michels says that these arose because Squillace " in true South Italian enthusiasm did all his work in his little native town, Catanzaro, far from all auxiliary scientific resources." [69]

Sociology as a Discipline. — In the chapter on British sociology, we said that in " the tight little isle " professors of sociology are almost as rare as snakes in Ireland; the same might have been said of Italy. Inquiries made for the purpose of this chapter [70] have disclosed the fact that although in 1906 fifty-six professors signed a petition for the establishment of chairs of sociology, only one now exists, that at the University of Padua. It was established about 1920; the first occupant was Filippo Carli, recently succeeded by Aldo Crosara, both *chargés de cours*. At Genoa there is a chair of general theory of the state and sociology, held by Romeo Vuoli, *chargé de cours* (about like the German *Privatdozent*). In the *Istituto Cesare Alfieri* at Florence, devoted to training in political and social science for the diplomatic and consular services, Giovanni Lorenzoni gives courses, varying from year to year, on general sociology, rural sociology, and Italian sociology, all of which have the reputation of being popular and interesting. At Rome Corrado Gini, professor of statistics, teaches courses having sociological implications, and there is a chair of criminology there as well. Several professors of the philosophy of law, among them Felice Battaglia and Alessandro Levi, include sociological material in their courses, but dissociate themselves sharply from sociology as a science because of its positivistic ancestry. The following statement by Battaglia, written in 1931, is typical of the attitude of many if not most Italian scholars:

Sociology as a unifying discipline flourished during the positivistic period, i.e., during the last twenty years of the nineteenth century. At the beginning of the twentieth its assumptions were vigorously and successfully attacked by Neo-Kantian criticism, nor has the immanent idealism of Croce and Gentile been more favorable to it. The philosophy of spirit [Mind, *Geist*], while respecting naturalistic positive science within the proper bounds, resents the claims of sociology, for it brings to bear upon facts of the moral and historical order methods proper only to the empirical sciences. Academically speaking, sociology has not been able to displace the philosophy of law, for law, being as it were the connective tissue of social life, is the most obvious expression of sociality. This is the reason why Italian universities have hardly any chairs of sociology; the one or two that exist are held only by *chargés des cours*. Note that political science has developed richly in the last twenty years. It does not use the empirical basis which in our eyes discredited sociology.[71]

Since the advent of Fascism, a little sociology is taught in the high schools as a substitute for religious instruction, but it is insignificant in both quantity and quality. The fact that Fascist politicians continually demand the " purification " of all university faculties, meaning thereby the elimination of non-Fascists or " critical elements," makes it highly unlikely that any sociology of a really fundamental nature could be taught even if by some miracle it found its way into the list of courses offered.[72]

Very few books bearing the title of sociology are now published in Italy. For over twenty years (1891–1920) one of the best sociological journals in the world was the *Rivista Italiana di Sociologia*, edited by Guido Cavaglieri and Giuseppe Sergi. When Cavaglieri died it passed off the scene. From 1927 to 1935 a *Rivista di Sociologia* appeared, edited by Sincero Rugarli, but it was published in Paris, printed its contributions in several languages other than Italian, and finally united with the *Archives de l'institut international de sociologie* and disappeared. It can scarcely be regarded as an Italian journal. Francesco Cosentini edited semi-sociological journals called *La Scienza Sociale* and *Vox Populorum* for a number of years (1898–1910), but they contained hardly anything of fundamental theoretical importance. Corrado Gini edits the statistical and demographic periodical *Metron*, and *Scientia* occasionally prints sociological articles, but neither of these journals fills the place of an autonomous sociological publication. Perhaps the closest approach to such an organ is the Catholic *Rivista Internazionale di Scienze Sociali e Disciplini Ausiliarie*, but virtually everything in it is in the field of what was once called " applied sociology," and the papal encyclicals supply the theory.

Since 1910, Italy has had a sociological association, with the criminologist Raffael Garofolo at the head, but it is chiefly an honorific organization, and its activity is restricted to Rome. In fact, the word " activity " seems not quite *à propos,* for the society has never conducted Italian meetings, although in 1912 (!) it helped to organize the eighth congress of the *Institut international de sociologie.* In 1920 a new *Istituto Internazionale di Sociologia* was founded by Cosentini on the basis of local institutes which he had established in Milan, Genoa, Palermo, and other Italian cities. A number of international congresses have been held, but since the resumption of international activities by the older institute founded by Worms, Cosentini's project has languished; it held its last conference in 1928 in Havana. Moreover, he became engaged in a bitter controversy with Worms regarding the name of his institute, and eventually had to capitulate by adding *e di Riforme Politiche e Sociali* to the title of the new organization.[73]

Sociology in Italy languished for a long time after World War II, but since the middle 1950s has not only regained its health but is rapidly growing. Moreover, this has been accompanied by a notable diminution of influence deriving from Pareto. Ferrarotti and many other contemporary Italian sociologists, while making full use of the valid aspects of Pareto's work, are anything but faithful disciples. Still further, organismic demographers such as Gini today have little following.

The 1959 portion of the Appendix makes considerable reference to sociology in Italy. Another perspective is afforded by Ferrarotti's article in the MSTICAC symposium mentioned on pp. 814 and 877.

It is worth noting that although chairs of sociology in Italian universities are still prominent by their absence, public figures now and again make known their interest in sociology. For example, Amintore Fanfani, a leader in Italian political life, refers every so often to his work on the Calvinism-capitalism issue. He may well be pardoned for this in view of the fact that the study in question is important from the social-scientific standpoint; any defender of Weber's position must take account of Fanfani's searching critique.

CHAPTER XXVI

Russian Sociology

T HE PERSISTING INFLUENCE OF AUTOCRACY. — Even more than in other nations, sociology in Russia has been closely bound up with social philosophy and all sorts of political programs. As Hecker [1] rightly points out, by far the greater number of Russian sociological theories can be fully understood only when placed in the context of Russia's social and political life. In other words, most sociology in Russia is Russian sociology.

Until very recent times, certainly, and perhaps at the present moment, autocracy in an extreme form has colored Russian social thought. Through the open doors of the great plain, unprotected by any strong natural barrier, entered the elements that were to lend Russian autocracy its long-enduring character. From the northwest came the Norsemen, who set up the first dynasties of the Russian Slavs; from the south came the Greek orthodox religion, borne by Byzantine missionaries; and out of the east rode the Mongol nomads, who established that iron despotism which, when adopted by the Muscovite Czars, constituted a peculiar but stable combination of Tartar tyranny, Teutonic militancy, and Byzantine otherworldliness. In spite of the weight of the yoke laid upon them, however, various sections of the Russian population revolted from time to time, always in the hope of abolishing those phases of autocratic control that seemed especially irksome and of bettering their own social and economic lot.

The leaders of these rebellious classes, particularly in the eighteenth and nineteenth centuries, frequently sought to work out their own programs of action and to lend them rational justification by enlisting the aid of philosophy and the social sciences. The social-philosophical and sociological systems thereby called forth were of course rationalizations, but as we noted when discussing the theories of Auguste Comte, we take the position that sociological generalizations are valid or invalid regardless of their origins. The fact that a theory has been developed to justify a practical program does not excuse us from the scientific duty of examining it on its own merits. Here, as elsewhere in this book, evaluation must be subordinated to exposition, but even though we are unable to test the validity of the generalizations made by the various authors examined, we can at least proclaim that, until such tests are made, the mere circumstance that rationalization has demonstrably occurred is not in and of itself warrant for a negative judgment. This warning expressed, we shall continue to sketch in the historical background, halting from time to time to present the theory of one or another writer in detail. (It will be recalled that in earlier chapters we have discussed the theories of Kropotkin, Novicow, Bakunin, Lilienfeld, and others who either did not write in Russian or exerted more influence abroad than at home. They will therefore receive no extended consideration in this chapter; mere mention must suffice.)

I

POLITICALLY ORIENTED SOCIOLOGY

Light from the West. — Pushkin once wrote in a eulogy on Peter the Great that he cut a window through to Europe. Pushkin neglected to add, however, that Peter did not permit anything to come through but the diffused grayish light of the practical arts and sciences. It remained for Catherine II to grant the access of French and English liberal thought to the embryo intellectual class. Posing as an enlightened despot, she disseminated the ideas of Montesquieu and invited *philosophes* to instruct her in the wisdom of the Encyclopedists. The works of Voltaire, Adam Smith, and Diderot were greedily absorbed by many young Russians eager for knowledge and the favor of their sovereign. Further, the mystic idealism of the German *Illuminati* was taken up by the Russian nobility, and bore fruit in the early Masonic movement. The Masons helped to develop the first popular literature, organized schools for the masses, and engaged in philanthropy.[2] Journalism appeared, and conflicting currents of thought began to generate public opinion.

Catherine watched this flourishing intellectual activity with interest and approval, but suddenly reversed herself when the French Revolution began to get under way and popular uprisings disturbed her own domain. Rigid censorship was imposed, the leaders who sided with the people were imprisoned, and the Masons were forced to disband. Apparently Catherine had enough of Western illumination; henceforth she remained a despot without the effulgence of enlightenment.

Alexander I (of Holy Alliance fame) for a time encouraged

ideas of rational reform, especially those of his trusted adviser, Mikhail Speransky (1772–1839). But when the latter advocated measures that inspired the furious opposition of the conservative nobility, Alexander sent him into exile, and although he was allowed to return after some years, was never fully restored to favor. To be sure, Nicholas I permitted Speransky to collect and compile all the extant laws of Russia, but he never regained his place as confidant of a Czar.

Russia had not remained entirely isolated, however; the Napoleonic wars brought many army officers in contact with French liberal ideas, and when Alexander I abandoned their cause for the sake of the Holy Alliance, the eventual consequence was the Decembrist movement, which took its name from the unsuccessful military insurrection that occurred in St. Petersburg during December, 1825, when Nicholas I came to the throne after the death of Alexander I.[3]

The social theory of the Decembrists followed the social contract pattern of the English and French doctrines of the period. Among the most prominent of the Decembrists was Nicolai Turgeniev (1789–1871); his three-volume work, *La Russie et les Russes,* written during his long years of exile, provided the basis for many reform programs throughout the first three quarters of the nineteenth century. Turgeniev's views of society were strongly influenced by the ideas of Montesquieu and Adam Smith, and his political program was built on Western lines. The abolition of serfdom, reform of the legal and educational machinery, and a national constitution were among his demands. In accord with the ideas of his Western models, he was a champion of private property, of the rights of the individual, and of freedom of conscience.[4]

With the triumph of the Holy Alliance and the failure of the Decembrist revolution came a determined effort on the part of Nicholas I to eradicate liberalism; he established a rigid censorship of the press, and an iron discipline in the army, the bureaucracy, and even the universities. Forced out of political life, the intellectual class sought refuge either in literature, philosophy, or abstract schemes for the liberation and regeneration of Russia. The University of Moscow became the center of this more or less futile kind of intellectual activity, and in its academic atmosphere the study of German Romantic philosophy and French utopian socialism was diligently pursued.

Holy Russia and the Chosen People. — By no means all the intellectuals regretted the turn events had taken. In fact, for many of them the loss of freedom after the victory over Napoleon was more than made up by the pride they took in his defeat. Poets and novelists vaunted themselves upon their Russian nationality, and turned their faces away from the West. In the halls of the University of Moscow the new national sentiment was zealously fostered, and a convenient vehicle was discovered in the German Romanticism of Schelling and Hegel. Slavophilism and Russophilism developed, soon becoming influential in the affairs of the nation.

The Slavophils took over Hegel's chant of thesis-antithesis-synthesis and his notion that the Absolute incarnates itself in the life of nations (discussed in the chapter on theories of progress), but they naturally could not follow him in his conclusion that the wanderings of the *Weltgeist* had led it by way of Greece and Rome to its final haven in the Prussian state. For the Slavic races the cycle of the mystic transmigration of the Absolute had to be differently constructed. The Muscovite philosophers therefore asserted that the Western peoples were in a state of decay, hence the *Weltgeist* had to make one more jump to complete the circuit. The Slavic peoples, and preëminently the Russians, were set apart to be the final embodiment of the Rational made Real. Diligently searching for something characteristically Russian as the final avatar of the Absolute, they found it in the combination of the Russian Greek Orthodox Church, the autocratic régime of the Czars, and the parish land-commune of the Russian peasantry. Soloviev (1853–1900), whom Miliukov calls the founder of Neo-Slavophilism, the left wing of the Slavophil movement, varied this recipe by putting the Roman hierarchy in the place of the Greek Church and by diminishing the importance attached to the Slavic common people. But in spite of the absurdities into which the Slavophil writers often fell, it must be granted that their interest in their own land and people led to collections of historical and ethnographic material which, when purged of untenable interpretations, are highly valuable.

Danilevsky and Pobyedonoscev. — After the decline of the Hegelian school, other Slavophils arose who sought to reëstablish their principles through the aid of sociology and the natural sciences. Nikolai Danilevsky (1822–1885) is by far the most important of this group, and his theories, although erroneous in the light of present knowledge, were remarkable products for his day.[5] Indeed, they have been revived in recent years by the German writer Oswald Spengler, who, however, steadfastly avoids any mention of his debt to his Russian predecessor. The parallelism is too close to be accidental. Presuppositions, method, and conclusions are almost exactly the same in both — so much so, in fact, that Spengler the German, whose *Decline of the West* was completed before the outbreak of the World War, took over Danilevsky's mystic reverence for the mission of the Slav, and saw in Russia (of the pre-Revolution variety) the youthful culture that is to flourish after the effete West has sunk to the *fellaheen* level.[6]

In addition to the Slavophil school of thought, there developed, under the same set of influences, the Russophil movement, best exemplified by Katkov, Leontiev (who has also been called a Byzantophil),[7] and Pobyedonoscev. The latter was especially influential, for during his lifetime (1821–1901) he dictated the policies of two Czars, Alexander III and Nicholas II. His sociological system, although a primarily autochthonous product, also represents a Russian adaptation of Berkeley, Adam Smith, Montesquieu, Burke, DeMaistre, the early organicists, Hegel, Savigny and Puchta, and particularly of LePlay. It may be summed up as follows:

Society originates in the natural moral gravitation of individuals toward each other, and within the resulting social organism there necessarily develops a centralized authority for the administration of justice. This authority must be the manifestation of one will, unerring and sacred. The more primitive or concentrated the social organism is, the better it is able to protect itself against changes coming from without, and hence to survive. Foreign ideas are especially pernicious, because all historic institutions are the product of the spirit of a people and alter only through an *inner* law of growth. As long as the social organism can defend itself from external innovation, life within it is happy, for reason, emotion, and desire are harmoniously coördinated. Western culture tends to split up this harmonious relation, and hence it is the duty of the state to shield society from such disintegrating forces. Genuine betterment in society is the result only of the inner unfolding of life in harmony with tradition, inspired by the divine spirit and truth that is guarded by God's instrument for the realization of his will, the church.

Among other practical outcomes of this exaltation of orthodoxy, autocracy, and nationalism was Pobyedonoscev's campaign for the preservation of tradition among the peasantry; he was convinced that the masses would gain nothing by a type of teaching destructive of the stable balance of reason, emotion, and desire, of the " emotional halo " of the sacred. He was therefore a determined opponent of rationalism and innovation, of secularization.[8]

The Westernists, Emancipation, and Narodnik Subjectivism. — The Slavophils and Russophils soon found themselves opposed by a group of thinkers who believed that Russia had much to learn from the West, and who placed individualism and humanitarianism in the forefront. This point of view is generally called Westernism, and may be subdivided into three relatively distinct trends: (1) the theocratic notions of the 'thirties, with Chaadayev [9] as their most outstanding representative; (2) the humanitarian ideas of the 'forties, with Belinsky [10] as their leading exponent; and (3) the Narodnik or Populist philosophy of the 'sixties, for which Herzen and others paved the way in the previous decade, but which was most closely associated with the name of Chernishevsky. All these currents of thought were strongly influenced by Western contacts: the first, with its strongly Catholic bent, bore the marks of Jesuit philosophy; the second, with its appeal to the newly-risen intelligentsia, was a blend of German idealism and French rationalism; and the last, with its definitely non-religious, scientific, and revolutionary attitude, was closely in harmony with German materialism and French positivism.

The general effect of Westernism was to keep alive the tradition of independent thinking and of sympathy with the common people among the intellectual class that had been deprived of its former educational advantages by Nicholas I. In addition, Westernism was largely responsible for the outburst of emancipatory fervor that followed the collapse of Nicholas's régime after the disastrous Crimean war. His successor, Alexander II, was confronted by a tremendous clamor for radical reforms. Emancipation was the cry of the day: emancipation of the peasant from serfdom, of the citizen from the state, of the woman from patriarchal tyranny, of the thinker from authority and tradition. There was a demand that the new order not only improve existing conditions but also reconstruct the very foundations of society on positive scientific principles. This effort called forth whole schools of sociology, of which the subjectivist variety was in the lead. This theoretical trend had its practical counterpart in reformist political organizations, ranging from moderate liberalism to utopian socialism. The promises made by Alexander II were only partially kept; witness the fact that the serfs were freed but were still forced to pay tribute to the great landowners, inasmuch as the latter were permitted to exact abnormally high prices for the land they ceded or rented to the peasants. The intellectuals organized numerous revolutionary societies, at one extreme represented by the anarchisms of Bakunin and Kropotkin (described in an earlier chapter), and at the other the "educational revolutionary" movement of Lavrov and Mikhalovsky. The two writers last named were also prominent as subjectivist sociologists, sharing with Kareyev and Youzhakov the leadership of the school, the doctrines of which we shall shortly examine in detail.

The Russian subjectivists were in a sense the heirs of the early Narodnik or populist movement associated with the names of Chernishevsky, Dobrolubov, and Pissarev — which, during the early seventies, was largely responsible for the remarkable emancipatory crusade called "going among the people." In many respects this was like a great religious revival: the bulk of the educated class, not only students but many teachers, judges, officers, and physicians, went out to preach the doctrine of liberty to the people at the cost of great hardship. The peasants could not understand their would-be deliverers, in many instances turning them over to the authorities. It became quite clear to some of the political evangelists that, before any radical action by the peasants could be expected, they would have to be organized for and schooled in revolutionary objectives by an "unselfish, critically-intellectual" class.[11]

Lavrov, Father of "Subjectivism." — The first and one of the most able advocates of this propagandism was Peter Lavrov (1823–1900).[12] He it was who introduced the terms "anthropologism," "subjective point of view," and "subjective method." Exactly what he meant is a bit difficult to say briefly, but the following quotations give some indication:

In sociology and in history there are truths which are as unalterable and absolute as are the truths of all other sciences. These truths are objective, they may be unknown at one epoch and discovered at another. . . . But sociology and history also contain other truths which cannot be discovered before certain epochs, not because of any objective inadequacy in the material to be known, but in consequence of the subjective unpreparedness of society to understand the question in its active setting.[13] . . .

To make this somewhat abstruse idea clear Lavrov used several examples, of which the following is one:

Until in the laboring class there was aroused the desire to take part in public historical life in their own interest, there was no necessity for the historian to understand the past which had laid the foundation for this desire, and a multitude of facts recorded in annals and memoirs were well known, but did not enter and could not enter into a scientific understanding of history.[14]

The drift of these considerations is that Lavrov believed it necessary to ask not only the Aristotelian questions How? In what way? but also the questions What for? and Why? Sociology was conceived as a science closely bound up with ethical considerations, i.e., as a normative science. Lavrov also held that subjectivism reveals the individual as the only real factor of society and that to disregard him and his interests, the common practice of the organicists, is to overlook the most important social phenomena.

Like his animal forefathers, man begins with the hedonistic calculus, the pursuit of pleasure and the avoidance of pain. Eventually, however, the purely egoistic gratification of elementary needs yields to altruistic effects: justice, mercy, self-sacrifice, critical thought. Primitive human societies are held together by sacred bonds. These bonds constitute *culture,* which progresses toward *civilization* only through the operation of critical thought. The bearers of this thought make up the intelligentsia, membership in which is a high privilege capable of being repaid to society only through devotion to social ends. " *Intelligence oblige.*"

Such devotion helps to make the human individuality the real agent of the historical movement, for although the course of history is determined by objective forces, the individual, acting upon his own necessarily subjective interpretation of the historical process, sets his own goals and chooses his own means, *thereby transforming the objectively inevitable into acts of personal will.*[15] Here is a close tie-up with Marx and his " Circumstances may be altered by men" and " Revolutions are the locomotives of history." It is impossible to understand Lenin's interpretation of Marx without taking into account the fact that he grew up at a time when Lavrov's subjectivism was the standard theme for discussion. Lenin's orientation led him to search for and find in Marx's writings those parts in essential agreement with Lavrov's theory of the historical process.

Lavrov devoted a great deal of thought to a definition of sociology and to the difference between it and history, and also worked out theories of social solidarity and social control, of individuation and personality, and of social progress. His system shows the influence of Kant, Hegel, Comte, Proudhon, Feuerbach, Marx, Buckle, Darwin, and Spencer. Lavrov applied Kant's criticism, which lacked historical background, to Comte's positivism, which was historical but lacked the criticism generally believed to be the peculiar merit of Kant. He also sought to reconcile the evolutionism of Darwin and Spencer with the historical approach utilized by Comte, Hegel, Buckle, and others. As might be expected from this list of names, his attempt at synthesis resulted only in an eclectic mixture, and in addition, his epistemological foundations were shaky. His early philosophical training was Hegelian, and the Hegelian trilogy ambles through all his work, for his basic concepts are solidarity the thesis, individuality the antithesis, and social progress the synthesis. It is interesting to note that the " critically-minded individuals " who effect the fusion of the polar opposites and thus become agents of social progress are those young Russian revolutionists who made up Lavrov's following, opposing Bakunin on the one hand and Marx on the other.[16]

Nevertheless, Lavrov should be credited with a penetrating critique of the fallacy of biological analogy in sociology, and with a great deal of insight into the rôle of psychical factors in social life. His emphasis on the critically-minded individual as a social force and as a creator of new standards was strongly resented by his ultra-naturalistic contemporaries, largely because of his unfortunate use of the terms " subjectivism," and " anthropologism," but after all he meant by them only what Ward later called " psychic factors in civilization," " social telesis," and the " anthropoteleological method."

Mikhalovsky, Systematic Subjectivist. — The fact that Lavrov was forced in 1870 to go into exile gave him much influence on later exiles, such as Lenin, but it also deprived him of most of the direct influence he might otherwise have exerted on his contemporaries, and the task of spreading the doctrines of subjectivism within Russia itself fell to Nikolai Mikhalovsky (1842–1904),[17] one of the most original of Russian sociologists. He held fast to the doctrine that sociology and ethics are inseparably connected, and also maintained that an unbiased attitude toward social facts is impossible. " Tell me," he said, " what are your social bonds and I will tell you how you look at things " (virtually as radical as Marx's " It is not the consciousness of men that determines their being, but, on the contrary, their social being determines their consciousness ").[18] He rejected the evolutionism of Darwin and Spencer because of his belief that the individual should be rescued from the " degrading encroachments of social control," and maintained that there is a ceaseless war between the individual and society, attempting to support his position by biological analogies, the use of which by other writers he elsewhere criticized.[19] At the same time, his effort to safeguard the individual was responsible for some of his most significant work: he turned his attention to the mass movements so frequent in Russian history, and showed how imitation, suggestion, and prestige influence social conduct, thus covering the same ground as that later taken possession of by Tarde and LeBon. Some interesting anticipations of Freudian and Adlerian psychoanalysis are to be found in his treatment of the processes of individuation and the functions of libertinism and asceticism. He also anticipated Durkheim in his analysis of the division of labor; but took a much more pessimistic view of it. This pessimism was largely rooted in Mikhalovsky's latent Slavophilism; he exalted the parish land-commune and opposed the inroads of Western individualism.[20]

One of his followers, Kolosov, has carried further Mikhalovsky's distinction between the " technical " and the " social " division of labor, and shows how the latter, with its tendency to make workers mere cogs in an industrial machine, thereby warping their personalities as well, is necessarily destructive. Kolosov also shares Mikhalovsky's preference for " simple coöperation " based on the technical division of labor, which safeguards the individual's physiological complexity, and looks with disfavor on " complex coöperation," which makes extensive use of the social division of labor and thereby degrades man to a mere tool. Whatever one may think of Kolosov's more extreme conclusions, there can be no doubt that he has performed a signal service in developing further Mikhalovsky's distinction between the technical and the social division of labor.[21]

Youzhakov, Subjectivist Critic of Subjectivism. — Sergey Youzhakov (1849–1910) appeared in the Russian sociological arena as a critic of the subjectivist method in sociology, attacking both Mikhalovsky and Lavrov. The peculiarity of the method, says Youzhakov, is that it is based on an evaluation of the relative importance of social phenomena and on the personal views of the investigator as to what relations of members of society to each other and to society as a whole are normal. Youzhakov thinks there is nothing in this to warrant its being labeled subjectivism, for it reduces to the sociological proposition that society is based upon individuals and develops through and for individuals. This proposition Youzhakov thinks of vital importance, but says that it does not warrant the study of subjective and ethical phenomena by methods other than those hitherto used in the social sciences. He therefore proposes to drop the term subjectivism, and instead to use "the Russian school of sociology," holding that the Russians were the first to give due heed to the psycho-sociological and ethical phases of the science. It seems clear that this is a mere terminological squabble, and that for all practical purposes

Youzhakov can be classed as a member of the subjectivist group, for he follows in the footsteps of the writers he criticizes.

The chief points of interest in his theories (he did not develop a comprehensive system) are: (1) the socializing process has for its end the equilibration of the inner and outer relations of life and environment; (2) in this process life is first forced to adapt itself to environment, but later, through what Youzhakov calls social culture, it adapts the environment to itself; (3) the control over nature thereby resulting yields a surplus of material goods that sets limits to the operation of natural selection among men, thus permitting ethics to break the sway of biological laws in human relations; (4) the surplus, when large enough, also emancipates the individual from a too rigid social control and from the harmful consequences of a too minute division of labor.[22]

Academic Subjectivism: Kareyev. — Nikolai Kareyev (1850–1931) [23] was the only member of the subjectivist school to hold professorial rank; he occupied the chair of history in the University of Petrograd, and also lectured on sociology. His major interest was the development of a philosophy of history, but he wrote a great deal on sociological subjects (he was influenced by Simmel and Dilthey), and published an introduction to sociology in 1897 that ran through three editions. He was undoubtedly the most thorough and erudite scholar of the whole subjectivist group. In the field of methodology he did something to clarify the position of the subjectivists concerning the relation of sociology to other sciences and to philosophy, and concluded that " Neither the general logic of the social sciences, nor the methodology of history, political economy, law, and politics, is sufficient to take the place of a sociological methodology, which still awaits its complete development by sociologists." [24] His various analyses of the nature of society yielded the conclusion that it is not organismic, but that it is a complex product of biological, psychical, and environmental factors, with the psychical functioning through the individual units of society in such a way that all the other factors are dominated and organized. Like the other subjectivists, Kareyev took special interest in the rôle of the individual in history, and the result was the theory that although tradition, with its imitative repetition, is the primary constituent of the super-organic environment, individual initiative is responsible for innovation. Outer conditions may either curb or develop the capacity for independence and creativeness, but they can never call it into being. Quite in line with his chief objective, the formulation of a philosophy of history, Kareyev directed virtually all of his sociological analyses toward the development of an idea of progress.[25] Here his latent Hegelianism came to the surface, although he attempted to disavow it, and in attempting to express the idea that the end of social development is the product of "critically-intellectual" Narodnik reformers, he evolved this crystalline formula:

Thesis is the self-conditioning of the individual in the face of social and cultural forms; antithesis is the subjection of the individual's self to ideas and institutions of superorganic environment; synthesis is the subjection of the superorganic environment to the individual and the self-conditioning of the individual with the aid of culture and social organization.[26]

Wherein the Subjectivists Agreed and What Their Influence May Have Been. — With this we may close our exposition of the subjectivist school, for although there were other members, notably Rasumnik and Bulgakov, the four authors discussed represent the full range of ideas expressed. They have a number of elements in common. For example, they all believed themselves to be empiricists and positivists, and that there was no inconsistency in being at the same time advocates of an ethically directed sociology. Lavrov was the most extreme in the latter regard, for he held that he had discovered a socially evolved categorical imperative. (In this he seems to have anticipated the American sociologist, Ellwood.) Again, all four adopted Comte's classification of the sciences, except that they held psychology and ethics to be transitional and relatively independent sciences lying, as it were, between *and* above biology and sociology. Once more they all rejected, in principle at least, the deductions of the organicists and the social Darwinists, and also took exception to the impersonal mechanistic view of the crasser economic determinists. Further, all agreed that the driving force in social life is a complex of influences — biological, economic, and what not — but all emphasized the part played by psycho-social activities as manifested in the dynamic functions of the critically-intellectual individual.[27]

Although most Marxian scholars look with disdain on the work of the subjectivists, primarily because of Plekhanov's "destructive" critique, it is entirely possible that Lenin's emphasis on the ideological factor and the rôle of the intellectual in the revolutionary process was stimulated by them, as we pointed out in our discussion of Lavrov. It is true, of course, that Marx also emphasized the active part played by psychical factors, but under the spell of the rigid economic determinism attributed to him, this was almost entirely overlooked when Lenin was a young man.

Perhaps the subjectivists were not " totally eclipsed by the triumph of historical materialism in Russia " if through Lenin they helped to bring historical materialism into power.[28]

But be this as it may, the clash between the Narodniks (most of them were romantic idealists from the middle classes, with a sprinkling of " penitent aristocrats ") and the militant Marxists was fundamental and could not be averted. The Narodniks held to the utopian notion that Russia could avoid the scourge of capitalistic industrialism, that the surviving remnants of the parish land-commune could furnish the basis of a communistic social order, and that coöperative home industries would be able to provide all necessary manufactures. In short, the Narodniks wanted to overthrow the Czar and establish a republic on democratic lines that would give the peasant control of his own land, but that would not follow in the track of Western capitalism. The Marxists, on the other hand, held that Russia would have to undergo the pangs of industrialism, and that the proletarian class thereby developed would bear the brunt of a radical revolution which would overthrow not only the Czar but the bourgeoisie as well.

Unprepared for the actual inroads of industrialism in the last quarter of the nineteenth century, the Narodnik movement became a chaos by the beginning of the twentieth. It included extreme anarchists as well as moderate liberals, and rapidly split up into a number of more sharply defined parts. Among these was the nucleus of Russian Social-Democracy which, through the division into Bolshevik and Menshevik factions and the stresses of war and revolution, became the powerful Russian Communist party of today. Another fragment, with a strong terrorist bent, eventually gave rise to the Social Revolutionaries, the party of Kerensky and Chernov. A third party, owing relatively little to the Narodnik movement, was that of the Constitutional Democrats (the so-called Cadets). This was moderately revolutionary for a time, but after the Constitution was granted in 1905 it ceased to be radical, and even endeavored to preserve the monarchy after the February revolution of 1917. The chief Cadet ideologists were Milyukov and Struve.[29]

Chernov, Critic of the Dialectic. — To begin with the anti-Marxian sociologist, Victor Chernov (1873–), heir of Lavrov and Mikhalovsky: although he was an active Social Revolutionary, we shall confine ourselves to his less partisan theories. He attacked the Marxian dialectic, using as his weapons the empirical criticism of Avenarius, Mach, and Riehl. On this basis he discards the notion that economic factors can in any sense be regarded as primary in social processes, and substitutes the functional view, in which any social factor can be taken as an independent variable and all others treated as dependent. The resulting analysis is not in terms of cause and effect, but simply of the relation of one aspect to a whole, or of antecedent to consequent.[30] (This standpoint has found favor with many other sociologists, notably Max Weber, Vilfredo Pareto, and Pitirim Sorokin.) Chernov also adapted a position akin to Weber's theory of *verstehende* or interpretative sociology: he asserts that sociology must add " to the objectively constructed combinations, further constructions out of materials from the inner, subjective, psychological world." [31] On the basis of this subjectivism he hoped to construct a valid formula of progress by following these three rules:

(1) Utilize elements which constitute the inner subjective world of the investigator in order to construe out of them — on the basis of similarities to subjective phenomena or of difference from them — the subjective psychological world of other persons. (2) Construct rationally an ideal of normal social life, which shall present the highest unity of all active tendencies and interests of the human mind; the concrete content of the ideal being conditioned by scientific knowledge of the relation between the subjective requirements of man and the objective means of satisfaction. (3) Utilize this ideal as a criterion for (a) the classification of social phenomena according to the degree of their importance, and (b) the evaluation of phenomena and their division into progressive or regressive, normal or pathological, healthy or ailing. The ideal appears here as the formula for progress.[32]

In addition to the problem of progress, Chernov believed that sociology had to solve the problem of the relation of all social forms — institutions and the like — to the healthy, normal development of the individual. In harmony with his doctrine that there is no " first cause " of social change, he rejects determinism of every kind, maintaining that in " the interaction of natural environment with the quantitative and qualitative growth of man may be found the origin of the social process." Man is not a passive being exposed to the actions of nature; his feeling and will are dynamic forces (especially stressed by Chernov), and his intellect directive; on the other hand, he must interact with the natural environment in order to create the culture that gives him control over that environment.

Chernov, like his subjectivist predecessors, felt it incumbent upon him to defend both the strong individual and social solidarity, and maintained that these polar opposites can be harmonized only by a particular type of ethics, sociologically based, which will lead to the subordination of all lesser values to a supreme ideal.

The anti-Marxian strain in Chernov's sociological work becomes especially apparent when we are aware of the fact that he granted little or no place to classes in his theory of social development; in spite of his " functional " view, strong individuals were assigned the leading part. Whether or not this is theoretically justified does not at present concern us; suffice it to say that in the turbulent years of the World War and the Revolution Chernov's leadership of his party was not particularly effective, for the compromises to which his theory led him were disastrous, and were of a type which a keener realization of the nature of conflict between interest-groups would have avoided.[33]

Plekhanov, Lenin, and the Dialectic. — In the chapter on revolutionary socialism we have already discussed some of the theories of Marx and Engels at length, hence we need not go over this same ground again. Little attention was paid to the dialectic, however, and inasmuch as this enters into all Russian derivations and applications of Marxian theory, we shall deal with it here by setting forth the theories of Plekhanov. In so doing we shall also be expounding that particular interpretation of the dialectic to which Lenin subscribed, although it may well be, as Eastman and others maintain, that this was mere lip-service.[34] In any case, however, Lenin was Plekhanov's pupil, and in spite of later cleavage between Plekhanov the Menshevik and Lenin the Bolshevik, the latter continued to pay high tribute to his former teacher.

As is well known, the notion of the dialectic was taken over from Hegel. Marx simply seized the general idea of thesis, antithesis, and synthesis and, as he said, stood it on its feet. Instead of regarding Mind (*Geist*) as the basic factor in the cosmic process in general and historical development in particular, he maintained that Matter is fundamental. Thus Marx was a materialist for, as Lenin put it, a materialist is one who " takes matter as the *prius,* regarding consciousness, reason, and sensation as derivatives." [35] The dialectic operates in and through the interpenetration of material forces which approach a unity and then sharply separate; there is continuity and there are spontaneous, periodic breaks. As evidence that this process pervades all of nature, recent Communist theorists point to the phenomenon of mutation in biology and the behavior of the electron and the proton in physics. In both these instances there are sudden transitions which cannot be regarded as mere quantitative charges. Each of these periodic breaks indicates the beginning of a new synthesis and the resumption of continuity, but inevitably contradictions are generated and the process repeats itself. As Plekhanov asserted, " Every phenomenon sooner or later is inevitably transformed into its own opposite by the activity of those very forces which condition its existence." [36] Thus revolutions arise : any given social order generates class antagonisms, and these eventually pass from the quantitative to the qualitative stage, and thesis and antithesis eventually merge in a new synthesis. Plekhanov, echoing Marx, goes on to say that when Communism dawns, " the kingdom of necessity " will end; " freedom is sovereign, liberty itself has become a necessity." [37] The meaning of this cryptic utterance seems to be that the dialectic process will conveniently stop when the Communist ideal has been achieved, although elsewhere, in attacking the subjectivists, he insists that " dialectic thinking excludes every utopia and in fact any formula of progress with a set goal." [38]

Plekhanov also maintained that the " relations of production " determine ideologies, and as a consequence of the latter can never play any genuinely effective part in developing a new economic order. It is true that a number of scattered utterances can be collected in apparent contradiction of this interpretation of his theory, but when his actual practice is taken into account, it seems clear that such an interpretation is correct. For example, he did nothing to help organize the class struggle and even opposed those who did, vehemently attacked the theory of revolutionary mass-action advanced by Lenin and Trotsky, denied that the proletariat should lead the peasants toward the revolutionary objective, refused to accept the dictatorship of the proletariat, and supported the Imperial Russian government in the World War. In short, his opposition to the subjectivists led him to underestimate the rôle of the intellectual and the ideological factors generally; for all his emphasis on the dialectic, his theory tends toward a passive fatalism.

From Marxism through Revisionism to Subjectivism: Struve. — After the failure of the Russian Revolution in 1905 and the rise of Revisionism among the German Social Democrats, Marxism in Russia underwent a severe crisis. This is well exemplified in the theories of Struve, Tugan-Baranovsky, and Bogdanov.

Peter Struve was at first a follower of Marx, accepting all the essential doctrines, but at the beginning of the twentieth century he became a severe critic of them. In particular, he rejected the dialectic and the Marxian theory of social evolution, concluding that the latter proceeds not by cataclysmic leaps of antagonistic opposites, i.e., by revolution, but rather by gradual compromise and reform. He denied that capitalist society was developing the necessary contradictions that would lead to its own dissolution in a revolutionary synthesis, pointing out that there was no sign of any increase in the misery of the proletariat but rather a diminution, no progressive concentration of ownership, and no increase in the "anarchy of production." Marx, said Struve, based his theories on conditions existing in the middle of the nineteenth century, and by the beginning of the twentieth these had fundamentally changed.[39] Struve also criticized the dialectic on philosophical grounds, pointing out that it is constructed on the metaphysical principle that the laws of logic are also the laws of the external world. Logic thereby becomes ontology. Eventually Struve aligned himself with the subjectivist school; in a book written in 1906 he took the position that the political betterment of society depends upon the education of the individual, not upon class antagonism and revolution.[40]

From Materialism to Subjectivism: Tugan-Baranovsky. — The most scholarly and objective of the Russian Revisionists was M. I. Tugan-Baranovsky (1865–1919).[41] Subscribing to the materialistic conception of history, he analyzed it from three different aspects: (1) the nature of human interests as the dynamic force of social evolution; (2) the relation of economic activities to the rest of social life; and (3) the character of social classes and the class struggle.

Human interests are classified by Tugan-Baranovsky in five principal groups: physiological (food, shelter, etc.); sexual; sympathetic; ego-altruistic (power for the self and for groups with which the self is identified); and play, religion, and the other nonpractical interests. This list reminds one somewhat of Ratzenhofer, Loria, and Small. Tugan-Baranovsky maintains that *all* these interests, not merely those falling in the physiological category, are of great importance in social life, but holds that the physiological, ego-altruistic, and non-practical, particularly the religious, have been the most powerful in social development. He then asks whether this recognition of a fairly wide range of interests makes the economic interpretation of history untenable, and replies that it does not if the Marxian definition of economics is broadened to include "the coördination of human activity directed upon the outer world — having for its end the creation of a material environment necessary for the satisfaction of human needs." [42] Economics is central in social life at present, but as man steadily acquires more control over his environment, its direct importance will diminish. This same view was held by Lester F.

Ward and Simon N. Patten, and it may be said that in this respect Tugan-Baranovsky is as close to American sociology as he is to Marx.[43]

Turning to social classes and the class struggle, Tugan-Baranovsky held that although in one sense history may be regarded as the history of class struggles, this does not apply to those phases of human life outside the realm of the economic interests. Inasmuch as the economic interest is not the only human interest, economic antagonism does not necessarily lead to antagonism within the whole range of social existence.

The upshot of these considerations is that Tugan-Baranovsky closely approximates the position of the subjectivist school, although he insisted upon regarding himself as an adherent of the materialistic conception of history. Present-day Communists reject his doctrines as having little resemblance to historical materialism as they understand it.

Bogdanov, Bolshevik Revisionist. — Perhaps the most original and daring of all the Russian revisionists was Alexander Bogdanov (1873–1928).[44] He began by completely accepting Marxian doctrine, but early in the twentieth century, under the influence of the " energetic " philosophy of Ostwald and the empirical criticism of Avenarius and Mach (which, it will be recalled, also influenced Chernov), he developed an elaborate philosophical system to which he gave the name of tectology (from *tectonomai,* to build or construct). This in general conforms to the Neo-Kantian idea that man *makes* so-called " natural " laws by organizing his experience in accordance with his categories of time, space, cause, effect, and so on. The task of the philosopher is not to *discover* the principle of the unity of the external world, but to transform it into a unity by *constructing* such a principle. This doctrine runs counter to the dialectic theory that man can know the objective world because the latter is controlled by the same laws as those operating in the human mind — the processes of the dialectical logic, say its devotees, are the same as the processes of nature. But, although Lenin, among others, was sufficiently alarmed by Bogdanov's departure from dialectic materialism to devote much effort to refuting him,[45] tectology is of secondary interest to us here. More important is Bogdanov's earlier work in sociology (1900–1910), as outlined in his essays on the " psychology of society " and the " science of social consciousness." [46]

Here he attempts to give a psychological bent to the Marxian theory of evolution and to bring it into agreement with the Darwinian theory of adaptation. Holding that social adaptation is not essentially different from biological adaptation, he goes on to show how changes in the natural environment continually produce variations in social forms, the majority of which prove unfit to survive. Those that do win in the struggle for existence may be regarded as adaptations, as products of natural selection. This phase of Bogdanov's theory bears a close resemblance to Keller's attempt to apply Darwinian categories to the " evolution of the mores," and was set forth a decade earlier.[47] Bogdanov distinguishes two main types of social adaptation, technical and ideological, the technical being primary and the ideological dependent upon it. Both types of adaptation become social in the extent to which they are permeated by the " social instinct." This, in essence, is the force that urges man to remain with others and to act like them, being most clearly manifest in imitation. All the ideological forms are " organizing adaptations'" of the technical forms; language and mimicry, for example, are ideological forms, and serve as tools of mutual adaptation in social effort. Social progress is the increase of such mutual adaptation, and becomes apparent in idealism, which is the victory of the social in man.

Bogdanov also attempted to work out a theory of social evolution, and in so doing paid particular attention to the development of historic types of society and their ideologies, concluding with a sketch of the " collectivist society of the future." This will have as its general characteristics: (1) power over nature; (2) homogeneous organization of the whole productive system, conjoined with " a highly developed mental equality of the workers as universally developed conscious producers "; and (3) " complete freedom of consumption," abolition of coercion and compulsion of every kind, emancipation from all mysticism and metaphysics, and the " high development of comradely ties between men." [48]

In this closely condensed exposition of Bogdanov's doctrines it has been impossible to make their divergence from the Marxian point of view clearly evident. To begin with, Bogdanov differs from Marx by maintaining that social existence and social consciousness are the same, inasmuch as the social struggle is directed toward a goal determined by social consciousness, whereas the Marxian position is that social consciousness reflects social existence (or the social order) and is determined by it. To quote again from the famous passage, point of departure for so much *Wissenssoziologie*, in Marx's introduction to his *Critique of Political Economy:* " The mode of production of material life conditions the social, political, and mental life processes in general.

It is not the consciousness of men that determines their being, but, on the contrary, their social being determines their consciousness." [49]

The second point of difference is that according to Bogdanov classes develop because of " organizational experience," the ruling class being that which does the organizing of the society; for Marx, on the contrary, classes arise because of the ownership of the means of production and the use of this ownership in exploitation.

The third point of difference is with regard to the process by which classes " will be abolished." Bogdanov held that this would occur through the " socialization of organizational experience," brought about by the ideological education of the working class, i.e., by what he called proletarian culture. Bearing marked traces of subjectivism, this runs directly counter to the Marxian theory that the all-sufficient cause of the abolition of classes is the capture of the economic system through a proletarian revolution.

In this last deviation from the Marxian point of view, Bogdanov seems to have been influenced by subjectivism, although like many conjectures regarding unacknowledged influence, proof is difficult. Nevertheless, there are numerous features of Bogdanov's theory that are part of present-day Communist practice. This may be partly due to the fact that, although inactive in the 1917 Revolution, Bogdanov had been a Bolshevik since 1903, and after the party came to power coöperated with it in the departments of education and scientific research. [50]

The Sociology of Revolution: Lenin. — It is now time that we pay some attention to the work of the greatest Bolshevik theorist, Vladimir Ilyich Ulyanov, known to history as Nikolai Lenin (1870–1924). As already noted, he was an ardent adherent of the dialectic method, but it is doubtful whether this was sufficient to lead him to make his special contribution; namely, the stress on the rôle of the ideologist as the active element in revolution. [51] Certainly Plekhanov, who initiated Lenin into the mysteries of the dialectic, attached little importance to the ideologist. Perhaps, as we have several times suggested, the despised subjectivists were not without influence. But be this as it may, it cannot be denied that Lenin's theoretical interests were primarily in matters of revolutionary tactics and the structure of concrete social organizations rather than in more abstract and remote problems — his book on materialism and empirio-criticism to the contrary notwithstanding. (Significantly enough, the latter was written at a time when Lenin could not engage in direct revolutionary effort.)

The results of his studies in tactics and related matters may be summed up under the following heads: (1) the refutation of the doctrine of the so-called Economists that revolutionary political action should be wholly subordinated to the " spontaneous " economic struggle; (2) in close conjunction with this, the assertion of the vitally important part played by the " active element," i.e., the class-conscious proletarian vanguard led by skillful ideologists; (3) the further conclusion that these ideologists must make revolutionary activity their sole occupation and must undergo special " professional " training — this is the famous theory of the " professional revolutionist "; (4) the development of the theory that the state is an instrument of class dictatorship; and (5) the unflinching espousal of the principle of the dictatorship of the proletariat — or, more exactly put, of the dictatorship of a small class-conscious proletarian vanguard acting *for* the proletariat in accordance with the plans of revolutionary ideologists.[52]

All these contributions, with the exception of the notion of the professional revolutionist, can be found clearly foreshadowed in the writings of Marx and Engels, and inasmuch as we have stressed these very points throughout most of Chapter Seventeen, there is no warrant for working through them again. We shall content ourselves with calling attention to the fact that although Lenin took over these ideas from his forerunners, the way in which he combined, elaborated, and applied them gives him an independent and important place in the history of social thought. By collecting and relating his various utterances, one could present a completely integrated sociology of revolutionary tactics.[53]

Although it might be possible to glean a few sociologically relevant ideas from the works of Leon Trotsky, particularly from those phases dealing with the theory of " permanent revolution," it seems that enough space has already been devoted to matters of this kind. The same holds true with regard to the doctrines of Nikolai Bukharin and Joseph Stalin; furthermore, the former has contributed nothing particularly new — he simply wrote a textbook on Marxian sociology — and the latter is primarily interested in showing that he is the only lineal descendant of Marx and Lenin.

II

SOCIOLOGY WITHOUT DIRECT POLITICAL ORIENTATION

We shall therefore turn our attention to those varieties of contemporary Russian sociology which we could not consider in the chapter so far because they could not be fitted into the pattern of political development. That is to say, we shall now deal with Russian sociology that is not so specifically Russian, that is less directly connected with the persisting background of autocracy and revolution. This means that all the theories discussed will fall in the period from 1875 onward; indeed, most of them saw the light in the twentieth century. Sorokin says that the following changes began to become apparent about 1900: first, philosophical and highly general treatises lost favor and more concrete and specific analyses came to the fore; further, methods of research became less speculative and more exact; again, enthusiasm for the Marxian and subjective schools of sociology notably diminished; and finally, as sociological research became more specialized, the number of schools increased.[54] He distinguishes a large number, but we shall here deal only with the following: (1) general and historical sociology; (2) juristic sociology (or sociological jurisprudence); (3) psychological sociology; and (4) systematic sociology.

General and Historical Sociology. — One of the first writers in the general field of historical sociology was Vladimir Antonovitch (1834–1908), an Ukrainian who utilized his comprehensive historical, ethnological, and archaeological knowledge in the study of crowd behavior, social structure, psycho-sociological types, and the factors of social development. His work lacked the solid foundation of scientific research, but for its day was remarkably penetrating.[55] Another Ukrainian, M. Dragomonov (1841–1895), did important work in general sociology, applying his knowledge to the sociological analysis of the literature and social structure of the Ukraine. Most of his writing was done abroad, for in 1876 his boldness in announcing himself as a sociologist led the Russian government to regard him as a socialist, and he had to take refuge abroad, first in Geneva, where he edited the periodical *Hromada* (*Society*) from 1878 to 1882, and then in Bulgaria, where he taught at the University of Sofia until his death. Dragomonov advanced an intellectualistic theory of social development that in some respects is like the " three-stage " doctrine of Comte.[56]

Perhaps the earliest attempt at a comprehensive sociological system was T. Osadchy's book on *The Life of Society,* which he regarded as a sketch of a science of society. This appeared in 1901–1902, and shows the influence of Spencer, Giddings, Ward, Durkheim, Gumplowicz, Menger, and others. In it Osadchy sets forth a synthetic theory of society from both the static and dynamic points of view, with primary attention to economic development, and with a large amount of material drawn from the field of what is today called rural sociology. Like Dragomonov, he accepts the contentions of Comte, Fouillée, and DeRoberty that the advance of knowledge is the fundamental factor in social evolution.[57]

Another Ukrainian (thoroughly " Russified," by the way) is Maxim Kovalevsky (1851–1916), who published a treatise on sociology toward the end of his life that systematized and carried further the theories he had already propounded in his works on jurisprudence, economic evolution, and the history of law. At about the same time he brought out a thorough, critical study of the sociological theories of Tarde, Giddings, Baldwin, Gumplowicz, Ratzenhofer, Simmel, Durkheim, Marx, and others. This, according to Sorokin, is perhaps the most comprehensive (up until 1905) and critical work of its kind.[58] Obviously, it could not be discussed here even if it were available in translation; we shall restrict ourselves to the methodological and historical aspects of Kovalevsky's sociology.

By and large, he follows Comte in his classification of the sciences, in particular agreeing that psychology, in so far as it is not a branch of biology, is merely a subdivision of sociology. The concrete social sciences, such as ethnography, statistics, political economy, and so on, all supply sociology with material, but in their turn these sciences must " base their empirical generalization upon those general laws of coexistence and development which sociology, as a science of the order and progress of human society, is called upon to establish." [59]

Kovalevsky did not follow Comte or the other writers just mentioned, however, in the belief that "ideas rule the world or throw it into chaos," for after a careful study of all the important systems of sociology, he arrived at the conclusion that there is no single all-determining social factor. " To talk . . . about a central fact which determines after itself all others, is to me the same as to talk about those drops of the waters of a river, which, by their movement, condition its current." [60] (Here Kovalevsky is in agreement with Chernov and other subjectivists.) Strangely enough, Kovalevsky exerted a great deal of influence on the development of the extreme sociological objectivism of Pavlov and Bekhterev.[61] We say " strangely " because, in spite of Kovalevsky's insistence on the functional point of view, the extreme objectivists attempted to trace everything to man's neurological makeup, and particularly to his " unconditioned reflexes," as we shall later see when this school is discussed.

In his historical or genetic sociology, Kovalevsky made use primarily of Russian ethnographic material, some of which he gathered through his own field work;[62] other genetic sociologists, among them Ziber, Sumcov, Chernisov, Vook, and Ochrimovitch, furnished a large part of the remainder.[63] Especially interesting is Kovalevsky's argument that it is impossible to draw valid conclusions about the primitive state of mankind on the basis of the study of present-day preliterates, inasmuch as the latter are almost as far removed from a genuinely primitive state as are the literate peoples. He therefore paid a great deal of attention to animal sociology in order to gain light on the problems of the origin of the family and the tribe (clan, gens). His conclusion was that the family took its rise from the mother and her offspring, and that the tribe did not develop from the family but was at first a horde which grew through the integrating influences of taboo, exogamy, and the elimination of blood vengeance within the group.[64] These hypotheses are closely similar to those adopted much later by Robert Briffault in *The Mothers*. Kovalevsky also advanced an interesting theory of private property, holding that it was at first a result of magical " contagion." His theory of religious origins is animistic, and his analysis of political development something like that presented by Schmidt and Koppers. None of these theories, however, was first advanced by Kovalevsky, although he was a trail-blazer among the Russian social scientists. Perhaps the only original contribution he made was his theory that the growth and density of population are the most important influences in social development.[65] He was followed in this by a number of social biologists and demographers, notably Adolphe Coste and other French writers.

Kovalevsky's ethnographic interests have been continued on a grand scale in present-day Russia; a host of trained workers are gathering information about the manners and customs of the numerous exotic peoples within the confines of an area comprising one-sixth of the total land surface of the globe. To be sure, Kovalevsky has had little or no direct influence on this research, and most of it is done with practical ends in view — collectivization and what not — to say nothing of the distorting influence of dogma. Nevertheless, the sheer quantity of the data, and the fact that they are gathered from peoples rarely studied with thoroughness heretofore, will make acquaintance with them essential not only for ethnologists but for historical sociologists as well. Some of this work is being done with a more or less sociological orientation; for example, Tan-Bogoraz,[66] Fenomenov, and Jaklovev are studying Russian villages by what they call the " sociographic method." [67] This seems to indicate some German influence, perhaps that of Tönnies. LePlay and Steinmetz may also have parts. Unfortunately, however, the method of most of the ethnographers is the old-fashioned " comparative " variety of the nineteenth century.[68]

Highly significant work in historical sociology has been done by Alexander and Eugen Kulisher, sons of I. M. Kulisher, for a long time professor of economic history at the University of Petrograd. In 1932 there appeared a book entitled *Weltgeschichte als Völkerbewegung,* which set forth the hypothesis that the major trends of world history can be interpreted as aspects of migrations of various kinds. Although the two younger Kulishers are the authors of this work, the hypothesis itself was long a major interest of their father, and he accumulated a mass of evidence which the sons were able to utilize. The same idea has of course occupied many other thinkers, as our chapters on theories of culture contact have perhaps done something to show. Nevertheless, the Kulishers were among the first Russians of modern times to attribute major sociological significance to migration and its attendant phenomena, and the historical sociologist cannot afford to overlook their particular contribution.

Among the historical sociologists might also be placed a few of the philosophers of history such as Berdiayev, Frank, Karsavin, and Bulgakov, but they are so religious or even mystical in their approach to social problems that it seems hardly worth while to discuss them in the present context. For quite different reasons, we shall also be compelled to pass over the significant work of Lappo-Danilevsky and Shpett in historical methodology; [69] although interesting and important, it falls slightly outside the field of sociology proper.

Juristic Sociology. — Also outside the central field of sociology, but a little closer than the type just mentioned, is Russian juristic sociology or sociological jurisprudence. It began with Nikolai Korkunov [70] (1853–1904), who was professor of law at the University of Petrograd. His contribution was not in the form of an independent sociological system, for he borrowed most of his sociological ideas from Spencer, Fouillée, Kareyev, Gumplowicz, and others. His importance derives from the fact that he succeeded in developing a system of law from sociological postulates, thus demonstrating that the jurist need not confine himself to logical acrobatics, precedent-chasing, or scholastic delvings into Roman law. Korkunov's sociological jurisprudence was much appreciated, particularly outside of Russia, and his chief work, a general theory of law, was translated into a number of languages. He was followed by many other jurists, some of them pushing his point of view further, and some working out theories of their own. One of the most important was Nogorodtsev, whose *Social Ideals,* a survey of plans for " social reconstruction," is like Pareto's *Les Systèmes socialistes,* except that the Russian writer is incomparably superior as logician and dialectician. We may also name Trubetzkoy, Kistiakovsky,[71] Taranovsky, Dnistriansky, Cherchenevitch, Starosolsky, Pokrovsky,[72] Lasarevsky, and Kokoshkin.[73]

In the field of criminology and penology or, more strictly speaking, the sociology of crime and punishment, a great deal of work has been done by Russians in establishing correlations between various types of crime and their social, psychical, and biological conditioning factors. Further, the general social phenomena of crime, disgrace, social and personal dishonor, and the like, have been sociologically analyzed. The most important writers in this field are Gernet, Chubinsky, Foynitsky, Charykov, Kosin, Posnytchev, Timasheff, and Teranovsky.[74]

Psycho-Sociology: Petrazycki and Emotion. — Closely allied with juristic sociology is the unique psycho-sociology of the famous Russo-Polish writer Leo Petrazycki (1867–1931), before the revolution professor of legal philosophy at the University of Petrograd, and thereafter at the University of Warsaw. This, according to Sorokin, is quite different from the psycho-sociology of the subjectivists. Petrazycki developed his theory in conjunction with a trenchant criticism of traditional logic and traditional psychology as applied to theories of the state, law, morals, and society. Sorokin says that his work in the field of logic and psychology is among the most important accomplished in the twentieth century, but also says that it is impossible to give a brief version of it or of its sociological implications, inasmuch as it is so thoroughly integrated that it must be studied as a whole. We can therefore do no more than hint at some of the characteristic features of Petrazycki's theory. Among other things, he lays great stress on the rôle of emotion as an autonomous and truly normative agent in behavior. It is the driving force of animal activity and the chief factor in human conduct, for it makes possible adaptation to the environment and dominates all social processes. This would at first glance seem to bear a marked resemblance to the psycho-sociologies of Lester F. Ward or Simon N. Patten, but it is fundamentally different, inasmuch as it does not incorporate a " sensualistic " psychology of emotion. Some writers compare Petrażycki's conception of emotion with Pareto's notion of " residues," but if his theory is as original as is commonly claimed, such a comparison does not do him justice. As applied to morals and law, Petrażycki's theory bears the earmarks of " emotional intuitivism," and seems to have a strong resemblance to the " emotional phenomenology " of Max Scheler and the " empirical psychology " of Franz Brentano.[75]

On the basis of his " emotional sociology " Petrażycki developed a comprehensive analysis of all types of social process, structure, and development, but in particular dealt exhaustively with legal and political institutions. His influence before the revolution was great. Jurists, social philosophers, psychologists, biologists, economists, and sociologists joined his school, and at that time it seemed probable that his influence in Russia would be comparable to that of Durkheim in France. The revolution put a stop to these developments, however, for Petrażycki had to go into exile, and although a few of his remaining Russian disciples tried to carry on their work after 1920, the arrest of many of them again brought matters to a standstill. But in any event, says Sorokin, those works which Petrażycki has already published are so significant that his influence will sooner or later make itself felt among the sociologists of all countries.[76] (We shall later note his influence in Poland.)

Psychological Sociology: Objectivism. — Another school of psychological sociology that has recently arisen in Russia, directly antithetical to the once so popular subjectivism, is the objectivistic or behavioristic, which took its rise from the psycho-neurological work of Pavlov and Bekhterev. This school seeks complete objectivity by rigidly excluding all non-quantitative data and by concentrating on external social phenomena that are repetitive and hence subject to " genuinely scientific observation and control." [77]

Zeliony, one of Bekhterev's students, has presented a systematic outline of a " socio-physiology " along objectivist lines which, although extreme, has the merit of consistently adhering to its announced principles. No " speech-reactions " and no influences from outer states to inner are taken into account, and one can at least see where an absolutely consistent behaviorism leads the sociologist.[78] Bekhterev himself (1857–1927) recently wrote on the theory of " collective behavior," but in so doing did not notably further the cause of scientific sociology. Like many laboratory scientists who make excursions into fields not their own, Bekhterev failed to see that hypotheses which have proved useful under the controlled conditions of the laboratory are easily reduced to absurdity when applied in other ways. To talk, as Bekhterev did, about reflexes of property, reflexes of liberty, and the like, is not only to ignore the influence of culture on human behavior but to imply, by constantly confusing conditioned and unconditioned reflexes, that culture has no particular influence. Such theories are open to all the objections which American sociologists have rightly made to the licentious application of the notion of instinct.[79] Other members of the school are Vassiliev, Protopopov, Hakkebush, Wagner, Lenz, Ivanov-Smolensky, Savitch, Orbelly, Babkin, Frolow, and Sorokin.[80]

The sociologist last named has applied the behavioristic method in a less extreme way than Zeliony and Bekhterev. In his works on general sociology, and particularly in his studies of the effect of hunger on human behavior, of the sociology of revolution, and of social mobility, considerably more caution than is manifested by other objectivists is in evidence.

We shall here discuss only his *Social Mobility* (1927) which, although published in English five years after his flight from Russia, bears within it evidence that it is a continuation of earlier trains of thought. Dividing the concept of mobility into horizontal and vertical, Sorokin defines the former in terms of actual change of location in physical space, such as emigration, whereas the latter is conceived in more or less figurative terms as change in social status, i.e., "movement up or down the social ladder." This movement varies in rate and type with varying types of society, and in all societies there are recognized "elevators" by means of which social ascent or descent is effected. Classical examples are the army, the school, the bureaucracy, professional bodies, ecclesiastical organizations, the acquisition of wealth, and so on. All these "elevators" are selective in their action, and "they are as inevitable a part of the social body as the organs of control of blood circulation in a complex biological body." Analyzing the different strata, Sorokin finds that except in times of decadence the upper classes are on the average physically and mentally superior to the lower. The more permanent causes of this are to be sought in biological factors, although changes in the "anthropo-social environment" are also of some importance. The psycho-sociological effect of mobility is brilliantly dealt with by Sorokin, and his general conclusion is that mobility furthers mental plasticity and versatility, facilitating invention and discovery and the intellectual life generally, but also produces scepticism, cynicism, pathological isolation, moral disintegration, and suicide — here the reader will recall our numerous references to mental mobility. There are many other phases of Sorokin's work that are of great interest to sociologists, but we cannot devote space to them here, more especially as we have paid some attention to Sorokin in the chapters on historical sociology and on sociology in the United States. It is sufficient to say here that his study of social mobility is an excellent demonstration of the possibilities of " an objective, factual, behavioristic, quantitative sociology." [81] In one study at least the objectivist point of view has yielded results.

Analytic Sociology. — So-called formal sociology, better termed systematic or analytic sociology, has had few adherents in Russia. The works of Simmel and, to some extent, of Tarde, directed attention to types of social interaction such as contact, conflict, domination, etc. Struve in his earlier writings, when he was still primarily a Marxian, attempted to enlist the doctrines of Simmel in support of historical materialism, and Tachtarev has made a similar attempt. All in all, however, it must be said that Russian analytic sociology has brought forth nothing comparable to the work of Simmel, Ross, Park and Burgess, or Wiese.[82]

Russian Sociology as an Academic Discipline. — Although a great deal of sociology was current in Russia during the nineteenth century, both under its own name and in the guise of history, economics, and the like, it was not introduced in the universities until after the revolution of 1917. This was in part due to the extreme tenacity with which the traditional pattern of instruction resisted innovations, and in part to the attitude of the government toward anything that by its very name seemed to indicate socialistic leanings. As an example of the latter obstacle to the progress of sociology may be instanced the fact that the whole Russian edition of Ward's *Dynamic Sociology* was confiscated because of its supposedly terroristic (dynamite!) and revolutionary (socialism!) nature.[83]

In spite of opposition, however, sociology gradually won its way, and when Bekhterev included it under its own name in the courses offered at the Psycho-Neurological Institute of Petrograd, founded in 1919, the new discipline seemed certain of victory in the near future.[84] Prospects looked even brighter when Kovalevsky, who had induced Bekhterev to incorporate sociology in the plan of his institute, became the editor (with DeRoberty and Sorokin) of a series of sociological symposia appearing about every six months. These were entitled *New Ideas in Sociology,* and contained translations of the most significant sociological contributions appearing outside Russia, as well as studies by Russian sociologists. From 1913 to 1915 four volumes were published: the first was devoted to the problem of sociology as an autonomous science, the second to the relations of psychology and sociology, the third to the question of progress, and the fourth to various conceptions of the nature of primitive society. The World War and the death of Kovalevsky and DeRoberty put an end to this publication, but it nevertheless helped to gain general recognition for sociology in the Russian academic world.[85]

In 1916 a number of the leading Russian sociologists, biologists, and economists founded the Russian Sociological Society, with Lappo-Danilevsky as president and Sorokin as secretary. A comprehensive program of research was adopted, but the Revolution and the death of various members, including the president, brought the work to a standstill. In 1920 the society was again revived, this time with Kareyev, the well-known subjectivist, as president, and Sorokin again as secretary. At about this time, however, the Bolsheviks began to reverse their former favorable opinion of sociology. Immediately after the revolution they thought so well of it that all the Russian universities had to install departments of sociology, but when it gradually became apparent that the new discipline was not necessarily a prop for Communist doctrine, it fell from its high estate. Moreover, the arrest, exile, or forced flight of various members of the Russian Sociological Society, because of alleged counter-revolutionary activities, was not especially helpful to sociological research, and when in 1922 the teaching of sociology under that name was prohibited in all Russian universities, the society died a somewhat unnatural death.[86]

For a time it seemed as if sociology would be permanently extinguished in the Soviet Union, but according to the reports of Shapoval, an Ukrainian *émigré* who certainly had no reasons for excessive optimism, there has been a marked revival. To be sure, much of the sociological research and writing now going on does not bear the label, and Communist dogmas hinder the free search for truth, but the situation is far from hopeless. Demographic, ethnographic, psycho-neurological, and historical institutes are to be found that grant a large place to problems essentially sociological, and there is a great deal of public interest that reflects itself in volume of publication and eagerness of students.

As is well known, instruction in social affairs with particular reference to the tenets of the Marxist-Leninist-Stalinist ideology is obligatory in all the secondary and higher schools — technical-industrial, economic-social, pedagogical, and even those devoted to the fine arts. Among the textbooks used are the following: Kushner, *Outline of the Evolution of Social Structures;* Lozovik, *History of Society;* Christyuk, *History of Class Struggles and Socialism;* Zaluzhny, *Theory of Collective Behavior;* Friche, *Sociology of Art;* Lunacharsky, *Sociology of Music;* Hordon and Zotin, *Manual of the Science of Society;* Wolfson, *Outlines of the Science of Society;* Farforovski and Kochergin, *Sociology;* and Nikolai Bukharin, *Historical Materialism, or the Development of Marxian Sociology.* Let us quote Shapoval regarding the nature of these volumes:

Obviously the content and character of all these textbooks is prescribed by the prevailing régime; for the most part they give only the elementary notions of Marxism and some explanation of the economic processes of society. But, in spite of this, it must be admitted that even under the sway of these propagandistic aims the sociological knowledge of the . . . population is raised to a higher level. No " politics " can forever oppose the development of true science: even in the highly orthodox text by Bukharin there are some pages which show that the contributions of sociology in the world outside have penetrated the USSR. . . . In the textbook by Farforovski and Kochergin, *Sociology,* a list of necessary books for the pupils in the higher classes of the secondary schools is given, and the index of names includes Marx, Engels, Lenin, Kautsky, Plekhanov, Bogdanov, Lunacharsky, Rozhkov, Ziber, Tachtarev, Cherchenevitch, Isayev, Weil, Bücher, Spencer, Kareyev, Barth, DeGreef, Giddings, Ward, Gumplowicz, Sorokin, Loria, and others. Note, however, that the names of Comte, DeRoberty, Lavrov, Mikhalovsky and Durkheim are missing, and that Giddings is the only American sociologist mentioned.[87]

We therefore seem justified in concluding that although Russian sociology is feeble and provincial, it is by no means dead, and that there is hope for the future. At the same time, it would be folly to deny that Russian sociology is now markedly different from the types taught elsewhere. Moreover, the persisting influence of autocracy must still be taken into account, whether for good or bad. Under the Czars a great many Russian sociologists were known abroad at least as well as at home; one need only recall the names of Dragomonov, Novicow, DeRoberty, Kovalevsky, and Kropotkin. Under the Soviets it seems probable that a good deal of Russian sociology will continue to be written outside of Russia.

The 1959 portion of the Appendix gives ground for modifying the remarks made above, but before shouting for joy the reader should consult the 1960 aftermath. Dolefully, the writer has concluded that in an intellectual realm so crucial as that of sociology, uninhibited teaching and research in the Soviet bloc will be a long time coming.

CHAPTER XXVII

Sociology in Eastern Europe, the Balkans, and Turkey

SENSITIVE SPOTS. — Among the countries included in this chapter are several which were once parts of the Dual Monarchy or the empire of the Czars or of Germany before 1918, so that many of the men whom they now claim as their leading sociologists of the past have already been considered. Gumplowicz is usually dealt with as an Austrian sociologist, but the Poles now count him as one of them, and they also place Petrażycki in their ranks. Lindner is regarded as a Czech in spite of his Germanic affiliations. Those Ukrainians who are *émigrés* or autonomists assert that Tugan-Baranovsky and Kistiakovsky, although they wrote in Russian, belong to their would-be nation. Other countries which have not so recently been subjected to larger units but which are forced to make use of foreign languages in order to win an international audience are also in an equivocal position: for example, the Roumanian, Drăghicescu, wrote in French, and the Greek, Eleutheropoulos, writes chiefly in German and taught in Switzerland until 1926.

Whatever we do, therefore, we are likely to offend some ardent nationalist, and we can only hope that as Americans we shall not be suspected of ulterior motives. In giving the examples of conflicting claims, we have called the roll of nearly all the countries to be dealt with in this chapter: Czechoslovakia, the Ukraine in emigration, Poland, Hungary, Yugoslavia, Roumania, Greece, and Turkey.[1]

I

CZECHOSLOVAKIA

Before Masaryk. — Modern sociology in Czechoslovakia may be said to begin with the work of the man who until recently was president of the Republic, Thomas Garrigue Masaryk (1850–1937), but, as elsewhere, a number of important forerunners are to be found.

Škrach takes us as far back as the time of the Reformation, pointing out that Huss [2] and Chelčický [3] advanced definite theories of social relations even though they were bound up with theology. He also says that the great Czech scholar Comenius,[4] well known in the history of pedagogy, can be regarded as an early sociologist. Škrach does no more than present " the calling cards of these three thinkers," to use his own metaphor, but announces his intention to justify his action by detailed historical studies.

Other forerunners of Czech sociology, says Škrach, are to be found among the students of comparative philology and literature, historians of Czech culture, and followers of Hegel. Here we may mention Josef Dobrovský (1753–1829), " an enlightened Catholic priest and Mason," who was the founder of comparative Slavic philology as well as a rationalistic advocate of the Czech national renascence. He propounded a definitely sociological theory of language. One of his followers, Josef Šafařík (1795–1861), not only elaborated this theory but also did much to further the study of Slavic cultural history, thus providing valuable sociographic material.[5] A Romanticist, Josef Jungmann (1773–1841), applied the *Volksgeist* theories of Grimm and others to Czech language and literature, and also made a sociological diagnosis of the nationalist aspirations manifest at the beginning of the nineteenth century.

These aspirations were nourished by the various philosophies of history represented by Herder, Kant, and Hegel. Herder in particular made a strong appeal to the Slavophils, among whom we may name Jan Kollár (1793–1852), a Slovak Protestant who wished to further literary interrelations among the Slavs for Pan-Slavic purposes. He was also influenced by Kant's disciple, Fries, and by the *Naturphilosoph,* Oken.[6] The most important Czech historian, František Palacký, wrote a history of Bohemia along Hegelian lines, stressing the religious tendencies manifested during and after the Reformation.[7] The philosophy of history espoused by Masaryk is in some respects only a further development of that set forth by Palacký. Other Czech Hegelians were Augustin Smetana (1814–1851), Jan Hanuš (1812–1869), František Klácel (1808–1882), and Karel Štorch (1812–1842). The writer last named was also influenced by Comenius and by Krause (see pp. 1108–1113).

When the eager and gifted followers of the idealistic Hegelian philosophy tried to apply it toward the solution of their pressing national problems, however, its highly speculative and intellectualistic character made it unsatisfactory. By the time the Young

Hegelians of the Left appeared, a reaction set in which was furthered by the Austrian government and the Catholic Church, both of which suppressed Hegelianism by every device possible.[8] The complete antithesis of the " radical rationalist " Hegel was sought and found in the empirical philosopher-psychologist Herbart, to whom we have already referred in the chapter on sociology in the Germanic languages. A strong Herbartian school soon developed, among the earliest members of which were Gustav Adolf Lindner (1828–1887) and Emanuel Makovička (1851–1890). The latter was also influenced by Comte and Mill.

Lindner followed Herbart in his emphasis on psychology, and in 1871 published his *Ideen zur Psychologie der Gesellschaft als Grundlage der Sozialwissenschaft*.[9] The guiding principles of this work came from Herbart and much of its material from Lazarus, as noted in Chapter Twenty-Three but nevertheless all that Lindner borrowed was worked over in the light of his own ideas. The Herbartian influence is especially manifest in the fact that Lindner was largely concerned with the sociology of education. The valuable feature of his work was the attention it focused on the psychical phases of social life, with the consequence that bio-organismic notions have never taken root in Czechoslovakia.

The Sociology of Masaryk. — Lindner's psycho-sociology was nevertheless highly speculative, and we may date the emergence of sociology from the early writings of Masaryk, one of the first of which, a statistical study of suicide, appeared in 1881. This was written at a time when Masaryk had no direct knowledge of Comte's writings, but it is positivist in spirit. Later Comte exercised a strong influence on Masaryk (especially manifest in his logic), and in an unpublished aphorism he remarked that had he known nothing of Comte he would himself have worked out a similar sociological system.[10]

Masaryk's youth disclosed this bent toward positivistic and realistic sociology quite plainly. He studied statistics and geography, and evidenced preference for the natural sciences. The influence of the Czech renascence turned him toward philosophy " on a scientific basis " and in harmony with human needs. In particular, he hoped that such a philosophy might contribute toward the reorganization of Czech life, both individual and social. The work on logic already mentioned was written with a national aim; Masaryk desired to systematize the thinking of his compatriots in order that they might be able to make headway against the Austrian autocracy. All his sociological studies show the same preoccupation: not merely scientific knowledge for its own sake, but also for the reform of Czech society.

Although Masaryk learned much from Comte, he rejects the epistemological doctrines commonly identified with positivism, and also refuses to regard religion as a stage of human thought certain to be superseded by science. Further, he criticizes Comte's political doctrines, maintaining that in the end they are as reactionary as those of DeMaistre, by whom the great author of the *Philosophie positive* was so early influenced. Again, Masaryk differs from Comte in his classification of the sciences, for he includes psychology, which, as is known, was left out of the hierarchy by Comte. In harmony with this, data of consciousness such as ethical perceptions, religious emotions, and what not, are included in Masaryk's sociological analysis, thus continuing the Herbart-Lindner tradition. It is for this reason that he qualifies the Comtean conception of *consensus;* although he grants it a central place in his sociological system, he does not identify it with the idea of physical equilibrium. Once more, Masaryk does not follow Comte in the contention that society alone is real and the individual an abstraction. His critical realism places him midway between extreme individualism and extreme collectivism, although some critics maintain that he is a subjectivist much like Kareyev (cf. pp. 1039–40). At any rate, he maintains that even though society must be regarded as a dynamic organization composed not of individuals but of configurations of organized individuals, a social consciousness does not exist, and in the last analysis individuals are therefore the basic elements of society. Hence, psychology is the direct foundation of sociology.[11]

These theoretical postulates set forth in Masaryk's early writings on the nature and methods of sociology pervade his studies of religion, revolution, Marxism, Russian culture, and the like.[12] Much space might be devoted to a discussion of these more concrete and popular presentations, but for our purposes it is enough to note that they are all directed toward the upbuilding of Czech society. Bláha says that Masaryk was always both a philosopher and a propagandist. To quote:

In fact, he never philosophizes for philosophy's sake. Philosophy was to him always a function of life, directed particularly to the pressing problems and needs of life in general and national life in particular. As soon as he became interested in philosophy, he felt that there could be no rest until he had made this philosophy, which had brought order and reason into his own life, a principle of collective direction and organization.[13]

Masaryk's Chief Disciples. — The influence of the first president of Czechoslovakia has been enormous: problems of democracy and theocracy, nationalism and internationalism, pacifism and war, leadership and revolution, the interpretation of cultures, public and private morality, and countless others have been dealt with by his pupils and followers along lines suggested by him, so that it is possible to say with Škrach that " all Czech sociology is oriented toward Masaryk." [14] Three of his most important pupils are Břetislav Foustka (1862–), Eduard Beneš (1884–), and Innocenc Arnošt Bláha (1879–).

Foustka has done little in the field of theoretical sociology, having been most attracted by the humanitarian and reform elements in Masaryk's doctrines; at the same time, we should mention that an excellent study of the sociology of Turgot (1891) has come from his pen. He has been especially useful as a popularizer of sociology.[15]

Beneš, formerly minister of foreign affairs and now president of Czechoslovakia, has been too much absorbed by the pressing needs of national life to devote himself to pure theory, although his studies of the party system, the city, morals, and child life are excellent theoretical treatises. His sociology of politics bears the stamp of both Comte and Masaryk, and his work as foreign minister has demonstrated that it will bear the test of application. An upholder of democracy in spite of a keen realization of its difficulties, he defines politics as a social activity which has for its purpose the shaping of the social milieu so that through it all men can so far as possible satisfy their varying needs and desires. Reckoning with both the individual and the social factor, he regards himself as a critical realist of the school of Masaryk. In his analysis of the individual factor he grants full weight to irrational tendencies, and utilizes suggestions coming from Freud, Pareto, and Michels.[16]

Bláha has attempted to show certain similarities between Masaryk and Ward in his treatise on the former's " synergetic" philosophy. His articles on contemporary Czechoslovakian sociology have done a great deal to acquaint outsiders with the valuable work now being done, and his systematic treatise on the sociology of morals has established his reputation as a sociologist in his own right. Bláha is also the author of two valuable monographs, one on urban sociology and the other dealing with social stratification as exemplified by the industrial worker and the peasant.[17]

Chalupný the Voluminous. — One of the most prolific of Czech sociologists is Emanual Chalupný (1879–), a pupil of Masaryk's who dared to disagree with the master. His books on Jungmann and Havlíček were directed against Masaryk's estimate of these two prominent figures in the history of the " Bohemian question," and his other writings on the character and mission of the Czech people were also out of line with Masaryk's ideas. Chalupný's sociological significance is not merely that of a heretic, however, for he is the first Czech to have written a systematic introduction to sociology (1905), and is now at work on a massive sociological treatise which is planned in fifteen parts, some of them occupying several volumes. Five volumes have thus far appeared: " Foundations " as the first part of the general division, and " Human Evolution " as the fifth part. Both of these he classes as sections of social statics. " Social Factors " and " Social Products " form parts three and four. The first volume of the second part is a history of sociology up to Comte. Whether or not Chalupný will live long enough to complete his grandiose project is perhaps doubtful, but his courage and industry may carry him through. Certainly his volume of publication is far greater than that of any other Czech sociologist, and its quality is often high. We shall discuss here only his classification and methodology of sociology.

Chalupný's originality is evident in the place he assigns sociology in the hierarchy of the abstract sciences, for he puts it between biology and psychology. The object-matter of sociology represents a union of that dealt with by psychology on the one hand and the natural sciences on the other. This reverses the usual relation of psychology and sociology; only the followers of Durkheim and the bio-social school represented by DeRoberty and Izoulet take a similar position. Even they fail to pursue their doctrine to its final consequences, as Chalupný does. For him the

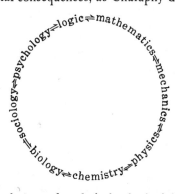

abstract sciences form a closed circle; logic follows psychology, and logic is in turn the connecting link with mathematics.

His sociological methodology is the noëtic type — that is, he does not base it upon hypotheses taken over from any of the other sciences, natural or social, but insists that sociological phenomena must be dealt with on their own terms. In this standpoint he has probably been influenced to some extent by Masaryk's critical realism, although he does not show the inclination toward subjectivism traceable in the latter.

In addition to the works already mentioned in the field of general sociology, Chalupný has published a number of more specialized studies. Those having to do with the problems of Czechoslovak national life have been noted above; he has also written on the legal philosophy of Soloviev, the study of sociology in the United States and in Czechoslovakia, the lawyer and the legal profession, and so on.[18]

Other Schools of Sociology. — Giddings has had a number of followers, among whom may be mentioned O. Jozífek (1880–1919) and Ladislav Kunte (1877–). Both of these men are journalists who have applied Giddings's consciousness-of-kind formula to the problems of Czechoslovak unification, religion, social problems, and the like.[19]

Durkheim has found an ardent disciple in Antonín Uhlíř. In his book on social philosophy, written in 1912, he takes over the idea of a collective consciousness and applies it to the categories of knowledge, arriving at the conclusion that the basis of all " true " thinking is provided by impersonal, objective, necessary, and uniformly valid concepts.[20]

The influence of Tarde and other " psychologistic " thinkers is evident in the work of Josef Fořt, a specialist in the sociology of economics, Antonín Klosse, a criminologist, and J. L. Fischer, a sociological analyst of political phenomena who has also done excellent work in the history of sociology.[21] Organismic social thought has a representative in J. Dušek, and even the mechanistic school has one supporter in Ivan Žmavc. Subjectivistic sociology something like that earlier identified with the Russian Lavrov is defended by Emanuel Rádl (1873–), whose philosophy of nature has won wide acclaim. Most of the younger Czech sociologists, however, hold that sociology should be free from value-judgments of every kind. Nevertheless, a great many social problems are subjected to sociological analysis in contemporary Czechoslovakia: the literature is voluminous (see notes).[22]

The Official Status of Sociology. — Before the World War, sociology in the universities was taught only under the protecting wing of philosophy. For example, Masaryk was professor of philosophy "with special attention to sociology" at Prague. Now all three universities (Prague, Brno, and Bratislava) have full professorships and subsidiary posts in sociology occupied by Král, Bláha, Chalupný, Fischer, Galla, and Machotka. In addition to this, sociology has a recognized place in various agricultural schools, theological seminaries, and commercial academies, and is even beginning to penetrate the Czechoslovak equivalent of the high school.

In 1920 the Republic founded a "social institute," but this comprises all the fields in which the social sciences can be applied, and serves propagandistic as well as scientific purposes. Its organ is the *Sociální revue.* In 1924 the Czechoslovakian Agricultural Academy was established; it includes a flourishing section devoted to rural sociology. The following year the Masaryk Sociological Society was organized; this is a scientific body like the American Sociological Society, and has been of particular service through its sponsorship of a series of sociological books, some of them translations and some of them domestic products. An important step in the development of Czechoslovakian sociology was taken in 1930 when the *Sociologická revue,* an excellent periodical given over primarily to theoretical questions, began to appear under the editorship of the sociological seminar of the Masaryk University of Brno. In 1932 this was supplemented by a journal focusing chiefly on matters of immediate concern, as is indicated by its title, *Sociální problémy.*

In conclusion, it may be said that there is no country anywhere of equal size that can display so impressive a list of contemporary sociologists or such a range and intensity of sociological activity. Here is another bright spot on the sociological map.[23]

II

ÉMIGRÉ UKRAINIAN SOCIOLOGY

Refuge in Austria and Czechoslovakia. — In the chapter on Russian sociology we have already discussed the work of such "Ukrainian" writers as Kovalevsky and Tugan-Baranovsky. They all wrote in Russian before the World War, so there is no reason for considering them here.

After the war and the revolution, the Ukrainian nationalists hoped to set up an autonomous state.[24] The Czarist régime had held them sternly in check — in 1863 and again in 1876 the publication of books in the Ukrainian language was forbidden — and there was a veritable flood of publications in Ukrainian when the barriers were torn down. This new-born nationalism was intensified by the Wilsonian doctrine of self-determination, and when various Czarist generals and foreign interventionists attempted to restore the old régime in 1918–1920, many Ukrainians turned against Soviet Russia, and proclaimed the short-lived Ukrainian republic. With the expulsion of the White and Allied Armies by the Red forces under Trotsky, there also came the expulsion of a large number of these autonomists. They found refuge in neighboring states, among the most hospitable of which were Austria and Czechoslovakia.

The first attempt at organizing Ukrainian sociological effort in emigration took place in Austria, where in 1919 the eminent social historian, M. Hruševsky, tried to found a Ukrainian institute of sociology. The project was not realized, but Hruševsky did succeed in having the writings of a number of Ukrainian authors published, among them three sociological treatises: one of his own on genetic or historical sociology (1921); another by Starosolsky on the theory of nationality (1922); and one by Shraha on the relation of the state to socialist society (1923).[25]

Hruševsky's treatise is of some interest. In the first part he surveys and analyzes earlier theories of social development and attacks what we have called the " single-factor fallacy," maintaining that a plurality of factors is always operative. He then shows their influence in a large number of cycles and trends. His analysis is carried out in terms of social processes, and has the unusual merit of being highly generalized and at the same time solidly buttressed by historical evidence. The second part treats of the successive forms of development of human associations, ranging from elementary types to the most complicated political structures. Hruševsky here succeeds in achieving systematic unity without falling into the grosser errors of evolutionism. The third part of the treatise is a review of Ukrainian work in historical sociology: the theories of Kovalevsky, Ziber, and others are expounded and critically evaluated. (It may be mere coincidence, or there may be a determining cultural situation, but for whatever reason the Ukrainians seem to have displayed an especial fondness for historical sociology.)

Czechoslovakia has been especially generous in its provision for Ukrainian refugees, and it has proved possible to establish two higher schools: the Ukrainian Agricultural Academy at Poděbrady and the Ukrainian Pedagogical Institute at Prague. In the socio-economic faculty of the Academy, chairs of sociological theory, social politics, social statistics, etc., have been established, and at the Institute courses in sociology are obligatory. In 1924 M. Shapoval, well-known Ukrainian sociologist, founded the Ukrainian Sociological Institute at Prague. This has for its purpose the organization of scientific research in sociology with special reference to the Ukraine; the training for qualified Ukrainian students for the doctorate in social science; the popularization of sociological knowledge among Ukrainians; and the publication of translations and original works in the Ukrainian language. The Institute possesses a rather large library and sponsors a review, *Suspilstvo* (*Society*), in which there have appeared articles by Bláha, Chalupný, Wiese, Ellwood, Chapin, Sorokin, Michels, and a great number of Ukrainian writers.

Shapoval himself died in 1932, leaving behind him a large treatise on general sociology that testifies to his great erudition. Unfortunately it remains unfinished. His work in the institute he founded is carried on by L. Bilecky and N. Hrihoriiv.

III

POLAND

The Nation Minus the State. — Ideas about man's conduct and institutions have been particularly numerous in Poland.[26] One reason for this was the peculiar character assumed by the Polish commonwealth in the early modern period: it was a free republic of nobles with an elected king, and all the decisions of its legislative body had to be unanimous. As can readily be imagined, a host of problems arose in connection with this type of organization, and as a consequence the Polish political literature of the sixteenth century is probably richer than that of any other country. This fact soon acquired great sociological significance, for when Poland was torn apart by Germany, Austria, and Russia (1772–1794), the Polish state disappeared and yet the Polish national group continued to exist, to develop, and to manifest solidarity in action. Here was a phenomenon in obvious conflict with the traditional view identifying the nation with the state; sociological reflection was stirred and the whole *corpus* of traditional political theory acquired a fundamentally altered significance. The shock of the dismemberment was analogous to the effect of the French Revolution on the thinkers of Western Europe, and if circumstances had been favorable to detached scientific thought, Polish sociology might have outstripped that of other countries by half a century.

As it was, however, sociological reflection was not and could not be disinterested; all efforts were concentrated on the struggle for freedom and self-preservation.

Consequently most writings in what we may call the first period of Polish quasi-sociology, i.e., from the first partition of 1773 to the abortive revolution of 1863, had an eminently practical character. A year after the first partition, for example, a commission of national education was organized at Warsaw, and after ten years of labor brought in a report that may justly be classed as a treatise in educational sociology with a strong national aim. After the complete loss of independence in 1794, this nationalistic tendency asserted itself still more strongly: numerous researches in folklore and ethnography attempting to demonstrate the essential solidarity of the Polish folk, and others directed toward the discovery of the " origins " of the Polish nation, were undertaken. Slightly later (1807) S. Staszic, a Polish " statistician " of the Achenwall type — that is to say, a sociographer — described the socio-economic life of Poland and attempted to draw certain economic conclusions from a comparison of the number of inhabitants with the extent of the territory occupied. In addition to the work just mentioned, Staszic wrote an important treatise in social philosophy having less directly national bearings. Also somewhat detached in character was the remarkably erudite book by St. Potocki, in which the influence of Aristotle on the thought of Machiavelli is clearly demonstrated. In 1822, J. Wybicki published an analysis of the social influences back of representative government, and V. Surowiecki wrote on the decadence of industry and village life in Poland. A startlingly modern note is introduced into Polish sociology of this period by J. Śniadecki, for what he termed the "philosophy of human thought, or the analysis of intellectual forces and actions " is really a demonstration of social compulsives in social thought, i.e., a study of one aspect of the sociology of knowledge.

But perhaps Śniadecki's achievement, remarkable though it was, is itself explicable as a reaction against certain social compulsives of his time. At any rate, Mochnacki,[27] Wroński-Hoene,[28] Trentowski, Kremer, Libelt, Cieszkowski,[29] and Królikowski afforded vivid examples of the effect of intense national feeling on social thought. Long before Durkheim, and apparently without any direct influence from Herder or Hegel, they reveled in discourse about the " national soul," the " collective soul," or the " collective consciousness." Nevertheless, whatever one may think of such manifestations of *Geist,* these social philosophers did much to turn the attention of the philosophical guild generally toward things of this earth, with fruitful results in literary criticism by J. Ossolinski and in historical criticism by A. Beilowski. Moreover, psycho-sociology made its bow at about this time; in 1836 M. Wiszniewski brought out a Polish treatise that was later translated into English under the title *Sketches and Characters, or the Natural History of the Human Intellect.* V. Majewski and J. Rzewvski exploited a similar view, but with somewhat more attention to the demands of national feeling.[30]

The Era of Revulsion. — Still, " the whirligig of time brings his revenges "; the nationalistic fervors that were repeatedly raised to the heights by the revolutions of 1794, 1831, 1848, and 1863, only to be plunged into the lowest depths by failure and inexorable suppression, finally brought on a genuine hatred of the Romanticism held responsible. A new generation of bitterly disillusioned Polish youth turned toward the positivism and materialism offered by France and Germany, and this reversal of mood had definite repercussions in the social sciences. Comte, Spencer, Darwin, Buckle, and Bagehot were zealously translated and studied, and under their influence the first school of thought definitely bearing a sociological label made its appearance.

Mirek calls this school "biologistic," but at least two of its members, Winiarski and Heryng, made quite as much use of categories borrowed from the physical sciences as they did of biological conceptions. Indeed, we might devote considerable space to Winiarski as an example of mechanistic analogizing: notions such as inertia, mass, attraction and repulsion, the law of least resistance, equilibrium, and the like are applied to social life (see notes).[31] Heryng used the physical concept of energy as the basis for his variety of analogy, and believed that he could trace transformations such as from friction to heat, from combustion to light, and so on, in man's conduct. To the present writers, at least, explanation of the respectful attention such absurd thinking attracted remains both difficult and fruitless, and we shall not attempt it. J. Potocki may properly be classed among the biologistic writers; he translated Spencer and published a book of his own in which he maintained that society is an organism in the strict sense. B. Limanowski set forth a complete system of biological sociology in his bulky two-volume work, which he began to write before 1870 but did not publish until 1919. Other sociologists who to a certain extent followed this biological blind alley are E. Majewski and Kasimierz Krauz-Kelles.[32]

The Beginnings of "Sociologism." — The only biological lead that proved valuable in Polish sociology was that which issued in social Darwinism of the type represented by Ludwig Gumplowicz, whose theories we have already discussed at length. He is usually classed as an Austrian sociologist, for he taught at the University of Graz and wrote in German almost exclusively. He was born in Austrian Poland, however, and seems to have sympathized with Polish aspirations toward independence.[33] Ironically enough, he is now claimed by the Poles in spite of the fact that the social ostracism under which he suffered at Graz was in large measure the reflection of Polish anti-Semitism, which until very recent times was far more extreme than anything found in the Germanic countries.

Gumplowicz has also been classed among the sociologistic writers,[34] i.e., among those who attempt to explain social phenomena by other social phenomena rather than by reference to physical, biological, or psychological principles. This sociologistic tendency may go so far that the notion of a collective mind is defended. We have encountered this untenable thesis before, *ad nauseam,* and Poland also furnishes flagrant examples. S. Krusiński reacted against the organismic analogy of Spencer in 1886 by expounding the doctrine of collective mind, thus jumping from the frying-pan into the fire,[35] and in 1900 L. Kulczycki stirred together the ideas of Gumplowicz, Fouillée, and Durkheim to produce a " sociological " gruel of his own.[36] Sigismund Balicki has gone to the extreme limit of social realism, far exceeding even that of McDougall in his *Group Mind.* Balicki assumes a collective psyche which possesses all the essential characters of individual consciousness and is capable of being studied by means of the same psychological categories.[37] Less extreme than this, but nevertheless strongly sociologistic, is the work of Jan Kanty Kochanowski, professor of history in the University of Warsaw, who teaches that " society " is a " whole " of a higher order that constrains the individual by means of " social facts " of essentially the same character as those analyzed by Durkheim.[38] Kochanowski's most important work was published in German under the title *Urzeitklänge und Wetterleuchten geschichtlicher Gesetze in den Ereignissen der Gegenwart* (1906); he is also the author of a number of works in Polish in which he " attempts to work out a basis for a comparative and revolutionary psychology of nations on the background of various forms of leadership, social action, and social organization." [39] Still closer to the Durkheim point of view is Stephan Czarnowski, author of a classic treatise on hero worship, *Le Culte des héros et ses conditions sociales: Saint Pat-*

rick, héro national de l'Irlande. His bold generalizations are based upon the most painstaking historical and ethnographical research. He is professor of the history of religion at the Free University of Warsaw.

Ethnography and Sociology. — In spite of the list of names, many of them distinguished, that we have adduced, it must be granted that until recent times sociology has been rather unpopular in academic circles. In Poland, as almost everywhere else, this was due to puerile analogies, premature generalizations, and unwarranted ambition to be the fundamental science of all culture. Before the World War it was only in connection with the firmly-grounded disciplines of ethnography and ethnology that sociology gained recognition in the universities. We have already mentioned Czarnowski in this connection, and we should also name Ludwik Krzywicki, "Nestor of Polish sociology," who, on the basis of voluminous ethnographic data, has sought to sustain the theory of thoroughgoing economic determinism in social life.[40] Another representative of this trend is Jan St. Bystroń, professor of ethnology at the University of Kracow who, as Mirek says, is an ethnographer by profession and a sociologist by predilection. Chief among the Polish ethnographers of sociological bent, however, is Bronislaw Malinowski, professor at the University of London. His numerous and brilliant works, with the exception of his first book, are all in English, but he is a Pole by origin and training. The various monographs on the borderline of ethnology and sociology of which Malinowski is the author — *Argonauts of the Western Pacific, Sex and Repression in Savage Society, Coral Gardens and Their Magic,* and several others — are fascinating, but they are nearly all marred by the attempt to derive sweeping generalization from one-man studies of limited areas.[41] But this fault is characteristic of virtually all field workers; they have great contempt for the comparative method of the old-time "book ethnologists," but when they themselves attempt to generalize, they sometimes do not show as much caution as the forerunners they denounce.

Study of the Psychical Aspects of Social Life. — Psychosociology has distinguished representatives in Poland. One of the first was E. Abramowski, whose rigorously scientific method and precise observations have set an excellent example. Some of his works are available in French, e.g., *Le Matérialisme historique et le principe du phénomène social* (1898). Abramowski was singularly free from dogmatic prepossessions (although, like every scientist, he worked with the aid of definite hypotheses). The book in French noted above provides an instance of this freedom from bias: by simply comparing his own critical analysis of human conduct with vulgar Marxism, he succeeded in demonstrating the mythical character of the latter without once forcing the argument or disputing the social utility of the myth. He was one of the most consistent of psycho-sociologists; for him, as for the Russian subjectivists and the German school of *Verstehen*, a social phenomenon is first of all a psychical phenomenon.[42]

Sigismund Balicki, to whom we have already referred in connection with " sociologism " or social realism, may also be classed as a psycho-sociologist. One of the interesting points in his work is the distinction between crowd psychology and " social psychology." The former deals with the psychical aspects of relations between individuals in the crowd, whereas the latter does not study relations between individuals or between individuals and groups, but studies the group as such in so far as it is an " organic whole." The distinction of course roots in Balicki's social realism.

Diametrically opposed to this is the point of view basic to the work of Leo Petrażycki. This writer has already been dealt with in the chapter on Russian sociology, but as he was born in Poland and taught at the University of Warsaw after the Russian Revolution, he should also be mentioned here. For him social phenomena have no objective reality as they have for Balicki; " they are mere combinations of psychological elements actually occurring in individual consciousness." [43] His fundamental psychological category is emotion, but his definition of this is quite different from that commonly adopted, for he includes in it elements of volition, sentiment, and intellect. (For further details consult pp. 1054–55.) Petrażycki is also of importance in the sociology of economics. In no sense an encyclopedist, drawing a sharp line between the provinces of sociology and economics, he nevertheless is unwearied in demonstrating that economic phenomena are closely linked with social phenomena generally, and that they can be dealt with satisfactorily only with the aid of psycho-sociology. Supinski and Grabski also take this position. The latter is the author of a German work, *Zur Erkenntnislehre der volkswirtschaftlichen Erscheinungen,* in which the explanatory value of psycho-sociology in economics is upheld with almost the tenacity of a Veblen. Other names that may be cited in this connection are those of Milewski, Czerkawski, Karo, Wójczicki, Zimmermann, A. Szymánski, and A. Mytkowicz. The jurists have also come to recognize the sociological, or at least the psycho-sociological, influence in the genesis of norms, and some of them, notably Ehrlich, expound a type of sociological jurisprudence. Ehrlich's chief work has recently been translated into English under the title of *Fundamental Principles of the Sociology of Law,* and may exert some influence in the United States and elsewhere.

Revival of Interest in National Reconstruction: Znaniecki. — In an earlier section we had occasion to say something about the disillusionment apparent after the revolution of 1863, and pointed out that this had much to do with the fervor with which positivism and materialism were embraced. We failed to call attention, however, to the fact that this disillusionment did not long endure. Beginning as early as the 'nineties, a pronounced reaction against the crude biologism of the early positivistic sociologists and against their infantile epistemology became manifest — a reaction of which we have implicitly taken account in our discussion of a number of the ethnographically grounded sociologists and the students of the psychical aspects of social life. A border province of sociology also gave evidence of this anti-positivistic trend and its correlated revival of more or less idealistic nationalism: the whole broad field of " social problems " came under cultivation. Social work, population policy, social hygiene, rural welfare, and the like were tilled, in many instances for the first time. The tools used were frequently primitive; a sort of " hoe-culture " of social problems developed, and the crop of scientifically valuable products was scanty. In a few instances, however, the plowing was deep, the cultivation careful, and the yield bountiful, as Bujak's study of the Polish village bears witness.

But the outstanding instance of a strong interest in national reconstruction which did not vitiate the conclusions achieved is provided by the remarkable monograph which Florian Znaniecki, in collaboration with W. I. Thomas, wrote on *The Polish Peasant in Europe and America* (5 vols., 1918–20; 2 vol. ed. 1927). There has arisen a regrettable tendency to overlook Znaniecki's highly significant part in the production of this monograph, perhaps because it is written in English and the fact that Thomas's name has alphabetical priority and is easier for Americans to pronounce. Judging by the other published works of both men, it seems fairly clear that Znaniecki had at least an equal and perhaps a major share of responsibility for the formulation of the epoch-making " Methodological Note," as well as of many other abstract portions of the work, and it is generally conceded that his intimate knowledge of Polish language and culture must have played a large part in the concrete sections.

The methodological note just referred to is placed at the beginning of the monograph. In it the authors state their conception of the nature of science in general and of social science in particular, and distinguish between social science of the idiographic type on the one hand and the nomothetic on the other. This is the familiar Windelband-Rickert distinction. History, for example, is idiographic, for it describes the unique, the non-recurrent, whereas sociology is nomothetic, for it formulates general laws in which the unique phenomenon is a mere member of a class. With the validity or invalidity of this distinction we are not here concerned; suffice it to say that it pervades the whole treatise. Other matters of importance discussed are the difference between scientific procedure in social control and " ordering-and-forbidding," between sociology and " social psychology," and between attitudes and values. The latter distinction is of great importance in the history of recent sociology, for it has had much to do with the overthrow of instinct psychology and the widespread adoption of the concept of social attitude as a fundamental tool of sociological analysis (partially replaced by " tendency " in Znaniecki's later work). Other important contributions are the notions of temperamental attitude and character attitude, situation and definition of the situation, and life-organization. In other parts of the book occur remarkably penetrating discussions of the scientific status and utilization of the life-history; social disorganization and reorganization; Philistine, Bohemian, and creative personality types; and the rôle of the parish, mutual-aid organizations, and similar bodies in maintaining or rebuilding the solidarity of Polish communities in America. Within present space limits it is impossible to give more than a fragmentary idea of the wealth of fertile suggestions to be found in this work; it is a monograph with universal significance.

In addition to this collaborative product, Znaniecki is the author of four other works in English: *Cultural Reality* (1919), *The Laws of Social Psychology* (1925), *The Method of Sociology* (1934), and *Social Actions* (1936). All of these testify to the extraordinary merits of his thought: the first is one of the ablest philosophical statements of historical relativism or culturalism (*Historismus*) yet produced; the second goes a long way toward making psycho-sociology a cultural science; the third shows, among other things, the unimpeachably scientific character of the life-history technique; and the fourth applies concepts schematically stated in earlier volumes to the problem of social action in so arresting a way that it will soon supersede *The Polish Peasant* as the chief example of Znaniecki's thought. His writings in Polish include a book on the problems of values in philosophy, another on the sociology of education, and an introduction to sociology.[44]

Sociology as an Academic Discipline. — Znaniecki occupies at Poznań one of the three chairs of sociology in Poland; the others are at Warsaw and Cracow. In 1922 an institute of sociological research was organized at Poznań under Znaniecki's leadership. " The working conception of the Institute is that sociology cannot be a general science of culture, but must be a special science, analytic and nomothetic, parallel to and independent of economics, theory of religion, linguistics, etc., and dealing exclusively with those activities of which human individuals and groups are the objects." [45] This admirably clear statement shows that Znaniecki's institute is aligned with the work now being done at Cologne, Columbia, Chicago, and, with some slight differences, at Wisconsin. There seems little doubt that the analytic or systematic trend represented by the departments mentioned is the one that promises most for at least the immediate future, and the Poznań institute therefore has bright prospects before it. Znaniecki has succeeded during the fifteen years of his leadership in gathering about him a number of promising sociologists, most of whom have undertaken monographic studies.[46] It should also be noted that Theodore Abel of the University of Columbia has been much influenced by Znaniecki.

At the University of Warsaw, L. Krzywicki, who has recently published (in English) *Primitive Society and Its Vital Statistics,* is active in the teaching of sociology, and at the Free University in the same city L. Kulczycki and S. Czarnowski represent the new discipline. (It is officially new in Poland, for it was not recognized by the state until 1919.) In the theological faculties of the Universities of Lublin, Lvóv, Wilno, and Warsaw there are chairs of " Christian sociology." [47] These are chiefly devoted to the study of social problems from the point of view of Catholic solidarism, and therefore are more concerned with the application of what are assumed to be sociological principles than with the further extension of the domain of theoretical sociology.

In conclusion, it may be said that Polish sociology, as represented by the schools of Petrażycki and Znaniecki, is on a theoretical level quite as high as that of any other country. The amount of monographic publication is still rather slight, but this is only to be expected in a country having a relatively small number of students. And after all, Znaniecki has exerted tremendous influence in the United States, and will exert much more when his monumental system of sociology, most strikingly represented in his *Social Actions,* becomes generally known.

IV

Political Liberalism and Public Law. — Sociology in Hungary [48] has had a checkered career that is quite unintelligible unless set against the background of the nation's political and economic life. No country in Europe, with the possible exception of some of the Balkan states, manifests so thoroughly a feudal type of structure. The Magyar landed gentry have successfully dominated Hungarian life for many centuries; only the short-lived revolutionary régime established after the War by Bela Kun even temporarily wrested power from them. The fruits of the French Revolution — political democracy, freedom of speech and press, parliamentarism — hung beyond the reach of most of the Hungarian populace. Outside of cities such as Budapest, where the suffrage was limited to about a quarter of the adult male population, there was either no voting of any kind or the simple show of hands which affords the ruling classes such splendid opportunities for ferreting out malcontents.

The consequence of these conditions was that the early Hungarian sociologists — they began to put in their appearance about the middle of the last century — nearly all used their science as a springboard from which to plunge into the seething waters of political strife. The political and economic liberalism they championed was far from radical when judged by the standards of their Western European contemporaries, but in their setting these sociologists were a bloody crimson.

Not only was sociology pulled into the political arena by forces of this kind, but in addition certain other elements in the Hungarian social heritage dragged it before the seat of Caesar. In even greater measure than the Italians, the Hungarians are a nation of jurists. Encamped among ethnically alien peoples, the Magyar landholders whose delegated agent the Hungarian government was could maintain themselves in power only by constant struggle in which law often served as a convenient substitute for the sword. Another reason for the preoccupation with the juristic disciplines so evident in Hungarian public life was the eternally problematic political relationship with the other half of the Dual Monarchy before the World War, and since then the revival of the fifteenth-century regency and the ceaseless to-and-fro of relations with the Succession States and the powers upholding or opposing the Treaties of Trianon and Versailles have certainly not diminished the attention given to public law.

Ethnography and Early Sociology. — With such a background, it goes without saying that not only sociology but its sister disciplines assumed outlines specifically Hungarian. Ethnographical research, for example, has been and still is markedly influenced by the prevalence of customary law. In addition, it has not yet shaken off the influence of the long controversy over the racial origin of the Hungarian people. The Turko-Tartar hypothesis was generally abandoned in the last half of the nineteenth century when Hungarian comparative philology cast its vote in favor of the Finno-Ugric, but the provenance of the Magyar overlords is still far from settled, and the passions evoked by revelations that cast doubt on cherished genealogies do not always respect the person of the scientist responsible. Folklore is also affected by racial and national considerations, and physical anthropology is seldom wholly free from bias or the pressure bias can exert.[49]

The preoccupation with juristic and political matters already noted is evident in the work of Beöthy de Bessenyo (1839–1886), one of the first of Hungarian sociologists.[50] He attempted to solve inductively the problem of social origins and, characteristically enough, set to work with the hypothesis that chieftaincy, well exemplified in the relations of Magyar overlord and semi-serf tenant of nineteenth-century Hungary, was the primal type of social organization, far antedating the patriarchal family. Not only did he demonstrate this, to his own satisfaction at least, but he also arrived at the conclusion that the development of all social institutions is largely although not wholly conditioned by the degree of political organization. But — and here liberalism raises its seditious head — the evolution of society may outstrip that of the chief political organization, i.e., the state, and when this occurs, the latter inevitably deteriorates and is replaced by a form more in harmony with the changed conditions. If only Bessenyo had made use of the alliterative lilt of " cultural lag " !

Also an apostle of liberalism and the doctrine of evolution was the sociological jurist, Agost Pulszky (1846–1901), founder in 1900 of the Hungarian Sociological Society.[51] The marks at which he hoped this organization would aim were the unbiased study of social problems and the gradual reform of the Hungarian social order. An unkind critic might be disposed to say that nobody could aim at both these marks at the same time, but that is neither here nor there. The lively interest in public law and social reform manifested by the Hungarian Sociological Society involved it in political struggle almost from the day of its foundation, a fact which accounts for the complete absence of chairs of sociology in the ultra-conservative universities.[52]

Another liberal democrat of sociological persuasion was Sándor Giesswein (1856–1923). Vámbéry says that he was a forerunner of Paul Barth, the German author of the well-known treatise on the philosophy of history as sociology. Giesswein coined the formula, " History contemplates the flux of things, sociology the achievement." [53] This would seem to bear some resemblance to the Windelband-Rickert contention that history is idiographic and sociology nomothetic (see pp. 759, 1076). Giesswein also might possibly rank as a predecessor of Cooley if we had more information about his theory that atomistic individualism and social realism are equally fallacious because individual and society condition each other and are but different aspects of the same thing. In conjunction with his defense of political liberalism, Giesswein also entered the lists on behalf of pacifism, feminism, and the anti-alcohol movement, thus ranking as a male reincarnation of Teréz Brunswick, the great Hungarian woman reformer of the early nineteenth century.[54] An unswerving opponent of the reaction that followed the post-War revolution, Giesswein died in exile.

The Exiles and Those Who Remain. — Exile has also been the lot of most of the surviving members of the first Hungarian sociological society. Oscar Jászi, author of a book on Austro-Hungarian nationalisms that was painfully disillusioning to many of his compatriots, found refuge in the United States and Czechoslovakia; Rusztem Vámbéry, one of the pioneers in the juvenile court movement in Hungary, had to flee; and Lajos Pikler, who was active in the effort to introduce economics and sociology into the secondary schools, is also out of the country. These and other members were responsible for a respectable amount of good sociological work during the eighteen years that the society was in existence, and higher scientific standards were gradually being attained. Since the forced dissolution of the organization, nothing of importance has been written by Hungarian sociologists (unless one excepts Kármán's studies in juvenile delinquency). The new sociological society that has taken the place of the old has as one of its cardinal requisites for membership the solemn promise to devote all sociological effort to national ends. Such a policy must check much thoroughgoing research. The only exception to

the general stagnation of sociological effort is found in the sociological division of the quarterly sponsored by the Hungarian Ethnographical Society, *Társadalomtudomány* (*Social Science*).
Here too " the vital needs of the Hungarian nation" are placed
uppermost, but the editor apparently nods occasionally and a few
of the contributors seem to yield primary allegiance to science.[55]
The journal was established in 1920.

Among the research institutes supported by the government is
one devoted to sociography, but as its aims are almost all immediately and narrowly practical, little of fundamental scientific
value results. This is also true of the institute of social politics,
which investigates living conditions among factory workers and
like social problems; it might make contributions of major importance, but its obsession with the demands of the day prevents it
from being *genuinely* practical. Only in some branches of public
health and economic statistics has government-supported research
made real progress;[56] it has worthily built upon the work of
József de Szántó Kőrösy,[57] Károly Keleti, and Lajos Láng, the
founders of Hungarian statistics.

V

YUGOSLAVIA

Ground Broken for Sociology: Ethnography. — There is relatively little sociology as such in Yugoslavia,[58] for reasons which
will become apparent as we proceed, but a great deal of preparatory work has been done in the fields of ethnography, human geography, and cultural history.

One of the earliest and most important of the ethnographers
was Baltazar Bogišić, for a time professor at the University of
Odessa, later minister of justice in Montenegro, and toward the
end of his life a private teacher of sociology.[59] He had been
trained in the historical school of law, and was particularly influenced by Puchta, the successor of Savigny at Berlin.[60] During
Bogišić's lifetime (he died in 1908), the southern Slavs in Serbia
and Montenegro were freed from Turkish domination, and gradually made the transition from customary or common law to the
more formal varieties. Familial and tribal relations that had en-
dured for many centuries began to disintegrate, and in so doing
called the attention of the learned world to them for the first
time. Bogišić, heir of the Romantic historical tradition, became
intensely interested in the " tradition-saturated patriarchal world

of the Slavic south," and in 1866–67 published an introduction
to the study of the customary law of the region which evoked the
enthusiastic approval of Henry Sumner Maine. Later he became
editor of an important collection of monographs on the same
theme, and his influence extended to other Slavic peoples, especially to the Poles, Russians, Czechs, and Roumanians. In 1876
one of Bogišić's associates, F. Demelić, attracted the notice of
Western European scholars by his report on *Le Droit coutumier
des Slaves meridionaux d'après les recherches de Bogošić*. As a
result of these and other publications, the forms of the Slavic
family known as the *inokosna* and the *zadruga* were widely studied. The *inokosna* is a type of particularistic marriage-group,
whereas the *zadruga* is a large family-group something like the
Greek *genos,* the family of the East Indian village community, or
the Polish peasant communal family described by Thomas and
Znaniecki. The *zadruga,* because of its relative unfamiliarity and
novelty, excited especially lively interest, and the number of books
and articles dealing with it can be compared only with the number
of those devoted to the Russian *mir*.[61] Students of the community
(in the sense of *Gemeinschaft* or of what we have called the
sacred society) have ready for them an exceedingly valuable mass
of material in these *zadruga* studies, more especially as they are
highly detailed, moot points are settled, and they lack only psycho-
sociological and sociological analysis. But with the exception of
Tihomir Gjorgjević, professor of ethnography at the University of Belgrade,[62] who has learned much from the modern British
functionalists, almost no one has shown any appreciation of the
sociological potentialities offered by the *zadruga*. Margaret
Mead's *The Changing Culture of an Indian Tribe* tries to do
with an American minority group what should be done with many
tribes in Montenegro and Herzegovina. Selection of leaders,
adoption and assimilation, overlapping of settlement areas, tribal
conflicts, increase in the division of labor, and the gradual disintegration of sacred bonds offer abundant opportunity for study,
and the results might be as sociologically relevant, to say the least,
as accounts of the Arunta or the Tlingit.

An Indispensable Substratum: Human Geography. — Another
rich source of sociological data is to be found in Yugoslavian anthropogeography. Jovan Cvijić, head of the geographical institute at the University of Belgrade, has supervised the gathering
and publication of a vast body of material concerning the forms
of settlement, migrations, psychical and cultural differentiation,
and economic life of the Balkan peoples as part of a comprehen-

sive " geographical " survey. In 1918 Cvijić brought out his own synthesis of these data under the title *La Péninsule.balkanique.* This is an indispensable foundation for any sociological study of the Balkan peoples, but it is to be regretted that Cvijić's assistants were not trained in economics and sociology; many vitally important matters are slighted or have received no consideration.

Cvijić's human geography was not only recognized by social scientists throughout Europe, but also became noteworthy in his own land, for he repeatedly made reference to the " floating situation " of the Macedonians. The nationalistic Serbs, who wished to deprive Bulgaria of all claims to Macedonia, bitterly attacked their countryman for intimating that the inhabitants of the latter country could be allotted to Bulgaria quite as justifiably as to Serbia. Cvijić was later proved to be right when Macedonia was divided after the Peace Conference, but his work was seriously hindered by withdrawal of funds, and his academic liberty was curtailed.

We have referred to this only for the purpose of directing notice to the most important reason for the slight amount of Yugoslavian sociology. In a country so feverishly tribal and nationalistic the detached social scientist is almost an anomaly, and when such a *rara avis* does turn up, he runs a real risk of being shot, as was the Croatian historian, Milan Šufflay.

The Help of History. — Šufflay was an outstanding student of marginal areas among the southern Slavic peoples, and in particular revealed a number of unpleasant truths with regard to Albanian and Yugoslavian relations. He made use of ethnological and anthropogeographical methods, and Kosić says that he approached historical problems from the sociological standpoint. Another sociologically oriented historian is Ljudmil Hauptmann, who has specialized in the ethnic backgrounds and migrations of the Slovenes. Processes of association and dissociation among the Serbs and Croats have been analyzed by Racki and Novaković, but their work is too deeply distorted by political biases to be of much sociological use.

Far and away the most important of Yugoslav historians, for our purposes, is Slobodan Jovanović. Thoroughly prepared in constitutional law, economics, and sociology, he has done more to establish genetic or historical sociology in Yugoslavia than all others combined. In his writings he describes in a fascinating manner how the Yugoslav nomad becomes a trader and in later generations advances from thence to a military and diplomatic career, how modern democratic and bureaucratic institutions are plastered on top of patriarchal tribal relations, transforming and being transformed thereby, how the primitive egalitarian democracy of the tribes forces outstanding individuals to the wall or hamstrings them with compromise, and how patriarchal families collapse through internal and external friction when they pass over to a traditionless *bourgeois* status. Jovanović's works will also some day be a rich mine for a typological psycho-sociology of the Serbs during their period of transition from a simple barter economy to urban capitalism, from the communal life of the peasant *zadruga* to urban individualism, from patriarchal despotism and oligarchy to universal suffrage and parliamentary democracy, and from Byzantine religiosity to modern scepticism.

The Impact of Ideologies, and the Fragile Shoots of Sociology. — The first genuine ideological innovations in Yugoslavia came through the introduction of Marxism; the *Communist Manifesto* was translated into Serbian in 1871. At about the same time the forerunners of the Russian Narodnik movement — Chernishevsky, Dobrolubov, and Pissarev (see pp. 1034–35) — gained a following with their internationalistic and individualistic antibourgeois doctrines, but the romantic exaltation of the peasantry which they fostered prevented them from gaining any real power. Svetozar Marković [63] was the outstanding propagandist for this peasant populism, but in spite of his enthusiasm and talent he was unable to attract disciples among the intelligentsia, the majority of whom went over to Marxism. In a relatively short time Marxist doctrine became fashionable, and with the aid of the rising tide of political democracy its advocates floated into professorial and ministerial posts. This did not hinder them from being glowing patriots or even aggressive chauvinists — professors of economics taught the Marxian theory of value and at the same time supported the bourgeoisie in their demands for *laissez faire* and national expansion. Marxism has remained the only consistently propagated social ideology among the Yugoslavs, and as recently as 1924 a compilation of theories lifted from textbooks by Bukharin and Bogdanov was published by Filip Filipović under the title *Evolution of Society.* This dominance of Marxism is in part the result of the stresses produced by the over-rapid industrialization of a backward peasant country, and in part the outcome of the rigidity of the academic system. Sociology has never been taught in any effective way, and those doctrines most highly spiced with value-judgments make a much greater appeal to the populace.

However, a compilation of extracts from Comte's writings was published in Serbian in 1880, and at about the same time Spencer's sociological system became known. Social Darwinism was introduced through an essay entitled *The Social and National Struggle for Existence* (1885) by a former minister of finance, Vladimir Jovanović. During the eighties there also appeared translations of Buckle's *History of Civilization,* Ihering's *Das Zweck im Recht,* Foustel de Coulanges's *La Cité antique,* Bagehot's *Physics and Politics,* and the like. These foreign products were supplemented by several able works on the positivistic philosophy of history by Boza Knežević, all of which appeared in the period from 1898 to 1901.[64]

In addition to nationalism and revolutionary socialism, several other social movements have manifested themselves since the beginning of the twentieth century that have helped to engender an interest in social affairs, if not in scientific sociology. (As previously noted, however, Marxism still provides the answers most satisfactory to the intelligentsia.) Feminism and agrarianism developed some following, and notably swelled the literature dealing with social problems. It was also at the turn of the century that nationalism received fresh nourishment from Gumplowicz's theory of intra-group conflict and Masaryk's so-called " realism " (which his Yugoslav followers transmuted into *Realpolitik*). During the time when these two sociologists became widely known, i.e., from 1900 to the beginning of the World War, LeBon's psycho-sociological works were translated and eagerly read. Kosta Stojanović, an erstwhile professor of mathematics and several times minister of finance, worked out a strictly mechanical theory of social relations along lines similar to those followed by Winiarski, Haret, and Barcelo, but his misguided analogizing fortunately proved unattractive. Zivko Jovanović, a disciple of Loria, was also active at about this time; he later became an ardent Marxian and " gave up his life for the cause." Christian-Socialist theories were propagated by the Catholic clergy of Slovenia and Croatia, and in 1910 Fr. Ušeničnik published a Slovenian handbook of " sociology " of almost nine hundred pages; two years later a smaller Croatian work of the same general type by Fr. Anderlić appeared. These works dealt with social problems from the Catholic point of view as laid down in Thomistic philosophy and the papal encyclicals, and were used in courses in theological seminaries, but otherwise remained virtually unknown.

Sociography and Scientific Sociology. — The Greek Orthodox clergy took little interest in " sociology " of the kind noted above, but more than made up for it by the numerous excellent monographs on the sociography of the village which they wrote or sponsored. Particularly valuable are the monographs dealing with the area known as the *Vojvodina* which, along with the southern Slavic majority, contains minority groups of Germans, Magyars, Roumanians, Slovaks, Ruthenians, and Jews. Not only are there these ethnic divisions, but the Germans, southern Slavs, and Magyars are divided along confessional lines, and many portions of each of the latter two also cling to widely varying tribal allegiances. Students of minority-group relations the world over have much to learn from an area like this, and Mihajlo Avramović has done something to synthesize the monographs dealing with it in his work on peasant economy (1928).[65] Many of the monographs mentioned also contain valuable material on the social biology of various peasant strata. In Bosnia, F. Geremić has made sociographic researches of the same kind, and Dragiša Lapčević and C. Mitrinović have made illuminating sociological and ethnographic studies of the Mohammedans of Herzegovina.

Sociology of a rather modern type is expounded by Mirko M. Kosić, professor at the University of Belgrade. Beginning his sociological career about 1912, Simmel, Hobhouse, Durkheim, Pareto, Oppenheimer, and Wiese have engaged his interest; at present he may be classed as a Neo-Simmelian. In countries without a heavy domestic production of sociological material, translation is always a very important activity, and Kosić has not neglected it, for through his efforts some of the writings of Sombart, Oppenheimer, Tönnies, Vierkandt, Michels, and Lederer were made available to the Yugoslavian public. His own researches fall in three groups: (1) problems of national solidarity and the technique of national conflict; (2) the sociological bases of the falling birth rate; and (3) the rural sociology of the southern Slavs. He has also written on the sociology of the Magyar revolution, the idea of progress in contemporary sociology, and problems of leadership.[66]

Sociological Publications and Academic Posts. — After 1918 interest in sociology became stronger, and Croat translations of LeBon, Sighele, Eisler, and Giddings were published. In the Serbian language, Kjellén's treatise on the state as an organism [67] and portions of Ostrogorsky's volume on democracy were brought out, but interestingly enough, Michel's drastically disillusioning work on the sociology of political parties could find no publisher.[68] Here again we see the influence of the violent internal strife so characteristic of Yugoslavia.

The paucity of sociological translations is of course accountable for in several additional ways. To begin with, the educated Yugoslavs are strongly polyglot: in the case of many German, French, and Italian books translation therefore is not necessary. Second, wide educational differences limit the market for books in the native tongues, for those acquainted only with their own language are frequently illiterate — that is, those who do receive education receive a great deal and can read foreign works; the others get crumbs or nothing at all. Finally, the Yugoslav people, numbering less than twelve millions, is split into two language groups, the Slovenian and the Serbo-Croatian, and the latter in turn makes use of two different alphabets, which are so divergent that one can justifiably speak of a Serbian and a Croatian written language.

The only sociological periodical in Yugoslavia, *Društveni Život*, has not appeared regularly; 1921, 1922, and 1930 have been its only years of publication, although Kosić, the editor, maintains that it is not yet extinct. In Zagreb there has been for many years a sociological society of encyclopedic character, i.e., it includes economics, social politics, social work, social pedagogy, social history, social philosophy, social economy, and what not. It admits everyone who can pay the dues, which is only natural in view of the fact that the group to which it can appeal is at best limited.

As an academic discipline sociology is represented only at the University of Zagreb, where a chair of sociology and criminology has been in existence since 1906. It was occupied until 1928 by Ernest Miler, who adhered to the theories of Spencer, Gumplowicz, and Giddings. Since that time it has been unoccupied, but has not yet been abolished, and now that Alexander's dictatorship is at an end, may be filled in the near future. At the University of Ljubljana, Kosić taught general sociology for some years after the War, but only in conjunction with statistics and economic policy. Both these universities are in the Croatian part of Yugoslavia, where vulgar Marxism has never gained quite the ascendency over those interested in the nomothetic aspects of social life that it has in the Serbian portion. Otherwise even this slight amount of academic sociology would probably be reduced to the vanishing point, for in the Serbian region there are no chairs of sociology or even officially sanctioned courses.

In view of the scanty opportunities for the academic sociologist in Yugoslavia, enterprising younger men emigrate. Radosavljević and Altaraz, for instance, are in New York, and Radaković in Graz (Austria). Others follow the example of Baltasar Bogišić, who in an earlier day chose to teach sociology privately

rather than thwart his interests by officially lecturing on subjects
of no overwhelming importance to him. The time cannot be far
distant, however, when sociology will assume its rightful place.
With opportunities for research in cultural and folk sociology
second to none, the Yugoslavs may eventually make their neighbors look to their laurels.[69]

VI

ROUMANIA

Heraclitus and Vico Revived; Goethe and Hegel Adored. —
The first faint notes of the sociological theme in Roumania [70] are
echoes of far older strains. Peter Depasta, a member of the
eighteenth-century school of Greek philosophy that flourished in
Roumania under the régime of the Phanariots, expounded a
doctrine of recurrent cycles in social development that his bi-
ographer, Scraba, believes to have been derived from Heraclitus
the Obscure, that embittered noble of Ephesus who declared that
cultures wax only to wane, and that " all things pass away, nothing remaineth." [71]

We have also encountered this notion of historical undulation
in the theory of Vico, whose *corsi* and *ricorsi* have left their mark
on so many social thinkers. The conception is not necessarily pessimistic, for in the mind of Goethe, the idea of the cycle was
given an optimistic twist by adding to it the notion of spiral development: every culture necessarily returns to a condition much
like that with which it began, but on a higher level. The same variant of the cyclical theory was adopted by Joan Heliade-Rădulęscu
(1802–1872), one of the leading figures of the Roumanian renascence that set in after the revolution of 1848 and the ensuing
union of Moldavia and Wallachia. He seems to have been
markedly influenced by German thought, for not only do we find
what seems to be traces of Goethe's ideas but also rather strong
evidences of Hegelian formulas. For example, both his historical
and social-political writings are pervaded by the theory that all
being is constituted by the interaction of an active and a passive
principle; to use his own words, it is "the equilibrium between
antitheses." This has a Hegelian ring, and in still closer accord
with the high priest of Prussianism, the equilibrium is not static
but dynamic. World history can be compared to a series of circles
that in their union form a spiral. Every people advances in each
generation, but the advance is not equal, and mankind progresses

under the changing leadership of those peoples which successively climb higher than their fellows. The culminating point of each section of the spiral is a state of equilibrium, so that progress may be regarded as passage from equilibrium to equilibrium. This being the case, the most desirable state of society is "Freedom without anarchy and order without despotism." [72]

We need not stop to criticize this pious wish. Let us see what later generations made out of the theory as a whole. Our best example is provided by Vasile Conta (1846–1882), who in his short lifetime won the distinction of being the first systematic philosopher produced by Roumania. In his formative years, cultural contacts with France and Germany were extraordinarily intense and numerous, and of course the vogue of evolutionism rapidly familiarized the educated world with Spencer and Darwin. Markedly influenced by these English thinkers and by Comte, Büchner,[73] and Moleschott, Conta nevertheless was primarily a follower of Heliade-Rădulescu, as the title of his chief work, *Théorie de l'ondulation universelle,* intimates. Adopting Spencer's cosmic evolutionism in part, he nevertheless vigorously attacked the corollary that dissolution is an integral part of the process. He justified his divergence by pointing to what he believed to be the difference between evolutive and non-evolutive forms, and maintained that world history is an interlinking of the former. This interlinking takes place in such a way that the spiral path already discussed is followed. Conta never worked out a sociological system, but he left a short plan for one bearing the suggestive title, *L'Art de se conduire et de conduire dans la société.* (*The Art of Conducting Oneself in and of Leading Society*). His interest in sociological matters was so great that as minister of education he took the then unprecedented step of proposing chairs for the philosophy of history and sociology in the two universities existing at that time, Jassy and Bucharest.[74]

Conta's proposal came to nothing, and sociology did not win its way until much later. A. D. Xenopol (1847–1920), appointed to a professorship at the University of Jassy a year after the death of Conta, finally took up the study of the relations of the philosophy of history and sociology with great zeal. Some scholars, notably Sorokin, rate Xenopol very highly; he has been classed with Windelband and Rickert as a founder of the logic of the historical sciences.[75] Xenopol restricted sociology to the study of facts of coëxistence and repetition, e.g., to the relations between the family, the church, and like social structures in a given society at a given time and a comparison of these relations with those found elsewhere, and in addition, the recurrence of these and like phenomena at other times and places. History, on the other hand, deals with facts of succession, with " historical series " in their full particularity. A cardinal error of sociology is the confusion of repetition with succession and the consequent attempt to generalize about matters that can be understood only when traced from the particular to the particular. This is not to deny the possibility of sociological laws of development, but these laws necessarily neglect the differences which constitute the essential character of facts of succession, and they therefore are of little or no value in prediction. Whatever one may think of Xenopol's theory (Barth was highly critical), there can be no doubt that had more attention been given to some phases of it he might have performed a signal service to Roumanian sociology by steering it away from premature generalizations and by focusing its attention on phenomena that " repeat themselves " in time and space and are thus more easily subjected to scientific analysis than are facts of succession.[76]

Hegelian speculations may have influenced Xenopol, however, for Mind or *Geist* plays a large part in the evolution of his " historical series," and Conta also may have had a rôle, for these series are arranged in an interlocking hierarchical pattern. The Hegelian turn of thought is evident in another Roumanian philosopher of history, H. Nicolae Jorga, but the fact that he studied under Lamprecht should not be overlooked, for the latter conceived of the historical process as a sequence of psychical tensions and relaxations.[77] Lamprecht of course gave great weight to economic phenomena, and would have spurned any attempt to class him with Hegel, but in many respects their theories of history are quite similar. The chief difference is that Hegel's dialectic is logical whereas Lamprecht's is psychological. But to return to Jorga: he has recently published a four-volume work, *Une Synthèse de l'histoire de l'humanité,* in which " the Idea " is dealt with as the creative principle in historical development.

From the Turn of the Century to the World War. — Such notions, whatever their truth or falsity may be, are of course far beyond the confines usually assigned to scientific sociology. A somewhat less ambitious venture is represented in the work of D. Drăghicescu. This writer may be classed with the bio-social school of which DeRoberty and Izoulet are members. Drăghicescu is a staunch exponent of Neo-positivism, i.e., of the thesis that sociology is directly based on biology, and that psychology is either " subjective sociology " or physiology. He is also of importance for the sociology of knowledge, for in one of his most interesting books, *La Réalité de l'esprit* (1927), he skillfully expounds the thesis that "consciousness is the daughter of the social milieu." Unfortunately, Drăghicescu does not avail himself of the mass of data that the Durkheim school, the American cultural sociologists, and the German exponents of *Wissenssoziologie* could put at his disposal. All that he offers is dexterous argument, which of course is not to be despised, but which ought to be supported by tangible evidence.

Although Drăghicescu's latest work appeared in 1934, he enjoyed a more receptive audience from the beginning of the twentieth century to the War. His recent enthusiasm for "Neo-Augustinism" may account for the wane in interest.[78] This loss of popularity is also evident in the case of G. D. Scraba, author of various interesting studies of the relations of philosophy and sociology and of history and sociology, as well as of several monographs on the history of Roumanian sociology, and of a treatise on general sociology.[79] Others active in this same period were C. A. Popescu (Spulber), V. Madgearu, M. Rakovsky, M. Porsena, C. Dobrogeano Gherea, H. Fundăteanu, T. R. Constant,[80] and Spiru C. Haret. The writer last named we have already mentioned in our discussion of the mechanistic analogy elaborated by Winiarski. Haret was a mathematician, and he wrote a *Mécanique sociale* (1910) in which he developed the concept of "social" space" (also propounded by Descartes, Berkeley, Hobbes, Leibniz, Weigel, Ratzel, Simmel, and Durkheim), and added to it other essentially analogical notions, such as that of "social mass." Like all attempts to subject social phenomena to categories developed in conjunction with sciences other than those dealing with the social world, Haret's ingenious use of mathematics and mechanics proved a mere *tour de force;* he founded no school, and his work crumbled under the impact of criticism.[81]

The New Burst of Energy: Gusti. — Sociology in Roumania after the War is bound up with the work of Dimitri Gusti. Trained in Leipzig and Berlin, he was made professor of sociology and philosophy at the University of Jassy in 1910, and from then until 1918 he worked steadily toward the goal of establishing a great institute of the social sciences under the aegis of sociology. A large number of enthusiastic young scholars looked to him as their leader, and the preliminary association, founded in 1918, manifested such energy that it has taken permanent form and has dominated Roumanian research in the social sciences since 1921, when Gusti was called to a professorship in Bucharest. The

Roumanian Social Institute, as it is now called, has become an integral part of the Roumanian state, enjoying a subvention from the government (although most of its funds come from private sources), and compares favorably with the Solvay Institute of Sociology in Brussels and like bodies.[82] It has branches at Timişoara and at Kishinau.

Gusti's activities have not been confined to the field of organization, however, for he is the author of several important studies in sociology, among them works on the sociology of war, social reform, the sociology of political parties, the relation of sociology to ethics, and many philosophical and pedagogical articles and books. Gusti's conception of sociology is that it is a non-normative, autonomous, general science of social life, coordinating and systematizing the elements common to all the other social sciences. Sociology should not be wholly derivative, however, but should practice direct observation of social life in conformity with its own frame of reference, incorporating the results in monographic studies meeting the most exacting standards of modern methodology.[83]

Guided by this program, the Roumanian Social Institute has sponsored a remarkable series of monographs on the sociology of the Roumanian village. These monographs not only make the fullest possible use of diagrams, photographs in the text, maps, and statistical devices, but are also supplemented by sound films of all the important ceremonials and daily activities of the respective villages.[84] Moreover, these monographs have not been written as if there were no body of systematic social science to provide hypotheses and significant questions, as has been the case with one or two American studies in related fields (*Middletown* is an example). In addition, the Institute has seen to it that important foreign articles and books dealing with methodological questions are made available through translation, and also furthers domestic publication in this and kindred fields.[85]

Other Contemporary Sociologists. — The disciples and collaborators of Gusti are many, and we cannot possibly discuss them all. Those who agree closely need not be dealt with; we shall confine ourselves chiefly to those who differ with him in some measure. One of the most important is P. Andrei, his successor at the University of Jassy, who apparently finds the type of sociology advocated by Gusti somewhat too much inclined toward encyclopedism. Andrei therefore works along analytic-systematic lines, conceiving of society as an *ensemble* of interhuman relations rendered objective and concrete in institutions. Sociology is the study of general types of institutions or of typical forms of human relations which are crystallized in mores, laws, and similar " exteriorized " structures. Here it is plain that the Simmelian school has gained an adherent. Andrei is also interested in the sociology of knowledge, as his book, *Die soziologische Auffassung der Erkenntnis* (1923), bears witness.[86] Somewhat more distant, but still in Gusti's orbit, is Traian Brăileanu, professor of sociology at the University of Cernauti. His conception of sociology is far more encyclopedic than Gusti's. Comte and Spencer dictate a large part of his terminology, and he regards society as an organism, although he opposes Durkheim's " collective mind " and stresses the rôle of the individual, as is clearly shown in his *Ethik und Soziologie: Ein Beitrag zur Lösung des Problems "Individuum und Gesellschaft"* (1926).[87]

The tolerance and catholicity of Gusti is attested by the fact that he is able to attract collaborators who differ with him on many important points. One of these, M. Saint-Zeletin, was before his premature death in 1934 the outstanding academic Marxian of present-day Roumania. Penetrating analyses of the Roumanian bourgeoisie, Neo-liberalism, social history, the psycho-sociology of Periclean Hellenism, and Marxism and agrarianism have come from his pen.[88] In spite of what seems an undue confidence in " the dialectic," there can be no doubt that Zeletin was in the front rank of Roumanian sociology.

Other important sociologists or specialists in other fields who take an interest in sociological problems are: M. Ralea, an adherent of the Durkheim school who has made significant contributions to the sociology of revolution; [89] C. Rădulescu-Motru, author of a number of interesting psycho-sociological writings as well as of several studies of trends in contemporary European culture; [90] Virgile Bărbat (died in 1931), professor at the University of Cluj (Klausenburg), well known for his work on American imperialism; [91] Nicholas Petrescu, sociological opponent of race prejudice and nationalism; [92] J. C. Filitti, chiefly interested in the history of social classes in Moldavia and Wallachia; [93] G. Antipa, specialist in the sociology of class conflict; [94] Petre Trisca, critic of " social mechanics " and student of social problems; [95] and many others.[96]

Periodicals. — The Roumanian Social Institute sponsors the *Archiva peutru ştiinţa şi reforma socială* (*Archives of Social Science and Social Reform*), which is now (1937) in its twentieth year. Inasmuch as Gusti, its founder, conceives of sociology as the synthesis of the special social sciences, the journal necessarily contains a great deal that in countries with more ample publication facilities would be divided among periodicals specializing in social legislation, social work, statistics, human biology, and theoretical sociology. A sample table of contents (eighth year) shows this clearly: Gusti has an article, primarily historical, celebrating the tenth anniversary of the founding of the new Roumanian state; G. L. Duprat writes on the physiology of the mores (*physiologie des mœurs*); Edmund E. Day discusses trends in social science; Leopold von Wiese presents his conception of sociology as a field of teaching and research; Sabin Manuilă deals with the demography of the villages and ethnic minorities of Transylvania; Tudor Vianu traces the rationalist and " historicist " conceptions of culture from Rousseau to Nietzsche; C. Sfintzesco outlines a city plan for Bucharest; N. Vasilesco-Karpen has a study of centralization and decentralization in higher education; P. P. Panitesco writes on the unity of the Roumanian nation; and H. H. Stahl makes a contribution to the solution of the problem of private property in the village of Nerej. This is a list only of the articles long enough to be graced with the title of *études;* there are also numerous shorter notes and documents ranging from a description of an institute for the culture and fermentation of tobacco to a digest of laws concerning public libraries.[97]

At Jassy there is a Sociological and Philosophical Society with a research program of its own. For a time it also possessed an excellent periodical, *Minerva* (which ceased publication in 1930). The Jassy society is very active, and as it has among its members three of the most promising of the younger professors with sociological inclinations — Andrei, Ralea, and Scraba — it may eventually become a real rival of the Roumanian Social Institute at Bucharest.[98] Just before his death in 1931, Virgile Bărbat of the University of Cluj established a *Revista de Sociologie,* but only seven numbers have appeared to date, and it is probably defunct.

The Roumanian Philosophical Society has as its organ the *Revista de Filosofie,* edited by G. Rădulescu-Motru, whose psychosociological interests we have already noted. In addition to the space it devotes to social psychology, the journal also is of service to sociology through the numerous philosophical studies it publishes; in particular, the epistemology and methodology of sociology are frequently examined. The Roumanian economists and historians also have their own technical periodicals, and in them much material of sociological interest is to be found. At Cluj a popular weekly, *Societatea de mâine* (*Society of Tomorrow*), does a good deal to arouse interest in the social studies; this is the definite policy of its editor, H. J. Clopoţel.

In conclusion, we quote the following characterization of contemporary Roumanian sociology by Brăileanu:

A definite school or tendency has not yet taken form. The preliminary stage of zealous construction still endures. The prediction may be ventured, however, that critical selection will soon set in, and the way will thus be cleared for an organic development on the basis of the foundations laid by Conta and Xenopol. In particular, scientific sociological research will be separated from practical social interests. Here many sins are committed, for, in the words of Pareto, much is held to be true that seems to be useful, and much is thought to be useful because it is believed to be true.[99]

VII

GREECE

The Twentieth Century: Social Reform. — Ancient Hellas certainly had no lack of social thinkers, as we have seen, and in the eighteenth century the Greek scholar, Peter Depasta, working in the comparative freedom of Roumania, successfully revived the doctrines of Heraclitus, but modern Greece, which won its freedom from the Turk only in 1830, and thereafter underwent a long and painful reconstruction period, had nothing in the way of significant social thought to show until well into the twentieth century.[100] Moreover, the sociological aspects of such thought were at first so closely bound up with immediately practical considerations and encyclopedic aspirations that sociology was little more than a vague label, a what-have-you like the Yankee peddler's trousers, "large enough for any man, small enough for any boy." For example, the first sociological society in Greece, founded by Alexander Papanastasion in 1909, expended almost all its energy in securing modern labor legislation and in organizing trade unions.[101] This is all very well, but it hardly constitutes sociological investigation. It must be granted, of course, that the rapid transformation which the economic life of Greece was undergoing at that time almost irresistibly forced labor questions on the attention of sociologists, more especially as most of them had been trained in Germany under the *Kathedersozialisten.* The journal of the society, which existed for only a year, printed just two articles that can be brought within the range of theoretical social science : one by Papanastasion on methodological problems of economics,

and the other by Eleutheropoulos on historical materialism *à la*
Marx — this in spite of the fact that the journal was labeled a
review of the juristic and social sciences. The short-lived sociological society was followed some seven years later by a similar
organization, also headed by Papanastasion, that tried to take
in all the "social and political sciences." This still attempts to
function, and although it must be regarded as a failure when
judged by the goal it has set for itself, the society has done something to arouse interest in the social sciences in general. Like its
predecessor, the official organ of the new association lasted only
a year, and an article on nationalism by Papanastasion was its
sole sociological contribution. Since 1926 it has sponsored the
Archives of Economic and Social Science, in which sociological
discussions occasionally appear.[102]

Parallel to the liberal-democratic efforts of these early social
science bodies went another, chiefly identified with the names of
Skleros, Kordatos,[103] and Glinos, all of them representatives, in
varying shades of orthodoxy and heterodoxy, of a Marxian interpretation of history. These writers are distinguished by the
fact that they apply their Marxian conceptions to the solution
of problems more or less peculiar to modern Greece — that is
to say, their historical materialism as actually applied is cast in
terms much less general than is customary among other Marxian
thinkers. It is therefore possible to speak of a Greek school of
Marxian interpretation that differs markedly from those found
elsewhere.

This preoccupation with contemporary phases of national development has not been confined to the Marxists, as witness the
recent analysis of modern Greek social and economic activity by
Danielides[104] and the lectures on the same topic by Kanellopoulos
at the University of Athens. Both these men utilize the most
modern types of sociological methodology, especially those made
available by Max Weber and Werner Sombart.[105]

Academic Sociology. — Like most countries whose national
renascence is not far in the past or is still going on, Greece has
drawn largely on the theories of foreign social thinkers. In addition to translations of Marx, Engels, and the Russian revolutionists, some of the writings of Durkheim, Loria, Ludwig Stein,
Richard, Max Weber, Sombart, and Wiese have found their way
into Greek. Further, there are numerous articles by Greek sociologists on one or another aspect of the works of Alfred Weber,
Kohler, Tönnies, Oppenheimer, Comte, Wiese, Sombart, Freyer,
Durkheim, Max Weber, Loria, and several others.[106]

It must not be assumed, however, that Greek sociological writing has been wholly restricted to translation and exposition of the theories of leading figures in other lands. In addition to the political scientists [107] and students of pedagogy [108] who approach their problems from a sociological standpoint, numerous practitioners of sociology conceived as a science in its own right are to be found. We may name Zissis, interested chiefly in methodology and epistemological presuppositions; Lempessis, sociological analyst of public opinion, economic problems, and the typology of personality; Saounatsos, contributor of a sociological theory of the origin and development of the family; Eleutheropoulos, determined opponent of the doctrine of collective mind and student of social origins; [109] and Kanellopoulos, social philosopher and exponent of a type of analytic sociology strongly resembling recent German varieties.[110] The last two writers in this list are occupants of the two chairs of sociology in Greece. Eleutheropoulos, for by far the greater part of his career a professor at Zürich, has since 1926 been at the University of Salonika; and Kanellopoulos, for several years *Privatdozent* for sociology at the University of Athens, was in 1933 made full professor.

Sociology Embedded in Social Philosophy. — Kanellopoulos is one of the editors of a new (1929–) philosophic and scientific periodical representing the modern Greek approach to German critical idealism of the general types identified with Natorp, Rickert, and other Neo-Kantians.[111] On the epistemological basis thus provided, Kanellopoulos has written numerous articles and books of sociological import, and three of the books can be regarded as largely sociological in character: *Modern Society: a Critique of Its Constitutive Elements* (1932); *History and Progress: an Introduction to Historical Sociology* (1933); and *Man and His Social Antagonisms* (1934). In the first of these volumes Kanellopoulos deals with questions of nationalism, individualism, public opinion, and style, concluding that the modern European-American period of world history, with its emphasis on " individualism," has done more to extinguish genuine individuality than any other period of which we have knowledge, precisely because of the way in which the campaign of extinction has been camouflaged. In the 1934 publication Kanellopoulos analyzes the concepts of class, station or estate (*Stand*), and caste, considers the question of social compulsives in social thought (and in so doing presents a critique of Mannheim's theory), works out a typology of social apostasy (the Bohemian, the renegade, the *déclassé*, and so on), compares modern theories of class struggle with similar doctrines current in Greek antiquity, and finally, deals with " the problems of the asocial world of absolute poverty and crime." [112]

These various topics may seem disconnected, but a unifying principle is to be found in Kanellopoulos's theory of individuality and sociality. Following Simmel, he maintains that there are two main classes of human actions: those which express intelligible meanings because their psychic concomitants can in some sense be evoked in the minds of others, and those which constitute the absolutely individual component of every human being because they necessarily remain unintelligible. In the first class fall all the elements of " civilization " (as defined by Alfred Weber) — for example, economic and political activities; in the second, the elements of " culture " (again in Weber's sense) as instanced by art and religion. On the one hand are the typical and rational webs of meaning which are socially communicable and subject to some measure of prediction and control; on the other are the wholly individual portions of consciousness, which in their outward manifestations show no progress and always express something absolute and ahistorical. Individuality being defined in this way, it therefore follows that "the individual lives alone and apart; the path which he travels is followed by no second wanderer, for his footsteps lead beyond the confines of historical and social space." From this it is easy to see that Kanellopoulos's sociology is integrally united with his epistemology and metaphysics; he is first of all a social philosopher and only secondarily an analytic-empirical sociologist. (This is by no means to decry the value of his social-philosophical work; it is of high quality and vital significance.) [113]

Our survey of sociology in Greece leads to the conclusion that it is still in the formative stage. Influences coming from the world outside have been so powerful that Greek sociology tends to be derivative. Those writers who have to some extent succeeded in asserting their intellectual independence have done work worthy of close study by sociologists everywhere, but they have not yet succeeded in presenting their contributions in such a way that they have won an audience in other countries, perhaps because these contributions are not in forms that can be readily assimilated and utilized.

VIII

TURKEY

From Aristotle to Rousseau. — The development of sociology in Turkey [114] provides still another illustration of the fact that mental and social life are under certain circumstances closely bound together; crises in the body politic have usually been accompanied by sweeping changes in social thought.

The old Ottoman Empire had as its dominant philosophy a Moslemized version of Aristotle, although Fārābi (*c.* 879–950) tried to harmonize this with the theories of Plato, and Hellenistic and Arabic science also played prominent parts. [115] After Fārābi, who was an organismic thinker, interpretations of the classical Greek writers along the lines he laïd down followed one another until the fifteenth century.

Somewhat more direct influence on modern sociology was exercised by the Turkish historians, particularly by those who failed to hold steadily in mind the orthodox Mohammedan conception of continuous divine intervention. Their theory of historical causation was largely drawn from Ibn Khaldūn (see pp. 265–78, 706–708), although some of them unfortunately turned his cyclical theory of the rise and fall of social structures such as the tribe and the dynastic state into full-fledged organicism, with its biological sequence of growth, maturity, and decay.

Slowly, however, the yeast of culture contact leavened the Turkish lump, and as the ever-increasing disorganization of the Ottoman Empire became apparent to thinking men, remedies were eagerly sought. First seized upon was army reform, which eventually brought with it knowledge of the Western physical sciences. Soon it was seen that this was not enough, and demands for political reform, becoming more insistent with each grudging concession by the autocracy, were formulated *à la* Locke, Montesquieu, Voltaire, and Rousseau. Before long constitutional government was openly advocated by outstanding nineteenth-century figures such as Shinasi, Ziya Pasha, and Kemal. These, with many others, were soon forced to seek refuge abroad. [116]

Should East Go West, Stay East, or Both? — The struggle between the Ottoman autocracy and the constitutional liberals led to the gradual crystallization of two main types of social thought: Pan-Islamism and Westernism. (Here we cannot but be struck by the close parallel with the Pan-Slavism and Westernism that emerged in the struggle with the Russian autocracy.)

The conflict between the two ended in the early twentieth century with the defeat of the first, but the Westernizers soon discovered that it was by no means easy to fuse European and Ottoman institutions. In fact, so many difficulties arose that intense interest was taken in studies designed to surmount them: (1) investigations of the foundations of Western civilization; and (2) researches into the genesis and growth of Turkish culture.

Later sociological developments have without exception been guided by one or both of these trends. Among those interested in the West we find Ahmed Riza, an émigré who adopted the positivism of Comte; Prince Sabahaddin, follower of LePlay and advocate of individualism; Riza Tevfik, exponent of Spencerian philosophy; and Abdullah Djevdet, belligerent disciple of LeBon. All these writers advocated the adoption or imitation of Western institutions. Diametrically opposed to them and also to the earlier Pan-Islamic thinkers were those social scientists interested in Turkish culture. They formed a school associated with the politico-cultural movement called Pan-Turanism, which strove for the ascendency of the Turkish nation over the Islamic faith.[117] Leader and most influential exponent of this school was Ziya Gökalp (1875–1924).[118]

First Academic Sociologist: Gökalp. — This vigorous thinker based his sociological system largely upon that of Durkheim, but added so much of his own that the resulting product may almost be termed original with him. Influential enough to have the first chair of sociology in Turkey established for him at the University of Istanbul (1912), nearly all the Turkish sociologists of recent times are his direct or indirect disciples.

In addition to his Durkheimian equipment Gökalp made use of the notions of civilization and culture in a way much like that followed by Alfred Weber, but with markedly nationalistic emphases not found in the work of the German writer. Western civilization, said Gökalp, can be assimilated by the Turks only to the degree in which its original characteristics are suitably changed by incorporating it in a specifically Turkish culture. The slogan he proclaimed was " Turkify, Islamize, and Modernize." In his various writings he attempted to show just what elements should constitute Turkish culture, and on this basis, to exactly what extent elements of the Islamic and the Western civilizations should be incorporated or excluded. His proposals were not of a merely speculative character; he and his assistants collected a rich body of ethnographical and historical materials as foundation for his generalizations. Further, he was more than a mere follower of

Durkheim, for he was well acquainted with the works of Ibn Khaldūn, Darwin, Comte, Spencer, Fouillée, Worms, LeBon, and Tarde, and intelligently utilized their relevant insights.

Consolidation of Victory. — Gökalp died only a year after the establishment of the republican régime in 1923, but he had accomplished so much that sociology has gained wide attention as an academic discipline. The college and normal school programs include it, and numerous textbooks, chiefly along Durkheimian lines, have appeared. (French is still the *lingua franca* of the Levant.) Mehmed Izzet, a leading sociologist, did much, however, to extend the scope of the science beyond the bounds of the Durkheim school, for he drew heavily on Simmel and Max Weber. Unfortunately, he died in 1930.

Forecasts and Hopes. — A short-lived *Journal of Sociology* was established in 1917, and another bearing the same name and containing chiefly methodological articles and translations struggled along from 1927 to 1930. The University of Istanbul has since 1934 issued a quarterly journal of sociology under the title of *Action;* this reflects the social-political and reform interests of Gerhard Kessler, a German sociologist who now holds Gökalp's chair of sociology there. Berkes, a Turkish writer, summarizes the characteristics of Turkish sociology as follows:

(1) It has been under the influence of political movements for a long time. . . . (2) The French school of sociology became . . . influential in shaping the scientific outlook of Turkish sociologists. (3) Its chief concern after the World War became endless methodological discussions; and for that reason it did not contribute anything to scientific research worthy of mention, while more interesting research studies have been made rather in other social sciences, such as anthropology, history, economics, and folk lore. . . . (4) The lack of financial support is one of the factors which prevent the development of a research program, the carrying-out of a plan of translations of foreign literature, the publication of journals, and the continuation of the sociological associations.[119]

This seems unduly pessimistic in the light of the remarkable progress Turkish sociology has made since the collapse of the Ottoman Empire. Moreover, even the virtual dictatorship of Mustafa Kemal Ataturk has not yet suppressed free inquiry; a larger measure of hope than some Western countries can entertain appears to be quite permissible.

Work now going on at the universities of Istanbul and Ankara warrants the optimism expressed above. To be sure, the passing of Ataturk did not at once lead to the elimination of the handicaps mentioned, but advances continue to be made. They would be more rapid were it not for the heavy military burden that the Turks feel compelled to carry.

CHAPTER XXVIII

Sociology in the Iberian Peninsula and Latin America

I

SPAIN [1] AND PORTUGAL

T HE BACKGROUND. — The Iberian Peninsula, with its climate and topography ranging from conditions like those of the Russian steppes to the desert plains of Africa, has had a no less varied history. Upon the early inhabitants — the so-called Celts, Iberians, and Celto-Iberians [2] — fell the impact, now crushing, now invigorating, of the Phoenicians,[3] Greeks, Carthaginians, and Romans. With the latter came the Jews, and no sooner had these children of the Diaspora adjusted themselves to their new dwelling-place than they were confronted by the swarming Vandals and the conquering Visigoths. Then up from the south swept the Moors, ignominiously ousting the Visigothic kings and kinglets, and making of Spain a center of learning when the rest of Europe was in the Dark Ages. But in the tenth century the Moslems began to lose ground, and in an ever greater number of the mosques of Spain the host was once more adored. The Crusades came as a welcome alliance with the rest of Europe to Spaniards who had been crusading for centuries, and the fourteenth century saw the virtual end of the Moorish dominion north of the Pillars of Hercules.[4]

Long before this the Christian church had been busy at the task of consolidating its power. The rise of the mendicant orders in the thirteenth century, Franciscans laboring among the poor and Dominicans among the rich, had a far-reaching influence on the life of Spain. Charitable, philanthropic, and learned institutions flourished, and morals took on a somewhat more Christian tinge. At about this same time, the monks of Cluny helped to extend the sway of the papacy over the Spanish church, and the king lost ground in ecclesiastical affairs. Personal immunities of the clergy were extended, the mendicant orders began to acquire wealth, and the stage was set for the future struggles between the priestly and lay politicians.[5]

These did not become serious, however, until the end of the sixteenth century, for the tremendous era of Hispanic expansion released energies and relieved stresses that might otherwise have generated domestic upheavals. The merchant adventurers of Spain and Portugal pushed out to the Canaries, the Azores, Madeira, down the African coast and around the Cape of Good Hope, across the Atlantic, and around the world. The flood of wealth that the daring seamen of Spain and Portugal let loose upon their homelands was ultimately to overwhelm them in disaster, but when the torrent was first rising it bore upward with it the art and learning of the whole peninsula. There were eight universities in the peninsula at the beginning of the sixteenth century; when it ended there were twenty-nine. This century, with its manifold culture contacts and its seemingly inexhaustible wealth (at least for the upper classes), was the high noon of Hispanic greatness; as Costa puts it, " That century of Spanish excellence, in which our nation locked with a golden key the Middle Ages and unlocked the modern." [6]

Vives, Daring Social Worker. — There were many Spanish social thinkers before this time — among others, Isadore of Seville with his theories of the origin of society and the natural state of man — but the sixteenth-century theorists far surpassed their predecessors. Witness the intellectual boldness of the learned Juan Luis Vives (1492–1540), who long before the time of Francis Bacon (1561–1626) declared that the observation of nature rather than the study of Aristotle and the Fathers is the path of knowledge.[7] Also anticipating many phases of the program of Vincent de Paul, Vives outlined, in his book on the relief of the poor, *De subventione pauperum sive de humanis necessitatibus* (1526), a whole system of charity organization and relief work which in its emphasis on constructive prevention of dependency is startlingly modern.[8] Attacking the feudal nobility and the higher clergy for their callous indifference to the needs of the poor, he asserts that the state should control relief work:

> They have no conception of the duty of a government who wish to limit it to the settling of disputes over money or the punishment of criminals. On the contrary, it is much more important for the magistrates to devote their energy to the producing of good citizens than to the punishment and restraint of evil doers. For how much less would there be to punish, if these matters were rightly looked after beforehand.[9]

Still more similar to the precepts of modern relief work are his two general rules of giving:

(1) Nor must we take into consideration what a man would like to have, but what is good for him to have; not what pleases him, but what is expedient for him; . . . (2) let us treat them as experienced physicians treat delirious patients, or wise fathers their young children; let us seek their true good, however much they fight and cry out against it. . . .[10] [Forms of help should consist] primarily in contributions of moral excellence and character. Intelligence, learning, and good sense, are of primary importance. . . . All material help in the way of benefactions is beneficial only as it contributes to the upbuilding of body, mind, morals and character.[11]

Vives's general plan for indoor and outdoor relief can be summarized under the following main heads: (1) registration of all those receiving aid of any kind; (2) visitation and investigation of all institutions; (3) state appointment of superintendents; (4) inspection and control of beggars; (5) special training for the blind, curative care for the mentally ill, and segregation and treatment for those afflicted with contagious diseases; (6) special provision for the education and upbringing of abandoned children and poor boys and girls; (7) the appointment of " censors " or supervisors to inquire into and regulate the life and morals of poor boys, youths, and old men; (8) strict control of public gambling and drinking; (9) punishment adapted to the particular circumstances; (10) the giving of aid to but the withholding of the names of certain classes of " unfortunates," i.e., sufferers by flood, fire, disease, and girls driven to prostitution; and (11) gathering of funds for the work from bishops, abbots, and other rich ecclesiastics, from wealthy hospitals, from state appropriations, and from gifts and loans made by the prosperous.[12]

Public Ownership of Land, and the New History. — These proposals were certainly novel and daring enough for their time to establish Vives's fame as an original social thinker, but still more striking was his radical proposal that all immovable property, particularly land, should be taken away from private owners and redistributed under the control of the state, which should retain title, giving only the use of such property to individuals.[13]

These, however, are all more or less concrete proposals for remedying contemporary situations; in the realm of more abstract social theory Vives was less gifted or less interested. He should, however, be recognized as one of the ancestors of the " new history," for he held that history should not confine itself to the doings of kings and queens and generals in armor, but should include all of the manifestations of social life.[14] Another sixteenth-century writer, Paez de Castro, followed in the footsteps of Vives, declaring that the history of a country should take in the " study of its geography, of the language of its peoples, of the dress, laws, religions, social institutions, general customs, literature, arts, sciences, and even the aspects of [the] nature of the land in so far as these things affect the actions of men." [15]

Vitoria, Internationalist in a Nationalist World. — As might be expected from his interest in the relief of the poor, Vives speaks indirectly of a law of nature, affirming that it is natural to bestow kindness and that this law has cemented all men together, thus expressing an idea which was also hit upon by many other social thinkers, particularly by Berkeley with his theory of moral gravitation, and Adam Smith with his famous doctrine of sympathy.

Another Spanish advocate of theological and legal reform, Francisco de Vitoria, professor in the University of Salamanca, took up a similar strand and wove it into an elaborate doctrine of international relations in his *Reflectiones theologiae* (1557).[16] Discussing natural society and natural communication, Vitoria asserts that nature has established a relationship between all men which, following Aristotle, he says is best exemplified in the bond of friendship. Thus grounded on Aristotelian principles, Vitoria goes on to cite the New Testament in condemnation of the resort to force in settling disputes between nations. With an audacity astonishing for the time of ruthless expansion in which he lived, he declares that neither the desire for the aggrandizement of one's own country nor the glory of princes can justify hostilities. Having taken this unequivocal position, it is not to be wondered at that Vitoria can find no language scathing enough to denounce the killing of children and non-combatants, and the burning of towns and other measures which were regarded as regrettable, perhaps, but unavoidable,[17] by the military leaders of the time. And not of that time only. . . .

The Wars of Religion and the Monarchomachs. — The impassioned denunciations of Vitoria had a bearing not only on the Hispanic conquest of the New World but also upon the religious strife of the Old. For some quarter of a century (1530–1545) the Protestant revolution seemed likely to carry all before it, not only in the Germanic but also in the Latin countries. Faced with the need of desperate measures, however, the menaced church carried through long-needed reforms, and under a series of popes very different from those of the Renaissance, began the work of the Counter-Reformation. In 1534 the Spanish soldier Ignatius de Loyola formed his band of Jesuits to combat the new heresies; at about the same time the Index began to regulate the reading of the faithful; the Inquisition undertook its task of wiping out the unfaithful; and in 1563 the doctrines of Roman Catholicism were recast, the better to furnish missiles against the heretical sects, by the Council of Trent.[18]

These measures proved effective. Before the close of the sixteenth century much of the ground lost by the church was under its rule once more. The victory was not won without terrific struggle, however, and until the middle of the seventeenth century the religious wars went their fanatical way, characterized by a sanguinary ferocity unknown in earlier strife with the infidel. Social thinkers on both sides were busy at the task of forging intellectual weapons. One of the first to be hammered out was the doctrine of resistance to tyrants — a tyrant being any ruler who did not happen to hold with the subject's form of religion. The French Calvinistic writer Duplessis-Mornay, with his *Vindiciae contra tyrannos* (1519), advocated a number of grimly consistent doctrines, as we noted in an earlier chapter, and not the least drastic of these was that kings, who are mere executive agents of the people, may properly be " removed " if they break the governmental compact through tyranny or wickedness. On the Catholic side, the Jesuits administered strong purgatives, and the Spanish writer Juan de Mariana concocted one of the strongest in his *De rege et regis institutione* (1599). This too has been discussed in previous pages; here we need only direct attention to his sanction of assassination of anti-Catholic rulers. It was a social theory with peculiar appeal to devout maniacs, and kings had new need of bodyguards.

Amid the fumes of such intellectual drugs as these it is amazing to find another Jesuit, Francisco Suarez, serenely proclaiming the doctrine of the solidarity of nations, i.e., the necessity of mutual support as the basis of international law. It may be that Suarez's treatise, *De legibus ac deo legislatore* (1613), was designed to convince the Catholic princes of their responsibility for each other's welfare, which is to say the welfare of Holy Church, but it was couched in terms that make it applicable, like Vitoria's earlier work, to any international situation.

Ethnography and Human Geography. — While the Old World was tearing at its own vitals, the New was called upon to aid in the bloody work. Mexico and Peru were drained of gold and silver, thousands of Indian slaves died under the lash in the mines and plantations, and the Spanish Main was hazy with the smoke of burning towns and galleons. But even under such conditions, historians and geographers busied themselves with the life of the natives and the lands they occupied; the works of Diaz del Castillo, DeZarato, Cabeza de Vaca, DeCastellanos, and many other savants provided information that might have been used to establish Spanish ethnography and human geography as sciences far ahead of all competitors in other nations. However, the work of the pioneers was not followed up, and it was left for the scholars of the Latin American republics to emulate their great predecessors.

National Exhaustion and Mercantilism. — The reason for the collapse of Hispanic Europe in these fields is to be found in the material and intellectual isolation, impoverishment, and political decadence that set in after the religious wars and the over-hasty expansion of domain. Even as early as the reigns of Charles V and Philip II, in the sixteenth century, there was a definite tendency toward a mercantile policy, and as the national depression made its full consequences felt in the seventeenth, many mercantilists appeared who clamored for economic reforms, ranging from anti-export laws for raw materials and metals to protective tariffs as a means of encouraging manufactures. The measures taken proved ineffective; the economic-political slump continued, and when the Bourbons superseded the Hapsburgs in 1701, the conviction of the necessity for economic reform passed from the realm of the academic to that of everyday talk. Soon there emerged a thinker who knew how to give persuasive form to the ideas then current; Jeronimo de Uztariz, in his famous *Teorica y practica de comercio y de marina* (1724), presented the most consistent plea for mercantilism that had yet appeared.

But nothing resolute and systematic, whether for good or bad, was undertaken by the decrepit government, and the depression dragged along until the opening years of the reign of Charles III (1759–1788). Charles was an enlightened despot who, though unwise in his foreign policy, was sufficiently liberal in domestic affairs to release the latent energies of the men of industry and science by following Physiocratic teachings. A general national revival got under way, and this was highly significant for the social sciences. University studies were reformed, and philosophy and law were brought somewhat abreast of the times. Economics, however, had no recognized place in the university system, and became an intellectual power only through the interest taken in it outside the halls of learning.

Unfortunately Charles III was succeeded by a ruler equally despotic but not at all enlightened — indeed, it has even been said that Charles IV (1788–1808) was a semi-imbecile. Frightened by the liberal movement to which his father had given rein, and by the spectacle of the French Revolution, Charles permitted the Inquisition to resume some of its power, and the consequence was the proscription of such relatively innocuous works as Adam Smith's *Wealth of Nations*.[19]

Liberalism Wins and Loses a Few Skirmishes. — The fears of Charles were justified: war with France of the Consulate and the Empire brought humiliating defeats, squalid dynastic machinations, and a virtual revolution in which the bourgeoisie gained the upper hand. The privileges of the clergy and the nobility were curtailed, and the Inquisition was effectively suppressed. Dissensions in the ranks of the supporters of the new order of things soon arose, however, and the son of Charles, Ferdinand VII, was restored in 1814. Supported by the nobility, the clergy, and the masses, Ferdinand succeeded in setting aside the middle-class Constitution of 1812. The next twenty-odd years were characterized by confused struggles between the liberals and the adherents of the old order, pretenders to the throne and the ruling dynasty. A liberal general, Espartero, was finally declared regent and held office until 1843, when he was expelled by a coalition of conservatives. His government had nevertheless held office long enough to do what later proved to be a very significant thing: just before its overthrow, a young scholar, Julio Sanz del Rio, was commissioned to go to Germany and study the Krausist movement.[20]

The Gospel According to Krause. — But what was the Krausist movement and who was Krause? Why should the liberal Spanish government commission anyone to study Krausist social thought?

Let us take the last question first. The defeat of Protestantism in Spain had left the Catholic church in almost undisputed control of the sentiment-creating symbols and rituals of Spanish life. The only organized body that dared to contest the sway of the church was the Masonic order, child of the Enlightenment, with its own colorful and impressive ceremonies. Many of the liberal bourgeoisie were Masons, and although direct evidence is lacking, it seems permissible to infer that the first steps toward *Krausismo* in Spain were taken by Masons who were attracted by Krause's reputation as a Masonic philosopher. In later life Krause indiscreetly revealed certain Masonic secrets and was expelled from the order and subjected to a considerable degree of mild persecution, but many of his Masonic disciples apparently dissociated the doctrine from the man, for the Krausist movement flourished. The movement was virtually non-existent during Krause's lifetime, but a few of his students got it under way after his death, and in France and Belgium it attracted much attention during the eighteen-thirties. Among its adherents were Ahrens,[21] Von Mohl,[22] Roeder, Schliephake, Bouchittée, Duprat, Tiberghien, Leonhardi, and Froebel, the founder of the kindergarten, who claimed to have been only less influenced by Krause than by Pestalozzi.[23] In spite of this array of names, the Krausist philosophy is now virtually unknown except in Belgium, where it is dying, and in Spain, where its great days are long past.

"*Spiritual Organicism.*" — Now that we are a little less in the dark about the movement, we can fix our gaze on the man and his teachings. Karl Christian Friederich Krause (1781–1832) was a contemporary of Fichte, Schelling, and Hegel, and during his lifetime was almost wholly obscured by these greater luminaries. In fact, his *general* influence has been so slight that when considering Hegel and other German writers in the chapter on theories of social progress we merely listed Krause's name. His system, although relatively original, bears the stamp of the mystic, exalted German idealism of the time.[24] He worked out a complete theology and metaphysics on the basis of his own alleged intuition, and in conformity therewith constructed an elaborate philosophy of history. The general nature of Krause's system is best described in his own terms as an *allgemeine Biotik,* a universal biotism or life-science. His basic concept is that of organism (of which he seems to have been one of the chief modern exponents) ; as Flint puts it, " With Krause the notion of organism was an *idée fixe,* and he probably sometimes fancied he saw ' organic totality ' and ' organic development ' where they had no existence." [25] Although not so crude as Bluntschli, Lilienfeld, or other crass exponents of organismic analogy — Krause simply used organismic labels — he indulged in many flights of fancy in attempting to show that society is " a spiritual organism."

His array of *Grundselbwesen* or fundamental social organisms is made up of the family, the neighbor-community, the tribe, the people, the association of peoples (here he seems to have the nation in mind), the union of association of peoples (analogous to the League of Nations), earthly mankind, and the grand totality of earthly mankind and mankind on " other worlds than ours." Krause also ascribed qualities of personality to each of these organic entities; he called them " social persons " (*moralische Personen*).[26] This is social anthropomorphism; groupings of all kind are regarded as homologous to human beings. (Had Krause's view prevailed, we should not now speak of " soulless corporations.") Absurd as such doctrine may seem, it must not be forgotten that a number of contemporary sociologists hold that groups are of a "higher order" than the single person; we may name among others Spann, Davy, Gini, Mukerjee, and Takata. This listing of present-day exponents of thoroughgoing "social realism" is of course no proof that Krause was correct, but it at least shows that his point of view is by no means extinct; his Spanish followers can find kindred spirits elsewhere. Moreover, in thus baldly stating some of the basic notions of Krause's social philosophy, we have failed to do justice to the all-pervading ethical note that is characteristic of him. It would be quite impossible to explain the influence he exerted on his Spanish liberal followers if this were passed over. The corroding ideas of class struggle, clashes of interest, and conflict as the lever of progress had not yet tarnished the symbols of nineteenth-century humanitarianism, parliamentary democracy, economic liberalism, and cosmopolitanism, more especially as these were treasures gleaming from afar to Spaniards living amid the wreck of feudalism and the relics of a once all-powerful Church. Flint has thus summarized this aspect of his thought:

> Each individual is called to realise in his own fashion the whole idea of man, — each is an end in himself, — all are essentially equal. The individual, however, can only become his true self, and fully attain to what he is called, through association and intercourse with his fellows. And, on the other hand, the whole society of mankind is to be viewed as one vast individual man, and each smaller society as a lesser individual. The end of these societies is, as collective moral persons, to develop and cultivate all the elements of human nature, and to realise all the aims of human life in an orderly and harmonious manner. The humanity of the universe, and, of course, the humanity of the earth, must become increasingly organized and increasingly conscious of their social unity. All the nations of the earth will ultimately be drawn closely together by association and confederation.[27]

In describing the stages by which this end is achieved, Krause unfolds his philosophy of history, which conforms to the organismic schema of infancy, youth, and maturity. The stage last named is the final one, and Krause thus describes the glorious day when it comes to pass:

> [Men] will not only become conscious of their unity in God and in humanity, but they will practically and outwardly realize it in every sphere of life, — the ethical, the political, the industrial, the aesthetic, the scientific, and the religious. Science and art, religion and morals, law and policy, will all become, when they have reached their maturity, cos-

mopolitan, and will all contribute to bind together, to unify, our earthly race into a city and kingdom of God. And even this will not be the end. . . . The humanity of earth may . . . enter into connection with the humanities of many a planet and sun, and thus bring nearer the day when all humanity will be one; when men not only of all countries, but of all solar systems, will know and love one another, and will work together in union of spirit.[28]

We should be arrogantly rationalistic if we were to allow the fantastic elements in this picture to distort our estimate of the effect its moral fervor had on men of the early nineteenth century. To the Spanish liberals groping for a coherent system that would supply the need for religion, philosophy, and a foundation of science, Krause had a tremendous appeal, more especially as it was quite possible to reconcile his doctrines with the Deism of the Enlightenment which is still powerfully represented in Continental Masonry. Moreover, the emphasis on the " spiritual " character of the bonds between men shielded the followers of Krause from the crudities of organismic speculation such as that perpetrated by naïve biologistic thinkers; as we shall later see, the psychical factors in social life received due attention. It will be recalled that we have distinguished between organismic and organic theories in an earlier chapter. Now, in spite of unguarded phrases, the drift of Krause's doctrine is distinctly organic. In saying this we by no means imply agreement with him, but we do wish to be fair to a man who is all too easily misunderstood.

The Fate of the Disciple and the Successful Apostle. — Sanz del Rio studied the teachings of Krause diligently; although he returned to a Spain torn by conflict between would-be absolutism and a growing passion for parliamentarism, he became a professor at the University of Madrid and succeeded in founding a school of *Krausistas*. In 1868, just before the mutiny which led to the expulsion of the Bourbon queen, Isabella, the aged DelRio had the temerity to translate Krause's *Urbild der Menschheit,* and the horror and indignation it evoked in Catholic circles led to DelRio's discharge. Shortly thereafter the conservative Bourbon system collapsed, and the Constitution of 1869 was enacted. This set up a limited monarchy, and was very liberal indeed for Spain of that period, but DelRio died before he could resume his work.

Fortunately for the cause, he had a devoted follower in Francisco Giner de los Rios (1839–1915), also a professor at the University of Madrid. He helped to make that institution a center of reform through liberal courses and the university organ *Rivista,* but in 1876, when the Bourbons were restored and the liberal constitution of 1869 was cast into the discard, the government sharply limited academic freedom and a great number of recalcitrant professors were expelled. Under the leadership of Giner, these men founded the *Institución Libre de Enszeñanza,* which became the home of the Spanish intellectual revolution (at least as far as the middle classes were concerned).[29]

Giner was the author of works on Schäffle, Spencer, and Wundt which became widely and favorably known, and he left a profound impression upon many of his contemporaries. His sociological doctrines may be summarized under the following heads: (1) society is an organic and persistent unity with psychical as well as physical division of functions; (2) society is not an organism in the crude physiological sense, for this would mean that its chief unifying relations, instead of being psychical (as they are), would be biological; (3) ethical considerations cannot be ignored in sociology, for the essential bonds of human society, being psychical, have inseparable ethical aspects; (4) society is a spontaneous product growing out of the very nature of man, and originates primarily in the sex instinct; (5) law, which provides a large part of the framework of social relations, grows out of custom, which in turn develops out of psychical processes; (6) the struggle for land well suited to agriculture has been one of the most important factors in social development.[30]

Giner's writings plainly show that the sobering influence of positivism eliminated many of the more fanciful and Romantic elements in the Krausist school of thought, but Giner himself never went over wholly to positivism — which, in view of the disregard of psychical factors in social life peculiar to some types of mechanistic and biologistic positivism, was perhaps just as well. Certainly the theories of Antonio Portuondo y Barcelo, a " social mechanist," and of Santa Maria de Paredes, who wrote shortly after biological terminology became fashionable, are examples of what might have happened to Giner.[31] DeParedes, for example, is simply a Lilienfeld on a small scale. (He and the other organismic theorists were promptly and caustically criticized by Gonzalez Serrano in *La Sociologia Cientifica* [1899], and the " social mechanists " have been forever laid to rest by Petre Trișcă in *Prolégomènes à une mécanique sociale* [1922].)

The Krausist Reformers. — Giner's capacities as a teacher were of a high order. Posada, writing in 1902, says that " threefourths of the interest of Spanish youth in matters sociological is due to the teaching of Giner."[32] His influence on his colleagues was also great. Among those trained or inspired by him may be mentioned a president of the *Instituto de Reforma Sociales,* Azcárate, and the criminologists Dorado Montero and DeQuiros.

Gumersindo de Azcárate (1840–1917) did not write any systematic treatise on sociology, but he gave it a large place in his lectures on comparative law at the University of Madrid, acknowledging his debt to Giner, Krause, Schelling, Savigny, Spencer, and Mackenzie. He conceived of sociology as a positive philosophy of history, regarded society as an organic structure, and, more influenced by biology than Giner, granted a large place to the biological factor in social causation. At the same time, he retained his allegiance to *Krausismo,* declaring that " the laws of evolution of society," the study of which he understood to be the peculiar task of sociology, cannot resemble the laws of physics, since they govern a " spiritual organism." Azcárate was a professorial socialist like Brentano, Wagner, and Schmoller, and was so highly esteemed by all classes of society that he had great success as an arbitrator in industrial disputes.[33]

Pedro Dorado Montero (1861–1919), one of Giner's pupils, was also greatly influenced by Karl Roeder, a Heidelberg professor of jurisprudence who was an enthusiastic follower of Krause. Roeder's works in criminology and penology were translated by Giner and Giron at the request of the liberal Spanish régime of 1873. Dorado Montero also studied in Italy for a time, probably at the suggestion of Giner, who was greatly impressed by the ethical and social aspects of the work of the Italian school of criminal anthropology, particularly the radical environmentalist wing led by Enrico Ferri. As a result of this varied experience, Dorado Montero inaugurated a new era in Spanish penal science. Following the Krausist lead, he put great stress on the ethical standards of society as incentives to or deterrents of crime, and by the same token insisted that society at large bears a heavy responsibility for criminal behavior. Nevertheless, Dorado Montero did not overlook the individual criminal, and strongly advocated psychological study and examination, particularly with a view to determining the relation between mental instability and crime. He was also a vigorous propagandist for negative eugenics, thereby incurring the displeasure of the church.[34]

Bernaldo de Quiros (1873–) is a follower of Dorado Montero, and is well known for his treatise on criminological theories; it is an excellent and concise survey and critique of all the European writers on criminal science from Beccaria onward.[35] He is an advocate of corrective principles in penology, the indeterminate sentence, abolition of capital punishment, special treatment for juvenile delinquents, and the occupational training of penal inmates. He also is a convinced eugenist, emphasizing the importance of positive and negative eugenics as crime preventives. Here again Italian and German currents of thought are clearly traceable. The profound conviction that " we are all members one of another " derives from the Krausist emphasis on the organic nature of society. The equally positive belief that criminals are products of bad heredity and/or environment, not of willful perversity, is distinctly due to the Italian positive school of criminology. Another Spanish criminologist strongly influenced by the Italians was Rafael Salillas (1855–1923), for a long time head of the government school for prison personnel, *Escuela de Criminologia*. Salillas attributed some importance to the general social situation in the causation of crime, but was primarily interested in its genetic aspects, as his treatise, *El delincuente español* (1896–98) clearly shows. He was not particularly influenced by *Krausismo,* but was a thoroughgoing positivist.[36]

Stress on the Psychical Phases of Social Life. — A pupil of Azcárate, Adolfo Posada, is an excellent example of a far from objectionable tendency in Krausist thought, namely, the emphasis on psychical phases of social life to which a conception of " spiritual organism " easily leads. Posada was greatly influenced by a number of positivist thinkers, but the significant thing is that he selects from the writings of these men — Spencer, Ward, Tarde, Giddings, Ratzenhofer, Durkheim, Baldwin, Cooley, and others — those elements most thoroughly in harmony with the third-generation Krausist thought he represents. His leaning toward psychology is clearly manifest in his definition: " Sociology, a complex science, has many roots in other sciences, and one of the most important of these is psychology." [37] Again, he writes: " The whole schema of human society may be summed up in the biological-psychological conception of Spencer, in the imitation theory of Tarde, in the personal achievement theory of Ward, and in the consciousness of kind theory of Giddings." [38] Once more: " The social forces in the individual are psychic; these forces are altogether human, and as such we must consider them. These psychic forces should not be confused with physical or mechanical forces; they are consciousness, will, volition and intention. Sociological method concentrates its attention on that which is peculiar to society." [39] Finally, Posada enumerates the following postulates of scientific sociology as he conceives it: (1) " The social reality — that we live in society. That we are society."

(2) "That we were born into society — that we are social by nature." (3) "That society cannot be considered apart from the individual nor the individual apart from society." [40] Let it be noted that his last postulate is the same as the conclusion at which Cooley arrived (or the presupposition with which he started), namely, that society is an organic structure built of social personalities organically bound up with society.

Posada is the author of several useful treatises, among them a comprehensive survey of the literature and problems of sociology and a presentation of the systems of various modern sociologists. These have done much to carry Spanish sociology beyond the confines of Krausist speculation. At the same time, Posada himself, while utilizing suggestions gleaned from many contemporary writers, remains fundamentally Krausist in his initial assumptions and value-judgments.

Organic Theory Challenged in Its Own Stronghold. — The next writer with whom we shall deal is a rather equivocal figure. Sales y Ferre is termed by Posada " an independent disciple of Sanz del Rio," [41] who, it will be recalled, imported the doctrines of Krause into Spain. Posada goes on to say of Sales : " His philosophical ideas are entirely within the Krausista current." [42] This may be true, but it is none the less difficult to perceive, for the influence of positivism in its *anti*-organismic aspects is strikingly prominent in Sales's work. Indeed, he not only says that the study of animal society is a necessary part of sociology — a position which Krause expressly rejected — but he also attacks the *organismic* theories of his time in so sweeping a fashion that the *organic* notions of the Krausists do not escape unscathed. Witness the following :

Between the physical organism and society there does exist a general likeness ; both are systems of coördinated activities, and subordinated to a common direction, but only in this respect are they alike. . . . The organismic element is the cell ; the social element is the individual. The cell possesses only the rudiments of consciousness and mobility ; the individual has intelligence and will. The bond between the first is predominantly physical ; that between the second is largely psychic. The cells are united the one to the other in order to form the organism, they lose their individuality ; the individuals are related in order to form a society ; they not only conserve but augment their individuality. The cells are unconscious slaves of the organism ; the second (individuals) react against their likenesses, changing their position within society and repeatedly migrating from one society to another. The cells perform their functions where their organs place them ; the individuals work voluntarily, they conceive ends and carry out plans in order to achieve these ends. The cell performs only one function, that of the organ to which it forms a part, the individuals may perform several functions, successive and simultaneous. *These differences between the two transcend the respective likenesses.* In the organism unity rules and dominates; in the society the parts are dispossessed, the individuals only being active, causing all of the changes and progress, a unity of agreement of thought and will following. The organism lives subject to its immediate surroundings, it is a wheel of an immense natural machine moved by the cosmic force; society operates against the medium, the individual transforming it, changing the natural strength of an enemy into its faithful servant. The unfolding of the cell is limited and unfailing; the unfolding of the individual is indefinite and uncertain. We are able to tell precisely what form a given organism will take; we are not able to predict definitely what course society will take, nor what will become of a particular society, for who after fourteen centuries of national development is capable of predicting what the actual conditions of European nations will be tomorrow? Physical heredity is transmitted by the act of generation; social heredity by education, by the adaptation of the organism to the means, the means to social ends: coöperation, mutual aid, and pity. The organism is composed of organs which exercise spontaneous functions unconsciously; society consists of institutions which realize certain ends intentionally and reflexively.[43]

This is one of the most cogent criticisms, not only of the crude organismic conceptions of the biologizers, but also of the more rarefied theories of the "spiritual organicists," to be found anywhere. We are therefore inclined to think Sales was a Krausist in name only.

Of course, the emphasis on the psychical aspects of behavior characteristic of Sales is probably due to Krausist influence, just as in the case of Posada, but that is the most one can say. His psychological theories derive from a number of sources: Aristotle, Vitoria, Vives, Suarez, Mariana, Adam Smith, Tarde, Giddings, Kropotkin, and Durkheim. There is nothing particularly novel in the use he makes of them, and we shall merely say that they are applied in accordance with postulates much like those of Posada.

Sales also attributes considerable influence to topography and climate, but true to his conviction that psychical factors must never be disregarded, he usually asserts that such influences are seldom direct. His theories of social development were largely borrowed from the nineteenth-century evolutionists, and his conceptions of social organization were based on Giddings's distinction between component and constituent societies.[44]

Sociology and History. — One of Sales's less obviously derivative contributions is his discussion of the relation between history
and sociology:

With history we touch the domains of sociology; both study social
actions, but from distinct viewpoints. We discern three aspects in the
social actions: (1) the general or psychic; (2) the temporal; (3) the
individual. The psychic aspect corresponds to psychology, common to
both history and sociology; the individual who comprehends the actions
is the subject of history; the temporal, which is made up of likenesses
and unlikenesses, the object of sociology. . . . History studies peoples
one after another, each locality, period after period, action after action.
Sociology, on the contrary, takes a broader view; it studies the genesis,
elements, bonds, forces, structure and organisation of societies; it classifies them into types, and follows the evolution of each one of these, fixing
their laws and their causes, and with all the past in view attempts to
formulate laws for the present and future. The relation of history to
sociology is exactly equal to that of natural history to biology. History is
concrete science; sociology abstract science. It is clear that, since their
fields are closely related, these two sciences grow out of similar conditions. History is the purveyor of sociology; it supplies material for the
sociologist; and at times, sociology assists history, giving light and direction for a more accurate interpretation of social acts.[45]

This is an admirably clear statement of the positivist view of
history, but like so many people who point out the road to be
followed, Sales neither did actual historical research himself nor
made any considerable use of historical data. Perez y Pujol, professor at the University of Valencia, was for a long time the
outstanding representative of the sociological approach to history
in Spain. In addition to his works on the relation of sociology and
law, Perez y Pujol wrote a monumental treatise on the social institutions of Gothic Spain, in which he splendidly exemplified his
own theories of the relation of sociology and history.[46] His own
statement of this relation is as follows:

Each generation seeks in the tradition of the past the antecedents
which the necessities of the present demand. For us the critical and sympathetic character for the nineteenth century has demanded a new examination of all human institutions, and the relation between them. Out
of this movement has developed the science of sociology, which has come
to require of history a greater amount of knowledge than it has hitherto
exacted.[47]

War and Reform. — Partly as a result of the determined efforts of sociologists and other social scientists, and partly because
of the rebirth the Spanish nation underwent after the humiliation
of defeat by the United States in 1898, the opening of the twenti-

eth century saw much critical self-appraisal and unprecedented activity in social reform. Before this time there had been a few more or less successful efforts to eliminate some of the more brutal features of the penal code, notably those associated with the names of Manuel, reign of Charles III; Giutierrez, reign of Charles IV; Salas, reign of Ferdinand VII; and the great Spanish feminist, Dona Concepción Arenal, Inspector General of Prisons during the last four years of the reign of Isabella II (1864–68).[48] None of these reforms, however, not excepting those sponsored by Arenal, with her curious blend of eighteenth-century rationalism and nineteenth-century humanitarianism, brought Spain within hailing distance of the rest of Europe. Mechanical measures or ordering-and-forbidding held sway in spite of the zeal of a few leaders, and no one seemed to think that actual investigation as a preliminary to the development of reform measures was necessary. Moreover, there was very little determined effort to train minor penal and welfare officials, etc., for their tasks; common sense was thought sufficient, with good will as a desirable but dispensable ingredient. As noted, however, the early 1900's brought sweeping changes. In 1903 an institute for the investigation of social problems was established by the government, and on its board were placed not only Christian Democrats (analagous to the erstwhile Catholic Centrists of Germany), but also professorial socialists, notably the sociologists Azcárate and Posada. This institute later turned into a school of the social sciences designed for especially qualified workers, employers, and members of the bureaucracy. The Spanish elementary school system was also reorganized, and a great number of correctional and penal reforms were adopted. Academies of the social sciences sprang up, and the populace at large began to take a new interest in public affairs.

University Stodginess. — But as frequently happens, the universities took little active part in developing the new social discipline, and even before the civil strife which began in 1936 were doing next to nothing. The faculties of philosophy and law remained supreme, as in Italy, with the consequence that only one chair of sociology and another of social politics were established (at the University of Madrid). A new chair of municipal law was also set up, occupied from the beginning by the sociologist Posada. Here again we have the situation exemplified by the proverb, "They won't eat the devil, but they drink his broth."

To be sure, one must grant that the failure of the universities to adapt themselves to change may be due to the fact that change has been coming rather rapidly in Spain. Even before the World War the soothing see-saw of Conservatives down, Liberals up, and *vice versa,* began to be disturbed by the industrialization of the country. Syndicalism, anarchism, and socialism of various shades caused much concern to respectable citizens. After the War, the Morocco muddle, the Rivera dictatorship, the 1932 revolution, the aftermath represented by the 1934 reaction, and the present Fascist-Loyalist struggle have made Spanish life even more kaleidoscopic.

Dearth of Recent Spanish Sociology. — Very little of funda-mental importance in Spanish sociology has been written since 1910; again as in Italy, the reaction against positivism has damp-ened enthusiasm. A literary philosopher, José Ortega y Gasset, has produced a book on " the revolt of the masses " which is a mixture of LeBon, Pareto, Spengler, and his own excellent rhet-oric,[49] but for the discriminating sociologist such left-overs, even when plentifully spiced, are not appetizing. A posthumous work by Dorado Montero, *Naturaleza y Función del Derecho,* ap-peared in 1927, but it offers only a minor variation on the old Krausist theme; for Dorado Montero the state is " an organism essential to progress." [50] Nothing startlingly new in that.

Sociology in Portugal. — When the University of Coimbra was reorganized in 1902, a chair of sociology was established, but in general the Portuguese universities have treated sociology as an unwelcome foundling. Moreover, although it might have been supposed that the overthrow of the monarchy would favor ad-vances in the social sciences, nothing of importance has appeared since the revolution — in spite of the fact that Portugal has had outstanding sociologists. One of them, J. P. Oliveira, is the author of a work on Iberian civilization ranking even higher than Perez y Pujol's study of the social institutions of Gothic Spain; it is a splendid example of the cross-fertilization of sociology and his-tory. Oliveira also executed treatises of fundamental importance on the subjects of primitive institutions and comparative religion. He wrote in the late nineteenth century; unfortunately, since that time there has been no one to follow him even from afar.[51]

II

LATIN AMERICA

Following the example of Bernard, who says that the twenty Latin-American Republics are quite similar in the general culture pattern affecting the social disciplines,[52] we shall not deal with the various countries separately except when making occasional reference to deviations of special significance.

Ethnography and Human Geography. — The exploits of the Spanish and Portuguese conquerors in Latin America were appallingly destructive of the lives and the advanced material culture of the Indians, and the early priests and missionaries who followed in the wake of the brutal soldiery were in their own way perpetrators of irreparable damage to the higher values of their wards. Manuscripts were burned with holy glee, and the fairly well-developed literatures of Mexico and Peru were almost entirely wiped out. A few hardy spirits in succeeding generations did something to circumvent the priestly ban and recover what they could of the lore of the past, but most of it had vanished.

It is therefore impossible to say anything about the social thought of the time before the conquest. We have already referred to the histories written in old age by the more garrulous or curious survivors of the invading Spanish host; these contained a considerable amount of ethnographic and geographical material interspersed with highly-colored accounts of the glorious adventure.

Later on more formal treatises began to appear, most of them written by the clergy, and giving a good deal of space to the "curious customes of ye heathen," the zealous efforts of the priests to effect their conversion, and the more outstanding occurrences of the profane world. As Bernard remarks, these narratives do not differ markedly from those written during our own colonial period. It should be noted, however, that the Latin-American works usually devote more attention to both physical and human geography, for to newcomers in those semi-tropical and torrid latitudes nature presents an unfamiliar aspect, is exceedingly difficult to master, and strongly influences human behavior and institutions. Equador, Peru, Chile, and Cuba were all represented by writers of such embryonic ethnology and human geography.[53]

Public Law and Political and Social Philosophy. — The law of nature and of nations, well exemplified by the doctrines of Grotius and Pufendorf, and at bottom consisting of public law and political and social philosophy, began to emerge very early in Latin America. Its beginnings can be found in the works of the "apostle to the Indians," Bartolomé de las Casas (1474–1566), who wrote to show that his charges were not untutored savages before the Spanish conquest but had a well-developed civilization of their own. The reason for LasCasas's eagerness to prove this point lay in current theories of the law of nature, according to which savages might be deprived of all moral and civil rights but civilized peoples were to be handled a little more considerately. This attempt to make a radical application of the fruits of scholarly contemplation inspired virtually no sixteenth-century followers, however, and with the decline in Spanish learning its Latin-American imitators also became exceedingly conservative. The University of Salamanca, which trained most of the emissaries to Latin America, virtually gave up the teaching of public law, and in the private field ceased to teach Spanish law, limiting itself to the Roman and canon varieties; this example was of course widely imitated in the colonies. The clergy were among the most active in the reaction, and later also attempted to block the new ideas which began to appear about the middle of the eighteenth century. But under the more liberal reign of Charles III (1759–1788), the works of the contemporary European natural-law theorists began to be known, and Physiocratic ideas also took root. The Jesuits were expelled from both Spain and the colonies, and as less aggressive religious orders came in and enlightened viceroys took the helm, some of the old universities expanded their curricula by adding the law of nature and of nations — which, as we have already said, was really in the realm of political and social philosophy and public law — and also taught all three forms of private law (Roman, canon, and Spanish). To quote Bernard again: " It was the same sort of intellectual and university movement that was being developed at the same time and somewhat earlier, on a larger scale, in English North America by Franklin, Washington, Jefferson, and others.[54]

Revolutions and Counter-Revolutions. — The consequences of these " dangerous thoughts " were not long in appearing, for the University of Charcas in Bolivia and some of the northern universities, particularly in Venezuela, developed into underground headquarters for revolutionary movements. After many premonitory rumblings the upheaval came at both ends of the continent early in the nineteenth century; the favorable opportunity provided by the Napoleonic conquest of Spain was quickly seized. The Latin-American revolutionary leaders were all men of ability, and they had the experience of the French and American revolutions to guide them, but it took them much longer to consolidate their victories. The long dominance of the church and the large landholders, together with the racial and cultural differences between rulers and ruled, made it difficult to carry the revolutions below a very superficial level. Intelligent self-government is difficult enough under the best of circumstances; it is virtually impossible even now in those parts of Latin America most heavily burdened by the dead weight of the past.

After a short period of relatively liberal teaching in the first quarter of the nineteenth century, at which time the social sciences as such entered the Latin-American universities, the inevitable counter-revolutions got under way. Liberal leaders were pushed aside, exiled, or executed, and until well past the second quarter of the century tyrannical governments held sway which united the vicious features of the old Spanish régime with the brutalities of a disorganized New World. During this time the universities lost almost every vestige of the intellectual *élan* that had begun to appear before and during the revolutionary period, and some of them were actually abolished. Eventually, however, they began to win back their old position, particularly when constitutional régimes were reëstablished after the middle of the nineteenth century.

The Lawyers Succeed the Priests. — It is these régimes which in part account for a situation affecting both the teaching and content of Latin-American sociology, which is strikingly different from that found in most other countries (although Italy and Spain offer some analogies). This situation inheres in the close connection of the practice of law, government service, and the teaching of the social sciences. As we noted when discussing Italian sociology, parliamentarism nourishes lawyers, and nowhere has this been more clearly demonstrated than in Latin America. The practice of law was not popular before the middle of the eighteenth century, but under the liberal régime of Charles III and after the revolutions it became the leading profession. Moreover, the intensity of the struggle for self-government throughout all the first half of the nineteenth century and the ensuing constitution-making period engendered an interest in public rather than private law. Not only specific legal rules but also the philosophy of law and government held attention, and of course the persisting influence of natural law and canon law, as well as the practice of deduction from general principles inherent in Roman law, operated to favor the systematic and generalizing type of legal thought.

Now the consequence of this was that until very recently, and in most cases even now, Latin Americans do not make any marked distinction between their law and more abstract social sciences such as sociology, political science, economics (in the sense of political economy rather than business economics), and criminology and penology. For all of them they use the same generic term, *derecho,* simply adding an adjective to indicate the special field. *Derecho* is best translated as " right " or " justice," and is primarily ethical in significance. For the more narrow and formal rules of action and procedure, into which ethical considerations do not directly enter, the term *ley* is used. Thus sociology has its roots primarily in the old *derecho natural,* political science and government remain bound up with *derecho publico* and *derecho politico,* and criminology and penology are inseparable from *derecho criminal.*

This close connection with the law is strengthened by the fact that the lawyers have been the beneficiaries of the clerical tradition in teaching. In colonial times the more able priest in the larger centers taught a course or two along with his more strictly ecclesiastical duties; in modern times until quite recently, and even at present in some centers, the lawyer teaches one or more courses in the social sciences as incidental to his private practice or his government position. Although this has prevented specialization, it has also prevented the growth of the hard-shell academic mind. Law remains in close touch with life, and the teaching of law in its most general aspects necessitates a firmer grasp of basic philosophical and legal principles than is necessary in routine practice.

Sociological Jurisprudence. — Perhaps due in part to these circumstances, and certainly in large measure as a result of the positivist spirit spread by the writings of Taine, Spencer, and Buckle, Latin America developed a sociological emphasis in law which anticipated many phases of the similar movement in the United States a quarter-century later. The cordial reception which many cultured Latin Americans gave to positivism derived from the newness of their own culture, the relatively direct response which they found it necessary to make to their physical environment, and the opposition of the traditional church which developed during the struggle for independence (when the ecclesiastics either sided with Spain or rejected republican principles). Sociological enthusiasm was so marked that Huneeus Zegers, writing in 1889, declared that " modern positivistic science has delivered the study of legislation and law over to the study of sociology." [55] This was said with reference to Chile, where positivism found soil already prepared by the widespread study of Bentham and James Mill, but the other Latin-American countries also developed a sociological approach to jurisprudence, primarily through the subject called the philosophy of law. This has been taught in all universities for over half a century as an introduction to the study of law and legislation. At present Neo-Kantian and Neo-Hegelian tendencies, although not so strong as in Italy, are nevertheless strong enough to put sociology on the defensive, but the philosophy of law still retains many sociological implications.

The Emergence of Sociology. — The development of sociology in Latin America can now be made a bit more clear. The old courses in natural law began to be transformed into the philosophy of law early in the 'eighties of the last century. Soon the wide scope of the latter topic made subdivisions necessary, and by the 'nineties the philosophy of law split into two general types of course: on the one hand, institutional history and general jurisprudence, and on the other, sociology and anthropology. The first specific use of the term sociology appears to have been that applied to one section of a course in the philosophy of law given by Antonio Dellepiane at the University of Buenos Aires about 1895, and approximately five years later this was followed by a whole course entitled sociology, taught at the same institution by Ernesto Quesada.

Sociological Impetus from History and Geography. — Merely because the philosophy of law was godfather at the christening of academic sociology, however, it should not be assumed that other branches of knowledge played no part in its development. The philosophy of history, if at all positivistic, necessarily carries a heavy sociological content. Most of the historical writing of nineteenth-century Latin America has as its central concern the emergence of nationality in one or another of its aspects, and in treating this theme mere fact as fact is wholly subordinated to interpretation, much of it of a type that makes the line between history and sociology very difficult to draw. In addition to history as such, studies of history in the making, i.e., of special social problems, were largely freighted with sociological ideas. As Sarmiento said in 1845, the nations of Latin America were perpetually compelled to struggle for civilization against barbarism, and in works on popular education, war, economic reorganization, racial amalgamation, morals, and so on, there were persistent efforts at the interpretation of Latin-American history in the making that, viewed in *ensemble,* form a sort of local sociology, pervaded by the ideas of Taine, Spencer, Tarde, and LeBon. Finally, the continuing interest in social and political geography produced many treatises which can be regarded as at least contributory to the growth of Latin-American sociology, a point to which we shall later refer when discussing the sociology of Venturino.

The Waning of Positivism in the Twentieth Century. — During the twentieth century a number of changes have taken place that have markedly altered the nineteenth-century picture. One of the most important of these we have already noted, namely, the shift of the philosophy of law from a primarily positivistic and sociological standpoint to Neo-Hegelian and Neo-Kantian presuppositions. This is largely because of the uncritical way in which earlier sociological thinkers identified the advance of positive science with progress; the disillusionment created by the World War concerning the power of science for good has brought with it a type of legal philosophy that has very little in common with sociology. Another shift is away from the practice of broad deduction from general principles to case law, primarily as a result of German and American tendencies. The net result of these developments has been to deprive sociology of a former ally, but at the same time to render it more independent.

Latin-American Criminology and Penology. — There is still, however, a very close connection between sociology and law in the fields of criminology and penology. *Derecho criminal,* as commonly taught in the universities, is divided into two branches or courses, one general and the other special, which respectively correspond rather closely to (1) criminal law and (2) criminology and penology as taught in the United States. From the last quarter of the nineteenth century onward there have been two main trends in Latin-American criminology: one derives from the Italian schools of criminal anthropology and criminal sociology associated with the names of Lombroso, Garofalo, and Ferri, and so far as the Ferri influence is concerned, has not markedly diminished in strength; the other springs from the North American school of penology, with strong infiltrations from modern European theory and practice. Some valuable work in the therapeutic and constructive prevention of juvenile delinquency has been done under the leadership of Jorge Coll and also of Ernesto Nelson, both of the University of Buenos Aires. Special training for this and other types of social work is now being offered in a few centers.

Interpretive History and Sociology. — History has continued to sustain its interpretive interest, and the earlier concentration on Latin-American matters continues. Economic history manifests strong sociological leanings, as does also the history of Latin-American institutions. Further, there has developed a school of thought which is concerned with the defense of Latin civilization as against Anglo-Saxon, and although apologetics sometimes gets the better of sober analysis, the works of the school often contain very penetrating insights into the social processes and structures characteristic of each of these civilizations. Francisco García Calderón (the younger) and Alfredo Colmo are among its outstanding representatives. Interpretations of current Latin-American history in one or another aspect are abundant: questions of culture, nationality, race, immigration, standards of living, and child welfare are thoroughly examined and many practical programs have been proposed and set in motion. As is the case with attempts in other countries to describe and solve pressing social problems, however, a good many of the resulting proposals do not rank as scientific products, although they are sometimes labeled sociology. Only a few can justifiably claim this title, among them treatises by Francisco Bulner, Caso, Vasconcelos, Bustamente, Oliviera Vianna, Guerrero, Desvernine y Galdós, and Agustín Venturino.

Ecological and Anthropogeographical Interpretation: Venturino. — This writer's four solid volumes have won the unstinting praise of so well-informed a sociologist and connoisseur of Latin-American matters as Bernard.[56]

In his two-volume treatise on the sociology of the Indians of early Chile, *Sociología Primitiva Chileindiana* (1927, 1928), Venturino follows the long-established South American custom of explaining their life and culture primarily in terms of the physical environment, in which factors making for vicinal isolation play an important part. He is not content, however, with loose assertions about "geographical influences"; flora and fauna, for example, are dealt with in the same connection and with a degree of precision sufficient to satisfy all but the hypercritical. Moreover, the myths, tribal organization, industries, commerce, art, language, and the juridical, educational, sacerdotal, governmental, and other institutions related to the physical environment are described and analyzed in detail, although perhaps not so schematically as a North American or European sociologist would have described them.

Venturino is not a mere *littérateur*, however; if his literary style sometimes gets in the way of scientific exposition, it is not because he is vague about the facts. Years of careful study of the physical and cultural setting of the Indians and colonists in all the Americas have given him a background that lends depth and perspective to all his work. Moreover, his comparisons of Chilean culture with Mayan, Aztecan, and Incaic cultures are very illuminating, and open up lines of analysis that seem likely to be rewarding. In the second volume of this treatise on the Chilean Indians, Venturino takes up the story with the coming of the Spanish *conquistadores,* and draws a vivid picture of the clash of the two cultures and the effect of war and conquest upon the native institutions — a study to place on the same shelf with those by Pitt-Rivers, Mead, and MacLeod.[57] Venturino, however, continues his presentation to a stage not reached by any of the writers just mentioned (although through no fault of theirs) : he shows the part played industrially by the flora and fauna and socially by the native women in helping to reëstablish a cultural equilibrium after the conquest.

In his *Sociología Chilena* (1929), which carries the same trend of study through colonial and national times, Venturino makes his most original contributions to human ecology. In several brilliant chapters he shows how the early colonial civilization was dominated by the military city, and how in the nineteenth century this gave way to the commercial city. The Chilean set-up — indeed, the whole Latin-American situation — is of peculiar importance to those interested in dominance and succession, for there the city has always held sway over its rural hinterland in a manner and to a degree unknown in North America, largely because the rural inhabitants of the southern continent have been Indians, whereas in the northern they are for the most part of the same ethnic groups as the city dwellers. This book and the one shortly to be mentioned emphasize the rôle of culture much more than that of the immediate physical environment, but Venturino never lets the reader forget that nature always lies back of nurture in the development of peoples and their institutions, even those of the present day.

Sociología General Americana (1931), the third of our industrious Chilean's treatises, deals largely with the conflict of races and classes and their gradual accordance and amalgamation during the colonial and national periods. The influence of governmental, economic, religious, scientific, traditional, and like cultural factors in bringing about these slowly developing changes is made abundantly clear; those who study " conflict and accommodation groups " can reap much profit from it.

It may safely be said that Venturino, heir of " the profound ecological and anthropogeographic trend of sociology south of the Amazon for nearly a hundred years," [58] has greatly and worthily augmented his heritage.

Synthetic Sociology: Cornejo. — Not only are excellent sociological interpretations of specifically Latin-American conditions to be found, but there are also closely-integrated and dispassionate sociological works of a general character conforming to rather high standards of scientific excellence. Ernesto Quesada, who, it will be recalled, taught the first course specifically named sociology in Latin America, was also the author of a systematic theoretical treatment of the subject (*La Sociología,* 1904) which won the praise of so exacting a critic as Lester F. Ward. The next year this was followed by a work on the principles of sociology by Alfredo Colmo, and in close succession there then appeared many high-grade, well-balanced presentations by Martínez Paz, Bunge, Carvalho, García, Orgaz, Oliva, Letelier, and Cornejo (whose important *La Sociología contemporánea* we shall later examine more closely). Latin-American writers on general sociology have of course been greatly influenced by Comte, Spencer, Ward, Tarde, Giddings, Durkheim, and Wundt; more recent suggestions have come from Ellwood and other North American writers, Pareto, Simmel, Wiese, Vierkandt and Spengler. Many of the North Americans have become known primarily through translations, made by the eminent Spanish scholar, Adolfo Posada, and by others.

The above-mentioned treatise by the Peruvian sociologist, Mariano H. Cornejo, is an outstanding example of the cross-fertilization of a half-dozen types of sociology coming from other continents. First published in Spanish in 1908, it attracted the attention of René Worms, then director of the *Institut international de sociologie,* and appeared in French translation in 1911 as *Sociologie générale* (2 vols.). It is an amazingly erudite work of more than a thousand pages, thoroughly matured and skillfully organized. Worms wrote an enthusiastic preface for it, and his judgment, considering the date of the work, seems eminently justified.

It opens with a splendid survey of the historical development of sociology which is a masterpiece of condensation and erudition. Next follows an elaborate theory of cosmic evolution in which Spencer, Ward, Poincaré, Weismann, Clerk Maxwell, and many other scientists figure, and which states in no uncertain terms the necessity for the assumptions of mechanism and determinism " if any sociology worthy of the name is to be developed." [59]

Quite in conformity with this unabashed positivism, Cornejo

points out that sociality is not characteristic of man alone, but roots in the very nature of all the higher organisms, and goes on to show that social evolution is but a continuation of the processes operative in biological evolution. This was also the position taken by practically all later nineteenth-century sociologists; we need mention only Espinas and Waxweiler as especially relevant examples.

The Debt to Ward and Giddings. — Cornejo is careful to state, however, that human society is more complex than all other types because of the parts played by adaptation and the development of solidarity through coöperation, conflict, differentiation, and selection. Here he draws heavily on Darwin, Kropotkin, Gumplowicz, and Durkheim, and then says that all the factors making for solidarity can be summed up under Giddings's " consciousness of kind " as the subjective manifestation, and adaptation as the objective cause working through the development of a community of sentiments and ideas. These psychical influences, together with the desires and their accompaniments, pleasure and pain, account for the greater complexity of social evolution as over against biological, but do not make it fundamentally different — a conclusion which is also a distinctive feature of Ward's sociology. The debt to Ward is still more evident in the treatment of social synergy; this is in all respects essentially identical with that set forth in *Dynamic Sociology* and *Psychic Factors in Civilization.*

Superorganicism. — But in dealing with the nature of society, the clarity that characterizes other parts of the work is lacking. Cornejo's position is difficult to understand: he ridicules those who draw analogies between society and an ordinary animal organism, but he says that societies have individuality even though there is no collective sensorium, and uses the term " collective mind." To be sure, he later attempts to justify this usage by saying that mind is nothing that is separable from the organism, and as the mind of the individual is simply a function of his body as a whole, so the social mind is a function of society as a whole — it reduces to a coördination superior to individual coördinations. This being the case, progress may be defined as the form that evolution takes in societies; it is a movement toward more complete coördination, and renders society more and more independent of the natural environment.

Careful examination of Cornejo's treatise has failed to disclose any reference to Krause or his Spanish disciples, but one cannot help surmising that in addition to Fouillée and other organismic thinkers cited, the German Romanticist perhaps played some part. Be this as it may, there is nothing especially objectionable in the actual analysis of society offered by Cornejo; the "superorganismic" line of argument could be eliminated and a great deal that is now regarded as valid would remain.

Social Factors and Products: a Skillful Blend. — The reason for this is that Cornejo goes over to an analysis of social factors and products that is only verbally connected with his superorganicism. Factors are regarded as the active characteristics of social phenomena, and products as the passive, although the two terms are used almost interchangeably. Before launching on his extended discussion of factors and products, he raises the question as to the causal efficacy inhering in the physical factors on the one hand and the social on the other, and replies that although the forces of nature and man's biological traits are oftentimes of great importance, the social factors exercise an even greater influence as civilization advances, and are destined to bring the physical factors under complete control. This is the position taken by Ward, and Cornejo acknowledges his indebtedness both by frequent references and by use of the term "social telesis." [60]

In a series of excellent chapters, Cornejo next discusses the physical factors, dividing them into two main classes: the external and the internal. The external are comprised in nature in the customary meaning of that term — climate, topography, etc. — and the internal are listed as individual heredity, race, and population. The chapter on population is worthy of special attention; considering the state of knowledge in 1908, it is a surprisingly cogent treatment. The influence of French, German, and Italian demographers is quite marked.

The strictly social factors and products are likewise divided into two main categories: (1) primary products, of an exclusively psychic character, collectively created, and distinctively human, comprising language, myths, and morals; and (2) general processes that organize the primary products and extract other products from them, comprising imitation, education, division of labor, and war. Let us take the general processes first. In the treatment of imitation Tarde is closely followed, although Cornejo is at pains to point out that this is far from exhausting the possibilities of sociology. Ward and Giddings are the sources from which his discussion of education derives. The division of labor is analyzed in close accord with Durkheim's distinction between "mechanical" and "organic" types, although a few references are made to Roscher and Schmoller. It should be noted that Cornejo takes issue with Durkheim's contention that the " primitives " are more thoroughly dominated by the " collective mind " than are the " civilized," pointing out that numerous instances can be brought to show that the reverse is sometimes true. The chapter on war follows Gumplowicz, Ratzenhofer, Spencer, and Ward, particularly the latter, and recurs to the theme of synergy. The discussion of the four factors is concluded by an attempt to show that they all impel society toward a condition in which there will be an optimum of liberty, equality, and solidarity. A child of his time. . . .

In dealing with the primary products of social life, Cornejo introduced novel elements, namely, the contributions made by Wundt in his monumental *Völkerpsychologie*. No other sociologist so promptly incorporated them in a systematic treatise. Cornejo somewhat extends the list he first gives: as actually set forth it includes language, myth, religion, art, custom, morals, and law. Although well organized and buttressed by copious citations from other authors, there is nothing in Cornejo's adaptation that cannot be found in Wundt. The special contribution of the Latin-American writer is the way in which he has interwoven the doctrines of *Völkerpsychologie* with his own pattern of other sociological theories.

Cornejo's work concludes with a few chapters that do not quite fit into the general scheme: marriage and the family, the state, and science are separately considered. The treatment of the family follows the highly questionable formulas of the classical ethnologists (discussed in our chapter on social evolution) ; the analysis of the national state arrives at the conclusion that DeGreef's theory of its gradual transformation into a pacific world-state is probably correct, and the final chapter, on science, asserts that as sociology becomes more highly developed it will make extensive use of mathematics. The thoroughgoing application of the quantitative method is seen as the goal of a scientific sociology.

In spite of his vast erudition and remarkable skill in weaving numerous theories derived from others into a homogeneous structure, however, it is impossible to call Cornejo's work original in any fundamental sense. Moreover, the fact that he does not draw on Latin-American experience — thus contrasting unfavorably with Venturino, for example — makes the content of his theories rather standardized and academic, and deprives him of his best opportunity for presenting original contributions. A splendid example of synthetic sociology with encyclopedic leanings, it is simply a massive boulder that in all probability will never find a functional niche in the structure of modern sociology.

Analytic Sociology. — Here and there throughout Latin America, in the works of such men as Poviña, Orgaz, Oliva, and others, may be traced a vein of analysis that promises much for the establishment of sociology as "the grammar of the social sciences." American and German influences have been paramount in this: Giddings, Ellwood, Simmel, and Wiese, to name no others, are mentioned frequently in the literature.[61] As yet, however, methodological questions and surveys of the history of sociology attract most attention, although a few writers have dealt along analytic lines with concrete social phenomena such as revolutions and social disorganization.[62] When and if methodological precision unites with diligence in utilizing the splendid sources of sociological data that Latin America affords, we can hope for great things. Perhaps Bernard's adverse criticism, quoted below, can then be radically revised:

Never has there been wanting originality in the manner of handling characteristic Latin-American problems in social science, but the fact that this civilization was less well developed than those of Europe and North America has made the Latin Americans in large measure dependent upon their distant neighbors for much of the method and content of that part of their social sciences which is not of indigenous origin.[63]

The Teaching of Sociology. — We have been able to secure trustworthy information on the place of sociology in the universities for only two countries: Argentina and Brazil. Either it is virtually non-existent as a university discipline elsewhere in Latin America, which is quite incredible in view of the outstanding work of Venturino in Chile and Cornejo in Peru, or the range of our knowledge is pitifully narrow.

Argentina has long had a chair of sociology in the University of Buenos Aires; it is in the faculty of philosophy and letters. There is another professorship of sociology in the same university in the faculty of law and natural science, but it is held by an institutional historian who rules out the possibility of sociological generalization. Dependent upon both these professorships are assistant professorships held by younger men, and the significant innovations seem to be coming from them. The University of Cordoba has its chair of sociology in the faculty of law and social science; it is occupied by one of the first of Latin-American sociologists to manifest analytic tendencies: Raúl A. Orgaz. His assistants, Alfredo Poviña and Francisco Torres, are doing excellent work in acquainting their students with the most recent tendencies in systematic-empirical sociology, and much can be hoped for from them. The University of Litoral has two professorships of sociology, one held by José Oliva, who inclines toward a Durkheimian view of the relation of the social and the psychical, and the other by Alberto Baldrich, who is especially interested in the type of *Wissenssoziologie* set forth by Scheler.

In Brazil higher education is carried on almost exclusively in independent, uncoördinated professional schools; general education of the liberal arts type is all but unknown, and the specialized activity of graduate schools has been quite absent until very recently. Herein Brazil is representative of many Latin-American countries. At São Paulo, the industrial center, a school of sociology and politics was established in 1933, and in 1934 a university (in a sense a rival of the 1933 institution) incorporating a section called a school of philosophy, science, and letters was formed from professional schools and other fragments already existing. The resulting structure is a sort of liberal arts college and graduate school with a tail, made up of professional schools, that very nearly wags the dog. Rio de Janeiro also has had a university since 1935.

In all of these Brazilian institutions there is a marked conflict of culture patterns, primarily between French and American conceptions of the nature and scope of sociology (although German and Italian ideas are not wanting). It is unfortunate that the Americans imported as professors of sociology have apparently been of the aggressively " factual " type; they have consequently had great difficulty in establishing rapport with colleagues and associates of a somewhat more reflective or speculative turn of mind. On the other hand, there can be little doubt that the French influence in Brazil has often been of a doctrinaire variety that is beginning to be outmoded even in France itself. Its saving virtue has been emphasis on general erudition and *savoir faire* of a sort readily acceptable to Brazilians, who for a long time have looked to France as arbiter of the higher values of life and learning. The outcome of the struggle, it may be hoped, will not be a decisive victory for either side.[64]

Positivistic Sociology Wanes. — Certain salient features of Latin-American social and cultural development as related to sociological theory may now be noted by way of résumé. In colonial times, when the clerics had the upper hand, history, archaeology, law, and those aspects of political philosophy comprised in theology, canon law, and natural law (*derecho natural*) made up the social sciences in general. Whatever theoretical sociology existed was buried in these subjects. During the nation-making period in the nineteenth century, and particularly after 1850, history and law gave larger and larger scope to political and sociological generalization, and there is still an emphasis on sociological interpretation in the fields mentioned and in others as well. Nevertheless, as the impetus derived from revolutionary and democratic fervor diminishes, and as parliamentarism becomes a less vital tradition to the now predominantly commercial and financial educated class, private, civil, and international law and economics are capturing some of the interest once focused on *derecho político* and sociology.

Since this chapter was first written, there have been many excellent surveys of sociology in Latin America written by Latin Americans themselves. As the numerous articles from a wide range of periodicals drawn upon by *Sociological Abstracts* testify, a large amount of writing is being done. Some of this is derivative and bellettristic, but in proportion nowhere nearly as great as was the case thirty years ago. Carefully formulated theory and research closely linked therewith are beginning to make their appearance. Now and again, of course, those priding themselves on being among the *pensadores* theorize in thin air, as it were; even library research is viewed as being just a little too humdrum or even undignified to be worthwhile. Survey research, field work, and the like are delegated to aides who at times approach the status of menials. But the theory-research disjunction manifests itself less and less frequently. It is rarely evident at all in the pages of such journals as the *Revista Mexicana de Sociologia*.

Among the abler theorists, Mario Lins has come to the special attention of sociologists in the English-speaking world because, in addition to the high quality of his work, he writes in English. For a long time at Bahia, he is now at Rio de Janeiro, and is continuing to publish interesting and valuable theoretical analyses. Somewhat influenced by the Unity of Science movement, he has nevertheless kept himself refreshingly free from dogmatism. Even though he is at times a trifle eclectic, this can be viewed as a virtue in an intellectual situation where it might be all too easy to be doctrinaire.

CHAPTER XXIX

Sociology in India, China, and Japan

N O DISCRIMINATION. — Sociology *in partibus infidelium* has never received very much attention from Western writers. The social thought of Oriental antiquity has not suffered neglect, but treatises that stop short at about the beginning of our era cannot yield a great deal of information concerning the contemporary world. And there is a great deal of information available; the intellectual ferment that has been going on ever since the countries " east of Suez " have been exposed to civilizations differing fundamentally from their own has engendered a vast amount of social thought, and from the late nineteenth century onward a considerable part of this has either been labeled sociology or has confronted problems which may be called sociological. (Here as elsewhere in the present volume, however, we are compelled to be very catholic in our use of the term sociology; some of the strict definitions now current would exclude much that we are forced to consider.)

India, China, and Japan are the inevitable choices — indeed, no other countries of the Orient *per se* have much to offer. The order assigned this chapter and the position of each country within it have nothing to do with estimates of their importance; we are neither upholders of an arrogant Westernism nor advocates for one Eastern nation as against another; if one wished, one might apply the well-worn phrase, " Last but by no means least." Questions of convenience in organization, and those alone, have determined our chapter sequence.

I

INDIA

The Indian Social Reform Movement. — The congeries of psychically, if not physically, isolated sacred societies composing ancient India — which, like Germany before the Napoleonic wars, was " a geographic expression, not a nation " — was rudely jostled by the shock of British conquest. Confronted by the disquieting spectacle of what seemed superior social organization as well as superior material culture, Indian thinkers began to look at the family, law, education, and religion in ways different from those honored by century-old traditions. One of the first of these thinkers was Rajah Rammohan Roy (1772–1833), who started the *Brahmo Samaj,* a sort of Hindu Protestant movement accepting many if not most of the fundamental tenets of Brahmanism but reinterpreting them in ways oftentimes denounced as heretical by the traditionally orthodox. Rammohan Roy was a man of encyclopedic learning, well versed in both European and Indian thought. Never an uncritical admirer of Western civilization, he was nevertheless sufficiently stimulated by its contrasting example to demand many basic reforms in his own culture. Another pioneer was Swami Dayanand Sarasevati (1824–1883), founder of the *Arya Samaj,* who envisaged an ideal social order based on the teachings of the Vedas. The movement he initiated has stood for the equality of man and the consequent abolition of caste and sex discrimination, as well as for the cessation of "idol worship." [1] As can readily be imagined, these aims created tremendous excitement when first announced, and even now have not lost their power to evoke vigorous controversy.

At a somewhat later period essays and lectures bearing marked traces of French Encyclopedism were launched against time-honored customs by the economist Mahadeo Govind Ranade of the Bombay Presidency,[2] and at about the same time the English Utilitarianism deriving from Jeremy Bentham was applied to Hindu categories of conduct by Bankim Chandra Chatterjee, the father of modern Bengali literature, in his book entitled *Anusilan* (*Culture*). Other writers who may be classified among the social reformers ranging from mild to drastic were Bhudev Chandra Mukerjee, Iswar Chandra Vidyasagar, T. C. Das Gupta, Atulanandra Chakravati, Sushil Kumar De, Priya Ranjan Sen, Malabari, Bhandarkar, Telang, and Chandavarkar.[3] As the movement gained momentum a journal was founded to spread its ideals. This organ, *The Indian Social Reformer,* is now edited by M. Natarajan, who began to be active in the cause of social reform almost fifty years ago. A similiar journal, *The Modern Review,* under the able editorship of Ramananda Chatterjee, has long championed the cause of the socially oppressed and enthusiastically supports education and social reforms generally. Organizations with like aims, although of course stressing different phases, are the *Prarthana Samaj,* the *Servant of India Society,* and the *Social Service League.*[4]

The Opponents of Social Reform. — Efforts at social reform, especially in the direction of Westernization, have not lacked opposition. Not only are the masses passively resistant to changes in the ancient-ways, however slight, but they are at times aroused to violence by what they regard as some particularly flagrant bit of sacrilege perpetrated by the reformers. Moreover, intellectuals of many kinds have ranged themselves on the side of tradition, or at the very least have counseled preservation of Hinduism and Hindu social organization through making a necessary minimum of adjustment to the civilization of the West. Much labor has been expended in the reinterpretation of tradition by importing into it the conceptions of modern science and scholarship. Wholesale denunciation of Hindu life and thought by Christian missionaries has naturally aroused resentment, and the imperialism sometimes manifested by British administrators and military men has not been enthusiastically welcomed. Further, the borrowing from the West of individualistic notions and ideals of mechanical efficiency has aroused misgivings none the less keen because economic pressure and the apparently irresistible might of modern political and industrial organization has rendered such borrowing inevitable. Theosophists like Bhagwan Das, Annie Besant, and Subramanya Iyer; pandits like Sasadhar Tarkochuramani; and ascetics like Swami Vivekananda and Ram Tirtha have been in the forefront of the orthodox defense,[5] each differing in the specific ideals cherished, but all united against far-reaching reform.

Other leaders, desiring changes in certain aspects of Indian society, are opposed to seeing those changes made under Western guidance or along Western lines. For example, Rabindranath Tagore denounces the one-sided code of sexual ethics that so completely subordinates the Hindu woman, but at the same time cherishes "the subtle psychological adjustment between the sexes "[6] in the Indian joint family, scathingly rejects the European cult of nationality and the gospel of fitness and efficiency, and upholds the ancient ideal of the autonomous, self-sufficing rural commune or *sangha*. In this latter advocacy he was preceded by Aurobindo Ghosh, the exile at Pondicherry who for a generation proclaimed that the *sangha* was to be " the spiritual lever of social uplift "[7] that would eventually bring India's political freedom (although Ghosh now seems to have lost faith in regeneration through social organization). A paean of praise for the harmony which is said to have existed in India's village communities and city guilds was furnished by Ananda K. Coomeraswamy, whose *Essays in National Idealism* proclaimed the dangers of the social conquest of India by the West.

This is also the position of Mahatma Gandhi, who rejects industrialism *in toto* and regards the revival of the ancient handicrafts as one of the chief means of India's economic and spiritual salvation. In his zeal to protect the Indian masses, poor and susceptible to various forms of exploitation as they are, he also attacks Western education and even Western medicine. Like the woman poet Sarojini Naidu, Gandhi preaches unity between castes, creeds, and religions in India, even attempting to reconcile " the cow-killer and the cow-worshipper," i.e., the Moslem and the Hindu. In his zeal for Indian unity he has dared to strike at the caste system, and by the same token at Hindu religion, through his uncompromising championing of the untouchables. Passionately believing in manual labor as every man's supreme right and duty, Gandhi seeks to instil ideals of the honor of craftsmanship running counter to that worship of conspicuous idleness found in India as elsewhere. And yet with all his reforming fervor, Gandhi remains essentially an opponent of social reform as it has been understood in India, for the movement early acquired a Western character which time has not effaced. Hygiene, sanitation, technical education, material prosperity, a higher standard of living as the Occident conceives it — all these things are dross to the Mahatma, who at bottom is just another link in India's long chain of ascetic sages.

The extreme form his opposition takes may be judged adversely by some critics, but so far as opposition itself is concerned, it should be noted that two great British administrators, Henry Sumner Maine and Alfred Lyell, bitingly commented on the blunder committed by many of their predecessors and contemporaries in rashly destroying ancient institutions and overturning native principles of socio-legal and administrative policy without being able to replace them by equally effective modes of social control.[8] So vigorous was their protest that in the sphere of civil law a strong reaction was produced that even today exerts its effect.

Concrete Studies of Sociological Import. — Mukerjee has gone so far as to call Maine and Lyell " great pioneers of Indian sociology,"[9] but this seems too generous. Similarly, we cannot justifiably include any of the social reformers or their opponents; the most that can be said is that they isolated problems with which sociologists as such were later to occupy themselves. Again, the numerous studies of Hindu social life that have appeared in recent years cover too wide a field to be termed strictly sociological, although they provide materials indispensable to the sociologist. It is for this reason that we shall discuss them in succeeding paragraphs.

The problem of the origin and development of castes has challenged investigators for many decades, but the approach has been mainly from the side of ethnology. The reports of the Indian census are amazingly good in this field, and it is through such means, as well as through the regular channels of scholarly publication, that Occidental names such as Wilson, Senart, Nesfield, Risley, Ibbetson, Thurston, Crooke, O'Malley, Stanley Rice, Jackson, and Blunt have become known. Among the Indian writers on caste are Ketkar, Rama Prasada Chand, Ghurye, B. S. Guha, N. K. Dutt, Hayavadana Rao, and U. N. Mukerjee. Most of the work done on castes has been chiefly concerned with origins; the way in which they have developed and interacted down to the present day receives sufficient attention only in Ketkar's *History of Hindu Castes,* Blunt's *The Caste System in India,* and Dutt's *Origin and Growth of Castes in India.* U. N. Mukerjee has a valuable book in Bengali on the history of the lower castes of Bengal, and the social and economic changes they have recently undergone have been the subject of several monographs based on field work sponsored by the University of Lucknow. Closely related to these caste studies are Benoy Kumar Sarkar's *Folk Elements in Hindu Culture* and Slater's *Dravidian Element in Indian Culture.*

Since Maine's *Village Communities in the East and West* the Indian village community has received much attention, chiefly from economists,[10] although Radhakamal Mukerjee traces the racial-cultural elements in the Indian village constitution in his *Democracies of the East* and *Land Problems of India,* and much material of sociological importance is to be found in the numerous economic studies. More definitely sociological are Wiser's *Behind Mud Walls* (1930) and *The Hindu Jajmani System* (1935); the same is true of G. C. Mukhtyar's *Life and Labor in a South Gujarat Village* (1930). As was already intimated when dealing with the opponents of Westernization, and as we shall later see when the regional-ecological school is discussed, the village community or *sangha* is of great practical and theoretical importance, more especially as India remains overwhelmingly rural in spite of the inroads of industrialism.

The Indian guilds are also a favorite field of research, largely because of the significance assigned them in various schemes of social regeneration. They were first closely studied by Hopkins in his *India Old and New*. The guild organization at Benares was the subject of a survey by Mukandi Lal, and K. Rambhadram Shastry is the author of a monograph on Madura. Radhakamal Mukerjee has described the organization and functions of guilds in southern and western India in several of his books, largely as part of a plea for economic reconstruction along guild socialist lines, and the book on the *jajmani* system by Wiser is also *à propos*. Not without relation to such works are those devoted to pauperism and unemployment: D. N. Ghosh has recently analyzed the problem as it affects Bengal, and a significant contribution has been made by Captain J.W. Patanel in his book *Man and the Machine Power*.

In a country where famines are found outside of history textbooks and where plagues of all sorts are not merely Biblical allusions, population studies are of peculiar interest. Intensive population surveys of small agricultural regions have been undertaken by several doctoral candidates at the University of Lucknow, among whom may be mentioned Mathur, Misra, and Pant.[11] The latter's thesis utilizes the ecological method for the study of the distribution and migration of the Himalayan peoples in relation to the alternation of the seasons. Radhakamal Mukerjee, professor of sociology at the same university, has made two similar studies, in one of which he seems to have found, for some areas of the Ganges plain at least, an interesting corroboration of Pearl's demographic S-curve hypothesis.[12] Mukerjee has also set forth a theory of human migration and settlement on the basis of the ecological principles of distribution and succession.[13] Shorn of terminology it runs as follows: just as plants and animals invade (or thrive when artificially introduced into) regions similar to those in which they have already worked out a successful adjustment, so do human groups succeed best in those frontiers of settlement which are similar to the homelands. Accordingly, he contends that ecological research more systematic than any hitherto undertaken may help to solve problems of acclimatization or of economic rivalry of immigrants and natives in the same region. In two interesting papers [14] the same ecologist has shown, on the basis of birth and death rates in densely settled sections of India, that the Malthusian checks of war, famine, disease, and death are not the only ones at work. When optimum density is exceeded, birth rates tend to become lower, and migration also plays a part in restoring the balance of numbers. This leads him to make a distinction, based on his studies in animal ecology, between optimum and equilibrium density; this he then applies to human groups and their food supplies. Benoy Kumar Sarkar is the author of a monograph comparing natality and mortality in India with other countries; he then ranks them in an order of precedence and forecasts lower birth rates for the Orient. A relatively comprehensive treatise is furnished by Wattel and Brij Narain's *The Population Problem of India.*

Criminology has not received much attention,[15] perhaps because crime in India is rather different from crime in the West. As might be expected, fraud, embezzlement, and the like, presupposing as they do a highly developed financial machine, are not much in evidence. Organized crime is virtually unknown. Moreover, as a general thing there are fewer crimes of violence. In another respect India is unique: it has castes or tribes, such as the *Thugs,* among whom crime is a hereditary calling with an elaborate code of etiquette, discipline, and ritual. The problem of reforming members of such a group presents serious difficulties, as is shown by the field work and investigations of B. S. Haikerwal, author of *Economic and Social Aspects of Crime in India.*

The subject of marriage and the family is the center of a voluminous literature; little of it, however, is of scientific quality. Wadia's book on *Feminism and Social Progress* was an early and learned treatment, but was almost exclusively concerned with Western social ethics and ideals. It and many others like it called forth defenses of the Hindu system of which Tagore's essay in Keyserling's *Book of Marriage* is characteristic. Radhakamal Mukerjee and N. N. Sen Gupta, sociologist and psychologist respectively, have published a non-propagandist work on *Sex, Marriage, and Love,* and in several recent articles [16] they use the materials and methods of modern studies in sex behavior for a psycho-sociological analysis of marital adjustment and family organization.

The Emergence of Sociology: Scientific Comparison. — The preceding pages have made it plain that Indian sociology in the narrower sense has not had a long history. As one Indian sociologist has said, " Sociology has so far emerged in piecemeal fashion, now obscured by current political issues, now losing its balance in the din and bustle of religious and social reform. It is not before sociology finds its place in the curriculum of studies in the University that it becomes scientific in method and coördinate in its treatment. As the newest among the subjects which have been introduced into an Indian University, it is taught systematically only in the Universities of Calcutta, Lucknow, and Mysore." [17] Or as another writer puts it, " Sociology in India as an academic discipline is in its teething stage. For the past fifteen years the departments of economics in some of the outstanding colleges have been giving a course in sociology. The full consciousness of sociology as a distinct and unique discipline in social studies does not date farther back than 1920. . . . The reason for Indian sociology being in such an infantile state must be attributed to the fact that the Indian educational system has been taking its cue for about a century from England — and since England itself is backward in the development of sociology, India cannot be expected to develop it independently." [18]

Other writers have not always been so frankly anti-British as the one last quoted. It is nevertheless interesting to note that the man who first drew the attention of the university world toward sociology was actively engaged in refuting unilinear evolutionary doctrines according to which Indian society in its various aspects represented the lower rungs of a ladder leading to early twentieth-century European civilization, the highest point thus far reached in the ascent of Progress. Sir Brajendra Nath Seal, now vice-chancellor of the University of Mysore, provided this defense of Indian culture through his studies in what he calls "comparative sociology," first expounded in his lectures and discourses while George V Professor of Philosophy at the University of Calcutta in the first quarter of the century, and later through a number of important papers.[19] He has published relatively little, but his influence on Indian sociology has been far greater than the number of his printed contributions might lead one to assume.

Seal's chief effort has been to introduce certain qualifications and corrections into the historical method of treatment. Opposing social evolutionism, he points out that piecemeal comparisons are of little value and that what some American sociologists now call culture case studies afford the only valid method. Similar types of social conduct and structure must be compared in the light of their history and growth and of their stage therein. Unless the compared customs, rites, institutions, and dogmas are taken in their full context, atomistic comparisons such as those perpetrated by some statisticians, for example, may be made to yield the most absurd results. And even when comparison works in its proper sphere, says Seal, "its application must be limited by considerations of organic growth and development, so that, for example, it would be worse than idle to assimilate the forms of divorce in such widely differing stages of society as those in Burma, Ancient Rome and Revolutionary France, or of local self-government in Indian village communities and English or Scotch vestries." [20]

A strong bias in favor of Indian institutions is evident in most of Seal's utterances, but, as we have several times remarked, a bias may occasionally be useful. Indignantly rebelling against the bland belief of the British conqueror that his subjects represent a lower stage of social evolution, Seal and his followers rightly point out that social development is multilinear and that in most cases judgments of superiority or inferiority are wholly out of place.[21]

Defense of the Economic Order. — Inasmuch as the impact of West on East has been exceedingly important in the economic field, the multilinear theory there found one of its first applications. While the blows of industrialism steadily chipped away the pillars of the joint family, caste distinctions, and the village community, efforts were made to show that these institutions represent aspects of the total social environment to which Western modes of economic activity can under no circumstances be adapted. Support for this point of view was soon forthcoming from the British followers of LePlay, whose Place-Work-Folk formula lends support to a kind of organic regionalism well suited to the defense of Indian traditions. Patrick Geddes, to whom we have already referred in the chapter on British sociology, organized civic and town planning exhibitions in different cities of India, and wrote some valuable reports on education and town development from the regional standpoint, with special emphasis on social problems. He also furnished descriptions of south Indian temple-cities and several reports on Indore which show a keen awareness of the processes of social change appearing under new urban conditions.[22]

During this same period several Indian writers, profiting by the sharpening of issues produced in the controversy between the social reformers and their opponents, as well as by the leads offered by Seal's critiques of social evolutionism and by the Le-Play Place-Work-Folk formula, provided a coherent system of apologetics for the native economic order. The following excerpt is characteristic:

The attempt to force systems and methods of industrial organization, economic arrangement, and institutions which have admirably suited a different geographical environment, will always be futile. In the first place, the people will not be able to work them successfully. Thus the struggle and pain during the period of transition will be severe. Secondly, the institutions cannot be adapted to the geographical and historical conditions. Thus economic progress will be retarded, and in many cases economic activities will be paralyzed. Lastly, the particular physical and social environment which requires its characteristic type of economic organization for perfect adaptation will re-evolve the type after a period of forced interference and substitution, and consequent stagnation and degeneration. . . . [Again,] racial differences are the product of adaptation to different environments, and every race, even the most backward, can progress indefinitely, under favorable conditions of environment, physical and social, unfolding a phase of universal humanity, and playing no small part in the development of humanity.[23]

In the face of utterances like these it is easy enough to exclaim " Rationalization! " or " Over-compensation! " but that does not solve the problem. This is not the place for a discussion of the sociology of knowledge, but we must again point out that the psycho-sociological origin of a theory proves nothing about its logical validity. We shall therefore go on to an extended exposition of the regional-ecological method in sociology to which such protests ultimately led.

Regional-Ecological Sociology. — In order to classify types of society more accurately along multilinear lines, a distinctively Indian method of regional analysis was developed. Not only was economics broadened to take account of " ethnic and national variations in different cultural regions," [24] but the same regional and comparative methodology was applied to the entire body of the social sciences. Indian sociology thereby became encyclopedic and synthetic, and for good measure took on most if not all the aspects of a complete social philosophy. Some of its more important doctrines, in addition to those directly traceable to Seal and the LePlay school, are as follows:

(1) The usual division of labor in the social sciences is directly attacked. Inasmuch as the effort is to achieve a complete description and analysis of man's entire organic and social equipment in a particular region, it is claimed that ethnology, economics, political science, systematic sociology, and like disciplines are too abstract to be of much use. As Mukerjee presents the case:

This is especially brought to light by regional studies in which the walls which keep the different social sciences in water-tight compartments crumble down. For the region is a reality and cannot be made to fit in with abstract theories. In a regional and concrete study, the first truth that emerges is that there is an agreement between stages and types of economic and political evolution with those of social development. Economic, religious and social norms and standards do, indeed, correspond. . . .

A more intimate coördination of the social sciences in the interpretation of the region will be a prelude to a classification of social types, so essential for a comparative study of civilisation. A scientific study of the forces which govern social growth-formations in different regions will also be accompanied by a more purposive control and selection, the necessity of which is felt now more than ever in this age of the substitution of cultures in the east. . . . The conflict between marriage and economic mores, between communal rights in land and individualistic notions in property, between traditions of village government and the tendencies of centralisation, between education for social service and education as a means of livelihood, between communal property and the passion for individualistic recreation, all these exhibit unintended social metamorphoses in India, with corresponding deterioration in the character of the people.

These have to be analysed and understood region by region, group by group. And for this social surveys must be initiated and introduced into new fields, . . . [furnishing] us with results that will be exactly measured for comparison and estimate in conflicts between old and new.[25]

(2) These regional surveys and all other studies (psycho-sociological and the like) are pervaded by an emphasis on the principle of coöperation. The rôle played by coöperation is traced through various developmental stages, in a fashion at times suspiciously reminiscent of the social evolutionism so decried (and rightly) by Indian sociologists, to the " communalism " exemplified in the *sangha* or village community. This communalism is regarded as the supremely desirable goal, although it is conceded that various types of society will have to follow different roads in attaining it: India is simply peculiarly fortunate in needing only to preserve, extend, and purify one phase of its traditional social order.[26]

The Western doctrine that society is a balance of class conflict is regarded as applicable only to the industrialized Occident; it is held that the communalism of the East represents an *integration,* rather than a conflict, of occupational and other functional interests in neighborhood groups of the sort described by Mary Follett in *The New State.* This pluralistic type of polity is favorably contrasted with the monistic variety, formed through conquest, of which Oppenheimer's *The State* provides so excellent an analysis.

As part and parcel of this advocacy of communalism goes an attack on the pleasure-pain principle in psycho-sociology. It is contended that the urges potent in group life lie much deeper than the merely hedonic level, and that only communalism permits a balanced functioning of all human capacities. N. N. Sen Gupta and Radhakamal Mukerjee have provided a systematic statement of this point of view in their *Introduction to Social Psychology*. Dhurjatiprasad Mukerji has presented a personalistic interpretation of the social process in which the interlocking and interpenetration of group impulses and will in a system of communalism guided by traditions of voluntary coöperation (again the *sangha!*) is the supreme medium for the development of personality.[27]

(3) This emphasis on mutualism is extended beyond the strictly human realm in the doctrine of symbiosis. Inasmuch as it is contended that the tendency in animate nature is to establish interrelations between organisms, " to link lives together in reciprocal service and adaptation," [28] social progress is interpreted in terms of plant and animal as well as of human well-being. It is simply " the complex interwoven growth of biological mutuality which continuously has evolved reciprocal service to the uplift of the entire living community." [29] The midge, the cobra, the mongoose, the tiger, the dense tangle of jungle vegetation, and man all form parts of one vast fellowship.

Given this standpoint, it is easy to see how the ecological interest that so strongly marks Indian sociology has developed. With an entire consistency, the Indian sociologists treat climate, soil, topography, plant and animal communities, and man himself, together with all his material and non-material culture, as interdependent parts of ecologic configurations known as regions.

Radhakamal Mukerjee, the outstanding exponent of social ecology as an integration of " geography, social anthropology, and economic history," [30] says that it has before it a threefold task: (a) " to trace the adaptations of inter-acting human beings and inter-related human institutions to the region, including in the latter term not merely climate, soil, and land form, but also plant and animal communities "; (b) " to investigate the spatial and food relations in which human beings and activities are organised in a natural area in terms of the *ensemble* of ecologic forces "; and (c) " to measure the balances and mutual pressure of human, along with other living and non-living [*sic*] communities in the region and discover whether they prove favorable or unfavorable for man's dominance and permanence." [31]

A great deal of attention is paid to distribution of population, herein resembling American ecology; a further resemblance is the borrowing of concepts such as " balance," " organization," " succession," " disturbance," and " regression " from plant and animal ecology.[32] Unlike most if not all the American ecologists, however, the Indian investigators take the postulated interrelation of human communities with plant and animal in deadly earnest; for example, meticulous studies have been made of the pressure of human and cattle population on the total ecological complex found in the crowded Ganges region, and the conclusion reached is that " symbiosis, organic and social, is the key to the permanence of man's civilisation, his works and experiences on the earth." [33]

(4) As should be amply evident by now, sociology is not regarded as a science having nothing to do with value-*judgments,* but on the contrary is charged with the responsibility of providing a comprehensive formulation of the goal of man's collective effort and aspiration.[34] The trend of development which many Indian sociologists explicitly state to be the guiding norm of their work is " for the pattern of life to attain greater solidarity and permanence through friendly and intimate and subtle linkages. What is organic in Nature and shapes her ends blindly and haphazardly becomes purposive in human society, and thus the pattern of life, spiritually and teleologically progressive, crosses the boundaries of time and space." [35]

Whatever else one may think of this statement, it is clear enough. Sociology not only absorbs social philosophy but also takes over the philosophy of values and a very large portion, to say the least, of the philosophy of religion.[36] The writings of Indian sociologists bear witness to this: one finds them making pleas for the reconciliation of the mechanical and the ideal, of the evolutionary and the spiritual, for the religion of social solidarity, for mysticism. Far from regarding this as a weakness, it is contended that the strength of sociology in India lies precisely in " its linking up of social with ethical and spiritual values." [37]

Conclusion: the Religious Roots of Indian Sociology. — Just as the influence of evangelical Protestantism is recognizable in the writings of many American sociologists, so the " climate of opinion " formed by elements basic to Brahmanism, Jainism, and other cults — which we continue as heretofore to call Hinduism (see Chapter Two) — exercises sway over Indian sociological thought. The conception of *dharma,* for example, has much to do with the espousal of communalism, for *dharma* is supposedly the fundamental law of the cosmos, assigning a functional niche to every human being in which he works out his ultimate destiny.[38] Not only does this notion make it possible for the Hindu to say that the caste system is not socially discriminatory, being merely the social framework of *dharma,* but in addition the advocacy of symbiosis in the whole organic world thereby reveals its deeper meaning. The different grades of human society each have their functions to carry out within a community of which the *sangha* provides so important an example, and over and above this the human community has a function in relation to the plant and animal communities in which it is set. The whole cosmos is thought of as a circling chain of reciprocal functioning, and rights have no meaning apart from duties.

Closely related, of course, is that doctrine of transmigration of souls which makes the Indian, whether Brahman or Sudra, so reluctant to take the life of even the humblest creature except under ritually sanctioned circumstances. Similarly akin is that conception of the identity of self with other, and thus with the all-pervading cosmic being, expressed in the dictum *Tat twam asi* — " That also art thou." Emerson put it well:

> If the red slayer think he slays,
>   Or the slain think he is slain,
> They know not well the subtle ways
>   I keep, and pass, and turn again. . . .
>
> They reckon ill who leave me out;
>   When me they fly, I am the wings;
> I am the doubter and the doubt,
>   And I the hymn the Brahmin sings. . . .

And here, for the purposes of the present volume, the matter rests.

II

CHINA

From Social Thought to Sociology. — Even the miserably inadequate amount of space we have been able to devote, in an earlier chapter, to Chinese thought in antiquity is enough to support the assertion that the Celestial Kingdom never lacked profound and original ideas concerning man's conduct and institutions. Like early Western social thinkers, however, Confucius, Lao Tse, and the host of other sages (perhaps equally important from the theoretical point of view) were exponents of closely interwoven philosophies that do not admit the separate, rigidly scientific treatment of any one aspect. In what we have called Sinism the social is inextricably intermingled with the metaphysical and even the religious phases of thought. (To be sure, one finds a certain intermingling of the same kind among modern scientists as well, but the union is not so organic in character and this or that section can more readily be singled out for treatment.) Further, the Chinese sages were on the whole much more concerned with practice than with theory. How to bring about celestial and social harmony, how to govern a state, how to rule oneself, how to inculcate the filial sentiments, how to ensure a good harvest — these, and not " idle contemplation," were the important things, as Granet has clearly shown.[39]

After the classical period — which is to say, after the first century of our era — these traits of Chinese mentality became self-perpetuating through the examination system, the stress on feats of memory and exegesis, and the mandarinate. Not until the 'forties of the last century, when British commercial enterprise forced China to open its doors to Indian opium, did effective culture contact with the West begin. Trading had already gone on for a long time, of course, and missionaries had been at work for centuries, but the real breakdown in China's isolation began with the Opium War.

Since that time every Western nation that could jam a foot through the Open Door has done so; " spheres of influence," gunboats, kerosene, missionaries, and educators have spread the culture of the Occident far and wide, and China has been gripped in the throes of a material and non-material transition that is still far from finished. Add to this the famines, floods, and plagues that have swept over the unhappy country, place in the same column the ravages of civil war, banditry, peasant uprisings, Communism, and Japanese aggression, and the sum, it will readily be seen, does not make for " the passionless pursuit of passionless intelligence." To arrive at the final staggering total, multiply these woes by a struggle between native reformers and traditionalists as relentless as that waged in India, and then ask why modern China has not been conspicuous for the development of detached, dispassionate sociological theory. Whitehead, thinking primarily of mathematics and epistemology, declares that " the great ages have been unstable ages," but he also says that " there is a degree of instability which is inconsistent with civilization." [40] Yet more may come out of China's anguish than is immediately apparent from an examination of her recent sociology. The most that should be said just now is that practical considerations are still uppermost in sociological research, teaching, and training in China; with the possible exceptions offered by social anthropology and cultural sociology, disinterested theory is not strongly represented.[41]

From this let no one infer that there is a lack of interest in sociological theory in China — on the contrary. Western thinkers have been avidly read and translated, but chiefly in the hope that something can be learned that will help solve China's problems. Precisely here, however, the pressing needs of the moment and the traditions of Chinese scholarship combine to thwart the development of native theory. Pushed by the desire to glean something immediately practicable, on the one hand, and on the other still dominated by an undue reverence for the written word of reputed sages, Oriental or Occidental, the Chinese sociologist has only in the last year or two begun to look directly at the scene about him and to put the results of his observations into theories that are not distorted by the frog's-eye perspective of what to do tomorrow.

The history of the relevant literature begins with Yen Fuh (1853–1921), the pioneer Chinese translator of Western sociological literature. He early acquired a firm foundation in the Chinese classics, and having been successful in the great competitive examinations through which the members of the bureaucratic mandarinate were selected, was sent to England as a young man to study naval affairs. True to the tradition of the Chinese *literati,* he found such crassly mundane matters unattractive, and upon his return did little to improve the scanty opportunities offered in the moribund Chinese navy to utilize what smattering of technical knowledge he had acquired. Instead, he devoted his energies to making Western thought directly accessible to his countrymen through translations of important books. Ta Chen has high praise for him: " Lucid in style, precise in meaning and elegant in form, Yen is easily the foremost translator of modern China." [42]

Beginning with John Stuart Mill's *On Liberty* in 1899, he brought out other translations in rapid succession, and in 1902 Spencer's *Study of Sociology* came from his pen. It is interesting to note that Yen Fuh translated sociology as " the study of groups " rather than as " the study of society," the rendering now generally accepted by the Chinese.[43] This was probably the result of his almost exclusively literary training, but a good case might be made for his version if one takes into account the present-day drift away from the grandiose synthetic conception of sociology toward the analytic, systematic conception.

Yen Fuh proved to be but the foremost of a whole swarm of translators and mediators. The works of British, American, French, German, Italian, and Russian social thinkers were dressed in Chinese garb,[44] and in addition numerous articles and books expounding and interpreting Western social theories appeared.[45] Of recent years the modern sociologists of Europe — Max and Alfred Weber, Pareto, Wiese, Mauss, and their like — have been quite as thoroughly studied in China as in the United States, if not more so.

As already pointed out, however, the effort has been primarily to apply the teachings of Western social thinkers and scientists to Chinese conditions, not to develop a body of original theory and research. A striking exception is of course furnished by the political doctrines of Sun Yat Sen, but these hardly come within the range of sociology proper, and in addition they were formulated either with the Chinese revolution of 1911 in view or during the throes of that struggle; their theoretical content is therefore implicit rather than explicit. The recent attempts to find in the thought of the ancient sages (particularly of the " heretics ") teachings applicable to modern conditions are similarly difficult to place in the sociological category, and for our purposes (but for our purposes only) may safely be omitted.

The Teaching of Sociology. — In 1905 the first chair of sociology in China was founded at St. John's University (Episcopal) in Shanghai with Professor Arthur Monn as the occupant. Bagehot's *Physics and Politics* was the textbook first used. The first Chinese student to receive a doctorate in sociology from a Western university was Y. Y. Tsu, a Columbia Ph.D., whose dissertation was on " The Development of Chinese Philanthropy " (1912). He returned to China and became professor of sociology at St. John's.[46] Even in its academic beginnings under Western auspices, therefore, the melioristic trend inherent in Chinese sociology was reinforced.

The first department of sociology was established at Shanghai Baptist College in 1913, and has been headed successively by James Quayle Dealey, Daniel Kulp II, and H. S. Bucklin. Since that time many other professorships and departments of sociology have been established, in both Christian and other private schools as well as in a few of the governmental establishments. American sociologists have been numerous in China, both as visiting professors and in regular posts.[47]

Christian colleges lead in the attention given to sociology.[48] At least two reasons may be assigned for this: (1) they are predominantly American, and sociology is more widely taught in the United States than elsewhere; and (2) the strongly humanitarian, social-ethical bent of recent Christianity makes for interest in sociology of the type represented by Ellwood, Hayes, and other exponents of normative theory. Because of this, the already over-practical tendency of Chinese mentality in general has been reinforced. Only with the slow waning of the missionary impulse and the "For-God's-sake-let's-do-*something*-immediately" attitude can one expect a union of sound theory and sound practice that will lead to the doing of the *right* thing eventually. There is already some evidence of this change for the better. Take, for example, the work done in Yenching University at Peiping. This Christian school is the only one offering graduate work in sociology in China, and also has the largest department, the greatest number of courses, and a relatively strong theoretical bent. A random sampling of theses written ten to fifteen years ago yields primarily normative efforts: Reconstruction of Country Life; A Survey of Peking Patients; A Study of the Social Life of Village Women in China; A Social Survey of Peking Churches; Social Thought of the Biological School after Spencer; Charitable Institutions in Peking; Child Labor in Shanghai; A Study of Soup Kitchens in Peiping.[49] It can readily be seen that social welfare interests guided the choice of the majority of thesis topics. Contrast with this a list drawing on the five-year period just elapsed: An Analysis of Some Aspects of the Concubinage System in China; Marriage and Funeral Customs as Recorded in Local Chronicles; A Socio-Psychological Study of the Personality of an Adolescent Hawaiian-Chinese Girl; The Study of Huang's Sib-Organization in Foochow; Sumner's Conception of Society; Social Organization of the "Flower-Basket" Yao Tribes. Here, it is true, the influence of ethnologists or "comparative sociologists" like Radcliffe-Brown has been predominant, rather than sociologists of the stricter sect, but of the scientific advance represented by the change there can be little doubt. Moreover, although the Yenching department is one of sociology *and* social work, there is some effort to classify the courses in the two main divisions, and the degrees granted indicate the special field of study. Again, social work majors must have thorough foundation work in general sociology before turning to their special field, and graduate work is confined to sociology majors alone. At the same time, it should be said that the greater number of students choose to study social work and find positions in it;[50] the department necessarily adapts its offerings to the demand in some measure.

It should be said, by the way, that social work as it developed under private auspices in the United States prior to the Franklin D. Roosevelt administration never flourished in China, for obvious reasons. The kind of social work referred to in this chapter has most to do with general social economy, social planning, and community reconstruction, on the one hand, and special techniques such as scientific disaster relief, medical social work, penology, and child welfare on the other.[51]

Tsing Hua University also has a leading department, and like Yenching, inclines in the direction of social anthropology — or at least did so until Shirogokoroff, the eminent Russian ethnographer, left that institution in 1935. Tsing Hua still possesses, however, one of the most productive sociological departments, in terms of individual achievement, in all China. Central University in Nanking also emphasizes social anthropology and cultural sociology, but the department has been "closed down" by the Ministry of Education for at least the current academic year (1936–37), and with the exception of Sun Pen-Wen, editor of the World Book Company's excellent Chinese sociological series, all the members of the staff have been obliged to leave. A number of other institutions have suffered the same curtailment or suppression, among them Fuhtang University of Shanghai, which had an outstanding department. This is largely because of the anti-Marxian bent of the New Life Movement sponsored by Chiang-Kai-Shek, and sociology has gained the reputation of being Marxian, or at least radical. Witness the following general criticism, by an eminent Chinese sociologist, of Chinese sociology as currently taught (particularly in the smaller schools) :

First, in one or two institutions socialism and radical economic principles are the exclusive subjects treated in an introductory course in sociology. Evidently the teacher has been unable to distinguish between sociology and socialism. Secondly, in several institutions an elementary course in social problems and advanced courses in applied sociology are offered, but theoretical courses such as general sociology, social theory, social progress, etc., are notably lacking. The third represents the other extreme, that is, sociology is taught as the philosophy of history. Consequently the students learn nothing about an objective science of society. . . .

The absence of a well-defined policy, the reckless use of foreign texts and materials without due emphasis on Chinese materials, and the lack of the spirit of original research are also very serious defects in the present system of teaching sociology in China.[52]

Recent Sociological Research and Publication. — Numerous sociological or quasi-sociological analyses of Chinese life have been published in recent years by Americans and Europeans resident in China for longer or shorter periods, and have received much attention (listed in the notes).[53] An important place must also be granted to the articles published in the United States by Chinese students and professors. Some of them deal with conditions in China itself, others with Chinese social life in America: organization and mentality, adjustment to the American culture pattern, village relationships in China, the stabilizing power of Chinese folksong, and like topics.[54]

Chinese sociologists writing primarily for a Chinese audience have themselves accomplished much in recent years — so much, in fact, that it is impossible to list their publications and research in the text (see notes). The most we can do here is to list alphabetically a number of the more prominent (American-trained unless otherwise noted) and indicate their chief interests: S. C. Chen, social and political philosophy; Ta Chen, labor and population problems; C. M. Chiao, population problems and rural sociology; Chen Han-Sen, Marxian analysis, research for the Institute of Pacific Relations; L. S. Hsü, Chinese social changes, and population problems; C. M. Hu, ethnography, French-trained; W. S. Huang, cultural and historical sociology; Yang Kun, French sociological thought; Franklin C. H. Li, social surveys and mass education; S. C. Liu, ethnography; Quentin Pan, eugenics; L. K. Tao, ethnologist trained in England by Hobhouse, Westermarck, and Seligman, head of the division of the social sciences of the *Academia Sinica,* and regarded by many as the greatest Chinese sociologist; P. W. Sun, historical development of Chinese culture and general sociology, author of the best Chinese textbook in sociology; Cato Young, Chinese rural community organization and ecological description and analysis; W. L. Wei, ethnography, trained by Mauss and Bouglé; C. C. Wu, social economics and urban sociology; Charles Wu, psychical aspects of social life; and W. T. Wu, comparative functional analysis of culture, chairman of the excellent department of Yenching.[55] This list might be considerably augmented, but enough names have been given to introduce a few of the leading Chinese sociologists to their Western colleagues.

Attention must be called to the fact, however, that professionally-trained sociologists have not had much influence on the thought of contemporary Chinese youth. Here the most important writers are the Marxian social historian, H. S. Tao, and the great poet and Marxian analyst of ancient Chinese thought and society, M. S. Kuo, now in exile in Japan. Kuo's chief work, *Studies in Chinese Ancient Society* (1930), is regarded even by those who condemn its methodology as the most brilliant book published in China during the past twenty years. Whether the New Life

Movement can counteract this Marxian trend remains to be seen, and even if it does, no good for sociology is likely to result, if one may judge by the " temporary " closing down of departments that has already taken place.

In the first flush of sociological enthusiasm in the 'twenties, numerous institutes for research in the social sciences were set up, the first at the University of Amoy in 1921. In rapid succession thereafter many others were established, but the number of those exclusively devoted to or even granting a prominent place to sociological research, however loosely interpreted, was never very large, and nearly all of the institutes have since given up the ghost. Among those remaining the only ones of any importance for sociology are the Yenching University Committee on Social and Population Research, and the Institute of the Social Sciences of the *Academia Sinica*.

The Chinese Sociological Society, having more than two hundred members, has been in existence since 1931. It publishes a quarterly, *The Chinese Sociological Review*. Two journals are sponsored by Yenching: *The Sociological World*, a quarterly now in its ninth year; and *Social Research*, a weekly replacing an older journal, devoted to the promotion of sociological field work from the comparative and functional point of view, and now in its third year. Ta Hsia University in Shanghai issues a monthly of somewhat the same type as the late lamented *Social Science Abstracts*, except that it is of course much smaller. This publication is now two years old. Others are the *Journal of the Social Sciences* of the *Academia Sinica; The Social Sciences* of Tsing Hua University; and the *Nankai Social and Economic Quarterly* (in English). Fairly adequate means of scholarly communication are provided by these growing-points of Chinese sociology. Here and there in their pages can be discerned, with increasing frequency, tendencies away from mere following of Western cues, and genuine interest in the profounder questions of sociological methodology rather than in ready-made techniques.

When once the dawning doubt that the reputed sages of either East or West have said the last word on things sociological becomes fully articulate, the travail through which China has passed, is passing, and will pass will not have been in vain — it will really be possible to say, " *That* unstable age was a great age." With intellectual capacities second to none, as their magnificent history abundantly demonstrates, Chinese observers and thinkers will eventually make their own contribution, in their own right, to the sociological theory of the world.

III

JAPAN

Upheaval and Transformation. — Social thought in the broadest sense has never been lacking in the Empire of the Rising Sun; the researches of Japanese scholars have incontestably shown that not only was the mainland heritage of Confucian and like ideologies zealously perpetuated, but that in addition new departures bearing a strictly indigenous stamp were abundant. This holds true for that earlier period when Nippon was open to culture contacts of all sorts, and for the later era (1550–1865) of feudal isolation and xenophobia as well. Unfortunately, however, Japanese treatises in this field have not been translated and Occidental scholars have made almost no researches of their own, so that we are compelled to pass over what is undoubtedly a most interesting body of social lore with this bare reference.[56]

It is now a commonplace to say that no nation in recorded history underwent so sudden a transition from agrarian feudalism to highly developed industrialism as did Japan after the Meiji Restoration of 1868. Keeping at least equal pace with the march of material culture went a host of new ideas from England, Germany, France, and the United States that challenged and in many instances overcame the sway of ancient lore and immemorial usage.[57] Had it not been for the remarkably farsighted policies of the Elder Statesmen the country might have lost all semblance of unity, but the sedulous preservation of certain key mores and the revival of Shinto as a national faith did much to counteract the disorganization that would otherwise have been the inevitable sequence of sudden high accessibility. In other words, the vitally important centers of Japanese existence retained, in all essentials, many of the traits impressed upon them in the days when Japan was an extreme example of an isolated, sacred society. Secularization has gone a long way, but there are barriers which it does not seem likely to pass in the foreseeable future. The seeming miracle of grafting West upon East and of retaining the vigor of both has been accomplished, and we are now witnessing a new and amazing variant in the results of culture contact.

Soon after the middle 'fifties, when the opening of Japanese ports ended three centuries of isolation, the leaders of the island empire made every effort to avoid the fate of China by taking over those portions of Western culture valuable for national strength and unity. Dreadnaughts, power looms, and lathes —

yes, and also comparative philology, botany, physics, and the social sciences. The Imperial University of Tokio underwent a drastic reorganization in 1871, and among the courses introduced were law, economics, political science, and statistics. As these disciplines had previously been unknown — at least in their Western garb — instructors were imported from France, England, and the United States, and at the same time numerous students were sent to Europe and America who afterward returned to fill professorships.

The intellectual ferment was tremendous, and rival schools of thought quickly arose. The utilitarianism of Jeremy Bentham and John Stuart Mill was espoused by Yukichi Fukuzawa and Keiu Nakamura; the notions of Montesquieu and Rousseau were upheld by Chomin Naki; and some aspects of Hobbes's and Spencer's political doctrines attracted Hiroyuki Kato, later privy counsellor to the Emperor, who also absorbed, as time went on, a good deal of German authoritarian social philosophy. Students of political science and law, counting among their number Nobushige Hozumi, Kencho Suematsu, Kenjiro Ume, and Nariaki Tomii, first went to England or America, but later German schools began to acquire greater prestige and attracted a large proportion of Japanese scholars. The constitution promulgated in 1889 was based on the authoritarian phases of the social philosophies of Stein and Gneist, with but scattering traces of Spencer and other liberals.[58]

Sociology Appears: the First Epoch. — Sociology at first found no place in the universities, although some knowledge of the new social science had already reached Japan. It was first translated as a virtual duplicate of " socialism," as " the study of shifts in public opinion," and also as " the study of social intercourse," [59] but when in 1882 Kotaro Noritake published his translation of Spencer's *Principles of Sociology* [60] an exact Japanese equivalent was found and has since been consistently used.

Before the translation appeared, Shoichi Toyama (1848–1900), holding a knowledge of sociology to be indispensable for the historian, used the English original as a text to accompany his lectures on Spencer which formed part of his course on the history of Europe at the Imperial University of Tokyo.[61] Toyama had gone to England in 1866, and the Spencerian social evolutionism he then acquired dominated all his later work. He had also been in the United States as a government official, and in 1872 entered the University of Michigan.[62] After his return to Japan, he gave the lectures mentioned above in 1880, only four years later than Sumner's first lectures on Spencer's sociology at

Yale.[63] When the chair of sociology was established at the Imperial University of Tokyo in 1893, Toyama was the first occupant. He was the author of several works dealing with ancient Japanese society as reflected in mythology, and also of a history of Japanese social thought that is still considered useful in spite of its excessive social evolutionism.[64]

None of his writings bore the title of sociology, however; here priority must be assigned to Nagao Ariga, who in 1883 published the first of his projected six-volume system of sociology. Only three appeared; these dealt with the evolution of society, religion, and the family, and in addition to Spencerian influence also showed marked traces of MacLennan and Morgan.[65]

Among the first to be borne along by that other powerful current of biologized sociology, social Darwinism, was Hiroyuki Kato, already mentioned as having been one of the students sent abroad in the early days of the Meiji Restoration. He returned to introduce French theories of natural law and the rights of man in his two volumes on *True Politics* and *A New Theory of the State*. But, after a thorough study of the evolutionary conceptions then current, he became an ardent supporter of social Darwinism, and in 1882 brought out his *New Theory of the Rights of Man,* in which he expounded an extreme form of the doctrine. He also inclined toward the authoritarian, state-supremacy doctrines of Gneist and Stein, and had much to do with their influence on the constitution of 1889. None of Kato's writings carried the word sociology on the title page, but his social Darwinism is clearly evident in his *Conflict and the Right of the Stronger* (1894) and *Evolution of Morals and Law* (1900).[66]

Any list of the pioneers of Japanese sociology must include the name of Nobushige Hozumi who, although known chiefly for his work in jurisprudence, passed beyond the bounds of his discipline to contribute several treatises of high sociological value: *Essay on Seclusion* (1891), *Evolution of Law,* and *Ancestor-Worship in Japanese Law.* Pervading all these works is Hozumi's theory that groups cluster about interests — indeed, that all groups are interest-groups. This, it will be recognized, is closely akin to the teachings of Ratzenhofer, Small, Bentley, and others. Interest Hozumi defined in accordance with social Darwinism: that which aids in the struggle for survival.[67]

During this early phase of the Japanese social sciences a great number of Western writings were translated. In addition to Spencer we find Malthus, Hegel, Quetelet, Jevons, Maine, Lubbock, Carey, Bagehot, Ward, John Stuart Mill, Marx, Engels, Kidd,

Fouillée, Giddings, Mayo-Smith, Small, Guyau, Karl Pearson, Westermarck, and many more.[68] Nearly all these writers bore some relation to sociology, and enthusiasm for the new science ran high. Japanese intellectuals referred to it with great although perhaps unwarranted frequency, and even " practical " men began to take account of sociology after the address delivered by Hiroyuki Kato on the occasion of his reception into the Imperial Academy, when he declared that everyone active in politics possesses sociological knowledge needing only to be systematized to be of high scientific value.[69]

The Second Epoch: Organicism and Psychologism. — In 1898 Nobuta Kishimoto published two works bearing the title of sociology. Like many of his predecessors and contemporaries, Kishimoto devoted part of his efforts to the exposition and criticism of various Occidental theories, but unlike everyone before his time, also systematically developed the doctrine of organicism.[70] Not otherwise important in the history of Japanese sociology, he nevertheless marks the beginning of what we here call its second period, which was primarily one of far-reaching closed systems of organicism or, in reaction thereto, of psychologism. Kazutami Ukita, Momoyo Oka, Wataru Totoki, Kôjirô Tatsumi, and many others might be chosen to exemplify these trends, but for our purposes the most important are Tongo Takebe and Ryukichi Endo.[71]

Takebe, who was Toyama's successor in the chair of sociology at the Imperial University of Tokyo, was a thoroughgoing organismic theorist who also held Comtean conceptions.[72] For the quarter-century from 1898 to 1922 he was perhaps the most influential single sociologist in Japan. Not only was his position in the chief governmental institution of high strategic value, but in addition he gathered about him a corps of collaborators for his *Sociological Miscellany* (1906–1912), presided over the Japanese Institute of the Social Sciences from 1912 to 1922, and edited the ten volumes of its annals. Moreover, he was an indefatigable worker; his *General Sociology* (4 vols., 1904–1918) took account of all the important sociological theories developed in the West up to his time.[73] Unfortunately, however, the critical abilities he displayed when dealing with the theories of others were not applied to his own work, and he fell prey to a kind of organismic doctrine almost as fanciful as that of Lilienfeld. He not only regarded " society " as a multicellular organism, but also endowed it with consciousness and personality.[74]

Although strongly influenced by Spencer, Lilienfeld, and Schäffle, he was primarily a follower of Comte — probably, as

Matsumoto has pointed out, because of the normative and practical features of the *Positive Polity*. These made a strong appeal to the political sympathies of Takebe who, like Confucius, believed his function to be that of teaching " how to govern the country well and how to rule beneficently over the world under heaven." [75] He explicitly announced his goal to be the establishment of the positive laws of human society in order that they might be applied to the ends of government. The system he developed, in addition to its resemblance to those of his predecessors listed above, might be compared to the early theories of René Worms or the organismic aspects of the work of Guillaume DeGreef. Takebe did not restrict himself to theoretical researches; he attempted to apply sociology as he conceived it to the contemporary problems of war, international relations, modern civilization, and education.[76] Occupant of his post until 1922, it is probable that he had a large part in the formulation of the declaration made by the faculties of the Imperial University of Tokyo when an independent department of sociology was established in 1920 (before that time it was an appendage of the department of philosophy in the Faculty of Letters) :

Recent social relations, especially the economic, have undergone many radical changes since the World War. . . . In order to promote the betterment of present-day society, the intellectual class must assume the duty of studying social relations scientifically in order to solve social problems most effectively. This cannot be accomplished without advanced education . . . and the University of Tokyo therefore takes the step of establishing a department of sociology. These are its aims: (1) to study the phenomena of the universe and formulate the principles of a synthetic philosophy; (2) to analyze economic problems and their relation to society — economics; and (3) to study the essential elements of social organization — sociology. These are to be regarded as basic sociological courses. Other subjects, such as ethics, law, politics, and history, we highly recommend to students of sociology in order that they may acquire sufficient knowledge for the solution of sociological problems and at the same time equip themselves for greatest efficiency as leaders in the work of civilization. . . .

The faculties of this University are greatly pleased by the rapid progress of science and education in recent times. On the other hand, recent social changes . . . [have brought] danger to uneducated people, who may be misled by false doctrines leading them to destroy our cherished national culture. We therefore establish this department of sociology . . . with the idea of cultivating the minds of students so that they in turn may offer their invaluable services for the betterment of society. . . .[77]

Whatever may be the ultimate judgment of sociologists concerning the permanent value of Takebe's work, there can be no doubt that his career as university professor was successful. In this he offers a marked contrast to Ryukichi Endo, who had to content himself with courses at the Tokyo Graduate School for Professorial Training and in several private institutions.[78] None gave him much opportunity for influencing students, and as a consequence he remained relatively unknown throughout his career. Only in recent times has there been any appreciation of his contribution to Japanese sociology.

In his first works Endo championed organicism, but after his translation of Giddings's *Principles of Sociology,* and his study of Simmel and Tarde, he turned against it (and therefore, be it noted, against Takebe). His *Modern Sociology* (1907) is representative of the psychologistic trend, and he has been called the Japanese Tarde. For him society is the willed association of human beings, using " will " in the very broad sense popularized by Wundt, whose voluntaristic psychology treats will and apperception as different aspects of the same function. All meaningful actions have will as their nucleus, and consequently the *Gebilde* or plurality pattern called society is a voluntary association. But if association, the preëminently " social " type of conduct, is voluntary, is voluntary dissociation non-social and therefore not an object for sociological study? (Space forbids that we concern ourselves with the confusion clearly manifest in this usage of " social," etc.; detailed criticism must yield to exposition.) Endo avoids this difficulty, to his own satisfaction, in a way reminiscent of Giddings. He asserts that dissociation is simply the rebound, as it were, of association, and, being altogether exceptional and occupying only a limited domain, it is not of great sociological importance. Association, which reigns in the major part of life in society, is the proper focal point of sociological research.

The modes of relation sustaining voluntary grouping are constraint, imitation, consensus, and the like. The principal voluntary associations forming the elements of social organization may be classed, according to Endo, as the government and the state, the public, the family, and groups united by mode-imitation, by friendship, by function, by tradition, by succession, and similar bonds. It should be noted, however, that, true to his particular variety of voluntaristic psychology, Endo regarded the fundamental bond of union in all social groups as conscious coöperation in the attainment of common goals.[79]

We now know that the explanatory rôle thus assigned con-

sciousness is far too weighty and that the naïve individualistic
voluntarism forming the basis of the system grants too little place
to the influence of genuinely collective phenomena. This mare's-
nest of errors must not, however, divert our attention from the
valid elements in Endo's doctrines, and we must also in justice
grant that most of the psychologistic theories of his day were at
least equally distorted. Moreover, Endo's very one-sidedness
helped to save Japanese sociology from complete domination by
Takebe's organismic dogmas, and that was no small service.

Finally, the fact must not be overlooked that Endo did not
confine himself to psychologistic speculation. Oriental philosophy
and ethics were considerably illuminated by his concrete studies,
and he was profoundly versed in the culture of China and Korea
as well as in that of his own land.[80] Perhaps his most lasting work
will not be any of his general sociological treatises but his penetrating analysis of *The Development of Japanese Society and the
Transformations of Its Social Thought* (1903).

The Third Epoch: Preparation and Transition. — Dissatisfaction with the vague and sweeping notions too frequently found in
the writings of Takebe, Endo, and other writers of the second
epoch did not at once become articulate, but it soon began to show
itself indirectly. For example, Ryukyo Higuti published an excellent history of sociological theories in 1911 in which he clearly
showed that Japanese sociology was eventually likely to incline
toward a psychological rather than a biological interpretation of
social phenomena, but he himself refrained from adopting the extreme psychologism of Endo. His position was much akin to that
of American psycho-sociology of the same period.

This likeness becomes still more striking in the work of Kaoru
Kobayashi, whose *Psychological Sociology* and *Study in Social
Psychology* appeared in 1909 and 1910 respectively. Portions of
these books remind one of Ellwood's *Sociology and Social Problems,*[81] and the resemblance is still more pronounced in Kobayashi's *General Sociology* (1923). Here, while partially avoiding
the worst consequences of those instinctivistic, psychologistic explanations that make social behavior a mere function of the individual's native equipment, he applied psycho-sociology to the
analysis of social processes, and at the same time showed how the
theoretical results achieved could be applied to the solution of
social problems.[82]

But the most important influences in the rejuvenation of Japanese sociology did not come from the United States. France and
Germany, particularly the latter, provided the stimuli that helped

to start the march toward the high level now occupied. The most important leader was Shotaro Yoneda, for the past quarter-century professor of sociology at the Imperial University of Kyoto. He studied under Giddings and Tarde,[83] and very early in his career was influenced by Simmel, the net result being that he was never an adherent of organismic theory. At the same time, he maintained an extreme catholicity — so great, in fact, that he has been charged with having no opinions of his own. This is unfair, for his general position can be inferred from his expository studies, and with regard to the logic and methodology of sociology he leaves no room for doubt as to what his own convictions are.

It must be granted, however, that the charge against him is superficially justified, for the great and indispensable rôle he has played in Japanese sociology has been that of transmitter of recent Western theories. He began before the World War to acquaint his students with all the various schools of sociology, and in spite of the difficulties of scientific communication during the decade after 1914, he succeeded in keeping pace with every new advance. An opponent of premature popularization and hastily constructed systems, Yoneda faithfully received, assimilated, and passed on in forms easily comprehensible to his countrymen the doctrines of the systematic-empirical or " formal " school, the sociographers, the sociologistic disciples of Durkheim, the cultural sociology of Alfred Weber and of some of the French social historians, the historical sociology of Max Weber and his co-workers, and the variegated but none the less stimulating notions promulgated by the more scholarly of the Marxists. Moreover, Yoneda continually emphasized the necessity of placing all these theories in their Japanese setting and of testing them by the use of materials derived from Japanese ethnography and sociography. His own interests tended toward psycho-sociology, and he paid much attention to fashion, reform, revolution, the crowd and the public, and the like. He has not yet published an exhaustive treatment of his own system, but in 1913 he set forth a lengthy outline that he has not since modified, and we may therefore take it to be representative of the views he now holds.

In the first part of this outline the logic and methodology of the social sciences are briefly expounded, and the first conclusion is that sociology is not a scientific variety of social technology but a strictly theoretical science having no direct concern with proposals for changing society. Second, he regards sociology as a special branch of philosophy based on the results of empirical investigation. Third, sociology falls into two main divisions: pure and synthetic, or abstract and concrete, or general and particular. By these antitheses he means that one branch of sociology is concerned with the formulation of general propositions drawn from the study of " social reality," which is primarily constituted by the web of intermental relations, and that the other or synthetic branch is occupied with the application of these generalizations, and of those of other sciences as well, to various configurations of social phenomena. To illustrate: pure sociology is based on the analysis of human conduct, viewed abstractly as mental interaction, in all its manifestations, whether among preliterates, Orientals, or Western peoples; synthetic sociology is the study of every phase of social life among, let us say, the Japanese, in the light of the theories of biology, psychology, pure sociology, and all other relevant sciences.

Let us repeat, however, in concluding this discussion of Yoneda, that his importance lies in his transitional and preparatory function as the great scholar whose erudition brought to his contemporaries a critical knowledge of all the important sociological theories formulated in the two decades before 1925.[84]

In a very real sense Yoneda was the Moses of the modern Japanese sociological movement; his unsurpassed erudition and indefatigable writing led the way to the Promised Land, but it remained for a Joshua in the person of Yasuma Takata to occupy it. He studied under Yoneda at Kyoto, and in 1919 published his *Principles of Sociology,* the culminating work of the transitional and preparatory period. In this and in later publications which supplement, modify, and qualify it, he develops a theory having the following significant features:

(1) Sociology is a special social science. The encyclopedic sociology represented, for example, by Comte, Oppenheimer, or Cornejo, and the synthetic sociology espoused by Branford, Dunkmann, or Bureau are brushed aside. Sociology is the special study of the purely social phase of human conduct, which is neither more nor less general than the economic, political, and like phases.

(2) Sociology is the study of the willed *association* of human beings, for its object is the social group. Dissociation is therefore of no importance in the *definition* of sociology, although of course it is present in all societies. This limitation of sociology to the study of association is probably due to the influence of Endo, although Tönnies has propounded a doctrine in all respects similar. Moreover, Endo and Tönnies are at one with Takata in the em-

phasis on *willed* association — a contention, by the way, that finds another supporter in MacIver. Most Japanese scholars, granting little weight to the possibility that Tönnies or even Wundt may have been the source of Takata's voluntaristic tendency, regard him as the successor of Endo so far as this part of his theory is concerned.

To the present writers the whole discussion as to whether sociology is primarily the study of sociation, i.e., of association *and* dissociation, or primarily of association with dissociation as a merely " negative " phase, is a pure logomachy of no particular scientific importance, serving only to whet the strife of " schools " of interactionism (Simmel, Wiese, Park and Burgess) on the one hand and of associationism (Tönnies, Heberle, Takata) on the other. This view finds some justification in the fact that Takata is forced to make a place for the study of dissociation in his " third view of history," i.e., in his system of social dynamics, which he apparently does not include in his conception of sociology. The so-called third view gets its name by contrast with Marxian historical materialism and Hegelian historical idealism; for Takata the clue to the presumed thesis – antithesis – synthesis (association – dissociation – re-association) of social development is found in the structure and mobility of the population — a position closely akin to Durkheim's morphological theory of the historical process and Sorokin's stress on social mobility.

(3) Sociology, although not a normative science, finds its focus in the study of " mind " rather than " nature," and " mind " is primarily characterized by its relation to values. Takata, pressing the German distinction between *Naturwissenschaften* and *Geisteswissenschaften*, even goes so far as to maintain that nature and mind are quite different, a position which is tenable only if a conception of nature peculiar to an outmoded nineteenth-century type of science is postulated. Apart from this, however, the emphasis on values — which of course has nothing to do with value-*judgment* — is of great methodological importance, as Thomas and Znaniecki have already shown.

(4) Since sociology is not a natural science, it follows that its generalizations have not the status of natural laws. With Max Weber, Takata asserts that only ideal-typical generalizations can be made, and that these ideal types (Takata says " genus-types ") have relevance only because they are oriented in the direction of values of one kind or another. The recurrent regularities in social behavior that are given meaning by these ideal types have merely

the status of probabilities: the social relationship of friendship, for example, exists merely in the probability that given such and such circumstances, conduct of a friendly character will ensue.

Here again there seems much ado about nothing. It was well enough to emphasize the merely probable nature of social regularities at a time when "the laws of nature" were thought to be absolute, but that time has passed. The element of statistical probability enters into all modern scientific generalizations. There can be no doubt, however, that Takata is quite right in upholding ideal-typical generalization as the only type valid for sociology — in fact, for all the social sciences.[85]

We may well agree with the Japanese historians of sociology who hold that Takata is a figure of great importance. Whether his theory is right or wrong, it represents a Herculean effort to raise Japanese sociology to a level of international significance, and that effort has been successful. The era of preparation and transition gives way to the period of maturity.

The Fourth Epoch: the Struggle of the Schools. — A whole school of sociology soon developed as a consequence of Takata's work. All its members continually take his theories into account, although of course this is not to say that he receives unqualified approval. Those most closely agreeing are Sakae Sugiyama and Uichi Iwasaki. Somewhat more critical are Shodo Shinmei and Teizo Toda. Definitely opposed to one or another phase of Takata's theory, but accepting his definition of sociology as a special social science, are Tomoo Otaka, Makato Igarashi, Kantaro Komatsu, and Kanrei Inoue.[86] The latter's critique of Takata is particularly interesting:

To begin with, says Inoue, it is futile to try to define sociology as "the study of society," for society is only the static, associative aspect of interhuman sociation, whereas social relations of all kinds, associative and dissociative, form the object-matter of sociology. On this point Inoue is in complete agreement with Wiese. Again, Inoue maintains that Takata's limitation of sociology to the static aspect of social life is a fundamental error; sociology alone cannot be the exception to the general rule that statics and dynamics are relative and therefore indispensable parts of any science. As already noted, the only way in which Takata has attempted to meet this telling objection has been by throwing the study of social processes bodily out of sociology into the philosophy of history.

Another interesting phase of Inoue's work is his attempt to synthesize German systematic sociology with the theories of the

Durkheim school by defining social relation as psychical relation, on the one hand, and on the other as normative relation comprising folkways, mores, and laws, thus making it possible to study the phenomena of society and of culture with the same set of concepts.[87]

The criticism of the systematic-empirical or " formal " school implied by this attempt at synthesis early became explicit in the work of Unosuke Wakamiya, who in 1924 pointed out that the study of Japanese society was being too much neglected in the zeal for methodology, classification, and logical analysis.[88] Allied with Wakamiya are a number of avowed exponents of Durkheim's theories, as well as several advocates of that type of social history pervaded by sociological analysis characteristic of some of the writers grouped around Henri Berr. In some respects, of course, it is false to place systematic and Durkheimian sociology in radical opposition, for they simply represent respectively the abstract analytic and the concrete synthetic methods of dealing with the same realm of social reality. But for all that the complaint grows that systematic sociology cannot describe and explain actual social life because the unique configuration represented by each particular culture cannot be dissected by the systematic method without losing the very characteristics that make it worthy of study. Representatives of the French concrete emphasis in ways ranging from partial acceptance to unqualified approval are Shizuya Akasaka, Junichiro Matsumoto, Yoshihiko Yamada, Tatsumi Makino, and Hisatoshi Tanabe.[89]

The most drastic critics of systematic sociology, however, are found among the cultural sociologists who follow the lead of Alfred Weber and other German scholars. They are akin to the Durkheim school in their insistence that the cultural characteristics of social phenomena cannot be caught within the meshes of systematic sociology, however finely woven they may be, but they go beyond the Durkheimians in the importance they assign to historical data and treatment. This school is not yet far advanced in Japan, but a number of interesting studies have appeared. Seki Eikichi has described and analyzed the relation between various cultural totalities and a few of the social configurations, such as nation and class, found within them. Kazuta Kurauchi follows Wakamiya's lead in concentrating on Japanese culture. Jun Tosaka, Ikutaro Shimizu, and Toshio Kaba have collaborated in a cultural critique of systematic sociology by means of studies in the theory of ideology and the sociology of knowledge, thus following the path marked out by Karl Mannheim and, to a certain extent, by Hans Freyer. The three Japanese writers just mentioned owe their urge to overcome systematic sociology to the Marxism so widely current in Japanese intellectual circles. Indeed, one of them, Shimizu, has recently become so zealous an advocate of Marxism that he uses it not merely to combat systematic sociology but sociology of every sort.[90]

Thus there are at present three prominent tendencies: the systematic, the Durkheimian, and the cultural, occasionally coöperating but usually competing. The unkind critic might be disposed to assert that the resulting chaos spells the doom of Japanese sociology, but it is probably more correct to say that the present stage will be followed by one in which irreconcilabilities will be eliminated or minimized and the materials for fruitful special studies directly available in Japanese culture more extensively used.

The Fifth Epoch: Coördination. — A first step in this direction has been taken by Junichiro Matsumoto, already mentioned in other connections, who attempts to harmonize the different schools. He summarizes his theory thus:

Sociology is the " total science " of " social facts," i.e., of social groups, social processes, and social products. The words society, social, and others like them have many meanings, but there is one sense common to all: they signify relations between human beings. These relations constitute the distinctively social part of " human facts," and comprise the three domains above mentioned. The social group is the real or possible " state " [static condition] in which individuals communicate with each other or are in preparation so to communicate. The social process is the " act " engaged in by individuals when they communicate — or, in Simmel's words, psychical interaction. The social product is the " normal behavior pattern " which, as Durkheim has said, is characterized by its constraining power.

The social group has three objective principles: reciprocal contact, community (*Gemeinschaft*), and society (*Gesellschaft*). These are not types of social organization, as the latter two are, for example, in Tönnies's theory, but " structural principles," and the most fundamental of these is reciprocal contact. This has three phases: social act as contrasted to individual act, social relation, and group action. Finally, the social product can be viewed under three aspects: culture, sociality, and " consciousness of the self of society " (this last means simply an ideology, unique to a given society, playing the rôle of its central, dominating principle).

The association theory defended by Takata can deal only with the social group because of its essentially static character; the interaction theory has to do only with social processes because it is limited to the dynamic phases of social life; and the social product or " social consciousness," which is the subject-matter of the cultural and Durkheimian schools, is only one phase of the social fact and therefore loses its significance if isolated from the social group and the social process.

Sociology must deal with all three of these, and therefore is a " total science." This total sociology, however, must be rigorously distinguished from the encyclopedic and·synthetic varieties because it has to do only with the social fact as " form," leaving the study of " content " to economics, political science, etc. . . . It is therefore a " special " science as well, and as it is not merely abstract and theoretical but also historical and normative, its full set of qualifying adjectives includes total, special, and *systematic*. [It will be noted that " systematic " as used by Matsumoto has a meaning different from that assigned it throughout the present work.] This being the character of sociology, its parts may be classified as follows:

1. Pure sociology, or the abstract study of society.
2. Empirical sociology, or the concrete study of society:
    a. Historical sociology, or sociological analysis of the history of society.
    b. Sociography, or descriptive study of society, comprising statistics, verbal description, and other techniques.

These two divisions are the central domains of sociology; the three following are complementary:

3. Applied or practical sociology:
    a. Study of social purposes or controlling directives.
    b. Study of social technology, or social politics, social work, etc.
4. History of sociology:
    a. History of social thought.
    b. History of sociological theories.
5. Logic and methodology of the social sciences.[91]

With this comprehensive schema before us, it should be easy to agree with Matsumoto's contention that if it were accepted as a working basis, however temporary, needless argument would be avoided and a fruitful division of labor instituted. The struggle of the schools is still too violent, however, for this or any other conciliatory proposal to meet with complete or even widespread approval. The most that can be said is that tendencies are here and there apparent which indicate that some such plan of coördination may eventually gain at least tacit acceptance. These tendencies are most clearly evident in the numerous special studies that have recently been made by Japanese sociologists, and in taking account of them we shall follow the order of Matsumoto's schema.

Special Studies. — Pure sociology is of course best represented by the various theories of the systematic-empirical or "formal" school, but most of these are in the form of comprehensive systems rather than special studies. There are, however, some analyses of community and society by Otaka, Takata, and Komatsu that should be mentioned here, as well as a few treatments of social classes by the two writers last named and by Matsumoto. Relatively little attention has been devoted to the state, this being usually left to the political scientists, but we should nevertheless mention the sociological or quasi-sociological work of Shigeru Nakashima, Tetsuji Kada, Shinichi Fujii, and Takata.

In the second division, that of empirical sociology, the family furnishes the most important and interesting object-matter for concrete study, but up-to-date economists like Shiro Kawata and moralists like Kimio Hayashi have almost monopolized the field. The only sociological treatments worth noting are Teizo Toda's *Studies of the Family* (1927) and *Family and Marriage* (1935). When we take account of the fact that the family is one of the most important, constant, and universal of groups, and that Japan offers a rich profusion of family types, this neglect seems hard to justify. We have already noted that Wakamiya, writing in 1924, charged his colleagues with servile imitation, aimlessness, and historical discontinuity. Such strictures are too severe, but if Toda's lead is not followed they will certainly be justified eventually. Fortunately Toda himself has expounded the method necessary for concrete family observation in his *Social Surveys* (1933), and he should not long lack collaborators. An exponent of sociography who has devoted much attention to method but who has so far restricted his researches to Russia is Tokio Imai.

But if the Japanese family has been neglected, the Japanese village has not. Takeo Ono, primarily a student of rural economic institutions, was a forerunner of rural sociography, which later came into its own when social survey techniques were generally adopted. Eitaro Suzuki is at present the outstanding student of rural society in Japan; his work in the Rinchu region, which is situated in the valley of the Gifu River, is a model of method. Beginning with the portion most subject to urban influence, he gradually went up the valley, at each step finding more definitely rural institutions, until in the most remote district the most simple and primitive of all were located and described. In this study he was obliged to make the most extraordinary efforts, now developing new methods and techniques and now setting them aside for others better adapted to the changing situations uncovered as the work progressed. Strongly influenced by the Le-Play school, his various writings nevertheless constitute a monument of *Japanese* ingenuity and resourcefulness. Other outstanding practitioners of rural sociography are Takashi Koyama and Seiichi Kitano. The latter has made much use of the excellent data of the Japanese census, placed on so firm a foundation by Kyoji Sugi and the disciple of Von Mayr, Iwasaburo Takano.

Primitive institutions in remote districts of Korea have been dealt with by Takashi Akiba with primary attention to religious practices, and Yuzuru Okada has studied the hill tribes of Formosa in an attempt to describe the whole range of social phenomena they exhibit. Two excellent histories of Japanese society, serving as indispensable auxiliaries for sociological analyses of the development of Japanese institutions, have been furnished by Eijiro Honsho and Kamejiro Takikawa.

Urban sociology is represented only by social surveys and by advocates of the *rapprochement* of sociology and various types of social politics and social service. Toshio Koyama, Eiichi Isomura, Myosen Furusaka, Toyotaro Miyoshi, Fuhutaro Okui, and Tomio Yonebayashi have made urban surveys; Kotoku Unno, U. Iwasaki, Kimio Hayashi, T. Yamaguchi, E. Isomura, and I. Abe are the outstanding practitioners of the *rapprochement* mentioned above. (The latter writers, by the way, might well be placed under the head of social technology.) There is certainly plenty of room for urban sociology of the types set forth by Sorokin and by the Chicago school.

The methods of human geography are turned to account by Michitoshi Odauchi, who correlates folklore with its geographical setting, and Seikan Kawanishi, who began with economic geography and found that it changed under his hands into what he now calls geographical sociology — closely akin, be it noted, to Mukerjee's regional-ecological sociology.

Population studies are made by Eizo Koyama, who calls himself a student of " racial sociology," and by Takata, who, as we have seen, bases his " third view of history " on the age distribution, mobility, and other characteristics of the population. A curious variant is provided by Ekai Hayashi, who has attempted to correlate population phenomena with psycho-sociology along lines at least superficially similar to those followed by Corrado Gini.

Concrete studies in collective psychology, mixed with a good deal of abstract theory, were made by Kobayashi, to whom we have already referred in our discussion of the " third epoch " of Japanese sociology. He inclined somewhat too strongly toward explanations on the basis of instinct, in which he is followed by Kisoburo Kawabe, who has a further point of resemblance to Kobayashi in that he strongly stresses the duty of the sociologist to contribute to the solution of social problems. Other students of collective or group psychology are Tokutomi, Teho, Tanimoto, Shinmei, and Oishi, all of them mentioned elsewhere in this chapter.

Skipping the division of applied or practical sociology, we turn to the history of social thought. Here is where the cultural sociologists and the Durkheimians have done the most valuable work. Hisatoshi Tanabe has written a *Sociology of Language* (1933) that is of the utmost significance for the analysis of such widely differing types of social thought as that found in China, with its ideographic writing, on the one hand, and in the Western countries, with their phonetic systems, on the other — an antithesis also stressed by the Frenchman, Marcel Granet (*La Pensée chinoise*) and by the German, Leo Jordan (*Schule der Abstraktion und Dialektik*). Tetsuo Watanuki has employed the Durkheim method in his unique studies of social thought during the most striking era of Japanese history, namely, the Meiji Restoration, and M. Shimoide and Seien Nunokawa have dealt with the same period. Religious influences on social thought are analyzed by two Durkheimians, Enku Uno and Seijin Furuno. Some outstanding writers in the general field of the sociology of knowledge have already been noted, but we should also mention the Marxist, Kiyoshi Miki; the expositor and commentator, M. Shinmei; the vigorous critic, K. Komatsu; and the thorough student of Japanese ideology, K. Kurauchi.

As might be expected from the general Japanese interest in everything concerning the West, the history of Euro-American sociology is heavily represented by translations (so numerous that they cannot be listed here), monographs, and general surveys. No other modern nation is so well informed with regard to the work that has been and is being done elsewhere. German sociology has been studied by U. Hayashi, K. Okada, Rikuhei Imori, Shodo Shinmei, E. Seki, and Makoto Igarashi. French sociology is surveyed and expounded by Sotaro Takasi, Yoshihiko Yamada, and several others. English and American sociology finds expositors in M. Furusaka, I. Kobayasi, M. Yamaguchi, and Toshio Hayase. The history of Japanese sociology is not so popular a subject, but it has been studied by K. Kada, Teizo Toda, Unasuke Wakamiya, and T. Simoide. General surveys of all these fields are provided by Shinmei and Matsumoto, the latter of whom has also written excellent monographs on the sociology of each of the countries mentioned.

The logic and methodology of the social sciences are best represented by the sociologists Takata, K. Komatsu, and Matsumoto, but the economist E. Soda and the Marxist Sakae Sugiyama (who, curiously enough, is also a disciple of Takata) cannot be overlooked.[92]

Sociological Publications, Research Institutes, and Societies. — Many of the special studies mentioned in the preceding section are of course too short or too technical to find commercial publishers. Fortunately, however, there are enough sociological journals and monograph series to make it possible for really good work to reach the learned world, although as in all other countries there is no over-abundance of such facilities. The first publication in the field was *The Journal of Sociology,* which appeared from 1897 to 1899. It was followed by *Society,* of which five volumes were published; this afterward became heir to the title of its predecessor, and as *The Journal of Sociology,* new series, ran through seven volumes. In imitation of Durkheim's *L'Année sociologique* a Japanese annual bearing a closely similar title came into print shortly after its French forerunner, and existed for ten years, afterward becoming *The Study of Sociology,* which struggled along for only four — the early postwar period proved too difficult to traverse.

In 1924, however, an ambitious venture was undertaken: *The Japanese Sociological Monthly,* drawing on the interest and good will built up by the earlier publications mentioned, began its phenomenally successful career. The economic difficulties of the early 1930's forced it to become a quarterly, and then a yearbook, but it still is exceedingly vigorous. *The Sociological Review,* a quarterly, entered the field in 1934; this is an excellent journal that shows every sign of continuing. Articles of sociological interest also appear in *Social Work,* a monthly, *The Yearbook of Japanese Social Work,* and *The Labor Yearbook;* these are the successors of *The Proceedings of the Society of Social Politics* which in 1919, when it ceased to appear, numbered twelve volumes. There are in addition two valuable auxiliaries: the monthlies *The Journal of the Anthropological Society of Tokyo* and *The Journal of Statistics.* Not quite of the same high quality as the publications already listed but none the less worthy of mention are *Sociological Research, Social Thought, The Study of Social*

Problems, and *Social Policy* (from the information available it is difficult to determine whether these are still published).

Research institutes are not so plentiful; apart from those attached to university seminars the only one of importance is the Ohara Institute for Social Research, and this is confined largely to the study of labor problems and Marxism.

Sociological societies and kindred bodies, however, flourish. The pioneer was the Society of Sociology (1896–1898), which later became the Society of Sociological Studies (1898–1904). The name was revived in 1931, and the society bearing it is quite active. From 1904 to 1912 there was a lull, but in the latter year Takebe founded the Society of Japanese Sociological Studies, and this held the stage until 1922, when Takebe's retirement brought disagreement among his followers and the organization broke up. The following year, however, the Society of Sociology in Japan got under way, and the year after a rival body, the Japanese Sociological Society, came into the disputed territory. At present, therefore, there are three active organizations of nation-wide membership, to say nothing of several smaller groups confined to various universities.[93]

Conclusion: The Sun Still Rises. — There seems every reason to be optimistic concerning the future of Japanese sociology. Wakamiya's first critique of sociology in Japan, written over ten years ago, is no longer valid. The stage of *undue* attention to the theories advanced in other nations is quickly drawing to a close. Moreover, Japanese sociologists are not only rapidly developing their own distinctive systems, but are also turning their energies toward the investigation of their own society. This offers opportunities for research unparalleled anywhere else in the world, and Western sociologists will soon be forced to look to their laurels. It is to be hoped that a realization of the importance of Japanese sociology will eventually lead Occidentals to a serious study of the language, at present an almost insuperable barrier.

This chapter began with the statement that questions of convenience in organization, and those alone, determined the order assigned to the different nations we have considered, and as the volume draws toward a close, we can reiterate the maxim, " Last but by no means least."

Only in Japan have there been any notable recent advances in sociology. India has proceeded slowly, and China has moved backward.

For Japan, see the able survey by Kunio Odaka in MSTICAC, noted on pp. 814 and 877. He regards the newer tendencies as: (1) growing importance of sociology in higher education; (2) greater emphasis on empirical research; (3) increasing popularity of statistical techniques; (4) development of new fields in empirical research; (5) closer association with neighboring sciences; and (6) beginning of international collaboration.

Epilogue

THE journey has been long; let us take our bearings.

"For to admire and for to see" the countries of the mind is in itself worth while, not to say fascinating, but few of us are content with this alone. We want to plot the course we have traveled, to appraise our varied experiences, and to envisage more clearly the task that lies immediately before us.

In the early stages of our journey we often slipped quietly into murky, mysterious caverns. Here we peered long and steadily through the shifting smoke while shaman, priest, or prophet stirred together scraps of lore and weird fancies from which he brewed potions of social thought for himself and his wide-eyed fellows. More, we saw the effects of the queer mixtures on those who imbibed them, and were able to gain inklings as to the outcome of certain sacred exaltations produced by lores of race, destiny, and force in our own day and generation. To choose the most striking examples: We watched the seething and bubbling of mores, ceremonials, myths, and charismas out of which oozed the sacred essences of *mana, tao, maât, dharma, religio, mishpat, logos,* and the like. When our steps led us among partially secular societies, we found that our senses had been sharpened through our sojourn in the caverns where the sacred showed its power. Familiar fumes betrayed the presence of fermenting residues of sacred essences lending potency to supposedly secular compounds known as the golden ages of past or future, the social contract, the normative conception of nature, natural rights, "the war of each against all," the capitalist mentality, organicism, inevitable progress, "the dialectic," racial mission, totalitarianism, and other heady draughts.

Here and there on the long road we toiled through scorching deserts, where utopian mirages danced before our eyes and the winds of doctrine beat upon us. More than once we came upon rocky defiles of fantastic sand-carved analogies that presented society in the guise of Leviathan, or the circling planets, or the many-hued pattern of the changing seasons. To him who can reckon only by the harvests of the oases and the fertile river-bottoms, it may seem that our labor in the barren regions was lost. But may it not be that the futilities of social thought are quite as instructive as the sight of the ravages of erosion or the havoc wrought upon topsoil by unwise tillage and windy drought? Must we not be thoroughly aware of aberrations in the interpretation of social processes, not to mention derangements of the processes themselves, that ruin the intellectual harvest?

And apart from all this, does not the history of science show that a false theory may have great utility? Not merely that an error sufficiently flagrant is sometimes a burial cairn warning later explorers of the fate that lurks in the wastelands – more than this is involved. A wrong theory may lead to the discovery of stretches of reality that otherwise would never have been stumbled upon: men sought for a route to the Indies and found a New World. Our much-denounced unilinear evolution is a case in point. The doctrine inevitably involved detailed comparison, and as time went on it became more and more detailed. When as a consequence relevant new data stood out more sharply amid the concealing thickets, vigorous efforts were made to set them up along the unilinear path at predetermined points. Soon, however, it was found to be impossible to wrench these data free from the dense tangle of other social and cultural phenomena with which they were intertwined. Bends and even loops were therefore made in the trail in order to link up the stubborn facts, but in the process of clearing these bypaths many more culture complexes revealed themselves, and it was seen that no single route, however meandering, could possibly bring all the evidence into orderly sequence. The result was the adoption of the hypothesis of many lines of development, some parallel, some divergent. The axemen of the doctrine of unilinear evolution had hacked out the first clearings from which their successors ran their branching roadways. While struggling through the slashings and down-timber and stumplands that the social evolutionists left behind we often spoke of them in ways less than respectful, but never without the feeling that even this stage of the toilsome journey was worth while.

From time to time, as we slowly plodded out of the forest wilderness or the desert, we feasted our eyes on variegated fields tilled by scientists, natural and social, in the days when one plot might be sown with a half-dozen kinds of seed and when one man might try to do work now assigned to a half-dozen different specialists. Gradually we learned to recognize unity in the diversity; the sociological harvest took discernible form amid the profusion of multifarious fruits and grains heaped up by cultivators calling themselves geographers, economists, philosophers, historians, ethnologists, or whatnot. Eventually the task of recognition grew somewhat easier, for the boundaries of the fields became more sharply marked, each of the various labors of tillage was allotted to men highly skilled in one rather than adaptable to many, and the seed was sorted and sifted with care.

True, we saw that old folkways persisted in many of the countries through which we passed, that an appalling number of fields had been trampled down or were overgrown with weeds, and that in once promising lands prospects for rich harvests were darkened by sudden blight. None the less, our travels through even these desolate and neglected regions, near and far, taught us much, for we saw that the sociologist must ever be on his guard against sloth, ignorant or malicious destruction, and the deadly scourge of anti-scientific and arrogant power that scatters abroad the all-supplanting dragon's teeth of ethnocentrism, obscurantism, and rationalization. We cannot remain free from the biases of lore if we do not foster a bias in favor of science.

In the happier acres our slowly-acquired facility in recognizing strips and patches bearing the crops of the different social sciences also gave us eyes to see the corners and borders as yet improperly cultivated. Much can still be done in even the most closely-covered regions by giving heed to what lies on the edges of the fields. Further, what we have already seen with regard to the newer varieties of our science, such as psycho-sociology, the sociology of knowledge, and culture case study, has borne in upon us the fact that the traditional plantings are not the only possibilities. Cross-fertilization may increase many times over the yield of new knowledge about man's life with his fellows. Perhaps this very cross-fertilization will also yield varieties that are not so entirely dependent as many now are on " climates of opinion," the peculiarities of national soil, and the traditional types of scholarly cultivation. Perhaps we may some day have a sociology, to name no other science, that will take root and flourish anywhere.

At any rate, our wanderings have clearly shown us that no such sociology now exists except as a tender growth that has still many vicissitudes to meet. We have seen that the development of social theory is linked not only with the theory of social development but also with its facts. Our garden cannot be cultivated in the clouds; we must plant and harvest on the earth, and tender growths must become hardy or perish. Will the knowledge gained along the crooks and turnings of our toilsome path enable us to sow with knowledge and reap with confidence? Need we answer the question with the well-worn " Only time will tell "?

Beyond doubt time will tell us much, but we need not passively await its answer. Through the powerful aid of ideal-typical method, and on the basis of what we now know, we can pose crucial questions that may speed the pace of the seasons. For example, our new border-province, the sociology of knowledge, can be dealt with in such manner that the hardy theoretical fruits of the experience of past centuries may perhaps be reaped in the few decades immediately before us; " Ibn Khaldūn, Turgot, or Durkheim may yield more than learned footnotes and the prideful preening of the erudite." This is a task which cannot be left to the history of philosophy, intellectual and cultural history, or the history of science as such. The sociologist need not fear that he is working in forbidden precincts or using forbidden methods when he endeavors to discover the social causes of or conditions for valid sociology, nor when he inquires into the validity of the sociological theories dealing with those social causes or conditions. He alone knows the full scope and bearing of his problem, and he need apologize to no one for cultivating his own garden in his own way.

The abiding worth of our journey at last appears; it has taught us what we must do in the here and now if our science is to flourish in the future. Only when and if we transcend the relative, only when and if we uproot the thorny barriers of ancient lores, the weeds of limited and partial logics, the entangling biases of nation and class, and the cherished illusions by which we have tried and failed to live with our fellows, can we find sociological theories valid for all men as men.

Twenty-two years after, with wars and rumors of wars intervening, what was said in this Epilogue still seems worth reiterating. But there is more to be said: time is running out, and there is "no place to hide." Without abandoning our essential values, we must learn to live with our fellows, and our fellows, also cherishing supreme values, must learn to live with us. Science as such cannot save us, but without science we cannot be saved. And as Florian Znaniecki (now so little read) so clearly showed, there is cultural as well as natural science. Sociology is part of the science, or one of the sciences, of culture. The sociologist—and I say this in defiance of the "professionalizers" — has a mission. In all humility, and yet with full awareness of his indispensability as a cultural scientist, he must *serve* today's mankind in the hope that he can help *save* today's mankind. If he and his fellows fail, they need not worry about their mission, for there will be no tomorrow.

1937-1960 Appendix on Sociological Trends

THE LAST CHANGES in the original text of this treatise, rewritten, as noted elsewhere, "on the margins of the galleysheets" from 1935 onward, were made in the summer and early fall of 1937. The preface was completed on January 1, 1938, and in the spring the bound volumes finally made their appearance, bearing the date of that year on their title pages.

In 1941 the editor-coauthor (hereinafter called the writer) was asked by Walter Yust, of the *Encyclopaedia Britannica,* to contribute an article to the *Yearbook* on the trends in sociological writing and research during that year. The request was gladly complied with, and has been renewed and fulfilled every year since. Then, in 1945, plans for a large four-volume *Britannica* special project were launched; this was to cover the events of the period just before, during, and just after World War II; viz., 1937-1946. In early 1947 the volumes came out with the title *Ten Eventful Years;* included was a long article on sociology by the writer.

Hence, when in 1951 a new and enterprising publisher suggested that, in view of the persisting demand, *Social Thought from Lore to Science* be reprinted (the initial publishers let it go out of print, in part because the plates were melted for war metal), it was also suggested that it be brought up to date. Extensive alterations in the original text seemed neither possible nor desirable, and it was decided to ask for permission to use the *EB* articles as the basis for the Appendix now before the reader. Mr. Yust graciously granted permission; therefore, it was possible to provide a year-by-year account from 1941 to 1950, together with a general summary covering 1937 to 1946. As can be seen from the above, it was great good luck that the dates dovetailed perfectly!

Then, for the 1960 edition to be brought out in convenient form by Dover Publications, the request was repeated, and the same much-appreciated response was forthcoming. The writer had continued to prepare the yearly articles (with the exception of the one for 1958, which is here provided for the first time), so that everything for 1951 through 1959 has now been added, together with a preliminary statement about prospects for 1960.

The articles are offered in the order in which they were written. This accounts for the fact that 1941-1946 is presented in yearly sequence, followed by an interlude dealing with 1937-1946 in the form of a ten-year retrospective summary, with resumption of the yearly procedure for 1947-1960. It seemed best to retain this order, in part for the purpose of avoiding charges of "second-guessing" with regard to some of the major trends foreseen in their early stages. *Comparison with the original articles is hereby expressly invited.*

Here and there a few grammatical constructions are manifest that the writer feels to be somewhat infelicitous, most of them the result of the frequent use of the past, perfect, and pluperfect. The *EB* Book of the Year rules call for a kind of "historical" statement that makes it necessary, in many instances, to speak of events that have just occurred or are still going on without the use of the present or progressive. Consequently some authors may feel that they or their works are being referred to as "has-beens"; this is definitely *not* the writer's intention.

Coverage of all important authors, articles, books, and researches was naturally impossible. The writer undoubtedly has his blind spots and biases, and even if he had somehow attained perfection, the space limits imposed on him would still have prevented proper consideration of much that was and is of importance. Most readers will probably feel that he has said enough anyway.

A good deal of material that appeared in the *EB* has been omitted, some of it dealing with matters of detail now more adequately covered in Howard W. Odum's *American Sociology* (1951). Major omissions are indicated by . . . . Journal abbreviations are given in the Notes, pp. cxix.

In the bibliographies at the end, books and articles presenting complementary or contrasting views of the period dealt with are listed, and a good deal of what has been deliberately or unwittingly left out may be found in them. There have been several sectarian surveys of recent developments in sociology; the writer can only hope that he has not perpetrated another. If he has, at least the remedies are available. *Medice, cure te ipsum.*

1941

Indecision and Pearl Harbor

DURING THE YEAR sociology made definite progress; it went still further on its way toward becoming "the grammar of the social sciences." Less figuratively put, it was vigorously carrying out its task of the comparative study, looking toward prediction, of social personalities, processes, and structures—the analysis of social interaction as such.

Many of the trends apparent in previous years continued. Before World War I, sociology had little recognition as an academic discipline except in the United States; elsewhere it was in the hands of brilliant amateurs or university men whose official positions were in quite different fields: philosophy, history, economics, and so on. Immediately after World War I, however, there was a tremendous expansion of sociological teaching and research throughout the whole civilized world, notably in Czechoslovakia (whose first President, Masaryk, had held the first chair of sociology at Prague—later occupied by Beneš), Germany, Japan, and Latin America. Elsewhere sociology grew steadily, but not at so remarkably rapid a rate. (One country of the first rank, however, failed to respond to the new stimulus; in Britain the humanists of the Oxford-Cambridge tradition continued to cherish the belief that sociology was either the flatulent evolutionism of Herbert Spencer or the study of "drink, drains, and divorce.")

With the coming of World War II, social scientists of every variety were expelled from the totalitarian countries, and many of them found final refuge in Britain, Latin America, and the United States. . . . In Germany, the few sociologists who remained were either men whose age and silence prevented them from being disseminators of "dangerous thoughts," or they were young Nazis whose glib talk about "folk-fellowship" and the "mission of leadership" endeared them to those in power. In France, the shift from "liberty, equality, fraternity" to "family, country, work" was paralleled by totalitarian trends in the universities. The important Durkheim school, which counted among its numbers the majority of French sociologists, suffered the triple disadvantage of a Jewish founder, sponsorship of lay education (and therefore of anti-clericalism), and devotion to the Third Republic. The great sociological tradition of France was not dead under the Vichy regime, but it was certainly quiescent, and relatively few French sociologists were able to make their way to other countries.

In Britain the influence of the émigré sociologists, most of them German, was salutary; Karl Mannheim, Adolf Lowe, and a host of others did much to reinforce the forlorn heirs of the Hobhouse school, and sociology of knowledge, sociology of religion, and several other branches of the science were introduced. The LePlay tradition represented in the *Sociological Review* and LePlay House was likewise rejuvenated and in some measure divested of its sectarian character.

These were not the only influences at work in Britain. The success of the Gallup polls in the United States led to a British variant of them in the late 1930's. Even before this, however, the Mass Observation movement had started. Tom Harrisson, one of the founders, was initially trained as an anthropologist; another, Charles Madge, had extensive experience as a journalist specializing in the human-interest story. . . . Mass Observation became a force to be reckoned with in Britain, for it had a staff of whole-time field investigators plus a nation-wide panel of over two thousand voluntary observers. Getting under way in 1936, largely because of the unusual phases of public opinion evoked by the abdication of Edward VIII, it made pioneer studies of various phases of folk life such as football pools, all-in wrestling, public-house conviviality, and the Lambeth Walk. Its most important project before the final outbreak of World War II, however, was its intensive social survey of Bolton, Lancashire, but unfortunately the four large volumes resulting were never published. When war began in September, 1939, Mass Observation . . . at once turned to the rich new field of changing social habits. Books, bulletins, newspaper articles, and radio broadcasts resulted, and even The Thunderer took notice in these words: "How pleasant to find serious sociologists who are also first-rate journalists."

In 1941 Mass Observation work was largely concentrated on problems of morale, and many important studies in towns that suffered heavily under the German assault were made.

Other subjects of investigation were saving habits, attitudes toward joining the Women's Services, clothes rationing, housing, and neighborhood attitudes. Along with the professional field work, the national panel of voluntary observers contributed important material on a wide range of subjects, ranging from religious attitudes to personal fears. Not the least important of Mass Observation's wartime activities was its war library, which collected ephemeral documents such as local newspapers, circulars, menus, and house journals. These were not at that time systematically collected by any other organization, basic though they were for the sociological analyses of wartime Britain that might later be written. Some of Mass Observation's collection was made available in duplicate at the University of Chicago, although of course much necessarily remained in Britain. . . .

Latin America had long had its own distinctive varieties of sociological thought. In earlier years the strongest influences from abroad, some flowing in the ordinary channels and some issuing from émigrés, were German and French—indeed, it is quite safe to say that sociologists such as Scheler, Alfred Weber, Bouglé, and Richard were better known south of the Rio Grande than in the United States and Canada. Moreover, there could be little doubt that Latin American sociologists were quite well informed as to what their colleagues farther north were doing, whereas, the reverse, unfortunately enough, was not the case. Those North American sociologists who attempted to remedy their deficiencies in this matter found that Professor Alfredo Poviña of the University of Cordoba, Argentina, in his *Historia de la Sociología Latino-Americana,* had provided an informative account.

German influence seemed to be strongest in Argentina; Brazil had a considerable admixture of French along with German, perhaps because of the fact that French rather than Spanish was the chief language of scholarship in this Portuguese-speaking nation. In Chile during the year North American sociology had one of its first representatives, Professor W. Rex Crawford of the University of Pennsylvania; another North American, Professor Donald Pierson, had for some time been identified with the Escuela Libre de Sociología y Politica of Sao Paulo, Brazil.

In Mexico there was a flourishing institute of social investigation in conjunction with the Universidad Nacional

Autónoma de Mexico at Mexico City. There was also an editorial organization called Fondo de Cultura Economica, which published the book by Poviña referred to above and was also responsible for several treatises, notably José Echavarría's *Sociología: Teoria y Tecnica,* as well as several translations of fundamental North American and European works. The institute of social investigation sponsored by the University of Mexico issued an excellent sociological review, the *Revista Mexicana de Sociología.* This ran to over five hundred pages yearly and was very well illustrated with line drawings, photographs, and other visual aids. The same institute also issued an interesting monograph entitled *Los Tarascos,* dealing with the Tarascan Indians of Michoacan.

Implied in the reference just made is a fact worth noting; namely, that throughout all of Latin America there was little or no distinction between anthropology and sociology. This probably was as it should have been, for in the United States during 1941 the *rapprochement* of social anthropology and sociology was a striking development. . . . Ralph Linton and Bronislaw Malinowski, both social anthropologists, addressed the American Sociological Society at its December meeting, and the works of Arensberg, Redfield, and Warner, likewise anthropologists, dealt with topics and peoples previously handled by sociologists exclusively. To be sure, sociology was usually characterized by greater precision and methodological sophistication, albeit at the cost, occasionally at least, of a frog's-eye rather than a bird's-eye view of social phenomena.

This sociological myopia, engendered by technical over-enthusiasm, was slowly disappearing, but even in 1941 it was responsible for the fact that the social anthropologists had to perform tasks which the sociologists ought to have done better—if they had been less limited in their viewpoint. . . .

Perhaps the most well-marked 1941 trend in the field of sociology *per se* was in "sociometry." This specialty, christened by the émigré psychiatrist-sociologist J. L. Moreno, oscillated between a kind of socio-therapy of mental ills, called the psychodrama, and a quantitative-graphic method of describing social processes and social structures. The journal of the movement, *Sociometry* (*S*) in 1941 came under the editorship of Professor George A. Lundberg of Bennington College, who gathered about him a wide array

of sponsors and contributing editors. Some articles of fundamental importance appeared in the new publication. . . .
Undeniably there was much faddishness in the sociometric
movement; the mixture of a method of healing mental ills
by acting out thwarted impulses combined appealingly, for
most Americans, with the graphing and measuring of social
conduct. In spite of uncritical enthusiasm, however, there
was a sound sociological core in sociometry, for some
aspects of it went back to the work of Simmel, Wiese,
Cooley, and Mead, as Moreno freely acknowledged.

This sociologist or, more strictly speaking, sociometrist,
could not properly be classed among the recent émigrés, for
he came to the United States from Vienna in the late 1920's.
Later arrivals from many parts of Europe were legion, but
among the most prominent might be named: the amazingly
erudite Paul Honigsheim, interrelation of anthropology
and sociology, sociology of religion, and several other fields;
Godfrey S. Delatour, sociological training of administrators; Georges Gurvitch and N. S. Timasheff, sociology of
law; Eugen Kulischer and Rudolf Heberle, sociological
aspects of migration; Henry Jordan, Sigmund Neumann,
Franz Neumann, Otto Kirchheimer, Herbert Marcuse, and
Hans Speier, interrelations of sociology, history, and political science; H. H. Gerth, Ernst Kris, and Paul Lazarsfeld, public opinion studies and other varieties of psycho-
sociology; Hans von Hentig, criminology and penology;
Werner Landecker, Henrik Infield, Erich Franzen, Albert
Salomon, and N. C. Leites, systematic sociology and researches based thereon; Kurt Wolff and Ernst Manheim,
sociology of knowledge. Most of these men were promptly
placed on the staffs of universities, research institutes, or
specially-created schools such as the University in Exile, but
several of them had not yet found suitable posts in 1941.

In general, it could be said that the émigrés did not exert
much influence at first. Reasons were numerous: first, slow-
ness of assimilation to North American modes of thought
and instruction; second, reserve or lack of appreciation on
the part of native sociologists, many of whom literally
did not know what the émigrés were talking about;
third, ultra-conservative editorial policies in the learned
journals; fourth, the textbook pattern of publishing in the
United States—treatises with small sales prospects had to
be subsidized; fifth, occasional manifestations of arrogance
by émigrés who over-valued their European training in the

changed situation; sixth, jealousy and fear among those native sociologists who felt insecure against "outside" competition; seventh, strong aversion, on the part of some of the émigrés, to certain research methods beloved in the United States; and so on.

The widespread American interest in quantification received further impetus during 1941, largely because of the well-advertised prospective publication of S. C. Dodd's *Dimensions of Society*. Dodd spoke before the Committee on Conceptual Integration and the Sociological Research Association in December, and won a respectful hearing (because of his obvious sincerity and dispassionateness) from those who on methodological grounds might be most opposed.

In some respects related to the quantifying trend, but in others independent thereof, was the interest in sociological prediction manifested during the year. In part deriving from the 1939 Burgess and Cottrell *Prediction of Marital Adjustment* was the symposium, *Prediction of Personal Adjustment,* edited for the Social Science Research Council (hereinafter referred to as the SSRC) by Paul Horst. The Michigan Sociological Society, in its meeting of November, devoted a great deal of attention to predictive assumptions. In general, it may be said that this trend bade fair to become stronger as time went on, more especially as its concrete applications to problems of probation, parole, the family, personnel work, and similar matters were likely to secure the interest of the ubiquitous practical man.

Almost diametrically opposed to the varieties of North American sociology thus far noted was the *Social and Cultural Dynamics* (4th and final volume) of P. A. Sorokin. This was an arresting attempt, Spengler-like in its sweep, to chart the future of civilization. Sorokin's proclamations of the decadence of Western civilization were sharply challenged by eminent sociologists such as R. M. MacIver of Columbia—in fact, the Harvard writer obtained only a small but loyal following. Likewise with only a few adherents but of striking scientific penetration was F. J. Teggart, the republication of whose *Theory and Processes of History* would do much, it was thought, to counteract emotionalism and loose generalization in the sociologist's approach to world history.

Analytic or systematic sociology markedly contrasting with the all-inclusive researches of Sorokin was represented by the publication of Leopold von Wiese's articles, written for Vierkandt's sociological encyclopedia, as a book, *Sociology,* translated by Franz Mueller. This little volume, drawing heavily for its terminology on the present writer's treatise, *Systematic Sociology on the Basis of the* Beziehungslehre *and* Gebildelehre *of Leopold von Wiese* (1932), was the most concise presentation of sociology as a science of social interaction available in English. Also of great significance for analytic sociology was the completion during 1941 of the Henderson-Parsons translation of Max Weber's *Wirtschaft und Gesellschaft,* chapters I-IV. Although not at the time available as a book, this translation promptly circulated in mimeographed form among American sociologists, and promised when published to elevate Max Weber to the rank of a sociologist not only great in reputation but also in influence.

During the year, however, there was no monograph of any importance utilizing Weber's mode of analysis. A much less gifted theoretician, Vilfredo Pareto, provided the conceptual tools for George C. Homans' *English Villagers of the Thirteenth Century.* If all adherents of Pareto had written books like Homans', however, the curse of the faulty conceptual scheme centering about "residues" and "derivations" would have been lifted. . . .

Although the Bureau of the Census employed many sociologists, and although population courses were frequently given by departments of sociology, it does not seem either justifiable or expedient to include demographic studies in a survey of sociology during 1941. Likewise marginal was social psychology, even though Steuart Henderson Britt's *Social Psychology of Modern Life* was definitely of sociological as well as psychological derivation. Similarly, George Kingsley Zipf's *National Unity and Disunity: The Nation as a Bio-Social Organism* was only quasi-sociological—in addition to being a regrettable instance of bio-mathematical analogizing and fantasy-thinking. Far sounder, although distinctly less "scientific" in appearance, was another work on essentially the same topic: R. C. Angell's *The Integration of American Society.* This writer stemmed from the Cooley school, and exemplified both its merits and defects. Chief among the former was the focus on the relevant and the willingness to be vague when the evidence did not admit of precision; among the latter, the failure to provide sufficient documentation at certain vital points and a nostalgia for a kind of "democracy" that had never existed anywhere.

The nostalgic shortcoming just noted could not be attributed to James Burnham, for his *The Managerial Revolution* was a bitterly or even cynically disillusioned effort to show that the structure of American society, and especially of American industry, was already controlled by small non-democratic interest groups, and that these "managers" would rapidly extend their power at the cost of the rest of the populace. Burnham was a former Marxist, and, as might be expected, he dispensed a *mélange* of economics, political science, and journalistic psychology; nevertheless, such significant border-line studies could not be overlooked.

The *ASR* continued as the official publication of the American Sociological Society. The *AJS,* an organ of the University of Chicago, continued its aggressive editorial policy, already exemplified in timely special issues such as that dealing with war, in January, and the one on national morale, in November. The *JSP,* sponsored primarily by members of the Columbia and the College of the City of New York faculties, continued as one of the most stimulating periodicals, although it perhaps could not be classified as sociological in the narrower sense. The *A* from time to time published issues of sociological import. Published at the University of North Carolina, *SF* retained its regional emphasis; clearly among the better sociological journals, it was primarily Southern in orientation. Similarly regional was *SSR,* published by the University of Southern California. A quite different journal, *SR,* was published by the University in Exile, and afforded a vehicle for some of the best émigré work. Sociology might be said to have had ample publication facilities in the United States where shorter articles were concerned; the major lack seemed to be an organ for longer presentations that were still too brief for book format.

In the United States the utilization of sociologists in the armed forces, in spite of totalitarian pioneering, was not extensively practiced; apparently we found it hard to learn from our opponents. In the governmental bureaus there was a somewhat better situation. Reporting to the American Sociological Society in December, 1941, George A. Lundberg showed that Washington took considerable advantage of the offerings of sociologists. Although these sociologists were placed primarily in the Bureau of the Census and the

Department of Agriculture, and although they were sometimes brought in under the protective cloak of "economist"
or "statistician," there was ground for a good deal of optimism. This arose from the fact that the sociologists scattered here and there in the various bureaus acquitted themselves so well that there was a steadily-increasing demand
for their services *as sociologists*.

1942

Confusion and the Slow Beginning of
All-Out War Effort

THE YEAR WAS characterized in part by the rising
awareness of possible Axis victory, and in part by the
demonstration of the minor nature of what had been
previously thought, in some quarters, to be major social-
scientific gains.

At the close of 1941, for example, hopes were high that
the type of systematic-positivistic sociology promulgated
by G. A. Lundberg and S. C. Dodd would lead to consolidation of the attested results of previous but presumably
less scientific researches. These hopes were misplaced, for
with the publication of S. C. Dodd's grandiose *Dimensions
of Society* early in 1942, it became apparent to many sociologists that a mountain had been in labor. Scathing critiques came from the mathematician E. T. Bell and the
sociologist Talcott Parsons (*ASR* book reviews), but these
were relatively brief; the most thoroughly destructive
analysis was an article by Ethel Shanas in the September
issue of the *AJS*.

Similarly disconcerting was the reception accorded the
first two volumes of W. Lloyd Warner's *Yankeetown* series.
Sociologists found them analytically inadequate because of
Warner's apparent lack of familiarity with, or wilful
ignoring of, the earlier literature in the class-status field,
while anthropologists objected to the extreme formalism
apparent, in particular, in the volume entitled *The Status
System of a Modern Community*. At the same time, it must
be said that, had it not been for the excessively optimistic
advance advertising that Warner's work received, it is likely

that criticism would not have been so severe; discrepancies between promise and performance are always harshly judged. Moreover, this advance advertising revived among American sociologists their interest in problems of social stratification, and this revived interest resulted in what virtually amounted to a special "stratification issue" of the *ASR* in June. The consequent contrast between Warner's loose concepts and more refined types of analysis could not fail to evoke further disapproval of his methods, exemplified in the trenchant although Marx-biased article by Oliver C. Cox, "The Modern Caste School of Race Relations," *SF* (December)....

These setbacks fortunately were not the whole story of sociology in 1942. Witness the great improvement in general sociological analysis registered by R. M. MacIver's treatise, *Social Causation*. In this work the author pointed the way to more circumspect and more fruitful sociological research. Sometimes considered a foe of quantitative method, it seemed fair to say that MacIver opposed only statistical dogmatism of the more belligerent type. If any fault at all was to be found with his treatise it was only with regard to emphasis: historical or unique time-series causation got too much attention, the role of language in what MacIver called "dynamic assessment" got too little, and there seemed little point in substituting "dynamic assessment" for the older and more useful "definition of the situation."

Similar but graver faults were immediately manifest in a work of widely differing character, Gordon W. Allport's *The Use of Personal Documents in Psychological Science*. From the standpoint of the social psychologist and sociologist, Allport unduly disparaged typological analysis because of his interest in the individual personality as developing in a unique time-series. Such an interest in the unique leads away from science and toward Gamaliel Bradford's psychography. A step in the right direction was taken by the social anthropologist Morris Opler in his *An Apache Life-Way*. He tried, with measurable success, to avoid mere psychography; his was a social-psychological presentation of sociological rather than psychological derivation. Such studies promised much for the future.

Of course, the guide-lines for such studies had been laid down long before by C. H. Cooley and G. H. Mead. Interest in Cooley was revived by E. C. Jandy's *Charles Horton Cooley: His Life and His Social Theory*. In spite of the

Cooley revival, however, it was clear that American social psychology was shifting more and more toward the Mead emphasis on the rise of the self in and through a role-taking process using significant symbols, especially those of language.

The year yielded no such crop of sociologically relevant work on language as did 1941, but the census of current research, published in the August issue of the *ASR,* plus other sources of information, showed that steady progress along this and other lines was being made.

But, if one were to have taken seriously A. G. Keller's *Net Impressions,* one would have been forced to conclude that little of social-psychological or sociological importance in any field had occurred since the death of W. G. Sumner. The biases of the Sumner-Keller school were fortunately well known; little discouragement resulted from Keller's charmingly written and reminiscent onslaught. (Interestingly enough, one of the most striking developments running directly counter to the ultra-conservative Sumner-Keller ideology occurred in Britain early in the war. An International Library of Sociology and Social Reconstruction, under the editorship of the German émigré Karl Mannheim, was announced by the publishers of the famous International Library of Philosophy and Psychology. That so extensive a venture should have been undertaken or even projected under the arduous conditions of war-time Britain did honor to all associated with it.)

Newly emerging fields of investigation made modest but none the less definite advances during the year. Sociology of knowledge was represented by Oscar Cargill's *Intellectual America: Ideas on the March,* the Beards' *The American Spirit: A Study of the Idea of Civilization in the United States,* and Logan Wilson's *The Academic Man.* The volume last named, more strictly sociological than the others, developed in detail one aspect of Florian Znaniecki's epochal *The Social Role of the Man of Knowledge* (1940), a pioneer study in *substantive* sociology of knowledge. Sociology of law was represented by the first number of the new *Journal of Legal and Political Sociology,* appearing under the editorship of Georges Gurvitch; the journal continued for several years thereafter in spite of Gurvitch's return to France. Sociology of religion found a distinguished exponent in Salo W. Baron, whose three-volume treatise *The Jewish Community* was a welcome complement of Max

Weber's studies. Sociology of economic life is notoriously hard to define, and some students would include much work on labor relations in the field. However this may be, it seems fair to say that F. J. Roethlisberger's *Management and Morale* was a valued 1942 addition to this area of investigation.

The traditionally-accepted varieties of sociological research were not neglected. Race relations had as outstanding contributions Graeber and Britt's *Jews in a Gentile World: The Problem of Anti-Semitism* (with a striking chapter by "Anonymous"), and Donald Pierson's *Negroes in Brazil*. So-called "social pathology" and "human ecology" were given a definitive synthesis in one research zone in Shaw and McKay's *Juvenile Delinquency and Urban Areas*. Nothing substantially new was provided, but all of the research on the interrelations of deviate social conduct among juveniles and locality patterns was neatly coordinated. A similar synthesis of closely related type was Ernest R. Mowrer's *Disorganization: Personal and Social,* although here adult phenomena were focused upon.

A text called *Principles of Anthropology,* but actually an amalgam of ideas gleaned from the social interactionists, both of social-psychological and sociological persuasion, was launched by E. D. Chapple and Carleton Coon. It marked another step, albeit a halting one, on the road toward the merging of sociology and social anthropology. Nevertheless, it almost immediately called forth charges of "academic kleptomania." Textbooks are the rearguard of a discipline, and although of no great significance in and of themselves, are nevertheless important because they establish the zone of academic acceptability and teachability.

Sociology, whether academic or not, underwent many shifts in personnel in 1942. The armed forces absorbed many younger men; war-time agencies in Washington and elsewhere accounted for many more. All in all, the shift from strictly academic to total-war pursuits more than kept pace with the dwindling of college and university enrollment. But in spite of the shift, many sociologists continued to dwell in ivory towers.

1943
Scientific Isolation Breaks Down

THIS YEAR BORE witness to the struggle of World War II in unprecedented degree, and sociology was one of the social sciences most affected.

Chief among the changes brought by the war was the introduction of area courses in over two hundred American colleges and universities. These were part of the Army Specialized Training Program, forming a major share of the subdivision called the Foreign Area and Language Study Curriculum. The area portion of the FA & LSC accounted for about one-half of the time of the student-soldier, and after several changes in prescribed content arrived at the point where sociology and social anthropology, together with their social-psychological correlates and other social sciences, had much to do with the instruction offered. The FA & LSC men were to be equipped for service as aides to civilian affairs administrators (military government), liaison and intelligence personnel, examiners of war prisoners, and so on. Not only was working knowledge of at least one foreign language necessary, but in addition extensive acquaintance with the physical and human geography, recent political, economic, and social development, and the basic features of the social processes, groups and institutions of the culture area or civilization concerned was demanded.

Teams of specialists—geographers, economists, political scientists, sociologists, social psychologists, etc.—were called together, in the larger schools, to provide the instructional staffs. In almost all cases knowledge of the languages concerned was asked of the area specialists, but in some instances the requirement could not always be met. Nevertheless, it is safe to say that those offering area courses ordinarily had reasonable linguistic competence as background of their knowledge of the peoples and countries studied. . . .

Interest in the area work of the FA & LSC was strong. The lay public was of course fascinated by the glamour of a program whose products were presumably to have much to do with the various undergrounds, revolutionary movements in the Axis countries and their satellites, the checking of sabotage and espionage, the relief and re-education of civilians, the control of defeated and demobilized armed forces, and the general task of "winning the peace." This interest was even more intense where the "big-brother" of the FA & LSC was concerned; namely, the Civilian Affairs Training Program. Whereas the former was designed for privates and non-commissioned officers, with a sprinkling of possible later entrants in officers' candidate schools, the latter, the CATP, was exemplified in the Charlottesville School of Military Government and the ten universities offering courses along parallel lines. Commissioned officers only made up the students of the CATP. Many of them were commissioned directly from civilian life as having skills and aptitudes fitting them for the administration of civilian affairs under military law: former legislators, executives, business men, and technicians. Sociologists and other social scientists had a large part in the training of these men as well, although some of the officers' time was absorbed by topics, such as military law, that did not enter the work of the FA & LSC.

As later developments showed, however, the FA & LSC program was robbed of full usefulness by the shortsighted policies of Army officers, who often used trained specialists to do routine duties that could have been performed by anyone. The CATP was likewise maladministered, and the melancholy results soon appeared in the partial breakdown of American military government, especially in Germany.

Army ineptitude not being foreseen, however, the popular interest in area work was shared by the administrators of foundations and by college and university leaders. During the summer of 1943 the SSRC began studies of the possibilities of "world regions" as instructional and research foci when peacetime higher learning could be resumed. The American Council of Learned Societies turned its attention in a similar direction. Deans and presidents began to assess the worth of area studies as possible means of vitalizing language and social science instruction and of eliminating needless overlapping of courses. . . .

Where the more strictly disciplinary aspects of sociology were concerned, the year was significant in only a few fields. Race relations received much attention, primarily because of the mounting antagonisms manifested in the "zoot suit" and Negro-White riots in Los Angeles and Detroit. Charles

T. Johnson's *Patterns of Negro Segregation,* Odum's *Race and Rumors of Race,* Lee and Humphrey's *Race Riot,* Ottley's *New World A-Coming,* and Strong's "Social Types in a Minority Group," *AJS* (March) were among the most significant publications. Studies of ideologies from the sociology of knowledge standpoint continued to appear; important were Kelsen's *Society and Nature* and DeGré's *Society and Ideology.* Social-psychological researches such as those conducted by Mass Observation in Britain and the American and British Institutes of Public Opinion continued; and an informative account of Mass Observation activities appeared in the *AJS* (January). The Gallup and similar polls continued; they were clearly on the way to becoming "big business." An important *Dictionary of Sociology,* edited by Henry Pratt Fairchild, made its bow; although abounding in faulty definitions, insufficiently systematized, and lacking in bibliographies and like reference aids, it served a useful purpose in recording contemporary sociological terminology and in pointing out the patterns future standardization would have to take.

The December program of the American Sociological Society was significant primarily for the attention paid to war and post-war topics; ivory-towerism was becoming more and more difficult. As was just beginning to be the case in the year previous, the records of the society showed a very large number of its members in the armed forces or in various administrative services connected with the war effort.

1944

Preoccupation with the Aftermath of Victory

THE WAR CONTINUED to force American sociologists to look beyond the limits they had previously set up or passively accepted. For example, the *ASR* brought out a special issue, edited by Joseph K. Folsom of Vassar, entitled "Social Trends in the Soviet Union," and the *AJS* had one number almost wholly devoted to the problems of the coming peace.

An ever greater number of sociologists went into agencies connected with the war effort: OWI, OSS, G-2, ONI, the

State Department, and so on. Not only did these agencies continue to be vitalized by the sociological "invasion," but the sociologists concerned were also vitalized by the agencies. New points of view, new data, new tasks, new insights into the functioning (and malfunctioning!) of the armed forces and governmental bureaus made it probable that with the return to civilian life there would be a higher level of relevance and directness in academic instruction and research. At the same time, however, many sociologists remained in their usual academic posts and, in the case of some younger men, succeeded in dodging war-time responsibilities. They doubtless hoped to forge ahead, academically at least, of their more zealous or less fortunate colleagues.

Lewis Mumford's *The Condition of Man,* written in the Patrick Geddes tradition, was published in 1944, and was considered by an enthusiastic handful of American sociologists to be one of the most stimulating works in general sociology since the appearance of Max Weber's *Wirtschaft und Gesellschaft* in 1920. The first good biography of Geddes was likewise published in 1944—P. L. Boardman's *Patrick Geddes, Maker of the Future.* Mumford's revival of the Geddes mode of analysis overtopped, in the estimation of some circles, Karl Mannheim's *Diagnosis of Our Time,* although the latter was a significant study, suffering, if at all, only by comparison.

Other important works of the year were: Joachim Wach's *Sociology of Religion,* a treatise that showed promise of eventually doing much to get American sociologists outside of the barren technological determinism with which most of them were still afflicted; and Gunnar Myrdal's *An American Dilemma: The Negro Problem in a Democracy,* a two-volume tract supervised by a Swedish moralizer that nevertheless had many sociological merits, particularly in the parts written by his aides.

Significant articles in the *ASR* were: George A. Lundberg, "Sociologists and the Peace"; T. Lynn Smith, "The Locality Group Structure of Brazil"; Carl C. Taylor, "Rural Locality Groups in Argentina"; H. W. Gilmore, "The Old Orleans and the New: A Case for Ecology"; Rudolf Heberle, "The Ecology of Political Parties"; Émile Benoît-Smullyan, "Status, Status Types, and Status Interrelations," and Erich Fromm, "Individual and Social Origins of Neurosis." In the *AJS:* George Katona, "The Role of the Frame of Reference"; Fred H. Blum, "Max

Weber's Postulate of 'Freedom from Value-Judgments' ";
Alfred Schuetz, "The Stranger: An Essay in Social Psychology"; and Wilson H. Grabill, "Effect of the War on the Birth Rate and Postwar Fertility Prospects." Other journals such as *SF* and *SSR* published several first-rate studies.

All in all, the year showed serious effects of the war where sociology was concerned; many publications were abandoned or postponed, classes were made up chiefly of women students without professional interests, and professional sociologists continued to be drawn away for service with the government or the armed forces. America's "all-out" effort was making itself felt, and prospects of success engendered much interest in what was to be done with the success when at last achieved.

1945
Enthusiasm for the Supposedly Reborn World

THE YEAR SAW a great increase in the amount of sociological publication—although whether this all represented fundamental research was in considerable degree doubtful. Apparently the imminence of victory in the early part of the year, and its decisiveness when it came, had something to do with the upswing. Publishers perhaps became more optimistic and were getting ready to capitalize on a postwar boom. On the other hand, the scholarly journals also showed a considerable increase in the number of significant articles.

"Problems of the postwar world" of course loomed large; among the more general treatises Thomas C. McCormick's (ed.) symposium deserved prominent notice.

More specific studies, many of them "postwar," fell into the general categories of military-civilian adjustment and readjustment, "the government of men" under wartime conditions of various types, social stratification, race relations and similar themes, critical analyses of currently accepted sociological doctrines, and family problems. Most of these studies used sociological modes of analysis, broadly defined, but sharper focus here and there would have been desirable, as various reviews and critiques that appeared during the year pointed out.

Military-civilian matters were dealt with by Robert A. Nisbet, "The Coming Problem of Assimilation," S. Kirson Weinberg, "Problems of Adjustment in Army Units," Alfred Schuetz, "The Homecomer"—all in the *AJS,* and by Wilbur B. Brookover, "The Adjustment of Veterans to Civilian Life" in the *ASR.*

The Government of Men, by A. H. Leighton, centered on the problem of Japanese relocation, but as the title indicated, many general considerations of social control were raised. Leighton was an anthropologist-psychiatrist by training, but like so many persons using such a perspective, his direction of attention and analytic interest was definitely although perhaps unwittingly sociological. Another study, much more clearly sociological because made with full awareness, was John Useem's "The Pattern of Military Government in Micronesia" in the *AJS* and his integrally related paper in the *AA.*

Useem and his wife, Ruth Hill Useem, contributed a significant analysis to the social stratification interest mentioned above as clearly apparent in 1945. "Minority-Group Patterns in Prairie Society," *AJS,* dealt with the acculturation and concomitant secularization of a Norwegian group, and showed how thoroughly the old-line "race relations" approach was outmoded so far as certain minority group phenomena were concerned.

Numerous reviews and commentary articles appeared in the wake of Myrdal's *An American Dilemma,* a race relations treatise in the narrower sense which, as was noted earlier, was first published in 1944. The general conclusion seemed to be that Myrdal was psychologically correct in his diagnosis of "impartiality" among many American sociologists dealing with the race problem. (This same point was made from another angle by Carey McWilliams, "Race Discrimination and the Law" in *Science and Society* —*SS.*) But although on the right track psychologically, Myrdal went badly astray in the logic of the attack on the "freedom from value-judgments" position. An interesting article on a little-known "race" group was Brewton Berry's "The Mestizos of South Carolina" in the *AJS.* A good general summary was provided by E. B. Reuter's "Racial Theory: Developments in the Past Fifty Years," in the *AJS.*

The occasion of Reuter's survey was the special semi-centennial issue of the *AJS*. This appeared in May, and although unduly devoted to exaltation of certain sadly parochial trends in American sociology, it nevertheless furnished a welcome benchmark. Especially noteworthy was Florian Znaniecki's article, "Controversies in Doctrine and Method." Another important collection of papers—not, however, grouped around a central theme—was the April issue of the *ASR*. Because of the fact that the annual meeting of the American Sociological Society was cancelled, the papers designed to be read at that gathering were printed under one cover. The presidential address, Rupert B. Vance's "Toward Social Dynamics," was a statement of the point of view that equates "social dynamics" with "social progress." Postwar optimism was in evidence.

This same collection was also important, however, because of the critical tendency it manifested; one of the many straws in the wind was Melvin Tumin's "Culture, Genuine and Spurious: A Re-Evaluation." Other critical studies appearing in 1945 were Jessie Bernard's "Observation and Generalization in Cultural Anthropology," *AJS*, a kindly but trenchant discussion of Margaret Mead's neglect of evidence and loose conceptualization; Joseph Schneider's "Cultural Lag: What Is It?," *ASR*, an attack on W. F. Ogburn's carefree use of a dubious hypothesis; and Thomas C. McCormick's "Simple Percentage Analysis of Attitude Questionnaires," *AJS*, a proposal for the more frequent use of simple types of statistical analysis instead of apparently more precise but really only more complicated procedures.

Marriage and the family had a bumper crop of books and articles. The long-awaited text, *The Family*, by Ernest W. Burgess and Harvey J. Locke, bore the subtitle "From Institution to Companionate"—which raised afresh the problem of the nature of social institutions, if nothing else! Evelyn Millis Duvall and Reuben Hill brought out a lively presentation, *When You Marry*, designed for the general reader and for courses paying little heed to the larger contexts of marriage and the family; and Sidney E. Goldstein, in his *Marriage and Family Counselling*, provided the first complete manual combining the counselling experience of many specialists other than sociologists. Svend Riemer's studies, published in the *ASR* and elsewhere, continued to stress the role of housing in family relations—an emphasis particularly timely in view of the postwar crisis.

Among miscellaneous but important publications were Abram Kardiner's *The Psychological Frontiers of Society,* a book that Robert Merton rather generously characterized as "marking a turning point in the study of man." Rural sociology was enriched by the work of an anthropologically trained observer, James West (pseudonym), whose *Plainville, U.S.A.* was a sort of Missouri *Middletown* or *Small Town Stuff.*

In general, the year marked the return of more strictly academic interests, in part because of the widespread belief that although there were postwar problems, victory over the Axis had really settled all the major issues. It remained only to consolidate the gains the war had brought. "Readjustment" was the watchword.

1946

Waning Enthusiasm, Incipient Uncertainty,

Assimilation of War-Time Changes

TENDENCIES LONG APPARENT in American sociology became very obvious during the year. These tendencies were toward the merging of sociology, social and cultural anthropology, social psychology, and social psychiatry in what was coming to be called the science of social relations. Harvard brought the trend into the open by establishing a department of social relations, but essentially the same state of affairs existed at Chicago, Wisconsin, Yale, Columbia, and a number of other universities.

Up to the end of the year, however, clear theoretical formulation of the *de facto* merger was not forthcoming. Earlier systematic works in the various fields named were all lacking in sufficient appreciation of closely related approaches. A renewed interest in far-flung *and* closeknit theory was badly needed.

Unfortunately, many of the theorists active in the 1930's had either passed their peak or had their energies drained off by absorption in the day-to-day "application of theory to research." Such application put the cart before the horse. Scientific research worthy of the name is undertaken with the sole end of proving or disproving a given body of theory; all else is technology, highly useful but promising little for basic advance. The remarks by Franklin Frazier, Herbert Blumer, and Alfred McClung Lee at the December 1946 meeting of the American Sociological Society bore melancholy witness to this fact, as their critics, Melvin Tumin and William L. Kolb, were quick to point out.

The lagging of strictly theoretical interest was made worse, in a period of rising public appreciation of the importance of a potential science of human relations, by the great number of commercial opportunities awaiting the trained social scientist. Polling agencies, personnel departments, governmental bureaus, military government, and many other organizations competed for the services of social scientists, and the low rate of pay in the academic field, where theory as such had been most cultivated, lured many of them into positions of lucrative but, where theory is concerned, blind-alley character.

At the same time, it cannot be denied that immediate problems loomed so terrifyingly large that many social scientists felt called by duty to aid in their solution. For example, W. F. Ogburn contributed a significant although disheartening article, "Sociology and the Atom," *AJS*. The preoccupation with atomic problems resulted in an attempt to discover just how the scientists directly concerned viewed their responsibilities; Margaret Smith Stahl's "Splits and Schisms: An Analysis of Atomic Energy Factions" (unpublished dissertation, University of Wisconsin) undertook this task. Using sociology of knowledge as a guide, she showed that there was a basic cleavage between pure and applied scientists working on atomic energy projects, and that the resulting factions could be interpreted as following their special interests quite as much as their announced ideals.

A somewhat similar analysis, but focusing on sociologists rather than physical scientists, was provided by Kurt H. Wolff, "Toward a Sociocultural Interpretation of American Sociology," *ASR*. Wolff's contentions, which ran to the effect that marked class biases and sentimental attachments distorted the findings of many prominent American sociologists, were somewhat sweeping, and it is to be doubted whether he got much beyond the familiar *argumentum ad hominem*. Research comparable to Stahl's in its thoroughness was clearly necessary if Wolff hoped to be taken seriously. . . .

Studies of a German thinker, Max Weber, who opposed the vulgar Marxism of his day, became increasingly numerous. Among the most important were Reinhard Bendix's "Max Weber's Interpretation of Conduct and History," *AJS,* and Paul Honigsheim's "Max Weber as Rural Sociologist," *RS.* The vogue of Weber was furthered by the appearance of H. H. Gerth and C. Wright Mills' *From Max Weber.* This was a collection of important excerpts and articles prefaced by Gerth's fine introduction. This book made it abundantly clear that Weber was never an exponent of religious determinism *versus* economic, but rather an analyst stressing the interdependence of these and several other aspects of man's institutional conduct.

Coming from a quarter quite different from that represented by Weber, an implicit demonstration of the futility of rigid determinism of any sort in the interpreting of human conduct was offered by the anthropologist Morris Edward Opler, in "An Application of the Theory of Themes in Culture," *Journal of the Washington Academy of Science.* Opler showed how the "themes" or ideological patterns evident among even a primitive people, the Lipan Apache, divide into at least twenty main strands, among which no single one is dominant in all aspects of life. Relevance to general value-system theory was clearly apparent.

Nowhere, however, did Opler or any other responsible social scientist deny the very great importance of economic activity. Indeed, the preoccupation with immediate problems already noted brought forth a new specialty drawing upon economics, sociology, and social psychology. It bore the label "industrial sociology" but there were several other terms that could have been used just as well. It did, however, lay marked and justifiable stress on the importance of social groups and their interrelations within large factory organizations presumably modelled along strictly economic lines. Past efforts to deal with the worker either as a purely individual entity, as had so frequently been the case among industrial psychologists, or as a mere member of a collective bargaining unit, as had so frequently been the case among industrial relations specialists of economic derivation, almost wholly obscured the role of small cliques, factions, congeniality groupings, and the like in influencing workers' morale and, incidentally, output.

Centering on a somewhat different problem, but indirectly throwing much light on industrial sociology, was

Mirra Komarovsky's "The Voluntary Associations of Urban Dwellers," *ASR*. Here she showed that the working classes, in particular, had relatively few affiliations of "joining" character. Formally named clubs, lodges, churches, unions, and so on were shown to be much less significant than small informal clusters related to family, friendship, and similar "natural" groupings.

Testimony to the same effect was provided by the anthropologist Carleton S. Coon's "The Universality of Natural Groupings in Human Societies," *Journal of Educational Sociology*. Coon's evidence made it abundantly clear that social scientists had generally disparaged or ignored the influence of smaller clusters, from the pair or couple upward, in favor of larger but frequently less powerful modes of association. Among the influential small clusters are those set by the succession of generations; parent-child, grandparent-grandchild, and similar kinship dyads, as well as other small units in which age difference rather than kinship as such is significant. Many striking and hitherto out-of-the-way data were presented by Leo W. Simmons, in "Attitudes toward Aging' and the Aged: Primitive Societies," *Journal of Gerontology*.

The kind of sociological research and therapy rather inaptly christened "sociometry" had from the very beginning emphasized the part played by small groupings in social life, and during the year provided many studies.

Sociometry (*S*), the major vehicle of publication, produced an offshoot entitled *Sociatry,* which, as its etymology indicated, was devoted to "social healing." The founder and editor of both journals, J. L. Moreno, became famous through his "psychodrama" which he now began, perhaps in order to avoid misunderstanding, to call "sociodrama." This was a method of dealing with certain functional varieties of mental ill-health by means of a role-taking therapy involving the deliberate staging of social situations designed to facilitate the curative process. Sociometry or, better, sociatry, devoted much attention to mental difficulties attributable to family complications, in particular, and gained widespread acceptance among family counsellors.

More orthodox studies of family problems appearing in 1946 were: James H. S. Bossard and Eleanor S. Boll, "The Immediate Family and the Kinship Group," *SF,* Margaret Park Redfield, "The American Family: Consensus and

Freedom," *AJS,* and Austin H. Porterfield and H. Allison Salley, "Current Folkways of Sexual Behavior," *AJS.*

The article by Mrs. Redfield was interesting, not only in its own right but also because of its bearing on what Philip Wylie, followed by Edward Strecker, called "Momism." If it was true that the larger part of the mental difficulties in the American armed forces was attributable to maternal over-protection and under-discipline, Mrs. Redfield's article helped to set the matter in its proper perspective. She pointed out that American children had not suffered repression in any degree that would make psychoanalytic assumptions applicable, but on the contrary were deprived, in recent years, of adequate parental oversight and advice. These conclusions ran counter to those of Porterfield and Salley who, finding that premarital chastity among American youth in Texas was actually less frequent than was enjoined by prevailing ideals, argued that the latter should be relaxed. This argument was a *non sequitur;* the precise reverse could just as readily have been maintained.

The Porterfield and Salley contentions perhaps derived from absorption of popularized psychoanalysis—although in fairness to psychoanalysis be it said, its more circumspect advocates would have championed no such egregious conclusions. This was particularly true of the neo-Freudians: Abram Kardiner, Karen Horney, and Erich Fromm. But these too were sharply criticized; articles evidencing such a trend were: Judson F. Stone, "The Theory and Practice of Psychoanalysis," *SS;* Arnold W. Green, "Social Values and Psychotherapy," *S;* ———, "The Middle Class Male Child and Neurosis," *ASR;* ———, "Sociological Analysis of Horney and Fromm," *AJS.*

A searching application of psychoanalytic insights, reinterpreted from the standpoint of sociatry and social psychology, was Gustav Ichheiser's "The Jews and Anti-Semitism," *S.* This author broke new ground by advancing the well-attested hypothesis that frontal attacks on anti-Semitism were fruitless, essentially because the Jews themselves were afflicted by socially acquired attitudes which helped the anti-Semite to rationalize his prejudices. Another intertwining of psychoanalysis and social science was the book, documented with amazing thoroughness, by Gilberto Freyre, *The Masters and the Slaves: A Study of Brazilian Civilization.* Freyre made a radical break with the traditional geographic interpretations of Brazilian life, but he came dangerously close to espousing an equally fallacious sexual determinism. Nevertheless, the book was of great importance, if only for its documentation.

Studies of major civilizational entities along lines less questionable than those followed by Freyre were provided by: Dinko Tomasic, "The Structure of Balkan Society," *AJS,* and Hsiao-tung Fei, "Peasantry and Gentry: An Interpretation of Chinese Social Structure and Its Changes," *AJS.* Tomasic's article was a follow-up of earlier analyses of personality types published in *Psychiatry,* and foreshadowed the Yugoslav role in the Greek "civil war" and the later "cold war" with Russia.

Shifting from considerations of structure to the more orthodox quantitative presentations, it can be said that the year witnessed the publication of the first full-length treatment of an aggregate much talked about but little known, Ta Chen's *Population in Modern China* (book-size supplement of *AJS*). This marked a great step in advance; reasonably precise analysis supplanted guesswork. A similar advance was apparently manifested in John H. Burma's "The Measurement of Negro Passing," *AJS.* The old estimates of passing provided by Hornell Hart almost two decades ago were attacked as considerably too high. If Burma's conclusions were corroborated by other researchers, drastic revisions of prophecies about Negro-White intermixture would have to be made.

Race problems are of course not confined to the United States; World War II was sufficient demonstration of that. The way in which many persons, otherwise kindly, could think of another race as virtually non-human, and therefore suffer no pangs of conscience in committing or tolerating acts of the utmost cruelty, was set forth by Morris Janowitz, "German Reactions to Nazi Atrocities," *AJS.*

That these phenomena could not be regarded as peculiarly German was shown, by implication, in the exceptionally careful and thorough study by C. P. Loomis and J. Allen Beegle, "The Spread of German Nazism in Rural Areas," *ASR.* These authors produced evidence going far to prove that any group of comparable background subject to similar influences would have behaved in much the same way as did the German peasantry.

Like conclusions were reached in Clifford Kirkpatrick's "Sociological Principles and Occupied Germany," *ASR,* but over and above these he pointed out that many of the difficulties experienced in bringing Germans to appreciate democratic values were attributable to the fact that the American military should never have been assigned other than essentially police functions. Government and all related matters should have been handled by American civilians from almost the very beginning of the occupation. The Army and Navy were called upon to do a task for which they were never designed—a conclusion amply borne out by the special issue of the *AJS* for March, devoted exclusively to analysis of military process and structure in combat and noncombat periods and places. Most of the contributors to this issue were returned officers and enlisted men, and while doing full justice to the U. S. Army and Navy, unshrinkingly maintained their inability to attain other than strictly military objectives. Enthusiasm for the task of remaking the world was clearly waning. . . .

The postwar revival of the social sciences did not early manifest itself outside the United States until 1946, but it then became strikingly evident. The Belgian, J. Haesaert, professor at the University of Ghent, published a large theoretical treatise, *Essai de sociologie.* In France, Georges Gurvitch and his co-workers established a new journal, *Cahiers de sociologie.*

In Switzerland, René König of the University of Zürich began the editing of an important series of monographs on sociological topics; one by Klara Vontobel on the work ethic of German Protestantism, and another by König himself on various aspects of the family, promptly appeared. In Britain, the present writer's *German Youth: Bond or Free* and several other new volumes came out in the International Library of Sociology and Social Reconstruction, and Mass Observation, *plus* several British polling agencies, got into peacetime swing. The German Sociological Society held its first postwar meeting in September and, although feeble, showed some promise; publication, however, was sharply limited, although a volume of social-philosophical and sociological essays by Marianne Weber was independently published.

1937 - 1946
Retrospective Interlude on Selected Themes

THE COURSE OF SOCIOLOGY during the decade from 1937 to 1946 was one of consolidation and expansion rather than of innovation. No strikingly new variants in sociological theory, methodology, or techniques appeared, but extremes were either eliminated or crystallized into forms of lessening adaptability and influence, and modes of analysis and interpretation not marked by single-factor fallacies slowly gained the upper hand.

One of the most interesting developments was the full realization of the significance of values in social life. Indeed, the analysis of value-systems became a favorite approach.

This was the more surprising in view of the extreme behaviorism that had threatened to dominate the socio-logical scene in the 1920's and the earlier part of the 1930's, and according to which the more complex value-systems were mere "speech-reactions" of utterly insignificant or even epiphenomenal character. The impact of those value-systems popularly called ideologies and "isms" during the period immediately preceding World War II had doubtless done much to show the utter insufficiency of the sociological brand of white-rat behaviorism, but the actual scientific demonstration of its shortcomings was at least equally important. The extreme behaviorists and their followers no longer commanded respectful attention; reference to their work became increasingly superfluous.

In fact, social scientists arrived at the point where it was more and more necessary to insist that studies of total value-systems, particularly those delivered by social anthropolo-gists of psychoanalytic bent, be carried on with more stringency of method and technique; there was definite danger of reliance on casual impressions and the mistaking of the merely plausible for the demonstrably probable. The kind of analysis offered by Znaniecki, Opler, and G. C. Homans, with its careful dissection of value-systems into "themes," "life-policies," "sentiments," and the like, was expected to do much to counteract the suggestive but un-guarded writings of Sorokin and evangelical anthropologists such as Margaret Mead, Gregory Bateson, and Ruth Benedict.

Closely related to the increased attention given to value-system analysis was the changed emphasis in the study of sociation. Where once it was thought sufficient merely to classify and rank in order of intensity the various associative and dissociative relations, it became increasingly evident that social interaction of every variety had so large a value-component that very little predictive utility attached to researches that ignored it or treated it as secondary.

This was particularly obvious in the published work of the sociometrists clustering about Moreno, but fortunately practice seemed to be better than publication. If one were to take the articles appearing in S as they stood, instead of continually reading between the lines, one would have to conclude that the gyrations of so-called social atoms had as little reference to value-systems or fragments thereof as do the attractions or repulsions of uranium or lead.

The elaborate pretense involved in using the terminology of physics and chemistry, while actually dealing with conduct not susceptible of reduction to physical and chemical interactions alone, robbed the researches of many other students of sociation of their full effectiveness. Further, the perpetual intermingling of two differing analytic standpoints, viz., the situation as defined by the participant and the situation as defined by the observer, vitiated the great potential usefulness of several studies.

Among the most fruitful work in this field during the decade was that on the sociation of workers carried on at Harvard, but the criticisms just noted apply to these as well. When in F. J. Roethlisberger and W. J. Dickson's most elaborate study of pairs, triads, and similar sociative groupings among employees there was no single word of reference to union or non-union ideologies, the disregard of value-system orientation was glaring indeed. If one were attempting to predict typical group responses in strike situations, of what utility would these studies of "workers' morale" actually be?

Nevertheless, there can be no doubt that sociative analyses greatly advanced in relevance and precision during the ten years now being surveyed, and that Leopold von Wiese's conception of a sociology of economic life was well on its way toward realization through the work of investigators who knew little if anything of Wiese and had only a few general ideas about Simmel. (This was not true, of course, of the sociometrists, for Moreno admittedly owed as heavy a debt to Simmel and Wiese as he did to Freud; the "psycho-drama" or "sociodrama" as a process of "group therapy" was genuinely sociative in theory and practice.)

As a matter of fact, it seemed probable that the most definite theoretical influences on the Harvard analysts of workers' sociation derived from Durkheim and Pareto, particularly the latter. In general, it could be said that the stress on the non-rational aspects of conduct smacked of Pareto's "residues," and the ignoring of ideologies had more than a little flavor of "mere derivations." Pareto's vogue enormously declined during the decade, but some of its most doubtful benefits still remained in 1946. Incidentally, it should be noted that Homans' treatise on the English villager likewise leaned heavily on Pareto, but that the use made of his ideas was rather discriminating and advan-tageous. "Derivations" need not be treated as epiphe-nomenal unless the researcher is as fanatical a "positivist" as the notoriously inconsistent Pareto sometimes was.

A worthwhile phase of Pareto's analysis—by implication, at least—was the inseparability of social psychology and sociology. The development of social structures was closely bound up, all through Pareto's work, with on-going changes in social processes and the concomitant shifts in dominant personality configurations. Talcott Parsons was too chari-table an interpreter, in his *Structure of Social Action* (1937), of the great Italian, but there can be little doubt that Parsons' zeal for the merging of sociology and social psychology stemmed as largely from Pareto as it did from Max Weber and Durkheim.

A clearer case for the merger, however, was afforded by the writings of G. H. Mead and the neo-Freudians such as Horney, for here it made abundantly clear that man be-comes human, in the social-psychological sense, only in society. Only in and through interaction with his fellows who themselves as personalities have been woven from threads forming part of societal patterns does *Homo sapiens* take on the attributes of man defined as man in any society of which we have knowledge. Differently put: Physiolog-ical psychology is a branch of biology; social psychology is inextricably linked with sociology; and so-called indi-vidual psychology incessantly fluctuates between these equally necessary poles. Still otherwise: Man's experience as man is essentially dramatic; he learns to play roles in a cast of societal characters, takes parts in a *dramatis personae,* responds to his own actions as others respond to them, and develops an array of mirrored selves that are eventually integrated in some socially acceptable way.

The contribution of the neo-Freudians to this essentially Meadian (G. H.) analysis was the reinterpretation of Freud's conceptions of id, ego, and super-ego. The id became the more crudely biological phase of Mead's "I"-actions; the ego represented those social roles of the "me" with which the person could feel himself identified (*plus* those "I"-actions of necessarily unique and less directly biological character consonant with such social roles), and the super-ego was taken to signify "me"-actions and assigned roles with which no genuine identification takes place and which therefore remain somewhat external—even though this externality may become manifest only in schizoid states or extreme demoralization.

Unfortunately, many neo-Freudians sometimes failed to analyze their vague referents, "society" and "culture," in terms of specific roles and their accompanying rights and duties; the result was the belligerent championing of the "environment" pole of the false "heredity *versus* environment" dilemma. Further, where Mead and his followers were wisely reluctant to catalog a detailed list of "basic needs," the neo-Freudians ordinarily substituted an instinct for security for the orthodox Freudian instinct of sexuality; the derived arguments were just as circular in the one case as in the other.

The importance of the value-system approach was also evident in the renewed attention to social stratification. Twenty-five or thirty years before, sociological interest in class struggles was well-marked; Albion W. Small's most famous course dealt with precisely this topic. The waning of ideological analysis during the 1920's and the early 1930's, perhaps because of behavioristic prepossessions or intimidations, was counteracted from the later 1930's onward by several factors. Among these was the assimilation of numerous émigré sociologists whose experiences with Nazism and Fascism had rendered them keenly aware of the crucial role of class mentalities. Moreover, the 1929-'34 depression and its aftermath made even the most obtuse and optimistic of American social scientists realize how sharply class lines had come to be defined in even so relatively open-class a country as the United States.

The result was a flood of articles and books on stratification topics—a flood that showed little sign of abating among sociologists even during the war period. Further, the "Spissies" (members of the Society for the Psychological Study of Social Issues) generated a good deal more heat than light about American class discrimination, but here and there valuable insights were achieved. As matters stood in 1946, sociologists insufficiently aware of social stratification and its ideological accompaniments would have been hard to find.

Another trend of the decade, the inaptly christened "sociology of knowledge," was closely bound up, as ordinarily presented, with stratification ideologies and their analysis. Although he had many forerunners of much greater intrinsic importance than himself, Karl Mannheim was largely responsible for the burst of interest in the field because of the strong appeal his books made to those of left-wing political allegiance or imbued with the ideology of social planning. His severest critic, Alexander von Schelting, pointed out the untenability of any theory in which all knowledge is class-bound except the variety possessed by the promulgator of the theory—Mannheim made the "free-floating intelligentsia," to which he himself presumably belonged, the court of last resort.

It must not be imagined, however, that "sociology of knowledge" is necessarily embroiled in epistemological quarrels, for it is quite possible to show the functional relations of idea-systems, on the one hand, and social processes and structures, on the other, without assuming one-way "causal" flow in either direction. Some of Mannheim's own substantive work was consequently above the epistemological battle, as was likewise that of Wilson, Merton, Cargill, and several other writers. Znaniecki, in his *Social Role of the Man of Knowledge,* pointed the way to effective research and showed how to evade the many fatal thrusts awaiting the unwary.

Even greater "skill at running cannily among the spears" was needed in another field that greatly expanded during the ten years surveyed; namely, sociology of religion. Nevertheless, such skill was frequently in evidence; Wach, Honigsheim, and Mecklin, among others, provided excellent articles, treatises, and monographs. The basic reason for the success of these studies was close adherence to the practice of taking the religious belief in question as given and proceeding to the analysis of its functional inter-dependences with the social world *per se*. Questions of the validity or invalidity of the belief itself were not raised.

During the war, and especially after the entry of the United States, much of the earlier work in social psychology and sociology having to do with minority groups, leader-ship, public opinion, population, and related matters found a new focus in the area courses sponsored by the armed forces. Social scientists who carried out the area training job were brought to a vivid realization of the artificiality of most of the traditional boundary lines between many of their respective disciplines and of the consequent necessity for a regrouping of the social studies. True, there had been much effort long before the war to stimulate "interdepart-mental projects" on the part of the foundations aiding research, but the projects were usually quite poorly con-ceived along "big business" lines, and the results frequently superficial from any social-scientific standpoint. There is no merit in the crossing of departmental boundaries as such, but when there is a genuinely common problem or a close grouping of definitely related social sciences, the usual lines of academic jurisdiction can and should be ignored.

Area studies were not the only zone of operation for social scientists during the war, for they were on the staffs of a great number of the government bureaus and branches of the armed services. The I and E division of the War De-partment used many, as did likewise WLB, BEW, the State Department, USSBS, OSS, OWI, and scores of other agencies. After the V-days most of them returned to their peacetime posts, but IRO and UNO absorbed a number, and the occasional restaffing of the occupation groups with civilian personnel at the "expert" levels accounted for a few more.

A substantial part of the social-psychological and soci-ological work done for the armed forces was of "poll" character. There were studies of food preferences among the troops, ratings of uniforms, conceptions of fairness in redeployment and demobilization, attitudes of civilians in liberated areas toward Allied forces, and so on. Although the ideal method for gathering data is to collect them with a highly specific research problem in view, the great mounds of "poll" and similar material still held under security restrictions contain thousands upon thousands of recorded observations utilizable by all but the most hypercritical. World War II can still be of some benefit to social scientists in general and to sociologists in particular if there is sufficient effort—and opportunity—to extract that benefit.

Thus far attention has been focused chiefly on those developments in sociology and related fields discernible by an American observer—and after all, sociology is far better represented in the United States in terms of personnel, number of courses, and volume of publication than it is at any other place in the world. Hence, although the exposition now shifts to a country-by-country summary of the major developments of the decade, there seems fair warrant for again referring to the American scene at the very beginning.

The American Sociological Society underwent many changes, most important of which were: (1) the displacement of the *AJS* as the official journal in favor of the newly-founded *ASR;* (2) the splitting off of the rural sociologists from the parent body; (3) the establishment of mail voting for officers of the Society and the adoption of a new constitution of considerably more flexible character than the old. Regional sociological societies, some of them in almost open competition with the national body, continued to spring up, grow, and flourish. . . . The last stronghold of resistance to sociology on the West Coast surrendered in 1946; the University of California at Berkeley finally installed a Department of Sociology and Social Institutions.

The former supremacy of Argentina in Latin-American sociology gave place to a triangular situation in which Brazil and Mexico figured as the other peers. Numerous books and periodicals were published, and university instruction grew rapidly. The activities of the Pan-American Union and of the State Department of the United States, as well as of the Rockefeller and other foundations, facilitated exchange of personnel, and prospects for further development were bright.

In Britain the movement known as Mass Observation gave much promise of developing into a base outside the universities for a science of social relations, but in the later war years enthusiasm seemed to wane. Only the provincial universities and London had any persons on their staffs calling themselves sociologists. . . . Most war. and postwar interest in sociology in Great Britain probably stemmed from two sources: (1) the earlier influx of refugee scholars who brought with them the Continental familiarity with sociology; and (2) the drastic alterations in social structure resulting, among other things, in the new Labor Government and making most persons acutely aware of social relations they had formerly taken for granted.

France underwent an almost complete elimination of sociology during the war, for it had come to be identified, in the popular mind, with the ideology of the Third Republic. Its representatives either quietly submerged as did Marcel Mauss, fled as did Georges Gurvitch, or were killed as was Maurice Halbwachs. After liberation, however, there was a genuine resurgence. . . .

The Nazis hated no intellectual enterprise more deeply than the sociological; consequently the German Sociological Society was among the first of the learned societies to be liquidated. Most sociologists lapsed into silence, fled, or were imprisoned and exterminated; a few, however, seized the opportunity to rise to positions of some influence. As noted above, some of the sociologists fled, reached the United States and Britain, and in many instances gave valuable assistance to governments and armed forces; others who remained in Germany and survived took over important parts in the postwar regime—e.g., Hanna Meuter became chief councillor for public welfare in the Aachen district, and Leopold von Wiese, although advanced in years, resumed his duties as professor of sociology at Cologne and Bonn and president of the re-constituted German Sociological Society. Unfortunately, the postwar Nazi murder of E. Y. Hartshorne, the MG officer most conversant with sociology and eager to aid in its re-establishment, temporarily reversed the forward movement.

Another Central European country, Czechoslovakia, actively resumed sociological teaching, research, publication, and organization. President Beneš was a sociologist of repute, as was his predecessor Masaryk. The Masaryk Sociological Society, official organization of Czechoslovakian sociologists, renewed contact with the other sociological societies throughout the world, and there seemed reason to believe that the high level of productivity and quality of research formerly shown by its members would once more be achieved if political conditions permitted.

Unfortunately very little was known, in 1946, about the state of sociology in Italy, the Balkans, and Russia. The same was true of India, China, and Japan; the accounts and bibliographies published in the present treatise in 1938 badly needed supplementing, but apparently more time would have to elapse.

1947

Continuing Hesitation, But Also Signs of Consolidation and Fresh Advance

UNCERTAINTIES IN DOMESTIC and international affairs, manifest the world over during 1947, were reflected in sociology. Few if any *sharply* marked tendencies were evident.

Among the eddies and shifting currents, however, it was possible to trace: (1) the continuing drift toward an inclusive science of social relations; (2) some evidence of return to the past in attempted revivals of thinkers who in some quarters were recently regarded as of historical relevance only; (3) interest in philosophy of history, theory of history, or historical sociology, stimulated by Somervell's summary of Toynbee's *A Study of History;* (4) the more or less hasty writing of a wide array of books and articles of somewhat *ad hoc* character, dealing as they did with matters in the forefront of public attention; and (5) studies in the methods and techniques of the social sciences in general and of sociology in particular. Taking these in order, the outstanding literature included the following:

(1) What was called "the anthropological approach" within the framework of a comprehensive science of social relations was evidenced in the monograph by Leighton and Kluckhohn, *Children of the People,* a follow-up of their earlier work, *The Navaho.* Field observation and a series of tests provided the data, but the loosely-integrated theoretical scheme lacked adequate empirical support at several places. A not altogether dissimilar approach, presented under a different name, was evidenced in the four special symposium issues of *S,* although the testing apparatus was more elaborate and was focused on a number of additional points.

Single articles of general "social relations" type were very few; the only one of importance was that by Homans, "A Conceptual Scheme for the Study of Social Organization" in the *ASR*. Deriving primarily from Henderson's interpretation of Pareto, and drawing heavily on the work of other Henderson-influenced researchers at Harvard, Homans' article failed to make the maximum impact because it made the usual Harvard error of not taking into account similar studies in the same field. In fact, it was somewhat myopic, and marked a recession from the point reached in the concluding chapter of Homans' earlier and promising book, *English Villagers of the Thirteenth Century*.

Textbooks in this field were published by Cuber, Hiller, and Sorokin. The first offered little that was essentially new or penetrating; Cuber's attempt to write down for the presumed benefit of undergratuates robbed his book of dignity and precision. Hiller's work was much better.

Sorokin's textbook was really a treatise systematizing the theoretical framework that pervaded his other voluminous writings. Reviews tended to be unfavorably critical, but if the un-English style had been left out of account, judgments would certainly have been less adverse. Whatever its limitations, the Sorokin volume reached a high level of abstraction, was carefully integrated, and made readily available a number of novel insights and formulations.

Competing with Sorokin's contribution, however, was the massive work of Max Weber, entitled in English *The Theory of Economic and Social Organization*, finally printed in translation by Henderson and Parsons.

(2) The revivals of thinkers judged to be of current sociological significance were best exemplified by Max Horkheimer's *Eclipse of Reason*, in which Hegelianism was persuasively recommended. Horkheimer's political leanings toward the German Social-Democratic tradition, with its attention to Hegel as interpreted by Marx, accounted in large measure for his special emphasis. In the pages of the Stalinist journal, *SS*, numerous articles of related type appeared—with, of course, a Communist rather than a Social-Democratic orientation. The Communist line of analysis, which also enjoyed some vogue in Britain although not popular among "intellectuals" on the Continent, was slashingly attacked by Lundberg in his "Sociology versus Dialectical Immaterialism," *ASR*. Lundberg was

undoubtedly nettled by Communist attacks on his positivism, but altogether apart from the intruding personal note, the article was an acute appraisal and rejoinder.

(3) Historical sociology enjoyed much although probably short-lived public interest because of the Toynbee fad. Dating from 1934-36, his six-volume treatise came to current attention because of an adroitly advertised one-volume abridgement, a *Life* feature article, and a *Time* appreciation. The work was hailed as a crushing refutation of Marx, but that obscured the genuine social-scientific importance of Toynbee's work. Real significance lay in his masterly descriptions and analyses of various ethnic and cultural groups such as the Spartiates, the Jews, or the Turks, rather than in his comprehensive but highly speculative theodicy. In the midst of a welter of enthusiastic reviews and commentaries, those by Hicks (*Harper's,* February), and Barnes (*ASR*) preserved balanced judgment, although Barnes was perhaps too harshly adverse.

(4) Among the publications dealing with contemporary problems having some sociological relevance, probably the most attention-compelling were those having to do with housing. "The American Family and its Housing" was the title of an entire issue of the *ASR,* and a similar emphasis was reflected in the programs of several sociological conventions.

Juvenile delinquency and family instability brought forth the usual large crop of texts, monographs, and articles. Surveying the mass of undigested fact and offhand opinion in this field, it was clear that basic theory was sadly lacking.

Ethnic conflicts ("race problems") caused much uneasiness, and the SSRC financed a well-meaning bulletin entitled *The Reduction of Intergroup Tensions.* A new series of books on "Peoples of America," aimed in a similar direction, was inaugurated by Arnold Mulder's *Americans from Holland.* The traditional melting-pot theme was used to integrate the facts. Frazier's article, "Sociological Theory and Race Relations," was one of the few good guides for analysis. Among the more definitely factual studies, McCormick and Hornseth's "The Negro in Madison, Wisconsin," *ASR,* offered several interesting conclusions.

Industrial unrest and related matters, crystallized for the public in the Taft-Hartley Bill, were scientifically discussed in Warner and Low's *The Social System of the Modern Factory,* subtitled *The Strike: a Social Analysis.* Well-financed and well-written, it nevertheless made no mention of Hiller's earlier study of the strike nor, indeed, of any other important work of similar focus. This was a short-coming of all the studies appearing under Warner's sponsor-ship, i.e., work done by others was ignored or overlooked.

Somewhat belatedly following the wave of general inter-est, there appeared a study entitled *Public Reactions to the Atomic Bomb and World Affairs*. Almost twenty-five thousand dollars were spent on this by the SSRC; it con-sisted essentially of a public opinion poll of six hundred individuals who were interviewed before and after the Bikini bomb tests. There was some attempt at explanation of the answers elicited. Cantril, Herring, Likert, and Cot-trell, the last as chairman, formed the research committee.

Some light was thrown on the nature of large-scale research of the kinds just mentioned in Bendix's article, "Bureaucracy: The Problem and its Setting," *ASR*. It concluded as follows: ". . . we cannot profit from the effi-ciency of large-scale organizations unless we succeed in making the initiative of the individual one of our principles of organization."

An article evidencing much individual initiative, but unfortunately not backed up by polling techniques that could easily have been applied (given the funds!), was Davis's "Some Sources of American Hostility to Russia," *AJS*. Abounding in analytic leads, it could probably have been turned into a large-scale research project that might have avoided bureaucratic handicaps. Perhaps its faintly discernible pro-Russian bias, which could readily have been eliminated or counterbalanced, made the finding of founda-tion sponsorship difficult. A study of large-scale type that was markedly successful was a White House report on civil liberties in the United States, *To Secure These Rights*.

Evidence of widespread uneasiness at the postwar turmoil could be inferentially gleaned from the large number of books and articles extolling the small community, with its presumable neighborhood cohesion, as a cure-all for a wide variety of symptoms of social disorganization. The draw-backs of the small community when it is extremely isolated were interestingly pointed up in the outstanding article by Peter Munch, "Cultural Contacts in an Isolated Com-munity: Tristan da Cunha," *AJS*. Studies of other com-munities in which isolation was in some sense disrupted were to be found in a report covering South Seas natives under American rule, *Economic and Human Resources of Micronesia,* United States Commercial Company. As a mine of empirical evidence and suggestions for further analysis, it had high likelihood of future use. Much the same, *mutatis mutandis,* could be said of the ten volumes of the *War Relocation Authority Monographs.*

(5) Turning away from work in the general field of social relations in large part inspired by current exigencies, and hence at times of small scientific utility, research and writing of more technical and/or less transitory interest may be surveyed.

Timasheff's "Definitions in the Social Sciences," *AJS,* was a much-needed corrective of the loose practices now widely evident, and Adler's "Operational Definitions in Sociology," *AJS,* was an amusing but trenchant attack on the basic absurdity of some varieties of operationism. Winch's "Heuristic and Empirical Typologies," *ASR,* was an interesting albeit over-ambitious effort to show that factor analysis might be of value in type construction and use.

Valuable mathematical innovations, focusing on a highly relevant problem, were presented in Guttman and Suchman's "Intensity and a Zero Point for Attitude Analysis," *ASR.* These writers are sociologists as well as genuine *mathematical* statisticians, and are keenly aware of the pitfalls as well as the possibilities of polling techniques.

In Latin America, sociological teaching and research was vigorously pushed forward. The quarterly journal edited by Laszlo Radvanyi, *The Social Sciences in Mexico and South and Central America,* and written in English, made its first appearance in May. It contained, among other things, valuable articles on the history of the social sciences in Latin America. The *ASR* also had a good article on sociology in Peru. The present treatise appeared in Spanish translation. Sociology in France was furthered by the continued functioning of the *Centre d'Études Sociologiques* at Paris. Sociology in Germany made progress through the resumption of publication of the *Cologne Journal of Sociology* under Wiese's editorship, and the establishment of a series of sociological sourcebooks and monographs—the *Civitas Gentium* series—edited by Solms of Marburg. In Britain the year was signalized by the publication of Ginsberg's *Reason and Unreason in Society,* Marshall's *Society at the Crossroads,* and the first issue of a new journal, *Human Relations,* published jointly by the Tavistock Institute of Human Relations, London, and the Research Center for Group Dynamics, Massachusetts Institute of Technology. A useful brief survey of the social sciences in the Soviet Union was presented by Barrington Moore, Jr., in the *ASR*. In Japan, the reconstruction of sociology was made tangibly evident by the publication of the first postwar number of the journal *Social Research*.

1948
Steady Development and Self-Criticism

TRENDS EVIDENCED DURING the year were in many respects continuations of those already clearly manifest. Among these were: (1) the gradual fusion of sociology and related social sciences into a more inclusive or at least more functionally differentiated whole; (2) the steady albeit slower growth of industrial sociology; (3) the continuing preoccupation with "race relations" and with "family problems"; (4) the analytic working over of war experience, oftentimes personal, with bureaucratic and similar structures; and (5) the slow *rapprochement* of methods and techniques once thought mutually exclusive but now seen to be complementary. Among the trends not previously quite so well marked were: (6) attention to international relations and area studies; and (7) sharp criticism of both the techniques and presuppositions of public opinion polling (well in advance of the November débacle). *Seriatim:*

(1) The trend toward fusion of sociology with certain other social sciences was demonstrated in Stuart Chase's *The Proper Study of Mankind*. Excessively popular, in many respects appallingly naive, and sadly restricted in its scope, it nevertheless served a useful purpose in showing the general public that "academic" analyses may have fruitful concrete applications. Those most frequently coupled with the sociologists in Chase's book were the anthropologists, and justifiably so.

Kluckhohn's *Mirror for Man,* winner of the Whittlesey House award for 1948, here and there contained exaggerated claims that might have caused other social scientists to shout "academic imperialism!" but even the most vociferous critics would not have denied its considerable merits. Among textbooks the anthropological-sociological merger was most effectively demonstrated by Bennett and Tumin's *Social Life: Structure and Function.*

(2) Industrial sociology, perhaps better termed the sociology of industrial organization, continued to grow in popularity, as attested by the year's Census of Research, *ASR.* A stimulating article taking this interest as its point of departure, but having many implications of more general character, was Philip Selznick's "Foundations of the Theory of Organization," *ASR.* Moore's article, *ASR,* showed awareness of the criticisms of industrial sociology advanced by Blumer and Dubin, and in particular admitted the distorted perspective that the ignoring of union organization initially introduced.

(3) The theme of the yearly meeting of the American Sociological Society was racial and cultural conflict. Many of the papers maintained this focus, although naturally other interests received their customary recognition. It must be said that the meeting did little to advance knowledge of either empirical evidence or abstract analysis; the familiar man from Mars might have supposed that racial and cultural conflict occurred only within the United States. . . .

The outstanding treatise in the field was Tomasic's *Personality and Culture in Eastern European Politics.* This sociological study of Balkan problems broke new ground. It was adversely criticized as "propagandistic," however, by Kossitch in the *Cologne Journal of Sociology,* "Aus den Tiefen des Balkans." The best textbook of the year, Schermerhorn's *These Our People,* was not so parochial as most, but in any case it made no claim to thorough coverage outside the United States, and dealt with American minorities in a *very* effective and attractive way.

"Family problems" continued to elicit much interest, but the analysis remained superficial and/or conventional. Even Bossard's new departure, *Sociology of Child Development,* suffered from the pangs of undigested theory. One of the few articles striking a new note was that by William L. Kolb, "Sociologically Established Family Norms and Democratic Values," *SF;* another was Bossard and Boll's "Rite of Passage," *SF,* a study of the debutante. The *AJS* published a special issue on "The American Family," but it had no articles transcending the customary modes of description and analysis. . . .

(4) Sociologists, both as civilians and as members of the armed forces, oftentimes became acquainted with bureaucracy outside textbooks for the first time during the war. The flood of articles thereby produced showed few signs of abatement in 1948. These were nearly all somewhat impressionistic reports by participant observers; what the future should bring forth is a systematic treatise based on all the varieties of evidence available.

(5) Methodology and techniques of research continued to receive much attention. Ellis's "Questionnaire *versus* Interview Methods in the Study of Human Love Relationships," *ASR*, compared anonymous responses to questionnaires with interviews in which the subjects were identified, and arrived at the startling conclusion that more self-revelatory or unfavorable responses were elicited by the former than by the latter. The triviality of the questions asked and the statistical naivete of the analysis called forth biting comment from Jessie Bernard, *ASR*. Hollingshead's "Community Research," *ASR*, provided an excellent review, but was unfortunately marred by occasional errors. . . . Dodd's "Developing Demoscopes for Social Research," *ASR*, was most interesting as a sample of contemporary positivistic ideology pushed to a very extreme degree. Foreman's "The Theory of Case Study," *SF*, showed a refreshing awareness of the need for coming to grips with the empirical data.

Possibilities of bringing together the less extreme points of view were tellingly set forth by Merton, "The Bearing of Empirical Research upon the Development of Social Theory," *ASR*. In general, it seemed clear that belligerent antitheses of method and techniques were losing ground in favor of more conciliatory approaches which, if the dangers of facile eclecticism could be avoided, promised much.

(6) Sociological aspects of international relations and of area studies were brought into focus in a way that perhaps represented the start of a new trend. State Department, Military Government, and foundation officials had long been outspokenly aware of the sadly limited scope of American sociology as compared with several neighbor disciplines, but little attention on the part of sociologists was evidenced, even during the war. Two articles showing keen realization of the situation appeared in professional sociological journals in 1948, however: Crawford's "International Relations and Sociology," *ASR*, and Smith's "Needed Emphases in

Southern Sociology," *SF.* The discussion that followed Crawford's paper, in particular, showed the vast scope of teaching and research opportunities available to sociologists prepared to take advantage of them. Chief among the kinds of preparation needed was of course the linguistic, English not yet being a universal language even when shouted nasally.

(7) Several sociologists and social psychologists were among the few social scientists not discredited by the results of the presidential polls. In the *EB* Book of the Year for 1947 attention was called to the critical article by Guttman and Suchman; in 1948 similar skepticism was expressed, from a quite different standpoint, by Robert E. Myers and, at considerable length, by Herbert Blumer. The latter's article, "Public Opinion and Public Opinion Polling," *ASR,* was formulated in 1947 but did not appear until October, 1948. Newcomb and Julian Woodard attempted to rebut Blumer's attack, but without marked success. Faith in such techniques, however, was still so strong that not even the November reversal did much to weaken it among the orthodox; only "the whirligig of time" seemed likely to do that—and there was always the chance that the techniques might improve. Few critics were completely negativistic.

Outside the United States several developments of considerable significance took place, but few if any seemed to be of crucial or even novel character.

1949

Some Fads Wane, Older Emphases Revive

AMONG THE YEAR'S trends most clearly apparent were: (1) waning of the "child training" emphasis in the "personality and culture" field; (2) emergence of the study of small groups as a field of major interest; (3) greatly increased interest in general sociological theory; (4) continuing attention to social stratification; (5) stronger interest in sociology of religion, albeit with primary reference to religious conflict; (6) sharp focus on the social-psychological problems dealt with in studies of American troops during World War II; (7) prolonged discussion of "the polls"; and (8) evidences of a possibly developing "Americanization" of sociology in Europe and elsewhere.

(1) During the postwar years a number of investigators, chiefly of anthropological background and psychoanalytic bent, had laid heavy stress on the presumably crucial importance of childhood feeding and toilet habits for the determining of adult character traits. In this emphasis they were followed by many social psychologists and sociologists. Merely secondary importance, if that, was assigned to religious belief, political doctrine, class position, and the like.

So extreme did this trend become that a British anthropologist, Geoffrey Gorer, attributed certain basic features of Pan-Communism and Pan-Slavism to the aggression-inciting effect of the tight swaddling clothes worn by Russian infants. Confronted by "diaper determinism" of this type, many of the previously gullible began to question the conclusions about "Japanese," "German," "American," or "Irish" character that they had formerly accepted, and the result was a precipitate retreat, in some instances, from a position leading to such patent absurdities. Nevertheless, the effect of persuasive anthropological accounts laden with the charm of the exotic, combined with the effect of a variety of psychoanalysis presented, like most other varieties, with missionary fervor, sufficed to keep a number of believers within the fold, particularly when they were sociologists taking their anthropology and psychoanalysis at second hand. The most that could be said was that there was a distinct decline in enthusiasm and the voicing of distressing doubts. Alistair Cooke, reviewing Gorer's book on the American character, was a pungent critic: "It makes you wonder how accurate Malinowski's study of the Trobrianders was."

(2) The study of small groups has had a long history, and in recent times the names of analysts, systematists, and empirical researchers such as Georg Simmel, Leopold von Wiese, Kurt Lewin, Eliot Chapple, and Carleton Coon have been well known. Most recently students of "group dynamics," the majority of them trained in psychology, together with "sociometrists," of whom the majority are psychiatrically-sociologically oriented, have attracted the lion's share of attention.

In 1949, however, the American Sociological Society established for the first time a section on the study of small groups, and R. F. Bales, active in the Laboratory of Social

Relations at Harvard, gained attention for his interesting research. It was interesting because a definite, readily transmissible method for the study of social interaction in small groups was developed; before that, with the possible exception of Chapple's study, only sterile "field theory" and "topological" analogies, or elaborately diagrammed verbalisms relying on terms filched from other sciences, had been available as guides for the empirical researcher. In other words, the suggestive leads provided by Simmel, Wiese, and others had been ignored. Bales' work not only took advantage of these leads, but explored and exploited new approaches. It was still too early to say whether the kind of description and analysis represented by Bales was likely to prove fruitful, more especially as key problems of cultural differentials were not directly confronted, but it unquestionably provided a basis on which research leading to acceptance, rejection, or modification of the method on grounds other than those of personal preference could be carried out.

(3) General sociological theory had long been a stepchild of sociology, particularly in the United States, where raw empiricism had been in vogue since the middle 1920's. It was still in vogue in 1949, but the theoretical work of a new generation of American sociologists, notably Talcott Parsons and his students, had started a counter-vogue. True, this counter-vogue, using the ambiguous slogan of "structural-functional" theory, had a host of uncritical followers, but it nevertheless represented a useful shift in emphasis. Given this shift, it was apparent that earlier and equally significant theoretical work done in the United States and abroad would eventually emerge from stepchild status also and receive due although belated consideration.

The major obstacle to theoretical advance—namely, the unwillingness of American publishers to issue treatises having little prospect of extensive textbook use—was partially overcome by the appearance of small, venturesome organizations such as the Free Press of Glencoe, Illinois, the Norman Paul Press of Gary, Indiana, and the Harren Press of Washington, D. C. How long such enterprises could survive was perhaps questionable, but in 1949 they had already rendered great service to American sociology.

Although the two American sociological journals with the widest circulation, the *ASR* and the *AJS,* granted increased space, all things considered, to theoretical articles, the greatest proportional increase was registered by the North Carolina journal, *SF*.

(4) Social stratification studies, when beyond the journalistic level, necessarily lean heavily on general sociological theory. During 1949 W. Lloyd Warner's long-heralded book on social stratification appeared, but it unfortunately was pervaded by a kind of home-brewed theory that did little to integrate it with other work in the field. A. B. Hollingshead's study of "Elmtown," in spite of its limited focus, had a more readily adaptable theoretical framework. There were no journal articles of crucial importance in the stratification field, but continuing interest was apparent. This was particularly evident at the Christmas meeting of the American Sociological Society, where three long papers on social stratification in Russia, England, and Germany were presented in a two-hour session.

(5) A field of much significance, sociology of religion, had until the late 1940's received little notice in the United States (except in conjunction with the economic analyses of Max Weber and R. H. Tawney). Sociologists in Britain, and particularly on the Continent, on the other hand, confronted by clericalist-anticlericalist movements, novel sects, State churches, *Kulturkampf, laïcisme,* ecclesiastically-sanctioned governments such as those of Dollfuss, Salazar, and Franco, and many related matters, had long regarded sociology of religion as of the highest scientific import. The pages of the recently revived *L'Année sociologique* and the *Cologne Journal of Sociology (Kölner Zeitschrift für Soziologie),* as well as *Cahiers sociologiques,* the British *Sociological Review, Psychologie des peuples,* and several other journals testified to this. Further, the elaborate bibliography by Daniel Warnotte which appeared posthumously during 1949 in *RDIS* was studded with books and articles on sociology of religion.

American interest, however, had begun to appear, but, characteristically, in textbooks and collections of readings for students rather than in systematic treatises. This interest may have been evoked by the same series of events that brought forth Paul Blanshard's *American Freedom and Catholic Power,* but in any case it had become definitely apparent. Whether it would result in impartial, unbiased— i.e., genuinely scientific—studies could not yet be foreseen.

(6) A major effort at a genuinely scientific approach to prediction of military conduct was made in *The American*

Soldier in World War II, a four-volume treatise (liberally financed by the SSRC) by Samuel Stouffer of Harvard and other major researchers. Opinions about its merits differed sharply. The *Nonpartisan Review* and *Commentary* published bitter attacks, and Herbert Blumer proclaimed, "No new theory, no new methods, no new conclusions." Some journals published laudatory reviews, most of them by persons identified with the project itself or already committed to the methods it represented. Stouffer, on the other hand, pointed out that one of his most severe critics, Arthur Schlesinger, Jr., was a young historian whose writing showed strong political bias and reliance on "one-man intuition," and that Blumer, quoted above, was a habitual negativist, "the chief mortician of American sociology."

In spite of the special session of the Sociological Research Association devoted exclusively to discussion of the treatise at the Christmas meeting, it seemed clear that its merits and demerits had not yet been thoroughly assessed, and that controversy would continue for some time. This was perhaps as it should be; in the realm of the mind, at least, "Conflict is the father of all things." Certainly the work, good or bad, of Stouffer and his collaborators was too important to be passed over lightly.

(7) Similar controversy surrounded the aftermath of the polling débacle of the 1948 election. The SSRC financed a large meeting at Iowa in the spring of 1949 for discussion of "what went wrong with the polls." No definite conclusions were reached, but most of the discussants were sympathetic with the pollsters' plight, although at the same time critical of certain techniques. Definitely unsympathetic and sweepingly critical, however, was Lindley Rogers, who brought out *The Pollsters,* a sharp and telling attack on the presuppositions, methods, tactics, and political orientations of Gallup, Roper, and other leaders in the polling movement. Here also it seemed obvious that impartial assessment had not yet been achieved.

(8) Through the operation of the Fulbright grants, researchers on the staffs of the occupation forces in Germany and Japan, general North American influence in Mexico, Central, and South America, and in other ways, a trend toward the "Americanization" of sociology seemed to have emerged. Nels Anderson, with the German occupation, secured the services of American experts to carry out a study of the Darmstadt community, using younger German

sociologists as field workers, tabulators, etc. J. H. Kolb of the University of Wisconsin carried out a rural community research project in Norway for the University of Oslo. The chair of sociology left vacant by Wiese's retirement at the University of Cologne was filled by René König of Zürich, who had been directly influenced by sociologists at the University of North Carolina. Jean Stoetzel of Bordeaux, trained at Columbia, continued to head the French Institute of Public Opinion. John Bennett and Herbert Pessin of Ohio State University did much to influence developments in Japanese anthropology and sociology. Several British universities were endeavoring to secure the services of American sociologists on short- and long-term bases, and the University of Ceylon did likewise. Louis Wirth of the University of Chicago was elected first president of the new International Sociological Society, sponsored by UNESCO. (It would be regrettable, however, if this extension of American influence were to go too far; doubtless the United States has much to contribute, but it has also much to learn.)

1950

Drift Toward Unity

A T THE MID-CENTURY POINT, sociology was just about one hundred years old, both with regard to its name and its strictly scientific study. True, the history of social thought, as distinct from the history of sociology, had a record going back to Hammurabi and beyond, and the history of sociology since 1850 included much that did not conform to the canons of science. Nevertheless, 1950 could be regarded with some warrant as a sociological centennial.

The trend most clearly apparent in this year was the continuing merger of sociology with a vaguely general social science as yet unnamed. The merger was the result of drift; there was certainly little semblance of planning. In fact, the various foundations supporting research and advanced training, and the governmental agencies directly and indirectly carrying out similar financing functions, had done a great deal to make planning difficult if not impossible. They inclined to support almost at random nearly anything to which the label "social science" could be applied by its promoters, and the universities were not much more discriminating. The result was an all-pervasive overlapping of effort, concealed by competing terminologies and esoteric techniques. Close examination of work done in human or cultural geography, social history, and numerous other specially labelled fields would reveal a great deal that was being done in other fields as well, and *vice versa.* This would not have been disadvantageous had it been the result of concerted endeavor to achieve a balanced perspective; in multitude of counsel there is sometimes wisdom. The trouble was that the members of the multitude did not take counsel with one another, but carried on what amounted to a string of miscellaneous monologues.

Sociology itself, particularly in the United States, had contributed to this planless drift. Rightly objecting to the *pot-pourri* of schemes for "uplift," substitutes for religion, concealed political programs, and random speculation on "social affairs" that sometimes passed as sociology, professional sociologists had turned toward the analysis of concrete evidence by means of standardized and readily transmissible techniques. This was a turn in the right direction, but it went too far. All general theory that could have served as a guide for concerted effort was not so much rejected as ignored. The resulting vacuum was filled, albeit unsatisfactorily, by investigators in other fields who tried to devise, bit by bit, "the grammar of social relations" that they found so strangely lacking, from about 1925 to 1950, in the works of most sociologists.

Only in the writings of a few Europeans, and of Americans in some measure influenced by them, was concern for general theoretical orientation shown. Among the more recent American treatises could be mentioned Talcott Parsons' *Essays in Sociological Theory, Pure and Applied* (1949), Robert K. Merton's *Social Theory and Social Structure* (1949), and the present writer's *Through Values to Social Interpretation: Essays on Social Contexts, Actions, Types, and Prospects* (1950). These authors, and several others who might well have been listed, quite clearly did not constitute a group sufficiently influential to bring about, in the near future, a reorientation of North American sociology, much less of the science of social relations. They represented a possible nucleus of sociologists who might some day join forces with other social scientists in filling the existing theoretical vacuum with less oddly assorted fragments, but that was the most that could be said.

Moreover, the systematic filling of the vacuum would have to wait on the development of bodies of coherent theory in related fields that, together with existing and to-be-developed sociological theory, could be integrated into a general theory, or closely interlinked set of theories, within which all of the activities of "the sciences of man" would find their appropriate places. . . .

Among the fields in which work was going on during 1950 that, albeit overlapping with prior and contemporary effort in sociology, was capable of being linked up with an eventual general theory of the social sciences, was social psychology. The studies of Muzafer Sherif on social norms, of H. A. Murray and Norman Cameron on abnormal personality, of L. S. Cottrell and others on "subjective" aspects of social interaction, and of the followers of Kurt Lewin on "group dynamics" were all relevant.

In particular, Cottrell's revival of attention to the phenomena loosely called "empathy" promised much, for it gave some assurance that the almost-forgotten work of Max Scheler on "the forms of sympathy"—compathy, transpathy, mimpathy, empathy, unipathy, and propathy—would soon be integrated with current theory and research.

Further, the trends in group dynamics correlated not only with R. F. Bales' *Interaction Process Analysis* (1950), but also with the quasi-sociological studies carried on by the school centering around J. L. Moreno and his journals, and with the renewed interest, strongly manifest in 1950, in the study of small groups.

Among other ways in which this interest appeared was the translation, by Kurt H. Wolff, of *The Sociology of Georg Simmel* (1950) and the reissue of the present writer's *Systematic Sociology on the Basis of the* Beziehungslehre *and* Gebildelehre *of Leopold von Wiese* (Gary, Ind.: Norman Paul Press, 1950).

The field roughly described by the phrase "culture and personality" also gave some indication of eventual interconnection with general social science theory. Initially stimulated by grants from the SSRC in the early 1930's, and intended to serve as an "open court" for all the social sciences, "culture and personality" showed signs, in 1950, of profiting by contact with social psychology rather than with psychoanalysis only, and also of absorbing effectively the French sociological contributions of Emile Durkheim, Marcel Granet, Louis Gernet, and Maurice Halbwachs.

If this integrative trend were to continue, it would mean that sociology of knowledge, not only of French derivation but also stemming from the German varieties represented by Max Scheler and Karl Mannheim, would either incorporate "culture and personality" or be incorporated by it. The end product, moreover, would be readily assimilable into one important section of a general theory of the social sciences. (Incidentally, 1950 saw the posthumous publication of Mannheim's *Freedom, Power and Democratic Planning*, ed. by H. H. Gerth and Ernst K. Bramstedt.)

It was earlier noted that during World War II there emerged a strong interest in what might be called a concrete rather than abstract integration of the social sciences; namely, area studies. Following on this, interest in abstract integration soon developed. Werner J. Cahnmann, a sociologist, was among the first to advance a general theory of area studies, and in 1950 the SSRC published a monograph by Julian H. Steward, an anthropologist, entitled *Area Research: Theory and Practice*. Further, a considerable number of grants was made for area research training fellowships and travel. The Russian institutes at Harvard and Columbia continued to function essentially as centers of area studies, and other institutes dealing with the Far East, notably the one at Yale, were also established. The state of world affairs had again given a concrete emphasis to area studies, but in 1950 the abstract counterpart was not lacking, and might be expected to develop further.

Perhaps more important than any other 1950 development toward the integration of the social sciences, because clearly not of limited perspective, was the November Princeton Conference, sponsored by the American Council of Learned Societies, on "Uniformities in History." There had been previous conferences along related lines, but that in 1950 was particularly designed to take advantage of the presence in the United States of the famous author of *A Study of History*, the British writer A. J. Toynbee. In view of the fact that his work, vast in its sweep and implications, included far more than conventional history, philosophers, anthropologists, sociologists, and students of language and literature were brought together with a number of specialists in various historical fields. The topic was Feudalism, but might just as well have been called Methods for the Comparative Study of Social Structures, with Special Reference to Feudalism. Toynbee participated actively in the discussions, and all those present agreed that a definite step toward the integration of history (in certain of its aspects) with the other social sciences had been made.

1951

Reflections on Recent Developments

THE CONTINUANCE of the cold and Korean wars seemed to have accelerated in the United States the trend toward large-scale research. Funds in considerable amount became available for social-psychological and sociological investigation. The Department of Defense let numerous contracts; the Rand Corporation (an Air Force device for avoiding red tape) continued its "brains trust" program; the Central Intelligence Agency almost certainly had, under tight security, an extensive research setup; and the Department of State did a great deal of high-quality work under severe handicap. Field workers were sent to many areas at home and overseas by some of these agencies to deal with such problems as "how to avoid friction between American forces abroad and the indigenous population." Lecturers from the universities were called in to work along lines reminiscent of the FA & LSC and CATP of the Hitler war. The Point Four program, in which the Department of Agriculture necessarily played a large part, enlisted the research and field work services of many rural sociologists.

All in all, governmental agencies seemed to be sponsoring, supervising, or conducting general social-scientific research on a very large scale indeed, and the various specialties in the science of social relations came in for a good share of attention. Most of the work was done by teams or at least by "co-ordinated personnel," and was almost always anonymous and under security classification. Whether in the long run the social sciences could make basic advances under these conditions remained to be seen; at any rate, some of the contracts were for what some points of view regarded as basic social science research.

The private foundations, large and small, also fostered large-scale research. Some of them, notably the Ford Foundation, gave support to programs aimed not at specific researches but at staffing and otherwise organizing so that research could be done in what was judged to be the appropriate way. This promised much, although "the appropriate way" was occasionally determined by foundation officials who themselves had had relatively little if any research experience. Nevertheless, there could be no doubt that the prevailingly well-considered foundation attention to genuinely basic considerations rather than to highly specific projects was likely, if continued, to be most helpful. Large grants to individual researchers who then recruited personal assistants were also made, but not in most cases by the more conventional foundations.

The universities also showed signs of favoring large-scale research, especially on interdepartmental and teamwork bases. This was sometimes partially supported by the taking of contracts to do work for private concerns—advertising agencies, television and radio sponsors, industrial organizations, and so on. Over and above this, however, appeared the increasing practice of giving release from teaching and committee duties in order to do research, and also of the establishment of full-time research professorships. Mistakes in judgment were sometimes made, and intramural "politics" occasionally intruded, but with limited resources some universities achieved results quite as good as those coming from government or foundation projects.

Research of small-scale type, much of it carried out by individuals, continued to be of importance although relatively less prominent. Fulbright appointments, SSRC grants (especially for area training and investigation), university sabbaticals, special research leaves, reduced teaching schedules, provision for research assistants, Carnegie support, and self-financed projects accounted for a considerable flow of basic and applied work. Many men who would have chafed under even the mild regimentation that some large-scale projects involved were thus enabled to make important contributions, more especially when the projects they undertook did not lend themselves to the use of standardized methods or techniques. Most large-scale projects, however, had to proceed along fairly orthodox lines; too much money was at stake. The place to take chances was on the small-scale research; if it didn't pan out, no great damage was done.

The teaching function of the social scientist also received recognition from governmental agencies. For example, the Department of State brought in sociological and anthropological specialists for its summer and other staff courses; the Air Force College at Maxwell Field, Alabama, made use of social-science-trained lecturers on both permanent and visiting bases; the Central Intelligence Agency had university men on leave or "on career" who taught ordinary academic subjects slanted to the needs of the agency; and the Pentagon not infrequently utilized academic "consultants" in a teaching capacity.

In the colleges and universities the teaching of this or that branch of the science of social relations, at both undergraduate and graduate levels, still took up the greater part of the time of most staff members of those branches. (Included under "teaching" was the writing of the ubiquitous course syllabus and its end-product, the textbook.) This was not to be deplored; even research procedures had to be capable of being communicated—if not to the undergraduate, at least to the advanced graduate.

Some university administrators publicly proclaimed that they favored the teacher over the researcher, but in spite of occasional exceptions, budgetary practice usually belied commencement proclamation. If it had not been so belied in most cases, it was hard to see why such proclamation should have been made at all. Why should the research man have been verbally slighted except as a means of placating the teacher who was actually slighted? The plain fact was that other than routine advances in salary were most likely to come to the man who received offers from other institutions, and those offers necessarily had to be made with primary regard to the man's research attainments. There were too few ways of determining teaching success, and too few channels for making it known when it had been determined. Until such time as university administrators were to take seriously the task of searching for and rewarding genuinely good teaching, it would remain what it was—namely, the incomprehensible concomitant of undercompensated devotion to duty.

At both undergraduate and graduate levels, but particularly at the latter, the lessening of the effectiveness of teaching seems to have become particularly evident in the period from 1946 onward. It would have been a mistake, however, to place all the blame on the shoulders of the departments offering graduate work. The influx of veterans who were understandably eager to "get through and find jobs" meant that graduate study regressed to the undergraduate level with regard to the range of interest manifested by the student; he wished to learn and write only what would get him through the particular course or seminar successfully. Concentrated effort there undeniably was —in fact, it was far too concentrated. Sociologists and other exponents of the science of social relations who came into the forefront of attention from 1946 onward were almost the only ones known to the hatching or newly fledged Ph.D. Great works such as Thomas and Znaniecki's *Polish Peasant in Europe and America* (New York: Dover, 1958), remained unread—they were mere items in bothersome bibliographies.

Along with this, as might have been expected, professional jargon spread even more widely. Oftentimes harboring the uneasy feeling that he really didn't know very much, the sociological neophyte resorted to protective peroration, herein following the example of some established sociologists who on principle never said anything in plain English. It was amazing, in view of this, that so many really good theses and dissertations were produced; it may well be that the war experience and increased age of most graduate students helped to make up for the hasty and short-range character of their training. Moreover, there were many signs in 1951 that the handicaps of the postwar period were being overcome; in particular, there seemed to be a swing away from the practice of taking three pages of polysyllables to say, in effect, "the cat is in the hat."

Sociological and allied publication continued on its accustomed way. The usual flock of elementary textbooks made its appearance, but was peppered by the telling shots of A. H. Hobbs, whose *Claims of Sociology* (1951) showed clearly how much quoting of textbooks by other textbooks, and so on, was going on, and how flimsy some of the most widely accepted textbook generalizations were. The best textbook of the year, however, Don Martindale's and E. D. Monachesi's *Elements of Sociology* (1951), was not as vulnerable as others. There was a continuance of the translation vogue, but with at least one worthwhile result, H. H. Gerth's work on Max Weber's *The Religion of China*. In general, some sociologists were inclined to view translations from the major languages of scholarship with mixed feelings. On the one hand, they helped to foster the belief that if one only waited long enough, everything that was valuable would be translated, and therefore that remaining in a linguistic lubberland was justifiable. On the other, it was quite certain that many highly important studies would never be read by more than a handful if they were not translated; the whole drift of training at the graduate level in sociology, at least, was away from competence in any language but English, if that. The barefaced arrogance with which avowals of linguistic incapacity were made by many sociologists well established in the profession was revealing indeed. At the very time when we had become, for how long no one knows, *the* world power, some of our American specialists in the study of human conduct "the wide world around" were becoming so provincial that they were only a hair's-breadth away from the "gook complex" that wreaked such havoc to our prestige in the Far East. "Let the Yids and Krauts sputter around with German and translate it for us; let the Frogs, Dagos, and Spics scribble out their stuff in English if they want to make an impression; and who gives a damn what the behind-the-Iron-Curtain dimwits have to say anyway?" The notion that "if a man is really friendly he will learn your language, and that if he is an enemy you shouldn't demean yourself by learning his," might not have been properly attributable to American sociologists; the foregoing comments were perhaps unfair. But wherein did the unfairness lie? American sociologists just did not learn the languages; Ph.D. language examinations were farcical. Why? Were they lazy? But they worked hard enough at other things. Again, why? For the answer, a call should have gone out to the specialist in sociology of knowledge as applied to certain American sociologists.

Among important treatises published were Talcott Parsons' *The Social System* (1951) and a symposium edited by Parsons and E. A. Shils, *Toward a General Theory of Action* (1951). It was too early to assess the ultimate significance of these works, but it already seemed clear that they would call forth much comment. The careful student could readily determine where most of the theoretical insights came from. The university presses and the small, venturesome publishers continued to carry the burden of bringing out limited-market treatises and monographs that were courteously but definitely passed over by the big textbook houses. The *AJS* practice of printing special monographs was a great help; it should have been imitated by the *ASR*. The *A* issued useful symposia; this likewise was a welcome aid. The SSRC financed the publication of studies that it had sponsored or specially requested, as did the Russell Sage Foundation and several others; here again appreciation was due. But in the long run there was no substitute for a less crassly commercial attitude on the part of the major publishers.

In spite of these drawbacks, it seemed clear that sociology and its closely related disciplines in the United States led the rest of the world in 1951, but that did not necessarily mean "in 1952 and thereafter." The race was not over; if the United States stayed in the lead, it would only be because of learning from past mistakes and taking full advantage of whatever superiorities it may have possessed or acquired.

Where sociology beyond the United States was concerned, it could be stated, first of all, that the often-repeated assertion to the effect that sociology in Britain is as rare as snakes in Ireland was not as tenable in 1951 as it was in the 1920s and 1930s. Oxford and Cambridge remained as disdainfully aloof—barring exceptions noted later—as they had ever been, but some of the research institutions and the "red brick universities" (as the provincial institutions had come to be termed) were almost precipitately eager to make a place for social psychology, sociology, and social statistics. (Social anthropology had long been granted moderate elbow-room, although not as much as might have been assumed in view of the importance of the subject for the colonial administrator.)

Further, there was sound stress on field work and similar kinds of empirical research; if anything, the British student at some universities perhaps spent too much time in first-hand investigation before he had a thorough grasp of theory and method. Only at the University of London, where Ginsberg was still the only topflight sociologist— after the relatively short Mannheim interlude—was there a reverse emphasis. If choice had to be made, however, most sociologists would have reluctantly turned away from the London example.

At Birmingham, there had already appeared an impressive research publication following a social-cartographic method (so-called human ecology) that bore the title, reminiscent of Patrick Geddes, of *Conurbation;* Americans would have classified it as urban sociology. A survey of Banbury, with primary reference to neighborhood and similar clusterings, was in full swing, and a somewhat similar survey of Coventry was well advanced. Liverpool researchers were working on the sociology of housing. At Edinburgh, the Department of Anthropology was carrying on studies in remote Scottish parishes, small villages, and among minority groups, that were essentially sociological. Oxford had at least one anthropologist with strong sociological interests, and in the Institute of Agricultural Economics there researches were proceeding that seemed as clearly in the field of rural sociology as one would have been likely to find any place. The Tavistock Institute of Human Relations was conducting studies along "group dynamics" lines, with heavy injections of psychoanalysis, labor economics, and measurement techniques. An important new periodical, the *British Journal of Sociology,* made its bow.

Outside the British universities and institutes there was to be encountered some amazingly good sociological work that did not bear that label. The enthusiastic social-scientific amateur, who in frequency and conscientiousness seemed to be a peculiarly British phenomenon, was to be found in all walks of life. To take the single example of Shropshire: Slack in Shrewsbury, Hamar in Clun, and Lavender and Metcalfe in Bishops' Castle were veritable storehouses of sociologically relevant information, some of which they published in small local journals of high quality. Further, vast numbers of "county books" and similar publications dealing with manners, customs, and social institutions of all sorts abounded in the bookshops, to the undying credit of British publishers *and* bookbuyers. Studies of regional characteristics in "culture and personality" were numerous; familiarity with them would doubtless be of future help in breaking up some of the crude stereotypes cherished by those who should have known better.

If the British succeeded in disentangling "social science"—a label applied to what Americans would have called social work, public welfare administration, and a number of related matters—from social psychology, social anthropology, and sociology, it would redound to the benefit of all concerned. Signs of such progress were apparent, but further advances depended on the adaptability of British university authorities.

In France the break with the period prior to World War II was not so strikingly apparent as it was in the United States. There was no notable increase in the scanty number of professorial posts for sociologists. Durkheim and anti-Durkheim controversies, however, had fortunately diminished. It was freely granted by erstwhile Durkheim disciples that the master had not inscribed the Ten Commandments with regard to all things sociological, that *anomie* was a weasel word, and that the statistics of *Suicide* badly needed reinterpreting. Conversely, the opponents of Durkheimian doctrine were prepared to admit that many of the great advances in comparative law, linguistics, and allied fields that were so plainly apparent in the France of 1951 could not have taken place without the push given by Durkheim and his followers. Important French research centers were the École Pratique des Hautes-Études and the Centre d'Études Sociologiques (the latter a part of the Centre National de la Récherche Scientifique). Books and articles of significance were published by Georges Friedmann, Paul Maucorps, Georges Gurvitch, Roger Bastide, and Marcel Mauss, and there appeared posthumously Maurice Halbwachs's *La Mémoire collective*.

Germany was slowly recovering from the Nazi blight and the postwar confusion, but there was a deplorable dearth of younger men in important posts. Few chairs of sociology had been established; those that existed were sometimes occupied by men who were primarily philosophers, historians, journalists, or would-be political figures. At the same time, it was noted that good research institutes with some place for sociology were established at Frankfurt, Münster, Marburg, Giessen, Hanover, Darmstadt, and Göttingen, to name only a few at random. Further, the number of younger men who were sent abroad for sociological training was quite considerable, and if on their return they could find suitable positions before they were graybeards, much valuable instruction and research might result. During the year, an imposing *Festschrift* was published in honor of Leopold von Wiese on his 75th birthday, with contributions from sociologists from all over the world.

1952

Social Action Theory Commands Attention

THE OFTEN-NOTED TREND toward a merger of the social sciences continued in 1952, but with new fluctuations, some of them seemingly furthering the merger, and some retarding it. Trend and fluctuations were most plainly apparent in the United States, where sociology, in particular, was more strongly represented in amount of personnel and publication than anywhere else.

The numerous foundations—Ford, Russell Sage, etc.— had much to do with the fluctuations, notably the stress on the "behavioral sciences." These, comprising sociology, social anthropology and social psychology, received much attention. Social sciences not of "behavioral" type, such as political science, human geography and history, were not so directly favored—although by no means neglected. It was still too soon to say whether foundation policies were producing scientifically beneficial results, but the policies had already produced, clearly enough, another crop of would-be beneficiaries, all speaking the same language and making the same invocations. Fragments of an earlier language still survived, as witnessed by the continuing currency of "interdisciplinary," "cross-cultural," and so on, but had begun to sound slightly outmoded. British reviewers of "behavioral science" articles and books published in the United States were quick to note these facts, and to comment appropriately.

Efforts directed toward providing a sound basis in general theory for actual or potential merger continued, although without large-scale foundation support. This could hardly have been otherwise, for successful work in abstract theory is difficult to plan, to say the least. There was, however, one planned theoretical enterprise that made its effects felt in 1952; it took the form of a symposium by a Harvard group, and was published as *Toward a General*

Theory of Action, edited by Talcott Parsons and Edward A. Shils. The most important part of it was the monograph by the editors appearing as the introduction; this was primarily a stimulating treatment of motivation. At a time somewhat earlier than the symposium was published, Parsons brought out his *The Social System.* This one-man undertaking seemed to embody many of the merits of the symposium without its more serious defects. Notable among the merits was the somewhat boring but necessary "spelling out" of personality system, social system, and cultural system as analytically distinct although empirically intertwined.

One of Parsons' predecessors in the realm of social action theory as such was Florian Znaniecki, and in 1952 he in effect summarized, brought up to date, and strikingly advanced his 1918, 1925, and 1936 contributions. Znaniecki's 1952 work in action theory, *Cultural Sciences, Their Origin and Development,* was a landmark of great prominence; it did much to clarify concepts such as culture, social action, and definition of the situation or "humanistic coefficient," and to show how they interrelate in sociology as "the grammar of the social sciences."

Basic to the work of Parsons, Znaniecki, and many other theoreticians was stress on values. This ranged from the definition of all objects as values, through all social action as involving choice between value alternatives, to cultural systems as culminating in value systems. In other words, "stress on values" meant many things and the results were many: efforts at measurement of values on the one hand to unabashed espousal of value-judgments as scientifically necessary on the other. Plainly, the slogan of "through values to social interpretation" needed less enthusiastic reiteration and more hardheaded pondering.

Some observers felt that in 1952 there was especially evident, among students and established social scientists alike, a value-preference for the study of "social statics" as against "social dynamics." Attention to social structure and to the functions presumably maintaining it took precedence over interest in social change—except when change was viewed as "dysfunction." The uncertainties of the post-World War II period and particularly the defensive position of most western European and American nations vis-à-vis social changes from which it was believed that they would suffer disadvantage (at least initially) may have had something to do with this. Instead of a "generation on trial" that had once looked favorably on change, there appeared a "generation on tenterhooks."

This, if it was a conclusion representing something more than idle speculation, may have been an aspect of that "normative reaction to normlessness" that frequently becomes evident when social change has been so rapid as to be profoundly unsettling. Whether or not connected with this, it may also be noted that the study of power relations and systems of authority, from democracy to totalitarianism, had been popular among all social scientists of recent years, and that sociologists, directly or indirectly, had made some of their most notable contributions here. The vogue of Max Weber, who wrote much on "authoritative rule" (*Herrschaft*), did not wholly explain this, for many important works about authority took little or no account of him, perhaps because his vogue was based primarily on knowledge of his translated writings and those on authoritative rule had not been translated. (Incidentally, an excellent translation of Weber's *Ancient Judaism,* by H. H. Gerth and Don Martindale, appeared in 1952.) At best, Robert K. Merton and others, in scattered articles and collections of readings, dealt with bureaucracy from a standpoint akin to Weber's. There was needed a sustained systematic treatment of political sociology in general, with or without benefit of earlier writers.

In some ways linked with political sociology, social stratification studies continued to be made, and those sponsored by the University of London were definitely new in emphasis and important in results. Stratification analyses had clearly reached a point of diminishing returns, however, if they continued to be preoccupied with middle-class matters in the United States. Their significance had been much exaggerated anyway, largely because of the tendency of newly fledged "research men" to jump on anything that looked like a bandwagon. Much had been put forth as "the very latest" that in actuality was very old indeed, as was convincingly shown by W. C. Lehmann's article in the *British Journal of Sociology* on the work of John Millar in the eighteenth century, "On the Distinction of Ranks."

Neglect of the history of sociology, characteristic of the generation of graduate students completing their work since 1945, was partly the result of scarcity of convenient handbooks having adequate coverage. Few students could spare the time, or commanded the languages necessary, to read widely in the original sources. The handicap was to some extent overcome by the republication, with 1952 revision and expansion of a work that first appeared in 1938, *Social Thought from Lore to Science,...*

In England, worthwhile trends in sociological research, already manifested at Birmingham, Manchester, Liverpool, Nottingham, and similar "red brick universities" continued, as did the valuable work in social anthropology at Oxford and Edinburgh. The same was true of the social psychology intensively applied, albeit with almost psychoanalytic dogmatism, at the Tavistock Institute of Human Relations. One of the most important changes, generally speaking, in the approach to sociological research seemed to be the at least partial emancipation from the traditional social survey. A number of urban neighborhood studies, such as those at Banbury and Coventry, granted large place to intensive analyses of social relations in contrast to the customary survey focus on large numbers, sampling, and problems of planning.

Where the continent was concerned, the most noteworthy developments in 1952 were those in Germany. Western Germany continued its advance; rural and urban sociology, in particular, moved rapidly ahead. There seemed every likelihood, when publication facilities once more became adequate, of contributions so substantial that they would make a distinct impress on research being done elsewhere. Eastern Germany afforded an interesting contrast. Chairs of sociology, where they existed, were abolished; instead, "social science" instruction was installed. This was grounded, by decree, on "diamat" (dialectical materialism), and virtually all the newer social science instructional staff members not only imparted "diamat" in unmixed form but were also adherents of the S.E.D. (equivalent of the Communist party) and products of its training system. Here and there survivors of an earlier and less dogmatic although Marxist point of view continued to lecture, but were being steadily shouldered aside or replaced by exponents of "diamat" whose orthodoxy could not be called in question. Publication took merely polemic form; few or no basic researches, given the taboo on "objectivity" and "cosmopolitanism," could be carried out even if there had been any researchers so inclined. Here East Germany provided an interesting comparison with the Soviet Union itself; there was, understandably enough, even less freedom in the satellite than in the dominating country. In the latter some work in social anthropology was being done that permitted the "diamat" to be easily combed out, as it were; what remained was utilizable even by the despised bourgeois researcher.

1953

Confusion and Remedies Therefor

IN SPITE OF THE SECOND KINSEY REPORT, the year was not remarkable for novelty in sociology and its congeners.

"The new sociology" had in fact been declared by W. J. Goode and P. K. Hatt, in their *Methods in Social Research,* as having been in course of development during the past fifteen or twenty years only, and as consisting primarily in the introduction of more precise techniques. Basic innovations in theory, however, are necessarily rare, and the fact that they did not occur in a given year, or even over a considerably longer period, should not be taken as reason for profound discouragement.

Their absence may nevertheless be taken as a possible warning. Some observers of regional and nation-wide annual conventions of sociologists commented on the apparent need for change in emphasis. The meeting of the American Sociological Society, held at Berkeley in September, was said to be characterized by its *ad hoc, ad infinitum* program. The 1953 impact of foundation grants and the financing of research by the armed forces had seemingly shifted many sociologists even farther toward exclusive preoccupation with government contracts, research staffing, hasty publication, and "subsidy politics." Relatively little appeared on the September program mentioned, therefore, of fundamental theoretical or even long-range significance.

It would be going much too far, of course, to attribute this lack only to the immediate factors noted. Sociology in the United States has long inclined in the direction of social engineering rather than of pure science or scholarship, as caustically noted by A. H. Hobbs in his *Social Problems and Scientism*. The September convention of the National Council on Family Relations, held at East Lansing, presented evidence of this inclination, for even the sessions devoted to research findings were heavily weighted with immediate "answers" to immediate "problems." At the same time, it must in fairness be stated that the Council meetings were commendably fair, open and aboveboard in the presentation of hotly controversial issues.

Regrettably, the second Kinsey report had not appeared in other than predigested and popularly sensationalized form at the time of the East Lansing conference, for it would probably have been subjected to salutary and widely heeded criticism. Later published and unpublished adverse comments by many sociologists ran to the effect that: (1) the report was not comprehensively sociological, as was popularly assumed, but essentially limited and dogmatically biological; (2) it offered little that was new to those acquainted with the works of Havelock Ellis, Katherine Bement Davis, Magnus Hirschfeld, and scores of other investigators; (3) the sampling procedure was poor, and hence the report really had to do chiefly with college-educated, middle-class, mid-twentieth-century Midwestern American women having few current orthodox religious connections, and not with "the human female" in all the diversity of periods and peoples; (4) the interviewing technique was open to serious error; and (5) the insistent advocacy of reform legislation dealing with sex betrayed unscientific bias. Favorable comments stressed: (1) the large number (some 5000) of those interviewed; (2) the sober and restrained style of the report itself as distinguished from the journalistic skimmings; (3) the careful training of the interviewers; (4) the effort to elicit truthful responses by means less time-consuming than those used, for example, in much contemporary psychiatry; and (5) the earnestness, sincerity, and good intentions of Kinsey and his staff.

But to return to the main theme, the scarcity of new departures in the more basic aspects of sociology and its affiliates in 1953, it could be said that the United States was by no means the only nation thus deficient. The Second International Congress of Sociology, held at Liège in the latter part of August under the auspices of UNESCO and the Belgian government, with participants from most major and many minor countries, also seemed to have no coherent program, to be even more inconsequentially subject to the supposed needs of the hour, and even more strikingly to lack general theoretical orientation. Bureaucracies, however benevolent and however multi-national, had not yet learned how to domesticate the social scientist and still keep him scientifically fertile.

Part of the difficulty confronted by UNESCO and like organizations lay in the still unsolved problem of scientific communication. Until such time as the elaborate translation apparatus of UN could be set up, not merely for generally understandable political speeches and appeals to public opinion but also for elaborate specialized languages, international scientific congresses in fields not fully pervaded by mathematical, chemical, and similar standard symbolism would resemble Babel.

A step in the right direction would be the diminution of esoteric terminology in English, the most widely used social-scientific language. Justification for shorthand communication among experts there undeniably is, but such shorthand should not be carried to the point where it is unintelligible even to those in closely related sciences. In 1952 and 1953, under the auspices of the Wenner-Gren Foundation, there was conducted an interesting interdisciplinary experiment that involved, among other things, the avoidance of ultraspecialized English. Two sociologists, two anthropologists, and two social psychologists, called together by John P. Gillin, an editor of anthropological background also having considerable acquaintance with the two other fields, wrote about past, present, and possible future cross-fertilization of their disciplines. One sociologist dealt with anthropological contributions to sociology, the other with social-psychological; one anthropologist surveyed sociological contributions to anthropology—and so on around the circle. Before the writing began, editorial conference with each specialist, and then a meeting of all for the discussion of proposed outlines, determined how the collaboration would proceed in general. A concluding meeting, at which the nearly completed or completed portions of the symposium were critically reviewed with regard to final revision before publication, provided striking evidence of the fact that even the most recondite specialisms could be couched in language that, although not of primer simplicity, should be readily understood by most intelligent college graduates. The resulting volume, it was initially decided, was to bear the title of *Convergences among the Sciences of Social Man;* whether the publishers exercised their right to choose "something snappier" still remained to be seen.

Wise foundation policy having thus enabled seven social scientists to assert that they were intelligible to one another and hence that they should all be intelligible to any reasonably full beneficiary of higher education, it would be still wiser to increase the number to seventy times seven. At the moment, some tendency to foster competing "foundation jargons" is evident; a unified policy is needed. Perhaps a project that would enable those who allocate funds to various projects to understand one another well enough to avoid useless duplication, and themselves well enough to avoid playing favorites because said favorites have mastered the appropriate application lingo, would be suitable for some super-foundation. Failing such a federal facility, appropriate arrangements might even be made on a sort of confederate basis. The results might lead to fewer opportunistic undertakings and more basic theory and research.

The pressing necessity for fundamental work was shown by the confused condition of social psychology in 1953. Hubert Bonner, a psychologist by training, uncritically incorporated in his *Social Psychology: an Interdisciplinary Approach,* many of the most questionable propositions of the "child training—basic personality-and-culture" school represented by Margaret Mead, Geoffrey Gorer, E. H. Erikson, Gregory Bateson, *et al.* According to this school, the feeding and toilet habits taught to infants determine not only their personalities but also the major structural features of their societies. W. H. Sewell, in a devastating article published in the *American Sociological Review,* the year previous, had been among the most recent of a number of skeptics who for some time had been pointing out the untenability of this position. Sewell's critique went beyond any previously published in the care with which it had been based on intensive statistical study of a carefully selected sample, but could have profited by at least a few footnote references to "cross-cultural" evidence. For ex-

ample, Dutch, Norwegian, Swiss, and many other European families are quite as "authoritarian" (hesitantly to use
a wartime label) as the German, but their political life is
regarded as "democratic." It seems a little odd, to say the
least, that similar family structures should engender widely dissimilar political structures. It was significant that the
1953 "social-psychological" treatise (of overwhelmingly
strong sociological derivation) by H. H. Gerth and C.
Wright Mills, entitled *Character and Social Structure,*
made little or no use of the notions of the "diaper determinists," but drew on a great deal of historical evidence
to show that adolescent and even adult experience in certain types of social structure may go a long way to set so-
called basic character. Further testimony to social-psychological confusion in 1953 was provided by Muzafer
Sherif and M. O. Wilson, eds., in their *Group Relations at
the Cross-Roads.* Tidbits from nearly all of the social sciences were mixed together and arbitrarily christened "social psychology" and in so doing much of the relevant
literature was either ignored or overlooked. The development of a general science of social relations, so strongly
desired by so many social scientists, could only be hindered
by such exhibitions of academic imperialism. A suitable
division of labor, and careful cultivation of the soil one was
best fitted to till, seemed likely to go farther toward establishing the hoped-for cooperative social science than any
amount of "what is mine belongs to me, and what is yours
is mine."

But although lack of basic innovation and a certain
amount of confusion seemed to mark 1953, in the United
States at least, the adoption of American research techniques in Europe, Japan, and elsewhere proceeded apace.
At the Darmstadt Institute of Technology, a number of
detailed studies of German villages, small towns, and cities
had already appeared, and others were under way. In
Norway, at Oslo, a comprehensive study of nationalism
had been undertaken, utilizing the counsel of American
theoreticians and survey research technicians. An exchange
arrangement set up between the University of Caracas and
the University of Wisconsin, with the Venezuelan government footing the bill, promised much, and during the year,
with aid from other sources as well, a team of physical and
social scientists made an extensive study of the land re-

sources—including the people on the land—of certain parts of Venezuela. In Japan, interest stimulated by the 1948 translation of Ruth Benedict's *The Chrysanthemum and the Sword* (which reached its eighth edition in 1953!) led to examination of the techniques she had used and to proposals for a more valid analysis of Japanese characteristics on the basis of sounder techniques. So might the examples have been multiplied; during the year there was certainly no lack of effort, enthusiasm, and skillful investigation.

1954

Aftermaths and Outcomes

A NUMBER OF SIGNIFICANT HAPPENINGS in sociology and closely related disciplines took place during the year, although some of these were but outcomes, and occasionally aftermaths, of earlier developments—some of them many years earlier.

Among the aftermaths was a special issue of the sociological journal, *Social Problems,* that was devoted to critical analysis of the second Kinsey report, *Sexual Behavior in the Human Female.* All the adverse comments noted in the 1953 survey were reiterated with wealth of sustaining logic and evidential detail. Particularly impressive were the critiques by Manford Kuhn and Harriet Mowrer; these social psychologists showed how essentially naive and groundless many of Kinsey's supposedly scientific conclusions actually were. . . .

Another aftermath, less strikingly apparent but with many ramifications, was the drastic diminution of U. S. governmental funds available for research in the social sciences. The Eisenhower administration's fairly successful effort to limit budgetary allotments for the armed forces resulted, rightly or wrongly, in more sweeping cuts among social-science than among natural-science projects. Many sociologists, to name no other social scientists, found this distressing, for some of them had begun to build professional reputations as large-scale administrators of "teamwork" research, and others, not so skilled or so fortunate administratively, had nevertheless found research team positions that, although perhaps not lucrative, represented desirable employment. What the total organizational and personnel shifts resulting from the cuts would amount to, in the immediate future and in the long run, was difficult to estimate, but it was already clear, toward the end of 1954, that some serious dislocations had come about here and there. Optimists occasionally expressed the opinion that the slack would soon be taken up, in most cases, by the foundations making grants for behavioral-science research, and that a number of the remaining cases were only healthy diminutions or terminations of swollen or inappropriate projects.

Foundation plans for an Institute for Advanced Study in the Behavioral Sciences (anthropology, social psychology, sociology), with provisional location on the West Coast, began to crystallize during the year—in fact, sessions began in September. Other evidences of foundation backing for "interdisciplinary" enterprises were numerous, although here and there skeptics began to raise questions as to whether "old-fashioned" disciplinary specialization had been unduly disparaged in favor of modish "interdisciplinary" specialization with many of the drawbacks and few of the advantages of the earlier varieties. It was also pointed out that an "interdisciplinary" terminology having some of the traits of jargon was enjoying a flourishing vogue.

An "interdisciplinary" enterprise that had been launched in 1952-1953 was completed in 1954; this was a book, sponsored by the Wenner-Gren Foundation, entitled *For a Science of Social Man: Convergences in Anthropology, Psychology, and Sociology*. John P. Gillin of the University of North Carolina was the editor, and he seemed to have succeeded in inducing his collaborators to avoid jargon and to pay heed to one another's contributions; the symposium was readable and well integrated. Had other "interdisciplinary" efforts received such firm guidance and wholehearted collaboration, the critique by Adolphe Tomars, presented in September at the annual meeting of the American Sociological Society at the University of Illinois, would have been much less to the point. As it was, his remarks about "unity achieved only by the aid of the bookbinder" were wryly and widely acknowledged to be far from amiss.

At the same annual meeting, a renewed but perhaps temporary emphasis on sociological theory and its recent history was strongly in evidence. The program included at least fifty papers bearing witness to this, and a general evening session focusing directly on the topic, with opportunity for discussion from the floor, had been arranged for by the president of the Society, Florian Znaniecki. Stress was supposed to be laid on developments since World War I, but naturally enough, the period since World War II received most attention. Some section chairmen, notably Pitirim Sorokin, had secured papers sharply critical of current trends toward extensive use of measurement in sociological research, but except for these, most of the papers took little account of earlier "either-or" antagonisms between qualitative and quantitative investigation; their complementary character was generally taken for granted.

The Rural Sociological Society met at the University of Illinois slightly in advance of the American Sociological Society; the Society for the Study of Social Problems met slightly afterward, likewise at Urbana. The latter society followed up its earlier statement of concern at expressed or incipient opposition to freedom of social-scientific research and teaching by passing resolutions in defense of such freedom. During the discussion of these resolutions—and indeed, of the "Statement on Freedom and Responsibility in Research and Teaching"—it was pointed out by a minority that only *unbiased* social-scientific activities could properly be defended. This position was the same as that taken by A. H. Hobbs in his scathing and little-quoted indictment of "scientism" in the study of social problems. There seemed little doubt, to some observers, that a substantial proportion of the majority that eventually passed the resolutions above noted was anything but unbiased, and that this boded ill, in the long run at least, for the scientific standing of the Society for the Study of Social Problems. In the short run, it was doubtless worthwhile to defend social science, whatever its shortcomings may have been, against the unwarranted attacks of demagogues. Some social scientists may have been badly biased, but few if any of them were in any ordinary sense subversive or disloyal.

Among the year's more important outcomes of trends in sociological research evident long before was the publication of several articles, a fairly comprehensive bibliography, and a special issue of the *ASR* on "small group" theory and research. At least as early as the time of Georg

Simmel, small groups had been objects of sustained attention. C. H. Cooley, commonly regarded as among the "founding fathers," had made his analysis of primary groups central not only to his own version of sociology but also to that of virtually the entire succeeding generation of American sociologists. Leopold von Wiese, both in his original treatises of 1924 and 1929 and in the augmented American adaptation of these appearing in 1932 under the title of *Systematic Sociology,* had effectively revived Simmel's emphasis. J. L. Moreno, beginning his social-psychiatric work in the 1920s, built his entire theory and practice around the interaction of persons within small groups. There were many other forerunners—so many, in fact, that sophisticated sociologists blinked in amazement when they read some of the 1954 publications heralding this or that "new" development in the study of small groups. Incontestably, a few of the developments were new—certainly so in the application of recent techniques of research to older hypotheses—but many of them could have competed with Methusaleh. Where the application of techniques was concerned, much effort centered on procedures found effective in psychological laboratories, notably those dealing with the infrahuman animals. Critics of these techniques were quick to point out that even the infrahuman animals behave differently outside the cage than they do inside it, that the overwhelmingly larger proportion of man's significant conduct can take place only "outside," that laboratory researches, unkindly called "cage studies," can therefore tell the sociologist very little that he desires to know, that under any circumstances the cultural context of social action must be taken into account, and that the laboratory is only one kind of cultural context—and an insignificant one at that. Defenders of small-group studies in most instances pointed to the attested results of what may be called "field studies" of work groups, military groups, play groups, marital groups, and so on, under non-laboratory conditions. With this defense there was little quarrel.

Far removed from "microscopic" analyses, of either "cage-study" or "field-study" type, were the comprehensive culture case studies incorporated in the four concluding volumes of A. J. Toynbee's *A Study of History.* These brought to completion in 1954 an analysis, grandiose in its plan and execution, of evidence coming from the past of practically all the societies concerning which there are even remotely adequate archaeological and documentary sources, *plus* evidence from a very few of the many, many societies having practically no adequate records of any sort. Basically Toynbee's work was a theodicy finally assessable only by the trained theologian, heterodox or orthodox, Christian or non-Christian, as the case may be. In its implied attempt to discover and state recurrent regularities in social action, moreover, it was essentially sociological rather than historical in the idiographic sense. Of this latter fact Toynbee was apparently aware, for the work was not called a history but *a study* of history. Referring, however, to the idiographic aspects, inasmuch as these have been frequently discussed by professional historians, and inasmuch as their judgment as to the accuracy of the work was essential if its sociological significance was to be properly evaluated, it could be said that apart from calling attention to a few striking exceptions (such as the erroneous presentation of the relations of the Minoan and the Mycenaean societies—and here Sir Arthur Evans was really the person at fault), most historians would have agreed that Toynbee was amazingly close to correctness in his major outlines, and often highly precise in even the most minute details. They would have granted that he was compelled, by the very nature of the work, to make generalizations going far beyond the available evidence, and on occasion they have therefore complained that *A Study of History* was not sprinkled with a sufficient quantity of "perhaps," "later research may more clearly show," "if this were indubitably so, then this would be too," "by and large," "other things being equal," and just plain "maybe." Whether, given the audience to which the work was designed to appeal, such elaborate qualification was necessary, of course, remained a moot question. Where the nomothetic aspects, of primary concern to sociologists, were involved, it could emphatically be said that all future studies of social change not paying due heed to Toynbee's analyses would merit the verdict of "parochial." His work swept Oswald Spengler, Alfred Weber, and even Max Weber into subordinate rank. This was not to say that his schemas of social change were in all or even in most important respects free of flaws and distortions; here Toynbee would have profited greatly by fuller awareness of procedures such as those of constructive typology. It most strongly was to say, however, that by far the greater number of contemporary sociologists, in the United States and elsewhere, had much more to learn from Toynbee than he had to learn from them.

In countries other than Britain and the United States the year likewise brought little of outstanding importance other than "aftermath" or "outcome." In France, for example, the very considerable volume of sociological publication remained, generally speaking, within the confines of the pro- and anti-Durkheimian traditions. The few innovations consisted essentially of adoptions of research methods characterized as "American" for application to French data and hypotheses. In Western Germany the tendency to "Americanize" was similarly manifest, although it was to be doubted whether all those who climbed on the bandwagon did so with complete conviction that the vehicle was durable enough for a long journey. In Mexico, Brazil, Chile, and similar countries of the New World, American research techniques, if not American ideas, were likewise much in vogue. Some Americans were rendered uneasy by all this, feeling as they did that their imitators were putting too many eggs in one basket. As a means of correcting such uncritical mimicry, the opinion was voiced that the reading of Gisela and Roscoe Hinkle's *The Development of Modern Sociology* would be most helpful.

1955

Readjustment and Hopeful Advance

THE YEAR SAW NOTHING STARTLINGLY NEW in sociology and specialties closely related to it, but there were several minor developments of interest.

The lack of new vogues perhaps reflected the fact that readjustments, already evident the previous year, were still continuing. Cancellation or termination of research contracts by the armed services sharply limited the amount of large-scale team research, simultaneously releasing a considerable number of younger men for regular academic work.

Not only was there a lack of new vogues, but a number of old vogues continued to wane. For example, the psychoanalytic influence, once so popular in sociology, social psychology, and social and cultural anthropology, affected far fewer specialists in these fields with the possible exception of the last. Even here the earlier excesses of the child-training enthusiasts and the "national character" impressionists had begun to encounter somewhat more outspoken criticism than had hitherto been evident. Social psychology continued to be popular in the United States, and in Germany the *Cologne Journal of Sociology* added *and Social Psychology* to its title, but it was nevertheless clear that more resistance to all-inclusive sovereignty was being encountered. Structural-functional sociology was still much advocated, but it had begun to become plain that structure and function had long been sociological household recipes, so to speak, under less grandiose names. Small-group studies, as in the half-dozen previous, had many aggressive practitioners; nevertheless, there were noticeably fewer bandwagon jumpers.

One exception to the decline of old vogues should be noted, although it was in a certain sense an index of the decline of another vogue not yet mentioned; this was the transfer of the journal *Sociometry* to the American Sociological Society and the prompt addition of a subtitle, *a Journal of Research in Social Psychology*. Sociometry apparently waned whereas social psychology waxed. Inspection of the list of editors and subeditors showed, however, that no new names appeared; all those responsible for the new journal had long been identified with social psychology, and some of them had been consistent advocates of limited claims. Sociometry, moreover, retained its distinctive psychotherapeutic emphasis in other publications not transferred, although it was probably true that it no longer attracted as much attention even in that field as it had ten years before.

The absence of new and the decline of old vogues was accompanied, as might perhaps have been expected, by a lack of response to challenging issues. For example, although in 1952 and for a short time thereafter there had been some signs of strong reaction to A. H. Hobbs's forth right attacks on sociologists for their real or supposed lack of objectivity and scientific probity, by 1955 these signs had almost wholly disappeared. The attacks, in other words, remained unanswered.

Another issue, repeatedly although not sensationally raised, was the failure of sociologists, in the United States in particular, to make effective use of the data of history. In spite of the widespread public interest in A. J. Toynbee's *A Study of History,* for instance, few sociologists took the trouble, so it seemed, to acquaint themselves with his work, much less to conduct similar investigations. W. J. Cahnmann had tried for several years and especially in 1955 to get a place on the annual program of the American Sociological Society for a group of sociologists interested in the interrelations of sociology and history, but without success.

A hopeful note was introduced, however, by the successful continuation of *Sociological Abstracts,* a journal that for a time had seemed unlikely to survive; it reached its third volume in 1955. The wide range of articles and books abstracted might eventually, it was thought, broaden the horizon of its readers. The same was true of *Current Sociology,* a bibliographical journal published under the auspices of the United Nations Educational, Scientific and Cultural Organization, likewise in its third year. Further, the attention of sociologists was called to the *Journal of Social History,* beginning publication in Amsterdam in 1955, and having sociologists among the sponsoring board and the contributors to the first number.

Still another hopeful development was the new policy of the Ford Foundation with regard to research grants in the "behavioral sciences"—sociology, social psychology, social and cultural anthropology. Most Ford grants, in earlier years, had been for large-scale team research projects. In 1955 requests were solicited for grants-in-aid of projects of any kind; the researcher to whom the grant was made was given sole authority for the expenditure of the amount ($4,500) in any way he saw fit. This meant that many researchers previously reluctant to apply for team research projects now felt that individual enterprise had some likelihood of recognition.

A new and apparently worthwhile trend also appeared in conjunction with the Society for the Study of Social Problems. Doubts had previously been apparent about the policy of the society and of its publication, *Social Problems,* for it was felt that a certain lack of scientific detachment and impartiality prevailed. In 1955, however, the society announced a competition for the Helen DeRoy award, to be granted for the best paper on some social problem, this paper to be published in the society's journal. The contest judges were about as free from commitments to favorite causes as any persons having any interest in social matters were likely to be, and the award, divided because of their equal merit, was granted to two papers that were models of objectivity. One, on the sociology of work groups, was by Robert Dubin; the other, by Melvin Seeman, was on the creativity of marginal personalities. Many of the other papers submitted in the competition manifested similar objectivity; it was evident that the study of social problems was reaching a new and higher scientific level.

A meeting held at Fisk University, Nashville, Tenn., early in April, 1955 was likewise strikingly objective. The meeting was for the dedication of the Robert E. Park Memorial Social Science building at Fisk, and the occasion coincided with the lively popular interest in Negro-white relations stimulated by the desegregation decision of the U. S. Supreme Court a short time before. Under the guidance of Charles S. Johnson, president of Fisk, a number of Negro and white speakers representing the social sciences participated in the dedication addresses, and the tone of their remarks was almost uniformly sober and restrained.

Sociology in countries other than the United States continued to forge ahead, but at uneven rates. In Israel the work of S. N. Eisenstadt, Uriel G. Foa, and Louis H. Guttman was outstanding. Turkey showed strong interest, setting up plans for an Institute of Sociological Research at the University of Ankara and endeavoring to secure lecturers from abroad to supplement regular staff. In France sociological activity was everywhere evident, but was somewhat dominated by schools of thought and too diffuse. The sheer volume of publication, however, was impressive. Germany accomplished a good deal during the year, but continued to be handicapped by the dearth of properly trained personnel and the curious ignoring of much of the significant work done in the 1920s, the "classic" period of German sociology. Britain continued the advances evident earlier; there was still, however, a notable lack of recognition of sociology in other than the red-brick universities. Japan was very active, with a strong group of younger men who launched Japanese researches independently of hampering traditions and American occupation influence alike; Kunio Odaka was one of the most vigorous. Norway, Sweden, and Denmark made notable progress; the latter country brought out a new periodical, *Acta Sociologica,* the first issue of which was devoted to the work of Theodor Geiger of the University of Aarhus. The one exception to the generally hopeful picture was Italy, where except for Franco Ferrarotti and his associates little was being done that represented any marked departure from the older and basically sterile period immediately prior to World War II.

Popular interest in sociology in the United States was enormously stimulated by a special feature in *Time* magazine, devoted to the work of David Riesman, a University of Chicago sociologist whose book, *The Lonely Crowd,* was a stimulating analysis of changes in American character. His types of "other-directed," "inner-directed," and "autonomous" personalities were refreshing departures from the orthodox Freudian models that had previously monopolized the field. In a little-known book, edited by John Doby, *Introduction to Social Research,* John C. McKinney of Michigan State University, East Lansing, contributed the best analysis of the entire procedure of type construction to be found in English. Lacking the appeal of Riesman's book, it nevertheless provided a rationale for types of all kinds—of personality, social group, value system, and so on—that Riesman's brilliant but impressionistic treatment did not include. . . .

1956

Critiques, Revivals, New Procedures

G ROWTH IN FIELDS that had been lying fallow for some time or that had not been cultivated intensively was characteristic of the year. Most developments could be viewed as worthwhile, although sharp criticism was by no means lacking.

Sharpest was perhaps that offered by Pitirim Sorokin in his *Fads and Foibles in Modern Sociology and Related Sciences* (Hinsdale, Ill.: Regnery, 1956). His attack was over a wide front, but was chiefly centered on: (1) disregard of past achievements; (2) jargon; (3) operationism and natural-science imitation; (4) poorly conceived and misused tests; (5) over-elaborate mathematical procedures; (6) spurious experimentation; (7) trivial small-group studies; (8) platitudes hailed as epoch-making discoveries; (9) undue stress on prediction; and (10) failure to deal with societal and cultural systems as such. By no means all of the criticism could be viewed as relevant or valid, and much pique was unfortunately evident. Nevertheless, G. M. Sykes was quite right when he said in his review in the *ASR* for October, pp. 633-34, that although there "is no need for a young and vigorous discipline to be constantly engaged in self-flagellation, . . . a moment's modesty and self-examination is never harmful."

Criticism interspersed with a heavy load of value-judgment, and obscured for most readers by the fascinating content of the book, was contained in C. Wright Mills's *The Power Elite* (New York: Oxford, 1956). Clearly in the Mosca tradition of sociology of politics, neglected until recently, it evidenced the use of techniques of research about which the author apparently felt defensive; consequently, he offered a good deal of criticism of those who, it could be foreseen, were most likely to criticize him. He charged contemporary sociologists with absorption in trivial issues to which, because of their limited range, "rigorous" techniques of investigation could be readily applied —or putting it more drastically, with choosing topics for investigation not for their real importance, but for their amenability to currently approved card-punching practice. Whether right or wrong, Mills's book clearly focused on crucial matters, and although pervaded by a tone of personal hostility to those controlling political, financial, and other public affairs in the United States, offered food for disquieting thought. It received much attention in reviews and feature articles; professional sociologists were on the whole unfavorably inclined, whereas most of the "general reader" commentators seemed to like it.

Contemporary in emphasis, the procedures used in Mills's study could nevertheless be viewed as adapted, in their sounder aspects, to the use of historical evidence for sociological purposes—for the point at which the past begins is always a matter for more or less arbitrary decision. "History," in other words, is not exclusively the concern of the professional historian. Accordingly, the American Sociological Society, at its annual September meeting, devoted one section session to sociology of history. Historians having sociological inclinations, and sociologists utilizing data commonly viewed as historical, were among the participants. Issues were quite sharply drawn, one historian accusing sociologists of having little to offer because of unsuitable techniques, and one sociologist asserting that all generalization about social affairs, past or present, is the special preserve of the sociologist under whatever name. In spite of such contrasts, however, the section session proved worthwhile, and the hope was expressed that at future annual meetings such a section would not only be continued but also expanded. Mention was also made of the new publication medium, the *International Journal of Social History,* published in Holland, as a possible vehicle for at least some of the papers that might be presented.

Sociology of religion, a field of research and instruction to which relatively little effort had been devoted in recent years, showed signs of revival both in the United States and in France—to single out only two of the many countries concerned. Several significant articles, as well as the lists of research projects, theses, and dissertations, published in American sociological journals during the year, showed this plainly, as did also the very active French participation in journal publication and in the sections on sociology of religion held at the Third International Congress of Sociology meeting at Amsterdam in August. . . .

Pervading the various studies on sociology of religion was the effort to construct usable typologies of religious organizations; cult, sect, denomination, ecclesia, and the like all figured prominently. Similar concern with adequate typology was also to be observed in urban sociology. This field, after the decline of so-called human or social ecology, had suffered eclipse, but during the year many signs of renewed interest appeared. The sociology of work, chiefly as viewed in its urban setting, likewise enjoyed some popularity, especially at the University of Chicago under E. C. Hughes, where it was conveniently paired with the sociology of leisure under David Riesman. In the Chicago publication, the *AJS,* an interesting issue featuring sociology of work included an excellent article on the typology of work leadership. However, the use of "typology" as a mere substitute for "classification" pointed, in a few instances, to failure to observe the cardinal principle of good typological procedure; namely, to develop types *only* in conjunction with (1) a clearly posed question, (2) culture case study aimed at securing a tentative answer, (3) formulation of a definite hypothesis and its related types, and (4) proper validation of the hypothesis by all suitable methods of causal inference. Steps (2) and (4), in particular, were occasionally disregarded. It was interesting to note, in Herbert Blumer's otherwise excellent article, "Sociological Analysis and the 'Variable,' " *ASR,* December, 1956, pp. 683-90, apparent unfamiliarity with typological procedures, which avoid many of the criticisms leveled against the other procedures and techniques mentioned in the articles.

Fortunately, some of the year's work in rural sociology followed good typological practice; the article on Latin-American communities by C. P. Loomis and J. C. McKinney, in the March number of the *AJS,* was a commendable example, and there were several others. Not explicitly typological, but affording a good basis for reformulation in such terms, was the book by W. M. Williams, *The Sociology of an English Village: Gosforth* (London: Routledge Kegan Paul, 1956). The general topic of the Third International Congress of Sociology having been social change, it was quite natural that many studies of rural societies undergoing change were there presented. Several of these, in their orientation toward some more or less well-defined body of sociological theory, provided a refreshing contrast to the naive collections of raw rata passing as rural sociology in the United States a generation ago, and in some circles even in 1956. A Dutch book combining zeal for fact-gathering with sound theory in rural sociology was I. Gadourek's *A Dutch Community: Social and Cultural Structure and Process in a Bulb-growing Region in the Netherlands* (Leiden: Steinfert Kroese, 1956). The excellent German journal of rural history and sociology, *Zeitschrift für Agrargeschichte und Agrarsoziologie,* continued to present articles of high quality, although history rather than sociology got the lion's share of space.

Social change continued to hold the attention of sociologists everywhere; its choice as topic for the Third International Congress of Sociology was no accident. The many papers making up the *Proceedings* of the congress (published in advance) were of first-rate quality, with the exception of a few serving totalitarian propaganda purposes. The general theoretical papers, chiefly in volumes I and VI, were of much interest, particularly for their emphasis on the part played in social change by values. Volume III, dealing with changes in class-structure, was also significant, especially with regard to social mobility and classes.

Interestingly enough, the general interest in social change evoked defensive reactions among the adherents of structural-functional analysis, which is notoriously hard to apply to problems of social change without begging crucial questions. This defensiveness was especially evident in the article by Bernard Barber in the April number of the *ASR*. In the May *SF,* also, the structural-functional approach was the subject of an article; this, however, was not defensive but critical—"Position, Role, and Status: a Reformulation of Concepts," pp. 313-21, by Frederick M. Bates.

Among other important topics dealt with in *SF* was that of sociological field work, particularly in the October number, pp. 1-15. Anthropologists had long stressed the necessity of living as participant observer with the given people being studied, and in an earlier period sociologists had also followed this practice. Of recent years, however, sociologists had tended to restrict their efforts to the more formalized techniques. In 1956, as just noted, this restriction was challenged in two *SF* articles, both of them by sociologists who had themselves carried out extensive field investigations.

The year having been a Presidential one in the United States, various polls and highly publicized computing devices were much in evidence. Made wary by the debacle in 1948, when Truman triumphed in spite of poll predictions, most polling organizations so severely qualified their forecasts of an Eisenhower victory that the mountain-mouse metaphor came easily to mind. By contrast, the searching one-man analyses of Samuel Lubell, based on field studies, not only flatly predicted an Eisenhower sweep, but also correctly forecast in detail the anomaly of a Democratic House and Senate victory, district by district and state by state. Lubell's widely syndicated studies stood in marked contrast to the hedging presentations of the mass samplers and computers.

Sociological societies the world over were active, and several new organizations, some specialized, some regional, took shape; among them was the Scottish branch of the British Sociological Association. This branch held a two-day conference in Edinburgh in April, and issued an interesting report of its proceedings. The Third International Congress of Sociology provided a prominent place for reports on the teaching of sociology and the professional activities of sociologists; Austria, Belgium, Canada, Finland, the Netherlands, Poland, Turkey, and Venezuela were included in one collection, and research going on in Austria, Finland, France, Great Britain, Israel, Norway, Poland, and Sweden was considered in another....

1957

A Little Thaw

MANY DIFFERENT METAPHORS might have been used to characterize the year with regard to developments in sociology, but none of them would have fitted precisely; sociologists were busy over a remarkably wide range. "The year of increasing thaw" might have been fairly apt, however, for a number of trends already apparent speeded up their rate of flow, as it were, while at the same time the various orthodoxies that had checked such advances became slightly less rigid.

An instance of such accelerated thaw was afforded by the voicing of skepticism about the utility of structural-functional theory, dominant for nearly a decade. Several papers read at the annual meeting of the American Sociological Society not only expressed doubt concerning theory of this sort, but also challenged, directly or by implication, the basic equilibrium model. Further, alternative models or schemas were offered; the attack was not merely negative. A few books and a number of articles in the professional journals evidenced the same trend.

Further, the organismic analogy in terms of which some aspects of current varieties of equilibrium model were cast was also called strongly in question. At Northwestern University, for example, a symposium held in May featured both a forthright presentation of extreme organicism and a vigorous critique thereof. The latter drew heavily on "general systems theory" (a journal devoted to which had recently been established), and, as might perhaps have been expected, utilized suggestions stemming from cybernetics. The concept of "feedback," in particular, received renewed attention.

Another manifestation of thaw was provided by the notably increased prominence vouchsafed "historical sociology" at the annual meeting. Whereas 1956 was the first year in which there was so much as a section meeting on the program, a plenary session of a full evening's length was granted to historical sociology in 1957. Three substantial papers were presented, and the time allotted for discussion, in marked contrast to most sessions, was quite sufficient. Moreover, a regularly scheduled section was to appear on the program of the annual meeting in 1958, and if a sufficient number of high-quality papers were submitted, there were to be several sessions.

Additional indications of interest in historical sociology were provided by two leading articles in the July issue of the *AJS,* and by news of the establishment of a periodical, *Society and History: A Journal of Comparative Studies.* . . . Among sociologists, however, misgivings about the term "historical sociology" were occasionally expressed. It was pointed out that there had been confusion, stemming from writers as eminent as Howard Odum, between the sociological analysis of historical evidence bearing on well-defined hypotheses, on the one hand, and the history of sociology, on the other. Further, "historical sociology" was often erroneously identified, it was felt, with "social history." The latter had often been construed as meaning the history of residual topics not dealt with by political history, economic history, "cultural" history, and so on; namely, the history of the family, classes, and other "leftovers." Consequently, there were serious proposals for discarding "historical sociology" as designating the new (or newly rejuvenated) field of sociological interest, and replacing it with "sociology of history." It was still too soon to say, however, whether this or similar proposals would find a favorable hearing.

An excellent example of "social history" appeared in March in the *British Journal of Sociology,* I. Pinchbeck's

"The State and the Child in Sixteenth-Century England."
In another British publication, the *SR*, the July number
afforded an even better specimen, H. Tint's "The Search
for a Laic Morality under the French Third Republic:
Renouvier and the 'Critique Philosophique.'" But interestingly enough, this outstanding study of social history
was also of great interest for intellectual history and for
the history of sociology as well. In particular, it not only
showed the general context in which the work of Émile
Durkheim went on, but also used terminology making it
easier to discriminate between "laicism" and "secularization" than had previously been the case—in sociological
circles at least. The difficulty of discrimination had been
partially the result of the fact that "secularization," and
more especially "secularism," had frequently been used in
an invidious sense in pronouncements by religious leaders
of many persuasions. Tint's study, by merely following established French linguistic precedents, did much to introduce scientific neutrality.

Such neutrality was also evidenced in a new French
journal, *Archives de Sociologie des Religions,* as well as in
the continued activity of a new professional organization
with headquarters in the United States but with members
drawn from many countries, the Society for the Scientific
Study of Religion. The same dispassionate but by no means
anti-religious attitude was also evident at the annual meeting of the American Sociological Society in the three sessions devoted to sociology of religion. Although the sacred-
secular continuum, as it had been called for the past decade, figured prominently in several of the papers read at
these sessions, it was there made abundantly clear that the
continuum was not confined to the systematization of
strictly religious concepts, but on the contrary included
value-systems of non- and anti-religious character within
its broad scope.

Controversy about the nature of the sacred-secular continuum arose in conjunction with an article by L. C. Freeman and R. F. Winch, "Societal Complexity: An Empirical Test of a Typology of Societies," in the *AJS* for
March. Comment on alleged errors embodied in this article was published in the July number, with a rejoinder by
the authors. Controversy of this kind served a useful scientific purpose as long as it was restricted to the central issues

and did not degenerate into mere personal polemics.

Another controversy, also not unduly acrimonious, appeared in the February and April issues of the *ASR*. Peter Munch, in an article entitled "Empirical Science and Max Weber's *Verstehende Soziologie,*" took exception to a 1956 article in the same journal by Albert Pierce, "Empiricism and the Social Sciences." Pierce then offered a rebuttal. The debate, however, seemed far from satisfactory completion, for neither author quite adequately confronted the points raised by the other. Here again, however, a useful scientific purpose was served, especially for American sociologists, who tended to avoid or to gloss over crucial questions, or to use definitions so vague that almost anything could be included under them.

This vagueness was well illustrated in a February article in the *ASR* by G. M. Vernon and R. L. Stewart, "Empathy in the Dating Situation." Here empathy was equated with role-taking behavior in a very loose way—"Almost every conceivable social act involves this complex process . . ." Attention to the literature, even in English only, would have made it clear to the authors that empathy has a restricted albeit differentiated range of meaning. The first number of the first volume of the *International Journal of Sociometry,* for example, contained an article developing that meaning in some detail.

A refreshing contrast to such vagueness was provided, with reference to a different problem, by John C. McKinney in his outstanding article, "Polar Variables of Type Construction," *SF* for May. He showed, among other things, how indiscriminate was the presentation of types in a well-known article by R. F. Winch, and then went on to distinguish five variables in constructed types that must be taken into account when assessing their sociological utility. The article was a model of clarity.

A similarly lucid article appeared in the May number of *The Midwest Sociologist,* a journal that was distinctly worthy of attention, although modest in size and circulation. The article, by Harold O. Orbach, "Operational Definitions and the Natural Science Trend: A Methodological Note," was exceedingly brief, but it covered more ground, in strikingly effective fashion, than many lengthier efforts. The main point—that operationism was by no means the unassailable, generally accepted philosophy of

modern science, as it was recently represented to be by
George A. Lundberg—was made with devastating logic
and careful scholarship. The article was a fitting complement of A. Cornelius Benjamin's excellent book, *Operationism* (Springfield, Ill: Thomas, 1955). Here again
signs of a thaw in orthodoxy were in evidence.

Honesty, however, compelled the statement that few
such indications could be found in the brochure edited for
UNESCO by Hans L. Zetterberg, reviewed in the *AJS*
for September by Charles H. Page. As the latter noted,
". . . it accents a youthful semiorthodoxy." However this
may have been, "Sociology in the United States of America" was best read in conjunction with more inclusive
works such as the symposium, *Modern Sociological Theory in Continuity and Change* (New York: Dryden Press,
1957), and Joseph B. Gittler, ed., *Review of Sociology:
Analysis of a Decade* (New York: Wiley, 1957).

Shifting attention to work of more concrete character,
mention should be made of the informative article by
R. H. Wax, "Twelve Years Later: An Analysis of Field
Experience," in the September *AJS*. It was especially enlightening with regard to the reciprocity of field work: the
investigator not only learns from his informants but also
teaches them the role behavior that enables him to learn
from them. A vivid descriptive article, based on thorough
field work, was published in the July *Social Problems*. By
Harold Finestone, it was somewhat cryptically entitled,
"Cats, Kicks, and Color," and dealt with the young Negro
drug addict in contemporary Chicago as a constructed
type. Only by means of studies of this kind, it seemed, could
genuinely helpful recommendations be made to those officials directly charged with combating drug addiction.
Once more the thaw in orthodoxy was evident; of recent
years sociologists had begun to abandon their earlier interest in field work, and to relinquish it to anthropologists,
social workers, and the like. The articles noted above and
several similar ones showed that sociological attention to
field work was definitely reappearing.

A survey of American master's theses and doctoral dissertations completed and in progress during 1957 showed
a very high degree of concentration on "social problems,"
or their implicit equivalents, of more or less immediately
American concern, although here too signs of a thaw were

by no means absent. Most obvious among these signs, perhaps, was the fair number of projects having to do, in one respect or another, with value-systems viewed with some measure of scientific detachment. This was apparently true even of the studies in sociology of religion, which were relatively more prominent than in previous years.

Outside the United States, one of the most significant publications was the *Handbuch der Soziologie* (Stuttgart: Enke, 1955-57), edited by Werner Ziegenfuss and reviewed in the September *AJS*. German sociology was obviously reviving at a rapid rate. And, in the symposium on *Modern Sociological Theory in Continuity and Change,* the French sociologist Jean Stoetzel presented a truly impressive array of active younger French workers to the international audience; here also speedy sociological regeneration was apparent. Nevertheless, the same could not be said for all the countries of Europe, even when those in the Soviet bloc were left out of account; it would be some time, evidently, before intellectual rebuilding and expansion could bring sociology everywhere above and beyond the havoc wrought by World War II.

1958

Much Ado, but Sometimes about Something

THE CENTENARY OF THE BIRTHS of Durkheim and Simmel" was one of the ways in which sociologists labeled the year. Many ways were possible, for an amazing variety of activities in a wide range of countries became manifest.

The works of Durkheim and Simmel were given considerable attention: journals published special commentary issues; symposia dealing with their works were launched; their various writings were brought out in new editions and collections; translations were published; professional societies officially recognized the centenary; and younger social scientists intensified acquaintance with their stimulating theories. What was lacking, however, was fresh theoretical endeavor even remotely approaching the level reached, in their day and generation, by these outstanding men. In some instances, indeed, those who joined in the chorus of praise turned their backs, in effect, on the kinds of theoretical investigation for which Durkheim and Simmel had become famous, denouncing contemporary investigation of the same sort as "philosophical" or "essayistic."

But apart from such inconsistency, there were several lacks in the centenary observance. There was, for example, little or nothing in the way of sociology of knowledge analysis of the men and their works. Durkheim's role as Third Republic ideologist, his anti-clericalism, his pervasive and dogmatically atheistic value-judgments, his acceptance of the crude ethnology of his day, his intense nationalism, his continuance of the Comtean and DeMaistrean traditions—all these merited close study, but got none worth mentioning. Simmel's Bergsonian *Lebensphilosophie,* his highly debatable relativism, his special appeal for the rootless and *declassé,* his deep identification with urban life, his profound allegiance to the Germany of World War I, his seemingly spontaneous but actually calculated lecture technique—here again the sociologists who rendered him lip-service did little to help in the understanding of him.

The basic theories of Durkheim and Simmel, of course, could be neither validated nor invalidated by such scrutiny *per se,* but at the very least flaws in logic and deficiencies in factual evidence might have been pointed out. No science dare rest on past achievement *uncritically* accepted, and sociology least of all—but here looms danger of digression; matters other than centenaries must be surveyed.

Social stratification continued to receive much attention. Baltzell's work on the Philadelphia gentleman was noteworthy. Walter Buckley published a searching article in the *ASR,* pointing out that prevailing definition of stratification so loose that it was continually confused with mere differentiation invalidated many of its "functional" justifications. Hollingshead and Redlich's study of New Haven, Conn., published as *Social Class and Mental Illness,* was illuminating, as was also Floud, Halsey, and Martin's British analysis, *Social Class and Educational Opportunity.* From a different perspective, *Talent and Society,* by McClelland, Baldwin, Bronfenbrenner, and Strodtbeck, offered some new conclusions and many fresh suggestions. Closely linked with stratification and mobility studies are those of presumably disadvantaged groups, usually termed "minorities," etc. Here an excellent symposium appeared under the editorship of Marshall Sklare, *The Jews: Social*

Patterns of an American Group; it was based on a number of good empirical researches. Investigation of racial integration continued to be popular, and was especially timely; the appearance in the *Public Opinion Quarterly* of the study by Melvin Tumin and his associates, although harshly reviewed in at least one instance, evoked widespread notice.

Sociology of medicine, or "medical sociology," continued to forge toward the front, especially in conjunction with studies of aging, professionalization among nurses and physicians, increasing costs of hospitalization, "socialized medicine," and the like. The orientation toward what are commonly called social problems was clear, but most of the work conformed reasonably well to scientific standards.

Demography, although not always sociologically oriented, had never been moribund, but human ecology had earlier showed signs of very poor health. However, Hauser and Duncan edited an important work, *The Study of Population,* that seemed likely to bring demography more definitely into the sociological orbit while at the same time keeping it vigorous, and also to revive ecology in a creditable way. The work of Ryder and Schnore, among the younger exponents of the fields in question, began to attract favorable attention; this, of course, had previously been vouchsafed the studies by Kingsley Davis and his co-workers.

Interest in mathematical models of social systems, social structures, social processes, and such social actions as decision-making (e.g., "jury projects") continued to grow, often stimulated by the availability of rapid computing and data-processing devices. Along with this went some skepticism with regard to the usability, or even validity, of earlier techniques in the form of Guttman scaling and the like. Novel techniques of research, widely hailed as likely to be highly useful, were presented by Lazarsfeld and Thelen in *The Academic Mind,* although criticism of the presumably value-laden data-gathering instruments involved was not lacking.

Some British work in social stratification has already been mentioned; in addition, that done at the London School of Economics by Montague and others was especially noteworthy. Reference to Peter Townsend's *The*

Family Life of Old People: an Inquiry in East London is relevant here in view of the rather well-marked class lines encountered in the district studied, but it also has some bearing on sociology of medicine. Other developments in British sociology were thus characterized by Leo Kuper, for a time at Birmingham while absent from South Africa:

> . . . a number of urban neighborhood studies have been started. What is interesting about them is the partial emancipation from the social survey. . . . These younger sociologists [involved] are in a dilemma . . . [arising] from the difficulty of reconciling two rather different influences, the social survey . . . and the social-psychological deep level approach of the Tavistock Institute of Human Relations. I think for the moment that they are likely to get these thoroughly entangled with their interest on the one hand in sampling and large numbers, and on the other in depth and the analysis of social relationships. Still, it seems to me a promising sign, the beginnings of a revolt against the established system of research.
>
> In regard to the developments in sociological theory, I cannot see any contribution being made at the present time.

In France, the potential teaching of sociology made much headway through the establishment of a *licence de sociologie* based on certificates of proficiency in four fields: general sociology, social psychology, social and political economy, and one broadly defined as of sociological relevance by the particular faculty of letters concerned. The group of students of sociology at Paris looking forward to careers in teaching and research issued a bulletin as a vehicle for any of their studies worthy of publication; three numbers appeared during the year.

The extensive sociological investigations earlier initiated under the leadership of Jean Stoetzel at the National Center for Scientific Research (see MSTICAC, noted on pp. 814 and 877) continued, and two new teams took form, one on sociology of knowledge led by Georges Gurvitch, and one on automation led by Pierre Naville.

Among the more important publications on general sociology were those of Armand Cuvillier and Georges Gurvitch; on sociology of politics, Alfred Sauvy, J. Meynaud, Jacques Fauvet, and H. Mendras; on sociology of work, Georges Friedmann, Pierre Naville, J. Dofny, J. D. Reunaud, and A. Touraine; on cultural anthropology and history of civilization, J. Cazeneuve, Claude Levi-Strauss, Marcel Griaule, Lucien Febvre, and H. Martin; and on social ethnology, P. H. Chombart de Lauwe and L. Couvrier; on demography, J. Fourastié; on race relations, I. Meyerson; and on sociology of religion, Lucien Febvre. Obviously, sociology in France covered a wide field, but it must also be said that the coverage was thorough.

In Germany the tendency, so strongly evident in previous years, toward empirical research largely ignoring the "classical 1920s" showed signs of slackening off; indeed, reestablishment of continuity was here and there quite evident. In social stratification and industrial sociology, for example, this appeared in the publications of Heinz Popitz, a student of Jaspers', of Ralf Dahrendorf, a student of Josef König's, and of H. Paul Bahrdt, a student of Plessner's. Of course, these were not the only fields in which important books and articles appeared in 1958; for community studies, mention should be made of those by H. Croon and K. Utermann, René König, and R. Mayntz; for youth and age, Helmut Schelsky, L. von Friedeburg, F. Weltz, and K. M. Bolte; for social mobility, K. M. Bolte; for sociology of politics, W. von Baeyer-Kette, O. Büsch, P. Furth, Arnold Bergstraesser, W. Cornides, K. D. Bracher, W. Hirsch-Weber, K. Schütz, and E. Thier; for sociology of culture, W. Schulenberg, Helmut Plessner, and M. Schwonke; for social psychology, P. Heintz and H. Kluth; for social philosophy, Christian Graf von Krockow and Albert Salomon; and for methodology, René König, W. Bernsdorf, and Heinz Maus.

University institutes for research in various fields of sociology were relatively abundant: for community studies, Cologne; youth affairs, Hamburg; sociology of education, Göttingen; sociology of politics, Berlin; sociology of international relations, Freiburg; industrial sociology, Saarbrücken; demography, Kiel; general sociology with emphasis on the work of Max Weber, Munich; social anthropology, Mainz; and social psychology and related matters, Frankfurt.

All in all, the "economic miracle" was being paralleled by a sociological miracle in West Germany during 1958. In East Germany, alas, "social science" under the dictates of "diamat" still held sway; little except sterile polemics was in evidence.

In Israel, Bacchi, Bonne, Buber, Eisenstadt, Foa, Guttman, Patinkin, Taraktover, and others seemed to be carrying on in spite of repeated crises, but precise information was lacking, understandably enough.

Japan was enjoying a veritable boom in sociology, in part because of a spate of translations of Western writings, but in much greater measure because of important works being produced by Japanese themselves. These works, for 1958, included general lecture collections such as that by Fukutake, Hidaka, and Takahashi; a sociological dictionary of more than a thousand pages edited by the same trio; a systematic treatise with contemporary emphasis by Odaka; a full-scale study of modern Japanese society, based on surveys of stratification and mobility conducted by 45 cooperating Japanese universities and the Japanese Sociological Association Research Committee; several shorter publications, by a group of rural sociologists and land economists, dealing with Japanese villages; and an interim report of an ambitious attempt at the integrating of several social sciences, with sociology viewed as the co-ordinating discipline, in which Masamichi figures for political science, Nakayama for economics, and Odaka for sociology.

Here too there was much ado, and frequently about something!

1959

Rapprochement and Expanding Organization

THE APPEARANCE OF SOCIOLOGICAL WRITINGS that could at once be judged as having extraordinary importance was not characteristic of the year, although the general quality of publication in many countries was distinctly creditable. Further, the spate of reasonably priced reprints of meritorious earlier works, some of them long off the market, did much to diffuse sociological knowledge, not only among laymen and students at all levels, but also among professional sociologists who previously had been unable readily to acquaint themselves with what their predecessors had accomplished. Still further, translators were active, even for English into French or German and *vice versa,* and also for these three into and, less often, from the wide range of other languages in which sociological treatises, compendious or brief, had been less frequently evident. Once more, *Sociological Abstracts,* the excellent journal abstracting in English books and articles in many languages, continued to broaden its scope. A very considerable proportion of the works abstracted had initially been printed in English. Nevertheless, it seemed clear that however widespread the reading of English had been or would become, a substantial part of the *corpus* of sociological publication would continue to make at least its first appearance in other languages. Rapprochement in the form of terminological equivalences, however, was quite obvious.

Still, there was much evidence of terminological indecision. The painful dilemma of neologisms *versus* ordinary words adapted for analytic purposes was as painful as ever. Many sociologists showed impatience with cumbrous, platitude-disguising statements decked out in neologistic or unduly technical terms. Their impatience, however, did not always lead to appropriate action; namely, to careful discrimination among and suitable use of the extensive array of words available in any good dictionary, plus explicit, skillful, and *minimal* adaptation, were absolutely necessary for the purpose in hand, of this or that word. . . . Rarely indeed are neologisms unavoidable; when they are, it is primarily because of their great utility for what may be called "shorthand communication among specialists." To be sure, readers of social-scientific works are not always specialists in the particular field to which the neologism had reference; when they can be expected to be such, decision to take the risk of being called a "jargoneer" may then be made. For better or for worse, something will have been decided.

However, a number of quite important organizational developments were evidenced during 1959. For example, at the Fourth World Congress of Sociology, meeting at Milan and Stresa, Italy, in early September, there appeared the first representatives of the Sociological Association of the Soviet Union. There had been persons from the Soviet Union at the Third World Congress in 1956, but they did not represent any official sociological association, for there was no such association to which they or others like them could belong until late in 1957. The conduct of the U.S.S.R. official delegates at Milan-Stresa seemed to some participants from other countries to offer a discernible contrast with that of the persons earlier present at Amsterdam. This contrast was said to consist chiefly in the less aggressively propagandistic utterances of the Milan-Stresa delegates, together with their improved organization and presentation of papers, their greater curiosity about sociological developments outside the Soviet Union, their more overt and successful efforts to get in congenial touch with delegates from elsewhere (notably from the English-speaking countries), and their closer observance of time limits set by the Congress chairmen on presentation and discussion. In short, they may have been somewhat better sociologists and distinctly better propagandists than their Amsterdam predecessors.

Participants in the Milan-Stresa Congress from other countries in the Soviet bloc put in their appearance: Poles, Czechs, East Germans, etc. Several of the Polish papers, based on sound research, were well formulated and interesting. The East Germans, on the other hand, seemed to have been poorly selected and trained; their papers and discussions were seldom if ever above the secondary-school level.

Naturally, the bulk of work reported at the Milan Congress was that of sociologists from the "West," with Britain, France, Germany, Italy, and the United States (here listed with regard only to alphabetical order) in prominent positions. However, the Near and Middle East, the Far East, Africa, Latin America, the Scandinavian countries, and several other regions were well represented in quality, and sometimes in numbers as well. Sociology of work, of politics, of religion, and of the family were among the chief topics of interest, but procedures and techniques of research, together with sources of evidence such as historical documents, interviews, and so on, received due attention.

Another important organizational development was the meeting celebrating the fiftieth anniversary of the founding of the German Sociological Association; this was held at Berlin in late May. Although attended primarily by sociologists from West Germany, who flocked to the gathering in spite of the tense period during which it occurred, the more than four hundred professional sociologists and other social scientists present included a number from other countries, among whom were several representatives of their respective national organizations. In addition to the "professionals," there were at the meeting at least two hundred students, most of them from the Free University of Berlin. At least one or two of the addresses at the plenary sessions were characterized as "elegant soap-bubbles," but among the remainder were many of outstanding merit —focused on topics of importance, firmly based on relevant evidence that was closely analyzed, and with conclusions cautiously drawn. The papers read at the smaller section gatherings were on the whole excellent, especially those dealing with sociology of work and with what, following Thurnwald, might be called ethno-sociology. Unfortunately, there were indications of factional struggles within the Association, but these may not have been serious. Helmut Plessner of the University of Göttingen was re-elected as President.

Throughout Germany and Austria the year brought many new organizational developments, some of them representing culminations of earlier trends, at various universities: Munich, Göttingen, Kiel, Graz, and elsewhere. These developments were chiefly along the lines of research institutes devoted to sociology, much like those earlier established at Cologne, Hamburg, and so forth, and gave much promise for the future.

In Britain, there seemed to be less ground for optimism. Oxford and Cambridge appointed sociologists to their staffs, but although those chosen were of definite merit, they were not placed in positions of much influence or assurance of continuity. The sociologists attached to the London School of Economics had earlier done a good deal toward the advancement of their field, and these efforts were of course carried further; nevertheless, little of high significance occurred during the year. The "red brick" universities were sociologically active, but here again there were no outstanding developments. To one observer it appeared that the entrenched disciplines, particularly those among or linked with the so-called humanities, were continuing their resistance to sociology with considerable effect. Even Scotland provided no exception.

French work in sociology continued to be notably productive, both in quantity and quality, but there were no unusual organizational developments. The Italian Sociological Association, however, greatly expanded and intensified its activities; much of the success of the Milan-Stresa Congress was directly attributable to Italian initiative and provision of excellent facilities.

In the United States, organizational developments were considerable and important. The American Sociological Association (which during the year replaced "Society" with "Association" in its title) reached a membership total of more than 6,500, making it well over four times as large as any other strictly sociological body of national scope. Sheer size, together with increasing specialization, brought about the not altogether fortunate founding, within the general framework of the Association, of "established sections."

Such sections, electing their own officers and working with the general Program Committee in the setting up of annual programs, seemed likely to proliferate and to diminish further the already limited extent of mutual understanding among American sociologists. Three such sections were established in 1959—social psychology, methodology, and medical sociology—and several others were rapidly organizing. The section on social psychology threatened to be divisive because of the inclination of its leaders to define their specialty in a way such that infringement on the fields viewed as proper to most other specialists, and to general sociological theory as well, seemed inevitable. The establishment of the methodology section also had divisive possibilities because of the potential exclusion, foreshadowed in the preliminary organizational strategy, of all methods and procedures that did not follow operationist practices, narrowly defined. On the other hand, no particular exceptions could be taken to the establishment of the section on medical sociology (perhaps better phrased as sociology of medicine) except those of possible parochialism and triviality. The American Psychological Association, long familiar with its own established sections, had been attempting to check their imperialism, disintegrating tendencies, and extreme specialization, but with only partial success.

Hopeful, however, was the *modus vivendi* brought about among social psychologists of sociological derivation and those whose training had been primarily or even exclusively psychological. The American Sociological Association had for some time been trying to persuade the

American Psychological Association to exert restraining influence on state psychological bodies active in lobbying for legislation designed to restrict the use of the title "psychologist," with or without a qualifying adjective, to those approved by examining boards effectively controlled by psychologists only. The persuasive efforts were successful; the American Psychological Association finally agreed to recommend that social psychologists whose training was chiefly or even wholly sociological (and the first book entitled *Social Psychology,* without any other qualifying word or phrase, was published in 1908 with the sociologist E. A. Ross as the author) need undergo no examination or certifying procedure except as controlled by the American *Sociological* Association, and here only when practicing outside the confines of ordinary academic instruction and research. What the various state psychological groups (to which their national organization could merely make recommendations) would actually do toward changing their restrictive efforts remained to be seen, but it seemed probable that the *modus vivendi* would eventually extend from the national to the local level.

1960

A Very Short Look Ahead

WRITING IN THE SECOND WEEK of February, it is obvious that very little referring specifically to 1960 can be said. Still, that little may be worth saying.

The program of the annual meeting of the American Sociological Association, to take place in New York, grants reasonably adequate places to several topics not previously given much recognition—sociology of art, of literature, of music, and so on. Most of the standard topics have been accommodated, although in some instances altered terms have been employed to designate them. Herbert Spencer is to be the patron saint (how he would have writhed to hear himself called that!) of the gathering, for 1960 is the centenary of the publication of the prospectus of his great sociological treatise.

At about the same time that Spencer's canonization received approval, St. Louis, Missouri, was chosen as the site for the 1961 meeting, and Washington, D. C., for 1962. Washington was selected because it had earlier been decided that, barring a world crisis, the Fifth World Congress of Sociology is to be held there either just before or after the American assembly.

An unpleasant consequence of the meeting of the Fourth World Congress at Milan must here be mentioned, in part as correction of the over-optimistic tone of the 1959 comments about the Soviet Union and satellite delegations. One of the Poles who spoke with quite astonishing freedom has since been dismissed from his post, and the Polish Sociological Association has been dissolved.

So much for the specific and determinable; now for the general and speculative. At the beginning of the seventh decade of the twentieth century, sociology the world around seems to have prospects of increasing expansion, professionalization, and (if the uneasy "peace" endures) Internationalization. To what extent all this will be accompanied by genuine advance in explanatory and predictive power remains to be seen. Certainly there have been tremendous strides in technical proficiency, but as Leo Kuper has said, there is also evident "an increasing interest in virtuosity of method with little interest in the problem to which the method is applied." But may it not be possible that continuing growth of technical proficiency will inevitably bring with it a realization that just as "concepts without percepts are empty, and percepts without concepts are blind," so "problems without solutions are idle, and solutions without problems are vain"? If such realization were to come about, then what now sometimes seems to be much ado about nothing may prove to have been an unavoidable and salutary period of forging some of the specialized tools needed for the tremendous task of making a humane cosmos, in the old Greek sense of an orderly but endurable society, out of the present human-all-too-human chaos? "Now abideth hope. . . ." In that hope let each one of us honestly do what he knows he is best fitted to do, ignoring, like Dürer's Knight, Death and the Devil.

And so, with a short sermon, the end of this long book is almost reached. Now, except for the Bibliography, Notes, and Indexes, the journey is over. For a closing word, it seems fitting to call on the redoubtable Armstrong,

the Scottish Borderer who composed this farewell song
on his way to execution for killing the English Warden of
the Middle Marches:

> This night is my departing night,
>   For here nae langer must I stay;
> There's neither friend nor foe of mine.
>   But wishes me away.
>
> What I hae done thro' lack o' wit,
>   I never, never can recall;
> I hope ye're all my friends as yet;
>   Goodnight, and joy be with you all!

Supplementary Bibliography for Volume Three

It is of the utmost importance that the reader bear in mind the fact that this bibliography, as the items in the Prefaces, the Notes, the Third Edition Comments (in small type at the end of each chapter) the Value-System Commentary, and the Appendix on Sociological Trends, *is not indexed*. In other words, the Name Index and the Subject Index deal only with the names and subjects appearing in the First Edition (1938) text *as such,* and this text, with the exception of minor corrections, is presented unaltered.

Reviewers the world over evidenced remarkable kindliness in dealing with the 1938 version, in spite of the extremely wide coverage that the nature of the treatise made necessary. Only with such encouragement would the present writer have ventured to present the original text again in 1952; thereafter the earlier goodwill was once more manifested. Now, in 1960, the risk is once more taken, with the hope that tolerance, at least, will be encountered.

Given the tremendous amount of contemporary scholarly activity, full up-to-dateness could not conceivably be achieved within any reasonable space limits, even if the present writer felt competent to achieve it. The list here provided is intended merely to offer a means whereby the reader can delve deeper in the direction of his interests, guided by searching investigators, than this treatise alone would ever have made possible.

Stress is on the fairly recent, but a few references of earlier date are given when it seems obvious that they should have been included in the first place. Now and again, items listed elsewhere in this treatise are included here if the present writer's orientation is indicated or has been markedly influenced by them; some of his own books and articles, understandably enough, fall in this category! Apart from such considerations as these, preference has often gone to works that contains bibliographies, in footnotes or otherwise. Further, articles and books that survey the various works of given authors, grouped in "schools" and the like (albeit singly now and again), rather than the writings of the authors themselves, figure prominently—need for brevity forced this in *most* cases. In addition, there has been an effort to list convenient "paperpacks"; in some cases passages or entire books that would otherwise be hard to come by, will thus become available. Had it seemed advisable to list well-known standard writings, such as those of Plato, Hegel, Max Weber, and others, the bibliography would have been in some respects more useful (*many* "paperbacks" are in print), and certainly more lengthy—but a line somewhere was unavoidable.

Abbreviations of journals, etc., follow the keys at the beginning of the Notes; what is not to be found in the keys is not abbreviated. The abbreviations bib. or bibs. is used for bibliographies, n. for notes, fn. for footnotes, sel. for selected, I or II for "also very useful for Volume I" (or II); PB for paperback, ext. for extensive, and so on.

Abel, Theodore, "Sociology in Postwar Poland," *ASR,* vol. xv, 1 (Feb., 1950), pp. 104-106.

————————, "The Contribution of George Simmel: A Reappraisal," *ASR,* vol. xxiv, 4 (Aug., 1959), pp. 473-481.

Acquaviva, S. S., "La Sociologia della Pratica Religiosa," *Quaderni di Sociologia,* 22 (Autumn, 1956), pp. 182-189.

Alcorta, J. I., "Tipologias Sociologicas: Formalismo Sociologico," *Revista Mexicana de Sociologia,* vol. xi (Apr.-June, 1953), pp. 267-285.

Alihan, M. A., *Social Ecology* (New York: Columbia Univ. Press, 1938). Sharp crit. of assumpt. of hum. ecol. in U. S.

Allwood, M. S., *Eilert Sundt: A Pioneer in Sociology and Social Anthropology* (Oslo: Olaf Norlis Forlag, 1957).

Alpert, Harry, "Émile Durkheim: A Perspective and Appreciation," *ASR,* vol. xxiv, 4 (Aug., 1959), pp. 462-465.

————————, "France's First University Course in Sociology," *ASR,* vol. ii, 3 (June, 1937), pp. 311-317.

Andrieux, Cécile, "La sociologie polonaise," *Cahiers Internationaux de Sociologie,* 24 (Jan.-June, 1958), pp. 167-175.

Arendt, Hannah, *The Human Condition* (Chicago: Univ. of Chicago Press, 1958). Stim. II.

Aron, Raymond, *German Sociology,* trans. by Mary and Thomas Bottomore (Glencoe, Ill.: Free Press, 1957).

————————, *et al.,* *Les Sciences sociales en France,* Paul Hartmann, ed. Centre d'études de politique étrangère, 5 (Paris: 1937).

Bailey, R. B., III, *Sociology Faces Pessimism: Amidst a Fading Optimism* (The Hague: Martinus Nijhoff, 1958). Val. for "shift of mood." II.

Barnes, H. E., Becker, Howard, and Becker, Frances Bennett, eds., *Contemporary Social Theory* (New York: Appleton Century, 1940). Ext. bibs. for topical chaps. and in fn., also compr. gen. bib.

Baskin, M., "Soviet Evaluation of American Sociology," *ASR,* vol. xiv, 1 (Feb., 1949), pp. 137-143.

Becker, Howard, "British Sociology" (in Czech), *Sociologickà revue,* vol. v, 4 (1934), pp. 251-270.

————————, "Sociology and Suffering," trans. with introd., of section from Leopold von Wiese's *Beziehungslehre* (1924), *IJE,* vol. xliv, 2 (Jan., 1934), pp. 222-235. Does not appear elsewhere in Eng. II.

————————, "A new Classification of Culture" (discussion of paper by James W. Woodward) *ASR,* vol. i, 1 (Feb., 1936), pp. 102-104. Att. on cult. lag. doctr.

_____, "La Tipologia Constructiva en las Ciencias Sociales," *Revista Mexicana de Sociologia,* vol. i, 4 and 5 (Sept., Dec., 1939), pp. 65-98.

_____, "Sociological Analysis of the Dyad," *ASR,* vol. vii, 2 (Feb., 1942), pp. 13-26. With Ruth Hill Useem.

_____, "Befuddled Germany: A Glimpse of Max Scheler," *ASR,* vol. viii, 2 (April, 1943), pp. 207-211. In dram. form but based on direct ev. (interviews, etc.).

_____, "Interpretative Sociology and Constructive Typology," ch. IV in symposium, *Twentieth Century Sociology,* Gurvitch and Moore, eds. (New York: Philosophical Library, 1945), pp. 70-95.

_____, "Peoples of Germany," ch. XVI in symposium, *Problems of the Postwar World,* T. C. McCormick, ed. (New York: McGraw-Hill, 1945), pp. 342-390. "Personality and culture" desc. and analysis of 15 pre-World War II German regions. II.

_____, "Los Pueblos de Alemania," *Revista Mexicana de Sociologia,* vol. vii, 1 (Jan.-Apr., 1954), pp. 23-67.

_____, "Maurice Halbwachs," *ASR,* vol. xi, 2 (April, 1946), pp. 233-235. *In Memoriam* art.

_____, "Jugendpflege und Jugendbewegung einst und Heute," *Verhandlungen des neunten Deutschen Soziologentages* (Tübingen: Verlag J. C. B. Mohr [Paul Siebeck], 1949), pp. 47-82. Disc. of dev. in Ger. youth, affairs and soc. anal. thereof.

_____, "Die Entwicklung der soziologischen Forschung ausserhalb Deutschlands," *Verhandlungen des neunten Deutschen Soziologentages* (Tübingen: Verlag J. C. B. Mohr [Paul Siebeck], 1949), pp. 143-151.

_____, "Politische Gebilde und Aussenkonflikt," *Kölner Zeitschrift für Soziologie,* vol. i, 1 (1948/49), pp. 5-16. Imp. for comm. *re* Oppenheimer. II.

_____, "Die jüngste Entwicklung der Soziologie," *Universitas,* vol. iv, 7 (1949), pp. 793-799.

_____, *Systematic Sociology on the Basis of the* Beziehungslehre *and* Gebildelehre *of Leopold von Wiese* (1932; reissued Wisconsin edition with a 1950 preface, Norman Paul Press, 1148 St. Joseph St., Gary, Ind., 1950), "Historical Postscript." Appears in 1960 in abridged version, omitting "His. Postscr.," under some such title as *Systematic Sociology as Based on Wiese,* Dover PB.

——————————————, "Science, Culture, and Society," *Philosophy of Science,* vol. xix, 4 (Oct., 1952), pp. 273-287. Disc. of positiv., ubity of sci., soc. of kn., etc.

——————————————, "Vitalizing Sociological Theory," *ASR,* vol. xix, 4 (Aug., 1954), pp. 377-388. Att. to small groups, int. training, etc.

——————————————, *"Systematic Sociology* and Leopold von Wiese" in J. S. Moreno, ed., *Sociometry and the Science of Man* (New York: Beacon House, 1956), pp. 262-268. Also appears in *Sociometry,* vol. xviii, 4 pp. 518-524.

——————————————, "Empathy, Sympathy, and Scheler," *International Journal of Sociometry* (New York: Beacon House, Sept., 1956), pp. 15-22. II.

——————————————, *Modern Sociological Theory in Continuity and* and Boskoff, Alvin, eds., *Change* (New York: Dryden, 1957), ch. 6, "Current Sacred-Secular Theory and Its Development," by HB. I.

——————————————, *Soziologie als Wissenschaft vom sozialen Hendeln* (Würzburg: Holzner Verlag, 1959). Exc. trans. of chs. 1, 2, 3, 4, and 6 of *Through Values to Social Interpretation* (Durham, N. C.: Duke Univ. Press, 1950). Has inform. intro. by Prof. Burkart Holzner of Univ. of Pittsburgh. I and II, esp. ch. 3.

——————————————, "Werte als Werkzeuge soziologischer Analyse," ch. VII in *Gegenwartsprobleme der Soziologie: Alfred Vierkandt zum 80. Geburtstag,* Gottfried Eisermann, ed. (Potsdam: Athenaion, 1949), pp. 116-140. Variant but exc. trans. of 1st ch. of prev. item.

——————————————, "Das Deutschlandbild in Amerika," *Politische Studien, Heft* 115, 10. Jahrgang, pp. 740-757. (München: Monatsschrift der Hochschule für Politische Wissenschaften,Nov., 1959).

——————————————, "Deutsche Beiträge zu der amerikanischen Sozialpsychologie und Soziologie der Gegenwart,' "Soziologie und moderne Gesellschaft," *Verhandlungen des 14. Deutschen Soziologentages.* Alexander Busch, ed. (Stuttgart: Ferdinand Enke, 1959), pp. 90-99. II.

——————————————, "On Simmel's 'Philosophy of Money'," in Kurt H. Wolff, ed., *Georg Simmel, 1895-1918: A Collection of Essays, with Translations and a Bibliography* (Columbus: Ohio State Univ. Press, 1959), pp. 216-233.

——————————————, "Max Scheler's Sociology of Knowledge," *Philoso-* and Dahlke, Helmut Otto, *phy and Phenomenological Research,* vol. ii, 3 (Mar., 1942), pp. 309-322. Brief treat. of Scheler's assump.

Bellah, R. N., "Durkheim and History," *ASR*, vol. xxiv, 4 (Aug., 1959), pp. 447-461.

Benjamin, Cornelius, *Operationism* (Springfield, Ill.: Charles G. Thomas, 1955). Very usef.

Bernard, L. L., "Recent Work in Cultural Sociology in Brazil, Argentina, and Mexico," *ASR*, vol. ii, 2 (Apr., 1937), pp. 265-268.

Bernsdorf, Wilhelm, ed., in Verbindung mit Horst Knospe, *Internationales Soziologen Lexikon: Unter Mitarbeit zahlreicher Fachleute des In und Auslandes* (Stuttgart: Ferdinand Enke Verlag, 1959). Thor., bibs.

Bierstedt, Robert, "Sociology and Humane Learning," *ASR*, vol. xxv, 1 (Feb., 1960), pp. 3-9.

Bogardus, E. S., "Forty Years of 'Sociology and Social Research,'" *SSR*, vol. xl, 6 (July-Aug., 1956), pp. 426-432.

Borgatta, E. F., and Meyer, H. J., eds., *Sociological Theory: Present-Day Sociology from the Past* (New York: Knopf, 1956). Somewh. lim. and arb. sel.; some imp. auth. om. II.

Borkenau, Franz, *Pareto* (New York: Wiley, 1936). Best brief treat.

Bourricaud, Francis, "Sur la predominance de l'analyse microscopique dans la sociologie americaine," *Cahiers Internationaux de Sociologie,* vol. xiii (1952), pp. 105-121.

Brim, O. G., Jr., *Sociology and the Field of Education* (New York: Russell Sage Foundation, 1958). Contemp. emph.

Brunner, E. DeS., *The Growth of a Science: A Half-Century of Rural Sociological Research in the United States* (New York: Harper, 1957).

Buckley, Walter, "Social Stratification and the Functional Theory of Social Differentiation," *ASR*, vol. xxiii, 4 (Aug., 1958), pp. 369-375. Crit. of equil. theory and assoc. functionalism.

Burnham, J. C., *Lester Frank Ward in American Thought* (Washington, D. C.: Public Affairs Press [Annals of American Sociology], 1956).

Cantril, Hadley, ed., *Public Opinion 1935-1946* (Princeton: Princeton Univ. Press, 1951). Elab. bib.

Carroll, J. W., "Merton's Thesis on English Science," *American Journal of Economics and Sociology,* vol. xiii, 4 (July, 1954), pp. 427-432. Crit.

Chapple, E. D., "Research—Business or Scholarship?" *Human Organization,* vol. xi (Fall, 1952), pp. 3-4.

Chase, Stuart, in cons. with deS. Brunner, Edmund, *The Proper Study of Mankind,* rev. ed. (New York: Harper, 1956). Pop. and over-simp., but useful prelim. surv.

Chugerman, Samuel,   *Lester F. Ward, the American Aristotle* (Durham, N. C.: Duke Univ. Press, 1939). Bib.

Collard, E., *et al.,*   *Vocation de la sociologie religieuse et sociologie des vocations* (Paris: Éditions Casterman, 1958).

Cottrell, L. S., and Gallagher, Ruth,   "Developments in Social Psychology, 1930-1940," *Sociometry Monograph,* No. 1, 1941. Soc. psych. "acad. imperialism."

Cuvillier, Armand,   *Où va la sociologie française? Avec une étude d'Émile Durkheim sur la sociologie formaliste* (Paris: Librairie Marcel Rivière et Cie, 1953).

Dahrendorf, Ralf,   *Class and Class Conflict in Industrial Society* (Stanford: Stanford Univ. Press, 1959). Exc. treat. worthy sust. att.

——————————,   "Out of Utopia: Toward a Reorientation of Sociological Analysis," *AJS,* vol. lxiv, 2 (Sept., 1958), pp. 115-127.

Davis, Kingsley,   *The Population of India and Pakistan* (Princeton: Princeton Univ. Press, 1952). Sociol. as well as demog. anal. Bib.

DeVisscher, Pierre,   "La psychologie sociale des psychologues et celle des sociologues, analyse comparée des principaux manuels de psychologie sociale," *Bulletin de l'Institute de Recherches Economiques et Sociales,* vol. xx, 7 (Nov., 1954), pp. 707-748.

Doby, J. T., *et al.,* eds.,   *An Introduction to Social Research* (Harrisburg: The Stackpole Co., 1954). Exc. art. and bib. on constr. typ., early as well as rec. II.

Dohrenwend, B. P.,   "Egoism, Altruism, Anomie, and Fatalism: A Conceptual Analysis of Durkheim's Types," *ASR,* vol. xxiv, 4 (Aug., 1959), pp. 466-473.

Doob, Leonard,   *Social Psychology: An Analysis of Human Behavior* (New York: Holt, 1952). Frust.-aggr. stressed, explic. and implic.

Duncan, O. D.,   "Rural Sociology Coming of Age," *Rural Sociology,* vol. xix, 1 (Mar., 1954), pp. 1-12.

Eisermann, Gottfried,   "La Situation de la Sociologie en Allemagne," *Cahiers Internationaux de Sociologie* (Jul.-Dec., 1958), pp. 100-115.

——————————, in collaboration with Paul Honigsheim, Georges Gurvitch, Frederick Lenz and Allan Beegle,   *Die Lehre von der Gesellschaft: ein Lehrbuch der Soziologie* (Stuttgart: Ferdinand Enke Verlag, 1958). Remark. surv. high qual., exc. fn. bibs.

Endleman, Robert,   "The New Anthropology and Its Ambitions," *Commentary,* vol. viii (Oct., 1949), pp. 284-291. Ex. "acad. imperialism."

Farnsworth, P. R.,   *The Social Psychology of Music* (New York: Dryden, 1958). Some bib. with psych. emph.

Ford, J. B.,

"Sociology in Russia?" *ASR,* vol. xxiv, 2 (Apr., 1959), p. 255.

Furfey, P. H.,

The Scope and Method of Sociology: A Metasociological Treatise (New York: Harper, 1953). Bibs.

Gassen, Kurt, and Landmann, Michael, eds.,

Buch des Dankes an Georg Simmel (Berlin, Germany: Duncker and Humblot, 1958). Many letters, etc., not prev. available.

Gerard, Alain,

"Entwicklungstendenzen der Soziologie in Frankreich," *Soziale Welt,* vol. viii, 1 (1957), pp. 13-22.

Gillin, J. P., ed.,

For a Science of Social Man (New York: Macmillan, 1954). Useful for contemp. interrel. of sociol., anthro., and social psych. in U. S. and elsewhere, also for disc. of early treat. of culture (Pufendorf), pp. 115-128. II.

Gittler, J. B.,

Review of Sociology: Analysis of a Decade (New York: Wiley, 1957). Bibs.

Gurvitch, Georges, and Moore, W. E., eds.,

Twentieth Century Sociology (New York: Philosophical Library, 1945). sel. bibs. for topics and countries; latter exp. useful.

——————————, *Traité de sociologie,* vol. i (Paris: Presses Universitaires de France, 1958). Some ref. to 19th cent. auth. II.

Gutman, Robert,

"Cooley: A Perspective," *ASR,* vol. xxiii, 3 (June, 1958), pp. 251-256.

Hager, D. J.,

"German Sociology under Hitler, 1933-1941," *SF,* vol. xxviii, 1 (Oct., 1949), pp. 6-19. Bibs. in fn.

Halbwachs, Maurice,

Memoire et societé, 3rd ser., vol. i (Paris: Presses Universitaires de France, 1949).

——————————, *The Psychology of Social Class,* introd. by Georges Friedmann, trans. by Claire Delavenay (Glencoe, Ill.: Free Press, 1959).

Hauser, P. M., and Duncan, O. D., eds.,

The Study of Population: An Inventory and Appraisal (Chicago: Univ. of Chicago Press, 1959).

Hawkins, N. G.,

Medical Sociology: Theory, Scope and Method (Springfield, Ill.: Charles C. Thomas, 1958).

Hearn, Lafcadio,

Japan: An Attempt at an Interpretation (New York: Macmillan, 1904). Tuttle PB. I and II.

Henderson, L. J.,

Pareto's General Sociology (Cambridge: Harvard Univ. Press, 1935). Enthus. advoc.

Hertzler, J. O.,

"Edward Alsworth Ross: Sociological Pioneer and Interpreter," *ASR,* vol. xvi, 5 (Oct., 1951), pp. 597-609.

Hiller, E. T.,

Social Relations and Structures (New York: Harper, 1947). Oft. ignored but exc. syst. treat.

Hobbs, A. H., — *The Claims of Sociology: A Critique of Textbooks: A Critique, also, of Teaching and Teaching Methods* (Harrisburg, Pa.: The Stackpole Co., 1951).

Homans, G. C., — *The Human Group* (New York: Harcourt, Brace, 1950). Neo-Simmelian, Neo-Paretian, etc., Stim.

——————————, and Curtis, C. P., *An Introduction to Pareto, His Sociology* (New York: Knopf, 1934). Bib.

Horkheimer, Max, ed., — *Survey of the Social Sciences in Western Germany* (Washington: Library of Congress, Reference Dept., European Affairs Division, 1952).

Hoselitz, B. F., — *A Reader's Guide to the Social Sciences* (Glencoe, Ill.: Free Press, 1959).

Hoult, T. F., — *The Sociology of Religion* (New York: Dryden, 1958). Not first-rate treat., but recent and with some bib.

Hughes, H. S., — "Gaetano Mosca and the Political Lessons of History," in Hughes, H. S., *et al.*, eds., *Teachers of History* (Ithaca, N. Y.: Cornell Univ. Press, 1954), pp. 146-167. I and II.

Humphrey, Richard, — *Georges Sorel—Prophet without Honor: A Study in Anti-Intellectualism* (Cambridge: Harvard Univ. Press, 1951).

Kolaja, Jiri, — "The Contemporary Polish Sociological Review," *ASR,* vol. xxv, 1 (Feb., 1950), pp. 105-107.

Krech, Davis, and Crutchfield, R. S., *Theory and Problems of Social Psychology* (New York: McGraw-Hill, 1948). Good chap. bibs.

Kroeber, A. L., *et al.*, — *Anthropology Today* (Chicago: Univ. of Chicago Press, 1953).

——————————, and Kluckhohn, Clyde (with the assistance of Untereiner, Wayne and Appendices by Meyer, A. G.), *Culture: A Critical Review of Concepts and Definitions* (Cambridge: Peabody Museum, 1952). Coverage not thor., as exemp. by om. of imp. surv. by Joseph Niedermann. No ment. Pufendorf, *et al.*

Langer, S. K., — *Philosophy in a New Key,* 3rd ed. (Cambridge: Harvard Univ. Press, 1957). Mentor PB. Highly imp.

Lehmann, W. C., — "Tendenzen und Trends in der gegenwärtigen deutschen Soziologie," *Sociologus,* vol. vi, 2 (1956), pp. 115-126.

Lerner, Daniel, ed., — *The Human Meaning of the Social Sciences* (New York: Meridian, 1959). Meridian PB.

——————————, and Lasswell, H. D., *The Policy Sciences: Recent Developments in Scope and Method* (Stanford: Stanford Univ. Press, 1951).

Lerner, Max,   *America As a Civilization: Life and Thought in the United States Today* (New York: Simon and Schuster, 1957). Journ., but informative and usef.

Lindzey, Gardner, ed.,   *Handbook of Social Psychology,* vol. i, *Theory and Method;* vol. ii, *Special Fields and Applications* (Cambridge: Addison-Wesley Publishing Co., Inc., 1954). Int. as ind. diverg. between soc. psych. of psych. deriv. and soc. psych. of sociol. deriv. II.

Lins, Mario,   "Aspectos de la Sociologia en el Brasil," *Revista Mexicana de Sociologia,* vol. xvi.

Linton, Ralph,   *The Study of Man: An Introduction* (New York: Appleton-Century-Crofts, 1936). Very influent.

Lipset, Seymour,   "Jewish Sociologists and Sociologists of the Jews," *Jewish Social Studies,* vol. xvii, 3 (July, 1955), pp. 177-178.

Loomis, C. P., and Beegle, J. A.,   *Rural Social Systems* (New York: Prentice-Hall, 1950). Exc. for rur. soc., etc.

Lovejoy, A. O.,   *Essays in the History of Ideas* (Baltimore: Johns Hopkins Press, 1948). Capricorn PB. High qual. II.

Lowenthal, Leo,   *Literature and the Image of Man: Sociological Studies of the European Drama and Novel* (Boston: Beacon, 1957).

Lundberg, G. A.,   "The Natural Science Trend in Sociology," *AJS,* vol. lxi, 3 (Nov., 1955), pp. 191-202. Interp. of "nat. sci." interesting.

MacIver, R. M.,   *Social Causation* (Boston: Ginn, 1942). Esp. relev. for U. S.

——————————, *The Web of Government* (New York: Macmillan, 1947). Mature, val. book. II.

Mack, R. W., Freeman, Linton, and Yellin, Seymour,   *Social Mobility: Thirty Years of Research and Theory: an Annotated Bibliography* (Syracuse: Syracuse Univ. Press, 1957).

MacRae, D. G.,   "Social Theory: Retrospect and Prospect," *British Journal of Sociology,* vol. viii, 2 (June, 1957), pp. 97-105.

Mairet, Philip,   *Pioneer of Sociology: The Life and Letters of Patrick Geddes* (London: Lund Humphries, 1957).

Maquet, J. J.,   *Sociologie de la connaissance* (Louvain: Institut de Recherches Économiques et Sociales, 1949). Also avail. in Eng.; see below.

——————————, *The Sociology of Knowledge: Its Structure and Its Relation to the Philosophy of Knowledge. A Critical Analysis of the Systems of Karl Mannheim and P. A. Sorokin* (Boston: Beacon, 1951). Exc. bib., gen. as well as spec.

Meadows, Paul,   "Models, Systems and Science," *ASR,* vol. xxii, 1 (Feb., 1957), pp. 3-9.

Meisel, J. H.,   *The Genesis of Georges Sorel: An Account of His Formative Period Followed by a Study of His Influence* (Ann Arbor: George Wahr, 1951).

——————————, *The Myth of the Ruling Class: Gaetano Mosca and the "Elite"* (Ann Arbor: The Univ. of Michigan Press, 1958).

Merton, R. K.,   *Social Theory and Social Structure,* rev. and enlarged ed. (Glencoe, Ill.: Free Press, 1957). Esp. usef. for soc. of kn.

Meyerhoff, Hans, ed.,   *The Philosophy of History in Our Time* (Garden City, N. Y.: Doubleday, 1959). Anchor PB. Useful compend.

Mills, C. Wright,   *The Sociological Imagination* (New York: Oxford Univ. Press, 1959). Useful for curr. trends, alth. crit. extr. sharp.

Moreno, J. L.,   "Contributions of Sociometry to Research Methodology in Sociology," *ASR,* vol. xii, 3 (June, 1947), pp. 287-292.

Morioka, K. K., and Steiner, "American Sociology in Japan," *AJS,* vol. lxiv, 6
J. F.,   (May, 1959), pp. 606-609. See also Steiner-Morioka item listed below.

Newman, K. J.,   "Georg Simmel and Totalitarian Integration," *AJS,* lvi, 4 (Jan., 1951), pp. 348-353.

Norman, Albert,   *Our German Policy: Propaganda and Culture* (New York: Vantage Press, 1951). Usef. for interrel. of prop. and cult. with spec. ref. to cult. intricacies.

Northrop, F. S. C., ed.,   *Ideological Differences and World Order: Studies in the Philosophy and Science of the World's Cultures* (New Haven: Yale Univ. Press, 1949). Occ. vague, but usef. I and II.

Oakeshott, M.,   *The Social and Political Doctrines of Contemporary Europe* (Cambridge, Eng.: Cambridge Univ. Press, 1939). Sel. bibs.

O'Dea, T. F.,   "The Sociology of Religion," *American Catholic Sociological Society Review,* vol. xv, 2 (June, 1954), pp. 73-103.

Odum, H. W.,   *American Sociology: the Story of Sociology in the United States through 1950* (New York: Longmans Green, 1951). Very ext. bib. "who's who," etc. Useful.

Olmsted, M. S.,   *The Small Group* (New York: Random House, 1959). Brief but search.

Orlansky, Harold,   "Infant Care and Personality," *Psychological Bulletin,* vol. xlvi, 1 (Jan., 1940), pp. 1-48. Ext. bib.

Owen, J. E., — "Sociology in Finland," *ASR,* vol. xix, 1 (Feb., 1954), pp. 62-68.

Park, R. E., and Burgess, E. W., — *Introduction to the Science of Sociology* (Chicago: Univ. Press, 1922). Still maj. treat. in textb. guise. Exc. bibs.

Parsons, Talcott, — *The Structure of Social Action: a Study in Social Theory with Special Reference to a Group of Recent European Writers* (Glencoe, Ill.: Free Press, 1937). Esp. good for Weber.

Pellizi, Camillo, — "Gli studi sociologici in Italia nel nostro secolo," *Quaderni di Sociologia,* 20 (1956), Spring, pp. 67-89; Summer, pp. 123-141.

Pergolessi, F., — "Notas sobre la 'Ciencia Politica' de Gaetano Mosca," *Revista de Estudios Politicos,* 89 (Sept.-Oct., 1956), pp. 53-113.

Persons, Stow, ed., — *Evolutionary Thought in America* (New Haven: Yale Univ. Press, 1950). Useful compend. II.

Pipping, Ida, — "Sociology in the Netherlands," *Transactions of the Westermarck Society,* 3 (1956), pp. 114-121.

Popper, K. R., — *The Poverty of Historicism* (Boston: Beacon, 1957).

————————, *The Logic of Scientific Discovery* (London: Hutchinson, 1959). Utmost contemp. relev. for curr. soc. method.

Ranulf, Svend, — *Methods of Sociology,* with an essay, "Remarks on the Epistemology of Sociology," (Kφbenhavn: Universitetsforlaget i Aarhus Ejnar Munksgaard, 1955).

Rapport, V. A., Cappannari, S. C., and Moss, L. W., — "Sociology in Italy," *ASR,* vol. xxii, 4 (Aug., 1957), pp. 441-447.

Redfield, Robert, — *The Primitive World and Its Transformations* (Ithaca, N. Y.: Cornell Univ. Press, 1953). Great Seal PB. I.

Rose, Edward, — "The English Record of a Natural Sociology," *ASR,* vol. xxv, 2 (April, 1960), pp. 193-208.

Rossi, P. H., ed., — Durkheim-Simmel Commemorative Issue, various authors, *AJS,* vol. lxiii, 6 (May, 1958).

Rostow, W. W., *et al.,* — *The Dynamics of Soviet Society* (New York: Norton, 1953). Mentor PB. Sociol. anal.

Roucek, J. S., ed., — *Contemporary Sociology* (New York: Philosophical Library, 1958). Num. auth.; many bibs.

Schoeck, Helmut, — *Soziologie: Geschichte ihrer Probleme* (Munich: Karl Alber, 1952).

Segerstedt, T. T., — "The Uppsala School of Sociology," *Acta Sociologica,* vol. i, 2 (1956), pp. 85-119.

Shock, N. W.,   *A Classified Bibliography of Gerontology and Geriatrics: Supplement One, 1949-1955* (Stanford: Stanford Univ. Press, 1957).

Silbermann, Alphons,   *Introduction à une sociologie de la musique,* trans. by Pierre Billard (Paris: Presses Universitaires de France, 1955).

——————, *Wovon lebt die Musik: die Prinzipien der Musikosoziologie* (Regensburg: Gustav Bosse Verlag, 1957).

Simmel, Georg,   *Brücke and Tür: Essays des Philosophen zur Geschichté Religion, Kunst, und Gesellschaft,* ed. and with an introd. by Michael Landmann and Margarete Susman. (Stuttgart: K. F. Koehler, 1957).

——————, Various writings, trans., ed., and with an introd. by Kurt H. Wolff as *The Sociology of Georg Simmel* (Glencoe, Ill.: Free Press, 1950). Exc. bib.

Smith, W. Robertson,   *Lectures on the Religion of the Semites* (Edinburgh: A. and C. Black, 1889). Meridian PB. Outmod. but instr. as source of some Freud. assump.

Sorokin, P. A.,   *Social Mobility* (New York: Harper's, 1927). Imp. II.

——————, *Contemporary Sociological Theories* (New York: Harper, 1928). Outst. work, altho. occ. hypercritic. II.

——————, *Society, Culture, and Personality* (New York: Harper, 1947). Oft. ignored but imp. work.

——————, *Social Philosophies of an Age of Crisis* (Boston: Beacon, 1950). Value-judg. but stim. II.

——————, *Fads and Foibles in Modern Sociology and Related Sciences* (Chicago: Henry Regnery, 1956).

Sorre, Maximilien,   *Recontres de la géographie et de la sociologie* (Paris: Librairie Marcel Rivière & Cie., 1957).

Soviet Sociological Society,   "Annoted Publications on Sociological Problems in the USSR," *Moscow, USSR; Bulletin No. 1* (in French) (Volhonka: Institute of Philosophy, 1959).

Spykman, N. J.,   *The Social Theory of Georg Simmel* (Chicago: Univ. of Chicago Press, 1925). Best brief treat. of Simmel; abounds in good short trans. and paragph.

Steiner, J. F., and Morioka, K. K.,   "Present Trends in Japanese Sociology," *SSR,* vol. xli, 2 (Nov.-Dec., 1956), pp. 87-93. See also Morioka-Steiner item listed above.

Stern, B. J., ed.,   "The Ward-Ross Correspondence, 1891-1912," *ASR*, various issues, beginning with vol. iii, 3 (June, 1938), pp. 362-401, and ending with vol. xiv, 1 (Feb., 1948), pp. 88-119.

Strodbeck, F. L.,   "The Case for the Study of Small Groups," *ASR*, vol. xix, 6 (Dec., 1954), pp. 651-657.

Sumner, W. G., and Keller, A. G.,   *The Science of Society* (New Haven: Yale Univ. Press, 1927). Good examp. 19th cent. compar. approach.

Susato, Shigeru,   "La Sociologie Japonaise," *Cahiers Internationaux de Sociologie*, 19 (Jul.-Dec., 1955), pp. 147-156.

Tambiah, S. J., and Ryan, Bruce,   "Secularization of Family Values in Ceylon," *ASR*, vol. xxii, 3 (June, 1957), pp. 292-299.

Thomas, W. I., and Znaniecki, Florian,   *The Polish Peasant in Europe and America* (New York: Dover Pubns., Inc., 1958.) Still maj. work.

Thomas, W. L., Jr.,   *Current Anthropology* (Chicago: Univ. of Chicago Press, 1956).

Thrupp, Sylvia,   "History and Sociology: New Opportunities for Co-operation," *AJS*, vol. lxiii, 1 (July, 1957), pp. 11-16. Adv. nomothet. work by hist.

Timasheff, Nicholas,   *Sociological Theory: Its Nature and Growth* (Garden City, N. Y.: Doubleday, 1955).

Topitsch, Ernst,   "The Sociology of Existentialism," *Partisan Review*, vol. xxi, 3 (May-June, 1954), pp. 289-304.

UNESCO: Special Authors, Editors, Consultants, Staff, *et al.* Some sample names: LeBie, Hill, Levi-Strauss, Nuttin, Zetterberg.   Numerous Trend Reports, Compendia, Bibliographies, etc., on Sociology and Related Topics, many but not all in Current Sociology, vol. i to present. Lists available from UNESCO, 1950 onward, Paris 16ᵉ, 19, avenue Kleber, and Paris 7ᵉ, 27, rue Saint-Guillame. Also procurable from UNESCO Publications Center, 801 Third Ave., N. Y. 17, N. Y.

Van Doorn, J. A. A.,   "The Development of Sociology and Social Research in the Netherlands," *Mens en Maatschappij*, vol. xxxi, 4 (July-Aug., 1956), pp. 189-264.

Wadia, A. R.,   "Sociology in Relation to Other Social Sciences and Its Development in India," *Agra University Journal of Research* (Letters), 3 (Dec., 1955), pp. 18-27.

White, L. D., ed.,   *The State of the Social Sciences: Papers Presented at the 25th Anniversary of the Social Science Research Building, the University of Chicago, November 10-12, 1955* (Chicago: Univ. of Chicago Press, 1956).

Whorf, B. L.,   *Language, Thought, and Reality,* ed. and with an introd. by John B. Carroll, foreword by Stuart Chase. (New York: The Technology Press of Mass. Institute of Technology jointly with John Wiley and Sons, Inc. London: Chapman and Hall, Ltd., 1956).

Wiese, Leopold von,   "Bosquejo de una Historia de la Sociología," *Revista Internacional de Sociología,* vol. xiv, 53 (Jan.-Mar., 1956), pp. 5-18.

——————————, *Soziologie: Geschichte und Hauptprobleme* (Berlin: Walter de Gruyter and Co., 1954). Most recent ed.; "Hist. Postsor." conv. summ. II.

Williamson, R. C.,   "Sociology in Latin America," *SSR,* vol. xl, 1 (Nov.-Dec., 1955), pp. 24-30.

Wish, Harvey,   *Society and Thought in Early America* (New York: Longmans Green, 1950). II.

——————————, *Society and Thought in Modern America* (New York: Longmans Green, 1952).

Wolff, K. H., trans. and ed., *The Sociology of Georg Simmel* (Glencoe, Ill.: Free Press, 1950). Good coll., surpassed only by Spykman, now out of print.

——————————, "Sociology and History: Theory and Practice," *AJS,* vol. lxv, 1 (July, 1959), pp. 32-38.

Wollheim, R.,   "Vilfredo Pareto: a Case in the Political Pathology of Our Age," *Occidente,* vol. x, 6 (Nov.-Dec., 1954), pp. 567-577.

Young, Donald,   "Sociology and the Practicing Professions," *ASR,* vol. xx, 6 (Dec., 1955), pp. 641-648.

Yzerman, T. J.,   "Venster op de verenigde staten," *Sociologische Gids,* vol. i, 2 (1953-54), pp. 34-36.

Ziegenfuss, Werner, ed., *Handbuch der Soziologie,* 2 vols. (Stuttgart: Ferdinand Enke, 1955). Ch. by Heinz Maus good surv. Exc. bibs. other chs.

Zimmerman, C. C.,   *Patterns of Social Change: a Survey of the Main Ideas of the Greatest Sociologists* (Washington, D. C.: Public Affairs Press [Annals of American Sociology], 1955). I and II.

Znaniecki, Florian,   "European and American Sociology after Two World Wars," *AJS,* vol. lvi, 3 (Nov., 1950), pp. 217-221.

——————————, *The Social Role of the Man of Knowledge* (New York: Columbia Univ. Press, 1940). Caref. delim. field.

——————————, *Cultural Sciences, Their Origin and Development* (Urbana: Univ. of Illinois Press, 1952). Among most imp. treat. of 20th cent.

NOTES

The reader should be made aware of the fact that, as mentioned elsewhere, *names and topics occurring in these Notes are not indexed.* Valuable bibliographic resources will be overlooked if those wishing to make use of such resources do not pore through the Notes. The same is true of the comments at the ends of all chapters; references appearing therein are not indexed.

Other bibliographical resources are provided in the Supplementary Bibliography for Volumes I, II, III. These bibliographies contain references to other bibliographies. As DeMorgan said:

> Great big fleas have little fleas upon their backs to bite 'em,
> And little fleas have lesser fleas, and so *ad infinitum.*
> And the great fleas themselves, in turn, have greater fleas to go on;
> While these again have greater still, and greater still, and so on.

Levity aside, now, it may be well to direct attention to the present state of the history of social thought and, for that matter, of sociological theories. Less and less reading in these fields, to say nothing of research, is today being done by professional sociologists, and this might be viewed as justifiable if it were not for the fact that picayune notions are perpetually being swallowed as the latest novelties by the gullible. Perhaps no one need worry about the gullible; the poor, in our present economy of abundance, may not be always with us (although the writer here coughs discreetly), but the gullible certainly will. Nevertheless, there are good grounds for worry; the gullible sometimes control the sinews of research, with the result that the veriest quacks and/or ignoramuses inflict on us their pompously formulated trivialities. "Paper is patient; anything can be impressed on it"—but should not *we* begin to be impatient with the fools, charlatans, semi-literates, and "scientistic" dogmatists?

Apart from this, it seems clear that those who have recently become interested in sociology of knowledge might gain a good deal for us all by dealing with the history of social thought and of sociological theories from that standpoint. If sociology is ever to transcend its ethnic, religious, class, national, chronological, technological, and other limitations, there must be relentless probing into basic assumptions with a view to discovering what can be relied on as suitable foundations for research leading to conclusions that hold despite those ethnic...to the *n*th limitations. Circularity of this kind is the only way out of circularity of that kind; only sociology of knowledge can lay bare our basic assumptions thoroughly enough for the logic of science to be effectively applied to them. And what better materials for sociology of knowledge investigation can be found than man's ideas about life with his fellows, from the years when the sages whose very names have long since been forgotten dispensed their lore to the days when the columnists who have themselves forgotten what they said last year peddle their wares?

I pause for a reply, and not only from the columnists. "My fires are banked, but still they burn..."

Notes and Suggestions for Further Reading

LIST OF ABBREVIATIONS

A   *The Annals of the American Academy of Political and Social Science*
AA   *American Anthropologist*
AAS   *Archiv für angewandte Soziologie*
ADS   *Archives de sociologie*
AESS   *Archives of the Economic and Social Sciences* (modern Greek)
AFLB   *Annales de la faculté des lettres de Bordeaux*
AGA   *Allgemein statistisches Archiv*
AGPS   *Archiv für Geschichte der Philosophie und Soziologie*
AHR   *American Historical Review*
AIIS   *Annales de l'institut international de sociologie*
AJS   *The American Journal of Sociology*
APM   *Archives of Philosophy and Methodology* (modern Greek)
ARGB   *Archiv für Rassen- und Gesellschaftsbiologie*
ARW   *Archiv für Rechts- und Wirtschaftsphilosophie*
AS   *L'Année sociologique*
ASGS   *Archiv für soziale Gesetzgebung und Statistik*
ASPS   *Archiv für systematische Philosophie und Soziologie*
ASR   *American Sociological Review*
ASSSR   *Archives of Social Science and Social Reform* (Roumanian)
ASUP   *Archiv für Sozialwissenschaft und Sozialpolitik*
BMCPEE   *Bulletin mensuel du centre polytechnicien d'études économiques*
BNJ   *Byzantinisch-neugriechische Jahrbücher*
BSFP   *Bulletin de la société française de philosophie*
BSSR   *Bulletin of the Society for Social Research*

BWC   Harry Elmer Barnes, *History of Western Civilization*
CAH   *Cambridge Ancient History*
CH   *Current History*
CM   *Communist Monthly*
ConR   *Contemporary Review*
CR   *Cambridge Review*
CSPSR   *The Chinese Social and Political Science Review*
E   *Economica*
EA   *Encyclopedia Americana*
EB   *Encyclopedia Britannica*
EI   *Enciclopedia Italiana*
ER   *Educational Review*
ES   *Encyclopedia Sinica*
ESS   *Encyclopedia of the Social Sciences*
GE   *Grande Encyclopédie*
GGE   *Great Greek Encyclopedia* (modern Greek)
HERE   Hastings's *Encyclopedia of Religion and Ethics*
HO   *Historical Outlook*
HWBS   *Handwörterbuch der Soziologie*
IJE   *International Journal of Ethics*
JA   *Journal asiatique*
JAFL   *Journal of American Folk-Lore*
JAS   *Journal of Applied Sociology*
JASA   *Journal of the American Statistical Association*
JASP   *Journal of Abnormal and Social Psychology*
JCCL   *Journal of Criminology and Criminal Law*
JCP   *Journal of Comparative Psychology*
JDP   *Journal de psychologie*
JFS   *Jahrbuch für Soziologie*
JNCBRAS   *Journal of the North China British Royal Asiatic Society*
JP   *Journal of Philosophy*

JPE *Journal of Political Economy*

JPNP *Journal de psychologie normale et pathologique*

JPPSM *Journal of Philosophy, Psychology, and Scientific Methods*

JRAI *Journal of the Royal Anthropological Institute*

JRAS *Journal of the Royal Asiatic Society*

JRD *Journal of Race Development*

JSM *Japanese Sociological Monthly*

JSP *Journal of Social Philosophy*

JSPS *Journal of Social Psychology*

KVS *Kölner Vierteljahrshefte für Soziologie*

M *The Monist*

MEM *Mensch en Maatschappij*

MF *Mercure de France*

MP *Modern Philology*

MSOS *Mitteilungen des Seminars für orientalische Sprachen*

PA *Pacific Affairs*

PASS *Publication or Proceedings of the American Sociological Society*

PR *Philosophical Review*

PSM *Popular Science Monthly*

PSQ *Political Science Quarterly*

RASI *Reports of the Archaeological Survey of India*

RAST *Royal Asiatic Society Transactions*

RB *Revue bleue*

RDI *Rivista d'Italia*

RDIS *Revue de l'institut de sociologie*

RDP *Revue de Paris*

REO *Revue de l'Europe orientale*

RHES *Revue d'histoire économique et sociale*

RIS *Revue internationale de sociologie*

RMM *Revue de metaphysique et de morale*

RP *Revue philosophique*

RPP *Revue de philosophie positive*

RS *Rivista di sociologia*

RSe *Revue socialiste*

RSH *Revue de synthèse historique*

RSICP *Report at Sixth International Congress of Philosophy*

RUBB *Revue universitaire belge: Bruxelles*

RUS *Rural Sociology*

S *Sociologus*

SBKAWPH *Sitzungsberichte der kaiserlichen Akademie der Wissenschaften, philosoph.-histor. Klasse*

SF *Social Forces*

SJ *Schmollers Jahrbuch*

SLR *Slavische Rundschau*

SM *Scientific Monthly*

SPSSQ *Southwestern Political and Social Science Quarterly*

SR *Sociological Review*

SRE *Social Research*

SS *Social Science*

SSR *Sociology and Social Research*

SSSQ *Southwestern Social Science Quarterly*

UTQ *University of Toronto Quarterly*

VFWP *Vierteljahrsschrift für wissenschaftliche Philosophie*

VWPS *Vierteljahrsschrift für wissenschaftliche Philosophie und Soziologie*

ZP *Zeitschrift für Politik*

ZSF *Zeitschrift für Sozialforschung*

ZVS *Zeitschrift für Völkerpsychologie und Soziologie*

Each author is responsible for the notes bearing on the chapters or sections marked with his symbol in the Table of Contents, with two exceptions: (1) all references in Barnes's notes to books and articles dated 1927 or later have been inserted by Becker; and (2) all the notes have been edited by Becker.

Books and articles likely to be of interest and value beyond their specific reference function are marked with an asterisk.

CHAPTER XXI

1. *Ernest Bouldin Harper, " Sociology in England," *SF*, xi, 3 (1933), pp. 335–42. Earlier papers on the same topic are: *Vivien M. Palmer, " Impressions of Sociology in Great Britain," *AJS*, xxxii (1927), pp. 756–61; Harry Elmer Barnes, " The Fate of Sociology in England," *PASS*, xii (1927), pp. 26–46. Cf. the discerning article by *Gladys Bryson, " Early English Positivists and the Religion of Humanity," *ASR*, i (1936), pp. 343–62.

2. Cf. *H. Westergaard, *Contributions to the History of Statistics* (1932); J. Koren, *A History of Statistics* (1918); *F. H. Hankins, " Individual Differences: the Galton-Pearson Approach," *SF*, iii, 2 (Dec., 1925); A. Meitzen, *History, Theory, and Technique of Statistics* (trans. by R. P. Falkner, 1891); Helen M. Walker, *Studies in the History of Statistical Method* (1929); Raymond Pearl, " Karl Pearson, 1857–1936," *JASA*, xxxi, 196 (Dec., 1936), pp. 653–64.

3. For the whole field of anthropogeography and related topics, see *Franklin Thomas, *The Environmental Basis of Society* (1925); use index for all the writers mentioned. See also Harry Elmer Barnes, *The New History and the Social Studies* (1925), chap. ii. An excellent recent study having some relation to human geography is R. R. Marett's *Jersey: Suggestions toward a Civic and Regional Survey* (1932).

4. *F. H. Hankins, *The Racial Basis of Civilization* (1925); A. A. Tenney, *Social Democracy and Population* (1916); W. S. Thompson, *Population Problems* (1930). Sweeping attacks on the British eugenists have come from the pen of G. Spiller, particularly his *The Origin and Nature of Man* (1931).

5. Cf. the summaries of English psycho-sociology by *Harry Elmer Barnes, *AJS*, xxvii, 3 (Nov., 1921) through xxviii, 3 (Nov., 1922).

6. A. C. Haddon, *A History of Anthropology*; *Alexander Goldenweiser, " Cultural Anthropology " in H. E. Barnes, ed., *History and Prospects of the Social Sciences* (1925); Clark Wissler, " Anthropology " in E. C. Hayes, ed., *Recent Developments in the Social Sciences* (1928).

7. E. Fueter, *L'Histoire de l'historiographie moderne*; G. P. Gooch, *History and Historians in the Nineteenth Century*; W. Riley, *From Myth to Reason*.

8. There is as yet no adequate survey of British institutional and social economics. A few more or less fragmentary American appreciations have been written by W. C. Mitchell, Walton H. Hamilton, *et al.*

9. Cf. Ernest Barker, *Political Thought in England from Spencer to the Present Day*; L. Rockow, *Contemporary Political Thought in England*; *H. J. Laski, *A Grammar of Politics*; C. E. Merriam and H. E. Barnes, eds., *Political Theories in Recent Times*, chap. i; *R. M. MacIver, *The Modern State*.

10. Cf. H. E. Barnes, ed., *The History and Prospects of the Social Sciences*, chap. ix.

To Professor W. Y. Elliott of Harvard University we owe the following list of contemporary British writers whom he regards as having sociological relevance: John Strachey, H. S. Brailsford, C. DeLisle Burns, Keith Feiling, Clapham, Hayek, D. H. Robertson, Edgworth, P. Sargant Florence, Marriott, H. W. C. Davis, Kellett, Routh, J. A. F. C. Fuller, H. A. Needham, Lawrence Hyde, Wyndham Lewis, Rockhouse, Esmé Wingfield Stratford, Leonard Woolf, David Mitrany, and several others. Professor Elliott also points out that in such publications as the *Proceedings of the Aristotelian Society* one finds, where perhaps they would be least suspected, worth-while sociological contributions, although of course not under that name.

In fairness to Professor Elliott we should mention the fact that he regards our presentation of British sociology as somewhat too negative in tone.

11. *For a brief general survey, see Hugh Carter, *The Social Theory of L. T. Hobhouse* (1927).

12. J. A. Hobson and Morris Ginsberg, *L. T. Hobhouse: His Life and Works* (1931), pp. 123–77, and Ginsberg, " Obituary: Prof. L. T. Hobhouse," *Nature*, civ (July 27, 1929), pp. 153–54, quoted by Harper, *op. cit.*, p. 337.

13. *L. T. Hobhouse, *Social Evolution and Political Theory* (1922), p. 118.

14. *Ibid.*, p. 11.   **15.** *Ibid.*, p. 8.   **16.** *Ibid.*, p. 39.

17. Hobhouse, *Social Development* (1924), p. 243.   **18.** *Ibid.*, p. 87.

19. Hobhouse, *The Elements of Social Justice* (1916), p. 16.

20. Hobhouse, *Social Evolution and Political Theory* (1922), p. 156.

21. *Ibid.*, p. 163.   **22.** Harper, *op. cit.*, p. 337.   **23.** *Ibid.*, p. 338.

24. S. K. Ratcliffe, " Patrick Geddes," *The Nation*, cxxxiv, 3487 (May 4, 1932), pp. 513–14.

Branford's devotion to the LePlay tradition can be clearly seen in his article on " Sociology," supplementary volume, *EB*, 13th ed., reprinted in *SR* as " A Survey of Recent and Contemporary Sociology " (1926). Branford is also responsible for the " Sociology " in the 14th ed. of *EB*.

25. Morris Ginsberg, " The Scope of Sociology," *E*, vii (June, 1927), pp. 135–49, and unpublished lectures quoted in Harper, *op. cit.*, p. 338.

26. Harper, *op. cit.*, p. 339. Ginsberg is quite familiar with recent German sociology. See his *" Recent Tendencies in Sociology," *E*, Feb., 1933, pp. 21–39.

CHAPTER XXII

1. For the beginner, the most systematic and useful treatment of the whole field of recent French sociology is to be found in *Daniel Essertier's *La Sociologie* (1930). It treats individually most of the main French sociologists of this century, including excerpts from their writings, brief summaries and criticisms, and excellent bibliographical and biographical material. This book is very well supplemented by *Célestin Bouglé's recent *Bilan de la sociologie française contemporaine* (1935), which is particularly good on the post-war period and on the interrelations between sociology and the other social sciences. An intensive discussion of several members of the sociologistic school is to be found in Georges Davy's *Sociologues d'hier et d'aujourd'hui* (1931). Both Davy's and Bouglé's books are written from a Durkheimian point of view, and contrast sharply with Essertier's book, which adopts a moderately anti-Durkheimian view. The recent study of I. Benrubi, *Les Sources et les courants de la philosophie contemporaine en France*, contains brief summaries of the work of several leading French sociologists. *Pitirim Sorokin's *Contemporary Sociological Theories* contains summaries and criticisms of many of the men to be treated in this chapter, in particular of LePlay, DeRoberty, Durkheim, Tarde, Coste, Dumont, Bouglé, and Lapouge.

For brief sketches, see: Celestin Bouglé, " The Present Tendency of the Social Sciences in France," *The New Social Science* (L. D. White, ed., 1930); ———, " Philosophy in France and the Sociological Movement," *RSICP* (1926); ———, " La Sociologie française contemporaine," *ASSSR*, v, 1/2 (1924); Georges Davy, " Sociology," *M*, xxxvi, 3 (1926); G.-L. Duprat, " La Psycho-sociologie en France," *AGPS*, xxx (1925), pp. 133–60; ———, " L'Orientation actuelle de la sociologie en France," *RIS*, xxxiv, 11/12 (Nov.–Dec., 1926); Mabel Elliott and Francis Merrill, *Social Disorganization* (1934), appendix on social disorganization in contemporary French sociology; Paul Fauconnet, " The Durkheim School in

France," *SR*, xix (1927), pp. 15–20; André Joussain, " Les deux tendances de la sociologie française," *RIS*, xxxix (1931), pp. 266–70; *René König, " Die neuesten Strömungen in der gegenwärtigen französischen Soziologie," in *ZVS*, vii (1931), pp. 485–505; A. Koyré, " La Sociologie française contemporaine," *ZSF*, i, 4 (1932); Raymond Lenoir, " Sur la sociologie française contemporaine," in *RSH*, xlviii, n.s. xxii; Henri Lévy-Bruhl, " The Social Sciences as Disciplines: France," *ESS*, i (1930), pp. 248–58; *Robert Marjolin, " French Sociology: Comte and Durkheim," *AJS*, xlii, 5 (Mar., 1937), pp. 693–704; Robert K. Merton, " Recent French Sociology," *SF*, xii, p. 537; Daniel Parodi, " La Philosophie française de 1918 à 1925," *RP*, 1925; ———, *La Philosophie contemporaine*, chap. v; Gaston Richard, " Nouvelles tendances sociologiques en France et en Allemagne," in *RIS*, xxxvi (1928), pp. 647–49.

Relevant articles in the *ESS* should also be consulted. For bibliographical material, see the *Guide de l'étudiant en sociologie* (1921), by Celestin Bouglé and Marcel `Déat, the *Manuel bibliographique des sciences sociales et économiques* (1920), by René Maunier, and the above-mentioned *La Sociologie* of Daniel Essertier, as well as his *Psychologie et sociologie* (1927).

2. A sympathetic study of the LePlay school is available in English in Sorokin's *Contemporary Sociological Theories*, chap. ii, pp. 63–98. The most important part of LePlay's main work, *Les Ouvriers européens*, has been translated and is included in *Family and Society, by Carle C. Zimmerman and Merle Frampton. In French, the best source of information on LePlay is to be found in the studies of Demolins, Bouchié de Belle, and Champault in *La Science sociale*. See also the important work of Paul Bureau, *Introduction à la méthode sociologique* (1923).

3. LePlay, *Les Ouvriers européens*, 2nd ed., i, pp. 224–28. Quoted by Sorokin, *op. cit.*, p. 67.

4. Paul Bureau, *op. cit.*, pp. 185–88. **5.** Zimmerman and Frampton, *op. cit.*

6. Lucien Febvre, *La Terre et l'évolution humaine* (1922), pp. 447–48. Available in English translation as *A Geographical Introduction to History.

7. S. J. Holmes, *The Trend of the Race* (1921).

8. DeRoberty's chief sociological works are: *La Sociologie* (Russian edition 1879, French edition 1881); *Auguste Comte et Herbert Spencer* (1894); *Le Psychisme social* (1897); *Les Fondements de l'éthique* (1898); *Constitution de l'éthique* (1900); *Nouveau programme de sociologie* (1904); *Sociologie de l'action* (1908); *Sociologie et philosophie* (1914).

About DeRoberty see René Verrier's *Roberty: Le Positivisme russe et la fondation de la sociologie* (1934). See also the study by Sorokin, *op. cit.*, pp. 438–63; and the treatment of DeRoberty in *Julius Hecker's *Russian Sociology* (1934).

Note the following articles about DeRoberty: G. DeGreef, *Eugène de Roberty*, *RUBB* (1904); ———, " L'Œuvre de M. de Roberty," *MF* (1904); Hervé Blondel, " M. de Roberty et la sociologie," *RIS* (1904).

9. DeRoberty, three sociological " notes " in *RPP*.

10. Tarde, discussion at 5th Congress of *Institut International de Sociologie*, on June 6, 1903. See *AIIS*, 1904.

11. DeRoberty, " L'Évolution de la philosophie," *RP*, Mar., 1890. **12.** *Ibid.*

13. ———, *La Philosophie du siècle*, chap. xviii (1891).

14. ———, *La Sociologie*, pp. 7 ff. (1881).

15. Espinas, *Dés Sociétés animales*, 2nd ed. **16.** *Ibid.*, pp. 528 ff.

17. ———, *Origines de la technologie*, *passim*. **18.** *Ibid.*, p. 34.

19. Izoulet, *La Cité moderne*, 6th ed., pp. 163 ff. **20.** *Ibid.*

21. In addition to the works mentioned in the text, the following monographs, articles, and posthumous books of Durkheim must be indicated:

(1) Monographs in *L'Année sociologique:* " La Prohibition de l'inceste et ses origines " (vol. i, 1897) ; " Définition des phénomènes religieux " (vol. ii) ; " Deux lois de l'évolution pénale " (vol. iv) ; " Sur le totémisme " (vol. v) ; " De quelques formes primitives de classification " (vol. vi, in collaboration with Mauss) ; " Sur l'organisation matrimoniale des sociétés australiennes " (vol. viii).

(2) Articles: " Représentations individuelles et représentations collectives," *RMM* (1898) ; " Détermination du fait moral," *BSFP* (1906) ; " Jugements de valeur et jugements de réalité " (International Congress of Philosophy at Bologna, 1911, *RMM*, 1911.) These three studies have been compiled in *Sociologie et philosophie.*

" Introduction à la sociologie de la famille," *AFLB* (1888) ; " La Notion du matérialisme économique," *RP* (1898) ; " La Sociologie en France," *RB* (1900) ; " Sociologie et sciences sociales," *RP* (1903, in collaboration with P. Fauconnet) ; " Conférences sur la famille," *RP* (1920), etc. ; " Introduction à la morale," *RP* (1919).

(3) Posthumous books compiled by Marcel Mauss: *Éducation et sociologie* (1922) ; *Sociologie et philosophie* (1924) ; *L'Éducation morale* (1925). Professor Mauss is now preparing an edition of Durkheim's courses on the family, and on the " science of morals." Durkheim's theories of the family have been treated by Davy in *Sociologues d'hier et d'aujourd'hui* (1931). Durkheim's sociology of religion has been summed up by Halbwachs in *Les Origines du sentiment religieux en France d'après Durkheim.* There is a very capable English translation of Durkheim's *Les Formes élémentaires de la vie religieuse,* by Swain, and a translation of *De la division du travail social,* by Simpson.

A short sketch of Durkheim's work is to be found in Sorokin's *Contemporary Sociological Theories,* pp. 463–80. The best known English monograph on Durkheim is C. E. Gehlke's *Émile Durkheim's Contributions to Sociological Theory.* In a recent book, **Structure of Social Action* (1937), Talcott Parsons has given a profound and intensive analysis of Durkheim to which our section on Durkheim is heavily indebted. We must note also the recent analysis by *George Mariça: *Émile Durkheim: Soziologie und Soziologismus* (1932). The best short study in French is that of *Halbwachs, " La Doctrine d'Émile Durkheim," *RP* (1918). Cf. also G. Davy's *Durkheim, Introduction et morceaux choisis* (1911) ; his " Durkheim: l'homme et l'œuvre," *RMM* (1919–20) ; and Robert Marjolin, " French Sociology: Comte and Durkheim," *AJS,* xlii, 5 (Mar., 1937), pp. 693–704.

For French criticisms of Durkheim, see the relevant sections of this chapter, and the works of the men there referred to. The English criticism has in general been much less able. Cf., however, Alexander Goldenweiser's critique in *JPPSM* (Mar., 1917), as well as the section on Durkheim's theories in chap. xvi of his *Early Civilization.* Cf. also the section on Durkheim in Dennes's *The Methods and Presuppositions of Group Psychology* (University of Calif. Pub. in Philos. vol. vi, no. 1).

An excellent bibliography of the writings of the Durkheim school is that by E. Conze, " Zur Bibliographie der Durkheim-Schule," *KVS,* vi, 3 (1927), pp. 278–83.

22. Notably Daniel Essertier and Roger Lacombe.

23. This side of Durkheim's thought has been excellently worked out by Talcott Parsons, *ibid.*

24. Compare, however, a contrary estimate by Parsons, *ibid.*

25. G. Belot, *La Morale positive* (1907).

26. Notably by Paul Barth, in *Die Philosophie der Geschichte als Soziologie*, 3rd and 4th eds. (1922). Also see section on Richard.

27. See, e.g., Carr-Saunder's *The Population Problem* (1922).

28. Durkheim's social pathology and therapy is mainly to be found in his **Règles de la méthode sociologique* (1895) and in an introduction written for the second edition of the *De la division du travail social* in 1902. There is also a good deal of material bearing on the issues in *Le Suicide* and *L'Éducation morale.*

29. Durkheim, *Le Socialisme* (1928; Mauss ed.).

30. ——, *Le Suicide* (1897). Cf. Hanna Meuter's interesting group review, "Neue Literatur zum Problem der Selbstentleibung," *KVS*, xii, 2 (1933), pp. 200–202.

31. Charles Blondel has formulated some very serious criticisms of Durkheim's definition of suicide in **Le Suicide*, pp. 14–26.

32. **Halbwachs, Les Causes du suicide* (1930).

33. Durkheim, *Le Suicide*, 2nd ed. (1912), p. 173.

34. Halbwachs has submitted recent evidence which entirely controverts this assertion; see *ibid.*, chap. xii.

35. On this point, see **G. Belot, "Un Théorie nouvelle de la religion," *RP* (1913), pp. 329 ff. This article is an able criticism of Durkheim's whole sociology of religion.

36. Durkheim, *Elementary Forms of the Religious Life* (Swain's translation), p. 215.

37. See Durkheim's address to the International Congress of Philosophy at Bologna in 1911, reprinted in *Sociologie et philosophie.*

38. Durkheim, *Elementary Forms of the Religious Life*, p. 440.

39. See note 21 above.

40. Georges Davy, *La Foi jurée, étude sociologique du problème du contrat, la formation du lien contractuel* (1922), p. 83.

41. Mauss, "Essai sur les variations saisonnières des sociétés eskimos: étude de morphologie sociale" (written in collaboration with H. Beuchat), *AS*, vol. ix. For a discussion of the article mentioned in the text, see Howard Becker, review of *L'Année sociologique*, nouvelle série, tome ii, in *AJS*, xxxiv, 3 (Nov., 1928), pp. 538–41.

42. In addition to the one just mentioned, we may include: "Essai sur la nature et la fonction du sacrifice," *AS*, vol. ii, in collaboration with H. Hubert; "De quelques formes primitives de classification," *AS*, vol. ii (1903), in collaboration with Durkheim; "Esquisse d'une théorie générale de la magie," *AS*, vol. iii (1904), in collaboration with H. Hubert; "Essai sur le don, forme archaïque de l'échange," *AS*, n.s., vol. i, (1923–24). We must also note Mauss's article, written in collaboration with Paul Fauconnet, in the *GE*, entitled **La Sociologie*, which gives an excellent account of the main point of view of the Durkheim school. See also two interesting articles in the *JDP:* "L'Expression obligatoire des sentiments" (1921), and "Les Rapports réals et pratiques de la psychologie et de la sociologie" (1924).

43. Mauss, "Essai sur les variations saisonnières des sociétés eskimos," *AS*, vol. ix, p. 124.

44. Durkheim, "Deux lois de l'évolution pénale," *AS*, vol. iv.

45. Halbwachs, *Les Cadres sociaux de la mémoire* (1925), pp. 51 ff.

46. *Ibid.*, pp. 194 ff.

47. **Les Sciences sociales en Allemagne* (1896), pp. 147 ff.

48. Célestin Bouglé, *La Sociologie biologique et le régime des castes;* and

Le Procès de la sociologie biologique. Note also Bouglé's article in *RDP*, " Un Sociologue individualiste: G. Tarde " (1905).

49. This is the only book of Bouglé's available in English: **The Evolution of Values*, translated by Helen Stalker Sellars, with an introduction by Roy Wood Sellars (1926)*.*
In addition to the works mentioned in the text, Bouglé has written a useful bibliography: *Guide à l'étudiant en sociologie*, in collaboration with Déat (1921); a compendium, *Éléments de sociologie*, in collaboration with J. Raffault (1926); and a brief and popular presentation of his own central position, *Qu'est-ce que la sociologie?* (1907, 3rd ed., 1935). He has also written on Proudhon and Saint-Simon, and has helped to edit their works.

50. **Charles Blondel, *La Conscience morbide, essai de psychopathologie générale* (1913). **51.** *Traité* of George Dumas, II, *Les Volitions*.

52. See note 31. Also worthy of attention are Blondel's *Introduction à la psychologie collective* (1928), and his *La Psychographie de Marcel Proust* (1932).

53. On the subject of primitive mentality Lévy-Bruhl has written five books: *Les Fonctions mentales dans les sociétés primitives* (1923), *La mentalité primitive* (1925), *L'Âme primitive* (1927), *Le Surnaturel et la nature dans la mentalité primitive* (1931), and *La Mythologie primitive* (1935). The first three of these are available in excellent English translations by Lilian A. Clare. Lévy-Bruhl's science of morals is developed in *La Morale et la science des mœurs* (1900). Note also his *History of Modern Philosophy in France*, his *La Philosophie d'Auguste Comte* (1900), and his edition of the correspondence between Mill and Comte. Georges Davy is preparing a study of Lévy-Bruhl's sociology.

54. Lévy-Bruhl, *La Morale et la science des mœurs*, 10th ed., p. 14.

55. *Ibid.*, pp. 99–100.

56. See also Bayet's *La Moral scientifique* (1905), and *La Science des faits moraux* (1925).

57. Lévy-Bruhl, *How Natives Think*, p. 38 (translation of *Les Fonctions mentales . . .*). **58.** *Ibid.*, pp. 76, 77. **59.** See note 53.

60. Cf. **Durkheim and Mauss, " De quelques formes primitives de classification," *AS*, vi. **61.** Mauss, *BSFP*, 1923.

62. Brunschvicg, *Les Bases psychologiques de la vie morale* (1928), p. 83.

63. Tarde is the author of the following works: *La Criminalité comparée* (1886), *Les Lois de l'imitation* (1890), *La Philosophie pénale* (1890), *Études pénales et sociales* (1892), *Les Transformations du droit* (1893), *La Logique sociale* (1893), *Essais et mélanges sociologiques* (1895), *L'Opposition universelle* (1897), *Les Lois sociales* (1898), **Études de psychologie sociale* (1898), **Les Transformations du pouvoir* (1899), *L'Opinion et la foule* (1901), *Psychologie économique* (1902), *Fragment d'histoire future* (1905). His most important articles have been compiled in two books: *Études de psychologie sociale*, and *Essais et mélanges sociologiques*.

The most thorough exposition of Tarde's sociological system is to be found in Michael M. Davis's monograph, *Gabriel Tarde* (1906), which was incorporated in his later work, **Psychological Interpretations of Society* (1909). Other briefer discussions are to be found in Sorokin's *Contemporary Sociological Theories*, pp. 636–40; G. Tosti's article, " The Sociological Theories of Gabriel Tarde," *PSQ* (1897), pp. 490–511; Giddings's Introduction to E. C. Parsons's translation of **Tarde's *Laws of Imitation*; Bristol's *Social Adaptation*, pp. 185–92; Gault's Introduction and Lindsey's editorial preface to Howell's translation of Tarde's *Penal Philosophy*; and Small's review of Tarde's *Social Laws*, *AJS*, vol. iv, pp. 395–400. For an ingenious American adaptation of Tarde's sociological theories, see **Ross's *Social Psychology*, and for the most extended application of similar theories to psychology by an American writer, see Baldwin's *Social and Ethical Interpretations in Mental Development.*

64. For a brief survey of the salient points connected with Tarde's career, see Giddings's Introduction, cited above. The historic antecedents of Tarde's theories and the stages in the development of his system have been indicated by Davis in his *Psychological Interpretations of Society*, chaps. ii, vii.

65. Wiese-Becker, *Systematic Sociology* (1932), p. 235. See there also the criticism of Tarde's theories, pp. 233–37.

66. *Tarde, *Laws of Imitation*, translated by Elsie Clews Parsons (1903), p. 141. 67. Davis, *Psychological Interpretations of Society*, pp. 97–98.

68. Tarde, *Social Laws*, pp. 135–37.

69. Durkheim, *Le Suicide*, new ed., pp. 107 ff.

70. *Ibid.*, p. 113. 71. *Ibid.*, p. 115.

72. Tarde, *Études de psychologie sociale*, p. 64.

73. *Ibid.*, p. 65. 74. *Ibid.*, p. 46. 75. *Ibid.*, p. 73.

76. See Maunier's *Manuel bibliographique des sciences sociales et économiques* (1920).

77. Maunier, *L'Économie politique et sociologie* (1910), p. 4. 78. *Ibid.*, p. 6.

79. ——, *Introduction à la sociologie* (1929), p. 15. 80. *Ibid.*, p. 19.

81. ——, *La Construction de la maison en Kabylie* (1926); " Recherches sur les échanges rituels en Afrique du nord," *AS*, n.s., II, (1927).

82. Maunier, *AJS*, xv, pp. 536–48. This is a translation of the first part of *L'Origine et la fonction économique des villes.*

83. Richard, *La Sociologie générale et les lois sociologiques* (1912), p. 50.

84. *Richard, " La Pathologie sociale d'Émile Durkheim," *RIS*, xxxvi, pp. 648 ff. 85. Essertier, *Psychologie et sociologie* (1927), p. 23.

86. Lacombe, *La Méthode sociologique de Durkheim: étude critique* (1926).

87. See G. Belot, " L'Utilitarisme et ses nouveaux critiques," *RMM*, 1894, pp. 408 ff.; and " Une Théorie nouvelle de la religion," in *RP*, 1913, pp. 329 ff. Other articles in the *RP*: vol. 49, pp. 288 ff.; vol. 52, pp. 688 ff.; vol. 72, pp. 434 ff. Also *Études de morale positive* (1907), *passim.*

88. Léon Brunschvicg, *L'Expérience humaine et la causalité physique* (1922), chaps. ix and x: *Le Progrès de la conscience dans la philosophie occidentale* (1927), pp. 573 ff.

89. *Traité* of G. Dumas, vol. I, pp. 39–40. 90. *RP*, 1904, i.

91. The best source of information concerning the interrelations of the social sciences in France is the extremely lucid and thoughtful little study by *Celestin Bouglé, *Bilan de la sociologie française contemporaine* (1935). For a survey of the academic status of French sociology, see E. E. Eubank, " Sociological Instruction in France," *AJS*, xlii, 5 (Mar., 1937), pp. 705–708.

92. Léon Duguit, *Traité de droit constitutionel* (1911); *Le Droit social, le droit individuel, et la transformation de l'État* (1911); *Les Transformations générales du droit privé* (1913); *Les Transformations du droit public* (1913).

93. Hauriou, *Les Idées de M. Duguit.* We must also mention among the jurists Paul Huvelin, whose memoir, " Magie et droit individuel," *AS*, vol. x (1907), has become a classic; as well as Georges Gurvitch, whose recent *Idée de droit social* (1931) is an important contribution to juristic sociology.

94. Of M. Simiand, see *La Formation et les fluctuations des prix du charbon en France pendant vingt-cinq ans 1887–1912* (1925), *Salaire des ouvriers des mines de charbon en France* (1907), *La Méthode positive en science économique* (1912), and *La Salaire* (1932). Compare the article by Halbwachs, " Le Point de vue sociologique en science économique," *BMCPEE*, 35 (Feb., 1937), pp. 23–30.

95. Antoine Meillet, " Comment les mots changent de sens," *AS*, vol. ix.

96. The definitive study of DeGreef's social theory is that by *Dorothy Wolff Douglas, *Guillaume DeGreef: the Social Theory of an Early Syndicalist* (1925). Much of our discussion is drawn from this and from a summary later to be published.

97. Toward the end of his life DeGreef remarked in his autobiography (as yet unpublished) that his two little brochures, *L'Ouvrière dentellière* (The Women Lace-Makers) and *Le Rachat des Carbonnages* (The Re-Purchase of the Coal Mines) " have given me a satisfaction as great as — in fact greater than — the most substantial of my theoretical works."

98. The best discussion of the theories of Quetelet available in English is provided by *F. H. Hankins, *Adolphe Quetelet as Statistician* (1908). See also his " Quetelet's Average Man in Modern Scientific Research," *RDIS*, xv, 3 (1935). **99.** *Ibid.*, pp. 62–82.

100. Douglas does not give the source of this quotation, but in Hankins, *op. cit.*, some references are made which would lead one to conclude that it may be found in *Du Système social*, p. 259, or in *Sur l'homme*, Bk. IV, chap. i, sec. 3. Unfortunately the original is not now available for verification.

101. DeGreef, *Structure générale des sociétés*, ii, p. 126.

102. *Ibid.*, pp. 10–11. **103.** DeGreef, *L'Ouvrière dentellière*, chap. xiv.

104. Leopold von Wiese has made this criticism of Waxweiler's work. See Wiese-Becker, *Systematic Sociology* (1932), p. 81.

105. *Ibid.*, p. 80. **106.** *Ibid.*, pp. 178–79.

107. *Ibid.*, p. 80. Here the term used is " sociability," but examination shows that elsewhere in the same treatise it is translated as " associativeness," and the systematic implications of the latter make it more desirable.

108. *Ibid.*, p. 81. **109.** *Ibid.* **110.** *Ibid.*, p. 129. See also Table 2.

111. Anonymous, " Le XXVe Anniversaire de l'inauguration de L'Institut de Sociologie Solvay," *RDIS*, vii, 4 (Oct.–Dec., 1927), pp. 21–25.

112. *Ibid.*, pp. 14–15.

113. Raphaël Petrucci, *Non-comparabilité des sociétés animales*; M. Wodon, *Notes critiques sur quelques erreurs de méthode dans l'étude de l'homme primitif*; D. Houzé, *L'Aryen et de l'anthroposociologie*; M. Varendonck, *Les Sociétés d'enfants*.

114. For confirmation of this optimistic statement, consult Dupreél's article on Belgian sociology in *Le Livre d'Or du Centenaire de l'Independence Nationale* (1930), pp. 111–14.

CHAPTER XXIII

1. This is the division adopted by *Leopold von Wiese in his *System der Allgemeinen Soziologie* (1932). The skeleton of this division on German and Austrian sociology owes much to his presentation in chap. i of the book cited. Primary sources, however, have been extensively used. Useful secondary presentations are to be found in the following books and articles:

Abel, Theodore, *Systematic Sociology in Germany* (1929). Good for Simmel, Vierkandt, Wiese, Weber.
Aron, M., *La Sociologie allemande contemporaine* (1936).
Barth, Paul, *Die Philosophie der Geschichte als Soziologie*, 3rd and 4th eds. (1922).
Baxa, Jacob, *Gesellschaft und Staat im Spiegel deutscher Romantik* (1924).
Bouglé, C., *Les Sciences sociales en Allemagne* (1896).

Brinkmann, " The Present Situation of German Sociology," *PASS*, xxi (1926), pp. 47–56.

Eisler, Rudolf, article " Soziologie " in his one-volume *Handwörterbuch der Philosophie*, 2nd ed., by Richard Müller-Freienfels (1922).

Ellwood, C. A., " Sociology in Europe," *SSR*, xiii, 3 (Jan.–Feb., 1929), pp. 203–10.

Freyer, Hans, *Soziologie als Wirklichkeitswissenschaft* (1930). Contains analyses of Dilthey, Simmel, Wiese, Spann, Oppenheimer, Alfred Weber, Max Weber, Tönnies, Vierkandt.

Geck, L. H. Ad., " Social Psychology in Germany," Parts I and II, *SSR*, xiii, 6 and xiv, 2 (1929).

——, *Sozialpsychologie in Deutschland* (1929).

Ginsberg, Morris, " Recent Tendencies in Sociology," *E*, Feb., 1933, pp. 21–39.

Heinrich, Walter, *Soziologie und Geschichtsphilosophie der Gegenwart* (1932). Extensive bibliography.

Honigsheim, Paul, " Adolf Bastian und die Entwicklung der ethnologischen Soziologie," *KVS*, vi, 1 (1926), pp. 61–76.

Jacobs, P. P., *German Sociology* (1915).

*Karpf, Fay B., *American Social Psychology* (1932), pp. 7–88.

——, " The Development of Social Psychology," *PASS*, xxi (1926), pp. 71–81.

Kaufmann, Erich, *Geschichtsphilosophie der Gegenwart* (1931). Extensive bibliography.

Larenz, Karl, *Rechts- und Staatsphilosophie der Gegenwart* (1930). Good bibliography.

Lasker, Bruno, " Systematic Sociology in Germany," *SSR*, xiv, 1 (1929).

Lederer, Emil, ed., *Soziologische Probleme der Gegenwart* (1921).

Lehmann, Gerhard, table, " Soziologie der Gegenwart in Deutschland," in *Deutscher Kulturatlas*, eds. Lüdtke and Mackensen (1928), v, p. 67, Table 444.

Matsumoto, J., " The Cologne School of Sociology and von Wiese's ' General Sociology ' and Scheler's ' Sociology of Knowledge ' " (in Japanese), *JSM*, ix (Jan., 1925).

Mehlis, Georg, *Lehrbuch der Geschichtsphilosophie* (1915).

*Meuter, Hanna, " Einführung in die Soziologie," in *Die neue Volkshochschule*, 8th ed. (1928). Excellent survey by a member of the Cologne school.

Michaelis, Alfred, " Der ontologische Begriff der Gesellschaft," *KVS*, vi, 2, pp. 113–35. An analysis of various writers who view society as an ideal or quasi-ideal entity only partially manifested in the empirical world.

Oppenheimer, Franz, " Tendencies in Recent German Sociology," *SR*, xxiv, 1 (Jan., 1932), pp. 1–13.

*—— and Salomon, Gottfried, *Soziologische Lesestücke*, 3 vols. (1926).

*Parsons, Talcott, *Structure of Social Action* (1937). Good chapters on Weber.

Richard, Gaston, " Nouvelles tendances sociologiques en France et en Allemagne," *RIS*, xxxvi, 11–12 (Nov.–Dec., 1928), pp. 647–69.

——, " Nouvelles tendances sociologiques en Allemagne," *RIS*, xxxvii, 3–4 (Mar.–Apr., 1929), pp. 262–77.

Salis, Jean R. de, " Remarques sur le mouvement sociologique en Allemagne," *RSH*, Dec., 1930, pp. 57–69.

Salomon, Gottfried, Introduction to Lorenz von Stein's *Geschichte der sozialen Bewegung in Frankreich*.

Small, Albion W., *Origins of Sociology* (1924).

Sombart, Werner, ed., *Soziologie* (1923).

Spann, Othmar, *Gesellschaftslehre*, 3rd ed. (1930). Book I, survey of schools of present-day sociology from a "universalistic" standpoint.

Spranger, E., "Die Soziologie in der Erinnerungsgabe für Max Weber," *SJ*, xlix, 6 (1925).

*Squillace, Fausto, trans. by Rudolf Eisler, *Die soziologischen Theorien* (1911).

Stein, Ludwig, *Die soziale Frage im Lichte der Philosophie*, 3rd and 4th ed. (1923).

Steinmetz, S. R., "Recent German Sociology" (in Dutch), *MEM*, i, 1 (May, 1925).

Stoltenberg, H. L., "Geschichte der Soziologie," *HWBS*.

——, *Geschichte der deutschen Gruppwissenschaft (Soziologie) mit besonderer Beachtung ihres Wortschatzes*, I (1937).

Thon, O., "The Present Status of Sociology in Germany," *AJS*, ii (1897), pp. 567–88, 718–36, 792–800.

*Tönnies, F., "Entwicklung der Soziologie in Deutschland im 19ten Jahrhundert," *Soziologische Studien und Kritiken*, ii (1927), pp. 63–103.

Troeltsch, Ernst, *Der Historismus und seine Probleme* (1922).

Wiese, Leopold von, *Soziologie: Geschichte und Hauptprobleme*, 2nd ed. (1930).

——, "Current Sociology. II. Germany," *SR*, xix (1927), pp. 21–25.

*——, "Der gegenwärtige internationale Entwicklungsstand der Allgemeinen Soziologie," in *Reine und angewandte Soziologie: Eine Festgabe für Ferdinand Tönnies* (1935), pp. 1–20.

*Wiese-Becker, *Systematic Sociology* (1932), Part IV.

*Wirth, Louis, "Modern German Conceptions of Sociology," *AJS*, xxxii, 3 (Nov., 1926), pp. 461–70. For its date, the best topical bibliography on the subject available in English.

Young, Pauline V., "Contemporary German Sociology," *SSR*, xvi, 4 (Mar.–Apr., 1932), pp. 355–66.

2. How long sociology will retain its hardwon footing is difficult to say. Under the Nazi system of *Gleichschaltung* ("coördination") the German Sociological Society was absorbed in the Academy of German Law in 1934, and soon thereafter was strangled by the professors of the so-called *Staatswissenschaften* while its Nazi-dictated president, Professor Hans Freyer, stood dutifully by. For this reason, the picture given in the following article, accurate enough for its period, is over-optimistic now: Leopold von Wiese, "Soziologie als Lehrfach und Lehrberuf," *Vortrag in der Vereinigung der sozial- und wirtschaftswissenschaftlichen Hochschullehrer in Kissingen am 24. September 1929* (Hamburg: Broschek, 1929). The same author is distinctly pessimistic in his "Der gegenwärtige internationale Entwicklungsstand der Allgemeinen Soziologie," in *Reine und angewandte Soziologie: Eine Festgabe für Ferdinand Tönnies* (1936), pp. 1–20.

3. Albion W. Small, *Origins of Sociology* (1924), chap. xvi.

4. Wiese-Becker, *op. cit.*, chap. xlix.

5. H. L. Stoltenberg, "Geschichte der Soziologie," *HWBS*, p. 583. See also Karpf, *op. cit.*, pp. 43–45.

6. Stoltenberg, *loc. cit.*; Karpf, *op. cit.*, pp. 46, 50.

7. Stoltenberg, *loc. cit.*; Karpf, *op. cit.*, p. 68, note 1.

8. Wundt, *Logik*, 3rd ed., vol. iii, p. 281.

9. ——, *Kultur und Geschichte* (vol. x of the *Völkerpsychologie*), pp. 152–62.

10. This primacy of the emotional life is underscored repeatedly in the *Physiological Psychology* (1912) and elsewhere. In the *Elements of Folk Psychology*

(Schaub trans., 1916) the application to the " primitive mind " noted in the text is often made. **11.** ——, *op. cit.*, p. 3; *Die Sprache* (vol. i of the *Völkerpsychologie*), pp. 20 ff.

12. The final volume of the *Völkerpsychologie, Kultur und Geschichte,* contains a summary of the main conclusions of the preceding volumes. *Some* idea of the range covered can be gained from the *Elements of Folk Psychology* noted above. It cannot be too strongly emphasized, however, that the *Elements* does not by any means convey the profundity and psychological insight evident in the larger works. **13.** ——, *Logik,* 3rd ed., vol. iii, pp. 429–30.

14. Wiese-Becker, *op. cit.,* pp. 56–61. We have leaned to some extent on an unpublished Harvard thesis by George A. Morgan, as well as on his excellent article, *" Wilhelm Dilthey," *PR*, xlii, 4 (July, 1933), pp. 351–80. Of greater aid, however, has been a paper on Dilthey by Alexander Goldenweiser, later to be published elsewhere. **15.** Morgan, *op. cit.,* p. 374.

16. Heinrich Rickert, *Die Grenzen der naturwissenschaftlichen Begriffsbildung* (1921), p. 100. Here again aid has come from one of Alexander Goldenweiser's later-to-be-published papers. His discussion of Rickert is marked by a keen awareness of the relevant issues.

17. Rickert, *op. cit.,* pp. 272–81. **18.** *Ibid.,* pp. 281 ff.

19. Wiese-Becker, *op. cit.,* pp. 222–26, 701–703.

20. Ferdinand Tönnies, *Gemeinschaft und Gesellschaft,* 6th and 7th eds. (an 8th ed. appeared in 1935), 1926, pp. 55, 80–81, 163, 249.

21. ——, *Thomas Hobbes, der Mann und der Denker,* 2nd ed. (1912).

22. Rudolf Heberle, *Über die Mobilität der Bevölkerung in den Vereinigten Staaten* (1929), and other works.

23. The definitive work on Simmel is that by *N. J. Spykman, *The Social Theory of Georg Simmel* (1925). See also Wiese-Becker, *op. cit., passim.*

24. Articles by Simmel under these titles appeared in the *AJS* in the late 1890's and early 1900's. See the bibliography in Spykman, *op. cit.*

25. Wiese-Becker, *op. cit.,* p. 708.

26. Compare these, for example, with *E. L. Nussbaum, *History of the Economic Institutions of Modern Europe* (1933). This is a condensation of the six large volumes of Sombart's *Der moderne Kapitalismus.*

27. Wiese-Becker, *op. cit.,* p. 52.

28. Robert E. Park, review of Sombart's *Die drei Nationalökonomien,* *AJS*, xxxvi, 6 (May, 1931), pp. 1073–75. Compare the chapter on " *Die verstehende Soziologie* " in F. N. House's *The Development of Sociology* (1936).

29. This has been translated as *The Protestant Ethic and the Spirit of Capitalism* (1930) by Talcott Parsons.

30. Max Weber, " Über einige Kategorien der verstehende Soziologie," first published in 1912, and reprinted in the *Gesammelte Aufsätze zur Wissenschaftslehre* (1922), hereafter cited as *Wissenschaftslehre.* See the notes of Chapter Twenty for discussions of Weber's methodology.

31. Translated in Wiese-Becker, *op. cit.,* pp. 56–57.

32. Weber, *Wissenschaftslehre,* pp. 403–405. See also Wiese-Becker, *op. cit.,* pp. 57–58.

The concept of secularization is not frequently mentioned in Weber's writings, and yet it plays a very large part in them. This is particularly true of his *Religionssoziologie.* As a matter of fact, he never uses " secularization " in its German form of *Säkularisation*; his phrase is *Entzauberung der Welt,* the " demagification of the world." See his *Wissenschaftslehre,* p. 554.

33. Weber, *op. cit.,* pp. 405–408. Cf. Wiese-Becker, *loc. cit.*

34. *Talcott Parsons, review of Schelting's *Max Webers Wissenschaftslehre*, *ASR*, i, 4 (Aug., 1936), p. 676. See also Parsons's telling review of Robertson's *Aspects of the Rise of Economic Individualism: A Criticism of Max Weber and His School* (1933), in the *Quarterly Journal of Economics* (Harvard).

35. Wiese-Becker, *op. cit.*, pp. 3–7. Compare this with C. A. Ellwood's *Method in Sociology* (1933), esp. pp. 128–49, and with his " Emasculated Sociologies," *SSR*, xvii, 3 (Jan.–Feb., 1933), pp. 219–29.

36. Ernst Troeltsch, *Die Soziallehren der christlichen Kirchen und Gruppen* (3rd ed., 1923), pp. 704–22 (an English translation is available). For a brief biographical sketch and characterization of Troeltsch's basic position, see *Eugene W. Lyman, " Ernst Troeltsch's Philosophy of History," *PR*, xli, 5 (Sept., 1932), pp. 443–65. **37.** Wiese-Becker, *op. cit.*, pp. 624–26.

38. Barth. Landheer, paper on Spann written for this chapter. See also J. Baxa, *Einführung in die romantische Staatswissenschaft* (1931), and his *Gesellschaft und Staat im Spiegel deutscher Romantik* (1924). The original source, of course, is Adam Müller, *Elemente der Staatskunst* (ed. Fischer). For a Marxian critique of Spann, see Andrée Emery, " The Totalitarian Economics of Othmar Spann," *JSP*, i, 3 (Apr., 1936), pp. 263–77. Spann's most popular work is his *Haupttheorien der Volkswirtschaftslehre*. An English translation is available.

39. Landheer, " Othmar Spann's Social Theories," *JPE*, xxxix, 2 (Apr., 1931), pp. 241–42.

40. *Ibid.*, p. 243. See also Spann, " Ein Wort an meine Gegner," *KVS*, vi, 4 (1927), pp. 312–36; Karl Dunkmann, *Der Kampf um Othmar Spann* (1928).

41. Landheer, paper cited. Compare Spann, *Der wahre Staat* (1930 ed.), *passim*. **42.** Emery, *op. cit.*, p. 264.

43. *Ralph Barton Perry, *Philosophy of the Recent Past* (1926), pp. 205–11. The primary source is Edmund Husserl, *Ideen zu einer reinen Phänomenologie und phänomenologischen Philosophie* (English translation by W. R. Boyce Gibson under the title *Ideas: General Introduction to Pure Phenomenology*). The work first appeared in the form of articles in 1913. See also *Wilhelm Reyer, *Einführung in die Phänomenologie* (1926) for a simplified version and an excellent bibliography.

44. Troeltsch, *Der Historismus und seine Probleme* (1922), p. 609. Compare Leopold von Wiese, " Max Scheler: Einige persönliche Erinnerungen," *KVS*, vii, 3 (1928), pp. 359–63.

45. Howard Becker, " Some Forms of Sympathy: A Phenomenological Analysis," *JASP*, xxvi, 1 (Apr.–June, 1931), pp. 58–68. The present version has been slightly revised.

46. *Scheler, *Wesen und Formen der Sympathie* (1926 ed.), pp. 68–92. Applications of these doctrines are made all through the *Formalismus in der Ethik und die materiale Wertethik* (1916).

47. ——, ed., *Versuche zu einer Soziologie des Wissens* (1924); ——, *Die Wissensformen und die Gesellschaft* (1926).

48. ——, *Mensch und Geschichte* (1929); ——, *Die Stellung des Menschen im Kosmos* (1928); ——; *Die Formen des Wissens und die Bildung* (1925); ——, *Die Idee des Friedens und der Pazifismus* (1931); etc.

49. The greater part of this material on Vierkandt is due to the excellent analysis provided by *Theodore Abel, *Systematic Sociology in Germany* (1929), pp. 50–79.

50. William McDougall, *The Energies of Men* (1933), p. vi *et passim*.

51. Alfred Vierkandt, *Gesellschaftslehre*, 2nd ed. (1928), pp. 208–32; Wiese-Becker, *op. cit.*, pp. 709–10.

52. *Leopold von Wiese, *Zur Grundlegung der Gesellschaftslehre, eine kritische Untersuchung von Herbert Spencers System der synthetischen Philosophie* (1906). See also his autobiographical sketch in *Die Volkswirtschaftslehre der Gegenwart in Selbstdarstellungen* (1929), pp. 187–239. At the end of this sketch will be found a fairly complete bibliography of his scientific writings. He has also written a number of short stories and novels.

53. The Nazi invasion of the German universities has done a great deal to crowd Wiese into the background along with most of the other really eminent German sociologists. Consequently " front rank " here means in the estimation of the sociologists of the rest of the world, not of present-day Germany.

54. Cf. Wiese-Becker, *op. cit.*, pp. viii, 710–11.

55. *Leopold von Wiese, *System der Allgemeinen Soziologie* (1933), pp. 110–13.

56. Inasmuch as the terms " action pattern " and " plurality pattern " were introduced by the American collaborator, they have been omitted from the above schema. Cf. Wiese-Becker, *op. cit.*, pp. 118–19. It is interesting to note that E. S. Bogardus has incorporated the term " plurality pattern " in his *Contemporary Sociology* (1931), pp. 131–32, without taking account of the fact that it does not occur at all in Wiese's original work. *E. E. Eubank has used a similar term, " plurel." See his *Concepts of Sociology* (1932), pp. 117–19. " Plurel " derives from F. H. Giddings, who also used the term " action pattern."

57. See Wiese-Becker, *op. cit.*, Part III. In Wiese's *System* noted above, he has added a valuable chapter on the station, the class, and civil society — pp. 574–97.

58. A member of the Sumner-Keller school, Murdock, has made this assertion. See *AA*, xxxiv, 4 (Oct.–Dec., 1932), pp. 703–705. For concrete evidence of the factual nature of Wiese's work, see the volumes of *KVS* and the supplementary brochures. Monographs and articles by Latten, Gierlichs, and a host of other members of Wiese's seminars and survey tours attest the consistently empirical turn of Wiese's thought. **59.** Wiese-Becker, *op. cit.*, p. 16. **60.** *Ibid.*, pp. 57–61.

61. Abel, *op. cit.*, p. 159.

62. Kurt Breysig, *Vom geschichtlichen Werden*, 3 vols. (1925–28). See also his *Der Stufenbau und die Gesetze der Weltgeschichte*, 2nd ed.

63. Hermann Schneider, *Philosophie der Geschichte* (1923).

64. Franz Oppenheimer, *System der Soziologie*, 4 large volumes and index, complete. The last half-volume appeared in 1934.

65. Wilhelm Jerusalem, *Einführung in die Philosophie*, 10th ed. (1922). This is available in an English translation by Charles F. Sanders, of which see especially pp. 311–517, " Sociology and Philosophy of History," with its subdivision, " Sociological Theory of Knowledge," pp. 406–31.

66. See the articles by these writers collected in the volume edited by Max Scheler, *Versuche zu einer Soziologie des Wissens* (1924).

67. Mannheim, *Ideology and Utopia* (Wirth and Shils trans., 1936), p. 6.

68. Scheler, *Der Genius des Krieges und der deutsche Krieg* (1915), Appendix on " Cant."

69. Leopold von Wiese, " Max Scheler: Einige persönliche Erinnerungen," *KVS*, vii, 3 (1928), pp. 359–63.

70. Mannheim, *op. cit.*, *passim* (use index). Cf. Schelting's review and the citations therein (note 73). **71.** Mannheim, *op. cit.*, pp. 70–81 *et passim*.

72. *Ibid.*, pp. 270–75 *et passim*.

73. *Alexander von Schelting, review of Mannheim's *Ideologie und Utopie*, *ASR*, i, 4 (Aug., 1936), pp. 666–73. A survey of the general field is given by

*Ernst Grünwald, *Probleme einer Soziologie des Wissens* (1934). See also J. S. Roucek, " Ideology as the Implement of Purposive Thinking in the Social Sciences," *SS*, xi, 1 (Jan., 1936), pp. 25–34. The Wirth-Shils translation of Mannheim's *opus* has an excellent bibliography, unfortunately marred by the omission of some of the most significant critical literature.

74. Johann Plenge, " Zum Ausbau der Beziehungslehre," Parts I, II, and III, *KVS*, ix, 3 (1931), ix, 4 (1931), and x, 3 (1932). He established a sociological institute in Münster, where a large number of his tables were on display. Cf. Leopold von Wiese, " Bemerkungen zu Johann Plenges Ausbau der Beziehungslehre," *KVS*, x, 4 (1932), pp. 537–58.

75. See the twelve volumes of the *KVS* and the supplementary brochures.

76. *Max Graf zu Solms, *Bau und Gliederung der Menschengruppen* (1929).

77. Willy Latten, " Die Halligen," *KVS*, viii, 4 (1930), pp. 384–98; ——, " Die niederrheinische Kleinstadt," *KVS*, viii, 3 (1930), pp. 313–24; Willy Gierlichs, " Zwischenmenschliche Probleme des Ghettos," *KVS*, x, 3 (1932), pp. 364–86.

78. Leopold von Wiese, " Adolf Günthers Alpenwerk," *KVS*, viii, 4 (1930), pp. 421–30.

79. Max Rumpf, " Die Groszstadt als Lebensform und in ihrer sozialen Prägekraft," *KVS*, x, 2 (1931), pp. 200–19.

80. Rudolf Heberle, " Soziographie," *HWBS*. See also Leopold von Wiese, " Soziographie und Beziehungslehre," *MEM*, ix, 1 and 2, pp. 107–14, and note 110, this chapter.

81. Wiese-Becker, *op. cit.*, p. 66.

82. *H. L. Stoltenberg, " Gesellschaftliche Gefühle," *JFS*, iii, pp. 48–58.

83. For a survey and bibliography, see *Healy, Bronner, and Bower, *The Structure and Meaning of Psychoanalysis* (1930).

84. See *Read Bain, " Sociology and Psychoanalysis," *ASR*, i, 2 (Apr., 1936), pp. 203–16.

85. *Bernhard J. Stern, ed., " The Letters of Ludwig Gumplowicz to Lester F. Ward," *S*, supplement 1, pp. 8–12.

86. P. A. Sorokin, review in *A*, vol. 157 (1931), pp. 250–51.

87. Franz Oppenheimer, *op. cit.*, pp. ix–xx.

88. Franz Carl Müller-Lyer, *Phasen der Kultur* (translated by the Lakes as *The History of Social Development* (1921).

89. Karl Dunkmann, *Angewandte Soziologie* (1929); Dunkmann, Lehmann, and Sauermann, *Lehrbuch der Soziologie und Sozialphilosophie* (1931).

90. Max Adler, " Soziologie und Erkenntniskritik," *JFS*, i, pp. 4–34. At the end of this article there is a good bibliography of Adler's writings.

91. Mark Abramowitsch, *Hauptprobleme der Soziologie* (1930).

In concluding the notes of this section on German and Austrian sociology, it may be well to mention a few of the sociologists who could not be considered in the text: Alfred von Martin, historical sociology; Julius Bab, studies of Bohemians and like marginal groups; Georg von Lukacs, Marxian epistemology; Werner Ziegenfuss, systematic sociology and sociology of aesthetics; Franz Jerusalem, sociology of law; and a number of others, including Schücking, Cysarz, Rothacker, Korff, Richard Schmidt, A. Meusel, Josef Schumpeter, Fritz Strich, Gottfried Salomon, Rudolf Sohm, Lempicki, Hausenstein, and Eduard Spranger.

92. *S. R. Steinmetz, " Soziologie in Holland," *KVS*, iii, 2/3 (1923), pp. 203–207.

93. J. de Bosch Kemper, *Handleiding tot de Kennis van de Wetenschap der Samenleving* (1863).

94. *Barth. Landheer, " Dutch Sociology," *SF*, xii, 2 (Dec., 1933), pp. 191–98. See esp. p. 191.

95. J. D. J. Aengenent, *Leerboek der Sociologie* (1909). See Steinmetz, *op. cit.*, p. 206.

96. In particular, *Rerum novarum* of Leo XIII and *Graves de communire* and *Motu-proprio* of Pius X. *Quadragesimo Anno* of course had not appeared.

97. J. R. Slotemaker de Bruine, *Sociologie en Christendom* (1912). Cf. Landheer, *op. cit.*, p. 192.

98. Anne Anema, *De Grondslagen der Sociologie* (1900). Cf. Steinmetz, *op. cit.*, p. 203.

99. Steinmetz, " Een Calvinist over de Sociologie," *De Tydspiegel* (1901). For a sample of the Dutch Calvinist point of view as applied to American problems, see R. J. Danhoff, *The One and the Many* (Grand Rapids, Mich.: Eerdmans, 1935).

100. *Steinmetz, " Soziologie in Holland," *KVS*, iii, 2/3 (1923), p. 203.

101. Kieviet de Jonge, *Die politiek der toekomst* (1917). Cf. Steinmetz, *op. cit.*, p. 205.

102. W. A. Bonger, *Criminalité et conditions économiques* (1905); ——, *Geloof en Misdaad* (1913); ——, *De maatschappelyke factoren van de Misdaad* (1912). **103.** Steinmetz, review in *Weekblad van Recht* (1906).

104. J. van Kan, *Les causes économiques de la criminalité* (1903).

105. Dr. de Roos, *Aetiologie van de Misdaad* (1908).

106. Steinmetz, " Het goed recht van Ethnologie en Sociologie," Inaugural Address, Utrecht, 1895. See also his " Verwaarloosde Wetenschappen," *De Tydspiegel* (1898), and " Wat is Sociologie," Inaugural Address, Leiden, 1900.

107. Landheer, *op. cit.*, p. 196. See also the review by Sorokin in *AAA*, vol. 148, p. 249.

108. *Richard Thurnwald, ed., *Soziologie von Heute* (1932), chap. by S. R. Steinmetz, " Soziologie als positive Spezialwissenschaft," pp. 93–102, especially p. 93. **109.** Steinmetz, " Soziologie in Holland," *KVS*, iii, 2/3 (1923), p. 205.

110. *Steinmetz, " Die Stellung der Soziographie in der Reihe der Geisteswissenschaften," *ARW*, vi (1913). Cf. *Die Arbeitslosen von Marienthal: Ein soziographischer Versuch über die Wirkungen andauernder Arbeitslosigkeit. Mit einem Anhang: Zur Geschichte der Soziographie.* Karl Bühler, ed. (1933).

111. See the article by Steinmetz, " Soziologie in Holland," and also the one by Landheer, " Dutch Sociology," for a list of the writings of Steinmetz's pupils and also those of the ethnographers and sociographers who have not been associated with him. Among the latter, Van Hinte and Ter Veen should also be mentioned. Attention should also be called to the recent studies by A. N. J. Den Hollanden, *De landelyke arme blanken in het Zuiden der Vereenigde Staten* (The rural poor whites in the Southern U. S. 1933); and by B. Schrieke, *Alien Americans* (1936).

112. G. A. Wilken, *De verspreide geschriften*, 4 vols. (1912); A. Blonk, *Fabrieken en Menschen* (1929); W. R. Heere, *Frédéric Le Play en zijne volgelingen* (1926). **113.** J. H. Kohlbrugge, *Practische Sociologie* (1925).

114. Steinmetz, " Soziologie in Holland," *KVS*, iii, 2/3 (1923), p. 205. Visser's books, in the order given in the text, are as follows: *De psyche de menigte, De collective psyche in recht en staat, Karakter als cultuurelement.*

115. Steinmetz, *op. cit.*, p. 204.

116. C. Gerretson, *Prolegomena der Sociologie* (1911); see the review by Steinmetz in *De Gids*, 1912. P. Endt, *Sociologie* (1931).

117. N. B. DeNood, review of *Handelingen van de " Nederlandsche Sociologische Vereeniging"* (1936), *ASR*, ii, 1, pp. 131–32.

118. *Bertil Ohlin, " Scandinavia," *ESS*, vol. i, pp. 292–94.

119. *Sven Helander, " Soziologie in Schweden," *KVS*, iii, 1 (1923), p. 87.

120. *Ibid.*, p. 85. Chief works, *Bidrag till utredandet av samhällslärans begrepp* (1826) and *Filosofisk rätts- och samhällslära* (1839).

121. *Ibid.*, p. 86. Chief works, *Grundlinjer till filosofiska statslärans propadeutik* (1874) and *Grundlinjer till filosofiska statsläran* (1859).

122. *Ibid.*, Chief works, *Några tankar om människan och samhället* (1887) and *Översikt över det mänskliga samhällslivets huvudformer* (1911).

123. *Ibid.*, p. 87. Chief works, *Om nationernas sammanväxning* (1887) and *Om utvecklingsanarki* (1892).

124. *Ibid.*, p. 86. Chief works, *Samhälleliga tidsfrågor* (1871–81) and *Positivismen* (1879).

125. *Ibid.*, pp. 86–87. Chief work, *Slutliquid med Sveriges rikes lag* (1861–86).

126. *Ibid.*, pp. 89–90. Chief works, *Missbrukad kvinnokraft* (1896), *Barnets århundrade* (1901), *Livslinjer* (1903–06), and *Die Frauenbewegung* (1909). *See the article in *ESS*.

127. *Ibid.*, p. 91. Chief works (for our purposes), *Tjänstekvinnans son* and *Det nya riket* (1882). Cf. Leopold von Wiese, *Strindberg: ein Beitrag zur Soziologie der Geschlechter*, 2nd ed. (1920).

128. *Ibid.*, p. 89. Chief work, *Masskultur* (1916).

129. *Ibid.*, p. 86. Chief work, *Om vår tids inre samhällsförhållanden* (1844).

130. *Ibid.*, p. 90. Chief work, *Social teleologi i marxismen* (1909).

131. *Sven Helander, *Marx und Hegel* (1922).

132. E. H. Thörnberg, *Samhällsklasser och politiska partier i Sverige* (1917).

133. Gustav F. Steffen, *Världsåldrarna* (1918–20). Other important works: *Sociala studier*, 7 vols.; *Krig och kultur* (1914–16); *Den materialistiska samhällsuppfattningens historia före Karl Marx* (1914); *Utvecklingen av Karl Marx materialistiska samhällsuppfattning* (1914); *Bostadsfrågan i Sverige ur sociologiska och socialpolitiska synpunkter* (1918).

134. Oskar Montelius, *Sverige under hednatiden* (1873) and *Vår forntid* (1919).

135. *Cf. the references to Fahlbeck in Sorokin's *Social Mobility*. P. E. Fahlbeck, *Stånd och klasser* (1892); ——, *Sveriges Adel* (1898–1902; available in French); ——, *Klasserna och samhället* (1920, Part I only; available in German). *Cf. the article in *ESS*.

136. Helander, *op. cit.*, p. 90. Cf. also the article in *ESS*. Chief works, *Stormakterna* (1905); *Staten som lifsform* (1916; available in German); *Grundriss zu einem System der Politik* (1920).

137. *Walther Vogel, " Rudolf Kjellén," *ESS*.

138. There is a whole school of *Geopolitik*. The latest effusion is by Richard Hennig, *Geopolitik*, 2nd ed. (1931).

139. Ferdinand Tönnies, " Nachruf auf C. N. Starcke," *KVS*, v, 4 (1926), pp. 490–91. Our information about Lönborg derives from Thorsten Sellin of the University of Pennsylvania, who has also given us the benefit of his critical reading of this section.

140. Helander, *op. cit.*, p. 90. Chief work, *Språkets makt över tanken* (1880).

141. We say " Scheler-like " because of the similarity of Ranulf's conclusions to some of those set forth in *Scheler's famous essay, " Ressentiment im Aufbau der Moral," in *Vom Umsturz der Werte* (1922).

142. *Svend Ranulf, *The Jealousy of the Gods and Criminal Law at Athens* (2 vols., 1934), i, pp. 145, 161.

143. Thorsten Sellin, notes written for this chapter. Cf. Ragnar Numelin, *Studier i nordisk sociologi* (1918). Numelin's study of migrations is interesting: *Orsakerna till folkvandringarna på lägre kulturstadier* (1918).

144. Cf. Numelin, *Studier i nordisk sociologi.* **145.** *Ibid.*

146. Robert E. Park, "Murder and the Case Study Method," *AJS*, xxxvi, 3 (Nov., 1930), pp. 447–54.

147. D. S. Thomas, review of Edin and Hutchinson, *Studies of Differential Fertility in Sweden* (1936), in *ASR*, ii, 1 (Feb., 1937), pp. 126–28.

148. *Ibid.*

149. Helander, *op. cit.*, p. 89. Chief works: editor of *Sweden, Its People and Its Industry* (1904); *Aperçus statistiques internationaux;* and *Det svenska folklynnet* (1911).

In concluding this section on the Scandinavian countries, the work of the criminologist Johan C. W. Thyren (1861–) should be mentioned; *Straffrättens allmänna grunder* (The general foundations of penal law, 1907). A number of Norwegian and Danish sociologists concerning whom insufficient information was available should also be listed:

NORWAY

Thorvald Aarum, *The Social Studies Abroad and at Home* (1909).
Herman H. Aall, *Interest as a Guiding Standard and Normalizing Idea: a Philosophical and Sociological Treatise*, 3 vols. (1913); ———, *More Light on Sociological Questions* (1911).
K. V. Hammer, *The Development of Law in its Sociological Aspects* (1904).
A. Haug, *A Textbook in Sociology* (1902).
Sigurd Ibsen, *The Quintessence of Human Nature* (1911).
Mikael H. Lie, *Outlines of Sociology* (1913).

DENMARK

Joseph Davidsohn, *The Conditions and the Problems of Sociology* (1913).
K. A. Wieth-Knudsen, *Population Growth and Progress* (1908).
C. Wilkens, *The Fundamental Law of Society: Principles of Sociology* (1881).

CHAPTER XXIV

1. This chapter is based largely on examination of primary sources, but secondary sources have also played an important part. Among the most useful of the latter has been the splendid article by *L. L. Bernard, "The Social Sciences as Disciplines. XI. The United States," in *ESS*, i (1930), pp. 324–48. Other sources, some of which have been directly drawn upon and others merely consulted, are: *L. L. Bernard, ed., *Fields and Methods of Sociology* (1934); John L. Gillin, "The Development of Sociology in the United States," *PASS*, xxi (1926), pp. 1–25, and "Recent Sociological Trends," *SSR*, xv, 3 (Jan.–Feb., 1931), pp. 203–208; Howard Becker, "Distribution of Space in *The American Journal of Sociology*, 1895–1927," *AJS*, xxxvi, 3 (Nov., 1930), pp. 461–66, and "Space Apportioned Forty-Eight Topics in *The American Journal of Sociology*, 1895–1930," *AJS*, xxxviii, 1 (July, 1932), pp. 71–78; Harry Elmer Barnes, "American Sociology in 1925," *ASPS*, xxix, 3/4 (1926), pp. 289–98, *The New History and the Social Studies* (1925), chap. xx, "Sociology and History," "The Development of Historical Sociology," *PASS*, xvi (1921), pp. 17–50, and numerous articles, to be cited later, in *SR*, *AJS*, etc.; *Gladys Bryson, "Sociology Considered as Moral Philosophy," *SR*, xxiv, 1 (Jan., 1932), pp. 26–36, and *"The Emergence of the Social Sciences from Moral Philosophy," *IJE*, xlii, 3 (Apr.,

1932), pp. 304–23; G.-L. Duprat, " Revue critique de la sociologie américaine," *RIS*, xxxiv, 11/12 and xxv, 3/4 (Nov.–Dec., 1926 and March–April, 1927); Willy Gierlichs, " Soziologischer Brief aus den Vereinigten Staaten," *KVS*, xi, 3/4 (1933), pp. 463–68; *F. H. Hankins, " Sociology," in *The History and Prospects of the Social Sciences*, H. E. Barnes, ed. (1925), pp. 314–31; Floyd N. House, *The Range of Social Theory* (1929) and *The Development of Sociology* (1936), *passim*; *Lundberg, Bain, and Anderson, *Trends in American Sociology* (1929); Albion W. Small, " Evolution of Sociological Consciousness in the United States," *AJS*, xxvi, 2 (Sept., 1921), pp. 226–31, " Fifty Years of Sociology in the United States," *AJS*, xxi, 6 (May, 1916), pp. 721–64, and " Sociology," in *EA* (1919); Howard W. Odum, ed., *American Masters of Social Science* (1927); Pitirim Sorokin, *Contemporary Sociological Theories* (1928), *passim*, and *" Some Contrasts in Contemporary European and American Sociology," *SF*, viii, i (Sept., 1929), pp. 57–62; Frank A. Tolman, " Study of Sociology in Institutions of Learning in the United States," *AJS*, vii (1901–02), pp. 797–838, viii (1902–03), pp. 85–121, 251–72, 531–58; Andreas Walther, *Soziologie und Sozialwissenschaften in Amerika* (1927); Leopold von Wiese, " Fünfzig Jahre Soziologie in den Vereinigten Staaten," *KVS*, i, 1 (1921), pp. 77–79; and " Der gegenwärtige internationale Entwicklungsstand der Allgemeinen Soziologie," in *Reine und angewandte Soziologie: Eine Festgabe für Ferdinand Tönnies* (1925), pp. 1–20; and Wiese-Becker, *Systematic Sociology* (1932), pp. 689–92.

2. Bernard, " The Social Sciences as Disciplines. XI. The United States," in *ESS*, i (1930), p. 339. 3. Bryson, *op. cit.* 4. Bernard, *loc. cit.*

5. *Ibid.* Read Bain has kindly permitted us to read his unpublished MS on Bishop.

6. Bernard, *op. cit.*, p. 338; and " Henry Hughes, First American Sociologist," *SF*, xv, 2 (Dec., 1936), pp. 154–74.

7. Barnes, " American Sociology in 1925," *ASPS*, xxix, 3/4 (1926), pp. 290–92. 8. Bernard, *op. cit.*, p. 339. 9. Barnes, *op. cit.*, p. 293.

10. Bernard, *loc. cit.*

11. William Graham Sumner, *What the Social Classes Owe to Each Other* (1883), p. 155 *et passim*.

12. *Barnes, " Two Representative Contributions of Sociology to Political Theory," *AJS*, xxv, 1 and 2 (July and Sept., 1919), pp. 1–23, 150–70.

13. Sumner, *Folkways* (1907), chaps. i–ii, xv, xix–xx.

14. ——, art. in *AJS*, xv (1909–10), p. 209.

15. A. G. Keller, introduction to Sumner, *War and Other Essays* (1913), pp. xv, xvii. 16. Small, art. in *AJS*, xxi (1915–16), p. 732.

17. *Ibid.*, pp. 729–48; C. H. Walker, art. in *AJS*, xx (1914–15), pp. 829–30; Giddings and Tenney, " Sociology," in Monroe's *Cyclopedia of Education*; Bernard, *op. cit.*, p. 339.

18. Sumner, " Sociology," in *op. cit.*, pp. 167–93, and " Introductory Lecture to Courses in Political and Social Science," in *The Challenge of Facts and Other Essays* (1914), pp. 391–403, and " Sociology as a College Subject," *AJS*, xii (1906–07), pp. 597–99, and xv (1909–10), p. 209; Keller, Introduction to *War and Other Essays* (1913).

19. Keller, *op. cit.*, pp. xxiii–xxiv. 20. Subtitle of *Folkways* (1907).

21. *Ibid.*, pp. 30, 33–34, 59, 97–98, 173–74.

22. Sumner, " The Absurd Attempt to Make the World Over," written in 1894, reprinted in *War and Other Essays* (1913), pp. 195–210.

23. Sumner was an alderman in New Haven from 1873 to 1876. His **Forgotten Man and Other Essays* (1918) contains a bibliography of his works and an

index to the four volumes of essays. A complete bibliography of his published books and articles is also to be found in *War and Other Essays* (1913), pp. 377–81.

24. *Keller's *Societal Evolution* had been given at Yale in the form of lectures for several years before its publication in 1915 (2nd ed., 1931). Reviewed by L. L. Bernard, *AJS*, xxi, 2 (Sept., 1915), pp. 264–65.

25. Keller, *op. cit.*, p. 13.   **26.** *Ibid.*, pp. 1–16.

27. Keller prefers "societal" to "social" as more definite in meaning; *ibid.*, p. 15.

28. For a critical estimate of Keller's *Societal Evolution*, see the review by R. G. Smith in the *PSQ*, Dec., 1917, pp. 638–71.

29. These were Ward's *Dynamic Sociology*, 2 vols. (1883); *The Psychic Factors of Civilization* (1893); *The Outlines of Sociology* (1898); *Pure Sociology* (1903); *Applied Sociology* (1904). His *Pure Sociology* appeared in a reduced and clarified form in *Dealey and Ward's *Textbook of Sociology* (1905). Ward's minor works and notices of his major contributions are brought together in his "mental autobiography," *Glimpses of the Cosmos*, 8 vols. (1913 ff.).

Of these works *Dynamic Sociology* is the best extended exposition of his social philosophy, a briefer and clearer presentation of which is to be found in the second part of his *Outlines of Sociology*. *Pure Sociology* is the authoritative exposition of his sociological system, which again is more clearly presented in Dealey and Ward's *Textbook of Sociology*. His social psychology is best brought together in *Psychic Factors of Civilization*, while his *Applied Sociology* is the classic exposition of his conception of social telesis.

Ward's *Pure Sociology* is reviewed by H. H. Bawden in *AJS*, ix (1903–04), pp. 408–15; is criticized in detail by A. W. Small, *ibid.*, pp. 404–407, 567–75, 703–707; and is critically analyzed by J. M. Gillette, *ibid.*, xx, i (July, 1914), pp. 31–67. An excellent summary is the chapter on Ward in *J. P. Lichtenberger, *The Development of Social Theory* (1925). See also *Clement Wood, *The Substance of the Sociology of Lester F. Ward* (1930).

Estimates of Ward's significance for sociology by eminent sociologists appear in *AJS*, x (1904–05), pp. 643–53; xix (1913–14), pp. 61–78; xxi (1915–16), pp. 748–58, 824. See also Stuart A. Rice, "The Spirit of Ward in Sociology," *Science*, Aug. 28, 1936.

30. Ward's academic career was limited to lectures at several university summer-school sessions and six years (1906–13) as professor of sociology at Brown University.   **31.** Ward, *Pure Sociology*, p. 91.   **32.** *Ibid.*, p. 15.

33. *Ibid.*, pp. 3, 431.   **34.** *Ibid.*, p. 79.   **35.** *Ibid.*, p. 171.

36. Cf. Gillette, "Critical Points in Ward's *Pure Sociology*," *AJS*, xx (1914–15).   **37.** Ward, *Pure Sociology*, pp. 176–97.

38. ——, "The Sociology of Political Parties," *AJS*, xiii, 4 (Jan., 1908), pp. 440–41.   **39.** ——, *Pure Sociology* (1903), p. 555.

40. *Ibid.*, *passim*. Cf. Ward's own summary in the preface of his *Dynamic Sociology*, and Gillette, *op. cit.*

41. Ward, *Psychic Factors of Civilization*, pp. 316–23. See also Ward's article, "Plutocracy and Paternalism," in *Glimpses of the Cosmos*, v, pp. 231–40.

42. ——, *Psychic Factors of Civilization*, p. 311, introductory note.

43. ——, "Professor Sumner's *Social Classes*," in *Glimpses of the Cosmos*, iii, pp. 301–05; and "The Political Ethics of Herbert Spencer," in *ibid.*, v, pp. 38–66.   **44.** ——, *Dynamic Sociology*, ii, pp. 212–17, 231, 236–50.

45. Ward, "False Notions of Government," *Glimpses of the Cosmos*, iv, pp. 64–71. This was written in 1887!

46. Cf. Ward's review of Sumner's *Social Classes*, in *Glimpses of the Cosmos*, iii, pp. 301–05; the preface to *Dynamic Sociology*; *Pure Sociology*, pp. 551 ff.; *Outlines of Sociology*, p. 268; and *Glimpses of the Cosmos*, v, pp. 38–66.

47. Ward, *Psychic Factors of Civilization*, p. 309; *Pure Sociology*, pp. 568–69; *Dynamic Sociology*, ii, p. 545; *Outlines of Sociology*, p. 274; articles, "The Utilitarian Character of Dynamic Sociology," and "The Science and Art of Government" (1891), reprinted in *Glimpses of the Cosmos*, iv, pp. 309–15 and 322–24.

48. ——, "The Way to Scientific Law-making," in *Glimpses of the Cosmos*, ii, 168–71. **49.** ——, *Pure Sociology*, pp. 568–69.

50. ——, *Dynamic Sociology*, ii, p. 545. **51.** *Ibid.*, i, p. 70.

52. *Ibid.*, ii, pp. 632–33. Ward's best brief statement of the sociological significance of education is his "Education and Progress," in *Glimpses of the Cosmos*, vi, pp. 333–40. **53.** ——, *Dynamic Sociology*, ii, pp. 249–50.

54. ——, *Pure Sociology*, p. 135. Interesting sidelights are to be found in "Giddings, Ward, and Small, An Interchange of Letters," ed. by Bernhard J. Stern, *SF*, x, 3 (Mar., 1932), pp. 305–18.

55. Giddings, article in *AJS*, xix, 1 (July, 1913), pp. 67–68.

56. This point is amply supported by the various chapters in Odum (ed.), *op. cit.*; Gillin, *op. cit.*, pp. 6–15; Bernard, *op. cit.*, pp. 332–41.

57. Barnes, *The New History and the Social Studies* (1925), *passim*, and *History and Social Intelligence* (1926), *passim* (use index).

58. E. M. Patterson, "Patten," in *ESS*, xii (1934), pp. 29–30. See also R. G. Tugwell, "Notes on the Life and Work of Simon Nelson Patten," *JPE*, xxxi (1923), pp. 153–208; and the bibliography by Tugwell in "Memorial Addresses on the Life and Services of Simon N. Patten," *A*, cvii (1923), pp. 333–67.

59. F. H. Hankins, "Hall," in *ESS*, vii (1932), pp. 247–48.

60. Barnes, "The Sociology of J. H. W. Stuckenberg," pamphlet issued by the Lutheran Tract Society. **61.** Bernard, *op. cit.*, p. 340.

62. Lundberg, Anderson, and Bain, *op. cit.*, chap. ii.

63. Odum (ed.), *op. cit.*, chap. vii.

64. Barnes, "American Sociology in 1925," *ASPS*, xxix, 3/4 (1926), pp. 289–98.

65. Giddings's chief work, the one which laid down the guiding lines for most of his later research, is *Principles of Sociology* (1896). Important for his statistical emphasis is *The Scientific Study of Human Society* (1924). A compact summary of his chief doctrines is provided in the posthumous *Civilization and Society* (1932), and it is from this that the definition quoted is drawn. See the articles by Bernhard J. Stern, "Giddings," in *ESS*, vi (1931), pp. 654–55; and F. H. Hankins, "Franklin Henry Giddings, 1855–1931," *AJS*, xxxvii, 3 (Nov., 1931), pp. 349–67. For a bibliography of Giddings's writings, see *Bibliography of the Faculty of Political Science of Columbia University, 1880–1930* (1931).

66. Theodore Abel, "The Significance of the Concept of Consciousness of Kind," *SF*, ix, 1 (Oct., 1930), pp. 1–10.

67. See the bibliographies in L. L. Bernard, ed., *Fields and Methods of Sociology* (1934), chaps. by Leyburn and Bernard on cultural and folk sociology.

68. R. M. MacIver, *Community* (3rd ed., 1924).

69. ——, *Society: Its Structure and Changes* (1931), last chapter. See also *Society: A Textbook* (1937), chaps. ii, iv, xxv, xxvi, *et passim*.

70. Abel's *Systematic Sociology in Germany* (1929) is a good brief study of Simmel, Vierkandt, Wiese, and Weber.

71. As evidenced in Small's *General Sociology* (1905).

72. For a complete bibliography of Small's writings, see Floyd N. House, *AJS*, xxxii, 1 (July, 1926), pp. 49–58.

73. Faris has made his contributions to sociology through numerous articles, among which may be mentioned: *" Are Instincts Data or Hypotheses? " *AJS*, xxvii (1921), pp. 184 ff.; *" The Concept of Social Attitudes," *JAS*, ix (1924), pp. 404–409; " The Concept of Imitation," *AJS*, xxxii, 3 (Nov., 1926), pp. 367–78; *" The Nature of Human Nature," in *The Urban Community*, E. W. Burgess, ed. (1926), pp. 21–37; " The Primary Group: Essence and Accident? " *AJS*, xxxviii, 1 (July, 1932), pp. 41–50; *" Attitudes and Behavior," *AJS*, xxxiv (Sept., 1928), pp. 271 ff.; " Borderline Trends in Social Psychology," *PASS*, xxv, 2 (1931), pp. 38–40; and many others, now fortunately collected in his book, *The Nature of Human Nature* (1937).

74. Some of Park's most important writings are: *Masse und Publikum* (Heidelberg dissertation, 1904); *Introduction to the Science of Sociology*, with E. W. Burgess (1921); papers reprinted in *The City*, Park and others (1925) and in *The Urban Community*, Burgess, ed. (1926); *Old World Traits Transplanted*, with H. A. Miller (1921); *" Human Nature, Attitudes and the Mores," in *Social Attitudes*, Kimball Young, ed. (1931), chap. ii; *" Sociology," in *Research in the Social Sciences*, Wilson Gee, ed. (1929), chap. i; and numerous articles in *AJS*, *PASS, SSR, KVS, ASR*, etc.

75. *Nels Anderson, *The Hobo: the Sociology of the Homeless Man* (1923); *F. M. Thrasher, *The Gang* (1927); E. T. Hiller, *The Strike* (1928); R. D. McKenzie, *The Neighborhood* (1923); *Louis Wirth, *The Ghetto* (1928); *H. W. Zorbaugh, *The Gold Coast and the Slum* (1929); *Paul G. Cressey, *The Taxi-Dance Hall* (1932); Ruth Shonle Cavan, *Suicide* (1927); R. E. L. Faris, " Cultural Isolation and the Schizophrenic Personality," *AJS*, xl, 2 (Sept., 1934), pp. 155–64; Clifford Shaw and others, *Delinquency Areas* (1929); Shaw, *The Jack-Roller: a Delinquent Boy's Own Story* (1930); and *The Natural History of a Delinquent Career* (1931); E. R. Mowrer, *Family Disorganization* (1927) and other works on the family; *Albert Blumenthal, *Small-Town Stuff* (1932); *et al.*

76. Significant works by Ogburn are: " Bias, Psycho-analysis, and the Subjective in Relation to the Social Sciences," *PASS*, xvii (1922), pp. 62–74; " The Historical Method in the Study of Social Phenomena," *PASS*, xvi (1921), pp. 70–83; *Social Change* (1922); *American Marriage and Family Relationships* (with E. R. Groves, 1928); *The Social Sciences and Their Interrelations* (ed. with Alexander Goldenweiser, 1927); *" The Folkways of a Scientific Sociology," *SM*, xxx (Apr., 1930), pp. 300–306; and *Recent Social Trends*, ed. (1930).

77. *——, " Limitations of Statistics," *AJS*, xl, 1 (July, 1934), pp. 12–20. Cf. Morris R. Cohen, " The Statistical View of Nature," *JASA*, xxxi, 194 (June, 1936), pp. 327–451.   78. Wiese-Becker, *op. cit.*, p. 711.

79. In this connection Cooley's little collection of comments and aphorisms, *Life and the Student* (1927), provides a splendid example. His collected papers, *Sociology and Social Research* (ed. by R. C. Angell, 1930), give fresh evidence of his original turn of mind. See the articles by Walton N. Hamilton, " Cooley," in *ESS*, iv (1931), pp. 355–56, and the biographical notes there listed; *G. H. Mead, " Cooley's Contribution to American Social Thought," *AJS*, xxv, 5 (Mar., 1930), pp. 693–706; A. E. Wood, " Charles Horton Cooley: an Appreciation," *ibid.*, pp. 707–17; and R. C. Angell, " Cooley's Heritage to Social Research," *SF*, xiii, 3 (Mar., 1930), pp. 340–47. For a related thinker, see C. A. Ellwood, " The Social Philosophy of James Mark Baldwin," *JSP*, ii, 1 (Oct., 1936), pp. 55–68.   80. Cf. Dealey and Ward's *Textbook of Sociology* (1905).

81. *James G. Leyburn, " Cultural and Folk Sociology," in *The Fields and Methods of Sociology*, L. L. Bernard, ed. (1934); George Peter Murdock, *Our Primitive Contemporaries* (1934); *E. Wight Bakké, *The Unemployed Man* (1934); Maurice R. Davie, *Problems of City Life* (1932).

82. *J. P. Lichtenberger, *The Development of Social Theory* (1925); Stuart A. Rice, *Quantitative Methods in Politics* (1928) and *Methods in Social Science*, edited with introduction and comments (1931); J. H. S. Bossard, *Problems of Social Well-Being* (2nd ed., 1934); Thorsten Sellin, " Crime," in *ESS*, iv (1931), pp. 563–69, and numerous articles in *A*, *JCCL*, etc.; *Donald Young, *American Minority Groups* (1932); W. Rex Crawford, *Remy de Gourmont* and similar studies; J. P. Shalloo, *Private Police in Pennsylvania* (1934); Roy Abrams, *Preachers Present Arms* (1933); W. Wallace Weaver, *Natural Areas in West Philadelphia* (1932), etc.

83. *F. S. Chapin, *Cultural Change* (1928) and other books, also numerous articles in *SF*, *AJS*, *PASS*, etc.; *Malcolm M. Willey, " The Cultural Approach to Sociology," with M. J. Herskovits, *AJS* (1923), pp. 188–99; *Readings in Sociology*, with W. D. Wallis (1930), and numerous articles in *AJS*, etc.; W. D. Wallis, *op. cit.*, *Introduction to Sociology* (1927), and *Culture and Progress* (1930); *Max S. Handman, " The Sociology of Vilfredo Pareto," in *Methods in Social Science*, Stuart A. Rice, ed. (1931), pp. 139–53, etc.

84. Thomas D. Eliot, *The Juvenile Court and the Community* (1914); *" A Psychoanalytic Interpretation of Group Formation and Behavior," *AJS*, xxvi, pp. 333–52; " The Use of Psychoanalytic Classification in the Study of Social Behavior: Identification," *JASP*, xxii, 1 (Apr.–June, 1927), pp. 67–81; *" The Adjustive Behavior of Bereaved Families: a New Field of Research," *SF*, viii, 4 (June, 1930), pp. 543–49; *" A Step toward the Social Psychology of Bereavement," *JASP*, xxvii (Jan., 1933), pp. 380–90; *American Standards and Planes of Living* (1931), etc.

85. Robert E. Lowie, *Culture and Ethnology* (1917), *Primitive Society* (1920), *Primitive Religion* (1924), etc.; A. L. Kroeber, *Anthropology* (1923); *F. J. Teggart, *The Processes of History* (1918) and *A Theory of History* (1925).

86. Dartmouth has, among others, J. M. Mecklin and McQuilkin DeGrange; Smith, F. H. Hankins, Neil DeNood, Katherine Lumpkin, Dorothy Douglas, and Gladys Bryson; Vassar, Joseph K. Folsom; Bryn Mawr, H. A. Miller; Cornell, Dwight Sanderson; Oberlin, Newell L. Sims; Colgate, Norman E. Himes; Illinois, E. T. Hiller; Iowa, E. B. Reuter; Duke, C. A. Ellwood and H. E. Jensen; Kansas, Mapheus Smith and Mabel Elliott; Nebraska, J. O. Hertzler; New York University, Henry Pratt Fairchild; Pittsburgh, M. C. Elmer; Rochester, Luther Fry; Buffalo, Niles Carpenter; Indiana, U. G. Weatherly; Ohio State, C. C. North and J. E. Hagerty; Cincinnati, E. E. Eubank; Washington, F. J. Bruno and L. L. Bernard; Temple, James W. Woodard; *et alii!*

87. Cf. the remarks by L. L. Bernard in Lundberg, Anderson, and Bain, *op. cit.*, chap. i.

88. This is clearly demonstrated by the contributions to recent symposia: L. L. Bernard, ed., *Fields and Methods of Sociology* (1934); and Stuart A. Rice, ed., *op. cit.*

89. For other classifications, see C. A. Ellwood, " Sociology," in *Recent Developments in the Social Sciences*, E. C. Hayes, ed. (1927); *F. H. Hankins, " Sociology," in *The History and Prospects of the Social Sciences*, H. E. Barnes, ed. (1925), esp. pp. 314–41; Ogburn and Goldenweiser, *The Social Sciences and Their Interrelations* (1927); and L. L. Bernard, ed., *op. cit.*

90. C. A. Ellwood's chief works are *The Reconstruction of Religion* (1922), *Sociology and Modern Social Problems* (rev. ed., 1924); *The Psychology of Human Society* (1925 — this supersedes a number of earlier works); and *Methods in Sociology* (1933).

91. Kimball Young, *Readings in Social Psychology* (1927) and *Social Psychology* (1930); *Fay B. Karpf, *American Social Psychology* (1932); E. S. Bogardus, *Essentials of Social Psychology* (1920); A. G. Balz, *The Basis of Social Theory* (1924); F. H. Allport, *Social Psychology* (1924); J. K. Folsom, *Social Psychology* (1931); *Krueger and Reckless, *Social Psychology* (1931).

92. Excellent discussions of quantitative method in sociology are to be found in Rice, ed., *op. cit.*; Bernard, ed., *op. cit.*; *G. A. Lundberg, *Social Research* (1929); Lundberg, Anderson, and Bain, *op. cit.*; Ogburn and Goldenweiser, eds., *op. cit.*; L. L. Thurstone and E. J. Chave, *The Measurement of Attitudes* (1929). Cf. Wiese-Becker, *op. cit.*, pp. 52, 56–61, 69, 500; F. S. Chapin, " The Meaning of Measurement in Sociology," *PASS*, xxiv (1930), pp. 83 ff., and " Socio-Economic Status — Some Preliminary Results of Measurement," *AJS*, xxxvii (Jan., 1932), pp. 581 ff.; E. S. Bogardus, *The New Social Research* (1926), chap. x; S. A. Rice, *Quantitative Methods in Politics* (1928), chaps. x–xxi; *F. N. House, " Measurement in Sociology," *AJS*, xl, 1 (July, 1934), pp. 1–11; and *Morris R. Cohen, *op. cit.* (note 77).

93. Cf. the ecological studies listed in note 75; Park, Burgess, and others, *The City* (1925); E. W. Burgess, ed., *The Urban Community* (1926); and the article on human ecology, with bibliography, by James A. Quinn in L. L. Bernard, *op. cit.*

94. See the surveys and bibliographies by Leyburn and Bernard in L. L. Bernard, *op. cit.*

95. In addition to the excellent works noted in the text, one may list J. H. S. Bossard, *Social Change and Social Problems* (1937); J. L. Gillin, *Social Pathology* (1933); R. C. Dexter, *Social Adjustment* (1927); C. A. Ellwood, *Sociology and Modern Social Problems* (rev. ed., 1924); H. A. Phelps, *Contemporary Social Problems* (1932); and many others.

96. *Park and Miller, *Old World Traits Transplanted* (1921); W. B. Dubois, *The Souls of Black Folk* (1920); Donald Young, *op. cit.*; *E. Franklin Frazier, *The Negro Family in Chicago* (1932); *C. S. Johnson, *The Shadow of the Plantation* (1934); F. H. Hankins, *The Racial Basis of Civilization* (1925); Louis Wirth, *op. cit.*; E. B. Reuter, " Civilization and the Mixture of Races," *SM*, xxi (Nov., 1930), pp. 442–49; and *Henry Pratt Fairchild, *Immigration* (1924).

97. For a temperate and on the whole acceptable statement of the claims of eugenics, H. S. Jennings, " Eugenics," in *ESS*, v (1931), pp. 617–21 (bibliography). Among the authors cited in the paragraph in the text to which this note is appended, see the following: E. A. Ross, *Standing Room Only* (1927); E. A. Ross and R. E. Baber, " Changes in the Size of American Families," *University of Wisconsin Studies*, no. 10; H. P. Fairchild, *Immigration* (1924); *R. C. Kucynski, *The Balance of Births and Deaths*, 2 vols. (1928–31); ——, " Population: History and Statistics," *ESS*, xii (1934), pp. 240–48; L. I. Dublin, ed., *Population Problems in the United States and Canada* (Boston: Publication of the Pollak Foundation for Economic Research, no. 5, 1926); *W. S. Thompson, *Population Problems* (1930); *——, " Eugenics as Viewed by a Sociologist," *PASS*, xviii (1923), pp. 60–72; Raymond Pearl, *The Biology of Population Growth* (1925); *F. H. Hankins, " Social Biology," in Davis and Barnes, *Introduction to Sociology*, 2nd ed. (1931). For general bibliography, see the chapters by Read Bain and Sanford Winston on social biology in L. L. Bernard, *Fields and*

Methods of Sociology (1934), and the bibliography on population in *ESS*, xii (1934), pp. 253–54.

98. E. A. Ross, *Principles of Sociology* (rev. ed., 1930); C. A. Ellwood, *The Psychology of Human Society: an Introduction to Sociological Theory* (1925); L. L. Bernard, *Introduction to Social Psychology* — extends notion of social psychology so far that it takes in a large part of sociology (1926); Pitirim Sorokin, *Contemporary Sociological Theories* (1928), last chapter, and *" Sociology as a Science," *SF*, x, 1 (Oct., 1931), pp. 21–27; *Thomas and Znaniecki, *The Polish Peasant in Europe and America* (5 vols., 1918–20 — 2nd ed., 2 vols., 1927), " Methodological Note "; R. M. MacIver, *Society: A Textbook* (1937); Park and Burgess, *An Introduction to the Science of Sociology* (2nd ed., 1924); Reuter and Hart, *Principles of Sociology* (1933); C. A. Dawson and W. E. Gettys, *An Introduction to Sociology* (rev. ed., 1935); E. T. Hiller, *Principles of Sociology* (1932); and *N. J. Spykman, *The Social Theory of Georg Simmel* (1925).

99. L. L. Bernard, historical articles cited, in *ESS*, i (1930), pp. 310–20, 324–49; " An Interpretation of Sociology in the United States," *PASS*, xxv, 2 (1931), pp. 43–54; " Teaching of Sociology in Southern Colleges and Universities," *AJS*, xxiii (1928), pp. 491–515; " The Teaching of Sociology in the United States," *AJS*, xv (1909), pp. 164–213; " Schools of Sociology," *SPSSQ*, xi, 2 (Sept., 1930), pp. 117–34; " An Interpretation of Sociological Research," *AJS*, xxxvii, 2 (Sept., 1931), pp. 203–12; (see chapter on Spanish and Latin American sociology for bibliography of Bernard's writings in this field); Louis Wirth, " Modern German Conceptions of Sociology," *AJS*, xxxii, 3 (Nov., 1926), pp. 461–70; F. N. House, *The Range of Social Theory* (1929); *Pitirim Sorokin, *Contemporary Sociological Theories* (1928); Harry Elmer Barnes, *Sociology and Political Theory* (1924); *The New History and the Social Studies* (1925), chapter on " Sociology and History "; " Sociology before Comte," *AJS*, xxiii, 2 (Sept., 1917), pp. 174–247; " Some of the More Important Works Which Have Appeared in the English Language since 1914," *AGPS*, xxxiv, old series, xxvii, new series, 3/4 (c. Sept., 1922), pp. 101–17; etc.; *A. J. Todd, *Theories of Social Progress* (1918); *J. O. Hertzler, *The History of Utopian Thought* (1926); Gladys Bryson, *op. cit.*; *W. C. Lehmann, *Adam Ferguson and the Beginnings of Modern Sociology* (1930); McQuilkin DeGrange, *The Curve of Societal Movement* (1930), and " The Method of Auguste Comte: Subordination of Imagination to Observation in the Social Sciences," *Methods in Social Science*, Stuart A. Rice, ed. (1931), pp. 19–58; J. P. Lichtenberger, *op. cit.*; F. H. Hankins, " Sociology," in *The History and Prospects of the Social Sciences*, H. E. Barnes, ed. (1925), chap. vi; E. S. Bogardus, *A History of Social Thought* (2nd ed., 1928); *J. L. Gillin, " The Development of Sociology in the United States," *PASS*, xxi (1926), pp. 1–25, and " Recent Sociological Trends," *SSR*, xv, 3 (Jan.–Feb., 1931), pp. 203–208; *Howard A. Odum, ed., *American Masters of Social Science* (1927); and *Dorothy Wolff Douglas, *The Social Theory of Guillaume DeGreef* (1925).

100. See the bibliographies in the chapters by Becker and by Hertzler, *Fields and Methods of Sociology*, L. L. Bernard, ed. (1934).

101. *R. M. MacIver, *Society: Its Structure and Changes* (1931), last chapter; " Is Sociology a Natural Science? " *PASS*, xxv, 2 (May, 1931), pp. 25–35; comment on paper by G. A. Lundberg, " Is Sociology Too Scientific? " *S*, ix (Sept., 1933), pp. 298–322; C. A. Ellwood, *Methods of Sociology* (1934), with introduction by H. A. Jensen; *F. N. House, " Measurement in Sociology," *AJS*, xl, 1 (July, 1934), pp. 1–11, and *Herbert Blumer, " Science without Concepts,"

AJS, xxxvi (Jan., 1931), pp. 515–33; *Charner M. Perry, "Inductive vs. Deductive Method in Social Science Research," *SPSSQ*, iii, 1, pp. 66–74.

CHAPTER XXV

1. For this chapter our chief secondary source has been the article by Roberto Michels, " Elemente zur Soziologie in Italien," *KVS*, iii, 4 (1924), pp. 219–49, partially translated by *Mildred Hartsough, " The Status of Sociology in Italy," *SF*, ix, 1 (October, 1930), pp. 20–39. *Our references are to the German original throughout.* Another article by Michels has also proved useful, " Nachtrag zu den ' Elemente zur Soziologie in Italien,' " *KVS*, iv, 3/4 (1925), p. 331. For Italian criminology, E. D. Monachesi's " Trends in Criminological Research in Italy," *ASR*, i, 3 (June, 1936), pp. 396–406, has been useful. We have also had the benefit of letters, dating from 1928 to 1931, from Francesco Cosentini, M. Fanno, Felice Battaglia, Alessandro Levi, Guido di Ruggiero, Gualtiero Sarfatti, Gioele Solari, and Gaetano Mosca. Most of these were written in response to an inquiry by W. Rex Crawford of the University of Pennsylvania, and have been graciously placed at our disposal. Some slight assistance has come from the article by *Augusto Graziani, " The Social Sciences as Disciplines. V. Italy. I. Italy to the End of the World War," in *ESS*, i (1930), pp. 274–77. Of course the numerous special articles on Italian social scientists in the *ESS* have been used, as have also those in the *EI*. Ludwig Stein's *Die sociale Frage im Lichte der Philosophie* (1st ed., 1897) has been referred to occasionally, as have also Filippo Carli's *Le Teorie sociologiche* (1925), Achille Loria's *La Sociologia: Il suo compito — le sue scuole — i suoi recenti progressi* (1901), and Fausto Squillace's *Le Dottrine sociologiche* (1902). Although it has proved of slight value for this chapter, we should also mention the article by *Guiseppe Fiamingo, " Sociology in Italy," *AJS*, i (1895), pp. 335–52. Unfortunately we have not been able to consult books and articles by: Arcangelo Ghisleri, " Sociologia Italiana," *RDI*, ii, 4 (1919); Gaston Richard, " Le Mouvement sociologique en Italie," *RSH*, Dec., 1909; Pasquale Rossi, *Sociologia e psicologia collettiva*, (2nd ed., 1905); Fausto Squillace, *Dizionario di sociologia*, (2nd ed., 1911).

2. Cosentini, *J. B. Vico et la sociologie* (1899). See Benedetto Croce, " Giovanni Battista Vico (1668–1744)," *ESS*, xv (1935), pp. 249–50.

3. Graziani, *op. cit.*, p. 274.

4. Michels, " Elemente zur Soziologie in Italien " (hereafter cited as " Elemente," etc.), *KVS*, iii, 4 (1924), p. 220. See also Rodolfo Mondolfo, " Filangieri," in *ESS*, vi (1931), p. 231, and the unsigned article under the same head in *EI*. 5. Michels, *op. cit.*, p. 223.

6. Ghisleri, *op. cit.*, quoted in Michels, *loc. cit.*

7. *Ibid.*, p. 235. Romagnosi's culture-historical work is *Dell' indole e dei fattori dell' incivilimento* (3rd ed., 1835). See the estimate of Romagnosi by Alessandro Levi, *ESS*, xiii (1934), p. 419. 8. Michels, *op. cit.*, pp. 221–22.

9. *Alessandro Levi, " Ardigò," in *ESS*, ii (1930), pp. 181–82.

10. Michels, " Nachtrag zu den ' Elemente zur Soziologie in Italien ' " (hereafter cited as " Nachtrag," etc.), *KVS*, iv, 3/4 (1925), p. 331.

11. ——, " Elemente," etc., *KVS*, iii, 4 (1924), p. 222.

12. *Eugenio Rignano, " Sociology: Its Methods and Laws," Parts I and II, trans. by Howard Becker, *AJS*, xliv, 3 and 4 (Nov., 1928 and Jan., 1929), pp. 429–50, 605–22. Bibliography in footnotes.

13. Michels, *loc. cit.* Fragapane's chief work is his *Contrattualismo e sociologia contemporanea* (1892).

14. Enrico Altavilla, " Pessina," *ESS*, xii (1934), pp. 93–94. Pessina's most relevant book is entitled *Il Principio organico nella scienza sociale* (1894).

15. *Ibid.* Vadalà Papale's most important treatise is *Darwinismo naturale e Darwinismo sociale* (1893).

16. *Michels, " Colajanni," in *ESS*, iii (1930), pp. 625–26.

17. Our brief discussion of Vaccaro is in part based on a much longer paper, especially prepared for us, which will later be published elsewhere. The author is W. Rex Crawford of the University of Pennsylvania, one of the few American sociologists who readily commands the Italian language. He has also provided us with summary discussions of Pareto, Loria, and Gini, all of which will be published elsewhere after this book appears. We shall simply refer to his discussions as " Crawford, *op. cit.*" *We of course bear full responsibility for everything printed here.*

18. Vaccaro, *Genesi e funzione delle leggi penali* (1908). See H. E. Barnes, " Criminology," *ESS*, iv (1931), p. 588a, for brief mention of Vaccaro.

19. Vaccaro, *La Lotta per l'esistenza e i suoi effetti nell' umanità* (5th ed., 1920); *Les Bases sociologiques de droit et de l'État* (revised for French translation, 1898).

20. Crawford, *op. cit.*

21. Wiese-Becker, *Systematic Sociology* (1932), pp. 248–49; Michels, " Elemente," etc., *KVS*, iii, 4 (1924), p. 225. **22.** *Ibid.*, p. 243. **23.** *Ibid.*

24. *F. H. Hankins, " Atavism," in *ESS*, ii (1930); *C. Bernaldo deQuiros, " Lombroso," in *ESS*, vi (1931), p. 604. The book by *DeQuiros, *Modern Theories of Criminality* (translated by Alfonso de Salvio, 1912) contains good analyses of all the leading figures of the various schools and sub-schools of Italian criminology.

25. *C. Bernaldo deQuiros, " Ferri," in *ESS*, vi (1931), p. 188. His chief writings are *La Scuola criminale positive* (1885) and *Discordie positiviste sul socialismo* (2nd ed., 1899). Cf. Enrico Morselli, *Sociologia criminale e psicologia forense* (1907).

26. *Raffaele Garofalo, *Criminology* (1914: revised for the English translation to such an extent that this is virtually a new book; no revised Italian edition has appeared). A good bibliography and estimate of recent writers is provided in E. D. Monachesi, " Trends in Criminological Research in Italy," *ASR*, i, 2 (June, 1936), pp. 396–406.

27. A. Niceforo, *Les Classes pauvres* (1905). Essentially the same book is his *Anthropologie der nichtbesitzenden Klassen* (1910), from p. 37 of which Michels quotes in " Elemente," etc., *KVS*, iii, 4 (1924), p. 231.

28. *Ibid.*, p. 228. Sergi's most important books are *Le Degenerazioni umane* (1889), and *Problemi di scienza contemporanea* (1910).

29. Gina Lombroso-Ferrero, *I Vantaggi della degenerazione* (1904).

30. Pio Viazzi, *La Lotta di sesso* (1900).

31. Michels, *Sittlichkeit in Ziffern?* (1928); *I Limiti della morale sessuale* (1912). **32.** Cavaglieri and Florian, *I Vagabondi*, 2 vols. (1907).

33. Pietro Ellero, *La Tirannide Borghese* (1879).

34. Pasquale Turiello, *Governo e governati in Italia*, 2 vols. (2nd ed., 1889).

35. Michels, *op. cit.*, p. 226; article, " Genovesi," *EI*; Graziani, *op. cit.*, p. 274.

36. *Joseph J. Spengler, " Ortes," in *ESS*, xi (1933), pp. 498–99; Graziani, *loc. cit.*; Michels, *loc. cit.*

37. *Rodolfo Mondolfo, " Gioia," in *ESS*, vi (1931), p. 665; Michels, *loc. cit.*

38. Filippo Virgilii, *La Statistica nella odierna evoluzione sociale* (1913).

39. Lanfranco Maroi, *I fattori demografici del conflitto Europeo* (1919).

40. Filippo Carli, *L' Equilibrio delle nazioni secondo la demografia applicata* (1919).

41. Mondolfo, *loc. cit.*; Michels, *op. cit.*, p. 234. See Gioia, *Elementi di filosofia* (1833), pp. 57 ff.; *Del merito e delle ricompense* (1819), ii, pp. 96 ff.

42. Michels, *loc. cit.*

43. This was revised and incorporated in Sighele's larger work, *I Delitti della folla studiati secondo la psicologia, il diritto, e la giurisprudenza* (1910). See the article by Alessandro Levi, " Sighele," *ESS*, xiv (1934), p. 51.

44. Romagnosi, *op. cit.*, pp. 41–55, cited by Michels, *op. cit.*, p. 235.

45. Cattaneo, *Psicologia delle menti associate* (1859).

46. Sergi, *Psicosi epidemica* (1906).

47. Giuseppi Prato, *Il Protezianismo operaio e l'esclusione del lavoro straniero* (1910); Luigi Einaudi, *Un Principe mercante. Studie sull' espansione coloniale Italiana* (1900); Francesco Coletti, " L'Emigrazione Italiana," *Cinquanta anni di storia Italiana* (1911), iii. 48. Graziani, *op. cit.*, pp. 276–77.

49. Giuseppe Pecchio, *Dissertazione sino a qual punto le produzioni scientifiche e letterarie seguano le leggi economiche delle produzioni in generale* (1826).

50. Crawford, *op. cit.*

51. Chief of Loria's works is his *Analisi della proprietà capitalista* (1887). Of great importance, however, are *Le Leggi organiche della costituzione economica* (1889), *Le Forme storiche della costituzione economica* (1889), *Le Basi economiche della costituzione sociale* (3rd ed., 1902), *Verso la giustizia sociale*, 2 vols. (1st ed., 1904), and *Aspetti sociali ed economici della guerra mondiale* (1921). Concerning Loria, see *Ugo Rabbeno, *Loria's Landed System of Social Economy* (1892: reprinted from *PSQ*, vii, 2), Benedetto Croce, *Le Teorie storiche del Prof. Loria* (1897), and Enrico Leone, *Appunti critici sulla economia Loria* (1900).

52. Michels, *op. cit.*, p. 227.

53. Most of this section is based on Crawford, *op. cit.*

54. Michels, " Nachtrag," etc., *KVS*, iv, 3/4 (1925), p. 331.

55. ——, " Elemente," etc., *KVS*, iii, 4 (1924), p. 229.

56. Sergio Panunzio, *Il Socialismo giuridico* (1907); Cesare Vivante, *L' Influenza del socialismo sul diritto privato* (1902); Arrigo Solmi, *Elementi di storia del diritto Italiano* (1908).

57. Ettore Cicotti, *Montecitorio. Noterelle di uno che c' è stato* (1908) and *Psicologia del movimento socialista* (1903); Celso Ferrari, *I Partiti politici nella vita sociale* (1909); Vincenzo Gioberti, *Del rinnovomento d'Italia* (1851); Gaetano Mosca, *Elementi di scienza politica* (2nd ed., 1923); Vilfredo Pareto, *Les Systèmes socialistes* (1902; Italian ed., 1915).

58. This information about Pareto's life is drawn from Crawford, *op. cit.*; *G. H. Bosquet, *The Work of Pareto* (1928); and Franz Borkenau, *Pareto* (1936). The greater part of our discussion of his theories is based on a first-hand study of Pareto carried on in Ellsworth Faris's seminar in 1927–28, and on Crawford's summary. Talcott Parsons has an excellent article on Pareto in *ESS*, xi (1933), pp. 576–78, and his book, *Structure of Social Action* (1937), devotes much attention to him. See also his lengthy critical review, *ASR*, i, 1 (Feb., 1936), pp. 139–48. It may be worth noting here that sociologists were well informed about Pareto long before that Boanerges Blitzen, Bernard DeVoto, began to use the weapon that slew the Philistines. We have already mentioned Ellsworth Faris; let it also be noted that Carl Kelsey, of the University of Pennsylvania, studied Pareto in the Italian original early in the 1920's, and Crawford, to whose summaries we so frequently refer, prepared a *paragraph-by-paragraph* analysis of the *Trattato* for his seminar in social theory in 1929. Sorokin's knowl-

edge of Pareto became generally diffused among American sociologists after the publication of *Social Mobility* in 1927. DeVoto's childish exhibitionism makes this note necessary; he was by no means the first American to acquaint himself with Pareto's work, although it must be granted that he is the first sociologically naïve *littérateur* to make himself the ballyhoo man for the *Trattato* in the United States. But if we know the *littérateurs*, he will not be the last.

59. In the English translation of the *Trattato*, which appeared in the fall of 1934 under the title of *The Mind and Society: A General Sociology*, Pareto's wishes for the retention of the paragraph numbers have been complied with. Similar piety toward the title would have been edifying.

60. *Max Sylvius Handman, " The Sociological Method of Vilfredo Pareto," in *Methods in Social Science: A Case Book* (Stuart A. Rice, ed., 1931), p. 151.

61. *Ibid.*, p. 153.

62. Crawford, *op. cit.* The critique by Filippo Carli is similarly adverse: " Paretos soziologisches System und der Behaviorismus," *KVS*, iv, 3/4 (1925), pp. 273–85, esp. 280 ff. Amoroso and Sensini may be mentioned as disciples, and in 1912 one attempt was made to prop up in advance the unstable structure of the treatise — Marie Kobalinska wrote a thesis under Pareto entitled *Le Circulation des élites en France*. For summaries, consult the brochure by *Bousquet (*op. cit.*); Andrew Bongiorno, " A Study of Pareto's Treatise of General Sociology," *AJS*, xxvi, 3 (Nov., 1930), pp. 349–70; *George C. Homans and Carl C. Curtis, Jr., *Introduction to Pareto* (1934); Talcott Parsons, " Pareto," in *ESS*, xi (1933), pp. 576–78, review of *The Mind and Society*, *ASR*, i, 1 (Feb., 1936), pp. 139–48, and *the division on Pareto in *Structure of Social Action* (1937); *Ellsworth Faris, " An Estimate of Pareto," *AJS*, xli, 5 (March, 1936), pp. 657–68; articles by *McDougall, House, and others in the Pareto issue of the *JSP*, i, 1 (1935); L. J. Henderson, *Pareto*, etc. (1935); *Franz Borkenau, *Pareto* (1936); *Max Ascoli, " Society through Pareto's Mind," *SRE*, iii, 1 (Feb., 1936), pp. 78–89; Pitirim Sorokin, *Contemporary Sociological Theories* (1928), pp. 37–62; Malcolm Cowley, " A Handbook for Demagogues," *The New Republic*, lxxx, 1032 (Sept. 12, 1934); Gina Borgatta, *L'Opera sociologica e le feste giubilari di Vilfredo Pareto* (1917); various writers, *Festschrift jubilé du professeur Vilfredo Pareto* (1920); Umberto Ricci, *Politica ed economia* (1919); Pareto number of the *Giornale degli economisti* (Jan., 1924); the vehement articles and letters of Bernard DeVoto and others in *Harpers, Saturday Review of Literature*, etc., in the nonsensical Pareto controversy of 1933; *Carli, *op. cit.*; the lengthy summary by Sensini in the *Rivista Italiana di sociologia*, xxi (Mar.–June, 1917), pp. 198–258; and Pareto's own summary in *Fatti e teorie* (1920), pp. 314–26. For a bibliography of Pareto's writings see the *Giornale degli economisti e rivista di statistica*, 4th ser., lxiv (1924), pp. 144–53.

63. Gaetano Mosca, *Elementi di scienza politica* (1896; 2nd ed. 1923); Michels, *op. cit.*, p. 243. See Mosca's article, " Church Sects and Parties " (adapted from a chapter in his *Elemente di scienza politica*, 1895), *SF*, xiv, 1 (Oct., 1935), pp. 53–63.

64. Carmelo Caristia, *L'Analisi odierna del costituzionalismo* (1908); Michels, *loc. cit.*

65. Our discussion of Gini is based on Crawford, *op. cit.* Gini's justification of Fascism is exemplified in " The Scientific Basis of Fascism," *PSQ*, xlii, 1, pp. 99–115. His population theories are to be found in his *Nascita, evoluzione, e morte delle nazioni* (1930), and in English in the three lectures " The Cyclical Rise and Fall of Population," delivered on the Harris Foundation at the University of Chicago in 1929, forming part of a volume entitled *Population* (U. of Ch.

Press, 1930). He and others have recently produced an important treatise, *Demografia, antropometria, statistica sanitaria, dinamica delle popolazioni* (1930).
66. H. G. Duncan, quoted in Crawford, *op. cit.* A less vulnerable Italian student of population is M. Boldrini.
67. Fausto Squillace, *Le Dottrine sociologiche* (1902), augmented German trans. by Eisler, *Die soziologischen Theorien* (1911). Some of the classifications in Sorokin's *Contemporary Sociological Theories* were apparently borrowed from Squillace. **68.** Squillace, *Dizionario di sociologia* (2nd ed., 1911).
69. Michels, *op. cit.*, p. 244. **70.** Letters mentioned in note 1. **71.** *Ibid.*
72. *Herbert W. Schneider, "The Social Sciences as Disciplines. V. Italy. II. Italy under Fascism," in *ESS*, i (1930), pp. 277–79.
73. Ferdinand Tönnies, "Der internationale Soziologentag in Rom," *KVS*, iv, 1/2 (1924), pp. 118–21; Francesco Cosentini, letter to the present writer, and "Zur Vorgeschichte des internationalen soziologischen Instituts in Turin," *ibid.*, pp. 121–22.

CHAPTER XXVI

1. As elsewhere, we are here dependent on translations and secondary sources in languages we can read. (Unless otherwise noted, titles of books and articles by Russian authors given in English are Russian originals.) The source of which we have made most use is *Julius F. Hecker's *Russian Sociology: A Contribution to the History of Sociological Thought and Theory* (1934). This is a complete revision of his doctor's thesis of the same title, published in 1915, and is highly praised in a foreword by Sidney Webb. Another useful secondary source has been the *ESS*; its Russian articles are surprisingly numerous and full, and we have made use of the introductory chapter, *" VI. The Social Sciences as Disciplines: Russia," i (1930), pp. 280–291. We have also made use of the fragmentary remarks in Ludwig Stein's *Die sociale Frage im Lichte der Philosophie* (1st ed., 1897), pp. 20 ff., and Christian Rappoport's *Zur Charakteristik der Methode und Hauptrichtungen der Philosophie der Geschichte* (1896), pp. 40 ff. For recent developments the articles of Mykyta Shapoval have been valuable; these have appeared in Czech, and have been abstracted and translated into French for us by Antonín Obrdlík, one of the most promising of the younger Czech sociologists. Shapoval's articles appeared in the *Sociologická revue*, i, 1/2 (1930), pp. 101–106; ii, 2 (1931), pp. 195–202; 4 (1931), pp. 492–97; iii, 3/4 (1932), pp. 293–97; iv, 2/3 (1933), pp. 189–95; v, 1/3 (1934), pp. 70–75. Shapoval's writing was devoted primarily to the Ukraine, however; for modern, "Russian" developments in the strictly sociological field our chief prop has been the article by Pitirim Sorokin, "Die russische Soziologie im zwanzigsten Jahrhundert," *JFS*, ii (1926), pp. 462–83. This is also available in English in the *PASS*, xxi (1926), pp. 57–69. Another aid for the modern period has been the chapter by Zdenek Ullrich, "La Doctrine et l'enseignement sociologiques à l'étranger," in *Comment juger la sociologie contemporaine*, J. T. Delos and others (n. d., but apparently 1930), pp. 186–243. For general reference see *T. G. Masaryk, *Russland und Europa: Studien über die geistigen Strömungen in Russland* (1913), available in English translation. **2.** Hecker, *op. cit.*, p. 7.
3. *Ibid.*, p. 9. For Speransky, see V. Miakotin, "Speransky," *ESS*, xiv (1934), pp. 296–97.
4. Hecker, *loc. cit.* See also V. Gelesnoff, "Turgenev," *ESS*, xv (1934), p. 131.
5. *Nikolai Kareyev, "Danilevsky," *ESS*, iv (1931), p. 708. See also Hecker,

op. cit., pp. 33–39. For Soloviev, see Paul Miliukov, " Solovyev," *ESS*, xiv (1934), p. 256.

6. Oswald Spengler, *Untergang des Abendlandes*, trans. by Atkinson as *The Decline of the West*, ii, pp. 192–96. The connection between Danilevsky and Spengler may have been strengthened by their common knowledge of a predecessor, the German historian Heinrich Rückert, who in his *Lehrbuch der Weltgeschichte in organischer Darstellung* (1857) used the idea of " historical types of culture " that conform to organismic laws. We can only infer this, however, for neither of them acknowledges his debt. (Wörringer was also a predecessor of Spengler.) For the possible relation of Danilevsky to Rückert, see the article by Bestuzhev-Rasumnik, *Russky Vestnik*, Oct., 1894 (cited by Hecker). The likelihood that Spengler had direct knowledge of Danilevsky, however, is strong, for otherwise his Slavophilism would be hard to explain. Danilevsky's most important work is his *Rossia i Evropa* (*Russia and Europe*).

7. *I. V. Diones-Shkovsky, " Leontyev," in *ESS*, viii (1932), pp. 410–11. See also Hecker, *op. cit.*, pp. 39–42. Volumes v and vi of Leontiev's *Works* cover his sociological writings.

8. *A. Koyré, " Pobedonostsev," in *ESS*, xii (1934), pp. 177–78. See also Hecker, *op. cit.*, pp. 42–48. His chief work of sociological interest is his *Moscow Sbornik*.

9. *Paul Miliukov, " Chaadeyev," in *ESS*, iii (1930), pp. 320–21. See also Hecker, *op. cit.*, pp. 16, 53–55. Most important among his sociological writings are his " Lettres sur la philosophie de l'histoire," *Works*, I.

10. *Avrahm Yarmolinsky, " Belinsky," in *ESS*, ii (1930), p. 503.

11. Hecker, *op. cit.*, pp. 15–20.

12. Ludwig Stein, *op. cit.*, p. 20. See also *Nicholos Rusanov, " Lavrov," in *ESS*, ix (1933), p. 201, and Hecker, *op. cit.*, pp. 75–101. A bibliography of his most important works is to be found in the Rusanov article cited above, and also in Hecker, *op. cit.*, pp. 75, 304. His " Historical Letters " are available in German translation. **13.** Lavrov, quoted in Hecker, *op. cit.*, p. 76.

14. *Ibid.*, footnote 2. **15.** Rusanov, *loc cit.* **16.** Hecker, *op. cit.*, pp. 78–101.

17. *Nicholas Rusanov, " Mikhailovsky," in *ESS*, x (1933), pp. 445–46. See also Ludwig Stein, *loc. cit.*, and Hecker, *op. cit.*, pp. 102–133. Mikhalovsky wrote a tremendous amount; his works in the most recent edition fill ten large double-column volumes. Bibliographies are given in the Rusanov article cited above, and in Hecker, *op. cit.*, p. 304.

18. Mikhalovsky, *Works*, iv, p. 405, quoted in *ibid.*, p. 104.

19. *Ibid.*, pp. 107–115. For criticism, see p. 115.

20. *Ibid.*, pp. 116–28.

21. Pitirim Sorokin, " Die russische Soziologie im zwanzigsten Jahrhundert," *JFS*, ii (1926), p. 468. **22.** Hecker, *op. cit.*, pp. 134–48.

23. *Paul Miliukov, " Kareyev," *ESS*, viii (1932), pp. 545–46. His chief works are listed in Miliukov's article and in Hecker, *op. cit.*, pp. 149, 304.

24. Kareyev, *Introduction to Sociology*, (3rd ed., 1913), p. 222, quoted in Hecker, *op. cit.*, p. 155. **25.** *Ibid.*, pp. 159–73.

26. Kareyev, *Principal Queries of the Philosophy of History*, ii, p. 270, quoted in Hecker, *op. cit.*, p. 171. **27.** *Ibid.*, pp. 173–74. **28.** *Ibid.*, pp. 174, 259.

29. *Ibid.*, pp. 23–27.

30. Chernov, *Philosophical and Sociological Studies* (1907), pp. 307–309, cited in Hecker, *op. cit.*, p. 187.

31. ——, *op. cit.*, p. 309, quoted in Hecker, *op. cit.*, p. 188.

32. ——, *op. cit.*, p. 238, quoted in Hecker, *op. cit.*, p. 189.

33. *Ibid.*, pp. 189–93.

34. It will be recalled that our chapter on revolutionary socialism is based on the thesis by Frances Bennett Becker, *Violence the Midwife: a Comparison and Sociological Critique of the Revolutionary Theories of Marx and Lenin* (Smith College: 1934). This thesis also provides the backbone of our discussion of Lenin and the dialectic here. For Plekhanov, see *A. Potresoff, " Plekhanov," in *ESS*, xii (1934), pp. 181–82, and Hecker, *op. cit.*, pp. 253–64. **35.** *Ibid.*, p. 231.

36. *Ibid.*, p. 258. **37.** *Ibid.*, p. 263. **38.** *Ibid.*, p. 258.

39. Peter Struve, " Die Marxsche Theorie der sozialen Entwicklung," *ASGS*, xiv (1889), cited in Hecker, *op. cit.*, p. 267.

40. Struve, *Ideas and Politics in Contemporary Russia* (1906), p. 10, cited in Hecker, *op. cit.*, p. 269.

41. S. Solntsev, " Tugan-Baranovsky," *ESS*, xv (1935), pp. 128–29; Shapoval, *op. cit.* Tugan-Baranovsky's chief sociological work is *The Theoretical Basis of Marxism* (1905; available in German translation).

42. Tugan-Baranovsky, *op. cit.*, p. 53, quoted in Hecker, *op. cit.*, p. 274.

43. *Ibid.*, p. 275.

44. Bogdanov's chief works of sociological interest are his *Psychology of Society* (1904), *The Science of Social Consciousness* (1914), and *General Organizational Science: Tectology*, 3 vols. (1925–29). His *Short Course in Economic Science* is available in English translation (1923). See the article by J. F. Hecker, " Bogdanov," *ESS*, ii (1930), p. 617, and the book by the same author, *Russian Sociology* (previously cited), pp. 279–96.

45. In *Lenin's *Materialism and Empirio-Criticism*, vol. xiii of his *Works*.

46. See note 44. **47.** In Bogdanov's *Psychology of Society* (1904).

48. Here we have followed Bogdanov's summary given in the final chapter of his *Short Course in Economic Science* (English trans., 1923).

49. Marx, *Zur Kritik der politischen Ökonomie*, p. liv.

50. Hecker, *op. cit.*, p. 279, footnote 1.

51. Frances Bennett Becker, *op. cit.*, Part II, sec. 7 *et passim*. See also the article by Harold J. Laski, " Ulyanov," *ESS*, xv (1935), pp. 140–43.

52. *Ibid.*, sec. 15. **53.** *Ibid.*, Part III, *passim* and concluding section.

54. Sorokin, *op. cit.*, p. 466. **55.** Shapoval, *op. cit.* **56.** *Ibid.*

57. T. Osadchy, *The Life of Society: Outline of a Science of Society* (1901–1902), cited by Shapoval, *op. cit.*

58. Sorokin, *op. cit.*, pp. 480–81. The book deals with the theories of Tarde, Giddings, Baldwin, Gumplowicz, Ratzenhofer, Simmel, Durkheim, Bouglé, Coste, Kidd, Marx, Lapouge, Ammon, Vaccaro, Matteuzi, and others. See also the article by *E. Spektorski, " Kovalevsky," *ESS*, viii (1932), pp. 595–96.

59. Hecker, *op. cit.*, p. 201. **60.** *Ibid.*, p. 202.

61. Sorokin, *op. cit.*, pp. 462, 464. **62.** Hecker, *op. cit.*, p. 204.

63. Shapoval, *op. cit.* **64.** Hecker, *op. cit.*, pp. 203–204.

65. Sorokin, *op. cit.*, p. 480.

66. M. Povrovsky, " The Social Sciences as Disciplines: Russia, II, Soviet Russia," in *ESS*, i (1930), p. 291.

67. J. T. Delos and others, *op. cit.*, Appendix by Zdenek Ullrich, " La Doctrine et l'enseignement sociologiques à l'étranger," p. 227.

68. Shapoval, *op. cit.*

69. *Peter Bizili, " Lappo-Danilevsky," in *ESS*, viii (1932), pp. 169–70. See also Sorokin, *op. cit.*, p. 480.

70. *Georges Gurvitch, " Korkunov," in *ESS*, viii (1932), pp. 591–92. See also Hecker, *op. cit.*, pp. 194–200.

71. *Gurvitch, " Kistyakovsky," in *ESS*, viii (1932), pp. 575–76.
72. Sorokin, *op. cit.*, pp. 478–79.
73. F. Epstein, " Pokrovsky," in *ESS*, xii (1934), pp. 181–82.
74. Sorokin, *op. cit.*, p. 479.
75. Georges Gurvitch, " Petrazhitsky," *ESS*, xii (1934), pp. 103–104; Sorokin, *op. cit.*, p. 470. **76.** *Ibid.*, p. 471. **77.** *Ibid.*, p. 471–77.
78. I. Zeliony, " Über die zukünftige Sozio-Physiologie," *ARGB* (1912), pp. 405–30. See the abstract of Zeliony's theory given in *C. A. Ellwood's *Methods in Sociology* (1933), pp. 33–45.
79. J. R. Kantor, " Bekhterev," in *ESS*, ii (1930), p. 498. Bekhterev's chief works of sociological interest are his *Objective Psychology, Collective Reflexology* (1921) and *Foundations of Reflexology* (1928). The latter is available in English translation under the title of *Conditioned Reflexes*. See also Sorokin, *op. cit.*, pp. 472–73. **80.** *Ibid.* **81.** Sorokin, *Social Mobility* (1927), p. ix.
82. Sorokin, " Die russische Soziologie im zwanzigsten Jahrhundert," *JFS*, ii (1926), p. 477. **83.** *Ibid.*, p. 462. **84.** Kantor, *loc. cit.*
85. Sorokin, *op. cit.*, p. 463. **86.** *Ibid.*, pp. 463–64. **87.** Shapoval, *op. cit.*

CHAPTER XXVII

1. Inasmuch as some eight countries are bundled together in this chapter, we shall make a separate introductory note for each one. Here only the Czechoslovakian materials are listed. Chief among our scanty supply is the article by Innocenc Arnošt Bláha, " Die zeitgenössische tschechische Soziologie," *JFS*, ii (1926), pp. 441–61, translated by *Mildred Hartsough, " Contemporary Sociology in Czechoslovakia," *SF*, ix, 2 (Dec., 1930), pp. 167–79. *Our references are to the German original throughout.* Very useful also has been an article by Vasil K. Škrach, " Glossen über die tschechische Soziologie," *KVS*, v, 3 (1926), pp. 329–37. For the very recent developments, another article by Bláha has helped: " Der gegenwärtige Stand der čechischen Soziologie," *SLR*, Mar., 1934, pp. 77–86. For those who can read it, cf. Bláha's longer article: " Vspótezesna socjologja czeska," *Odbitka z Kwartalnika Socjologiczego*, nos. 2–4, 1931. Valuable information on moot questions has come from Profs. Antonín Obrdlík and J. S. Roucek. The *ESS* has again provided good supplementary data.
2. *Ernest Barnikol, " John Huss," in *ESS*, vii (1932), pp. 560–61; Škrach, *loc. cit.*
3. *Oscar Jaszi, " Anarchism," in *ESS*, ii (1930), p. 47; Škrach, *loc. cit.* Chelčický has been regarded as the " spiritual father " of Tolstoi.
4. *I. L. Kandel, " Comenius," in *ESS*, iii (1930), pp. 674–75; Škrach, *loc. cit.* Cf. the collection of Comenius's educational writings, esp. " The Great Didactic," edited by M. W. Keatinge, *Comenius* (1931).
5. *Ibid.*, pp. 332–33; *Joseph Hanuš, " Dobrovsky," *ESS*, v (1931), p. 187; Emanuel Rádl, " Šafařík," *ESS*, xiii (1934), p. 503.
6. *Emanuel Chalupný, " Kollár," *ESS*, viii (1932), p. 588; Škrach, *loc. cit.*
7. *Emanuel Rádl, " Palacký," in *ESS*, xi (1933), pp. 534–35; Škrach, *op. cit.*, p. 333.
8. Bláha, " Die zeitgenössische tschechische Soziologie," *JFS*, ii (1926), p. 441; Škrach, *loc. cit.*; *Helmut Wiese, " Herbart," in *ESS*, vii (1932), p. 325.
9. This first appeared in German; much later it was translated into Czech by J. Král as *Ideje k psychologii spolecnosti jakožto základ sociálni vědy*. Král has also written the best book on Herbartian sociology, *Herbartovská sociologie* (1922).
10. Škrach, *op. cit.*, p. 331.

11. Škrach, *op. cit.*, p. 331; Bláha, *op. cit.*, pp. 444–46.

12. Masaryk's works are in Czech and in German; the latter language was used for most of what he wrote before the war, and after the war German translations were made of some of his important Czech writings. As few of our readers are able to read Czech, we shall list the German first: *Der Selbstmord als soziale Massenerscheinung der modernen Zivilisation* (1881); *Versuch einer konkreten Logik: Klassifikation und Organisation der Wissenschaften* (1887); "Skizze einer soziologischen Analyse der sogenannten Grünberger und Königinhofer Handschrift," *Archiv für slawische Philologie*, x (1887); *Palackýs Idee des böhmischen Volkes* (1889); **Die philosophischen und soziologischen Grundlagen des Marxismus* (1899); *Ideale der Humanität*, trans. by Herbatschek (1902); **Russland und Europa: Studien über die geistigen Strömungen in Russland*, 2 vols. (1913 — available in English trans.); *Das neue Europa*, trans. by Saudek (1922); **Die Weltrevolution: Erinnerungen und Betrachtungen 1914–18*, trans. by Hoffmann (1925).

Počet pravdepodobnosti a Humeova skepse (1883 — *The Theory of Probabilities and Hume's Scepticism*); *V biji o náboženství* (1904 — *The Struggle over Religion*); *Přehled nejnovější filosofie náboženství* (1904 — *Survey of Recent Philosophy of Religion*); *Inteligence a náboženství* (1907 — *Intelligence and Religion*); *Věda a církev* (1908 — *Science and the Church*); *Česká otázka* (1895 — *The Czech Question*); *Naše nynější krise* (1895 — *Our Present Crisis*); *Jan Hus* (1903 — *John Huss*); *Karel Havlíček* (1896); and a number of other Czech writings of which the original titles and dates are not accessible to us: "Theory of History According to the Principles of T. H. Buckle," "Man and Nature," "Handbook of Sociology" (a collection of sociological articles), and numerous reviews, lectures, and shorter articles of sociological import.

It should not be necessary here to give a bibliography like this; a simple reference to the *ESS* should suffice — but the incredibly shortsighted policy of the editors of that publication permitted only articles about *dead* social scientists. Masaryk, although born in 1850, stubbornly insisted on staying alive until the middle of 1937. Unfortunately, we have not been able to make use of an article forthcoming in the *ASR*, by J. S. Roucek, "Thomas Garrigue Masaryk as Sociologist."

13. Bláha, *op. cit.*, p. 447, trans. by Hartsough, *op. cit.*, p. 170.

14. Škrach, *op. cit.*, p. 332.

15. *Ibid.*, p. 334; Bláha, *op. cit.*, p. 450. Foustka's most important work is *Slabí v lidské spolecnosti* (1905 — *The Weaknesses of Human Society*).

16. Bláha, *op. cit.*, pp. 453–57; Škrach, *op. cit.*, pp. 334–35. Beneš's chief works of sociological significance are: *Le Problème autrichien et la question tchèque: études sur les luttes politiques des nationalités slaves en Autriche* (1908); *Strannictví* (1912 — *The Nature of Political Parties*); *Válka a kultura* (1915 — *War and Culture*); and *Povaha politického strannictví* — (a supplement to the 1912 treatise). For a more comprehensive bibliography, cf. Bláha, *loc. cit.*

17. Škrach, *op. cit.*, p. 335; Bláha, *op. cit.*, p. 457. Bláha's most important writings are : T. G. Masaryk: *Philosophie du synergisme* (1924); " La Sociologie tchèque contemporaine," *RIS*, xxix (1921); *Mesto* (1913 — *The City*); and the study of the worker and the peasant mentioned in the text — cf. Škrach, *loc. cit.* Recently Bláha has published an interesting study of the rôle of the intelligentsia, *Sociologie inteligence* (1937).

18. In addition to Chalupný's *Introduction to Sociology* (Czech, 1905) and his large systematic work *Sociology* (Czech, 1915–), he has written a large number of books and articles, of which a few of the most important are: *Národni povaha česka* (1907 — *The Character of the Czech People*); *Havlíček* (1908);

Úkol českého národa (1910 — *The Task of the Czech People*); *Český stát z hlediska sociologie* (*The Czech State from the Standpoint of Sociology*); *Studium sociologie v Americe a u nás* (*The Study of Sociology in America and in Czechoslovakia*); etc.

19. Josífek's chief works of sociological interest are: *Sociologie; Společenské vědomí* (*The Social Consciousness*); *Vývoj charkteruvývoj společnosti* (*The Evolution of Character — the Evolution of Society*); etc. Kunte's major sociological writings are: *Sociologie a její pracktické použití* (*Sociology and Its Practical Applications*); and *Socialisace* (*Socialization*). Cf. Bláha, *op. cit.*, pp. 458–61; Škrach, *op. cit.*, p. 335.

20. Bláha, *op. cit.*, pp. 457–58; Škrach, *op. cit.*, p. 336. Uhlíř's book is entitled *Soziální filosofie* (*Social Philosophy*).

21. Bláha, " Der gegenwärtige Stand der čechischen Soziologie," *SLR*, March, 1934, p. 85.

22. Studies of " national character," amalgamation, acculturation, culture conflict, and marginal peoples have been made by V. Dvorský, J. Matiegka, E. Rádl, J. Kallab, F. Žilka, K. Hoch, A. Štefánek, F. Peroutka, J. Mahen, O. Vočadlo, F. V. Krejčí, V. Mathesius, V. Vohryzek, J. Korčák, J. Húsek, Pražák, Chaloupecký, Trávníček, J. Auerhan, and J. Kohn. Research in the natural history of the Czechoslovak family, family disorganization, and the like, has been done by Friedrich Vasek, Machotka, Vešek, and Bláha. Population problems engage the attention of Boháč, C. Horáček, D. Krejčí, J. Korčák, and Auerhan. Social stratification in its various forms has been studied by Bláha, Mertl, Hodža, Stefánek, Hertl, Ullrich, Paleček, Čep, Matula, Smetánka, Pohl, Ráliš, and Galla. Problems of economic life are subjected to sociological analysis by Maiwald, Potužil, Knížek, Stern, Nečasová-Poubova, Mertl, Fleischner, J. Maček, Kunte, Špaček, Kučera, Modráček, and Zwicker. The sociological foundations of theoretical politics have long been a favorite field of Czech sociology, as our discussion of Masaryk, Beneš, and others made plain; other investigators are Obrdlík, Kallab, Weyr, Zd. Peška, J. L. Fischer, Reyl, Uhlíř, Mertl, Stocký, and Sedmík. The sociology of revolution has been dealt with by Obrdlík and Ullrich. The function of technics in modern social life has been analyzed by Fleischner, Šmejkal, and Kroha. The sociology of morals and of law finds representatives in Chalupný, Krejčí, Bláha, Uhlíř, Chlup, Machotka, Fajfr, and E. Svoboda. Art as a social product having sociological functions is analyzed by Šalda, M. Novák, Václavek, Götz, Teige, Kroha, and others. The natural history of the newspaper and like problems are studied by Butter, Bláha, and Machotka. Regionalism is dealt with from the sociological standpoint by Chalupný, Fischer, and Bláha. Criminology is approached from a sociological angle by Procházka, Lány, and Ráliš. Social work theory and practice are provinces occupied by Foustka, Kalláb, Krejčí, V. Vostřebalová, Fischerová, Král, Uhlíř, Modraček, Bláha, F. Fajhr, Škrach, Osuský, Ullrich, Galla, and Fryček. Finally, the history of Czech sociology is studied by Nejedlý, Král, Kozák, Hromádka, Stefánek, Fajfr, Škrach, and Bláha. Cf. Škrach, *op. cit.*, pp. 335–37, and Bláha, *op. cit.*, pp. 81–83, as well as the articles cited in note 51 below.

23. See the excellent articles by Joseph Roucek, " Sociological Periodicals of Czechoslovakia," *ASR*, i, 1 (Feb., 1936), pp. 168–70; and Antonín Obrdlík, " Sociological Activities in Czechoslovakia," *ASR*, i, 4 (August, 1936), pp. 653–56.

24. For the Ukraine our only sources of information are the articles by M. J. Shapoval (or Šapoval), " Soziologie in der Ukraine," *KVS*, v, 1/2 (1925), pp. 187–90, and " Contemporary Sociological Thought and Work in the Ukraine " (in

Czech; abstracted for us in French by Prof. Antonín Obrdlík), *Sociologická revue*, i, 1/2 (1930), pp. 101–106; ii, 2 (1931), pp. 195–202; 4 (1931), pp. 492–97; iii, 3/4 (1932), pp. 293–97; iv, 2/3 (1933), pp. 189–95; v, 1/3 (1934), pp. 70–75. As the articles in Czech supersede the earlier German article, we cite only the latter. We have taken account, however, of the protests against Shapoval's interpretations made by Starosolsky and Botschkovsky in *KVS*, v, 4 (1926), p. 495. Too late to be of use was the article soon to be forthcoming in the *ASR*, by Yaroslav J. Chyz, " The Development of Ukrainian Sociology."

25. The titles of these works (all in Ukrainian) are *Genetic Sociology, Theory of the Nation*, and *The State and Socialist Society*.

26. For Poland we have had the advantage of an excellent résumé written especially for us in 1928 by Florian Znaniecki, and of a long article by F. Mirek, " Sociologie v. Polsku," Parts I and II, *Sociologická revue*, i, 1/2 and 3/4 (1930), pp. 96–100 and 301–306. Mirek's article has been translated into French for us by Prof. Antonín Obrdlík, whose generous services in connection with this chapter have placed sociology in his debt. Obrdlík has also given us valuable information about the interval between 1930 and 1935. A few articles in the *ESS* have also been helpful. Further, we have made use of the recent article by E. M. Znaniecka, " Sociology in Poland," *ASR*, i, 2 (April, 1936), pp. 296–98.

27. *Artur Śliwiński, " Mochnacki," *ESS*, x (1933), p. 564.

28. *Nathan Reich, " Wroński-Hoene," *ESS*, xv (1935), pp. 504–506.

29. *Francizek Bujak, " Cieszkowski," *ESS*, iii (1930), pp. 469–70.

30. Mirek, *op. cit.*, Part I.

31. To state Winiarski's theory a bit more connectedly: " Man is a pleasure machine," and his pleasure-pain reactions are mathematically measurable. The attraction and repulsion (essentially similar to gravitation) that constitute the economic and social equilibrium are the work of the two social forces, egoism and altruism. These forces subsume all others — sexual, power, and whatnot. Social evolution is simply a moving equilibrium of these forces. Winiarski's chief statements of his theory are: " La Méthode mathématique dans la sociologie et dans l'économie politique," *RSe*, Dec., 1894; " Essai d'une nouvelle interprétation des phénomènes sociologiques," *RSe*, Oct., 1896; " Essai sur la mécanique sociale," *RP*, Apr., 1898; " L'Énergie social et ses mensurations," *RP*, 1900 (cited in Petre Trişcă, *Prolégomènes à une mécanique sociale*, Part II [thesis, Poitiers, 1922] p. 16); and an article in a special issue of the *AIIS*, " Mécanique sociale," vii (1900), pp. 229 ff. Trişcă's thesis, cited above, is the best discussion of Winiarski's work. See also Pitirim Sorokin, *Contemporary Sociological Theories* (1928), pp. 23–29.

32. *Ludwik Krzywicki, " Krauz-Kelles," in *ESS*, viii (1932), p. 598; Mirek, *op. cit.*, Part I.

33. *E. and F. Znaniecki, " Gumplowicz," in *ESS*, vii (1932), p. 227.

34. Mirek, *op. cit.*, Part I. See also Mirek's book, *The Sociological System of L. Gumplowicz* (Polish; 1930), sponsored by the Polish Institute of Sociology.

35. Mirek, " Sociology in Poland " (in Polish), Part I, *Sociologická revue*, i, 1/2 (1930), pp. 96–100. Krusiński's book is *Sociological Sketches* (Polish; 1886).

36. Mirek, *op. cit.*, Part I. Kulczycki is the author of *Principles of General Sociology* (Polish; 1900, new rev. and enlarged ed., 1923).

37. Znaniecki, *op. cit.* Balicki's chief work is *Psychologja społeczna* (*Social Psychology* — 1910). He is also the author of a French treatise, *L'État comme organisation coercitive de la société*.

38. Mirek, *op. cit.*, Part I; Znaniecki, *op. cit.* In addition to the German work cited in the text, he is also the author of *Echa prawieku* (*Echoes from Prehistoric*

Times — 1910), *Nad Renem i nad Wisła* (*On the Rhine and on the Vistula* (1913), *Postęp Ludzkości* (*The Progress of Mankind* — 1917), and *Polska w świetle psychiki własnej i obcej* (*Poland in the Light of Its Own and of Foreign Psychology* — 1920). **39.** Znaniecki, *op. cit.*

40. Znaniecka, *op. cit.*, p. 296. Krzywicki's chief works are *Ustroje społeczne w okresie dzikości i barbarzyństwa* (*Social Organization in the Periods of Savagery and Barbarism* — 1914), and *Studja socjologiczne* (*Sociological Studies* — 1923).

41. Znaniecki, *op. cit.* We have stated this objection rather more forcibly than has Znaniecki.   **42.** Mirek, *op. cit.*, Part II.   **43.** Znaniecki, *op. cit.*

44. The titles of these works of Znaniecki's are: *Zagadnienie wartości filozofji* (*The Problem of Values in Philosophy* — 1910); *Humanizm i poznanie* (*Humanism and Knowledge* — 1912); *Wstęp do socjologji* (*Introduction to Sociology* — 1922); and *Socjologja wychowania* (*Sociology of Education* — 1928).

45. Znaniecki, special résumé already cited.

46. The writings of these associates of Znaniecki's are: J. Chałasinski, *Wychowanie w domu obcym* (*Education in a Stranger's Home*); W. Adamski, *Zarys socjologji stosowanej* (*Outline of Applied Sociology*); F. Mirek, *Elementy społeczne parafji rzymsko-katolickieji* (*Social Elements of the Roman Catholic Parish*); T. Szczurkiewicz, *Sugestja* (*Suggestion*); H. Erzepski, *Stosunki towarzyskie mężczyzn i kobiet* (*Social Relations of Men and Women*); and S. Orsini-Rosenberg, *Zagadnienia styczne polityki gospodarczej i technologji społecznej* (*Problems on the Borderline of Practical Economics and Social Technology*). Dobrzyńska-Rybicka is a *Privatdozent* in the University of Poznań who is developing a system of education for citizenship based on sociology, but none of the exact titles of his publications are at present available. Abel's paper, " The Nature and Scope of Sociology," *SF*, xi, 2 (Dec., 1932), pp. 176–82, is partially based on Znaniecki's definition of sociology. Other writings by associates of Znaniecki are contained in the publication of the Poznań institute, *Przegląd socjologiczny*, published semi-annually.   **47.** Mirek, *op. cit.*, Part II.

48. The secondary sources on which we have relied for our information about Hungary are very scanty indeed: our sole aids have been articles by Leopold von Wiese, " Notizen über die gegenwärtige Pflege der Soziologie in Ungarn," *KVS*, iv, 3/4 (1925), pp. 329–30; and Theo Surányi-Unger, " IV. Austria and Hungary. II. Hungary," in *ESS*, i (1930), pp. 269–73; and scattered articles and references by Vámbéry, Jaszi, Ferrière, Szél, Krisztics, and others in the *ESS*.

Unfortunately, Lewis Leopold's important *Prestige* (1913) was overlooked by every secondary writer consulted, and we became aware of his Hungarian affiliations too late to deal with him.

For our general evaluation of post-War developments, Wiese's article (cited above) has been determining.

49. Surányi-Unger, *op. cit.*, pp. 269–71.

50. *Alexander L. Krisztics, " Bessenyo," in *ESS*, ii (1930), pp. 520–21.

51. *Rusztem Vámbéry, " Pulszky," in *ESS*, xii (1934), p. 639.

52. Surányi-Unger, *loc. cit.*

53. *Vámbéry, " Giesswein," in *ESS*, vi (1931), p. 656.

54. *Adolphe Ferrière, " Teréz Brunswick," *ESS*, iii (1930), p. 21.

55. Wiese, *op. cit.*, pp. 329–30. See E. von Kármán, *Die Diebstähle der Kinder* (no. 13 of the collection, *Entschiedene Schulreform* — c. 1923 or 1924).

56. Surányi-Unger, *op. cit.*, pp. 271–72.

57. *Theodore Szél, " Kőrösy," in *ESS*, viii (1932), p. 592–93.

58. For Yugoslavia our data have come primarily from articles by Mirko M. Kosić, " Soziologie in Jugoslawien," *KVS*, iv, 1/2 (1924), pp. 112–13, and

" Star sociologického studia u Jiho-Slovanu " (Sociology in Yugoslavia), *Socio-logická revue*, ii, 2 (1931), pp. 190–94. As the Czech article supersedes the German, we cite only the latter. Prof. Kosić originally wrote this in German, and has kindly placed the MS at our disposal. Recently J. S. Roucek has published an article on sociology in Yugoslavia to which we later refer.

59. *C. S. Lobingier, " Bogišić," in *ESS*, ii (1930), p. 618; Kosić, *op. cit.*

60. *Hermann Kantorowicz, " Puchta," in *ESS*, xii (1934), p. 702.

61. *See the *ESS* article, " Mir," and also the bibliography furnished by Roucek, *op. cit.*, p. 983.

62. Gjorgjević has a two-volume work, *Naš narodni život* (1930 — *The Life of the Yugoslav Folk*). Cf. this with *Louis Adamić's *The Native's Return* (1933).

63. *Dragoljub Jovanović, " Marković," in *ESS*, x (1933), pp. 144–45.

64. Knežević's works are: *The Principles of History* (1898), *The Founding of History* (1898), and *The Proportions of History* (1901). From Kosić's MS it is impossible to tell whether these are in German or one of the Yugoslav languages.

65. The title of Avramović's book is *The Economic Activity of the Yugoslav Peasantry* (in Croatian).

66. Some of Kosić's chief works are in German: *Moderne Germania* (1912), *Die Südslavenfrage* (1918), " Der Geburtenrückgang in Ungarn," *ASA*, 1914, and " Die soziologischen Grundlagen der Geburtenbeschränkung," *ibid.*, 1917–18. Others, in Croatian, are *Agrarian Policy* (1925), *Sociology of the Magyar Revolution* (1920), *The Idea of Progress in Current Sociology* (1924), and *The Problem of Leadership* (1930).

67. See our chapter on Germanic sociology, p. 949.

68. *Arthur W. McMahon, " Ostrogòrsky," in *ESS*, xi (1933), pp. 503–504; Kosić, *op. cit.*

69. See the article by J. S. Roucek, " The Development of Sociology in Yugoslavia," *ASR*, i, 6 (Dec., 1936), pp. 981–88.

70. The fact that a large proportion of Roumanian sociologists write in French or have their works translated into that language considerably simplifies our task in this section. Our chief secondary sources are articles by Traian Brăileanu, " Soziologie in Rumanien," *KVS*, v, 4 (1926), pp. 491–95, and G. Vladesco-Racoassa (hereafter cited as Vladesco), " La Sociologie en Roumanie," *RIS*, xxxvii, 1/2 (Jan.–Feb., 1929), pp. 1–22, as well as his as yet unpublished article, " Quelques notes sur la sociologie roumaine depuis 1929." Vladesco's brochure, *L'Institut social roumain: xv ans d'activité, 1918–1933* (1933), has also been useful. There is an article on Roumanian sociology by a writer named Andrassy, but we have been unable to trace it. See also M. C. Sandulesco-Godeni, " Problemi e realizzazioni sociologiche a Bucarest," *REO* (1934); and G. Marica, " Dorf-soziologische Untersuchungen in Rumanien," *KVS*, xii, 2 (1933), pp. 127–38.

71. Brăileanu, *op. cit.*, p. 491. Cf. G. D. Scraba, *Joan Heliade-Rădulescu, Inceputurile filosofici și sociologiei române (J. H.-R. The Beginnings of Rou-manian Philosophy and Sociology — c. 1914)*; and Marin Stefănescu, *Filosofia Românească* (1922). **72.** Vladesco, *op. cit.*, p. 3.

73. *Sidney Hook, " Büchner," in *ESS*, iii (1930), p. 30. Büchner's most important book is his *Kraft und Stoff* (1855, 21st ed. 1904; trans. by Colling-wood, 1864, 4th English ed. from 15th German ed., 1884).

74. Vladesco, *op. cit.*, p. 4. Conta's chief works are: *La Théorie du fatalisme* (1877; Roumanian ed. somewhat earlier); *La Théorie de l'ondulation universelle* (with an introduction by Büchner, 1895; Roumanian ed. 1876); *Introduction* *à la métaphysique* (1880; Roumanian ed. 1879); *Premiers principes composant le monde* (1888); *Les Fondements de la métaphysique* (1890); and " L'Art de se conduire et de conduire dans la société," *ASSSR*, with notes and commentary by Gusti, i, 4 (1919), pp. 619–24.

75. N. Bagdasar, " Conceptia filosofiei istoriei la A.-D. Xenopol " (Xenopol's Conception of the Philosophy of History), *ASSSR*, vii, 3/4 (1928), p. 558, cited by Vladesco, *op. cit.*, p. 5. See also O. Botez, *Al. Xenopol, teoretician si filosof al istoriei, studiu critic* (1928).

76. Xenopol's most important work is *Les Principes fondamentaux de l'histoire* (1899; second ed. under title of *La Théorie de l'histoire* [1908]). Our discussion is drawn from this and from Brăileanu, *op. cit.*, p. 493, and Vladesco, *op. cit.*, pp. 4–7. Much that is relevant is to be found in N. Bagdasar, *Filosofia contimporană a istoriei*, i (1930).

77. *Kurt Breysig, " Lamprecht," *ESS*, ix (1933), pp. 27–28; *H. E. Barnes, *The New History and the Social Sciences* (1925), pp. 198–204.

78. Brăileanu, *op. cit.*, p. 493.

79. Vladesco, *op. cit.*, pp. 9–10; bibliography. Drăghicescu's most recent works are *La nouvelle cité de Dieu* (1929) and *Vérité et Révélation* (1934).

80. Vladesco, *op. cit.*, p. 10; bibliographies.

81. A determined assault on Haret and other expounders of " social mechanics " is made by Petre Trişcă, *Prolégomènes à une mécanique sociale* (thesis: Poitiers, 1922). Trişcă's book is a curious conglomerate; although he calls it a " prolegomenon to a social mechanics " to be presented in three parts, only two have appeared, of which the first is a miscellaneous collection purporting to be " a history of economic and social doctrines," and the second contains an almost pathologically savage attack on Haret, who as minister of public education made some rulings adverse to Trişcă, who was then a student. The second part is nevertheless extremely useful to the historian of sociology, for it deals with Winiarski, Barcelo, Ward, Groppali, and other representatives of this obscure trend in sociology.

82. Vladesco, *op. cit.*, pp. 10–17, and *L'Institut social roumain: xv ans d'activité, 1918–1933* (1933), pp. 3–5; Brăileanu, *op. cit.*, pp. 493–94. See also the article by Philip E. Mosely, " The Sociological School of Dmitrie Gusti," *SR*, xxviii, 2 (Apr., 1936), pp. 149–65.

83. Among Gusti's outstanding sociological writings are: " Die soziologischen Bestrebungen in der neueren Ethik," *VWPS* (1908); " Sozialwissenschaften, Soziologie, Politik und Ethik in ihrem einheitlichen Zusammenhang: Prolegomena zu einem System," *ZP* (1909–1910); *Un Séminaire de sociologie, de politique et d'éthique à l'Université de Jassy* (1910); *Studii Sociologici si etice. Din lucrarile Seminarului de sociologie din Jasi*, ed. (*Studies in Sociology and Ethics: Works of the Jassy Sociological Seminar* — 1915); *Sociologia războiului* (*Sociology of War* — 1915); *Realitate, stiinta şi reforma sociala. Cateva indicatii asupra metodei* (*Reality, Science, and Social Reform: Some Comments on Method* — 1920); *Partidul politic. Sociologia unnui sistem al partidului politic* (*The Political Party: the Sociology of a System of Political Parties* — 1923); etc., cited in Vladesco, " La Sociologie en Roumanie," *RIS*, xxxvii, 1/2 (Jan.–Feb., 1929), pp. 11–14. Recently he has published a collection of his shorter writings on political sociology under the title *Sociologia militans, Introducere în sociologia politică* (1934).

84. Vladesco, *L'Institut social roumain: xv ans d'activité, 1918–1933* (1933), pp. 9–11.

85. *Ibid.*, p. 13; and Vladesco, " La Sociologie en Roumanie," *RIS*, xxxvii, 1/2 (Jan.–Feb., 1929), p. 14.

86. In addition to the book noted in the text, Andrei is the author of *Das Problem der Methode in der Soziologie* (1927); *Sociologia revolutiei* (*Sociology of Revolution* — 1925); *Problème de Sociologie* (1927); etc.

87. See the review of Brăileanu's *Sociologia Generala* (1926), by Nicolaus Petrescu in *KVS*, v, 4 (1926), p. 458. His other noteworthy writings are *Despre condiţiunile conştiinţei şi umoştinţei* (*Of the Conditions of Consciousness and Knowledge* — 1912); *Die Grundlagen zu einer Wissenschaft der Ethik* (1919); and *Introducere in Sociologie* (1923).

88. Saint-Zeletin's principal works are: *Burghezia Română. Origina şi rolul ei istoric* (*The Roumanian Bourgeoisie: Origin and Historical Significance* —1925); *Neoliberalismul. Studii asupra istoriei şi politicei burghesiei romane* (*Neo-Liberalism: Studies in the History and Politics of the Roumanian Bourgeoisie* — 1927); *Istoria sociala* (*Social History* — 1925); *Inceputurile individualismului: incercare de psichologie socială a culturii elene din a dona jamatate a veacului al v^e A.C.* (*The Beginnings of Individualism: Essay in the Social Psychology of Hellenic Culture in the Second Half of the Fifth Century B.C.*); *Toranism şi marxism* (*Agrarianism and Marxism*). Cf. Vladesco, *op. cit.*, p. 16.

89. Ralea's significant sociological treatises are: *Révolution et socialisme: essai de bibliographie* (1923); *L'Idée de révolution dans les doctrines socialistes: étude sur l'évolution de la tactique révolutionnaire* (1923); *Contributii la stiinta societatii* (*Contributions to the Science of Society* — 1927); and *Introducere in Sociologie* (1926).

90. Rădulescu-Motru's chief books are: *Psichologia martorului* (*The Psychology of Testimony* — 1916); *Personalismul energetic* (*Energetic Personalism* — 1927); and *Cultura romana şi politicanismul* (*Roumanian Culture and " Politicianism "* — 1912–13). Cf. Vladesco, *loc. cit.*

91. Bărbat's noteworthy writings are: *Nietzsche: tendances et problèmes* (1911); *Imperialismul american: doctrine lui Monroe* (1920); and *Dinamism culturii* (1928). Cf. Brăileanu, " Soziologie in Rumanien," *KVS*, v, 4 (1926), pp. 494—95.

92. Petrescu has written three important books in English: *Thoughts on War and Peace* (1912), *The Principles of Comparative Sociology* (1924), and *The Interpretation of National Differentiations* (1929). See the review of the book second in this list by Leopold von Wiese, *KVS*, iv, 3/4 (1925), p. 294. His Roumanian works include *Fenomenele sociale in Statele Unite* (*Social Phenomena in the United States* — 1925); *Sociologia ca disciplină filosofică* (*Sociology as a Philosophical Discipline* — 1933).

93. J. C. Filitti, *Evolutia claselor sociale in trecutul Principatelor române* (1926).

94. G. Antipa's noteworthy treatises are: *Problemele actuale ale miscarii socialiste* (*Current Problems of the Socialist Movement* — 1922); *Lupta de clasà şi transformarea socialà* (*Class Struggle and Social Transformation* — 1923); and *Marxismul oligarhic* (*Oligarchic Marxism* — 1926).

95. Trişcă's study of social mechanics has already been listed. He is also the author of a number of books and brochures on miscellaneous topics, ranging from the function of the check in the banking system to the protection of the unmarried mother.

96. We may name T. Vianu, N. Bagdasar, M. Vulcanescu, H. H. Stahl, Eugène Sperantia, C. Sudeteanu, Ion C. Filitti, Petre D. Toma, George Em. Marica, N. N. Matheescu, Alexandru Papacosta, André Corteanu, Gromoslav Mladenatz, P. Juganaru, P. P. Negulescu, Ioan Lupu, Al. Claudian, V. V. Pella, Florin Manoliu, and Trian Herseni.

97. Vladesco, *L'Institut social roumain: xv ans d'activité, 1918–1933* (1933), pp. 41–43.

98. Brăileanu, *op. cit.*, p. 494; Vladesco, " La Sociologie en Roumanie," *RIS*, xxxvii, 1/2 (Jan.–Feb., 1929), p. 21. 99. Brăileanu, *op. cit.*, p. 495.

100. For Greece our sole primary sources are articles and books in German (we do not read modern Greek freely), by Eleutheropoulos, Kanellopoulos, and others. (Unless cited in languages other than English, everything in the bibliographies hereafter given is in modern Greek.) Only one secondary source has been directly used: a résumé especially written for us by Panajotis Kanellopoulos, professor of sociology at the University of Athens, " Die neugriechische Soziologie " (1934).

101. *Ibid.* Papanastasion later entered active politics; he has several times been minister and twice ministerial president. He is now leader of the Labor-Agrarian party. Other prominent figures in the society were: Th. Koutopis, now a publicist on economic topics; A. Delmousos, professor of pedagogy at the University of Saloniki; Th. Petimesas, professor of commercial law at the University of Athens; P. Aravantinos, until his recent death active in politics and several times minister; K. Triantaphyllopoulos, professor of civil law at the University of Athens, also interested in the philosophy of law; and A. Mylonas, now leader of an independent agrarian party.

102. This journal is edited by Demosthenes Kalitsounakis, professor of economics at the University of Athens.

103. The chief works of these two writers are:.G. Skleros, *Our Social Problem* (1907); Joh. Kordatos, *The Social Significance of the Greek Revolution* (1924), and *Political History of Modern Greece*, vol. i (1925).

104. Dem. Danielides, *Society and Economics in Modern Greece*, Bk. I, Part I (1934).

105. See Kanellopoulos's article, " Soziologisches Denken und soziologische Wissenschaft," *KVS*, vii, 3 (1928), pp. 277–89.

106. Most of these have appeared in the *AESS*, and the others in the *APM*: G. Charitakis, " Alfred Weber's Theories of Societal Evolution, Civilization, and Culture "; P. Byzonkides, " Joseph Kohler's Contribution to Sociology"; Joh. Lampiris, " Émile Durkheim and the French School of Sociology "; Panojotis Kanellopoulos, " Ferdinand Tönnies and Sociology "; " The Sociology of Comte and a Critique of His Epistemological Assumptions," " Alfred Weber and the Idea of Progress," " Leopold von Wiese's Sociological System," and " Sociology as a Science of Reality: the Theory of Hans Freyer "; Dem. Besanis, " Economic Science According to Franz Oppenheimer "; P. Zissis, " Tönnies's Contribution to Sociology "; Dem. Kalitsounakis, " Werner Sombart and the Systematization of Political Economy "; and the introductions to the translations of Loria's *Sociologia* by Ar. Sideris and of Max Weber's *Wissenschaft als Beruf* by Joh. Sykoutris.

107. Al. Svolos, professor of public law at the University of Athens, *The New Constitution and the Foundations of the State* (1928); and D. Besanis, *Theory of the State* (1932).

108. A. Charachristos, *Sociological Pedagogy* (1928); and G. Sakellarion, professor of psychology at the University of Athens, *Elements of Sociology* (1933). Sakellarion has been chiefly influenced by American sociology.

109. A. Eleutheropoulos taught at Zürich until 1926, when he was called to the newly-founded chair of sociology at the University of Saloniki. His chief work is *Soziologie: Untersuchung des menschlichen sozialen Lebens* (3rd ed., rev. and augmented, 1923). See the review of this work by Alfred Peters, *KVS*, iii, 2/3 (1923), pp. 188–90. See also Eleutheropoulos's article, " Einzelmensch

und Gesellschaft: Prinzipielle Erörterungen," *KVS*, v, 3 (1926), pp. 213–24; and his book, *Die exakten Grundlagen der Naturphilosophie* (1926).

110. Some of Kanellopoulos's sociologically noteworthy articles have already been listed (see note 106); others are: "The Individual as the Limit of the Social and of Knowledge," *AAS*, iii, 2 (1931); "Besprechung der materialistichen Geschichtsauffassung in Bezug auf Griechenland," *BNJ*, v (1926); "Die Grundrichtungen der Gesellschaftslehre Lorenz von Steins" *AGPS*, xxxix, 3/4 (1930); and "Observations historiques sur l'idée de la société," *RS* (Jan.–Mar., 1934). His chief books of sociological import are given in the text, with the exception of *Sociology* (brochure: extract from the *GGE* — 1930), and *History and Critique of Sociological Theories*, vol. i, Part I (1929). See the review of the *Sociology* by Charalambides, *KVS*, x, 3 (1931).

111. Kanellopoulos, special résumé already cited. The other editors are: Joh. Theodorakopoulos, professor of philosophy at the University of Saloniki; K. Tsatsos, professor of the philosophy of law at the University of Athens; and M. Tsamados, formerly Greek ambassador at Washington, now member of the Greek equivalent of the Supreme Court.

112. Quoted by Kanellopoulos, in the special résumé already cited, from his book *Man and His Social Antagonisms* (1934).

113. But compare Kanellopoulos's article, "Soziologisches Denken und soziologische Wissenschaft," *KVS*, vii, 3 (1928), pp. 277–89.

114. For sociology in modern Turkey our sole guides are an article by Niyazi Berkes, "Sociology in Turkey," *AJS*, xlii, 2 (Sept., 1936), pp. 238–46, and articles in the *ESS*. In extenuation we can only say that we decided at the last moment to include this section.

115. David S. Margoliouth, "Fārābi," *ESS*, vi (1931), pp. 100–101. His chief work has been translated into German under the title of *Der Musterstaat*.

116. Ahmet Emin, "Shinasi," *ESS*, xiv (1934), pp. 23–24; ———, "Zia Pasha," *ESS*, xv (1935), p. 526; ———, "Kamál," *ESS*, viii (1932), pp. 535–36.

117. See the articles listed in the index of *ESS*, xv, p. 655, under the headings of Pan-Islamism, Pan-Turanism, and Pan-Movements.

118. Ahmet Emin, "Gök Alp," *ESS*, vi (1931), pp. 687–88.

119. Berkes, *op. cit.*, p. 246. For a sociological analysis of present-day Turkey as a whole, see S. H. Jameson, "Social Mutation in Turkey," *SF*, xiv, 4 (May, 1936), pp. 482–96.

CHAPTER XXVIII

1. The writer reads Spanish, but haltingly, and has therefore been compelled to make much use of secondary sources. For the Spanish section of this chapter, our chief secondary source has been an unpublished doctoral dissertation by John Lord, *The Development of Sociology in Spain* (1921: Syracuse University). This contains an abundance of translated passages from the works of nearly all the authors quoted, so that the curse of a wholly secondary source is in part lifted. Another aid has been the article by *Fernando de los Rios, "The Social Sciences as Disciplines. VIII. Spain and Portugal," in *ESS*, i (1930), pp. 295–300, and of course the many excellent articles on individual authors in the same encyclopedia have been most useful. For the Latin-American section we have been almost wholly dependent on articles by L. L. Bernard, of which "The Social Sciences as Disciplines. IX. Latin America," in *ESS*, i (1930), pp. 301–20, has been most useful. In a few instances, such as Cornejo and DeQuiros, translations into French or English are available, and we have made use of them.

2. C. E. Chapman, *A History of Spain* (1918), p. 7.

3. U. R. Burke, *A History of Spain*, 2 vols. (1900), i, p. 10, footnote 1.

4. Chapman, *op. cit.*, pp. 10 ff.; Burke, *op. cit.*, pp. 12 ff.; Lord, *op. cit.*, pp. 4–38. 5. Chapman, *op. cit.*, p. 67.

6. D. J. Costa, *Colectivismo Agrario en España* (1912), p. 27.

7. *Ibid.*, p. 29.

8. Fernando de los Rios, *op. cit.*, p. 295; Costa, *op. cit.*, p. 28.

9. Vives, *De subventione pauperum*, etc. (1526) trans. by Sherwood as *Concerning the Relief of the Poor*, iv, p. 9.

10. *Ibid.*, p. 39. 11. *Ibid.*, p. 10. 12. *Ibid.*, pp. 11–34, *passim*.

13. *Ibid.*, p. 52. For comment see Chapman, *op. cit.*, pp. 344–45.

14. *Ibid.*, p. 345. 15. Paez de Castro, quoted in *ibid.*

16. Fernando de los Rios, *loc. cit.*

17. Vitoria, *Reflectiones theologiae* (1557), quoted in F. Kelly, *History of Spanish Literature* (1898), pp. 91–93.

18. F. J. C. Hearnshaw, " The Development of Social Thought and Institutions. VI. Renaissance and Reformation," in *ESS*, i (1930), pp. 96–97.

19. Fernando de los Rios, *op. cit.*, pp. 295–96.

20. *Robert Flint, *The Philosophy of History in Europe. I. The Philosophy of History in France and Germany* (1874), p. 475; Fernando de los Rios, *op. cit.*, p. 297; Lord, *op. cit.*, p. 81; Adolfo Posada, *Literatura y Problemas de la Sociologia* (1902), p. 173; *Francis W. Coker, *Organismic Theories of the State* (1910), references to Krause (use index).

21. *Coker, " Ahrens," in *ESS*, i (1930), p. 608.

22. *Ernst von Hippel, " Von Mohl," in *ESS*, x (1933), pp. 574–75.

23. Flint, *op. cit.*, pp. 474–75.

24. *Ibid.*, p. 474. *See also the brief anonymous article on Krause in *EB*, 14th ed. 25. Flint, *op. cit.*, p. 490.

26. Theodor Geiger, " Gesellschaft," *HWBS*, pp. 207–208.

27. Flint, *op. cit.*, pp. 480–81. 28. *Ibid.*, p. 485.

29. Fernando de los Rios, *op. cit.*, p. 297; *C. Bernaldo de Quiros, " Giner de los Rios," in *ESS*, vi (1931), pp. 662–63.

30. *Ibid.*; Lord, *op. cit.*, pp. 62–65, 83–85, 107, 128–30.

31. Antonio Portuondo y Barcelo, *Apuntes sobres mecanica social* (1900); Santa Maria de Paredes, *El Concepto del Organismo Social* (1896), *passim*; Lord, *op. cit.*, pp. 75–76.

32. *Ibid.*, p. 65. One might also mention Ricardo Macías Picavea (1847–99). See the article by *B. Sánchez Alonso in *ESS*, x (1933), pp. 26–27.

33. *Fernando de los Rios, " Azcárate," in *ESS*, ii (1930), pp. 371–72; Lord, *op. cit.*, pp. 69–72, 85–87, 151–52.

34. *Bernaldo de Quiros, " Dorado Montero," in *ESS*, v (1931), pp. 218–19; Lord, *op. cit.*, pp. 77–79, 88–89, 108, 159.

35. *——, *Las Nuevas Teorias de la Criminalidad* (1908), trans. by Alphonso de Salvio as *Modern Theories of Criminality*; Lord, *op. cit.*, pp. 79, 89–90, 162–64. 36. *Ibid.*, pp. 91 ff.

37. Adolfo Posada, *Sociologia General* (1908), p. 406, quoted in Lord, *op. cit.*, p. 103. 38. ——, *op. cit.*, p. 68, quoted in Lord, *op. cit.*, p. 104.

39. ——, *Principios de Sociologia* (1908), p. 396, quoted in Lord, *op. cit.*, p. 74. 40. ——, *op. cit.*, p. 401, quoted in Lord, *op. cit.*, pp. 74–75.

41. ——, *Literatura y Problemas de la Sociologia* (1902), p. 188, quoted in Lord, *op. cit.*, p. 152.

42. ——, *op. cit.*, p. 189, quoted in Lord, *op. cit.*, pp. 152–53.

43. Sales y Ferre, *Sociologia General* (1912), pp. 6–12, quoted in Lord, *op. cit.*, pp. 85–87. **44.** *Ibid.*, pp. 98–104, 135–36.

45. Sales y Ferre, *op. cit.*, pp. 19–22, quoted in Lord, *op. cit.*, p. 154.

46. Fernando de los Rios, "The Social Sciences as Disciplines. VIII. Spain and Portugal," in *ESS*, i (1930), p. 297. Pujols's work is entitled *Historia de las Instituciones Sociales de la España Goda*, 4 vols. (1896).

47. *Ibid.*, i, "Introduction," quoted in Lord, *op. cit.*, p. 155.

48. René E. G. Vaillant, "Arenal," in *ESS*, ii (1930), p. 182; Lord, *op. cit.*, pp. 80, 165 ff.

49. José Ortéga y Gasset, *La rebelión de las masas* (1929; English trans., 1932).

50. Bernaldo de Quiros, "Dorado Montero," in *ESS*, v (1931), pp. 218–19.

51. *Fidelino de Figueiredo, "Oliveira," *ESS*, xi (1933), p. 465; Fernando de los Rios, *op. cit.*, p. 300.

52. L. L. Bernard, "The Social Sciences as Disciplines. IX. Latin America," *ESS*, i (1930), p. 301. This article provides the backbone of our discussion of Latin America, although we have also made use of a paper by S. N. Lowrie of São Paulo (forthcoming in an early issue of the *ASR*), an article by Alfredo Poviña, "A Brief History of the Teaching of Sociology in the Argentine Republic," *SSR*, xvii, 6 (July–Aug., 1933), pp. 503–509; a book review by E. Willems, "Delgado de Carvalho: *Sociologia*," *KVS*, xii, 3/4 (1934), pp. 404–405; book review by Annamarie Besantz, "Raúl A. Orgaz, *Estudios de Sociologia* (1915), *La Ciencia Social Contemporánea* (1932)," *KVS*, xii, 1 (1933), pp. 93–96; article by E. Willems, "Soziologie in Brasilien," *KVS*, xi, 3/4 (1933), pp. 468–69; Alfredo Poviña, *Notas de Sociologia* (collected articles and book reviews, 1935); and Bernard's other articles and book reviews, notably his "The Development and Present Tendencies of Sociology in Argentina," *SF*, vi (1927), pp. 13–27; "Sociology in Argentina," *AJS*, xxxiii (1927–28), pp. 110–17; "Peoples, Cultures, and Systems" (book review with J. S. Bernard), *SF*, xi, 4 (May, 1933), pp. 594–602; book review of Venturino's chief works, *AJS*, xxxviii, 2 (Sept., 1932), pp. 321–23; "Education and Society" (book review), *SF*, xv, 1 (Oct., 1936), pp. 127–30; and "Recent Work in Cultural Sociology in Brazil, Argentina, and Mexico," *ASR*, ii, 2 (Apr., 1937), pp. 265–68. Too late to be of use in the text was the excellent unpublished thesis of W. E. Moore, *Current Sociological Theories in Argentina* (University of Oregon, 1937).

53. See Bernard, "The Social Sciences . . ." etc. (note 51) for names and bibliographies of writers mentioned in text. **54.** *Ibid.*, p. 303.

55. *Ibid.*, p. 313.

56. Bernard, book review of Venturino's chief works, *AJS*, xxxviii, 2 (Sept., 1932), pp. 321–23.

57. We here refer to G. H. Lane-Fox Pitt-Rivers, *The Clash of Cultures and the Contact of Races* (1927); Margaret Mead, *The Changing Culture of an Indian Tribe* (1932); and W. C. MacLeod, *The American Indian Frontier* (1929). **58.** Bernard, *op. cit.*, p. 323.

59. Mariano H. Cornejo, *Sociologia General*, 2 vols. (1908), French translation by Émile Chauffard, *Sociologie générale*, 2 vols. (1911), with a preface by René Worms. **60.** *Ibid.*, i, p. 117.

61. Take, for example, the *Notas de Sociologia* of Alfredo Poviña (bibliographies) and other books and articles mentioned in note 52.

62. Orgaz provides a relevant example. We should also note the presence of several first-rate psycho-sociologists, e.g., Arthur Ramos, *Introducção á Psychologia Social* (1936).

63. Bernard, " The Social Sciences . . ." etc. (note 52), p. 320.

64. Information for this section has come chiefly from Bernard and Lowrie (see note 52). For Latin-American sociologists not mentioned or inadequately dealt with in the text, see these articles by L. L. Bernard: " Alberdi," *ESS*, i (1930), p. 613; " Alvarez," *ibid.*, ii (1930), p. 16; " Bunge," *ibid.*, iii (1930), p. 67; " Sarmiento," *ibid.*, xiii (1934), pp. 543–44.

CHAPTER XXIX

1. *See the articles dealing with the *Brahma Samaj* and the *Arya Samaj* in *HERE*.

2. Haridas T. Muzumdar, " Sociology in India " (paper written for this chapter).

3. Radhakamal Mukerjee, " Sociology in India " (paper written for this chapter). Unfortunately we went to press too soon to utilize Benoy Kumar Sarkar's chapter on " Sociology " in his *Creative India* (1937), pp. 650–69. See also his " Sociology in Bengal," *Mount Magazine*, Jan.–Feb., 1937 (Madras).

4. Muzumdar, *op. cit.*; Mukerjee, *op. cit.* 5. *Ibid.* 6. *Ibid.* 7. *Ibid.*

8. *See Henry Sumner Maine, *Village Communities in the East and West*, *passim*; William H. Wiser, *Behind Mud Walls* (1930); ——, *The Hindu Jajmani System* (1936). 9. Mukerjee, *op. cit.*

10. Shib Chandra Dutt, *Thirty-Five Years of Indian Economic Thought, 1898–1932* (Calcutta: The Insurance and Finance Review, Publishers, 1932); Mukhtyar, *Life and Labor in a South Gujerat Village*; Slater, *South Indian Villages*; Misra, *Social and Economic Survey of a Village near Cawnpore*; Radhakamal Mukerjee, ed., *Fields and Farmers in Oudh*.

11. Mathur, *Pressure of Population and Its Effects on Rural Economy in Gorakhpur*; Misra, *Over-population in Jaunpur*; Pant, *Social Economy of the Himalayans*.

12. Radhakamal Mukerjee, " The Environmental Control of Population Movement in Northern India," *P. C. Roy Commemoration Volume*; " The Gifts of the Ganges," *Malaviya Commemoration Volume*.

13. ——, *Migrant Asia* (Rome: Corrado Gini series).

14. ——, " Population Balance and Optimum," *Publication of the International Population Congress* (Rome: 1930); " The Criterion of Optimum Population," *AJS*, xxxviii, 5 (Mar., 1933), pp. 688–98.

15. There is, however, one important book on *Theories of Punishment*, by P. K. Sen.

16. Sen Gupta and Mukerjee, " Marriage and Personality," *SSR*, xviii, 2 (Nov.–Dec., 1933), pp. 115–22; " Binders of Marriage," *SF*, xii, 1 (Oct., 1933), pp. 88–93.

17. Mukerjee, " Sociology in India." 18. Muzumdar, *op. cit.*

19. *Brajendra Nath Seal, *Comparative Studies in Vaishnavism and Christianity*; " Race Origins," in *Inter-Racial Problems* (Spiller, ed.); *Comparative Studies in Vedantism and Christianity*. 20. *Ibid.*, p. 2.

21. Seal, *Address to the Fourteenth Meeting of the Mythic Society* (Bangalore: 1924); see also Radhakamal Mukerjee, *Foundations of Indian Economics* (1916), p. 328. 22. Mukerjee, " Sociology in India."

23. Mukerjee, *Foundations of Indian Economics*, p. 328.

24. ——, *Principles of Comparative Economics* (1921), Preface.

25. ——, Foreword, *The Indian Sociological Review*, i, 1 (Aug., 1923).

26. ——, *Democracies of the East* (London: 1923).

27. *Dhurjatiprasad Mukerji, *Personality and the Social Sciences* (1924); *Basic Concepts in Sociology* (1933).

28. Mukerjee, *Borderlands of Economics* (1925), p. 249.

29. ——, *Regional Sociology* (1926), *passim*.

30. ——, " Sociology in India."

31. *Ibid.* See *Mukerjee's articles: " Ecological Contributions to Sociology," *SR*, xxii, 4 (Oct., 1930), pp. 281–91; " The Ecological Outlook in Sociology," *AJS*, xxxviii, 3 (Nov., 1932), pp. 349–55.

32. ——, " The Concepts of Balance and Organisation in Social Ecology," *SSR*, xvi, 6 (July–Aug., 1932), pp. 503–16; " The Concepts of Distribution and Succession in Social Ecology," *SF*, xi, 1 (Oct., 1932), pp. 1–7; " The Broken Balance of Man and Region," *SSR*, xvii, 5 (May–June, 1933), pp. 404–408.

33. ——, " Relations between Human and Animal Communities," *ADS* (1934); " The Ecological Un-Balance of Man," *SR*, xxv, 3 (Oct., 1933), pp. 233–43.

34. ——, *" The Way of the Transcendentalist " (author's original title, " Religion as a Social Norm "), *SR*, xxi, 3 (July, 1929), pp. 197–207.

35. ——, " Sociology in India." **36.** *Ibid.*

37. *Ibid.* See also Mukerjee's articles: " The Way of the Transcendentalist," *SR*, xxi, 3 (July, 1929), pp. 197–207; " The Social Conception of Religion," *SSR*, xiii, 6 (July–Aug., 1929), pp. 517–25; " Roots of Religion," *SF*, viii, 1 (Sept., 1929), pp. 10–16; " Religious Experience," *SR*, xxii, 2 (Apr., 1930), pp. 97–107; " Sociology and Mysticism," *SSR*, xv, 4 (Mar.–Apr., 1931), pp. 303–10. **38.** Wiese-Becker, *Systematic Sociology* (1932), pp. 258–59.

39. Marcel Granet, *La Pensée chinoise* (1933).

40. A. N. Whitehead, *Science and the Modern World* (1926), p. 299.

41. See the articles by Leonard S. Hsü, " The Teaching of Sociology in China," *CSPSR*, xi, 3 (July, 1927), esp. pp. 11–17; " The Sociological Movement in China," *PA*, iv, 4 (April, 1931), pp. 283–307; and the article by Li Mon, " Le Mouvement sociologique dans la Chine contemporaine," *RIS*, xl, 1 (Jan.–Feb., 1932), pp. 64–68. We have also had the benefit of a paper written especially for this chapter by Ta Chen of Tsing Hua University. Unfortunately, we have not been able to consult the article by W. Ching-Chao and Lewis S. C. Smith, " Sociological Studies at the University of Nanking," *ER*, xxiii, 1 (Jan., 1934), pp. 61–66. **42.** Ta Chen, *op. cit.*

43. Hsü, " The Sociological Movement in China " (see note 41 above).

44. There appeared translations of works by Darwin, Huxley, Tylor, Bagehot, Wallas, Hobhouse, Ellis, MacDougall, Russell, Frazer, Malinowski, Cole, Radcliffe-Brown, Marett, Morgan, Dewey, Giddings, Robinson, Thorndike, Watson, Ellwood, Lowell, Seligman, Ogburn, Abel, Sorokin, Miller, Gillette, Snedden, Hayes, Blackmar and Gillin, Laidler, Bogardus, Marx, Engels, Bukharin, Lenin, Kropotkin, Durkheim, LeBon, Gide and Rist, Lombroso, Loria, Oppenheimer, Müller-Lyer, and many more.

45. These articles and books dealt with LePlay, Tarde, Mauss, Bouglé, Durkheim, Simmel, Tönnies, Wiese, Max Weber, Vierkandt, Pareto, Sumner, Park, Cooley, and several others. **46.** Hsü, *op. cit.*, p. 284.

47. Li Mon, *op. cit.*, pp. 65–66.

48. J. S. Burgess, report to the China Association of the Christian Higher Education, 1925; chart and abstract given in Hsü, " The Teaching of Sociology in China," *CSPSR*, xi, 3 (July, 1927).

49. " General Announcement of the Department of Sociology and Social

Work," *Publication of the Department of Sociology and Social Work, Yenching University*, Series A, no. 10 (Sept., 1932), pp. 40–43. **50.** *Ibid.*, pp. 52–59. **51.** Hsü, letter to the writer.

52. Hsü, "The Teaching of Sociology in China" (see note 41 above).

53. E. T. C. Werner, *Descriptive Sociology of the Chinese*; Arthur H. Smith, *Village Life in China*; Herbert F. Rudd, *Chinese Social Origins*; Gamble and Burgess, Peking: *A Social Survey*; Daniel Kulp II, *Country Life in South China*; Marcel Granet, *Fêtes et chansons anciennes de la Chine, Religion des Chinois, Danses et légendes de la Chine ancienne, La Civilisation chinoise*, and *La Pensée chinoise* (on which we drew so heavily in Chapter Two); S. M. Shirokogoroff, *Social Organization of the Manchus, Social Organization of the Northern Tungus, Anthropology of North China*, and *Anthropology of Eastern China and Kwangtung Province*; R. H. Tawney, *Land and Labor in China* (by far the best book on this phase of Chinese life in recent decades); Karl Wittfogel, *Wirtschaft und Gesellschaft Chinas*; S. D. Gamble, *How Chinese Families Live in Peiping*; J. S. Burgess, *The Guilds of Peking*; H. D. Lamson, *Social Pathology in China*; Father Schram, *Le Mariage chez les T'o Jen de Kan-sou*; O. Lattimore, *The Gold Tribe "Fishskin Tartars" of the Lower Sungari*.

There have also been several coöperative studies: one dealing with the 'rickshaw men of Peiping; others with the peasant family in various regions (supervised by Dittmer, by Malone and Taylor, and by Buck), with Peiping laborers (supervised by Blaisdell and others), and the like.

54. We may list: *Chieng F. Lung, "Social Order and the Concept of Harmony," *SSR*, xviii, 1 (Sept.–Oct., 1933), pp. 52–57; Francis Y. Chang, "An Accommodation Program for Second-Generation Chinese," *SSR*, xviii, 6 (July–Aug., 1934), pp. 541–53; *John Liu, "The Social Relationships of the Villagers in China," *SSR*, xiv, 5 (May–June, 1930), pp. 462–68; Betty Wang, "Folk-Songs as a Means of Social Control," *SSR*, xix, 1 (Sept.–Oct., 1934), pp. 64–69; Rowland J. Loh, "Dependency in Shengtu, China," *SSR*, xviii, 5 (May–June, 1934), pp. 477–79.

55. Works (in Chinese unless otherwise noted) by the writers listed in the text to which we have been referred by our informants are: S. M. Chen, *The Outlook of Chinese Culture* (1934); Ta Chen, *Labor Problems in China*; L. S. Hsü, *Population Problems in China, Culture and Politics*, and (in English) *The Political Philosophy of Confucius* (1934); W. S. Huang, editor of the first issue of the *Bulletin of Ethnological Studies* (1936); F. C. H. Li, *Social Survey of Ting Hsien*; L. K. Tao, *Life in China* (joint authorship with Leong) and *Livelihood in Peking* (both in English), articles in English in various collaborative works and periodicals — *Pacific Affairs*, volume dedicated to C. A. Seligman, and so on; P. W. Sun, *Principles of Sociology* (1935); Cato Young, *Methods of Social Research, Rural Policies, Rural Social Problems*, etc.; C. C. Wu, *Social Organization*.

56. Junichiro Matsumoto, *Outlines of Sociology* (1934), appendix on the history of sociology, abridged and translated for this chapter by Yoshihiko Yamada and Kanrei Inoue. Matsumoto has an article in German, "Soziologie in Japan," *KVS*, iii, 4 (1924), pp. 289–91, but it is superseded by the treatment just cited. (Unless otherwise noted or cited in languages other than English, all references in the section on Japan are to Japanese originals.) Personal discussion of various points and of the *ensemble* with Professors Yamada and Inoue has greatly aided in the writing of this division of the chapter, and we are deeply indebted to them.

57. *Teizo Toda, "The Social Sciences as Disciplines. X. Japan" (in English), *ESS*, i, Introduction, II, p. 321. **58.** *Ibid.*

59. T. Simoide, "A Contribution to the History of Sociology in Japan," *JSM*, nos. 18 and 23 (Oct., 1925 and Mar., 1926), translated for this chapter by the author. **60.** Matsumoto, *op. cit.*

61. Unasuke Wakamiya, paper written for the present chapter, based in part on his "The Meaning of Japanese Sociology," I and II, *JSM*, nos. 31 and 32 (Nov. and Dec., 1926), and his "Trends in Japanese Sociology," *JSM*, no. 8 (Dec., 1924).

62. Toda, *op. cit.*, p. 321. **63.** Matsumoto, *op. cit.*; Wakamiya, *op. cit.*

64. The titles of Toyama's sociological or quasi-sociological works are: *Japanese Women in the Age of Mythology, Marriage and the Family System in the Mythological Age, Political Thought and Institutions in the Mythological Age,* and *History of Japanese Moral Philosophy.* **65.** Matsumoto, *op. cit.*; Simoide, *op. cit.*

66. Matsumoto, *op. cit.*; Toda, *op. cit.* **67.** *Ibid.*

68. Wakamiya, *op. cit.*; Matsumoto, *op. cit.* **69.** *Ibid.* **70.** *Ibid.*

71. *Ibid.* **72.** Wakamiya, *op. cit.*; Toda, *op. cit.*

73. *Ibid.*; Matsumoto, *op. cit.* **74.** Wakamiya, *op. cit.*

75. Matsumoto, *op. cit.*

76. The titles of these applied studies of Takebe's are: *War* (1906), *Present-Day Great Powers and Their Present Condition* (1917), *Modern Civilization* (1919), and *Education* (1921). **77.** Simoide, *op. cit.* **78.** Matsumoto, *op. cit.*

79. *Ibid.*; Simoide, *op. cit.*; Wakamiya, *op. cit.*

80. Endo's works in these fields are: *History of Chinese Philosophy, History of the Development of Chinese Thought,* and *Orientalism.*

81. Simoide, *op. cit.* **82.** *Ibid.* **83.** Toda, *op. cit.*; Matsumoto, *op. cit.*

84. Practically all this discussion of Yoneda derives from Matsumoto, *op. cit.*, who has also furnished us with the following bibliography of Yoneda's chief works:

Methodology: *The Neo-Idealistic Philosophy of History,* 4 vols. (1920–21); *Rickert's Philosophy of History* (1922); *Problems of the Philosophy of History* (1924); *Systems of the Philosophy of History* (1924).

Psycho-sociological studies: *Psychology of Our Contemporaries and Modern Civilization* (1919); *Studies in Psychological Economics* (1919); *Sociological Considerations on Social Problems,* 2 vols. (1921); *Problems of Contemporary Population* (1921); *Psychology of Civilized Peoples* (1921); *Contemporary Culture* (1924).

85. Matsumoto, *op. cit.*, also furnishes a good part of our information about Takata, although we have made use of the latter's articles in German: "Der Weg zur Gesellschaft," *JFS*, iii (1927), pp. 22–37; "Eine dritte Geschichtsauffassung," *Reine und angewandte Soziologie: Eine Festgabe für Ferdinand Tönnies* (1936), pp. 309–20. **86.** Matsumoto, *op. cit.*

87. Personal discussions with Prof. Inoue have supplemented the information found in Matsumoto, *op. cit.*

88. Wakamiya, *op. cit.* **89.** Matsumoto, *op. cit.* **90.** *Ibid.*

91. Letter from Prof. Matsumoto, and material contained in his *op. cit.*

92. *Ibid.* Anyone wishing to get some idea of the extraordinary range of the special studies now being made should refer to the *KVS*, in successive issues of which are listed (in German) all the articles published in the *JSM* from 1924 to 1932. Western sociologists owe this list to the unfailing courtesy of Prof. Matsumoto.

At the last moment, just as these notes were going through the press, there came to hand a brochure by Matsumoto, Okada, and others, *Sociology Past and Present in Japan* (1937; in English) and a thesis by Yaemitsu Sugimachi, *The Social Thought of Ancient Japan* (University of Southern California, 1937). Needless to say, we have been unable to make use of the valuable aid they offer.

Name Index for Volume Three

Subject Index for Volume Three

Inasmuch as a very full Table of Contents has been provided, the Subject Index deals chiefly with matters not clearly recognizable in the section and chapter headings. For a full set of references, the Table of Contents, Name Index, and Subject Index should be used in conjunction. Moreover, account should be taken of the fact that subjects dealt with in the Notes are not indexed.

CATALOGUE OF DOVER BOOKS

Social Sciences

SOCIAL THOUGHT FROM LORE TO SCIENCE, H. E. Barnes and H. Becker. An immense survey of sociological thought and ways of viewing, studying, planning, and reforming society from earliest times to the present. Includes thought on society of preliterate peoples, ancient non-Western cultures, and every great movement in Europe, America, and modern Japan. Analyzes hundreds of great thinkers: Plato, Augustine, Bodin, Vico, Montesquieu, Herder, Comte, Marx, etc. Weighs the contributions of utopians, sophists, fascists and communists; economists, jurists, philosophers, ecclesiastics, and every 19th and 20th century school of scientific sociology, anthropology, and social psychology throughout the world. Combines topical, chronological, and regional approaches, treating the evolution of social thought as a process rather than as a series of mere topics. "Impressive accuracy, competence, and discrimination . . . easily the best single survey," Nation. Thoroughly revised, with new material up to 1960. 2 indexes. Over 2200 bibliographical notes. Three volume set. Total of 1586pp. 5⅜ x 8.
T901 Vol I Paperbound **$2.50**
T902 Vol II Paperbound **$2.50**
T903 Vol III Paperbound **$2.35**
The set **$7.35**

FOLKWAYS, William Graham Sumner. A classic of sociology, a searching and thorough examination of patterns of behaviour from primitive, ancient Greek and Judaic, Medieval Christian, African, Oriental, Melanesian, Australian, Islamic, to modern Western societies. Thousands of illustrations of social, sexual, and religious customs, mores, laws, and institutions. Hundreds of categories: Labor, Wealth, Abortion, Primitive Justice, Life Policy, Slavery, Cannibalism, Uncleanness and the Evil Eye, etc. Will extend the horizon of every reader by showing the relativism of his own culture. Prefatory note by A. G. Keller. Introduction by William Lyon Phelps. Bibliography. Index. xiii + 692pp. 5⅜ x 8. T508 Paperbound **$2.49**

PRIMITIVE RELIGION, P. Radin. A thorough treatment by a noted anthropologist of the nature and origin of man's belief in the supernatural and the influences that have shaped religious expression in primitive societies. Ranging from the Arunta, Ashanti, Aztec, Bushman, Crow, Fijian, etc., of Africa, Australia, Pacific Islands, the Arctic, North and South America, Prof. Radin integrates modern psychology, comparative religion, and economic thought with first-hand accounts gathered by himself and other scholars of primitive initiations, training of the shaman, and other fascinating topics. "Excellent," NATURE (London). Unabridged reissue of 1st edition. New author's preface. Bibliographic notes. Index. x + 322pp. 5⅜ x 8.
T393 Paperbound **$1.85**

PRIMITIVE MAN AS PHILOSOPHER, P. Radin. A standard anthropological work covering primitive thought on such topics as the purpose of life, marital relations, freedom of thought, symbolism, death, resignation, the nature of reality, personality, gods, and many others. Drawn from factual material gathered from the Winnebago, Oglala Sioux, Maori, Baganda, Batak, Zuni, among others, it does not distort ideas by removing them from context but interprets strictly within the original framework. Extensive selections of original primitive documents. Bibliography. Index. xviii + 402pp. 5⅜ x 8. T392 Paperbound **$2.25**

A TREATISE ON SOCIOLOGY, THE MIND AND SOCIETY, Vilfredo Pareto. This treatise on human society is one of the great classics of modern sociology. First published in 1916, its careful catalogue of the innumerable manifestations of non-logical human conduct (Book One); the theory of "residues," leading to the premise that sentiment not logic determines human behavior (Book Two), and of "derivations," beliefs derived from desires (Book Three); and the general description of society made up of non-elite and elite, consisting of "foxes" who live by cunning and "lions" who live by force, stirred great controversy. But Pareto's passion for isolation and classification of elements and factors, and his allegiance to scientific method as the key tool for scrutinizing the human situation made his a truly twentieth-century mind and his work a catalytic influence on certain later social commentators. These four volumes (bound as two) require no special training to be appreciated and any reader who wishes to gain a complete understanding of modern sociological theory, regardless of special field of interest, will find them a must. Reprint of revised (corrected) printing of original edition. Translated by Andrew Bongiorno and Arthur Livingston. Index. Bibliography. Appendix containing index-summary of theorems. 48 diagrams. Four volumes bound as two. Total of 2063pp. 5⅜ x 8½. The set Clothbound **$15.00**

THE POLISH PEASANT IN EUROPE AND AMERICA, William I. Thomas, Florian Znaniecki. A seminal sociological study of peasant primary groups (family and community) and the disruptions produced by a new industrial system and immigration to America. The peasant's family, class system, religious and aesthetic attitudes, and economic life are minutely examined and analyzed in hundreds of pages of primary documentation, particularly letters between family members. The disorientation caused by new environments is scrutinized in detail (a 312-page autobiography of an immigrant is especially valuable and revealing) in an attempt to find common experiences and reactions. The famous "Methodological Note" sets forth the principles which guided the authors. When out of print this set has sold for as much as $50. 2nd revised edition. 2 vols. Vol. 1: xv + 1115pp. Vol. 2: 1135pp. Index. 6 x 9.
T478 Clothbound 2 vol. set **$12.50**

Biological Sciences

AN INTRODUCTION TO GENETICS, A. H. Sturtevant and G. W. Beadle. A very thorough exposition of genetic analysis and the chromosome mechanics of higher organisms by two of the world's most renowned biologists, A. H. Sturtevant, one of the founders of modern genetics, and George Beadle, Nobel laureate in 1958. Does not concentrate on the biochemical approach, but rather more on observed data from experimental evidence and results . . . from Drosophila and other life forms. Some chapter titles: Sex chromosomes; Sex-Linkage; Autosomal Inheritance;; Chromosome Maps; Intra-Chromosomal Rearrangements; Inversions—and Incomplete Chromosomes; Translocations; Lethals; Mutations; Heterogeneous Populations; Genes and Phenotypes; The Determination and Differentiation of Sex; etc. Slightly corrected reprint of 1939 edition. New preface by Drs. Sturtevant and Beadle. 1 color plate. 126 figures. Bibliographies. Index. 391pp. 5⅜ x 8½.　　　　　　　　　　　S306 Paperbound **$2.00**

THE GENETICAL THEORY OF NATURAL SELECTION, R. A. Fisher. 2nd revised edition of a vital reviewing of Darwin's Selection Theory in terms of particulate inheritance, by one of the great authorities on experimental and theoretical genetics. Theory is stated in mathematical form. Special features of particulate inheritance are examined: evolution of dominance, maintenance of specific variability, mimicry and sexual selection, etc. 5 chapters on man and his special circumstances as a social animal. 16 photographs. Bibliography. Index. x + 310pp. 5⅜ x 8.　　　　　　　　　　　S466 Paperbound **$2.00**

THE ORIENTATION OF ANIMALS: KINESES, TAXES AND COMPASS REACTIONS, Gottfried S. Fraenkel and Donald L. Gunn. A basic work in the field of animal orientations. Complete, detailed survey of everything known in the subject up to 1940s, enlarged and revised to cover major developments to 1960. Analyses of simpler types of orientation are presented in Part I: kinesis, klinotaxis, tropotaxis, telotaxis, etc. Part II covers more complex reactions originating from temperature changes, gravity, chemical stimulation, etc. The two-light experiment and unilateral blinding are dealt with, as is the problem of determinism or volition in lower animals. The book has become the universally-accepted guide to all who deal with the subject—zoologists, biologists, psychologists, and the like. Second, enlarged edition, revised to 1960. Bibliography of over 500 items. 135 illustrations. Indices. xiii + 376pp. 5⅜ x 8½.　　　　　　　　　　　T786 Paperbound **$2.25**

THE BEHAVIOUR AND SOCIAL LIFE OF HONEYBEES, C. R. Ribbands. Definitive survey of all aspects of honeybee life and behavior; completely scientific in approach, but written in interesting, everyday language that both professionals and laymen will appreciate. Basic coverage of physiology, anatomy, sensory equipment; thorough account of honeybee behavior in the field (foraging activities, nectar and pollen gathering, how individuals find their way home and back to food areas, mating habits, etc.); details of communication in various field and hive situations. An extensive treatment of activities within the hive community—food sharing, wax production, comb building, swarming, the queen, her life and relationship with the workers, etc. A must for the beekeeper, natural historian, biologist, entomologist, social scientist, et al. "An indispensable reference," J. Hambleton, BEES. "Recommended in the strongest of terms," AMERICAN SCIENTIST. 9 plates. 66 figures. Indices. 693-item bibliography. 252pp. 5⅜ x 8½.　　　　　　　　　　　T1137 Paperbound **$2.00**

BIRD DISPLAY: AN INTRODUCTION TO THE STUDY OF BIRD PSYCHOLOGY, E. A. Armstrong. The standard work on bird display, based on extensive observation by the author and reports of other observers. This important contribution to comparative psychology covers the behavior and ceremonial rituals of hundreds of birds from gannet and heron to birds of paradise and king penguins. Chapters discuss such topics as the ceremonial of the gannet, ceremonial gaping, disablement reactions, the expression of emotions, the evolution and function of social ceremonies, social hierarchy in bird life, dances of birds and men, songs, etc. Free of technical terminology, this work will be equally interesting to psychologists and zoologists as well as bird lovers of all backgrounds. 32 photographic plates. New introduction by the author. List of scientific names of birds. Bibliography. 3-part index. 431pp. 5⅜ x 8½.　　　　　　　　　　　T1128 Paperbound **$2.00**

THE SPECIFICITY OF SEROLOGICAL REACTIONS, Karl Landsteiner. With a Chapter on Molecular Structure and Intermolecular Forces by Linus Pauling. Dr. Landsteiner, winner of the Nobel Prize in 1930 for the discovery of the human blood groups, devoted his life to fundamental research and played a leading role in the development of immunology. This authoritative study is an account of the experiments he and his colleagues carried out on antigens and serological reactions with simple compounds. Comprehensive coverage of the basic concepts of immunology includes such topics as: The Serological Specificity of Proteins, Antigens, Antibodies, Artificially Conjugated Antigens, Non-Protein Cell Substances such as polysaccharides, etc., Antigen-Antibody Reactions (Toxin Neutralization, Precipitin Reactions, Agglutination, etc.). Discussions of toxins, bacterial proteins, viruses, hormones, enzymes, etc. in the context of immunological phenomena. New introduction by Dr. Merrill Chase of the Rockefeller Institute. Extensive bibliography and bibliography of author's writings. Index. xviii + 330pp. 5⅜ x 8½.　　　　　　　　　　　S299 Paperbound **$2.00**

CULTURE METHODS FOR INVERTEBRATE ANIMALS, P. S. Galtsoff, F. E. Lutz, P. S. Welch, J. G. Needham, eds. A compendium of practical experience of hundreds of scientists and technicians, covering invertebrates from protozoa to chordata, in 313 articles on 17 phyla. Explains in great detail food, protection, environment, reproduction conditions, rearing methods, embryology, breeding seasons, schedule of development, much more. Includes at least one species of each considerable group. Half the articles are on class insecta. Introduction. 97 illustrations. Bibliography. Index. xxix + 590pp. 5⅜ x 8.   S526 Paperbound **$2.75**

THE BIOLOGY OF THE LABORATORY MOUSE, edited by G. D. Snell. 1st prepared in 1941 by the staff of the Roscoe B. Jackson Memorial Laboratory, this is still the standard treatise on the mouse, assembling an enormous amount of material for which otherwise you spend hours of research. Embryology, reproduction, histology, spontaneous tumor formation, genetics of tumor transplantation, endocrine secretion & tumor formation, milk, influence & tumor formation, inbred, hybrid animals, parasites, infectious diseases, care & recording. Classified bibliography of 1122 items. 172 figures, including 128 photos. ix + 497pp. 6⅛ x 9¼.
S248 Clothbound **$6.00**

MATHEMATICAL BIOPHYSICS: PHYSICO-MATHEMATICAL FOUNDATIONS OF BIOLOGY, N. Rashevsky. One of most important books in modern biology, now revised, expanded with new chapters, to include most significant recent contributions. Vol. 1: Diffusion phenomena, particularly diffusion drag forces, their effects. Old theory of cell division based on diffusion drag forces, other theoretical approaches, more exhaustively treated than ever. Theories of excitation, conduction in nerves, with formal theories plus physico-chemical theory. Vol. 2: Mathematical theories of various phenomena in central nervous system. New chapters on theory of color vision, of random nets. Principle of optimal design, extended from earlier edition. Principle of relational mapping of organisms, numerous applications. Introduces into mathematical biology such branches of math as topology, theory of sets. Index. 236 illustrations. Total of 988pp. 5⅜ x 8.   S574 Vol. 1 (Books 1, 2) Paperbound **$2.50**
S575 Vol. 2 (Books 3, 4) Paperbound **$2.50**
2 vol. set **$5.00**

ELEMENTS OF MATHEMATICAL BIOLOGY, A. J. Lotka. A pioneer classic, the first major attempt to apply modern mathematical techniques on a large scale to phenomena of biology, biochemistry, psychology, ecology, similar life sciences. Partial Contents: Statistical meaning of irreversibility; Evolution as redistribution; Equations of kinetics of evolving systems; Chemical, inter-species equilibrium; parameters of state; Energy transformers of nature, etc. Can be read with profit even by those having no advanced math; unsurpassed as study-reference. Formerly titled ELEMENTS OF PHYSICAL BIOLOGY. 72 figures. xxx + 460pp. 5⅜ x 8.   S346 Paperbound **$2.45**

THE BIOLOGY OF THE AMPHIBIA, G. K. Noble, Late Curator of Herpetology at the Am. Mus. of Nat. Hist. Probably the most used text on amphibia, unmatched in comprehensiveness, clarity, detail. 19 chapters plus 85-page supplement cover development; heredity; life history; speciation; adaptation; sex, integument, respiratory, circulatory, digestive, muscular, nervous systems; instinct, intelligence, habits, environment, economic value, relationships, classification, etc. "Nothing comparable to it," C. H. Pope, Curator of Amphibia, Chicago Mus. of Nat. Hist. 1047 bibliographic references. 174 illustrations. 600pp. 5⅜ x 8.
S206 Paperbound **$2.98**

STUDIES ON THE STRUCTURE AND DEVELOPMENT OF VERTEBRATES, E. S. Goodrich. A definitive study by the greatest modern comparative anatomist. Exceptional in its accounts of the ossicles of the ear, the separate divisions of the coelom and mammalian diaphragm, and the 5 chapters devoted to the head region. Also exhaustive morphological and phylogenetic expositions of skeleton, fins and limbs, skeletal visceral arches and labial cartilages, visceral clefts and gills, vacular, respiratory, excretory, and peripheral nervous systems, etc., from fish to the higher mammals. 754 illustrations. 69 page biographical study by C. C. Hardy. Bibliography of 1186 references. "What an undertaking . . . to write a textbook which will summarize adequately and succinctly all that has been done in the realm of Vertebrate Morphology these recent years," Journal of Anatomy. Index. Two volumes. Total 906pp. 5⅜ x 8.   Two vol. set S449-50 Paperbound **$5.00**

A TREATISE ON PHYSIOLOGICAL OPTICS, H. von Helmholtz, Ed. by J. P. C. Southall. Unmatched for thoroughness, soundness, and comprehensiveness, this is still the most important work ever produced in the field of physiological optics. Revised and annotated, it contains everything known about the subject up to 1925. Beginning with a careful anatomical description of the eye, the main body of the text is divided into three general categories: The Dioptrics of the Eye (covering optical imagery, blur circles on the retina, the mechanism of accommodation, chromatic aberration, etc.); The Sensations of Vision (including stimulation of the organ of vision, simple and compound colors, the intensity and duration of light, variations of sensitivity, contrast, etc.); and The Perceptions of Vision (containing movements of the eyes, the monocular field of vision, direction, perception of depth, binocular double vision, etc.). Appendices cover later findings on optical imagery, refraction, ophthalmoscopy, and many other matters. Unabridged, corrected republication of the original English translation of the third German edition. 3 volumes bound as 2. Complete bibliography, 1911-1925. Indices. 312 illustrations. 6 full-page plates, 3 in color. Total of 1,749pp. 5⅜ x 8.
Two-volume set S15, 16 Clothbound **$15.00**

CATALOGUE OF DOVER BOOKS

INTRODUCTION TO PHYSIOLOGICAL OPTICS, James P. C. Southall, former Professor of Physics in Columbia University. Readable, top-flight introduction, not only for beginning students of optics, but also for other readers—physicists, biochemists, illuminating engineers, optometrists, psychologists, etc. Comprehensive coverage of such matters as the Organ of Vision (structure of the eyeball, the retina, the dioptric system, monocular and binocular vision, adaptation, etc.); The Optical System of the Eye (reflex images in the cornea and crystalline lens, Emmetropia and Ametropia, accommodation, blur circles on retina); Eye-Glasses; Eye Defects; Movements of the Eyeball in its Socket; Rod and Cone Vision; Color Vision; and other similar topics. Index. 134 figures. x +426pp. 5⅜ x 8. **S924 Paperbound $2.25**

LIGHT, COLOUR AND VISION, Yves LeGrand. A thorough examination of the eye as a receptor of radiant energy and as a mechanism (the retina) consisting of light-sensitive cells which absorb light of various wave lengths—probably the most complete and authoritative treatment of this subject in print. Originally prepared as a series of lectures given at the Institute of Optics in Paris, subsequently enlarged for book publication. Partial contents: Radiant Energy—concept, nature, theories, etc., Sources of Radiation—artificial and natural, the Visual Receptor, Photometric Quantities, Units, Calculations, Retinal Illumination, Trivariance of Vision, Colorimetry, Luminance Difference Thresholds, Anatomy of the Retina, Theories of Vision, Photochemistry and Electro-physiology of the Retina, etc. Appendices, Exercises, with solutions. 500-item bibliography. Authorized translation by R. Hunt, J. Walsh, F. Hunt. Index. 173 illustrations. xiii + 512pp. 5⅜ x 8½. **S979 Clothbound $10.00**

FINGER PRINTS, PALMS AND SOLES: AN INTRODUCTION TO DERMATOGLYPHICS, Harold Cummins and Charles Midlo. An introduction in non-technical language designed to acquaint the reader with a long-neglected aspect of human biology. Although a chapter dealing with fingerprint identification and the systems of classification used by the FBI, etc. has been added especially for this edition, the main concern of the book is to show how the intricate pattern of ridges and wrinkles on our fingers have a broader significance, applicable in many areas of science and life. Some topics are: the identification of two types of twins; the resolution of doubtful cases of paternity; racial variation; inheritance; the relation of fingerprints to body measurements, blood groups, criminality, character, etc. Classification and recognition of fundamental patterns and pattern types discussed fully. 149 figures. 49 tables. 361-item bibliography. Index. xii + 319pp. 5⅝ x 8⅜. **T778 Paperbound $1.95**

Classics and histories

ANTONY VAN LEEUWENHOEK AND HIS "LITTLE ANIMALS," edited by Clifford Dobell. First book to treat extensively, accurately, life and works (relating to protozoology, bacteriology) of first microbiologist, bacteriologist, micrologist. Includes founding papers of protozoology, bacteriology; history of Leeuwenhoek's life; discussions of his microscopes, methods, language. His writing conveys sense of an enthusiastic, naive genius, as he looks at rainwater, pepper water, vinegar, frog's skin, rotifers, etc. Extremely readable, even for non-specialists. "One of the most interesting and enlightening books I have ever read," Dr. C. C. Bass, former Dean, Tulane U. School of Medicine. Only authorized edition. 400-item bibliography. Index. 32 illust. 442pp. 5⅜ x 8. **S594 Paperbound $2.25**

THE GROWTH OF SCIENTIFIC PHYSIOLOGY, G. J. Goodfield. A compact, superbly written account of how certain scientific investigations brought about the emergence of the distinct science of physiology. Centers principally around the mechanist-vitalist controversy prior to the development of physiology as an independent science, using the arguments which raged around the problem of animal heat as its chief illustration. Covers thoroughly the efforts of clinicians and naturalists and workers in chemistry and physics to solve these problems—from which the new discipline arose. Includes the theories and contributions of: Aristotle, Galen, Harvey, Boyle, Bernard, Benjamin Franklin, Palmer, Gay-Lussac, Priestley, Spallanzani, and many others. 1960 publication. Biographical bibliography. 174pp. 5 x 7½. **T1066 Clothbound $3.00**

MICROGRAPHIA, Robert Hooke. Hooke, 17th century British universal scientific genius, was a major pioneer in celestial mechanics, optics, gravity, and many other fields, but his greatest contribution was this book, now reprinted entirely from the original 1665 edition, which gave microscopy its first great impetus. With all the freshness of discovery, he describes fully his microscope, and his observations of cork, the edge of a razor, insects' eyes, fabrics, and dozens of other different objects. 38 plates, full-size or larger, contain all the original illustrations. This book is also a fundamental classic in the fields of combustion and heat theory, light and color theory, botany and zoology, hygrometry, and many other fields. It contains such farsighted predictions as the famous anticipation of artificial silk. The final section is concerned with Hooke's telescopic observations of the moon and stars. 323pp. 5⅜ x 8. **T8 Paperbound $2.00**

Psychology

YOGA: A SCIENTIFIC EVALUATION, Kovoor T. Behanan. A complete reprinting of the book that for the first time gave Western readers a sane, scientific explanation and analysis of yoga. The author draws on controlled laboratory experiments and personal records of a year as a disciple of a yoga, to investigate yoga psychology, concepts of knowledge, physiology, "supernatural" phenomena, and the ability to tap the deepest human powers. In this study under the auspices of Yale University Institute of Human Relations, the strictest principles of physiological and psychological inquiry are followed throughout. Foreword by W. A. Miles, Yale University. 17 photographs. Glossary. Index. xx + 270pp. 5⅜ x 8. T505 Paperbound **$1.75**

CONDITIONED REFLEXES: AN INVESTIGATION OF THE PHYSIOLOGICAL ACTIVITIES OF THE CEREBRAL CORTEX, I. P. Pavlov. Full, authorized translation of Pavlov's own survey of his work in experimental psychology reviews entire course of experiments, summarizes conclusions, outlines psychological system based on famous "conditioned reflex" concept. Details of technical means used in experiments, observations on formation of conditioned reflexes, function of cerebral hemispheres, results of damage, nature of sleep, typology of nervous system, significance of experiments for human psychology. Trans. by Dr. G. V. Anrep, Cambridge Univ. 235-item bibliography. 18 figures. 445pp. 5⅜ x 8. S614 Paperbound **$2.35**

EXPLANATION OF HUMAN BEHAVIOUR, F. V. Smith. A major intermediate-level introduction to and criticism of 8 complete systems of the psychology of human behavior, with unusual emphasis on theory of investigation and methodology. Part I is an illuminating analysis of the problems involved in the explanation of observed phenomena, and the differing viewpoints on the nature of causality. Parts II and III are a closely detailed survey of the systems of McDougall, Gordon Allport, Lewin, the Gestalt group, Freud, Watson, Hull, and Tolman. Biographical notes. Bibliography of over 800 items. 2 indexes. 38 figures. xii + 460pp. 5½ x 8¾. T253 Clothbound **$6.00**

SEX IN PSYCHO-ANALYSIS (formerly CONTRIBUTIONS TO PSYCHO-ANALYSIS), S. Ferenczi. Written by an associate of Freud, this volume presents countless insights on such topics as impotence, transference, analysis and children, dreams, symbols, obscene words, masturbation and male homosexuality, paranoia and psycho-analysis, the sense of reality, hypnotism and therapy, and many others. Also includes full text of THE DEVELOPMENT OF PSYCHO-ANALYSIS by Ferenczi and Otto Rank. Two books bound as one. Total of 406pp. 5⅜ x 8. T324 Paperbound **$1.85**

BEYOND PSYCHOLOGY, Otto Rank. One of Rank's most mature contributions, focussing on the irrational basis of human behavior as a basic fact of our lives. The psychoanalytic techniques of myth analysis trace to their source the ultimates of human existence: fear of death, personality, the social organization, the need for love and creativity, etc. Dr. Rank finds them stemming from a common irrational source, man's fear of final destruction. A seminal work in modern psychology, this work sheds light on areas ranging from the concept of immortal soul to the sources of state power. 291pp. 5⅜ x 8. T485 Paperbound **$2.00**

ILLUSIONS AND DELUSIONS OF THE SUPERNATURAL AND THE OCCULT, D. H. Rawcliffe. Holds up to rational examination hundreds of persistent delusions including crystal gazing, automatic writing, table turning, mediumistic trances, mental healing, stigmata, lycanthropy, live burial, the Indian Rope Trick, spiritualism, dowsing, telepathy, clairvoyance, ghosts, ESP, etc. The author explains and exposes the mental and physical deceptions involved, making this not only an exposé of supernatural phenomena, but a valuable exposition of characteristic types of abnormal psychology. Originally titled "The Psychology of the Occult." 14 illustrations. Index. 551pp. 5⅜ x 8. T503 Paperbound **$2.00**

THE PRINCIPLES OF PSYCHOLOGY, William James. The full long-course, unabridged, of one of the great classics of Western literature and science. Wonderfully lucid descriptions of human mental activity, the stream of thought, consciousness, time perception, memory, imagination, emotions, reason, abnormal phenomena, and similar topics. Original contributions are integrated with the work of such men as Berkeley, Binet, Mills, Darwin, Hume, Kant, Royce, Schopenhauer, Spinoza, Locke, Descartes, Galton, Wundt, Lotze, Herbart, Fechner, and scores of others. All contrasting interpretations of mental phenomena are examined in detail — introspective analysis, philosophical interpretation, and experimental research. "A classic," JOURNAL OF CONSULTING PSYCHOLOGY. "The main lines are as valid as ever," PSYCHO-ANALYTICAL QUARTERLY. "Standard reading . . . a classic of interpretation," PSYCHIATRIC QUARTERLY. 94 illustrations. 1408pp. 2 volumes. 5⅜ x 8. Vol. 1, T381 Paperbound **$2.50**
Vol. 2, T382 Paperbound **$2.50**

THE DYNAMICS OF THERAPY IN A CONTROLLED RELATIONSHIP, Jessie Taft. One of the most important works in literature of child psychology, out of print for 25 years. Outstanding disciple of Rank describes all aspects of relationship or Rankian therapy through concise, simple elucidation of theory underlying her actual contacts with two seven-year olds. Therapists, social caseworkers, psychologists, counselors, and laymen who work with children will all find this important work an invaluable summation of method, theory of child psychology. xix + 296pp. 5⅜ x 8. T325 Paperbound **$1.75**

Philosophy, Religion

GUIDE TO PHILOSOPHY, C. E. M. Joad. A modern classic which examines many crucial problems which man has pondered through the ages: Does free will exist? Is there plan in the universe? How do we know and validate our knowledge? Such opposed solutions as subjective idealism and realism, chance and teleology, vitalism and logical positivism, are evaluated and the contributions of the great philosophers from the Greeks to moderns like Russell, Whitehead, and others, are considered in the context of each problem. "The finest introduction," BOSTON TRANSCRIPT. Index. Classified bibliography. 592pp. 5⅜ x 8.
T297 Paperbound $2.00

HISTORY OF ANCIENT PHILOSOPHY, W. Windelband. One of the clearest, most accurate comprehensive surveys of Greek and Roman philosophy. Discusses ancient philosophy in general, intellectual life in Greece in the 7th and 6th centuries B.C., Thales, Anaximander, Anaximenes, Heraclitus, the Eleatics, Empedocles, Anaxagoras, Leucippus, the Pythagoreans, the Sophists, Socrates, Democritus (20 pages), Plato (50 pages), Aristotle (70 pages), the Peripatetics, Stoics, Epicureans, Sceptics, Neo-platonists, Christian Apologists, etc. 2nd German edition translated by H. E. Cushman. xv + 393pp. 5⅜ x 8.
T357 Paperbound $1.85

ILLUSTRATIONS OF THE HISTORY OF MEDIEVAL THOUGHT AND LEARNING, R. L. Poole. Basic analysis of the thought and lives of the leading philosophers and ecclesiastics from the 8th to the 14th century—Abailard, Ockham, Wycliffe, Marsiglio of Padua, and many other great thinkers who carried the torch of Western culture and learning through the "Dark Ages": political, religious, and metaphysical views. Long a standard work for scholars and one of the best introductions to medieval thought for beginners. Index. 10 Appendices. xiii + 327pp. 5⅜ x 8.
T674 Paperbound $2.00

PHILOSOPHY AND CIVILIZATION IN THE MIDDLE AGES, M. de Wulf. This semi-popular survey covers aspects of medieval intellectual life such as religion, philosophy, science, the arts, etc. It also covers feudalism vs. Catholicism, rise of the universities, mendicant orders, monastic centers, and similar topics. Unabridged. Bibliography. Index. viii + 320pp. 5⅜ x 8.
T284 Paperbound $1.85

AN INTRODUCTION TO SCHOLASTIC PHILOSOPHY, Prof. M. de Wulf. Formerly entitled SCHOLASTICISM OLD AND NEW, this volume examines the central scholastic tradition from St. Anselm, Albertus Magnus, Thomas Aquinas, up to Suarez in the 17th century. The relation of scholasticism to ancient and medieval philosophy and science in general is clear and easily followed. The second part of the book considers the modern revival of scholasticism, the Louvain position, relations with Kantianism and Positivism. Unabridged. xvi + 271pp. 5⅜ x 8.
T296 Clothbound $3.50
T283 Paperbound $1.75

A HISTORY OF MODERN PHILOSOPHY, H. Höffding. An exceptionally clear and detailed coverage of western philosophy from the Renaissance to the end of the 19th century. Major and minor men such as Pomponazzi, Bodin, Boehme, Telesius, Bruno, Copernicus, da Vinci, Kepler, Galileo, Bacon, Descartes, Hobbes, Spinoza, Leibniz, Wolff, Locke, Newton, Berkeley, Hume, Erasmus, Montesquieu, Voltaire, Diderot, Rousseau, Lessing, Kant, Herder, Fichte, Schelling, Hegel, Schopenhauer, Comte, Mill, Darwin, Spencer, Hartmann, Lange, and many others, are discussed in terms of theory of knowledge, logic, cosmology, and psychology. Index. 2 volumes, total of 1159pp. 5⅜ x 8.
T117 Vol. 1, Paperbound $2.25
T118 Vol. 2, Paperbound $2.25

ARISTOTLE, A. E. Taylor. A brilliant, searching non-technical account of Aristotle and his thought written by a foremost Platonist. It covers the life and works of Aristotle; classification of the sciences; logic; first philosophy; matter and form; causes; motion and eternity; God; physics; metaphysics; and similar topics. Bibliography. New Index compiled for this edition. 128pp. 5⅜ x 8.
T280 Paperbound $1.00

THE SYSTEM OF THOMAS AQUINAS, M. de Wulf. Leading Neo-Thomist, one of founders of University of Louvain, gives concise exposition to central doctrines of Aquinas, as a means toward determining his value to modern philosophy, religion. Formerly "Medieval Philosophy Illustrated from the System of Thomas Aquinas." Trans. by E. Messenger. Introduction. 151pp. 5⅜ x 8.
T568 Paperbound $1.25

LEIBNIZ, H. W. Carr. Most stimulating middle-level coverage of basic philosophical thought of Leibniz. Easily understood discussion, analysis of major works: "Theodicy," "Principles of Nature and Grace," "Monadology"; Leibniz's influence; intellectual growth; correspondence; disputes with Bayle, Malebranche, Newton; importance of his thought today, with reinterpretation in modern terminology. "Power and mastery," London Times. Bibliography. Index. 226pp. 5⅜ x 8.
T624 Paperbound $1.35

THE SENSE OF BEAUTY, G. Santayana. A revelation of the beauty of language as well as an important philosophic treatise, this work studies the "why, when, and how beauty appears, what conditions an object must fulfill to be beautiful, what elements of our nature make us sensible of beauty, and what the relation is between the constitution of the object and the excitement of our susceptibility." "It is doubtful if a better treatment of the subject has since been published," PEABODY JOURNAL. Index. ix + 275pp. 5⅜ x 8.
T238 Paperbound **$1.00**

PROBLEMS OF ETHICS, Moritz Schlick. The renowned leader of the "Vienna Circle" applies the logical positivist approach to a wide variety of ethical problems: the source and means of attaining knowledge, the formal and material characteristics of the good, moral norms and principles, absolute vs. relative values, free will and responsibility, comparative importance of pleasure and suffering as ethical values, etc. Disarmingly simple and straightforward despite complexity of subject. First English translation, authorized by author before his death, of a thirty-year old classic. Translated and with an introduction by David Rynin. Index. Foreword by Prof. George P. Adams. xxi + 209pp. 5⅜ x 8. T946 Paperbound **$1.60**

AN INTRODUCTION TO EXISTENTIALISM, Robert G. Olson. A new and indispensable guide to one of the major thought systems of our century, the movement that is central to the thinking of some of the most creative figures of the past hundred years. Stresses Heidegger and Sartre, with careful and objective examination of the existentialist position, values—freedom of choice, individual dignity, personal love, creative effort—and answers to the eternal questions of the human condition. Scholarly, unbiased, analytic, unlike most studies of this difficult subject, Prof. Olson's book is aimed at the student of philosophy as well as at the reader with no formal training who is looking for an absorbing, accessible, and thorough introduction to the basic texts. Index. xv + 221pp. 5⅜ x 8½. T55 Paperbound **$1.50**

SYMBOLIC LOGIC, C. I. Lewis and C. H. Langford. Since first publication in 1932, this has been among most frequently cited works on symbolic logic. Still one of the best introductions both for beginners and for mathematicians, philosophers. First part covers basic topics which easily lend themselves to beginning study. Second part is rigorous, thorough development of logistic method, examination of some of most difficult and abstract aspects of symbolic logic, including modal logic, logical paradoxes, many-valued logic, with Prof. Lewis' own contributions. 2nd revised (corrected) edition. 3 appendixes, one new to this edition. 524pp. 5⅜ x 8. S170 Paperbound **$2.00**

WHITEHEAD'S PHILOSOPHY OF CIVILIZATION, A. H. Johnson. A leading authority on Alfred North Whitehead synthesizes the great philosopher's thought on civilization, scattered throughout various writings, into unified whole. Analysis of Whitehead's general definition of civilization, his reflections on history and influences on its development, his religion, including his analysis of Christianity, concept of solitariness as first requirement of personal religion, and so on. Other chapters cover views on minority groups, society, civil liberties, education. Also critical comments on Whitehead's philosophy. Written with general reader in mind. A perceptive introduction to important area of the thought of a leading philosopher of our century. Revised index and bibliography. xii + 211pp. 5⅜ x 8½. T996 Paperbound **$1.50**

WHITEHEAD'S THEORY OF REALITY, A. H. Johnson. Introductory outline of Whitehead's theory of actual entities, the heart of his philosophy of reality, followed by his views on nature of God, philosophy of mind, theory of value (truth, beauty, goodness and their opposites), analyses of other philosophers, attitude toward science. A perspicacious lucid introduction by author of dissertation on Whitehead, written under the subject's supervision at Harvard. Good basic view for beginning students of philosophy and for those who are simply interested in important contemporary ideas. Revised index and bibliography. xiii + 267pp. 5⅜ x 8½. T989 Paperbound **$1.50**

MIND AND THE WORLD-ORDER, C. I. Lewis. Building upon the work of Peirce, James, and Dewey, Professor Lewis outlines a theory of knowledge in terms of "conceptual pragmatism." Dividing truth into abstract mathematical certainty and empirical truth, the author demonstrates that the traditional understanding of the a priori must be abandoned. Detailed analyses of philosophy, metaphysics, method, the "given" in experience, knowledge of objects, nature of the a priori, experience and order, and many others. Appendices. xiv + 446pp. 5⅜ x 8. T359 Paperbound **$2.25**

SCEPTICISM AND ANIMAL FAITH, G. Santayana. To eliminate difficulties in the traditional theory of knowledge, Santayana distinguishes between the independent existence of objects and the essence our mind attributes to them. Scepticism is thereby established as a form of belief, and animal faith is shown to be a necessary condition of knowledge. Belief, classical idealism, intuition, memory, symbols, literary psychology, and much more, discussed with unusual clarity and depth. Index. xii + 314pp. 5⅜ x 8. T235 Clothbound **$3.50**
T236 Paperbound **$1.50**

LANGUAGE AND MYTH, E. Cassirer. Analyzing the non-rational thought processes which go to make up culture, Cassirer demonstrates that beneath both language and myth there lies a dominant unconscious "grammar" of experience whose categories and canons are not those of logical thought. His analyses of seemingly diverse phenomena such as Indian metaphysics, the Melanesian "mana," the Naturphilosophie of Schelling, modern poetry, etc., are profound without being pedantic. Introduction and translation by Susanne Langer. Index. x + 103pp. 5⅜ x 8. T51 Paperbound **$1.25**

Teach Yourself

These British books are the most effective series of home study books on the market! With no outside help they will teach you as much as is necessary to have a good background in each subject, in many cases offering as much material as a similar high school or college course. They are carefully planned, written by foremost British educators, and amply provided with test questions and problems for you to check your progress; the mathematics books are especially rich in examples and problems. Do not confuse them with skimpy outlines or ordinary school texts or vague generalized popularizations; each book is complete in itself, full without being overdetailed, and designed to give you an easily-acquired branch of knowledge.

TEACH YOURSELF ALGEBRA, P. Abbott. The equivalent of a thorough high school course, up through logarithms. 52 illus. 307pp. 4¼ x 7.   T680 Clothbound **$2.00**

TEACH YOURSELF GEOMETRY, P. Abbott. Plane and solid geometry, covering about a year of plane and six months of solid. 268 illus. 344pp. 4½ x 7.   T681 Clothbound **$2.00**

TEACH YOURSELF TRIGONOMETRY, P. Abbott. Background of algebra and geometry will enable you to get equivalent of elementary college course. Tables. 102 illus. 204pp. 4½ x 7.
T682 Clothbound **$2.00**

TEACH YOURSELF THE CALCULUS, P. Abbott. With algebra and trigonometry you will be able to acquire a good working knowledge of elementary integral calculus and differential calculus. Excellent supplement to any course textbook. 380pp. 4¼ x 7.   T683 Clothbound **$2.00**

TEACH YOURSELF THE SLIDE RULE, B. Snodgrass. Basic principles clearly explained, with many applications in engineering, business, general figuring, will enable you to pick up very useful skill. 10 illus. 207pp. 4¼ x 7.   T684 Clothbound **$2.00**

TEACH YOURSELF MECHANICS, P. Abbott. Equivalent of part course on elementary college level, with lever, parallelogram of force, friction, laws of motion, gases, etc. Fine introduction before more advanced course. 163 illus. 271pp. 4½ x 7.   T685 Clothbound **$2.00**

TEACH YOURSELF ELECTRICITY, C. W. Wilman. Current, resistance, voltage, Ohm's law, circuits, generators, motors, transformers, etc. Non-mathematical as much as possible. 115 illus. 184pp. 4¼ x 7.   T230 Clothbound **$2.00**

TEACH YOURSELF HEAT ENGINES E. DeVille. Steam and internal combustion engines; non-mathematical introduction for student, for layman wishing background, refresher for advanced student. 76 illus. 217pp. 4¼ x 7.   T237 Clothbound **$2.00**

TEACH YOURSELF TO PLAY THE PIANO, King Palmer. Companion and supplement to lessons or self study. Handy reference, too. Nature of instrument, elementary musical theory, technique of playing, interpretation, etc. 60 illus. 144pp. 4¼ x 7.   T959 Clothbound **$2.00**

TEACH YOURSELF HERALDRY AND GENEALOGY, L. G. Pine. Modern work, avoiding romantic and overpopular misconceptions. Editor of new Burke presents detailed information and commentary down to present. Best general survey. 50 illus. glossary; 129pp. 4¼ x 7.
T962 Clothbound **$2.00**

TEACH YOURSELF HANDWRITING, John L. Dumpleton. Basic Chancery cursive style is popular and easy to learn. Many diagrams. 114 illus. 192pp. 4¼ x 7.   T960 Clothbound **$2.00**

TEACH YOURSELF CARD GAMES FOR TWO, Kenneth Konstam. Many first-rate games, including old favorites like cribbage and gin and canasta as well as new lesser-known games. Extremely interesting for cards enthusiast. 60 illus. 150pp. 4¼ x 7.   T963 Clothbound **$2.00**

TEACH YOURSELF GUIDEBOOK TO THE DRAMA, Luis Vargas. Clear, rapid survey of changing fashions and forms from Aeschylus to Tennessee Williams, in all major European traditions. Plot summaries, critical comments, etc. Equivalent of a college drama course; fine cultural background 224pp. 4¼ x 7.   T961 Clothbound **$2.00**

TEACH YOURSELF THE ORGAN, Francis Routh. Excellent compendium of background material for everyone interested in organ music, whether as listener or player. 27 musical illus. 158pp. 4¼ x 7.   T977 Clothbound **$2.00**

TEACH YOURSELF TO STUDY SCULPTURE, William Gaunt. Noted British cultural historian surveys culture from Greeks, primitive world, to moderns. Equivalent of college survey course. 23 figures, 40 photos. 158pp. 4¼ x 7.   T976 Clothbound **$2.00**

Miscellaneous

THE COMPLETE KANO JIU-JITSU (JUDO), H. I. Hancock and K. Higashi. Most comprehensive guide to judo, referred to as outstanding work by Encyclopaedia Britannica. Complete authentic Japanese system of 160 holds and throws, including the most spectacular, fully illustrated with 487 photos. Full text explains leverage, weight centers, pressure points, special tricks, etc.; shows how to protect yourself from almost any manner of attack though your attacker may have the initial advantage of strength and surprise. This authentic Kano system should not be confused with the many American imitations. xii + 500pp. 5⅜ x 8.

T639 Paperbound **$2.00**

THE MEMOIRS OF JACQUES CASANOVA. Splendid self-revelation by history's most engaging scoundrel—utterly dishonest with women and money, yet highly intelligent and observant. Here are all the famous duels, scandals, amours, banishments, thefts, treacheries, and imprisonments all over Europe: a life lived to the fullest and recounted with gusto in one of the greatest autobiographies of all time. What is more, these Memoirs are also one of the most trustworthy and valuable documents we have on the society and culture of the extravagant 18th century. Here are Voltaire, Louis XV, Catherine the Great, cardinals, castrati, pimps, and pawnbrokers—an entire glittering civilization unfolding before you with an unparalleled sense of actuality. Translated by Arthur Machen. Edited by F. A. Blossom. Introduction by Arthur Symons. Illustrated by Rockwell Kent. Total of xlviii + 2216pp. 5⅜ x 8.

T338 Vol I Paperbound **$2.00**
T339 Vol II Paperbound **$2.00**
T340 Vol III Paperbound **$2.00**
The set **$6.00**

BARNUM'S OWN STORY, P. T. Barnum. The astonishingly frank and gratifyingly well-written autobiography of the master showman and pioneer publicity man reveals the truth about his early career, his famous hoaxes (such as the Fejee Mermaid and the Woolly Horse), his amazing commercial ventures, his fling in politics, his feuds and friendships, his failures and surprising comebacks. A vast panorama of 19th century America's mores, amusements, and vitality. 66 new illustrations in this edition. xii + 500pp. 5⅜ x 8.

T764 Paperbound **$1.65**

THE STORY OF THE TITANIC AS TOLD BY ITS SURVIVORS, ed. by Jack Winocour. Most significant accounts of most overpowering naval disaster of modern times: all 4 authors were survivors. Includes 2 full-length, unabridged books: "The Loss of the S.S. Titanic," by Laurence Beesley, "The Truth about the Titanic," by Col. Archibald Gracie; 6 pertinent chapters from "Titanic and Other Ships," autobiography of only officer to survive, Second Officer Charles Lightoller; and a short, dramatic account by the Titanic's wireless operator, Harold Bride. 26 illus. 368pp. 5⅜ x 8. T610 Paperbound **$1.50**

THE PHYSIOLOGY OF TASTE, Jean Anthelme Brillat-Savarin. Humorous, satirical, witty, and personal classic on joys of food and drink by 18th century French politician, litterateur. Treats the science of gastronomy, erotic value of truffles, Parisian restaurants, drinking contests; gives recipes for tunny omelette, pheasant, Swiss fondue, etc. Only modern translation of original French edition. Introduction. 41 illus. 346pp. 5⅝ x 8⅜.

T591 Paperbound **$1.50**

THE ART OF THE STORY-TELLER, M. L. Shedlock. This classic in the field of effective story-telling is regarded by librarians, story-tellers, and educators as the finest and most lucid book on the subject. The author considers the nature of the story, the difficulties of communicating stories to children, the artifices used in story-telling, how to obtain and maintain the effect of the story, and, of extreme importance, the elements to seek and those to avoid in selecting material. A 99-page selection of Miss Shedlock's most effective stories and an extensive bibliography of further material by Eulalie Steinmetz enhance the book's usefulness. xxi + 320pp. 5⅜ x 8. T635 Paperbound **$1.50**

CREATIVE POWER: THE EDUCATION OF YOUTH IN THE CREATIVE ARTS, Hughes Mearns. In first printing considered revolutionary in its dynamic, progressive approach to teaching the creative arts; now accepted as one of the most effective and valuable approaches yet formulated. Based on the belief that every child has something to contribute, it provides in a stimulating manner invaluable and inspired teaching insights, to stimulate children's latent powers of creative expression in drama, poetry, music, writing, etc. Mearns's methods were developed in his famous experimental classes in creative education at the Lincoln School of Teachers College, Columbia Univ. Named one of the 20 foremost books on education in recent times by National Education Association. New enlarged revised 2nd edition. Introduction. 272pp. 5⅜ x 8. T490 Paperbound **$1.75**

FREE AND INEXPENSIVE EDUCATIONAL AIDS, T. J. Pepe, Superintendent of Schools, Southbury, Connecticut. An up-to-date listing of over 1500 booklets, films, charts, etc. 5% costs less than 25¢; 1% costs more; 94% is yours for the asking. Use this material privately, or in schools from elementary to college, for discussion, vocational guidance, projects. 59 categories include health, trucking, textiles, language, weather, the blood, office practice, wild life, atomic energy, other important topics. Each item described according to contents, number of pages or running time, level. All material is educationally sound, and without political or company bias. 1st publication. Second, revised edition. Index. 244pp. 5⅜ x 8.

T663 Paperbound **$1.50**

CATALOGUE OF DOVER BOOKS

THE ROMANCE OF WORDS, E. Weekley. An entertaining collection of unusual word-histories that tracks down for the general reader the origins of more than 2000 common words and phrases in English (including British and American slang): discoveries often surprising, often humorous, that help trace vast chains of commerce in products and ideas. There are Arabic trade words, cowboy words, origins of family names, phonetic accidents, curious wanderings, folk-etymologies, etc. Index. xiii + 210pp. 5⅜ x 8. T710 Paperbound **$1.25**

PHRASE AND WORD ORIGINS: A STUDY OF FAMILIAR EXPRESSIONS, A. H. Holt. One of the most entertaining books on the unexpected origins and colorful histories of words and phrases, based on sound scholarship, but written primarily for the layman. Over 1200 phrases and 1000 separate words are covered, with many quotations, and the results of the most modern linguistic and historical researches. "A right jolly book Mr. Holt has made," N. Y. Times. v + 254pp. 5⅜ x 8. T758 Paperbound **$1.35**

AMATEUR WINE MAKING, S. M. Tritton. Now, with only modest equipment and no prior knowledge, you can make your own fine table wines. A practical handbook, this covers every type of grape wine, as well as fruit, flower, herb, vegetable, and cereal wines, and many kinds of mead, cider, and beer. Every question you might have is answered, and there is a valuable discussion of what can go wrong at various stages along the way. Special supplement of yeasts and American sources of supply. 13 tables. 32 illustrations. Glossary. Index. 239pp. 5½ x 8½. T514 Clothbound **$4.00**

SAILING ALONE AROUND THE WORLD. Captain Joshua Slocum. A great modern classic in a convenient inexpensive edition. Captain Slocum's account of his single-handed voyage around the world in a 34 foot boat which he rebuilt himself. A nearly unparalleled feat of seamanship told with vigor, wit, imagination, and great descriptive power. "A nautical equivalent of Thoreau's account," Van Wyck Brooks. 67 illustrations. 308pp. 5⅜ x 8. T326 Paperbound **$1.00**

FARES, PLEASE! by J. A. Miller. Authoritative, comprehensive, and entertaining history of local public transit from its inception to its most recent developments: trolleys, horsecars, streetcars, buses, elevateds, subways, along with monorails, "road-railers," and a host of other extraordinary vehicles. Here are all the flamboyant personalities involved, the vehement arguments, the unusual information, and all the nostalgia. "Interesting facts brought into especially vivid life," N. Y. Times. New preface. 152 illustrations, 4 new. Bibliography. xix + 204pp. 5⅜ x 8. T671 Paperbound **$1.50**

HOAXES, C. D. MacDougall. Shows how art, science, history, journalism can be perverted for private purposes. Hours of delightful entertainment and a work of scholarly value, this often shocking book tells of the deliberate creation of nonsense news, the Cardiff giant, Shakespeare forgeries, the Loch Ness monster, Biblical frauds, political schemes, literary hoaxers like Chatterton, Ossian, the disumbrationist school of painting, the lady in black at Valentino's tomb, and over 250 others. It will probably reveal the truth about a few things you've believed, and help you spot more readily the editorial "gander" and planted publicity release. "A stupendous collection . . . and shrewd analysis." New Yorker. New revised edition. 54 photographs. Index. 320pp. 5⅜ x 8. T465 Paperbound **$1.75**

A HISTORY OF THE WARFARE OF SCIENCE WITH THEOLOGY IN CHRISTENDOM, A. D. White. Most thorough account ever written of the great religious-scientific battles shows gradual victory of science over ignorant, harmful beliefs. Attacks on theory of evolution; attacks on Galileo; great medieval plagues caused by belief in devil-origin of disease; attacks on Franklin's experiments with electricity; the witches of Salem; scores more that will amaze you. Author, co-founder and first president of Cornell U., writes with vast scholarly background, but in clear, readable prose. Acclaimed as classic effort in America to do away with superstition. Index. Total of 928pp. 5⅜ x 8. T608 Vol I Paperbound **$1.85**
T609 Vol II Paperbound **$1.85**

THE SHIP OF FOOLS, Sebastian Brant. First printed in 1494 in Basel, this amusing book swept Europe, was translated into almost every important language, and was a best-seller for centuries. That it is still living and vital is shown by recent developments in publishing. This is the only English translation of this work, and it recaptures in lively, modern verse all the wit and insights of the original, in satirizations of foibles and vices: greed, adultery, envy, hatred, sloth, profiteering, etc. This will long remain the definitive English edition, for Professor Zeydel has provided biography of Brant, bibliography, publishing history, influences, etc. Complete reprint of 1944 edition. Translated by Professor E. Zeydel, University of Cincinnati. All 114 original woodcut illustrations. viii + 399pp. 5½ x 8⅝. T266 Paperbound **$2.00**

ERASMUS, A STUDY OF HIS LIFE, IDEALS AND PLACE IN HISTORY, Preserved Smith. This is the standard English biography and evaluation of the great Netherlands humanist Desiderius Erasmus. Written by one of the foremost American historians it covers all aspects of Erasmus's life, his influence in the religious quarrels of the Reformation, his overwhelming role in the field of letters, and his importance in the emergence of the new world view of the Northern Renaissance. This is not only a work of great scholarship, it is also an extremely interesting, vital portrait of a great man. 8 illustrations. xiv + 479pp. 5⅝ x 8½. T331 Paperbound **$2.00**

Orientalia

ORIENTAL RELIGIONS IN ROMAN PAGANISM, F. Cumont. A study of the cultural meeting of east and west in the Early Roman Empire. It covers the most important eastern religions of the time from their first appearance in Rome, 204 B.C., when the Great Mother of the Gods was first brought over from Syria. The ecstatic cults of Syria and Phrygia — Cybele, Attis, Adonis, their orgies and mutilatory rites; the mysteries of Egypt — Serapis, Isis, Osiris, the dualism of Persia, the elevation of cosmic evil to equal stature with the deity, Mithra; worship of Hermes Trismegistus; Ishtar, Astarte; the magic of the ancient Near East, etc. Introduction. 55pp. of notes; extensive bibliography. Index. xxiv + 298pp. 5⅜ x 8.
T321 Paperbound **$2.00**

THE MYSTERIES OF MITHRA, F. Cumont. The definitive coverage of a great ideological struggle between the west and the orient in the first centuries of the Christian era. The origin of Mithraism, a Persian mystery religion, and its association with the Roman army is discussed in detail. Then utilizing fragmentary monuments and texts, in one of the greatest feats of scholarly detection, Dr. Cumont reconstructs the mystery teachings and secret doctrines, the hidden organization and cult of Mithra. Mithraic art is discussed, analyzed, and depicted in 70 illustrations. 239pp. 5⅜ x 8. T323 Paperbound **$1.85**

CHRISTIAN AND ORIENTAL PHILOSOPHY OF ART, A. K. Coomaraswamy. A unique fusion of philosopher, orientalist, art historian, and linguist, the author discusses such matters as: the true function of aesthetics in art, the importance of symbolism, intellectual and philosophic backgrounds, the role of traditional culture in enriching art, common factors in all great art, the nature of medieval art, the nature of folklore, the beauty of mathematics, and similar topics. 2 illustrations. Bibliography. 148pp. 5⅜ x 8. T378 Paperbound **$1.35**

TRANSFORMATION OF NATURE IN ART, A. K. Coomaraswamy. Unabridged reissue of a basic work upon Asiatic religious art and philosophy of religion. The theory of religious art in Asia and Medieval Europe (exemplified by Meister Eckhart) is analyzed and developed. Detailed consideration is given to Indian medieval aesthetic manuals, symbolic language in philosophy, the origin and use of images in India, and many other fascinating and little known topics. Glossaries of Sanskrit and Chinese terms. Bibliography. 41pp. of notes. 245pp. 5⅜ x 8.
T368 Paperbound **$1.75**

BUDDHIST LOGIC, F.Th. Stcherbatsky. A study of an important part of Buddhism usually ignored by other books on the subject: the Mahayana buddhistic logic of the school of Dignaga and his followers. First vol. devoted to history of Indian logic with Central Asian continuations, detailed exposition of Dignaga system, including theory of knowledge, the sensible world (causation, perception, ultimate reality) and mental world (judgment, inference, logical fallacies, the syllogism), reality of external world, and negation (law of contradiction, universals, dialectic). Vol. II contains translation of Dharmakirti's Nyayabindu with Dharmamottara's commentary. Appendices cover translations of Tibetan treatises on logic, Hindu attacks on Buddhist logic, etc. The basic work, one of the products of the great St. Petersburg school of Indian studies. Written clearly and with an awareness of Western philosophy and logic; meant for the Asian specialist and for the general reader with only a minimum of background. Vol. I, xii + 559pp. Vol. II, viii + 468pp. 5⅜ x 8½.
T955 Vol. I Paperbound **$2.50**
T956 Vol. II Paperbound **$2.50**
The set **$5.00**

THE TEXTS OF TAOISM. The first inexpensive edition of the complete James Legge translations of the Tao Te King and the writings of Chinese mystic Chuang Tse. Also contains several shorter treatises: the T'ai Shang Tractate of Actions and Their Retributions; the King Kang King, or Classic of Purity; the Yin Fu King, or Classic of the Harmony of the Seen and Unseen; the Yu Shu King, or Classic of the Pivot of Jade; and the Hsia Yung King, or Classic of the Directory for a Day. While there are other translations of the Tao Te King, this is the only translation of Chuang Tse and much of other material. Extensive introduction discusses differences between Taoism, Buddhism, Confucianism; authenticity and arrangement of Tao Te King and writings of Chuang Tse; the meaning of the Tao and basic tenets of Taoism; historical accounts of Lao-tse and followers; other pertinent matters. Clarifying notes incorporated into text. Originally published as Volumes 39, 40 of SACRED BOOKS OF THE EAST series, this has long been recognized as an indispensible collection. Sinologists, philosophers, historians of religion will of course be interested and anyone with an elementary course in Oriental religion or philosophy will understand and profit from these writings. Index. Appendix analyzing thought of Chuang Tse. Vol. I, xxiii + 396pp. Vol. II, viii + 340pp. 5⅜ x 8½.
T990 Vol. I Paperbound **$2.25**
T991 Vol. II Paperbound **$2.25**

CATALOGUE OF DOVER BOOKS

EPOCHS OF CHINESE AND JAPANESE ART, Ernest T. Fenollosa. Although this classic of art history was written before the archeological discovery of Shang and Chou civilizations, it is still in many respects the finest detailed study of Chinese and Japanese art available in English. It is very wide in range, covering sculpture, carving, painting, metal work, ceramics, textiles, graphic arts and other areas, and it considers both religious and secular art, including the Japanese woodcut. Its greatest strength, however, lies in its extremely full, detailed, insight-laden discussion of historical and cultural background, and in its analysis of the religious and philosophical implications of art works. It is also a brilliant stylistic achievement, written with enthusiasm and verve, which can be enjoyed and read with profit by both the Orientalist and the general reader who is interested in art. Index. Glossary of proper names. 242 illustrations. Total of 704 pages. 5⅜ x 8½.
T364-5 Two vol. set, paperbound **$5.00**

THE VEDANTA SUTRAS OF BADARAYANA WITH COMMENTARY BY SANKARACHARYA. The definitive translation of the consummation, foremost interpretation of Upanishads. Originally part of SACRED BOOKS OF THE EAST, this two-volume translation includes exhaustive commentary and exegesis by Sankara; 128-page introduction by translator, Prof. Thibaut, that discusses background, scope and purpose of the sutras, value and importance of Sankara's interpretation; copious footnotes providing further explanations. Every serious student of Indian religion or thought, philosophers, historians of religion should read these clear, accurate translations of documents central to development of important thought systems in the East. Unabridged republication of Volumes 34, 38 of the Sacred Books of the East. Translated by George Thibault. General index, index of quotations and of Sanskrit. Vol. I, cxxv + 448pp. Vol. II, iv + 506pp. 5⅜ x 8½.
T994 Vol. I Paperbound **$2.00**
T995 Vol. II Paperbound **$2.00**

THE UPANISHADS. The Max Müller translation of the twelve classical Upanishads available for the first time in an inexpensive format: Chandogya, Kena, Aitareya aranyaka and upanishad, Kaushitaki, Isa, Katha, Mundaka, Taittiriyaka Brhadaranyaka, Svetarasvatara. Prasna — all of the classical Upanishads of the Vedanta school—and the Maitriyana Upanishad. Originally volumes 1, 15 of SACRED BOOKS OF THE EAST series, this is still the most scholarly translation. Prof. Müller, probably most important Sanskritologist of nineteenth century, provided invaluable introduction that acquaints readers with history of Upanishad translations, age and chronology of texts, etc. and a preface that discusses their value to Western readers. Heavily annotated. Stimulating reading for anyone with even only a basic course background in Oriental philosophy, religion, necessary to all Indologists, philosophers, religious historians. Transliteration and pronunciation guide. Vol. I, ciii + 320pp. Vol. II, liii + 350pp.
T992 Vol. I Paperbound **$2.00**
T993 Vol. II Paperbound **$2.00**
The set **$4.00**

Dover publishes books on art, music, philosophy, literature, languages, history, social sciences, psychology, handcrafts, orientalia, puzzles and entertainments, chess, pets and gardens, books explaining science, intermediate and higher mathematics mathematical physics, engineering, biological sciences, earth sciences, classics of science, etc. Write to:

Dept. catrr.
Dover Publications, Inc.
180 Varick Street, N. Y. 14, N. Y.